THE COST OF
A REPUTATION

THE COST OF
A REPUTATION

Aldington versus Tolstoy: the causes, course
and consequences of the notorious libel case

Ian Mitchell

Topical Books

© Ian Mitchell, 1997

Published by
Topical Books
The Cogitorium
Lagavulin
Isle of Islay PA42 7DX

The moral right of the author has been asserted

ISBN 0 9531581 0 1

Printed and bound in Scotland by Bell & Bain Ltd., Glasgow

Cover picture: the Royal Courts of Justice
Back cover left: the Victims of Yalta Memorial
Back cover right: Brig. Low DSO MP, 1945 (*Blackpool Evening Gazette*)

This book is dedicated to my patron,
the Earl of Portsmouth

TABLE OF CONTENTS

FOREWORD
by Robert Harris

*T*HE COST OF A REPUTATION tells, in painstaking detail, the story of one of the greatest legal battles of the last half century: the libel case initiated by Lord Aldington against Nikolai Tolstoy and Nigel Watts that resulted, in November 1989, in the award to Lord Aldington of £1.5 million in damages.

That judgement was so devastating, the sum awarded so intimidatingly huge, that, eight years since, only a very few brave souls have dared re-enter the tangled thicket of historical documents, ancient loyalties, impassioned charges and counter-charges, not to mention legal man-traps, which the case engendered. One such brave soul is Ian Mitchell.

I first became properly aware of the great tragedy that lies at the centre of this book sixteen years ago when, as a young television reporter, I made a long film for BBC's Newsnight programme about the forcible repatriations of Cossacks and Jugoslav non-Communists from British-occupied Austria in May 1945. The horror of what happened was most forcibly brought home to me when I travelled to Cardiff to interview one of the principal British eyewitnesses, Major "Rusty" Davies of the Argyll and Sutherland Highlanders. His obvious and continuing anguish about what he had been required to do—to use pick helves and rifle butts to force thousands of screaming people into cattle-trucks—made a powerful impression. 'We couldn't understand,' he said, 'why everybody *en bloc* had to go back... Why *everybody* had to go back was beyond my comprehension.'

More than a decade and a half later, Major Davies's question remains unanswered. Why? Why did it happen? Why did 'everybody'—some 70,000 men, women and children—have to be handed over to the executioners, torturers and gaolers of Tito's Jugoslavia and Stalin's Soviet Union, when official Allied policy was that all except those Russians who were Soviet citizens—possibly half that total—should be given sanctuary?

The Cost of a Reputation does not pretend to be the definitive solution to this mystery, but it does, I think, bring us closer to an understanding of the precise chain of events. I would commend it in particular on four counts. First, by using documents which were not made available to the defence at the time of the libel trial, it brings fresh clarity to the complex story of what exactly happened in Austria in May 1945. The self-styled 'Cowgill Inquiry' of 1990 was widely canvassed—not least by its own members—as the final word on this subject. *The Cost of a Reputation* shows why it was not.

Secondly, Mr Mitchell raises some very disturbing questions—to put it mildly—about the way in which the last Conservative government discharged its duties as a custodian of historical documents. The official cover-up of the repatriations began as early as 1945, but there is evidence here which suggests that a similar kind of cover-up may still have been in operation until very recently.

Thirdly, the book exposes, better than any other I have ever encountered, the baroque absurdities and vast costs of British justice. Indeed, there are occasions when *The Cost of a Reputation* reads like *Bleak House* rewritten by Alexander Solzhenitsyn.

Finally, I think Mr Mitchell is, as far as anyone can be in this intensely polarized dispute, fair. Nobody really emerges as a hero or a victor from these pages; in this story everyone—except, of course, the lawyers—ends up damaged or impoverished to a greater or lesser degree. Nigel Watts went to prison. Nikolai Tolstoy has never produced the books he once planned to write. Even Lord Aldington, the ostensible winner, was in some senses a loser: he failed, in the end, to receive the money he was awarded, and still the litigation and the questions drag on, ruining the peaceful retirement he had hoped for.

But then how could it be otherwise? History did not stop at 4.24 p.m. on Thursday 30 November 1989 in the Royal Courts of Justice on the Strand. It is not a contract to be settled or a commodity to be parcelled up. It is a constant process of argument and inquiry, a freedom that belongs to all the citizens of a democratic state. As Winston Churchill put it in 1940: 'In one phase men seem to have been right, in another they seem to have been wrong. Then again, a few years later, when the perspective of time has lengthened, all stands in a different setting. There is a new proportion. There is another scale of values...'

If I were merely to draw one moral from this important book, it would be that history is too important—far, far too important—to be left to the lawyers.

Kintbury
Berkshire
August 1997

INTRODUCTION

T HE BACKGROUND to this book is the only serious crime which
the British Army has been widely accused of having committed in
World War II. It is a subject which has been well described by two
historians, Nicholas Bethell and Nikolai Tolstoy. In a sentence, 5 Corps,
a unit of the British 8th Army in Austria, handed over 70,000 Cossacks
and Jugoslavs to Stalin and Tito in May 1945, contrary both to the laws
and customs of war and to the intent of the British government and the
highest Allied military command. That story, however, is not the subject
of this book, which deals instead with the libel trial that took place in
London in 1989 after Tolstoy accused the Chief of Staff of 5 Corps,
Brigadier Low, now Lord Aldington, of having played a key role in
organising those handovers.

Tolstoy wrote that Lord Aldington had 'the blood of 70,000 innocent
men, women and children on his hands'. More than that, he was 'a war
criminal whose activities merit comparison with those of the worst of the
Nazi butchers'. If this was a *prima facie* libel of an uncommonly simple
and grave sort, the case did not turn out to be nearly so straightforward as
might have been expected. It lasted forty-one days, took evidence from
thirty-nine witnesses (excluding the litigants), considered a thousand
pages of documentary evidence and produced a transcript running to
nearly a million words. At the end of all this, an award of £1.5 million in
damages was made to Lord Aldington, against Tolstoy and his co-defendant, Nigel Watts, who had published Tolstoy's words.

But this did not put an end to the controversy. Since the verdict was
delivered, on 30 November 1989, to the time of this writing, there have
been a further fifteen cases fought on related matters by one or more of
the three litigants, and the end is not yet in sight. It is the aim of the courts
to provide finality in litigation. The Judge in the libel trial, Mr Justice
Michael Davies, expressed to the jury at the beginning of his summing-up
the hope that 'one side or the other, or preferably both, would shut up

about it all once you have given your decision.' Why this has not happened is, essentially, because the trial was conducted in such a way that the losing side, and a host of its supporters, some of them quite influential, have not felt the verdict to be the last word on the matter. Essentially it was due to the fact that critical evidence for the Defence was kept from the court by the Ministry of Defence and the Foreign Office. The essence of Lord Aldington's defence against Tolstoy's charges was that he was only obeying orders. The evidence in the files withheld from the court was that this was not true. Many people now feel that the verdict can no longer be regarded as either safe or satisfactory.

Some of the withheld evidence is quite explicit. The most important Foreign Office file contains an instruction to 8th Army to 'avoid entering into any signed agreements with Jugoslav commanders'. This was transmitted to 5 Corps on 17 May (copy in the same file). Two days later, Brigadier Low signed an agreement with a Jugoslav commander which provided for the handover of all the surrendered Jugoslavs in its control— about 25,000 of them—most of whom were murdered very soon after handover. This file also shows that it was purely due to 5 Corps' obstruction of the intentions of the higher Allied military command that the 45,000 Cossacks were delivered to the Soviet Army. Both the Supreme Allied Commander in the area, Field Marshal Alexander, and the British Prime Minister, Winston Churchill, were against this. Yet none of the evidence of 5 Corps' *dis*obedience to orders was seen by the jury.

Nonetheless, this file, together with some important corroborating Ministry of Defence ones, was used by Lord Aldington while preparing his case. He submitted numerous documents from them to the court. But he had consulted them, not in the Public Record Office where they would have been equally available to Tolstoy, but in, respectively, the Ministry of Defence and the Foreign Office, where they were not. When Tolstoy asked to see them he was told that would not be possible. The Ministry of Defence said one of the main files he needed was 'in use' and could not be released to him; the Foreign Office said the file referred to above was 'lost'. It remained 'lost' until the whole trial and appeals process had been exhausted, when it was mysteriously 'found'. It is now back in the Public Record Office, where anyone can consult it. Thus there is no dispute about the nature of the evidence withheld from the jury in 1989.

Immediately after he had issued his writ, Lord Aldington wrote to his friend and fellow Old Wykehamist, George Younger, now Lord Younger and then Secretary of State for Defence, asking if he would arrange for

Ministry of Defence files which he might need for preparation of his case to be withdrawn from the Public Record Office and sent to the Army Historical Branch in Whitehall. This was done. Closer to the trial, Lord Aldington asked another friend, Lord Trefgarne, then Minister of State for Defence Procurement, if he could use his Personal Service Record in court. Trefgarne said that the rules of Crown confidentiality forbade this, but that he would make an exception in Aldington's case if he agreed not to disclose the source of the document. The Foreign Office afforded similar facilities, all of which begs the biggest question of this whole story: does the Whitehall-Westminster establishment bend the legal processes to its own ends?

Whether or not what was done amounted to a conspiracy to pervert the course of justice is for the reader to judge—or, better still, the Director of Public Prosecutions. But it surely merits serious investigation, at least if public confidence in the judicial process is of any consequence to the nation at large. It is horribly ironic that the reason why the Cossacks and Jugoslavs were so happy to surrender to the British in May 1945 was because they had complete confidence in what they thought of as "British justice".

Map 1

This map shows the territory still under control of the Third Reich at the moment it surrendered on 7 May 1945. It makes in, graphic form, the important point that southern Austria (or Carinthia) was the largest area still unoccupied by the Allies. It was therefore temporarily home to an enormous number of refugees. Furthermore, soon after the British Army occupied this area, on 8 May, the contiguous area of German-held territory on Slovenia, immediately south of the Austro-Jugoslav border, was occupied by Tito's forces. Most of the Germans, Cossacks, Serbs and Slovenes, and many of the Croats, who had been crowded in there trekked north across the Karavanken mountains into Austria. The result was that Carinthia became, as one observer described it, 'the sump of Europe'—see p. 1. This was a major problem for 5 Corps, the British unit—a component of 8th Army—which was detailed to occupy southern Austria.

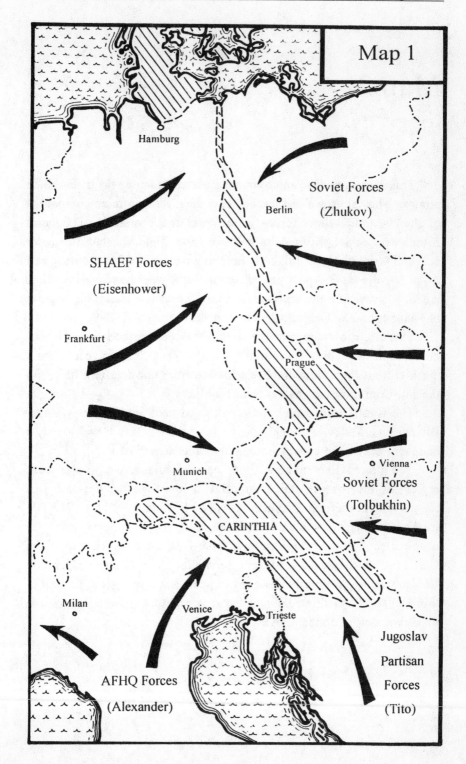

Map 2

This map shows the approximate areas occupied by the main Allied armies. They are separated by the heavy line. The northern component of the western Allies' forces were under the command of General Eisenhower, at SHAEF, and the southern under Field Marshal Alexander at AFHQ (see p. 17 for full command diagram). The Soviet Army had taken Vienna on 3 April, paused, then raced westward in early May, meeting British advance units at Judenburg, which was later to be the point of handover of the Cossacks by the British.

This map shows the routes by which the three main bodies of refugees made their way into Carinthia. The Cossack Cavalry came from north-eastern Jugoslavia, the Kazachi Stan from north-eastern Italy, and the anti-Communist Jugoslavs from Ljubljana.

The Croat Army which 5 Corps turned back into Jugoslavia near Bleiburg had followed roughly the route of the Cossack Cavalry, only a couple of days later, by which time the border was closed.

The dotted line running south past Ljubljana, but to the west, represents the pre-war Italian-Jugoslav border, and the dot-dash line zig-zagging north from Trieste the post-war boundary. In May 1945 Tito tried to claim territory to the west of this latter line, in Venezia Giulia, for a so-called "Greater Jugoslavia". Likewise, he also tried to claim Carinthia, which had a tiny Slovene population, from Austria. Operation Coldstream was primarily designed to push Tito's forces out of both of those areas. To facilitate this, the Cossack regufees in Carinthia were to be moved north into the SHAEF area.

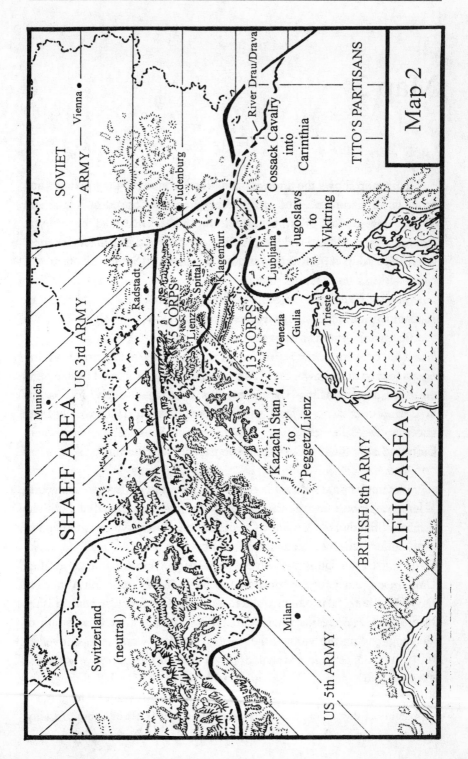

Map 2

Map 3

This map shows the three main settlement areas of the prisoners and refugees in Carinthia. The cross-hatched ellipse centred on Lienz and Spittal, and marked 'KS', represents the Kazachi Stan. Peggetz was outside Lienz. Shkuro and the officers invited to the bogus 'conference' with Field Marshal Alexander were kidnapped at Spittal. Both towns came within 78th Division' area.

The horizontally-lined, tear-drop-shaped area south-west of Judenburg, marked 'CC', represents the 15th Cossack Cavalry, which was camped within 46th Division's area.

The original evacuation plan for the Cossacks, proposed by Alexander to Eisenhower on 17 May, was that they be moved from Spittal north to Radstadt in the SHAEF area, thus 'clearing the decks' for 5 Corps in Carinthia prior to a push south against Tito (which never became necessary). At the same time, SHAEF forces would take over northern Carinthia and relieve 5 Corps of responsibility for guarding prisoners and refugees.

Eisenhower agreed to this on 19 May, but the route was changed to 'Lienz-Vipiteno-Innsbruck'. Despite this, 5 Corps handed both the Kazachi Stan and the Cossack Cavalry to the Soviet Army at the end of May. Judenburg was the handover point.

The third group, the Jugoslavs—in the speckled area marked 'Jugs'—was encamped at Viktring, south of Klagenfurt, in 6th Armoured Division's area. Alexander ordered that most of them be sent to Italy. Instead 5 Corps packed them into railway trucks at stations south of Viktring, giving the victims the impression they were being moved to Italy. Instead, as soon as the doors were locked, the trains were handed over to Tito's men. The people inside were then railed through the Karavanken mountains to Kocevje in southern Slovenia, where many thousands of them were murdered in circumstances of revolting brutality.

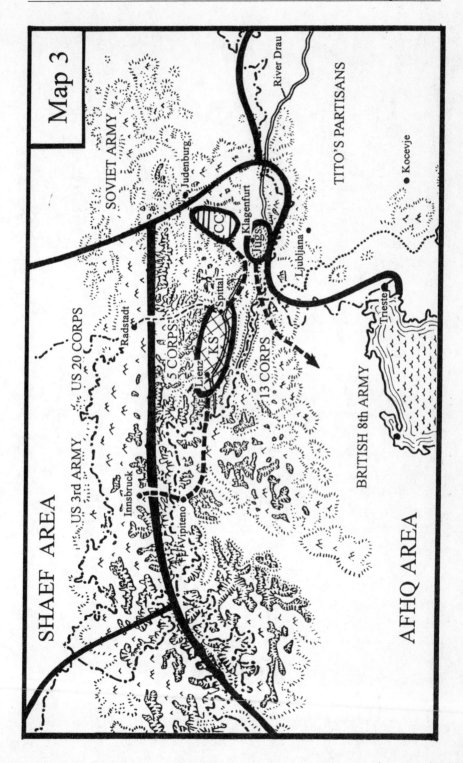

Map 3

SHAEF AREA

US 3rd ARMY

US 20 CORPS

Radstadt

Innsbruck

Vipiteno

Lienz

5 CORPS

KS

Spittal

CC

Judenburg

SOVIET ARMY

Klagenfurt

Jugs

13 CORPS

River Drau

Ljubljana

TITO'S PARTISANS

Kocevje

Trieste

BRITISH 8th ARMY

AFHQ AREA

Part I

The

HISTORY

'No Brigadier in the British Army could conceivably
have undertaken what Lord Aldington is accused of
doing.'

> —James Sabben-Clare
> Winchester College, 1987

1

The COSSACKS

A T THE TIME of the German surrender, on 8 May 1945, the western Allies had not yet crossed from Italy into Austria. The Soviet Army had already pushed past Vienna and were threatening to occupy the whole of Austria. On the day resistance formally ceased, elements of the British 8th Army crossed the mountains into the province of Carinthia (Kärnten) and raced east to Klagenfurt, the provincial capital. They beat the Soviets to it, but not Tito's Partisans. The British found small detachments trying to seize key installations. The Communists managed to occupy a printing works, but the British denied them the airfield. It was a close-run thing.

Carinthia was seething with refugees, prisoners of war and retreating troops, both of the defeated German Army and of the various Jugoslav anti-communist forces which had succeeded in escaping, often with their womenfolk and their children. Southern Austria was one of the largest areas still under German control at the time of the surrender (see Map 3). The Intelligence Officer of the 1st Guards Brigade, one of the first British units to enter Austria, Captain Nigel Nicolson, described the region at the time as 'the sump of Europe'.

> There seemed to be no limit to the number of nationalities which appealed to us for our protection. The Germans wanted to be safeguarded against the Tits [Titoists], the Cossacks against the Bulgarians, the Chetniks against the Croats, the White Russians against the Red Russians, the Austrians against the Slovenes, the Hungarians against everyone else and vice versa throughout the list. [1]

This presented a serious administrative problem to the arriving British. There were hundreds of thousands of these people, while 5 Corps, the 8th Army unit assigned to the occupation of southern Austria, mustered only 25,000 men at the time. The British problems were rendered more delicate by the fact that the Soviet Army had advanced a hundred miles beyond the agreed demarcation line between them and the western Allies. In the event no attempt was made to move the Russians back, only to limit their further advance. Within days, cordial relations had been established between the two commanders who faced each other.

The British task was eased by the fact that Carinthia had not seen any fighting and was largely untouched by war. Unlike other occupation zones in western Europe, food supplies were adequate. Not only was Carinthia a largely agricultural province, it had until a week before served as the supply base for the German campaign in northern Italy. The roads, railways and other public services were functioning almost normally. The only recorded emergency intervention by the British Army was the *demolition* of a length of railway track in order to impede a possible advance by Titoist Partisans.

Morale in the British Army was high. 'We were all young, supremely fit and confident and exhilarated by our victory,' Nicolson recorded. 'There had been very few battle casualties since we crossed the Po. We had entered one of the loveliest regions of Europe.' Generally speaking, the Austrian people received the British Army as liberators rather than as conquerors. 'We played cricket, rode horses, ran steeplechases, fished, swam, sailed,' another officer has said. 'There was no shortage of food for anyone.'[2] A Rifle Brigade Major spent time looking for a suitable cricket ground and 5 Corps' commanding General, Charles Keightley, took his Chief of Staff, Brigadier Toby Low, later Lord Aldington, sailing on the Wörthersee, a large lake on the north bank of which they had established Corps headquarters.

But Keightley and Low did have two serious problems to deal with, one caused by Stalin and the other by Tito. The latter was the more serious: Tito was claiming Carinthia as part of a Greater Jugoslavia. But the former was the more urgent: the Soviet Army wanted the British to

1   Nicolson *Operations of 1st Guards Brigade in Northern Italy and Southern Austria, April-May 1945* p. 20. See also Map 1

2   Lieut. Philip Brutton, Welsh Guards, letter to the author, 27 September 1993

hand over to them some of the refugees and prisoners of war in their zone. Stalin knew that amongst them was a large number of Cossacks, including some old enemies of his from the Civil War. The two most prominent personalities were Generals Peter Krasnov and Andrei Shkuro. In November 1917 Krasnov had commanded the Cossacks who, at the battle of Pulkovo just outside Petrograd (where St Petersburg airport is now), defeated a much larger force of Red Guards and nearly toppled the infant Soviet regime. Had it not been for a force of sailors from the Kronstadt naval base, the Bolshevik regime might not have survived.

After his defeat, Krasnov surrendered to the Bolsheviks, was given parole, broke it and fled south to the Don country where he was appointed Ataman (headman) of the Don Cossacks. He bartered wheat for rifles with the German Army then in occupation of the neighbouring Ukraine and declared his country independent of Red Russia. His forces and Stalin's crossed swords at the battle of Tsaritsyn (later Stalingrad) when the White Armies of southern Russia almost succeeded in linking up with those of western Siberia. The Volga was the Soviet life-line to the wheat and oil of the Caspian basin, and Stalin was sent personally by Lenin to organise the city's defence. Stalin's mission was successful. Krasnov's campaign ended in failure and in 1920 he went into exile. For many years he occupied himself writing long, romantic novels about Civil War battles. During the Second World War he helped the Germans in their efforts to establish an autonomous, anti-Soviet Cossack political entity in the Don country, but after Stalingrad came the German retreat. The Cossacks had to abandon their territory and Krasnov his dreams.

General Shkuro was an even more colourful character. He had commanded a force of Caucasian horsemen as part of the Volunteer Army in the Civil War to such effect that he had been given the nickname, 'the Wolf of the Kuban'. Shkuro's trademark was a wolf-skin cap, and he organised his headquarters in an armoured train which was decorated on the outside with brightly painted scenes of wolf-packs tearing prey to pieces. His men were all free-booters, living entirely off plunder. But they were so successful that, in the summer of 1919, they took the armament-manufacturing city of Tula, only 250 miles south of Moscow, and caused such panic amongst the Bolshevik leadership that Trotsky was compelled to devote almost the whole offensive strength of the Red Army to driving the Cossacks back south again. For this feat Shkuro was made a Companion of the Bath (CB) by King George V, on the recommendation, it is thought, of Winston Churchill, then Secretary of State for War and the leading proponent of the British intervention in the Russian Civil War.

The Red Army counter-attack was spectacularly successful, partly because the civilian population in the rear had been so mistreated by Shkuro's men that the Whites came to be thought of as being almost as lawless as the Bolsheviks. Within six months Shkuro was in exile. For the next twenty years he moved around western Europe, sometimes helping to organise underground resistance to the Soviet Union, at others leading a troupe of trick riders in a travelling circus.

Even in his hour of victory in 1945, Stalin had forgotten neither Krasnov nor Shkuro. He ordered the Red Army commander in Austria, Marshal Tolbukhin, to get hold of them. On 10 May Keightley had been entertained at Tolbukhin's headquarters where the question of the inter-Allied boundary was discussed inconclusively. Keightley refused to go back the next day himself. 'Too much vodka! Too many toasts!' he said, detailing his Adjutant and Quartermaster, Brigadier Edward Tryon-Wilson, to go in his stead. Tryon-Wilson was given a lavish lunch, preceded by sixteen toasts. As he left, he was handed a list of people who were "wanted" by the Soviet Army. Today, Tryon-Wilson remembers that there were twenty or so names on the list, with half a dozen typed in capital letters. He once told Tolstoy that he thought Shkuro's name was one of those, 'the old boy with the CB', he said. No further details of the list have survived.

Back at 5 Corps headquarters, Keightley's immediate reaction to this demand was to say, 'Over my dead body!' This was entirely in accord with 5 Corps' standing orders at the time. Allied policy on Russian refugees and prisoners of war had been settled at the Yalta Conference on 11 February 1945. Churchill and Roosevelt had committed their armies, in separate but identical agreements, to this principle:

> All Soviet citizens liberated by forces under British [or American] command ... will without delay after their liberation be separated from enemy prisoners of war and will be maintained separately from them ... until they have been handed over to the Soviet authorities.[3]

---

3   For a comprehensive treatment of the causes and consequence of this agreement, see Tolstoy's *Victims of Yalta.*

The problem for 5 Corps was that the Cossacks in southern Austria were not all Soviet citizens. Keightley knew this, having met some of the German officers who commanded the military units. Broadly speaking there were two groups. First, there was the 15th Cossack Cavalry Corps, a regular unit of the German Army which had been raised in 1943 and had fought mainly in Jugoslavia, against both Tito's Partisans and the Soviet Army. The main action against the latter had taken place over Christmas 1944 when they had encountered the Stalin Division which had just crossed the Drava north of Belgrade. The Cossacks drove their enemies, the Soviets, back across the river with heavy casualties in brutal, often hand-to-hand, fighting. As soldiers they had a very high reputation for courage and combat efficiency, marred somewhat by instances of casual brutality off the field of battle. Within days of the German surrender, they had been concentrated in a number of lightly guarded camps in north-east Carinthia, not far from the Soviet front line.

The other group was known as the Kazachi Stan, or Cossack Settlement, a civilian encampment which was quartered mainly at Lienz, sixty miles west of Klagenfurt, on the upper reaches of the Drau River (called the Drava in Jugoslavia). The bulk of these people had retreated with the Germans from the Don and Kuban country after the battle of Stalingrad. The Germans had tried to settle them in Byelo-Russia but, after the defeats of summer 1944, the Cossacks had been forced back on the road again, ending up in northern Italy. There they had successfully defended themselves against Italian Communist partisans. They were armed, but only as a militia, not an army. The majority of them were women, children and men over military age. As far as the British were concerned, whereas the Cossack Cavalry were prisoners of war, the Kazachi Stan were civilian refugees.

The Cossack Cavalry numbered about 25,000, of which about a tenth were German, mainly officers and senior non-commissioned officers.[4] The commander was General Helmuth von Pannwitz, the son of a minor Silesian nobleman. He had known Cossacks from the Russian army in Poland as a boy before the First World War, and he spoke their language. He loved his men, and they returned his affection. He encouraged the observance of their religion—Russian Orthodoxy—and wore Cossack

4   For a fuller description see Newland *Cossacks in the German Army*.

dress on ceremonial occasions. He went on campaign with a personal executioner and a body-guard of thirty fearsome-looking Cossacks who wore long beards, swords and daggers, and dressed in fur caps and buffalo-skin capes. He used them on one occasion to threaten an SS detachment which had come to his headquarters to arrest a German officer rumoured to be 'a quarter-Jew'. Von Pannwitz drew his bodyguard to attention in front of the SS men and said, 'You've got five minutes. If then you are still around, these men will hang you from this tree here.' They weren't.[5]

A high proportion of von Pannwitz's officers were Austrians (many of them anti-Nazi) and most were, like their Russian soldiers, enthusiastic horsemen. They were a proud and colourful unit. One of their German officers has estimated that 5% of the Russians were not Soviet citizens within the terms of the Yalta agreement. Of course, none of the Germans were.

Within the Kazachi Stan, the proportion of non-Soviet Russians was much higher—possibly a third, out of a total of about 20,000. They included Krasnov and Shkuro who had been citizens of the Russian Empire, but who had left their homeland in 1920. Since the Union of Soviet Socialist Republics only came into existence on 1 January 1923, they had never even set foot in it, much less taken its citizenship. They were no more Soviet than Anglo-Irish refugees in 1922 were citizens of Eire after they had fled to England. Many of these non-Soviet Russians had taken Jugoslav nationality after the King of that country, a Serb, had offered the remnants of the White Armies asylum in 1920.

In sum, then, of the 45,000 Cossacks who were eventually handed over to Stalin, probably about 10,000 were not Soviet citizens in terms of

---

5   Apologists for the forced repatriations have often tried to imply that the Cossacks were very much a Nazi unit, and therefore not undeserving of mistreatment. It is true that, as a result of office politics in Berlin, Himmler was given administrative control of the Cossack Cavalry in late 1944, but in the field they were always under Wehrmacht command. They were never part of the Waffen-SS and were not so described by the British in 1945. In fact, being Russian, they were not at all popular with the Nazis. On 27 January 1945, Hitler expressed his view to Göring and Guderian: 'People have got no pride. They'll put any old good-for-nothing into German uniform. I was always against putting the Cossacks into German uniform. They ought to have been given Cossack uniform and badges of rank. Much more romantic... The English let the Indians go around as natives.' (Quoted in Warlimont, *Inside Hitler's Headquarters*, p. 503)

the Yalta agreement. (No exact count was ever made.) Their handover was illegal. It is important to distinguish between this problem and the parallel controversy over Yalta as a whole. That was an agreement to hand over *Soviet* nationals to Stalin. The controversy over 5 Corps' actions in May 1945 relates to the fact that *non*-Soviets were handed over in large numbers with them. There is no disagreement about this, only about the reason why the principles of Yalta were ignored.

5 Corps' standing order, issued by 8th Army headquarters on 13 March, was quite clear.

(a) All Soviet Citizens, civilian or military, whether serving in the German Army or not, will without delay be separated from German PoW and shall be despatched to 373 PoW Camp [in Italy] under the care of a conducting party.

(b) The following definition of a Soviet Citizen is given in order to assist in determining nationality:

Under British law Soviet Citizens are all persons coming from places within the boundaries of the Soviet Union as constituted before the outbreak of the present war. All persons coming from west of such boundaries have Polish or Baltic State nationality unless there is evidence to show in particular cases that they have acquired Soviet citizenship by their own voluntary act. A man who has served in the Soviet Army is not a Soviet Citizen if he comes from territories west of 1939 boundaries of the Soviet Union unless he has acquired Soviet Citizenship.

All persons of undoubted Soviet Citizenship will be repatriated irrespective of their own wishes.

(c) In cases where nationality is in doubt, personnel concerned will be sent to 373 PoW Camp for adjudication.[6]

---

6   Although this was an 8th Army document, sent to 5 Corps, it is noteworthy, in the light of the later controversy, that no copy of this message survives in either the 8th Army or the 5 Corps war diaries. Many other similar documents have gone missing, some being found only in American archives. This one survives in the US National Archives and in a War Office file, WO 204/10449, which was kept out of Court, in the Ministry of Defence, throughout the whole period leading up to the libel trial. It was withdrawn from the Public Record Office on 18 February 1988 and returned on 31 October 1989, thus being available again round about 7 November. By then it was not usable by Tolstoy who had finished giving evidence on 3 November.

Thus 5 Corps' task was simple: they had to screen the Soviet from the non-Soviet personnel. This was what was done, admittedly often in a rough and ready way, in all other theatres. Yet within 5 Corps it was not. Every one of the 45,000 Cossacks, Soviet and non-Soviet alike, barring those who escaped or who were hospitalised during the round-up and handover operations, was delivered to the Red Army in an operation which was, administratively speaking, initiated by an order signed by Brigadier Low. The essence of Tolstoy's charge against Lord Aldington was that this was done contrary to both the Yalta agreement and superior orders. In Court Aldington denied both allegations.

2
The JUGOSLAVS

THE YALTA AGREEMENT covered displaced Soviet citizens only. Tolstoy's other allegation in Court in 1989 was that Lord Aldington had disobeyed superior orders in handing over 25,000 Jugoslav refugees to the victorious guerilla leader, Marshal Tito. The Jugoslavs who fell into 5 Corps' hands in early May 1945 were a more heterogeneous group than the Cossacks, but, like them, were all fiercely anti-communist. Tito wanted them all back: men, women and children. He claimed they would be tried by regular courts, but since his regime was no more than a military junta at that stage, entirely without regular courts, this assurance was valueless. The Jugoslavs themselves were well aware of their likely fate if they fell into the hands of Tito's communist Partisans, which is why they had abandoned their homes and fled to Austria. But, as Allied policy towards each of the groups was not identical, it is necessary to describe briefly the various national groups and military units 5 Corps found itself having to deal with.

After Hitler had invaded and partitioned Jugoslavia in April and May 1941, the main resistance offered came from the Serbs, historic enemies of the Germans and Austrians. After the young King Peter II had fled in rather undignified haste to London, General Drazha Mihailovic, Chief of Staff to the Jugoslav 4th Army in Bosnia, organised groups of Chetniks (an ancient Serbian term, dating from the period of Turkish occupation, for groups of resistance fighters) who harried the Germans, striking at their communications and, whenever possible, their troops. At the time, the Serbs were Britain's only militarily active ally on the Continent.

But German savagery soon put paid to Serbian resistance. The occupation forces announced that they would kill a randomly selected 100 people for every one of their soldiers murdered. This they did. One of the witnesses at the libel trial told how 46 Germans were killed just outside his home town of Kragujevac. The Germans surrounded the town and on 21 and 22 October 1941 shot 5,500 men. This was not an isolated incident. Soon it became apparent to the Serbs, just as it did to the British in the Channel Islands under the German occupation, that resistance unsupported from outside was futile.

This attempt to prevent useless slaughter was for a time defeated by Tito. Under orders from Stalin, he had initially co-operated with the Germans. But after the German invasion of the Soviet Union on 22 June 1941, Tito was ordered to change sides and attack the occupying forces. Tito recognised that he could kill two birds with one stone by doing so: he could inconvenience the invader and help his bid for power in the country at the same time by concentrating his attacks in Serbia, the stronghold of Royalist influence, where hostages would be murdered on a massive scale by the enraged Germans. The inevitable Serbian response was to form a body to drive Tito out of Serbia and therefore save the lives of Serbs. This body was called the Serbian Volunteer Corps (SVC). It was largely successful in its self-appointed task.

Did this kind of activity amount to collaboration or was it legitimate self-defence? It is hard for people who have never had to confront such brutality to judge. But it is possibly legitimate to observe, as it was by one of the witnesses at the trial in 1989, that if none of the British on the Channel Islands who helped round up Jews for "resettlement" were guilty of collaboration, then the Serbs were probably not either. Despite this, they were sneered at by Lord Aldington's Counsel for having weakly submitted to the German will. Members of the SVC had been 'serving in German forces'. Since, as will be seen below, these were the key words on which Lord Aldington based his attempt to justify their handover, this is a point of more than academic significance.

In the northern part of Jugoslavia, the consequences of the German occupation were different. Slovenia was dismembered and Croatia given a puppet Nazi government. Both countries also spawned resistance forces, although in neither did they match the strength or endurance of those in Serbia. Croatia added to the chaos by initiating a policy of ethnic cleansing against the Serbs. Hitler had given Bosnia to Croatia, and with it, a large Serbian population. The Croats declared they would kill a third of them, convert another third from Orthodoxy to Catholicism and expel the remaining third. The instrument for this policy was a para-military police force, run on SS lines, called the Ustache.

The result of all this was that, apart from resistance to the invader, there were two other wars in progress on Jugoslavian territory, Communists against Royalists and Serbs against Croats. Both were given a new impetus by the capture of Italian weaponry in occupied Slovenia and Dalmatia after Italy surrendered to the Allies on 8 September 1943. The Allied position was further complicated by the British government's changing sides, transferring its support from Mihailovic to Tito, but without either telling Mihailovic or immediately withdrawing the British liaison officers who were operating at his headquarters. Thus confusion was added to complexity. Within a year, Churchill realised that Tito was not to be trusted. He later considered this policy switch to have been his greatest misjudgment of the war.

At the end of 1944, the Soviet Army crossed into Jugoslavian territory and it became clear to all anti-communists that if they were not to be caught between Stalin's hammer and Tito's anvil they should move north immediately. They still hoped for British protection if they could break through to Allied lines.

By early May 1945, the exodus was concentrated in Ljubljana, the capital of Slovenia, sixty miles south of the Austrian border. There, too, were the remnants of the German occupying forces in the Balkans, under the overall command of General Löhr, and the local command of Oberst von Seeler. The Germans decided to move north with the idea of crossing the Karavanken mountains by way of the Loibl pass. This would have taken them directly to Klagenfurt, which was still in German hands. Most of the other refugees went with them.

By the time they arrived outside the Carinthian capital, the British were in occupation. From the point of view of the Jugoslavian refugees, this was the best possible outcome. They laid down their arms and allowed themselves to be concentrated in a largely unguarded camp at Viktring, just outside Klagenfurt. The women and children were lodged in a huge monastery which had been used as an armaments factory during the war, while the men camped in fields close by.

The total number of Jugoslavs at Viktring was about 35,000, of whom about 6,000 were in the civilian camp in the monastery. Of the remaining 29,000, approximately 13,000 were Slovenians, most of them members of the Home Guard ('Domobranci'), 4,000 Serbs of the SVC, 8,000 Croats and 4,000 men of a group known as the Russkii Korpus which was largely composed of the Russian Civil War refugees who had been given asylum by the Jugoslav Crown in 1920. Only a small proportion of this formation was Soviet and 5 Corps did not, in the event, include them in the handover scheme. Tolstoy has suggested that the reason might have been that none of them featured on Tryon-Wilson's list of "wanted" men, with the result that the whole group was spared. Since the list has never been found, this remains speculation.

All of the 25,000 people remaining in the military camp, after the Russkii Korpus had been moved, were handed to Tito. Not all of them had been in any of the military formations, indeed some were women and children who had stayed with their menfolk. In his order for their handover, Brigadier Low described all the non-combatants in the main camp as 'camp followers' and ordered that they be delivered to Tito, *pari passu* with the prisoners of war. In Court in 1989 he described this as a 'concession', made to avoid breaking up families.

The handover of the soldiers amongst them was controversial too. Lord Aldington's defence rested on the assertion that they had been 'serving in German forces'. As far as the Serbs were concerned, the SVC resistance to Tito was said to have put them into that category. The logic behind the inclusion of the Croats and Slovenians was that they had marched north from Ljubljana in a column organised by Oberst von Seeler. They had therefore been under German command, even if only for a few days, and therefore had also been 'serving in German forces'. Other arguments were adduced, like the fact that uniforms of the Slovenian Domobranci were made from cloth which came from Holland and therefore must have been given to the tailors by Germans. During the trial a Slovenian Domobranci hat was passed round so that the jury could see that the unfaded colour inside was similar to the sort of colour the Germans might have dyed an equivalent hat.

The reason history still debates the justice of these handovers is that most of the people involved were murdered in circumstances of horrifying brutality almost as soon as they crossed the border.

Not only that, outside 5 Corps' area, similar groups of people who surrendered to the British at much the same time were not handed over. At the beginning of May 1945, the total strength of the SVC in Ljubljana had been 15,000. Only 4,000 marched north into Austria: the other 11,000 marched west to Italy. There they were treated as legitimate refugees and were never handed to Tito. Since both groups surrendered to units of the

British 8th Army—13 Corps in Italy and 5 Corps in Austria—it is relevant that Lord Aldington argued in Court that he had at all times obeyed superior orders. As the main orders on which he relied applied to 13 Corps as much as to 5 Corps, this looks like a breakdown in the command chain. To assess whether this was simply the "fog of war", or deliberate insubordination, as Count Tolstoy alleged, it is necessary to understand the military hierarchy from which the orders and policies emanated.

3

The BRITISH

IN BRITAIN IN 1945, the top of the military hierarchy was the War
Cabinet, which was chaired by the Prime Minister, Winston Churchill.
He had had misgivings when, in the summer of 1944, Anthony Eden,
the Foreign Secretary, had first suggested a policy of forced repatriation
of Soviet citizens who had started falling into British hands as the German
armies retreated. In the long run, it was obviously going to be hard to
resist a policy of sending people back to their countries of origin once the
war had ended, particularly as Britain was anxious for Soviet co-operation
in the repatriation of British prisoners of war liberated by the Soviet Army
from German camps in eastern Europe. But there were humanitarian
objections, particularly as Stalin had specifically forbidden all troops to
allow themselves to be captured alive by the Germans. Their likely fate
on repatriation was dire. Many would surely not want to return home,
and a policy of repatriation could only be successfully conducted if Britain
were prepared to use force against these prisoners of war and refugees.
Churchill was against this. Moreover it was arguably contrary to the
spirit, if not the letter, of the Geneva Conventions on the treatment of
prisoners of war. But in the end Eden got his way, and Stalin got his men.
The agreement was formalised at the Yalta conference in February 1945.
A month later, the Foreign Secretary wrote to his friend the young
Brigadier Low at 5 Corps headquarters in terms which partly explain his
motives: 'Our great problem is the Bear,' Eden said. 'Can he be brought
to co-operate with us? I do not yet know this and on this point much, if
not all, depends.'[1]

Low and Eden had met in the Territorial Army in the 1930s and had corresponded throughout the war in affectionate tones. In March 1945, Eden was lobbying hard to have Brigadier Low selected as a Conservative parliamentary candidate in a safe seat for the election which would be fought immediately after victory in Europe. Low was therefore obligated to him and it is one of the critical, and still unanswered, questions about the forced repatriations whether this letter and any others like it show that the contact between the two men influenced 5 Corps policy.[2] There is only one clue: in 1985, Lord Aldington told Tolstoy that when he had successfully turned the Partisans back he got a personal message of congratulation from Eden. If their contact was that close, and if Low knew co-operation with 'the Bear' was so important, might he not have mentioned this to his Commanding Officer and close friend, General Keightley?

If Churchill's policy on Soviet citizens was what might be called Yalta-with-a-sigh, his policy on non-Soviet citizens was unambiguous: they were in no circumstances to be handed to the Soviets. Similarly with the Jugoslavs. His admiration for, and trust in, Tito had evaporated over the winter of 1944-5, and he now saw him as a land-grabber who had to be resisted for almost the same reasons as Hitler had been. The telegrams between London and Washington during the last two weeks of May make it quite clear that both governments were dead set against handing any of the Royalist Serbs or other anti-Communist Jugoslavs over to Tito. These people were, for convenience, all referred to as Chetniks, although far from all of them were, strictly speaking, describable as such. They were so described to differentiate them easily from the Croats, who the British Foreign Office was happy to hand to Tito. The reason was that they were seen as having collaborated actively with the Germans, not least because they had raised a substantial army which operated in concert with the Axis,

1   15 March 1945, Avon Papers
2   The question is still unanswered as the Trustees of the Avon Papers, Lady Avon, Sir Bryan Cartledge and Sir Nicholas Henderson, refuse to let Tolstoy see the correspondence, which is deposited at Birmingham University. (This author has also been refused access.) Within three working days of Lord Aldington's discovering the identity of the first researcher to disclose any details, that person, Adrian Liddell Hart, was banned from all departments of the University library for life. In a letter to Tolstoy in 1990, Liddell Hart commented on the correspondence: 'In general I was impressed by the intimacy and mutual regard—amounting on Low's side almost to adulation—and the freedom with which they referred to political and military matters given that Low was a subordinate officer while Eden was a member of the War Cabinet.'

often against the Serbs. But to complicate matters, Tito, the biggest thorn in the German side in the Balkans, was actually a Croat. In many of the documents of the time, all non-Tito Jugoslavs were referred to as either dissidents or quislings. The Chetniks (mainly Serbs) were the dissidents while the Croats were the quislings. Both were anti-communist, but only the Chetniks had been actively anti-Nazi.

The Americans objected to repatriating any Jugoslavs at all, Croats or Chetniks, and the British Foreign Office did not press the point. The policy eventually decided upon was that neither dissidents nor quislings should be handed over. But by the time the two governments had agreed this, 5 Corps, as will be seen below, had delivered every one of the 25,000 people in Viktring camp to Tito.

The War Cabinet operated, militarily, through the British Chiefs of Staff committee (COS), which liaised with the American Joint Chiefs of Staff (JCS) through the Joint Staff Mission (JSM), a British body based in Washington. Britain and the United States operated a unified military command through the Combined Chiefs of Staff (CCS). (To make it clearer how these and the inferior layers of the command related to each other, see the accompanying organisational diagram.)

On Germany's western front, there were two separate but equal Allied commands: the Allied Expeditionary Force in northern Europe and the Mediterranean command in southern Europe, the near East and north Africa. General Eisenhower was the Supreme Commander of the former and Field Marshal Alexander the Supreme Commander of the latter. Eisenhower operated from the Supreme Headquarters of the Allied Expeditionary Force, or SHAEF as it was known, and Alexander from Allied Forces Headquarters, or AFHQ. These acronyms will be used throughout. Alexander was referred to as Supreme Allied Commander, Mediterranean, or SACMED.

Field Marshal Sir Harold Alexander (later Earl Alexander of Tunis) was, like the other two best-known British generals in World War II, Bernard Montgomery and Lord Alanbrooke, an Ulsterman. He did not have Montgomery's ruthlessness, aggression or vanity. Neither did he have Brooke's brains or force of personality. Alexander's qualities were those of tact, honesty and human sympathy which earned him the respect of both Winston Churchill and his subordinates, as did his well-justified reputation for physical courage.

He had ended the First World War as a much decorated Brigadier in

UNITED STATES PRESIDENT	BRITISH WAR CABINET

Joint Chiefs of Staff (JCS)	Chiefs of Staff (COS)
(Washington)	*(London)*

Combined Chiefs of Staff (CCS)
(Washington)

Mediterranean	**Europe**
Allied Forces Headquarters	Supreme Headquarters Allied
(AFHQ)	Expeditionary Force (SHAEF)
F. M. Alexander	Gen. Dwight Eisenhower
Supreme Allied Commander,	Supreme Allied Commander,
Mediterranean (SACMED)	Europe (SACEUR)
(Caserta)	*(Rheims)*

Northern Mediterranean	**Other Mediterranean**
15th Army Group	various small forces,
Gen. Clark	e.g. in Greece

North-East	**North-West**
British 8th Army	US 5th Army
Gen. McCreery	Gen. Truscott

Southwestern Austria	**Northeastern Italy**
British 5 Corps	US 2 Corps, Polish 2 Corps,
Gen. Keightley	British 13 Corps

78th Division	6th Armoured Division	46th Division
Gen. Arbuthnott	Gen. Murray	Gen. Weir
Kazachi Stan, Lienz	*Jugoslavs, Viktring*	*Cossack Cavalry, various*

the Irish Guards. Immediately peace was declared he volunteered to go to Latvia as part of the British anti-Bolshevik mission. There he soon found himself in command of the *Landeswehr*, an anti-communist Territorial force officered by Baltic Germans. He liked both the people and the country. He learned to speak Russian and acquired a first-hand knowledge of the complexities of east European political migration, which was to re-surface as a problem in 1945. He was awarded the Baltic Cross of Honour by the Latvian government, and the Tzarist Order of St. Anne with Crossed Swords, by General Yudenich on behalf of the exiled White Russian "government".[3] As a return compliment, he had made for himself in London a cap modelled on the *Landeswehr* style which he wore until he retired from active service in 1945.

Some people have tried to suggest that Alexander turned a blind eye to 5 Corps' disobedience to his orders and was therefore partly responsible for the forced repatriations, or alternatively that he neither knew nor cared about eastern European anti-communists. It is therefore worth quoting his biographer, Nigel Nicolson, on the subject. Nicolson ends his chapter on the Latvian period as follows:

> In later years, Alexander attended several re-union dinners of the *Landeswehr*, and often corresponded with its officers. Then the Second War separated him from them. Many fought again on the German side... He met at least one of them in a prisoner-of-war camp in Italy. When the war was over he received pathetic appeals from survivors among them. Their country was once more destroyed by war, their independence once more lost. Alexander did what he could for them. [Later] as Governor-General of Canada he managed to secure immigration visas for a handful of Balts who had served with him.[4]

At AFHQ, Alexander had two main military assistants and two civil advisers, one of each appointed by the British and the American governments. The British adviser, formally titled British Resident Minister in the Mediterranean, was Harold Macmillan, later to become Prime Minis-

---

3   He wore his St Anne's Cross when he dined with the Soviet commander, Marshal Tolbukhin, who faced his forces in Austria in 1945. It is noteworthy that, 25 years after his Baltic service, he was still able to converse with Tolbukhin in Russian.

4   Nicolson *Alex*, p. 66

ter and the Earl of Stockton. Macmillan's American opposite number was
the plutocratic Alexander Kirk. Kirk combined the job of US Political
Advisor to SACMED with that of Ambassador to Italy. He had served in
the Berlin and Moscow embassies before America entered the war and
had conceived an implacable dislike of totalitarianism in any form. He
was not so clever a man as Macmillan, but neither was he as stupid as
Macmillan seems to have thought him. He was a resolute opponent of
both Stalin and Tito.

Alexander's two principal military assistants were General Sir William Morgan and General Sir Brian Robertson. Morgan was in charge of
the operational side of the headquarters and Robertson the administrative.
Morgan's title was Chief of Staff, and Robertson's Chief Administrative
Officer, or CAO. Morgan does not feature largely in this story, but
Robertson does. In his memoirs, Macmillan described him as 'the most
efficient "Q" officer since Marlborough's Cadogan'. His role in the
forced repatriations assumed particular importance because he took much
of the administrative burden from Alexander, who was notorious for his
dislike of paperwork.

Robertson's father was a self-made Scotsman of great distinction who
was the first ex-private soldier ever to be admitted to the Army Staff
College at Camberley. He went on to become the Chief of the Imperial
General Staff (CIGS) in the latter stages of the First World War. His son
seems to have inherited many of his qualities and went on to succeed
Sholto Douglas as military governor of the British zone in Germany. He
ended his career as Commander-in-Chief of Middle Eastern Land Forces.
He never was appointed Chief of the Imperial General Staff, as he wanted,
being vetoed by Field Marshal Montgomery on the ground that he was
known in the Army as a 'political General... He is first class at diplomacy
and political intrigue and is known in the Army as a political General.'[5]

Alexander's command comprehended all territories west of the Le-
vant, although the only one in which active fighting was in progress after
the German surrender was Greece, where Communist forces were attempting a *coup d'état*. By far the most important part of Alexander's
area of command was northern Italy and its extension, southern Austria,
all of which was the responsibility of 15th Army Group, commanded by

5   Quoted by Hamilton in *Monty: the Field Marshal*, p. 818

the American General Wayne Clark. (He preferred to be known as Mark Clark.) Clark's Army Group comprised two armies: the US 5th Army which occupied north-western Italy and the British 8th Army, which occupied north-eastern Italy and southern Austria. This was the formation which Montgomery had made famous in the western desert, and it was now commanded by General Sir Richard McCreery, a gangling Old Etonian of Irish Catholic stock. McCreery was an enthusiastic horseman who had become an armoured warfare expert and was highly thought of by Alexander, although not by Montgomery who considered him an 'amateur'. As to the question of whether 5 Corps was able to deceive 8th Army about its handover activities, it is perhaps relevant to note that McCreery's predecessor as Chief of Staff to the C-in-C, Middle Eastern Command, Brigadier Eric Dorman-Smith, called him variously 'a dolt', '"Dreary" McCreery' and 'the stupidest man in the Middle East'.[6]

In May 1945, 8th Army was organised into four Corps, three of which (12 US Corps, 2 Polish Corps and the British 13 Corps) occupied north-east Italy, and one, 5 Corps, southern Austria.

5 Corps was commanded by Lieutenant-General Charles Keightley. Keightley was not universally liked by his officers. General Murray of 6th Armoured Division, part of 5 Corps, described him many years later as 'very difficult'. 'I didn't get on with him at all,' Murray said. 'He thought that we as soldiers should carry out implicitly and without question any political order that came our way.'[7] General Sir James Wilson, one of Lord Aldington's witnesses at the trial, and in 1945 a Major in the Rifle Brigade at Klagenfurt, was not impressed by him either. He thought he was neither a particularly good general nor a particularly popular man. He was personally ambitious, Sir James thought, and more concerned with his superiors' opinion of himself than with the welfare of his subordinates.[8] Despite this, Keightley had a splendid war. At the time of his appointment as Lieutenant-General he was the youngest officer of that rank in the Army, and was younger than all three Major-Generals who commanded the Divisions which made up 5 Corps. He was very much a front-line soldier, on one occasion in Italy having his binoculars shot out

6   Quoted by Greacen in *Chink*, pp. 101, 194, 244
7   Imperial War Museum, Dept. Sound Records, tape 6208/2: General Murray
8   Interview with Tolstoy 30 July 1985, quoted in Court in 1989

of his hand.

After a spell in post-war Whitehall at the Ministry of Defence, Keightley was promoted further, finally succeeding Robertson as Commander-in-Chief of Middle Eastern Land Forces. There he planned and commanded the invasion of Suez in 1956, displaying the same lack of concern with the fate of civilians caught in a military cross-fire which he has been accused of in connection with the forced repatriations eleven years earlier. He wanted to open hostilities with a surprise naval bombardment of Alexandria which, given the density of population in that city, would have caused a bloodbath. It was only because of Mountbatten's objections that the focus of the attack was switched to the smaller and more open town of Port Said. Long before this, he had already acquired two unflattering nicknames, 'the smiling snake' and 'killer Keightley'.

Brigadier Austin Richard William ("Toby") Low was Keightley's Chief of Staff. Officially he was styled Brigadier General Staff, or BGS. The two men worked extremely well together, and remained close friends long after the war. Born on 25 May 1914, Low was educated at Winchester and New College, Oxford, where he read law. After leaving university he became a libel barrister and, in his spare time, joined the Territorial Army, where he met Anthony Eden. His regiment was the 12th London Regiment, part of the King's Royal Rifle Corps (in which Eden had served in World War I), which was based in Winchester.

In early 1939, Low was called away from the Bar to help administer the rapid expansion of the Territorial Army. He was embodied on 2 September and a year later promoted Major and sent out to the Middle East. He served in Greece, winning the DSO during the chaotic retreat south after the German invasion. He estimated that his own company, assisted by an Australian one, had killed '400 to 500 Germans' on Easter Sunday during their ultimately unsuccessful attempt to hold the Edhessa Pass near Salonika. Back in Egypt, Low's Battalion, the 9th, took part in the battle of Gazala during which, on 26 May 1941, he was briefly captured. But battle conditions were fluid enough that during a counter attack by elements of the South African Division, he was able to commandeer a truck and drive back to the Allied lines.

Shortly after that he was extracted from the front line and sent on a staff course. Three years and two promotions later he was the second-youngest Brigadier in the British Army. One study of the British Army in the later stages of the Italian campaign, singles out one of Low's soldierly qualities for special praise: 'No-one better appreciated the importance of strict camouflage discipline.'[9]

Low and Keightley co-operated very closely. The young barrister-Brigadier was very much the philistine General's amanuensis, as well as being his confidant and friend. Since the repatriations were conducted by troops under the command of the General but on orders drafted and signed by the Brigadier, this throws light on the issue of relative responsibility. On 13 June 1945, after learning that Low was leaving 5 Corps for good, Keightley wrote him a letter of thanks for his help. He called him 'the best Chief of Staff any commander ever had', and said, 'You played such a big part in our recent victories I can only say for an absolute certainty we should not have won our battles if I had anybody else. Thank you a thousand times for your wonderful patience, cheerfulness, hard work and efficiency.'[10]

While Low reported to Keightley on battle matters, the third man in the 5 Corps triumvirate, Brigadier Edward Tryon, looked after logistics. As "Teddy" Tryon-Wilson (as he now calls himself; the current name will be used below), he was to give evidence on Lord Aldington's behalf at the libel trial. During the repatriations, one of his duties had been to organise all the transport which conveyed the victims of 5 Corps to the Soviets and the Titoists.

5 Corps comprised three Divisions, 46th, 78th and 6th Armoured. 46th Infantry Division was commanded by a New Zealander, Major-General Cyril Weir, and was stationed in the north east of Carinthia. Within its boundaries most of the Cossack Cavalry Corps were camped after their surrender. 78th Infantry Division was commanded by Major-General Robert Arbuthnott and occupied western Carinthia, including Lienz where the members of the Kazachi Stan were quartered. Finally, 6th Armoured Division, commanded by Major-General Horatius Murray, and including 1st Guards Brigade, stood in the centre, linking the two. Viktring camp was in 6th Armoured Division's area.

To summarize: Arbuthnott (78th Div), Murray (6th Armoured Div) and Weir (46th Div) reported to Keightley at 5 Corps HQ, where he was assisted by Low (operations) and Tryon-Wilson (logistics). Keightley

9   Blaxland *Alexander's Generals*, p. 81
10   Richard Keightley's papers

reported to McCreery at 8th Army, who in turn reported to General Mark Clark at 15th Army Group, who in turn reported to Field Marshal Alexander at Allied Forces Headquarters, or AFHQ, at Caserta.

To the north of Alexander's area was Eisenhower's command, at SHAEF, which took in all of northern Europe. 5 Corps was on this boundary. Since it was Alexander's plan to rescue the Cossacks from handover to the Soviets by moving them north of this boundary into the SHAEF area, this is a fact of great significance to this story. His plan for saving the Jugoslav refugees from Tito was to move them south-west to Italy. 5 Corps frustrated both plans.

There are two Army orders which were central to the controversy which culminated in the libel trial in 1989. They initiated the handovers of both groups and both were signed by Brigadier Low. The first, issued on 17 May, dealt with the Jugoslavs. Since it ordered that those to be handed over be kept in ignorance of that fact, it has come to be known as the Deception Order. The other one, issued on 21 May, dealt with the Cossacks. Since it in effect defined various groups as Soviet for the purposes of handover, even though large numbers of them were not, it has become known as the Definition Order. As the Jugoslavs were despatched first, it is appropriate to start by considering the context and consequences of the Deception Order.

4

The DECEPTION ORDER

THE OVER-RIDING military problem for the Allies in south-central Europe in May 1945 was containment of Tito. This was the second of the two difficulties 5 Corps faced on arrival in southern Austria. It was a much more serious one than the Soviet request for the twenty elderly White Generals. Tito claimed the Italian province of Venezia Giulia as he did Carinthia. Until 1918, both, like the northern half of what became Jugoslavia, had been part of the Austro-Hungarian Empire. Both provinces had Slovenian minorities, although in the case of Carinthia it was a tiny one. In Venezia Giulia the Slovenian population was much larger. But the main prize for Tito was the port of Trieste. While the attempt to grab Carinthia was half-hearted, the lunge for Trieste was much more serious.

The attitude of the western Allies was initially ambiguous, but within days it had hardened into determined resistance. Shortly after Victory in Europe (VE) Day, Alexander was ordered to prevent Tito's forces seizing any more territory, and at the same time to make plans to eject them from all areas they had occupied outside the 1939 Jugoslavian frontiers. Territorial redistribution was to be a matter for the peace conference table. Tito threatened and blustered, but he was well aware of the disparity between the forces at his disposal and those of the Supreme Allied Commander, Mediterranean. Tito's only hope was that Stalin would back him with arms as well as words. For a couple of days, the Kremlin presented its enigmatic face. Then it decided for peace. Soon afterwards Tito's forces turned for home, and the crisis was over.

In Carinthia, the retreat started on 19 May. This was the day after 5

Corps delivered the first train-load of Croats to Tito. The handovers lasted until the end of the month. But from 20 May onwards, they had no possible justification in *realpolitik*, at least if that meant placating Tito with a blood-sacrifice, as has been claimed by some apologists for the repatriations. This is not Lord Aldington's case: he maintains that 5 Corps' actions were entirely legitimate within the terms of the orders which came down from AFHQ.

Brigadier Low's order for the handovers, issued on 17 May, had its origin in a request Keightley made on 10 May for permission to use force against the Titoist Partisans who were infiltrating Carinthia and treating the British military occupation authorities with contempt. 'It is now quite clear that I must be able to shoot at [Partisans] who categorically disobey orders from British commanders,' Keightley signalled McCreery at 8th Army.[1] McCreery passed this request up to Alexander at AFHQ who replied immediately that permission was *not* granted, since the political situation was very delicate. Nothing must be done which might provoke the Titoists. Alexander was unsure of morale in his multi-national force were he to embark on a war against Tito just a few days after finishing a very lengthy one against Hitler. Alexander said he would send Harold Macmillan, his political advisor, up to 8th Army to put McCreery in the diplomatic picture.

Macmillan flew north on 12 May and talked to McCreery at some length. The General saw the point but felt that Keightley should have a similar briefing. Accordingly, Macmillan flew to Klagenfurt the next day. It was at that meeting, on 13 May, that what Tolstoy has called the 'Klagenfurt conspiracy' was alleged to have been hatched.

Keightley and Macmillan talked for two hours about both Cossack and Jugoslav matters. It is not known if Brigadier Low was present. Macmillan records having met Keightley's staff, but gives no names. Before Tolstoy published his allegations about him, Lord Aldington maintained he could not remember whether or not he had been present; after publication he remembered clearly that he had not been.

The only contemporary record of the meeting is Macmillan's diary which, as far as the Jugoslavs are concerned (the Cossacks will be dealt with in Chapter 5), does no more than mention the different groups who

---

1   FO 1020/42, the 'lost' file. This signal has disappeared from all British military files.

were represented in the camp at Viktring.[2]

The following day Macmillan was back in Naples. That evening, General Robertson, Alexander's Chief Administrative Officer, issued an order which, according to Lord Aldington, gave authority for the handovers. For convenience, it will be referred to as the Robertson Order. The paragraph dealing with Jugoslavs reads as follows:

> All surrendered personnel of established Jugoslav nationality who were serving in German Forces should be disarmed and handed over to local Jugoslav forces.[3]

The key question is, what did Robertson mean by 'surrendered personnel ... who were serving in German Forces'? Since Lord Aldington maintained in Court that he had entire authority to hand over the whole Viktring camp to Tito—soldiers and civilians; men, women and children—on the basis of Robertson's wording, this is a question of fundamental importance to this story.

There are three possibilities. The first is that Robertson meant troops of the Croat Army, a force under almost direct German command but which was not as yet in Jugoslavia. It was known on 14 May that a column of 200,000 Croat soldiers ('quislings'), plus unknown but probably larger numbers of civilians, was advancing on Carinthia at that time from the south-east hoping to avoid the wrath of Tito by surrendering to the British. In the signals which Robertson was responding to when he composed his order, it was this column which was described as threatening the orderly British occupation of southern Austria. It is hard to imagine that his order was anything other than a response to this very obvious threat. In the event, the Croat Army was turned back at the border, near a town called Bleiburg, by a small force of the Royal Irish Fusiliers, on the following day, 15 May.

The second, and most likely, possibility is that Robertson meant all the people above plus those Croats who were already camped at Viktring. There were 13,000 of the latter, though far from all of them had been

---

2   See Macmillan *The War Diaries: the Mediterranean*, pp. 756-8
3   WO 170/4184. This is the 8th Army war diary; the signal has disappeared from the 5 Corps war diary. A copy exists in FO 1020/42, the 'lost' file.

'serving in German Forces'. In fact very few had, though some had served in Croat paramilitary forces such as the Gestapo-like Ustache.

The final possibility is the least likely, namely that Robertson meant all 25,000 Jugoslavs in Viktring, Croat or Chetnik, "quisling" or "dissident". In this view he would have meant the term 'surrendered personnel' to cover refugees as well as prisoners of war. Not only that, these people had all laid down their arms. Why would Robertson—'the most efficient "Q" officer since Marlborough's Cadogan'—order the disarming of people who had already been disarmed, not to mention those who had never borne arms in the first place, like the women and children?

The implausibility of this view is reinforced by the record of a conversation between Robertson and Alexander Kirk on 14 May. Kirk telegraphed the State Department in Washington that night as follows:

> This afternoon General Robertson requested us to concur in a draft telegram to CG British 8th Army ... instructing him to turn over to Jugoslav Partisans a large number of dissident Jugoslav troops *with the exception of Chetniks*... We asked General Robertson what definition he proposed to give to 'Chetniks' and he was very vague on this point. We then stated that we could not concur without referring the matter to our government. [Robertson] expressed disappointment ... but added that he was faced with a grave administrative problem with *hundreds of thousands of German POWs* on his hands and could not bother at this time about who might or might not be turned over to the Russians and Partisans and shot. (emphasis added)[4]

This surely implies, first, that Robertson had no intention of handing over anti-communist Chetniks to Tito and, secondly, that the people he had positively in mind were 'German POWs', a term which could be stretched to cover the Croat Army, and possibly the Ustache, but certainly not women and children and other civilians, even if they were Croat.

In Court in 1989, Lord Aldington had to defend the fact that he had ordered the handover of soldiers and civilians, both Croat and Chetnik. In doing so, he argued that because the whole group of people in Viktring had fled from Jugoslavia into Austria at the same time as, and in part

---

4   Quoted in Cowgill *Final Report*, p. 105, taken from US National Archives, Diplomatic State Dept. Control Italy

briefly under the command of, General von Seeler's retreating German troops, they had therefore been 'serving in German forces' and as such qualified for repatriation under the terms of Robertson's order.[5] Brigadier Low's order reads, in full, as follows:

> All Jugoslav nationals at present in Corps area will be handed over to Tito forces as soon as possible.
>
> These forces will be disarmed immediately but will NOT be told of their destination.[emphasis in original]
>
> Arrangements for the handover will be coordinated by this HQ in conjunction with Jugoslav forces.
>
> Handover will last over a period owing to difficulties of Jugoslav acceptance.
>
> Formations will be responsible for escorting personnel to a selected point notified by this HQ where they will be taken over by Tito forces.
>
> [signed] ARW Low, BGS.[6]

For an experienced lawyer, as Low was, there was a surprising ambiguity about this order. 'Jugoslav nationals', a term which embraces civilians, seemed to be used synonymously with 'these forces', a term which excludes them. Presumably questions were asked because, on the next day, Low issued a clarificatory rider to the effect that 'Jugoslav nationals will in this context comprise all non-Tito soldiers of Jugoslav nationality and such civilians of Jugoslav nationality as can be classed as their camp followers. The signal does not apply to Jugoslav civilians other than camp followers.'[7]

---

5   Some historians—Alistair Horne and Nigel Nicolson are amongst them—have suggested that the responsibility should be laid at Field Marshal Alexander's door since he knew about this order. The only evidence that he did is the fact that the order is 'Signed: SACMED'. This almost certainly refers to Alexander's office, since there are many messages in the files 'Signed: Alexander', and may well mean that he did not personally see the order. (There is no argument that it was composed and dispatched by General Robertson.) Alexander is known to have accepted that the Croat Army should not be allowed into Carinthia. Thus he would have understood Robertson to have meant the first of the three alternatives described above, or possibly the second, but certainly not the third. Later evidence of his attitude, as will be seen below, strongly confirms this view.

6   WO 170/4241

7   WO 170/4243

In retrospect this is odd on two grounds. The less important one, since the result was that the lives of the people concerned were spared, was that the Russkii Korpus were certainly describable as 'non-Tito soldiers of Jugoslav nationality'. They had been in Viktring until 16 May, and were still, at the time Low's order was issued, within 5 Corps' area, yet they were not handed back.

The more significant oddity was the apparent extension of Robertson's category to include 'camp followers'. Robertson had ordered the handover of those 'serving in German forces'; he had made no mention of camp followers. In Court in 1989 it was argued that the term was so vague that Robertson could have been thought to have intended this extension. This is not true. The term "camp followers" is precisely defined in British military law.

> It is expressly enacted that followers of armies—such as newspaper correspondents, reporters, sutlers [i.e. merchants], and contractors—who are captured and retained, can claim to be treated as prisoners of war, provided they can produce a certificate from the military authorities of the army they are accompanying.[8]

This definition is derived from that contained in the 1929 Geneva Convention, which was operative in 1945. Article 81 is the only one under the heading 'Application of the Convention to Certain Categories of Civilians'. In full, it reads:

> Persons who follow the armed forces without directly belonging thereto, such as correspondents, newspaper reporters, sutlers [i.e. merchants], or contractors, who fall into the hands of the enemy and whom the latter think fit to detain, shall be entitled to be treated as prisoners of war, provided they are in possession of an authorization from the military authorities of the armed forces which they are following.[9]

8   *Manual of Military Law 1929*, p. 282. Col. Vowles of the Directorate of Army Legal Services confirmed to this author (letter, 10 October 1994) that this edition (7th) of the *Manual* would have been the one current in 1945.

9   H.M.S.O. Cmd. 3941, 1931. It is hardly necessary to point out that the purpose of allowing these categories of people this level of protection was to *save* them from mistreatment rather than to permit their despatch to vengeful enemies.

There is an absolute contradiction between this wording and Robertson's term, 'serving in German Forces'. The whole point of both definitions is that the people involved are *not* serving in any forces. In Court in 1989 neither side introduced the *Manual of Military Law*, and evidence about the Geneva Convention was, as will be seen below, rendered inadmissible due to a technical argument about the status of the pleadings. Consequently, the only description of this term which the jury were given came from Brigadier Tryon-Wilson, who turned out to be ludicrously misinformed. He did admit that his only experience of camp followers came from his experience in the Indian Army in the 1930s. There, he told the Court, 'bearers' and 'cleaners' were considered camp followers. Initially he made no mention of women and children, so the Judge pressed him specifically. He then said they would also have been categorised in that way. Thus the Court was misled into thinking that the handover of women and children, and other non-combatants, with the Jugoslav soldiers was quite consistent with British and international military law. Since the allegation which Tolstoy was trying to justify was that the Plaintiff was a war criminal, this was a crippling handicap.

If neither military law nor the Robertson Order appear to have sanctioned the handover of the precise categories of people which Low's order covered, who is known to have wanted the people his order covered handed over? The uncomfortable answer is Tito. On 15 May, two days before promulgating the Deception Order, Low had met a Tito representative, Colonel Hocevar, with the purpose of co-ordinating the activities of the two armies. Hocevar had asked Low, amongst other things, for joint control of all camps where Jugoslavs were quartered. This was out of the question, and Low refused it. Since the people in the camps were violently anti-communist, and the camps were almost entirely unguarded, the arrival of communist guards would have resulted in either a mass breakout or a massacre. But Low did make one important concession: 'I agreed,' he minuted on 15 May, 'that we would, as soon as possible, send into Jugoslavia all the Croats (*sic*) in our area.'[10] How the uncontroversial proposal to return Croats—presuming he meant troops only—to Jugoslavia was translated into a plan to despatch every human being in Viktring camp has never been established. But on 17 May it was so translated, at the moment Brigadier Low signed the Deception Order.

The people to whom this order applied were, as Low ordered, kept in ignorance of their destination. Most believed that they would be sent to Italy. In the case of the Serbs, this was logical since the bulk of the SVC was already there. Moreover, that was where Alexander himself was shortly to order they be sent. Unaware of Low's scheme, they climbed on board Tryon-Wilson's trains with hope rather than fear in their hearts. Today Lord Aldington says that some British officers did explicitly tell the Jugoslavs that the trains would take them to Italy, but he denies having played any part in spreading that rumour, blaming his subordinates instead. 'The order [to keep quiet about the destination] was translated down the line into a statement to the Jugoslavs that they were going to Italy,' he told an audience at Winchester College in 1985.[11] He stood by that account in court. When asked why he had ordered that their real destination be kept from them, he said, 'If they do not know where they are going, they are more likely to get into the transport presented to them.'

Once inside the boxcars, the doors were locked. By this means, 25,000 Jugoslavs were kidnapped under trust.[12]

Within hours of Low's issuing his rider to the Deception Order, Alexander ordered the exact opposite. He wanted all 'Chetniks and dissident Jugoslavs' to be 'evacuated to British concentration area in Distone.' The term "Distone" was a contraction of "District One", an administrative district behind the lines in Italy. Because of the use of that term, this instruction has come to be known as the Distone Order.[13] Alexander noted that there

11 In 1990, shortly after the trial, Tolstoy finally tracked Hocevar down and interviewed him. (He has since died.) His memory was that 'he [Toby Low] told me that they [the British] would tell the prisoners of war, Jugoslavs, that they were going to be transported, transferred, to Italy.' 'This was Toby Low?' Tolstoy repeated. 'Toby Low,' Hocevar replied.

12 If they are considered to have been prisoners of war, then this act was another breach of the Geneva Convention, the aim of which is to minimise conflict by removing the fear of surrender. Prisoners must be kept safe from their enemies, not delivered to them, and if they are to be moved they must, under Article 26, be informed of their destination before departure. If they are to be thought of as having been refugees, then kidnapping is obviously illegal.

13 This signal has disappeared from the 5 Corps war diary though it is now accepted by the main apologist for the repatriations, Brigadier Cowgill, to have been sent to 5 Corps (see pp. 383-4). It can be found only in the Kirk Papers in the US National Archives and in the 'lost' file, FO 1020/42.

were 11,000 Jugoslavs already in Distone—this was the SVC contingent which had marched west rather than north—and said the balance to be moved would be about 24,000, almost exactly the total number in Viktring at the time, Chetniks *and* Croats (but excluding the Russkii Korpus, which had already been saved). The Robertson Order was now a dead letter.

The new instruction emphasised that the final destination of all these people was to be decided at government level. This was entirely in accord with War Cabinet policy which was already clear that none of these people were to be handed to Tito. The only decision yet to be taken was where they were to go. On 29 April, Churchill had given instructions that anti-Tito forces were to 'be disarmed and placed in refugee camps'. Alexander had repeated this for the armies in Italy and Austria on 2 May. 'Following surrender or after hostilities cease, [anti-Tito Jugoslavs] will be treated as disarmed hostile troops pending discharge to be administered and maintained by themselves as far as possible... Ultimate disposal will be decided on Governmental levels.'[14]

The next day, 8th Army passed this order down to 5 Corps as part of a broader instruction on the treatment of Prisoners of War and Surrendered Enemy Personnel: 'Chetniks, troops of Mihailovic and other dissident Jugoslavs, and any Italian adherents will be regarded as surrendered personnel and will be treated accordingly. The ultimate disposal of these people will be decided at Government levels.'[15]

This order does not mention Croats. It was the last order 5 Corps received in connection with the treatment of Jugoslavs before the arrival of the Robertson Order on the morning of 15 May. The text reinforces the view that Robertson intended only Croats be handed over to Tito. Of course, the Distone Order, coming from the Field Marshal on 17 May, should have removed any remaining doubt. *No* Chetniks were to be repatriated.

At about the same time as 5 Corps received the Distone Order, it received notice of another order, from 15th Army Group to 8th Army, forbidding any arrangements with the Titoists. 'Pending the outcome of present governmental negotiations with Jugoslavs you will avoid entering

14   WO 204/621. Since it was sent for information to 8th Army, it is noteworthy that it has disappeared from the 8th Army war diary.
15   WO 170/4182. This signal has disappeared from the 5 Corps war diary.

into any signed agreements with Jugoslav commanders.'[16] Since Lord Aldington's plea in Court was that he was at all times obeying orders, it is highly relevant that two days after 5 Corps received this signal, he himself, as Brigadier Low, made a signed agreement with a Jugoslav commander, Colonel Ivanovich, a colleague of Hocevar's. This committed 5 Corps to the delivery of all Jugoslavs, Croat and Chetnik alike, to Tito and must represent *prima facie* an act of serious insubordination.

On the day both the Deception and Distone Orders were issued, Alexander signalled London for urgent instructions on final disposal of both the Jugoslavs and the Cossacks because 'to return them to their country of origin immediately might be fatal to their health.' As noted above, Robertson admitted to Kirk that some of the victims might be shot after being handed over. More junior officers in 5 Corps talked after the deliveries had begun of Jugoslavs being 'en route for the slaughterhouse'. The Jugoslavs had trekked into Carinthia out of fear, as Low must have realised. Certainly he knew it would be easier to move them if he avoided letting them know the truth about their destination.

It is also worth remarking that the evening Low made his 'signed agreement' with Colonel Ivanovich, he and Keightley celebrated by giving Ivanovich dinner. 'Relations most cordial throughout,' Keightley signalled McCreery that evening by way of report. His signal describes their conversation but makes no mention whatever of the agreement Low had just signed. It took effect without 8th Army being aware of its terms.

In Court Lord Aldington denied that 8th Army had been kept in the dark. Tolstoy's Counsel questioned this. 'There is no document saying: "We are going to hand over Serbs and Slovenes and their camp followers", specifically, is there?' he asked.

Lord Aldington could only reply with bluster. 'No, and there's no document saying: "We're not", either... They're not fools in 8th Army Headquarters. They're not living on the planet of Mars. They're part of a combined team dealing with great military problems, and we knew what was in one's mind, and the idea that they didn't know what we were doing is really too ridiculous to contemplate.'

---

16 Since this signal was sent to 8th Army, and repeated by 8th Army to '5 Corps for Gen. Keightley', it is noteworthy that both have disappeared from both the respective war diaries. They survive only in the 'lost' file FO 1020/42, and were therefore not in Court in 1989. Their omission was surely of critical importance.

At 1st Guards Brigade headquarters, Captain Nicolson discovered that the truth about what was happening was something which his senior officers wanted to conceal immediately the handovers had started. On 18 May, the day the first Jugoslav 'consignment' was entrained near Viktring, Nicolson wrote, quite truthfully, in his daily situation report:

> The Croats have been given no warning of their fate, and are being allowed to believe that their destination is not Jugoslavia but Italy until the actual moment of their handover. The whole business is most unsavoury, and British troops have the utmost distaste in carrying out their orders.[17]

Having put this on the record, Nicolson was hauled up before a senior officer at Divisional Headquarters—he no longer remembers whom—and told that he should never have reported anything like that in a public document, and that the next day he was to 'correct' it. Weakly, as he now admits, he accepted this reprimand and the next day "recorded" that the Croats were 'kindly and efficiently handled [by the Titoists] and provided with light refreshments before continuing their journey into Jugoslavia.'[18] This was a downright lie, and one of the reasons Nicolson came to court to give evidence in 1989 was to make that point publicly. He said from the witness stand what he had wanted to say ever since that day in 1945, namely that the handovers were 'one of the most disgraceful operations British troops had ever been ordered to undertake'. Nonetheless, it is significant that within forty-eight hours of Low having issued his order, the British cover-up had begun.

On the night Low and Keightley entertained Ivanovich, a message was sent from the British Joint Staff Mission in Washington to the Chiefs of Staff in London reporting Washington's views about the situation in southern Austria.

> Chetniks should be disarmed and placed in refugee camps... [and] it would be wrong to hand Croats over to Jugoslav government until relations with that government are clearer. We suggest that in the meantime Croats should continue to be treated as prisoners of war.[19]

17   WO 170/4404
18   *Ibid.*

The reality was very different. It was described by one of the few people who escaped after being delivered to the Jugoslavs by the British. Joro Miletic, one of Tolstoy's witnesses at the trial in 1989, described in a pre-trial witness statement his reaction to the realisation that he had been kidnapped under trust.

> I felt completely stunned, amazed as if someone had told me I had come to the end of my life. I felt disgusted. My feeling was indescribable. The occasion was traumatic for me. We had fought so many battles and now we had been left without even a pen-knife... It haunts me even now to think of this and I know it will to the end of my life. In telling this I could cry at any time. There was a feeling inside the truck that we were all very close to the end of our lives. There was an intense feeling of helplessness and lost pride. We had pride as soldiers. We could have been killed in battle but to go out like this was utter humiliation.

On 23 May, by which time the handover of the Croats was almost completed, AFHQ despatched an urgent message to 8th Army, in reply to a query, confirming current policy: 'Agree that all Jugoslav Nationals in 8th Army area should be returned by you to Jugoslavia *unless this involves the use of force* in which case they should be dealt with in accordance with [the Distone order].' (my emphasis)[20] Shortly after this, AFHQ sent, for emphasis, a message to 15th Army Group.

> No Jugoslavs who have come into the hands of Allied troops will be returned direct to Jugoslavia or handed over to Jugoslav troops against their will. [This] includes Chetniks, Ustache, Croats, Slovenes and miscellaneous refugees and dissident civilians including women and children. All the above will be moved to suitable concentration areas and screened.[21]

Since this directly contradicted the Deception Order, it is of the

---

19 WO 32/13749. This was another file from the Public Record Office which was kept out of Court by the Ministry of Defence.

20 Both this signal and the one it was answering have disappeared from all the British Army war diaries, being found only in the US National Archives and in FO 1020/42, the 'lost' file.

21 This signal has disappeared from all the British Army war diaries, being found only in FO 1020/42, the 'lost' Foreign Office file.

highest significance that 5 Corps' policy did not change in response to it.

In Court Lord Aldington defended 5 Corps' actions on the ground that they had not used 'force' against these Jugoslavs. He accepted they had been misled, and had been locked up as a result in railway wagons, but denied that this amounted to a use of force. He was asked directly if the phrase 'do not use force' is not equivalent to saying 'do not send them back against their will'. He replied angrily to Tolstoy's Counsel, 'My goodness me, Mr. Rampton! It most certainly is not! If you do not understand the Queen's English, we cannot get much further.'

The war diary of 5 Corps shows how it reacted to those orders.

23 May: Handover of Croats to Jugoslavs continued.

24 May: Handover of Croats completed. Handover of Serbs began.

25 May: Further consignment of Serbs despatched by train via Rosenbach.

26 May: Further 1,500 Jugoslav nationals handed over.

27 May: 1300 Slovenes evacuated from Rosenbach.

28 May: 3000 Slovenes evacuated to Jugoslavia.

29 May: 2600 Slovenes and 500 horses evacuated from Rosenbach and Bleiburg.

30 May: 3000 Slovenes evacuated to Jugoslavia through Bleiburg and Maria Elend.

31 May: 1950 Slovenes and 50 Croats handed over to Jugoslavs, thus completing the evacuation as agreed [by Brigadier Low with Colonel Ivanovitch]. Total evacuated amounted to 26,339 persons.

Since one of the major arguments in favour of the handovers has been that they were necessary as a blood-sacrifice in a perilous military situation, it is worth noting that it was at the meeting with Colonel Ivanovich on 19 May that Keightley and Low were told that Tito had ordered his partisans to retreat from Carinthia. They had all gone by 21 May, by which time there was no justification for further handovers, even in cynical *realpolitik*. On 20 May Low had cancelled the operation he had planned to eject the Titoists from southern Austria. That day's situation report from 5 Corps to 8th Army read, 'All quiet in Klagenfurt.'

There is one final, unpleasant irony. Paragraph 2 of the Robertson Order dealt with Germans. It stipulated that all 'SS and other arrestable categories' should be 'disarmed and evacuated to Distone'. Had the Jugoslavs been sent to Distone, as Alexander ordered on 17 May, their lives would have been spared, just as those of the SS were. Given Low's interpretation of the third paragraph of the Robertson Order, the Jugoslavs at Viktring would actually have been better treated if they had been members of the SS, the vast majority of whom lived.

It is not unreasonable of historians like Tolstoy to press the surviving protagonists for answers. But it has been an uphill struggle. Tolstoy started investigating the Jugoslav handovers in 1983, before any of the acrimonious allegations had been made. At an early stage, he wrote to the ex-BGS asking for information. Lord Aldington replied very briefly: 'Thank you for letting me know you are preparing a piece on the handover of Jugoslav citizens to Tito in May/June 1945. I do not remember that problem arising in my time in Austria.'

5

The DEFINITION ORDER

I F THE POLICY of kidnapping Jugoslavs originated at 5 Corps HQ
some time after Low's meeting with Colonel Hocevar, the plan to hand
the Cossacks to the Soviets was first mooted during Macmillan's
meeting with General Keightley at Klagenfurt on 13 May. Macmillan
noted this in his diary that night:

> Among the surrendered Germans are about 40,000 Cossacks and "White
> Russians", with their wives and children. To hand them over to the Russians
> is condemning them to slavery, torture and probably death. To refuse is
> deeply to offend the Russians, and incidentally break the Yalta agreement.
> We have decided to hand them over, but I suggested that the Russians should
> at the same time give us any British prisoners or wounded he may have in
> his area.[1]

This entry is interesting because it was quite wrong to say that to
refuse to hand over 'White Russians'—if by that is meant non-Soviet
citizens—would be 'to break the Yalta agreement'. The Yalta agreement
provided for the handover of Soviet citizens and no others. There is no
question that Macmillan himself knew all about this, having been involved in the categorisation of German prisoners of war taken in the
Mediterranean theatre since early 1944. Some of them were Soviets who

---

1   Macmillan *The War Diaries: the Mediterranean*, p. 757

had been pressed into the *Wehrmacht* and it was Macmillan who formulated the policy that was adopted towards these people. On 26 July 1944 he minuted the Foreign Office as follows:

(a) Male Soviet nationals who fall into our hands while serving or having served in German military formations will be regarded as prisoners of war...
(b) Soviet civilians in Italy will be dealt with in accordance with the wishes of the Soviet representative on the Displaced Persons Commission...
(d) Men of Russian nationality who are not Soviet citizens and who are caught serving or having served in German military or para-military formations will be regarded as prisoners of war.
(e) Civilians and women of Russian nationality who are not Soviet citizens will be screened and dealt with by appropriate refugee organisations.
(f) In the absence of documentary evidence to show whether a person is or is not a Soviet citizen his own word will be regarded as conclusive, at least for the purpose of deciding his immediate disposal.[2]

In all essentials, this was the policy which was adopted seven months later at Yalta and which was codified by the 8th Army instruction to 5 Corps on 13 March 1945, quoted above (Chapter 3). The only difference was that the Soviets were to be returned to their home country after the cessation of hostilities. One thing is clear: Macmillan, Churchill and the British 8th Army all made a distinction between Soviet and non-Soviet citizens and ordered that the mass of "Russians" falling into Allied hands be screened into the appropriate category. Why, then, did Macmillan note that it would be to break the Yalta agreement to refuse to hand over the Cossacks and 'White Russians' to the Soviets as if they were all Soviet citizens?

The whole controversy about the forced repatriations in Austria has hinged on the answer to that question. Apologists have argued that the question never arose at Macmillan's meeting with Keightley, and both men assumed the whole group were Soviet citizens. Tolstoy has pointed out that Keightley had already met some German officers in the Cossack Cavalry who were clearly not Soviet citizens, and also that Macmillan himself used the term 'White Russians', which directly implies non-So-

2   FO 371/40444

viet nationality.

Though the truth will never be known, the best clue lies in Macmillan's note that 'to refuse is deeply to offend the Russians'. Why might that have been? The answer is because the Soviets had already asked, as noted in Chapter 1, for the twenty or so names on the list which Tryon-Wilson brought back from Tolbukhin to Keightley on 11 May, two days before Macmillan's arrival. If it is hard to resist the conclusion that the list was discussed by Macmillan and Keightley, it is equally hard to avoid thinking that it was talked about as some sort of guilty secret. Although Tryon-Wilson is quite clear today about its existence, the list is never again mentioned in any of the contemporary documents, not even by way of justifying the claim that the presence of the Cossacks in an area of British occupation was contentious. The correct response for Macmillan to have made to any suggestion that 'Cossacks and "White Russians"' be handed to the Soviets would have been to have referred Keightley to the 8th Army standing order of 13 March, which ordered that any refugees or prisoners of war be screened into two categories, Soviet and non-Soviet. The former were liable for repatriation, although that had not as yet been ordered, while the latter were not. Such screening would not have been a particularly long job. The Kazachi Stan were camped in an old German Army barracks at Peggetz, near Lienz. In order to control the demand for rations, every person admitted had to show a document given by the British which contained information on, amongst other things, their national status. (Ironically, in view of what later happened, the guards on the gate were there to prevent people coming *in* without permission, not leaving.) As far as the Cossack Cavalry were concerned, the German Army kept full records on everybody. One of the survivors of the handovers who came to Court to testify in 1989 had been responsible for keeping this information up to date and was able to give precise detail of what was known.

Late on the evening of 13 May, not long after Macmillan arrived back at AFHQ, 5 Corps sent 8th Army a description of what Macmillan had just witnessed. Very unusually, they repeated the signal to AFHQ itself, heading it 'Please inform Macmillan'. Macmillan then went to discuss the matter with Robertson, and the Robertson Order resulted. Since it was that which was used to justify the handover of the Cossacks, just as much as the Jugoslavs, the terms of 5 Corps' signal are of critical importance. Did it give any ground for thinking that all the Russians in 5 Corps hands were in fact Soviet?

> Approx 300,000 PW surrendered personnel and refugees in Corps area [5 Corps signalled]. Further 600,000 reported moving north to Austria from Jugoslavia... Should this number materialise food and guard situation will become critical. I therefore suggest that all possible steps be taken to dispose soonest of all surrendered personnel in this area whether German, Austrian or Russian by moving them to Northern Italy or their homes whichever may be the policy... *On advice Macmillan have today suggested to Soviet General on Tolbukhin's HQ that Cossacks should be returned to Soviets at once.* Explained that I had no power to do this without your authority but would be glad to know Tolbukhin's views and if they coincided with mine I would ask you officially. Cannot see any point in keeping *this large number of Soviet nationals* who are *clearly great source contention between Soviets and ourselves...* All relations with Soviets very friendly with much interchange whisky and vodka. (emphasis added)[3]

Nobody reading that would suspect that there were significant numbers of non-Soviets in 5 Corps' hands, nor that it was the *Soviets* who had asked for some of them back. The implication is the opposite. What was 5 Corps trying to cover up? If they were to comply with Tolbukhin's wishes and hand over the men named on Tryon-Wilson's list, they could hardly pluck them out individually and truck them across the lines, particularly so as the mention of Shkuro—'the old boy with the CB'—suggests that they would have been amongst the most prominent of the prisoners. There would have been an outcry. The only practical solution was to pretend the whole group were Soviet nationals and hand them all back 'under Yalta'. The Soviets would get the twenty men they wanted and the British would be disembarrassed of 45,000 prisoners and refugees. The only cost would be the 10,000 or so non-Soviets amongst the Cossacks who were sent 'to slavery, torture and probably death' when Allied policy was that they should not be.

Nobody knows if that really was the 'advice' that Macmillan offered to Keightley but, if it was, he was certainly unrepentant about it in later life. When interviewed by Ludovic Kennedy on television shortly after

---

3   WO 170/4241

publication of his *War Diaries*, Macmillan justified the handovers by saying the victims 'were rebels against Russia', adding 'the Cossacks were practically savages.'[4]

What must be true, though, is that for such a policy to be carried through it was necessary for 5 Corps to deceive the higher military command as to the national status of the Cossacks in Carinthia. That is just what the signal sent on the night of 13 May did. Since much of the libel trial turned on Lord Aldington's responsibility for the handovers, it is relevant to ask how much involvement he had in wording that signal. He has given two answers, one before any writs were issued and one in Court. In March 1985 he told the boys at Winchester College that this signal was one 'which I remember drafting myself'. However, four years later, in the witness box at the High Court in London, he no longer remembered things that way.

'Am I right that you drafted this signal?' Tolstoy's Counsel asked him.

'No,' Lord Aldington replied. 'You are right in saying that I *helped* in the drafting of this message.'

Lord Aldington went on to explain that he did not, in fact, remember who had composed the text and that, anyway, there was no intention to deceive 8th Army. Nonetheless, 8th Army *was* deceived, as were, much more importantly, AFHQ and through them, the War Cabinet in London and the State Department in Washington. It was a month after the Cossack handovers were completed that anyone in either of the Allied governments was aware that the Cossacks who had been handed over were not all Soviet citizens. By then they were all either dead or on their way to Siberia.

The Robertson Order was sent to 8th Army on the evening of 14 May, and transmitted by them to 5 Corps the following morning. The paragraph dealing with the Jugoslavs has already been discussed. There were two others. One dealt with German prisoners of war. This is the text of the one dealing with the Cossacks.

All Russians should be handed over to Soviet Forces at agreed point of contact established by you under local arrangement with Marshal Tolbukhin's Hq.[5]

4   'Macmillan at War', BBCTV 1982.
5   WO 170/4184

As with the paragraph about the Jugoslavs, this one is very ambiguous. What was the term 'all Russians' supposed to mean? It might have meant 'all Soviets', as, at that time, the word "Russian" was used by many people interchangeably with the word "Soviet", rather as some people used to say "England" when they meant "Britain". Alternatively, since 5 Corps had already received from 8th Army on 13 March the order which gave precise criteria on which "Russians" should be segregated into Soviets and non-Soviets, the Robertson Order could be read simply as legitimizing a change of plan whereby Soviet prisoners of war were to be handed over directly to the Soviet Army rather than transported to Italy and shipped to Odessa, as had been the practice up till that time.

In his published writings, Tolstoy lays the principal blame on Macmillan for what followed. Certainly, the Resident Minister was involved in the decision to send the Cossacks to 'slavery, torture and probably death', primarily by prompting the issue of the Robertson Order, and possibly also by influencing its wording. But it was 5 Corps which actually did the deed. As will be seen below, 5 Corps acted contrary to superior orders issued *after* Robertson and to contrary effect. If Macmillan was implicated in the promulgation of the Robertson Order, it was 5 Corps which continued to act on it after it had been countermanded. This was much as happened with the Jugoslavs. Macmillan's intentions may have been grim but, in the event, his responsibility for what ultimately occurred must be adjudged as small. Even Lord Aldington accepts this. Alistair Horne, Macmillan's official biographer, quotes him on this critical issue.

> Shortly before Macmillan died, in December 1986, Lord Aldington said to Julian Amery, and he repeated the statement several times subsequently, that the decision at Klagenfurt of 13 May had been purely 'military' and 5 Corps would have carried it out regardless of Macmillan's 'political advice'. Macmillan could 'have objected on political grounds, certainly', but the inference is that it might not have made much difference.[6]

The precise weight of responsibility for the Cossack handovers, as between Macmillan and 5 Corps, is arguable. What is unarguable is that

---

6   Horne *Macmillan Vol I*, pp. 279-80.

both the War Cabinet and Field Marshal Alexander were dedicated to the opposite policy. Both assumed that non-Soviet Cossacks would never be handed over; Alexander went further in that he tried to prevent even Soviets from being sent home immediately, hoping, it seems, for a change of policy at the highest levels.

In the paragraph of his order which dealt with German prisoners of war, Robertson presaged the policy Alexander was to adopt for the Cossacks. 'Movement to Italy of all Germans is NOT acceptable... We are approaching 12th Army Group immediately with request that they accept [them].' An hour after Robertson despatched his order, Alexander made the approach to 12th Army Group, which was part of SHAEF, and was in occupation of southern Germany. He did so through Eisenhower in a message which, unlike the Robertson Order, was definitely seen by the Field Marshal since it is not marked 'Signed: SACMED' but 'Signed: Alexander'.

> Refugee and prisoner of war situation in 5 Corps area becoming unmanageable and prejudicing operational efficiency of Corps. Essential to clear it immediately in view of political situation. Earnestly request your assistance by accepting concentration under your control in Radstadt area [within the SHAEF] or elsewhere more convenient to you. Information regarding numbers not definite, but total may be about 500,000. If you agree, request detailed arrangements be made directly with unit designated by you and headquarters 5 Corps.[7]

Alexander followed this request with another one the following day, 15 May, in which he asked Eisenhower to help him further by moving the SHAEF/SACMED boundary south, taking over the northernmost part of 5 Corps' area of occupation. This would have left 5 Corps in occupation only of the area immediately bordering Jugoslavia. Clearly Alexander intended 5 Corps to concentrate on resisting Tito, which is why he arranged for Eisenhower to take over the commitment to guard the prisoners of war in southern Austria, including the Cossacks.

Eisenhower was initially cool so, on 16 May, Alexander telegraphed Churchill personally saying that if he was to be ready to offer armed

---

7   WO 170/4183. This signal, though addressed to 5 Corps, has disappeared from its war diary.

resistance to Tito, he must disencumber himself of the prisoners of war and other refugees in Carinthia. 'I am trying to get SHAEF to accept them, so far without much success,' Alexander wrote. 'I must clear the decks in this area.'[8]

While Alexander was signalling London, Eisenhower replied to the Field Marshal's first message, of 14 May, saying he could *not* take the prisoners into his area as he did not have enough food.[9] The next day, 17 May, Eisenhower agreed to take over the northernmost part of 5 Corps' area, although he still said he could not accept the prisoners.

But Alexander persisted. He signalled London again (like the other messages in this sequence, this one was marked 'Signed: Alexander'), saying that he had three contentious categories of prisoner on his hands, Cossacks, Chetniks and Croats, and that in each case 'to return them to their country of origin immediately might be fatal to their health.'[10] Alexander described the first category in this way: 'approximately 50,000 Cossacks, including 11,000 women, children and old men. These have been part of the German Armed Forces and have been fighting against the Allies.' Under Macmillan's July 1944 formula, which was accepted by the Foreign Office, these people would have been disposed of as prisoners of war, and therefore within the terms of the Geneva Convention.

The same morning, Alexander had signalled Eisenhower again, this time with a more moderate request on the subject of prisoners. He did not ask him to take 500,000 Germans (this figure presumably included the 'German Croats' who had threatened to irrupt into Carinthia at Bleiburg, but were by then known to have been turned back by the Irish Fusiliers). Instead, he asked for haven only for 150,000 'German armed forces including Cossacks... I request urgently your agreement that these surrendered forces... be transferred to your area soonest... The only alternative is that as a matter of operational and administrative necessity I shall be compelled to disband them, which would produce confusion in contiguous German territory under your command.'[11]

It is relevant to the question of whether Alexander approved the

8   WO 101/4059
9   WO 170/4183
10   WO 106/4059. Note that Alexander sent this message on the same afternoon that Brigadier Low promulgated the Deception Order.
11   WO 106/4059

Robertson Order that he saw only two alternatives: send the Cossacks north or disband them. Nowhere did he say that if Eisenhower could not take them he would have to hand them over to the Soviets. Either Alexander was unaware of the Robertson Order or he thought it applied only to Soviet citizens and that the Cossacks were not primarily Soviet. Clearly he had not seen 5 Corps' signal to AFHQ of 13 May which prompted Robertson. It is also significant that Alexander's signal was copied to 5 Corps, as Lord Aldington admitted in Court. The fact that 5 Corps was aware of the Supreme Commander's larger policy objectives, casts an even more sinister light on its subsequent subversion of them.

Alexander broke down his figure of 150,000 'German armed forces including Cossacks' into 45,000 Cossacks and 105,000 Germans. Clearly, therefore, Alexander expected both the Cossack Cavalry and the Kazachi Stan would be moved north, in other words, *all* the Cossacks, or, in Robertson's words, 'all Russians'. Such numbers were manageable and Eisenhower agreed to take them. Arrangements were put in hand straight away.

On Saturday 19 May, Eisenhower agreed to Alexander's further proposal that the Cossacks should move before being disarmed. He would, he said, take

> 45,000 Cossacks still fully armed. The Cossacks may be expected to move more or less as organised bodies intact.[12]

This signal has disappeared from both 5 Corps' and 8th Army's war diaries; the copy in Court came from the 'lost' Foreign Office file, FO 1020/42. That copy has a manuscript addition saying 'Copy sent to 5 Corps', which was only to have been expected as the operations envisaged were to happen in their area. 5 Corps could therefore no longer argue they were ignorant of the higher command's thinking. As they would have seen from the copy they received, Eisenhower addressed his message to the Combined Chiefs of Staff and the British Chiefs of Staff, and copied it to AFHQ, 15 Army Group and 8th Army. It was clearly the accepted policy of the entire Allied political and military command in western Europe, and is therefore of the highest significance to this story. 5 Corps'

---

12   FO 1020/42. It was in Court because Tolstoy had made a copy in 1985 for other purposes.

subsequent handovers were in direct defiance of this policy.

The Eisenhower-Alexander evacuation plan was integrated with a larger one, emanating from 15th Army Group, which was designed to push Tito out of Venezia Giulia. Codenamed Operation Coldstream, it had three main aspects as far as events in Carinthia were concerned: first, five American Divisions were to move south to bolster 5 Corps' three Divisions for the defence of the Austro-Jugoslavian border; secondly, the SHAEF-SACMED boundary was to be pushed south, relieving 5 Corps of part of its territorial commitments and, finally, the prisoners in Carinthia were to be moved from the likely field of battle.[13] Operation Coldstream's main purpose, though, was to push Tito out of the whole province of Venezia Giulia and, in particular, out of Trieste, its main town. This was, in the event, accomplished on 22 May without a shot being fired.

Eisenhower put Churchill in the picture and on 20 May the Prime Minister sent a memo to General Ismay, his military secretary, asking for a 'report on the 45,000 Cossacks, of whom General Eisenhower speaks. How did they come into their present plight? Did they fight against us?' In manuscript at the bottom, he has added 'Ref... urgency of moving into 12th Army Group area [SHAEF] 150,000 surrendered enemy, including 45,000 fully armed Cossacks.'[14]

Within twenty-four hours of the Prime Minister's having scribbled this postscript, Brigadier Low at 5 Corps had issued the order which was to hand all 45,000 Cossacks, Soviet and non-Soviet alike, over to the Soviets.

Low's order has, from its declared purpose which was to define who was and who was not to be treated as a Soviet citizen, come to be known as the Definition Order. This is the full text:

> 1. Various cases have recently been referred to this HQ in which doubt has been raised as to whether certain formations and groups should be treated as Soviet Nationals in so far as their return to the Soviet Union direct from 5 Corps is concerned. Rulings in these cases are given below.
>
> Russian Schutzkorps [another name for the Russkii Korpus] will NOT be treated as Soviet Nationals until further orders.

---

13 Full details were given in a signal which was kept out of Court, in the 'lost' file FO 1020/42.
14 PREM 3/364/17

Following *will be treated as* Soviet Nationals:

Ataman Group [including Ataman Krasnov]

15 Cossack Cavalry Corps (incl Cossacks and Calmuks)

Res Units of Lt-Gen Shkuro

Caucasians (incl Mussulmen)

2. Individual cases will NOT be considered unless particularly pressed. In these cases and in the case of appeals by further units or formations, the following directive will apply:

(a) Any individual now in our hands who, at the time of joining the German Forces or joining a formation fighting with the German Forces, was living within the 1938 boundary of the USSR, will be treated as a Soviet National for the purposes of transfer.

(b) Any individual although of Russian blood who, prior to joining the German Forces, had not been in the USSR since 1930, will NOT until further notice be treated as a Soviet National.

(c) In all cases of doubt, the individual will be treated as a Soviet National.

[signed] ARW Low, Brigadier General Staff (emphasis added, capitals in original)[15]

The first point to emphasise is that Low does not say these people *are* Soviet Nationals, merely that they will *be treated as* such. Clearly he knew some were not. Secondly, despite all his later protestations to the effect that he was entirely ignorant of the presence of the old émigrés amongst the Cossacks, Low actually mentions General Shkuro *by name*. Furthermore, "Atamans" was a pre-revolutionary Cossack title, not a Soviet one. Since Keightley had personally met some of the Germans in the Cossack Cavalry, the only group which Low might have considered with some justification all-Soviet (although it wasn't) was the Caucasians. It is impossible to argue that Low did not know he was sending into the hands of the Red Army at least some people who should not have been. So why did he do it?

Lord Aldington's answer in Court was that he was, in essence, acting in conformity with the Robertson Order. But if that were so, the second paragraph, which gives rights of objection to the Cossacks on the ground of nationality, would constitute disobedience to Robertson. In fact that paragraph was a dead letter, since the whole order was kept secret from the people to whom it applied: they could not object to a plan of which they were in ignorance. Not only that, when they did protest, they were ignored. Both Generals Krasnov and Shkuro petitioned Alexander, whom they knew. But their letters went through 5 Corps headquarters where, it seems, they were destroyed.[16] Certainly there is no record that they ever arrived at AFHQ.

Precisely how it was 5 Corps went about frustrating the wishes of the high command and executing Low's order is clear only in the light of documents contained in the two main files retained by the Foreign Office and the Ministry of Defence in the period before and during the libel trial. In the event, the jury were to take their decision largely in ignorance of the unpleasant truth of events in Carinthia after Alexander had ordered the Cossacks sent north into Germany and Low ordered them handed over to the Soviets. The material remaining in the 5 Corps and 8th Army war diaries paints a very different picture from the one which emerges from FO 1020/42 and WO 32/13749 and other files.

On the evening of 21 May, when a copy of Low's text arrived at 8th Army headquarters, McCreery responded by sending an urgent message to AFHQ asking whether the Robertson Order was still current. He referred to that order—'stating that all Russians should be handed over to Soviet Forces'—and to Eisenhower's message to Alexander—'stating Cossacks [to be] accepted by 12th Army Group'—and then went on to ask for, 'earliest information whether approved policy is to despatch to SHAEF or to endeavour to secure direct return to Russians by 8th Army negotiations.'[17] That is a question which Brigadier Low ought to have asked before signing the Definition Order since 5 Corps had been sent a copy of Alexander's request to Eisenhower asking him to take the Cossacks into the SHAEF area. For some reason he did not.

The next morning, 22 May, 8th Army copied its message to AFHQ back down to 5 Corps, which ought to have alerted that unit to the fact

---

16   After an interview with Tryon-Wilson on 6 February 1985, Tolstoy noted, 'Krasnov's petitions were certainly destroyed at 5 Corps H.Q.'

17   This signal too has disappeared from all British military files and is extant only in the US National Archives.

that its current policy was not unquestioned. 5 Corps should then have stayed its hand pending McCreery's receipt of an answer to his question. But it did just the opposite: it pushed its policy through even harder and faster. Why?

Lord Aldington refuses to answer this question since, at this point, his defence changes: he was not there. Early on the morning of 22 May, he claimed in Court, he flew out of Klagenfurt *en route* for two weeks' leave in England. He says he should not be blamed for the application of the policy outlined in the Definition Order since he was not there when it was carried out.

There are two objections to this defence. First, there is only one Army signal which explicitly gives a date for his departure from 5 Corps and that records him as having left on 23 May.[18] Secondly, if by stating he was not there on 22 May, Lord Aldington implies that he bore no responsibility whatsoever for what was done on that day, it is relevant that he left on two weeks' leave, presumably after having briefed his stand-in, Brigadier Edward ("Dolly") de Fonblanque, on what to do in his absence. He might well have had to return and, in any case, he can hardly have expected that 5 Corps policy would be turned upside down the minute he was out of sight of headquarters.[19]

The actual sabotage of the Cossack aspect of Operation Coldstream began even before Low claims he left Austria. On the evening of 21 May, 5 Corps sent a startled message to 8th Army saying that 800 American vehicles had arrived from SHAEF in 78th Division's area.[20] Apparently they were for the 'evacuation of prisoners of war'. At 30 people per truck, they could have moved the whole of the Kazachi Stan in a day, and the

18   This signal comes from 2 GHQ Liaison Regiment—the 'Phantom' unit—the secure communication channel which the senior Generals in all theatres used to keep in touch with divisions. It had a high reputation for efficiency and reliability, despite being considered one of the "fun" units, possibly because, being a headquarters operation, officers seldom came under fire. Many subsequently distinguished people served in it, including David Niven, Peregrine Worsthorne and Maurice Macmillan. The message about Brigadier Low, which has come to be known as the 'Phantom' signal, was not discovered until after the libel trial.

19   General Keightley's son, General Richard Keightley, until recently Commandant of the Military College at Sandhurst and therefore some authority on military organisation, told this author in an interview on 14 April 1993 that a change of BGS would be less like a change of government, when the policy changes, than a change of personnel in the civil service, when the public policy remains the same.

20   This was another signal kept out of Court in the 'lost' file FO 1020/42.

whole of the Cossack Cavalry in another day. By 24 May all the Cossacks would have gone. What did 5 Corps do? Did it heave a sigh of relief that a tricky problem had been solved? No, it immediately moved to *prevent the Americans rescuing the Cossacks.*

Beyond the signals record, the nearest thing to eye-witness evidence of the suggestion that the major decisions were taken before Low left Austria comes from his colleague, Brigadier Tryon-Wilson, who told an Imperial War Museum researcher in 1990 that the decision not to allow the Cossacks to be moved north was in fact Low's.

> Probably when you spoke to Brigadier Low he would have told you that at the *moment critique* he decided that he didn't want that [American] help because operationally we were in a position to deal with it as we thought right and proper, which he did do.[21]

On the morning of 22 May, between the time Aldington claimed in Court to have left Austria and the time the Phantom signal records him as having done so, Keightley held a Corps Commander's conference at which it was agreed that Cossacks who tried to escape handover to the Soviets would, if necessary, be shot at. Since many were refugees, and all were defenceless, this amounted to a command to murder.[22]

Within an hour of Keightley's authorising the use of lethal force on the Cossacks, Alexander issued an order to precisely the opposite effect. This was his answer to McCreery's question whether current policy was that as laid down by Robertson on 14 May or the execution of the more recently conceived Operation Coldstream:

> All who are Soviet citizens and who can be handed over to Russians *without use of force* should be returned by 8th Army. Any others should be evacuated to 12th Army Group. (emphasis added)[23]

21 Imperial War Museum, Dept. Sound Records, tape 11738

22 In the *Manual of Military Law*, 1929 edition, Chapter 14, paras. 74 and 75 (p. 284) deal with the escape of prisoners of war. The former says they may be shot at, but the latter implies only to prevent their further participation in the war. Since, on 22 May 1945, the war had already ended, paragraph 74 was of doubtful effect. The case of refugees is simpler: in no circumstances may they be shot at to prevent non-criminal movement.

23 WO 170/4184

This signal was copied for information to 5 Corps (though no copy remains in the 5 Corps war diary). In Court Lord Aldington argued that 5 Corps had no obligation to obey it as it was sent 'for information' only. It was a direct order to 8th Army, not 5 Corps, he said, though of course 5 Corps was a part of 8th Army.

Later that evening, Alexander's Chief of Staff signalled 8th Army in equally unambiguous terms:

> Personal for General McCreery from General Morgan... You have authority to pass Cossacks direct to Russians *provided force has not repeat not to be used.*' (emphasis added)[24]

The policy was quite clear. Violence towards escaping prisoners was forbidden.

How did 5 Corps respond? *They objected!* Whatever the new circumstances were, 5 Corps was desperate to carry out the repatriations. Not only did it obstruct the attempt to find a safe haven for the Cossacks, it also insisted on being given the freedom to use force to implement its own preferred solution. The message, sent at 7.15 pm on Wednesday 23rd, was marked 'Personal BGS to Chief of Staff, Main 5 Corps to Main 8th Army', and it reads:

> As a result of verbal directive from Macmillan to Corps Command at recent meeting we have undertaken to return all Soviet Nationals in Corps area to Soviet forces. Macmillan mentioned no proviso about use of force and we have issued instructions that force may be used if absolutely necessary. Consider quite impossible to guarantee to return Cossacks and so honour our verbal agreement with Soviet forces unless we are allowed free hand in this matter. Cossacks will view any move with suspicion as to destination. Consider therefore may be necessary to use force to move Cossacks at all from present area. Longer they remain present area the more likely force have to be used. Request you confirm our freedom of action in this.[25]

---

24   Absent from the relevant war diaries, this signal is contained in the 'lost' file FO 1020/42.

25   This is another signal which has disappeared from the relevant war diaries, being contained in the 'lost' file FO 1020/42. Another signal in that file (which did not come to Court) suggests that Keightley had asked McCreery to ask Clark to ask Bradley to halt the movement south.

This message is as deceptive as the one of the 13 May which started the whole process. It, too, describes the Cossacks in such a way as to give the unwary reader the impression they are all Soviet nationals and therefore liable for repatriation under Yalta.

Pleading to be allowed to employ violence on the Cossacks was not sufficient in itself to enable 5 Corps to get the Cossacks delivered to the Soviets, it also had to stop the American forces from SHAEF rescuing them. In the late afternoon of 23 May, 5 Corps signalled 8th Army confirming an earlier telephone conversation between 8th Army Chief of Staff and 5 Corps BGS:

> Do NOT now consider it necessary for us to be relieved up to boundary suggested in our [message] dated 16th as situation in Lienz well in hand and can be organised by one unit. (emphasis in original)[26]

This signal is particularly interesting in the light of Lord Aldington's claim in Court that 5 Corps did not screen Cossacks into Soviet and non-Soviet nationals because it did not have time.

Later that afternoon, 5 Corps made doubly sure there would be no takeover of the camps where the Cossacks were quartered. A signal was sent to 20 US Corps (the unit from 12th Army Group which would have moved south), with copies to 78th Division, in whose area Lienz and Spittal were, and to 8th Army:

> Most grateful your prompt action in moving south but in view of improvement in local situation understand that higher authority is proposing to SHAEF no move your main bodies takes place south of Kleine Tauern [the mountain range separating the Mediterranean command from SHAEF, Radstadt is north of it] until further orders. Suggest therefore you confine movement in our areas to reconnaissance parties until then.[27]

26 WO 170/4184. This signal was not in Court. It is contained in the 8th Army war diary (it has disappeared from the 5 Corps war diary), which was held in the Ministry of Defence for the eight months leading up to the trial in 1989 (see Appendix B).

27 This signal exists in the 'lost' file FO 1020/42 and also in WO 170/4183, another part of the 8th Army war diary, which was also held by the Ministry of Defence for eight months in 1989. A copy exists in FO 1020/42, but that file was held in the Foreign Office for the four years immediately following Tolstoy's inclusion on the writ which gave rise to the libel action.

As a result of all this, while Operation Coldstream progressed according to plan and timetable in Venezia Giulia, where there was a substantial "enemy" presence, in Carinthia, where there was no enemy, only 5 Corps, it ground to a halt in muddle and confusion.

Four days after the thrust past Trieste had been launched and completed, the 3rd US Army had still not made its way past Mauterndorf and into Carinthia. A signal on 26th from SHAEF to AFHQ explains why.

At present only reconnaissance elements of 3rd Army have reached "Coldstream" objectives. These were informed *by 5 Corps units* that congestion and shortage of supplies made further build up in subject areas undesirable. (emphasis added)[28]

The desire to avoid congestion on the roads seems a less than adequate reason to prevent the rescue of 45,000 people from 'slavery, torture and probably death'. The shortage of supplies argument, anyway, was nonsense. The US 3rd Army brought its own food with it, so evacuation north would have *improved* the situation in Carinthia. There can be no doubt that 5 Corps had an agenda of its own which it kept secret from all superior formations and its American allies. The only military unit which was cognizant of its plans—and possibly of its motives—was Marshal Tolbukhin's Third Ukrainian Front.

As with the Jugoslav handovers, there are very profound and worrying questions about this whole operation. But, as with the Jugoslavs, Lord Aldington has not been forthcoming about his role. When Tolstoy first wrote to him in 1974 to ask for an interview, he refused saying, 'I am very much afraid I shall not be able to help you in your research about the handover of the Cossacks Divisions in Austria in May/June 1945... I do not remember myself being involved in any matters concerning the Cossack Divisions.'

---

28   WO 214/1615. This was another signal which was not in Court, but in this case purely because neither side thought to submit it. In any case, without the preceding ones explaining that Coldstream had failed, the reasons for that failure are meaningless.

6

The HANDOVERS

WHETHER BRIGADIER LOW left Klagenfurt on 22 or 23 May, it was common ground at the trial that he arrived home on 24 May, going straight to his mother's house in Roehampton, where he arrived at sundown. At the same moment other, less pleasant, homecomings were taking place south of the Austro-Jugoslavian border.

One of the witnesses who came to Court in 1989, Milovye Stankevich, has described how, that evening, he and a train load of Serbs found themselves in Kranj, a small town about half-way between the Austro-Slovenian border and Ljubljana. Separated from their men, the officers sang Orthodox Vespers and discussed death.

> In case we were going to die during the night [Stankevich wrote in his witness statement] we agreed all to do it in a dignified way, dedicating our last thoughts and words to the King and our country. However we also discussed ways of escaping. Late in the night, one of our soldiers managed to contact us. He told us what happened in their part of the camp. One Partisan political commissar came to tell them how they were misled and defeated. But a seventeen year old Volunteer stood up and said, 'Do not waste your time. You did not defeat us. This was betrayal and treachery.'

It is not known how Low spent the next few days since the story he gave in his own witness statement a month before the trial was disproved in dramatic circumstances in Court. He claimed to have dined twice with his friend the Foreign Secretary while that august gentleman tried to persuade the diffident young Brigadier to stand for parliament in the forthcoming General Election. In fact, Eden was outside London for the whole period. In any case, he had already persuaded Low that he should go into politics. On 15 March Eden had written to Low saying that he had been 'quite active' and spoken to Central Office on his behalf. 'I hope you won't be embarrassed thereby.' On 21 March, Low had replied saying, 'I am most grateful and I shall, of course, accept your advice unreservedly.'[1]

On Monday 28 May Low travelled up to Blackpool for a selection committee meeting. On the same day the bulk of the Cossack officers were kidnapped by 5 Corps. This operation had been fraught with difficulties. Apart from the threat of American help for their intended victims, the Soviets had proved sticky about Low's plan to hand entire formations over to them. The local command had no instructions to accept these large numbers and, apparently, no resources to receive them. In due course they wanted all the Soviet nationals, as per Yalta, and they would have liked the émigré Generals right away. But 5 Corps was short of time. The American forces might re-appear at any moment and move the Cossacks to safety. The only sure way to defeat the Alexander-Eisenhower plan was to move so quickly that the Allied High Command was presented with a *fait accompli*. All 45,000 had to be despatched at once. After several days of persuasion, the Soviets finally capitulated on 24 May. 'At a conference with representatives of 57th Russian Army at Wolfsburg,' the 5 Corps war diary states, 'Russians agreed to accept Cossacks from 6th British Armoured Division and 78th Division areas by train at Judenburg and those from 46th Division by march route at Voitsberg.'[2]

Within hours of 8th Army's issuing the "no force" order, 5 Corps sent out detailed instructions for the impending operation. The main target was to be the Cossack officers, a group which included the émigré

---

1   Avon Papers

2   WO 170/4241. The impression of reluctance on the part of the Soviets to receive such large numbers is given by several other records. For example, on 17 May, at a conference with a Major Skvortsoff, Major Taylor of 5 Corps (who reported to Tryon-Wilson and gave evidence in Court in 1989) noted: 'The question of the disposal of 75,000 (*sic*) Cossacks was raised, but Skvortsoff said he was only empowered to deal with those ex-PoW in the Wolfsberg area... the 1,500 in Spittal and Klagenfurt were *sold* to the Russians as being part of the Wolfsberg camp.' (emphasis added) FO 916/1202

Generals whose delivery Tolbukhin had originally requested.

It is of the utmost importance that all officers and particularly senior commanders are rounded up and none are allowed to escape. The Soviet forces consider this as being of the highest importance and will probably regard the delivery of the officers as a sign of British good faith.[3]

When the Cossacks were moved closer to the border, the order continued, the ordinary soldiers were to be escorted by 'guards', but the officers by 'strong guards'.

In the middle of these preparations, Alexander Kirk telegraphed the State Department in Washington assuring them that Field Marshal Alexander had, as indeed he had, instructed 8th Army that 'all persons who are Soviet citizens will be repatriated but any person who is not a Soviet citizen under British law will not be sent back to the Soviet Union unless he expresses a desire to do so.'[4]

At 5 Corps, things were being organised in quite a different spirit. On 25 May 78th Division noted in connection with the anticipated move of the Kazachi Stan and the Caucasians that, 'as these Divisions (*sic*) are both opposed to their return to Russia, it will be necessary to have strong military guards in attendance on their move.'[5] Three units were put on four hours' notice to move. The war diary of the 2nd Battalion Inniskilling Fusiliers, one of those units, noted that, 'The Battalion was to move as for battle with first line ammunition.'[6]

While Kirk's optimistic comments on the fate of the non-Soviet Cossacks were being digested in Washington, 5 Corps set to work to bring about the opposite result. 15th Army Group had sent a Colonel Gerrett up to Austria to arrange the move north of the Cossacks under the Alexander-Eisenhower plan and co-ordinate it with 12th Army Group, the command in SHAEF opposite 15th Army Group. When Gerrett asked about the national status of the Cossacks, he was lied to. He was told that 'approximately 42,000 Cossacks to be handed over to Russians are Soviet citizens (*sic*) ... Any not eligible for transfer to Russians will be [sent to

3   WO 170/4241
4   US National Archives. This signal was not in Court.
5   WO 170/4388
6   WO 170/5018

SHAEF].'[7]

In fact 5 Corps had no knowledge of the national status of the Cossacks, since it had refused to carry out any screening. Neither did 5 Corps ever transfer a single individual to SHAEF.

The next day, 26 May, instructions went down the line to the unit guarding the Cossack Cavalry, 138th Brigade, part of 46th Division under General Weir. The Brigade was to provide 'static picquets' along the route the Cossacks were to travel. The Brigade was told 'the return of the Cossacks to Russia is part of an international agreement and we are disinterested executors. A very large number of the Cossacks are wanted for war crimes. Any Cossack who escapes will be a menace to British troops stationed in the area.'[8] Consequently their orders were 'to capture or shoot any Cossack who attempts to escape'. To this end 'troops will have no hesitation in using firearms', but 'mass shootings will, if possible, be avoided'. The Welsh Guards, who had been temporarily detached to 46th Division to provide part of the guard along the road to Judenburg, were told, 'Shoot to kill if it becomes necessary.'[9] Such was 5 Corps' interpretation of Alexander's prohibition on the use of force.

Something of the guilty conscience which many officers felt at having to implement the Definition Order comes through in the orders of the time. On 26 May Brigadier Musson of 36th Infantry Brigade, which was guarding the Kazachi Stan at Peggetz camp and the Caucasians at Oberdrauberg, gave a message to the troops under his command about the operation they were about to embark upon.

> It has been decided by Higher Authority that all surrendered troops in the Brigade area will be disarmed today. After 1400 hours any surrendered troops found in possession of arms or ammunition will be arrested immediately and will be liable to the death penalty.... If it is necessary to open fire you will do so and *you must regard this duty as an operation of war.* (emphasis added)[10]

The following day Musson issued more detailed instructions. At the

7   WO 170/4241
8   WO 170/4473
9   Manuscript log of 1st Guards Brigade operations, now in the possession of Nigel Nicolson
10   WO 170/4396

top of the order, typed in block capitals, was a warning which revealed Musson's embarrassment:

THE CONTENTS OF THIS ORDER WILL NOT BE DIVULGED EXCEPT TO THOSE INDIVIDUALS FOR WHOM COMMANDING OFFICERS CONSIDER IS ESSENTIAL. IT SHOULD BE DIVULGED AT THE LAST POSSIBLE MOMENT AND ONLY THOSE PARTS WHICH AFFECT THE UNIT OR SUB-UNIT CONCERNED SHOULD BE COMMUNICATED TO THEM.[11]

In 46th Division, through which all the Cossacks would pass on their way to the handover point at Judenburg, General Weir gave the impression of being similarly uncomfortable.

It is of the highest importance that NO unauthorised disclosures of Allied practice on this and kindred subjects should be made in any form whatever, even now that hostilities have ceased. This applies to methods used in specific operations and to general policy. Any knowledge of the subject will continue to be treated as TOP SECRET. (emphasis in original)[12]

Even the existence of this order was to be kept secret as it must not 'arouse undue comment'.

Now the lies were everywhere. The plan was to tell the Cossack officers of the Kazachi Stan, which included most of the old émigrés, that they were being invited to a conference with Field Marshal Alexander at which their future would be discussed. This stratagem appealed to 5 Corps because they knew that both Krasnov and Shkuro had written letters to the Field Marshal asking for a meeting and emphasising that, under Yalta, they and many others were not due for "repatriation". They appeared to trust the British and the announcement of a meeting with Alexander might be plausible enough to lull them into a false sense of security.

Brigadier Musson ordered his officers to tell their men on 28 May, the day the Cossack officers were all kidnapped, that 'Troops concerned with the move of Cossack and Caucasian Officers ... will be told that the

---

11   WO 170/4461
12   WO 170/4352

officers are going to a conference.'[13] The rest of the British troops were to be told that the officers were being separated from the men 'in order to save trouble within unit areas'. This at least was true, but the fact that they were being returned 'in accordance with an agreement made by the Allied governments' was not.

British troops were to be lied to as well—presumably to prevent a mutiny provoked by the common sentiment that 'this was not what we fought the war for'. Musson ordered his officers to explain to all ranks why they were about to embark upon an operation in the course of which they would be ignoring the traditional, and legally binding, distinction between combatants and non-combatants. This was to be the substance of the talk.

> As there are so many women and children, some of you will feel sympathetic towards these people, but you must remember that they took up arms [women and children?] for the Germans. There is no doubt that they sided with the Germans because they hoped to regain power in Russia. When they saw this was not possible they tried to excuse themselves in our eyes... You have a very big task and a very unpleasant one. Let us try to carry it out firmly and without bloodshed, but if it is necessary to resort to force, do so promptly and without fear.

General Arbuthnott went further, including unborn children in his list of intended victims. Knowing the full extent of the violence which was about to be unleashed, he still issued an order to all units within 78th Division, paragraph 15(f) of which included in those to be forcibly handed over, 'lying sick *and expectant mothers*'. (emphasis added)[14]

There is no difference between this type of order and that on which many Germans were subsequently convicted as war criminals. Not one of these officers had the courage to challenge the legality of the orders they had been given.

One of the witnesses at the trial, Zoë Polanska, was with the Cossacks at Peggetz and described in her witness statement to the Court in 1989 seeing the consequences of Arbuthnott's order about expectant mothers.

---

13   WO 170/4461
14   WO 170/4388

When the British troops started beating the civilians, with pick-axe helves and rifle butts, and attacking with bayonets anyone who would not move towards Tryon-Wilson's transport, a group of young Cossack men tried, with futile but unblemished courage, to defend their womenfolk.

[These men were] leaping like hounds. Underneath their feet I saw a woman in what must have been the last month or so of pregnancy. She lay back in a most uninhibited fashion, her hands flung above her head and her legs parted, unable to protect the small life inside her.

Whatever the justice or lack of it of Tolstoy's phrase about Lord Aldington, that his activities 'merit comparison with those of the worst butchers of Nazi Germany', it surely applies without reservation to the man who ordered such an attack: Colonel (temporary Major-General) Robert Keith Arbuthnott CB, CBE, DSO.

While these operations were being planned in Carinthia, Low arrived in Blackpool and booked into the Clifton Hotel. *Arsenic and Old Lace* was showing at the Princess Cinema and *You Can't Ration Love* at the Waterloo; Feldman's Theatre featured a revue called *Soldiers in Skirts*. The *West Lancashire Evening Gazette* said that, after Mr Eden's intervention, 'the man for whom the Blackpool North Conservatives have been waiting' had arrived. He had been delayed in southern Austria, because 'despite the surrender of the Germans, things have since been more than "touchy" and the ability and experience of this officer was urgently needed on the spot.' Since the German surrender, 'he has been engaged in highly important work of a confidential nature. That story cannot yet be told.'

Years later the editor and owner of the paper, Sir Harold Grimes, described how the selection committee had made its decision. 'In five minutes we knew the choice was right: not on political grounds... but on the firmest grounds of all—character.' The qualities he perceived in Low were bluntness and 'uncompromising honesty'. Blackpudlians understand, Sir Harold said, 'that when a banker and a barrister forsakes the potential fleshpots of industry (*sic*) for the hard and thankless job of full-time politics, he is made of rugged stuff.'

On Tuesday 29 May Low celebrated his selection, and opened his campaign. His theme was individual liberty and the integrity of the family. 'We relied in the past for our greatness on the enterprise of the individual,' he said, 'and we must ensure that nothing we do ever denies us that.'

Things were not so easy in Carinthia. The war diary of the Welsh Guards recorded what happened when the kidnap scheme was put into effect.

> Rather trying day. Half of the Cossack officers, when they were informed that they were to embus refused to as they had tactlessly been informed that they were going to Russia. Thinking that their fate would be a desperate one they demanded to be shot or given firearms in lieu. By tactful negotiation and timely display of a Wasp flame-thrower they were induced to get into the [transport].'[15]

Then it was the turn of the German cadre of the Cossack Cavalry Corps. Their handover was the clearest violation of the Geneva Convention implicit in Low's Definition Order, not to mention the Yalta agreement. By no conceivable stretch of a barrister's imagination could these men be considered Soviet. Some had sniffed the wind and escaped, but about 1000 were handed over. Only 250 survived to return to Germany. One of those who did, Karl-Gottfried Vierkorn, came to London in 1989 to give evidence at the libel trial. This is how he described his handover in his witness statement:

> On the 28th an enormous number of heavy military lorries arrived outside the camp and we were ordered to board them. We were taken on a drive of 40 or 50 kilometres to Judenburg. We were accompanied by British guards who appeared to be heavily armed. During the journey I remember we stopped on two occasions, the second being many kilometres before Judenburg. We were allowed off the lorries to stretch our legs and "spend a penny". The British guards did not take any steps to ensure we returned and indeed I could easily have escaped and would have done so had I known at the time that we were going to be handed over to the Soviets.
>
> Gradually on either side of the road there appeared British guards and their frequency grew the further we travelled. During the last few kilometres British soldiers were lining the road every 100 metres or so and in the last

15   WO 170/4982

kilometre every 50 metres. To me escape now seemed impossible and I remember being extremely angry when I thought that I could easily have escaped soon after we surrendered to the British.

By now we were driving through the little town of Judenburg. The guard along the road had meanwhile been reinforced and now formed almost a human chain. No one in my lorry said a word. I remember looking at my comrades. I shall never forget those faces and the expressions reflected in them. Some showed iron self-control while others looked tremendously fearful. Everyone had ashen faces and I remember the skin on my comrades looking old and leathern, their eyes empty yet feverish. Some of my comrades were fiddling about with their baggage with a sort of deliberate concentration, others were hastily throwing their most valuable possessions to the civilian population who lined the roadside. Some were incapable of moving at all. Others became extremely agitated and I remember seeing some of my colleagues jump from other lorries and run amok in the crowds. I remember hearing gun shots and shouts. I remember seeing the British soldiers on my lorry fire their guns. The British soldiers did not seem to be firing merely into the air.

I then remember hearing a sudden disturbance in the corner of my lorry. I looked and I saw a young lieutenant whom I had always known to be a very calm and restrained person. He was trying to cut his arteries with a sharp knife. Quickly those around him fell upon him and wrenched the knife out of his hands.

Shortly after this, I remember the lorries of the convoy moving across the bridge in Judenburg separately. On the other side of the bank was the Red Army and we were handed over to the Soviets. Everyone in the lorry looked very wooden and motionless. When the lorry stopped we all knew we were in the hands of the Bolsheviks.

Hardly had the vehicle stopped than what appeared to be a wild pack of heavily armed Soviet soldiers and Commissars fell upon us. Many of them seemed to be under the influence of drink and presented a terrifying appearance. Their uniforms, in stark contrast to those of the correctly attired British, were filthy and ill-cared for; for example their boots and belts had not been polished. Their army shirts were mostly unbuttoned and wide open, revealing a variety of fantastic and obscene tattooings. With indescribable longing, I remember gazing after the British drivers as they turned their vehicles and drove back to the other side.[16]

On 1 June the worst of the violence on the part of the British took place in the barrack square at Peggetz. Whereas the officers were tricked, the other ranks and civilians were to be dealt with by brute force. Tolstoy has described at length the gruesome scenes of violence in *Victims of Yalta* and *The Minister and the Massacres*, as has Lord Bethell in *The Last Secret* and Zoë Polanska in *Yalta Victim*. There is no need here to do more than summarise the events of the day.

It dawned bright and sunny. The inmates of Peggetz had been informed of the fate which awaited them and had determined on passive resistance. They erected an altar in the barrack square and sung the Orthodox liturgy as the British troops formed up and fixed bayonets. An officer ordered them to prepare to move. They refused. Then some of the soldiers who had been armed with pickaxe helves started trying to drag individuals from the crowd, but it was several thousand strong and those at the edge linked arms, while the rest kept singing the Lord's Prayer. The women and children were moved into the centre of the crowd, which grew tighter together as the perimeter shrank under pressure from the troops. In the middle, people started climbing on top of one another. The soldiers tried to club their way into the throng with the aim of cutting off sections of it which could then be attacked from all sides until either they submitted or could be dragged wounded or unconscious to the transport.

As they did so, the crowd retreated and was pressed harder and harder up against the wooden barrack fence. Suddenly it burst and people scattered in all directions. Some ran for the forests, others across the River Drau. Others still thought this would be their only opportunity to commit suicide before the Soviets got hold of them. Women threw their babies and then themselves into the freezing river, which was flowing in spate with the spring meltwater off the mountains. Others hung themselves from trees, and Major Davies, the officer commanding the operation that day, found one Cossack who had shot his wife, then his three children and finally himself. Before committing suicide, the man, Pyotr Mordovkin, had laid out neatly on a grassy bank, side by side, the four corpses of his family, presumably hoping to bring at least a trace of dignity to their deaths.

16   Vierkorn was released from Siberia in 1954, by which time three-quarters of his fellow officers were dead. He has written a book (under the pseudonym of Karl Nork) about his experiences called *Hell in Siberia*.

Shortly after this, Major Davies himself broke down. Like many of his soldiers he was so revolted at what he was doing that he could issue no further orders to attack these defenceless people. At 11.30 a.m. the operation was called off in Peggetz. That morning 1,250 people had been loaded from that camp. A further 5,200 Cossacks were sent east from other camps in Carinthia that day, usually also after scenes of violence. In the days that followed, the dwindling remnants of the Kazachi Stan were handed over, but with progressively less resistance offered as the victims became resigned to their fate.

A British officer inspecting the trains at Judenburg noted that, once in Soviet hands, the Cossacks were treated 'coarsely but not brutally'. This was not at all the case as far as the Jugoslavs were concerned. Three of the Defence witnesses who gave evidence at the trial in 1989, France Kozima, France Dejak and Milan Zajec, were amongst the few who survived the savagery of the Partisans in what has come to be called the massacre of Kocevje.

Kozima's statement to the Court in 1989 starts by describing the mood of the anti-Tito Slovenians at the time of the handover.

> On 28 May I remember one of my officers informing me that the British had informed him that, the following morning, we should make ourselves ready as we were going to leave [Viktring] to go to the nearby railway station, and that we would all be taken by train to Italy. He also said the British would escort us on our journey and provide us with two days' rations. I remember I and my compatriots were very glad to hear this news. It never occurred to me at this point that the British would be handing us over to the Partisans. I still continued to trust the British.

They were locked into their carriages, the points were changed, and they were on their way to Jugoslavia. After passing through Ljubljana, their train took them on to the small town of Kocevje in the mountains of southern Slovenia.

Dejak remembers that, with about 800 others, he was confined to the second floor of a former blind-people's home. In groups of 30 they were taken downstairs where the guards wired their hands behind their backs and tied them together in pairs by the arms. So tight were the lashings that some fainted as their circulation was cut off. After an hour they were loaded onto trucks where we were compelled to kneel down with our heads toward the floor. In each corner of the truck a guard was stationed with an automatic weapon and a wooden club. My truck moved off. Because the area was close to my home I was able to detect the route even though I could not see where we were going. During the journey, I remember the guards walked all over us and kept beating us. There was blood all over the place.

After an hour's drive they stopped in the Kocevje forest where they were taken off the trucks and ordered to strip. Unlike most of the others Dejak managed to retain his underpants.

France Kozima was in another batch delivered to the same place. He told the court how they were made to walk the hundred yards or so from the trucks to the mouth of a large pit.

While still tied together in pairs, we had to pass between two lines of Partisans who were holding an incredible collection of instruments designed for killing and maiming, including axes, pitchforks and jagged knives fastened to poles. While we passed between the two lines of Partisans they attacked us with these weapons.

At the edge of the pit I was briefly interrogated by a man whom I knew as he had lived in our neighbouring village. His name was Karel Francelj. I remember he looked me straight in the face and asked me to give him my name (which he already knew) and my date of birth. He was standing extremely close to me and I realised he was trying to see if I had any gold teeth. I saw an ammunition box nearby which was filled with gold teeth, watches, rings etc. all swimming in blood which I assumed had come from smashed jaws and severed fingers. Francelj, who was holding a gun, then ordered me to squat down by the edge of the pit. As I did so his gun exploded and I felt a burning pain across my scalp. Instinctively I jumped down into the pit. As I fell I grabbed hold of a tree which was lying inside and this broke my fall. I then realised that by sheer luck I had not been injured by the gunshot.

Having landed I found myself scrambling across an enormous number of dead bodies. I remember as I slithered over them the skin on many bodies appeared to be slippery and often it became partially detached from the flesh beneath. A watery liquid flowed out where the skin was broken.

At the mouth of the pit, Dejak too had not waited for the gun to fire, but had jumped. Likewise, he slithered uninjured across the pile of corpses. 'I remember,' he wrote in his statement, 'seeing many of the bodies with their jaws broken and bloodied where their teeth had been wrenched out.'

Similarly with Milan Zajec.

> I landed on many bodies, most of whom were dead but some only wounded. Shortly I realised that I had not been shot. Immediately I felt that I wanted to die and I remember shouting up to the Partisans to kill me. However, I remember seeing someone else whom I recognised who was wounded. Seeing him gave me the urge to continue living.

It was extremely cold in the bottom of the pits. Kozima remembers dragging a few scraps of clothing which he found on a couple of the dead bodies. He also found a damp patch of stone which he licked to stave off thirst. He discovered a friend who had been in the pit for five days (he died the next morning). A dozen or so other survivors had dragged themselves to the edges of the kiln-shaped chamber. 'There seemed to be no possible escape as the top of the pit was higher than a telegraph pole. Also the sides slanted so that the bottom of the pit was much larger than the top.' All that day and the next, those at the bottom of the pit could hear screams and gunshots coming from above, followed by the sound of bodies flopping onto the slippery heap.

Zajec estimates that two thousand landed in the pit he was in (there were several of them). After a day of silence he and five other survivors started to try to climb out, clambering over rocks and trees. The first one up was met by a Partisan and knifed. He fell back, dead. The others retreated to wait for darkness. Soon the sound of digging came from the top. Then an enormous explosion: the Partisans had dynamited the mouth of the cave with the aim of covering up the evidence of their deeds. Earth and rocks cascaded onto the heap of corpses. But Zajec had crawled into one of the many tunnels leading off the main chamber, and he was not injured. Four more explosions followed. That night two of the four remaining survivors died of cold and starvation. The other two knew that if they did not eat soon they, too, would die. Zajec described how his compatriot, 'using a small knife which he had with him, cut the flesh from a dead body nearby and started to eat it. I tried to eat it but could not swallow as my mouth was completely dry. I had no saliva.'

The next night they *had* to climb out. Using the branches of a tree Zajec was able to do so but his friend was too weak to pull himself up.

There was nothing Zajec could do to help. He had to leave him there to die. Under a new moon, he made his way through the forest, sucking dew from the foliage for liquid. 'I walked to a valley which was full of strawberries which I was very pleased to eat. I then staggered to a village where I found some water near a barn. A woman brought me some food but I left after she asked me why I had not joined the Partisans.' Like Dejak and Kozima, who had also clambered out into the forest under the new moon, he felt it was not safe to push on to the border and freedom so, for the time being, he went into hiding.

It was to be three years before they were able to make their way out of Jugoslavia and thirty-three years before their story became public knowledge. Forty-four years later they came to Court in London to tell it in their own words. But the Judge did not want to hear any 'emotional' testimony. All he would allow them to say was that they had been 'badly treated' in Jugoslavia and that 'they had escaped'. It was a libel trial, he reminded the jury several times, not a war crimes investigation.

7

The COVER-UP

I N EARLY JUNE 1945, while the shootings in Kocevje forest were still in progress, a young Partisan officer, Branko Todorovic, defected to the West. He wrote a long statement covering the brutalities he had witnessed and which had led him to abandon the Communists. This statement came into the hands of the former Deputy Prime Minster of Jugoslavia, Dr Miha Krek, who wrote to Field Marshal Alexander on 7 June asking him to put a stop to the handovers and to impose temporary Allied control of his country to rescue those already repatriated and still unkilled. Krek attached Todorovic's statement to his letter to give weight to his plea.

Alexander responded by asking 8th Army to investigate. 8th Army passed the request down to 5 Corps under Alexander's heading 'War Crimes'. 5 Corps responded with a memorandum headed, 'Handover of Jugoslav Personnel'.[1]

5 Corps' reply enclosed a report signed by General Murray (also headed 'Subject: Handover of Jugoslav Personnel'), describing what happened at Viktring. To cover himself, Murray enclosed copies of Brigadier Low's two applicable orders: the Deception Order and the rider defining his use of the term "Jugoslav national". Murray started with a

---

1   This is another document which has disappeared from the British files, being extant now only in the Kirk papers in the US National Archives. Had AFHQ not been a joint American-British command, with papers deposited in both Washington and London, no record of this part of the cover-up would have survived.

brazen lie: 'No members of the Slovene National Army or any other Jugoslav forces hostile to [Tito] have been handed over to the Partisans.' His next sentence contradicted this. 'On the other hand, on instructions from 5 Corps, numerous nations (*sic*) who have been fighting the Allied Jugoslav troops under the command of Marshal Tito were handed over to the latter forces.'

Keightley attached Murray's document to a report of his own in which he did not comment on either of Murray's claims; instead he made a third one. Like Murray's, his document also contradicted itself. First, Keightley cited the Robertson Order, saying that all the Jugoslavs handed over—26,339 of them—were prisoners of war. He added, in an echo of Low's phraseology in the Definition Order, that they 'were *considered* to have fought for the Germans against Marshal Tito's forces'. (emphasis added) Keightley then said precisely the opposite:

On 24 May, orders were received from AFHQ that no Jugoslav nationals would be handed over to Tito if this involved the use of force. By this date, the evacuation of those who had borne arms against Tito was complete. This order was rigorously applied in evacuating Jugoslav Displaced Personnel, whose evacuation succeeded the evacuation of the Military Personnel.[2]

This implies that all those handed over were prisoners of war. Then Keightley says that those handed over before 24 May were, but those after that date were not.

In Court in 1989 Lord Aldington used Keightley's second argument. Since he claimed to have left on 22 May, and it was only Croats who had been handed over up to that date, this was easier to square with the Robertson order (assuming it had any validity after the Distone Order was issued on 17 May). He then disclaimed responsibility for what happened after 23 May on the ground that he was in England by that time.[3]

---

2   This report has also disappeared from all British files, being extant only in the Kirk papers in the US National Archives. Like Alexander's request, Keightley's report, including Murray's response, is in Cowgill's *Final Report*, Vol II, pp. 292, 299, 300.

3   This assumes that an officer has no responsibility for the execution of orders after he has left the scene. This might be fair, if circumstances changed dramatically after the officer left, but that did not happen in this case. Also Low expected to return from leave in a fortnight's time, presumably to find the policy he had ordered before departure successfully carried out.

The most casual glance at the 5 Corps war diary shows that the Keightley/Aldington argument is nonsense. The Jugoslavs were handed over by national categories, not by degrees of military involvement. The first group to go was the Croats. On 24 May, the diary records, 'handover of Croats complete. Handover of Serbs began.' The last five days of the repatriation, from 26 May, all involved Slovenes.

More importantly, none of this sophistical reasoning is relevant if it is accepted, as it now is even by the most vociferous apologists for the forced repatriations[4], that the Distone Order stated categorically that all the Jugoslavs in Viktring should be evacuated to Italy. The whole operation was clearly insubordinate. Keightley's report is as much a lie as Murray's. It is remarkable that they did not trouble to co-ordinate their stories.

On 31 July Dr Krek got a letter from General Morgan, Alexander's Chief of Staff, denying everything and inventing a fourth excuse for the Jugoslav handovers. Contradicting Keightley and Murray—both of whom had admitted that *some* Jugoslavs who had not fought Tito had been returned—Morgan said, 'no Jugoslavs who have not borne arms against the Allies and are classified as displaced persons have been repatriated to Jugoslavia against their will. It remains (*sic*) the Allied policy to allow such displaced persons a free choice as to whether they wish to return to Jugoslavia or not.'[5] Keightley had said that *everyone* handed over after 24 May was a displaced person. Murray's use of the phrase 'numerous nations' seems to have been designed to suggest, by contrast with 'Jugoslav forces hostile to the Allies', that only non-soldiers were handed over.

If Krek, whom the British Ambassador in Rome thought a nuisance, was not given the courtesy of an honest reply to his query, the situation was quite different when John Selby-Bigge, a senior officer with the Military Government in Austria, enquired. According to Lady Falmouth, head of the British Red Cross Relief Department in Austria at the time, Selby-Bigge met Keightley on 30 May at which he rehearsed the charges of brutality in connection with the Jugoslav handovers.

Keightley listened, but he would not agree to stop the handovers.

---

4   See Cowgill *Final Report*, Vol I, pp. 71-3 (published a year after the trial, in October 1990)

5   FO 371/48825. This emollient message still exists in the British files, unlike Keightley's and Murray's reports on which it is, falsely, based. Since the lies are revealed only in the comparison, this is perhaps not without significance.

Instead, and quite remarkably, *he asked Selby-Bigge to assist in the deception since he knew the Jugoslavs trusted him!* For once, a Briton refused to go along with the 'smiling snake'. Selby-Bigge flatly refused the General's request. Keightley then gave him an order. Selby-Bigge refused to obey it, pointing out that he was not under Army command, but that of the Allied Military Government. Keightley responded by ordering him back to England, as he had the power to do. Selby-Bigge said he would go, but he added that when he got home he would make a report to the Red Cross. With that he turned to leave. Suddenly Keightley gave in. Selby-Bigge could stay, Keightley said. Clearly, any embarrassment was preferable to having the truth spread around London by a well-informed man of principle.

In his memoirs, Selby-Bigge described the 'discreditable' methods 5 Corps had used and said, 'My workers got increasingly restless; one of my supervisors threatened to resign; the head of the Friends Ambulance Unit said his team would not continue to work under these circumstances. From our point of view as Red Cross workers the position was untenable.'[6] Finally, on 4 June, Alexander himself visited 5 Corps where he expressed shock at what had happened during the previous fortnight. He issued what he called the 'New Army Order', which stopped all Jugoslav handovers of any sort with immediate effect.

Selby-Bigge next protested to McCreery at 8th Army about the Cossack handovers, even though they had been completed by this time, barring stragglers. McCreery seemed to be unaware that the "no force" order had been disobeyed. Immediately he issued another order. 'On no account is force to be used in connection with any repatriation scheme.'[7]

But by then it was 13 June and the whole of Cossack Cavalry and the Kazachi Stan had already been in Soviet hands for nearly two weeks. But

6   Unpublished manuscript, kindly provided by Dennis Conolly, a Civilian Relief Worker with the Friends Ambulance Unit which was in Austria and worked with the Red Cross. Conolly was head of the Displaced Person's Information Office in Klagenfurt from 23 May onwards. Conolly has told this author of his only visit to Viktring: 'I was deeply impressed with the orderly state of the camp. The Slovene lady showing me around invited me to tea at their tent and the occasion took place as if we were in an English vicarage garden, not in a rudimentary camp whose inhabitants were in danger of being sent back to Jugoslavia and consequent torture and death.'

7   FO 1020/2838. This signal has disappeared from all British military records.

rumours were spreading: even if most of the intended victims were likely to be *incommunicado* for good, there were still many perpetrators from the British Army who did not like what they had seen being done, or had themselves done. What was called for was a long, flatly-worded, apparently dispassionate report which denied that anything wrong had been done. This 36th Infantry Brigade now proceeded to produce.[8]

Non-Soviet personnel *were* screened from Soviets, the report said— quite untruthfully—and, if a few mistakes were made, this was due to a 'lack of documents and the speed and secrecy with which the operations had to be carried out rendered a complete check impossible'. Today Brigadier (now General) Musson, the Battalion Commander, accepts that this was a lie. 'I don't honestly think screening in my area was really considered,' Musson has told Tolstoy. 'I think the over-riding thing of getting all the officers out of the valley and to Spittal overrode all that.'[9]

Musson also gave a more general warning against taking the written orders at face value. He had been given verbal orders, he said, 'which compelled him to return all the Cossacks under his control, irrespective of nationality.'[10] Musson said that he was told 'on more than one occasion that the order had come from Field Marshal Alexander's headquarters and was H.M. government policy.' Who told him? He will not say.

The cover-up took a different form in the regimental histories. As part of 36th Infantry Brigade, and therefore also 78th Division, it was the 8th Argylls who had had to carry out Arbuthnott's brutal orders at Peggetz on 1 June. But the *History of the Argyll and Sutherland Highlanders 8th Battalion, 1939-47* focuses on other aspects of the regiment's time in

---

8   It is in a PRO file, WO 204/10449, which was withdrawn to the Ministry of Defence on 18 February 1988 and not returned to the PRO until 31 October 1989, Day 25 of the trial. Thus it was kept away from the Defence. Nonetheless, it was used by the Plaintiff, Lord Aldington. In September 1989 the final bundles of evidence were prepared. The 36th Infantry Brigade report was not included. Part of it was inserted in the evidence, at the request of Lord Aldington, after the bundles had been prepared. Tolstoy was cross-examined on it, on Day 22, without the opportunity of seeing the whole file, or even the whole report.

9   Quoted in *The Minister and the Massacres*, p. 316. When Tolstoy made this point in Court, the Judge was aghast. With WO 204/10449 kept in the MoD, and no notice that the report was going to be included in the bundles, the Defence had no opportunity of laying before the Court evidence to counter this report, which even General Musson considers misleading.

10   *Victims of Yalta*, p. 318. Alistair Horne confirms this, quoting Brigadier Tryon-Wilson: 'verbal instructions to divisional and brigade commanders were in accordance with the decision not to screen formations to be sent back.' *Macmillan 1894-1956*, p. 267

Austria. This is the whole of the text relating to the handovers:

> The [Cossack men] were dispersed by units all along the fifteen miles of the
> Drau valley from Lienz to Oberdrauberg, and the women and children were
> in a hutted camp at Lienz. Major Davies was made liaison officer at Cossack
> HQ, and his responsibility was to try and get them to carry out British
> orders—not an easy task, because although the officers were willing to help,
> the discipline of the division was conspicuous only by its absence.[11] They
> remained in this situation until June (*sic*), when orders to send all the
> Cossacks back to Russia were received. This was the fate which they had
> all been dreading, and consequently there was considerable unrest and
> desertion. As these camps were neither wired nor guarded, it was not a
> difficult matter to escape into the mountains (as many did), but it did not
> simplify the Battalion's duty of entraining them. After some unpleasant
> days this duty was completed: the camps were cleared of their personnel,
> but their 5000 horses remained in the area, and Captain McNeill had to
> exercise considerable initiative to find grazing for this herd. It was event-
> ually disposed over the whole of Austria, but not before he had selected a
> fine string of animals for the 8th Argylls... A brown mare called Katinka
> carried the Battalion Colours to victory on ten occasions in the seasons of
> 1945 and 1946 at race meetings organised by 46th and 78th Divisions.

In 1946, General McCreery wrote the Foreword to *The Story of 46th Division 1939-45*. He did not make explicit mention of the forced repatriations in which the Division had played a leading part, but he did refer briefly to the period immediately after the end of the hostilities.

> In Austria the 46th Division has fully upheld its great reputation in battle.
> Since the end of the fighting a great variety of tasks has been undertaken,
> many of them unfamiliar. The British soldier has once again been a good
> ambassador for his country. By his cheerfulness, his high standard of
> soldierly bearing and his good behaviour to the civil population he has won
> the respect of the Austrians and has shown why we won the war.

---

11   Contrast this with 36th Infantry Brigade (of which the 8th Argylls were a part) report, as quoted
above. 'On the whole the Cossack forces were well organised. Discipline and morale were
surprisingly high.' That version, written in 1946, was categorised at the time, 'Closed until
2046'; the regimental history was available immediately on publication in 1949.

General Keightley himself added to the chorus when, on 18 July 1945, while back in London on leave, he went to see a senior Red Cross official, Lady Limerick, by way of countering any lingering problems arising from his conversation with Selby-Bigge. Keightley told Lady Limerick that the Cossacks had left for the Soviet Union quite willingly. After they were 'interviewed' they 'agreed to return to Soviet territory with their wives and children', although some of the women protested briefly 'under the instigation of their priest'. British troops only had 'to shoot twice' and in neither case did they hit anybody.

As far as the Jugoslavs were concerned, Keightley was equally dishonest:

> There was a considerable number of Jugoslav Displaced Persons (not soldiers) [Lady Limerick wrote], they were asked if they were prepared to return to Jugoslavia, and expressed themselves quite willing, in fact volunteered and were accordingly sent off by train and lorry. After they crossed a bridge they were all machine-gunned. On this information being received, no further evacuations to Jugoslavia were made.[12]

Keightley ended by giving a 'categorical assurance that there were no unwilling people being sent back'.

Despite General Morgan's dismissive reply to his letter to Alexander, Krek circulated Todorovic's statement as widely as he could. As a result, on 4 August, Alexander Kirk was outraged to learn that, quite contrary to Allied policy and without his concurrence, Croats, Serbs and Slovenes had been handed over by 5 Corps to Tito. The State Department in Washington told him to protest. He did, but to no avail.

A few days later, a British Member of Parliament, Major Guy Lloyd, tried to raise the matter with the Foreign Office. The query landed on the desk of John Colville who had been Churchill's private secretary during the war. Colville was able to say that, as far as he knew, no inkling of any of the events described had reached the Prime Minister's ears. He thought the incident so serious that the War Office should be asked to investigate. 'I think we can do no more than admit that a serious blunder took place and that the story does not reflect well on the officers immediately concerned.' But the Foreign Office refused to make these doubts known to Major Lloyd. Parliament was, in effect, misled and the enquiry died.[13]

Two years later Sir Charles Keightley (as he by then was) was given a rest from command in the field and appointed Military Secretary to the Secretary of State for War, Emanuel ("Manny") Shinwell. He had hardly started in his new job than a familiar problem landed on his desk. The Duchess of Atholl, a prominent anti-Communist, had been given Todorovic's statement about the Partisan crimes. She passed it on to an MP, Reginald Paget, who wrote to the War Office asking for an explanation. As luck would have it, it fell to Keightley to provide the briefing on which the reply was based. While Kozima, Dejak and Zajec were still living rough in the Slovenian hills, Keightley made the following points about the Jugoslav handovers:

- Each one of the hundreds of thousands of prisoners of war and displaced persons in Austria in May 1945 filled up a form to say where they wanted to go.
- Many of the Jugoslavs chose to go back to Jugoslavia. 'There was no question of these being sent to Jugoslavia against their will as has been suggested.'
- The British were especially careful not to send any Chetniks back. Instead they were routed to Italy.
- Senior Jugoslav (i.e. Partisan) officers denied the claims made in the Todorovic statement. 'My own feeling,' Keightley wrote, 'is that some Jugoslavs were killed, but for some specific reason and not in the least in the manner or numbers indicated in the report... We had at the same time many equally colourful reports on entirely different subjects which proved to be completely untrue.'
- After receiving the Todorovic report, the British 'allowed' more Jugoslavs to go back across the border.
- The Jugoslavs were not, he felt sure, ever told they were going to

---

13   It is noteworthy that Colville told Tolstoy in 1984 that he thought that Alexander could not have been responsible. 'It would have been wholly untrue to his form,' he said. 'Whether Harold Macmillan was responsible, I doubt if we shall ever know, for I expect orders were not committed to paper and it seems clear that the Chiefs of Staff, the Foreign Office and the Prime Minister were not informed.'

Italy. Both his and Field Marshal Alexander's concern was to get them down to Italy, but for some reason it was felt better not to give them this news.[14]

This was the most comprehensively dishonest account so far, yet it formed the basis for the parliamentary answer, which Keightley himself drafted:

> It can be categorically stated [Keightley wrote] that... no Jugoslav displaced persons were ever sent back to Jugoslavia against their will or under false pretences, nor were any Jugoslav prisoners once they came into British hands. It is understood that a certain number of Jugoslavs did return to Jugoslavia shortly after the ceasefire entirely of their own free will. Whether any of these were killed in Jugoslavia cannot be found out for certain, but it is certain that no mass killing as described ever took place.[15]

This is such a deceitful reply that it is almost impossible to conclude that Keightley was not the victim of a guilty conscience. That in turn may explain the weeding of the 5 Corps war diary, which was done while he was working in Whitehall. Whoever carried it out, and for whatever purpose, the scale of the weeding was enormous. It is best illustrated with reference to the selection of papers made by the principle apologist for the repatriations, Brigadier Cowgill (see below Chapter 12). Of the documents he reproduces in his *Final Report on the Repatriations from Austria in 1945, Vol II The Documents*, taking the period from the German surrender to the date of Alexander's New Army Order—8 May to 4 June—there are 232 "Key Papers" listed. Of these nearly a quarter, 52 of them, come from the US National Archives because they no longer exist in the British files. Of the messages he quotes from the AFHQ Message Centre (Caserta) 33 out of 42 come from America. Thus 78% of the messages which passed through Alexander's headquarters and

---

14 Quoted in Cowgill's *Final Report*, Vol I, pp. 170-1. Cowgill gives no bibliographic reference. When asked for it by this author, he replied saying, 'I am not going to do Tolstoy's research for him at third hand.' Christopher Booker, author of *The Looking Glass Tragedy* later said the Committee were lent the document by Alistair Horne. Horne initially agreed to allow access to his papers (letter to the author 5 January 1994), then later stopped replying to letters.

15 *Ibid.*, p. 171. The comments in the previous note apply.

which are required to understand the history even from a sympathetic point of view can only be found in foreign archives. There are two series of files, WO 228 and WO 229, listed in the PRO catalogue as 'Military HQ papers: AFHQ microfilm'. Yet both sets of files are closed. The result to date has been that, but for the passage of the Freedom of Information Act in the United States—an event which could not have been foreseen in 1946—the whole episode might well have gone completely unnoticed by history. 5 Corps would, in that case, have "got away with it". British historians of their own country's military past are, like Russian researchers in the Soviet period, dependant on foreign archives to keep a record of their government's misdeeds.

Lord Aldington's explanation for the paucity of material, given to Richard Keightley, the General's son, shortly before the trial opened, is bizarre. Neither his own nor the General's personal files had survived, Lord Aldington explained, because 'the office trucks of 5 Corps were squashed by falling walls on their way through Italy after the move of HQ from Austria at the end of 1945.'[16]

Another attempt to get at the truth, this time of the Cossack repatriations only, was made in July 1947 by another Member of Parliament, Tufton Beamish (later Lord Chelwood). He had been alerted to the events of 1945 by a Mrs Tiashelnikova who wanted the government to try to secure the release from the Soviet Union of some of the non-Soviet citizens who had been "repatriated". The enquiry found its way to the War Office, where Keightley was still at work. After four months, a reply was produced which drew almost exclusively on the 36th Infantry Brigade's account of the handovers at Peggetz.[17] The War Office recommended the inquirer be told two specific lies: everything was done to ensure to prevent non-Soviet nationals being included in those evacuated, they said, and over 2,000 of them were segregated and not dispatched to the Soviet Union.

This information was digested in Whitehall and, in December that year, Beamish received a reply to the effect that there was nothing that the

16   Letter from Aldington to Richard Keightley, 12 August 1989
17   Note that although the file was closed to the *public* until 2046, it was available for the government to use as it pleased. Its early release was due to the passage of the Public Records Acts of 1958 and 1967.

British government could or would do. 'We should not be willing to ask for [the people mentioned by Mrs Tiashelnikova] and the Russians would not be willing to let them go.' The most helpful suggestion the War Office could make was that relatives of the victims should write to the Union of Soviet Red Cross and Red Crescent Societies, Kuibyshev Street, Moscow.

With that, the rumours of forcible repatriations in Austria began to fade from the public memory. Other, larger issues cropped up, one of which, the Korean War, raised the problem of forcible repatriation of refugees and prisoners of war again. Should the North Korean or Chinese prisoners of war in United Nations captivity be handed over against their will to the North as part of any future armistice? By the time this question needed an answer, in 1952, the British Foreign Secretary was Anthony Eden once again. The man who had argued so ruthlessly in favour of forcible repatriations in 1944, now declared that he was against them. With the 1944 Cabinet papers still secret, he was able to take his stand, not on practical grounds but on *moral* ones. His answer was the opposite of what 5 Corps had done in Carinthia in 1945. The numbers involved were not dissimilar, 62,000 in this case. In the event, each man was interrogated individually and his wishes were respected. 'It would clearly be repugnant to the sense of values of the free world to send these men home by force,' Eden told the House of Commons on 7 May 1952. 'It would make a deplorable impression on fair and liberal-minded opinion all over the world and would go far to cancel out the effect made on world opinion by the evident firmness of purpose underlying the United Nations resistance to aggression in Korea.'

After that statement, there was only one man left in Britain who had the power to get at the truth: the Prime Minister, Winston Churchill. In February 1953, during his second term of office, Churchill tried. The occasion was a letter from a General Polyakov, a prominent émigré Russian, who wrote to the Prime Minister describing something of what had gone on at Peggetz on 1 June 1945 and saying that many of the people who were beaten up and handed to the Soviets had not in fact been Soviet citizens. Polyakov pointed out that the numbers involved were larger than those massacred at Katyn, already an international scandal. He asked Churchill to instigate an enquiry and try to find out who was guilty.

The matter was handed to the Foreign Office, which would not authorise any reply beyond 'a non-committal acknowledgement'. But, anticipating questions in the House of Commons, Churchill demanded further information.[18] The Foreign Office played for time, taking eight weeks to arrive at the provisional conclusion that the personnel referred to in Polyakov's letter were probably the '15th SS (*sic*) Cossack Cavalry Corps'.[19] These men had been repatriated, the Foreign Office said, as a result of an agreement signed by Field Marshal Alexander and the Soviet authorities in Vienna on 23 May 1945. They could not find a copy of that agreement, so they asked the War Office.

For some reason the enquiry was re-routed to the Cabinet Office and away from the War Office. It is not known who arranged this, but possibly the only person who would have had both the authority to do so and the motive to damp down the enquiry would have been Anthony Eden. A careful search of the files was made but no record of any agreement could be found. Since no such agreement had ever been signed, and Alexander had spent the whole of the latter part of May in southern Italy, this was not surprising. What was surprising was that they did not ask the Minister in charge of the War Office at the time, who was none other than *Alexander himself*. But, for some very peculiar reason, they did not. Churchill never received the answer he wanted.

18   Possibly he remembered his enquiry of General Ismay on 20 May 1945. Ismay had replied on 5 June, *after* the last of the Cossacks had been handed over by 5 Corps that they were living in Austria in fear of being handed over to Tito, against whom they had fought with 'savagery'. They came, Ismay said, 'from very backward and ferocious Cossack tribes of the north Caucasus and were reckoned excellent auxiliaries by the Germans.'

19   This is, as far as can be ascertained, the first recorded reference to the Cossack Cavalry as an SS formation. Like the Jugoslavs, they were in the ironic position that, had they actually been one, they would have been saved from the Definition Order by paragraph 2 of the Robertson Order and sent to Italy for individual interrogation. Both Cowgill and Horne refer to them as the '15th SS Cossack Cavalry Corps', though without giving any justification for the use of the term.

Part II

The *CONTROVERSY*

'I hope His Majesty's Government will do all they can to see that steps are taken in the peace treaty to show to the Japanese people as a whole that they are responsible for the foul treatment meted out by their soldiers and officers to our prisoners.'

—Brigadier A.R.W. Low, MP
House of Commons, 1951

8

The BUSY BARON

A T THE CONCLUSION of the libel trial in 1989, Lord Aldington was awarded £1,500,000 in compensation for the damage to his reputation caused by Count Tolstoy's allegations about his conduct as BGS 5 Corps in May 1945. This was then, and still is, by far the largest award ever made in a personal defamation suit in England. It is legitimate, therefore, to enquire into the nature of the reputation that the jury were presuming had been damaged. More than this, a brief examination of the subsequent career of the man who signed the Deception and Definition Orders might provide some clues to the greatest remaining mystery of the forced repatriations: why? Is it credible that Eden's March letter—'our great problem today is the Bear'—could have influenced 5 Corps' approach, especially so when reinforced by a ruthless pep talk from Macmillan? How desperate was Low to please the men he thought might be able to help him? One thing is certain: a sketch of Lord Aldington's career helps explain why he thought it worthwhile asking to have files moved from the Public Record Office to Whitehall with such disastrous consequences for the trial in 1989.

The first point to emphasise—and possibly it is the most important of all when considering the course of the litigation he undertook—is that to Lord Aldington the reputation which is the subject of this book was of absolutely vital importance to him. To a much greater extent than most men, even men in public life, Lord Aldington is sensitive to slights. Since his schooldays, he has devoted his best energies to building up a reputation with his peers and superiors. Like a lot of egocentric men with an exaggerated desire to be noticed by the world at large—of those who figure in this story, Winston Churchill, Anthony Eden, Harold Macmillan and Nikolai Tolstoy were in some degree affected—Lord Aldington suffered from a badly disrupted relationship with his father. The natural self-esteem which a boy develops from a conventional relationship with his father was not something Lord Aldington ever enjoyed. The hurt with which he responded to Tolstoy's attack on his war record is understandable, but the vindictiveness with which he has pursued his defeated adversary is explicable, it seems to this author at least, only in terms of a personality racked with inner insecurity.

Lord Aldington comes from a broken home. When he was fourteen his parents divorced in an unusually acrimonious atmosphere. 'Terrible, fearful scenes,' he recalled six decades later. 'They didn't talk to each other for another nine years.' The young Toby Low saw his father only infrequently after that, forming a closer bond with his maternal grandfather, the well-known judge, Lord Atkin.[1] Lord Aldington's father was lost at sea in 1942 when the ship taking him on a business trip to India was torpedoed.

Low had much more contact with his grandfather, Sir Austin Low. Sir Austen was the son of Stephen Philpot Low, who had joined Grindlay's Bank as a clerk in 1856 and risen to the top. Sir Austen in turn became Chairman of the Bank (for which he was knighted), as well as a director of the National Provincial Bank and the London Assurance. In all, he worked at Grindlay's for seventy years. He was a member of the Carlton Club as well as a freemason. His funeral, in 1956, was attended by no

---

1   James Atkin was born in Brisbane, Australia, of Irish immigrant parents from County Cork. His father died when he was young and his mother, who was Welsh, took the family to Wales. Atkin, who for the rest of his life regarded himself as a Welshman, became a barrister then a judge, finally being made a Lord of Appeal in 1928. He earned a considerable reputation for defending the rights of the individual against large and powerful organisations. He was the first judge to uphold a major claim for negligence against a manufacturer, in *Donoghue v Stevenson* (1932), when he awarded compensation to the purchaser of a ginger beer who found in it, after drinking the contents of the opaque bottle, the decomposed remains of a snail. One of Atkin's most famous judicial opinions was a dissenting one, in *Liversidge v Anderson* (1942), when he opposed "bureaucratic dictatorship", even in wartime. He held that the courts, rather than the Home Secretary, should have the final say about the legality of an alien detention order. 'In this country,' Atkin said, 'amidst the clash of arms, the laws are not silent.' A quarter of a century later Lord Aldington proudly quoted this noble dictum to the House of Lords (in Latin). Atkin married an Australian, had seven children—the boys were sent to Winchester—and died in the land of his mother's fathers in 1944.

less a dignitary than Vivian Elgood of the United Lodge, later to become Grand Treasurer General of the Supreme Council of the 33rd Degree.

Sir Austen sent his son, Stuart, to Winchester, the first of that branch of the family to receive a public school education, although the boy did not go on to university. Stuart Low trained as a solicitor then joined Grindlay's Bank. He served in the Gunners in the First World War, rising to become a Colonel and winning the DSO. He acquired the nickname "Punch" Low, which is why his son came to be called "Toby". Despite his wartime successes, surviving photographs give the impression of Stuart Low as a sharp, possibly bumptious, man.

Toby was sent, like his father, to Winchester where he became Senior Commoner Prefect (unofficial head boy: the nominal head boy is a Scholar) and won prizes for maths and English Speech. Out of doors, he rowed and won the school steeplechase twice. He capped his school career by winning an Exhibition to New College, Oxford, where he read Law.

Low was called to the Bar in early 1939 and, shortly afterwards, appointed Secretary to Lord Porter's Royal Commission on defamation law reform, a signal honour for a novice barrister. But the war interrupted his career at the libel bar and took him, as described earlier, into politics as Member of Parliament for Blackpool North.

On 21 April 1947, on the day of Princess Elizabeth's 21st birthday and three months after Generals Krasnov, Shkuro and von Pannwitz were hung in Moscow, Brigadier Toby Low married Mrs Araminta Bowman. They had met before the war, in a train on the way to a hunt ball. 'I fell in love with the whole manner, lovely shape, gorgeous eyes, the whole joy of life,' he recalled recently. 'Be kind to me,' he said to her at their first meeting, 'I've been hurt too much.' But Araminta disregarded his plea and married someone else. Today she says, 'I certainly did not fall in love with *him* at first sight. I wasn't interested in anyone who did not know one end of a horse from another and couldn't waltz. When you're seventeen those are the only two things that matter.'

Araminta went abroad, to Palestine, where her father, Sir Harold MacMichael, was the British High Commissioner.[2] Then she came back

---

2   Harold MacMichael, the son of a vicar, was educated at Bedford Grammar School and Cambridge, where he took a First in Arabic. He joined the Sudan Political Service in 1905

to Britain and became an announcer, known as Ann Bowman, on the BBC Forces radio. Her previous marriage was dissolved, and she met Toby Low again.

They were married in a register office in Kent, near the bride's parents' home. After a Church blessing service, the couple drove up to London for a reception at the Hyde Park Hotel. The *West Lancashire Evening Gazette* described the groom as a Director of Grindlay's bank and a barrister who 'was assigned to important work on the Continent after the German capitulation.'

On 22 June 1948 Araminta gave birth to a son, who, according to *The Times*, had no fewer than six godparents. The three godfathers were Mr John Hogg, who had been Low's best man, Colonel Charles Villiers, late of the 6th Special Force in Jugoslavia and Austria and whose best man the groom had been in 1938, and Mr Anthony Eden. According to the *West Lancashire Evening Gazette* there was one more. A short piece, under the headline 'Seven Godparents', listed those above but added 'Lieut.-Gen. Sir Charles Keightley KBE, CB, DSO'.

In the House of Commons, Low was the archetypal backbencher. He busied himself with his constituents' concerns rather than trying to build a reputation with the country at large. He wrote to the Minister of Labour asking what steps he had taken to assist sea-side laundries in finding the labour they needed to wash holiday-makers' clothes. He asked the Minister of Food if he had 'considered the regulations governing the allocation of fat to fish friers to bring them into line with the regulations covering the allocation of fat to caterers so that fat may be allocated to fish friers on the basis of numbers of fried fish sold rather than on the present basis of the 1939 figures?' He drew the attention of the President of the Board of Trade to the problems of a Blackpool manufacturer of

---

where he spent his spare time researching and writing about topics like the branding marks used on camels in northern Kordofan. His biggest literary achievement was a two-volume *History of the Arabs in the Sudan*, published in 1922. He rose high in the Sudan civil service, and later became governor of Tanganyika. In 1932 he was knighted and in 1937 he was appointed High Commissioner and Commander-in-Chief in Palestine. As an Arabist, he was disliked by the Jews. On 8 August 1944, the Stern gang tried to assassinate him. Lady MacMichael was slightly hurt, but Sir Harold was unscathed. He left Palestine a month later and spent most of the rest of his life in Britain. In 1919 he had married another child of the vicarage. They had two daughters and Sir Harold died in Kent in 1969.

false teeth: why had he 'authorised the expenditure of $502,702 on the import of luxury artificial teeth from the United States when Messrs. Hawtins Ltd. of Blackpool produce similar or better class teeth and export their teeth all round the world?'

It is noticeable that Low avoided contributing to debates on matters which touched, even peripherally, on the events of May 1945. In November 1945 a parliamentary delegation was sent to Jugoslavia to observe the country's first "elections" under Communism. The debate on the delegation's report veered off the subject of Jugoslav politics and on to war crimes. The Labour Member for Newcastle West, a Mr Popplewell, told the House that he had found the Jugoslavs suspicious of the position Britain was adopting about repatriating alleged war criminals.

> [They] had seen the Allies declare as part and parcel of their war aims the return of various war criminals. Jugoslavia has submitted applications, and asked for the return of a number of war criminals who committed atrocities in their country that take one's breath away, and yet they find these people away in Italy today as tourists.[3]

Why did Brigadier Low not try to add some clarity to a debate which descended at times to ludicrous levels? Major Macpherson (Dumfries), for example, felt it necessary to tell the House that he did not believe 'mass executions or deportations do anything but harm.' Apart from Brigadier Fitzroy Maclean, then Member for Lancaster and a friend of Low's, the Member for Blackpool North was possibly the only one in the House who had any first-hand experience of these problems. Yet he did not say a word.

The only occasion when Low spoke about war crimes was in a debate on the Japanese peace treaty in 1951. A Brigadier Smyth had moved that the government should ask the Japanese government for compensation for British troops who had endured Japanese captivity during the war 'for the brutalities, indignities and gross under-nourishment to which they were subject in flagrant contravention of the Hague (*sic*) Convention'. Low opposed this proposal, but on the grounds of bureaucratic logic rather than simple indifference to the fate of the men concerned.

---

3   *Hansard*, 22 November 1945

I wholeheartedly accept the principle which my Honourable and Gallant friend said was behind the motion—that everything should be done to see that in future no Power treats prisoners of war in the way our prisoners of war were treated. I hope that His Majesty's government will do all they can to see that steps can be taken in the peace treaty to show to *the Japanese people as a whole* that they are responsible for the foul treatment meted out by their soldiers and officers to our prisoners. (emphasis added)[4]

Despite the fact that many officers had been charged with war crimes by the International Tribunal sitting in Tokyo, 'the nation too has a responsibility,' Low said. 'International law is so often flouted that every opportunity should be taken of bringing home to the nation the fact that it cannot be flouted with impunity.'

Low went on to develop a subtle argument for not compensating British ex-prisoners of war. Instead the British government should ask for reparations, he said, even if it was clear that they could not be paid. Low's first premiss was that when the Crown declares war on a foreign enemy, it is the duty of His Majesty's government to act as the insurer of last resort against all injury done to British subjects in wartime. The correct agency for dealing with compensation was the Ministry of Pensions. 'The great value of the Ministry of Pensions is that through its excellent machinery it is able to deal with *each individual case separately* and compensate each individual for the damage he has suffered.' (emphasis added) Low went on to say that he was against any extra provision being made for those who had been through Japanese camps. What about those who had suffered in German captivity? What about those killed or wounded in action but who were never captured? It would be unfair to give extra compensation to one category and not the others, he said. This was 'the cold, hard logic of cold, hard principles'. Low ended by saying that 'the Foreign Office should take all possible steps to see that never again does any nation treat prisoners of war in the way these prisoners were treated.'

After his outstanding successes at school and the bar and in the Army, Low's post-war career has the feel of early promise not fully realised. Beyond parliament he obtained only two directorships: one with Grin-

4   *Ibid.*, 10 May 1951

dlay's, predictably—'heavily encouraged, I must admit, by my grand-father'—and the other with a Lancashire concern, the United Premier Oil and Cake Company. Likewise his political career, while perfectly respectable, showed no signs of taking off. When the Conservatives were returned to office in 1951, Low achieved office, it is true, but at the lowest possible rank, being appointed Parliamentary Secretary at the Ministry of Supply. Nonetheless, he played this break for all it was worth, telling the *West Lancashire Evening Gazette* that when he went to see Churchill to accept the job the Prime Minister 'literally bounded out of his chair, gave me a most hearty handshake and smack on the back, and said, "I am very glad you are going to join us".'

Low's most noticeable quality in government was his energy. 'There must be few people who can pack as many facts and comments into 300 seconds as Mr Low,' one reporter gushed after being granted a five-minute interview on the subject of a recent eleven-day trip to Finland, Norway and Sweden. This energy was rewarded when Low was made Minister of State at the Board of Trade in 1954. But there his career stalled. Even the appointment of his old mentor, Sir Anthony Eden, as Prime Minister the following year did not bring the expected offer of promotion to a position with some real power. Low hung on until January 1957, when Eden resigned. Low decided to go with him and told the incoming Prime Minister, Harold Macmillan, that he would not be available for government as he needed to make money to pay for the education of his son (at Winchester) and two daughters. Macmillan knighted him in his first Honours list, as he did Isaiah Berlin; Sir Thomas Beecham was made a Companion of Honour and J. Arthur Rank was elevated to the Peerage. The municipal fathers of Blackpool took this as a compliment to their town and Sir Toby Low KCMG, CBE, DSO, PC, MP received a formal telegram of congratulation from the Mayor, Councillor Grimbledeston BEM, JP.

Low's new goal was to capitalise on the contacts he had made while in government. Having been at the Ministry of Supply and the Board of Trade he was ideally placed to do that. But he started with old friends. After resuming his seat on the Grindlay's board, he was made a director of the Clyde shipbuilding firm of John Brown and Co., where the Chairman was an old Oxford friend, Lord Aberconway. (Aberconway was also a director of both the National Provincial Bank and the London Assurance, as Sir Austin Low had been.) Three weeks later Low was appointed to the board of the civil engineering group, Dowsett Holdings, soon being appointed Deputy Chairman under Field Marshal Sir Claud Auchinleck, who had earlier been a director of Grindlay's. Two months later Sir Toby joined the board of Dorman Long, a large steel-making and construction company based in Middlesborough.

Finally, and most significantly, he was appointed to the Board of Arnold Weinstock's aggressively expansionist industrial conglomerate, the General Electric Company (GEC). In the late 1950s GEC was trying to expand its nuclear power-generating interests and was keen to employ the man who, while at the Ministry of Supply, had overseen the Dounreay project in Caithness. This was then, as now, a field in which government patronage was all-important. Low was a consistent enthusiast for nuclear power, both civil and military.[5] It is perhaps significant that it was on 2 May 1957, only a fortnight after Low joined the firm, that Dorman Long announced that it, too, was going into the nuclear business. Five years in junior ministerial positions in trade- and industry-related departments had obviously made a tremendous difference to Low's reputation in industry. Although still on the lookout for other Directorships, he never went back to the United Premier Oil and Cake Company.

Five Directorships was not enough for the position-hungry Sir Toby. Within the year, he was appointed chairman of the Conservative Party Finance Committee, chairman of the Conservative Party's Commonwealth Affairs Committee and chairman of the all-party House of Commons Select Committee on Nationalised Industries. By all accounts he was an excellent committee chairman. Alfred Robens, the Labour MP and future chairman of the National Coal Board, said that 'congratulations are due to Sir Toby Low for his work as chairman [of the Nationalised Industries select committee]. So wisely did he guide the committee that it produced from the chairman and deputy-chairman of the Coal Board what is the best evidence I have ever seen in relation to the coal industry.'

Sir Toby's skill in this field derived partly from his ability to be all things to all men. When the Chancellor of the Exchequer, Peter Thorney-croft resigned, in January 1958, Sir Toby was, almost uniquely, able to

---

5   In December 1950, for example, at a time when the Korean War was going badly for the United Nations, Low had told the Sydenham County School for Girls that Britain should make it clear 'to all that immediately upon any Russian aggression in Europe, or any Russian inspired aggression, the atomic bomb will be dropped on Russia.'

defend *both* sides of the dispute. 'I know it is unpopular to sit on the fence or to try to back both horses,' Sir Toby said in the House, 'but it is likely that if Mr Thorneycroft was right to resign, the government were right to accede to his request.'[6]

This was a man who wanted to be liked. Part of his technique was his eternal optimism. Sometimes he took it to a ludicrous extreme, as, for example, when he told a meeting of manufacturers at the Gifts and Fancy Goods Fair in 1957 that he looked forward to the time when the value of their exports matched those of the British aircraft industry. Already, Sir Toby said, Britain 'led the world [in the] design and manufacture of powder compacts'.

At Christmas 1958, Low invited a rising young star of the Conservative Party, Edward Heath, to a bonfire party at Knoll Farm, the country home he had bought outside the village of Aldington, in Kent, on the heights above Romney Marsh (from where he was soon to be afforded a distant prospect of Dungeness power station, another GEC contract). Soon Heath was a regular visitor there. In the evenings Lady Low would sing while Heath accompanied her on the piano. Heath often preferred to spend Christmas or other holidays there, rather than with his own family in Dumpton Gap Road, Broadstairs. Ten years later, one of Heath's biographers described Lord Aldington, as Sir Toby by then was, as 'a wiry, very active man, always darting about, busy, yet thoughtful, even studious, and radical in outlook. The Aldingtons are both inclined to be blunt; they are as much in Heath's confidence as anybody.'[7] A recent book called Lord Aldington Heath's 'foul-weather friend'.[8]

In 1959 the glass was still rising for Sir Toby. But in terms of the fading memory of 1945, there was a cloud on the horizon, small and distant, it is true, but one which was destined to overshadow the sunlit years of retirement that he was later to look forward to in vain: on 1 January 1959 the Public Records Act came into force.

Hitherto, the decision as to which records should be made available for public scrutiny, to whom and when, was a matter for each of the

6   *Ibid.*, 23 January 1958
7   Hutchinson *Edward Heath*, pp. 157-8
8   Campbell *Edward Heath*, p. 655

departments of state. The Foreign Office, for example, had, until 1858, denied all public access to any of its records. In that year it took the considerable step of opening its archives up to 1688. This did not mean that a 170-year rule now operated: the open date stayed at 1688 until it was later brought forward to 1760. In 1891, the files were opened up to 1802, but a date so recent was thought to be risky and large categories of files were barred to the public. In effect, the Foreign Office acted as the owner of private papers rather than the custodian of public ones. Other departments did much the same. The danger for a government was that any department might, on its own initiative, make papers of any date, even recent ones, available to a researcher without the government being aware of the fact. To prevent any such disasters, the rules of record publishing had to be systematised. This the Public Record Act did by introducing the 50-year rule.

By this rule the army records for 1945 would be available to historians, not in 2046 as originally envisaged when they were archived, but in 1996. This was far enough away that no-one with guilty secrets need have worried unduly. Had he lived that long, Keightley would have been 95 years old by then; Macmillan would have been 102. The only foreseeable danger was that, once the government had reduced the issue to a simple figure, a demand might emerge for a lower figure. What was so sacred about 50? Why not 40? Or even 30? This was exactly what happened in the 1960s. Under Harold Wilson's Labour government the Public Records Act of 1967 was passed which amended the standard period to 30 years.

As a result, in the early 1970s researchers were able to study all the files on the Second World War. Crucially, this was long before the people involved were all dead. For the first time in British history, researchers had free access to both the official records of events and living witnesses to them. People like Zoë Polanska could match their memories of events in the barrack square at Peggetz on 1 June 1945 with the official report— the one which General Musson now says was a lie—of the same events prepared by 36th Infantry Brigade. History was about to come alive. For Lord Aldington, the consequences were to prove catastrophic.

But that was ten years hence. In the early 1960s Sir Toby took on more Directorships. He joined Lord Aberconway on the board of English China Clays and, after he had been elevated to the peerage, London Assurance (where Sir Austin had been a Director). This company was to merge in

1965 with the Sun Alliance Insurance company to become the Sun Alliance and London Insurance. Twenty-five years later, the company paid the costs of Lord Aldington's libel action.

In 1961, Harold Macmillan gave Sir Toby Low one of the last of the hereditary baronies 'for political and public services'. He became the 1st Baron Aldington of Bispham. In 1989, Aldington told the Court that the idea for the title was not his own. 'I was wondering what I should call myself,' he said, 'when the Chairman of the Parish Council came to see me and said that he and his friends would very much like it if I would take the title of Aldington.' Sir Toby graciously acceded to this request. He added Bispham in memory of the successes he had scored in Blackpool, of which Bispham is a part. The new peer's sponsors in the House of Lords were Lords Carrington and Crathorne.

Soon after being ennobled, Lord Aldington's career took a further step upwards when he joined Lords Runciman, Abergavenny, Bearstead, Beeching, Cobham, Franks, Kenyon, Lloyd, Luke, Neverthorpe and Waldegrave on the board of Lloyds Bank. Many debates in the House of Lords were attended by fewer peers than board meetings at 71 Lombard Street.

In 1962 he was appointed to one of his most influential positions, Deputy Chairman of the Conservative Party. Under the Chairman, Iain Macleod, he was in charge of party organisation. On at least one occasion, he revealed a streak of unprincipled ruthlessness which does him no credit. Once again, the evidence would not be available today had it not been for the Public Records Act of 1967.

The subject was Europe and the campaign, led by Macmillan and organised in detail by Edward Heath, to take Britain into Europe. After a promising start, by the middle of 1962 the campaign to persuade the country of the benefits of joining the EEC was faltering. What could be done? Iain Macleod suggested to his new deputy that support should be lent to the activities of a lobbying group called the Commonwealth and Europe League. Aldington was against this.

On 11 September he minuted Macleod on this subject. It was important to mount a media campaign against those who opposed entry, Lord Aldington said, but this could be done through newspapers sympathetic to the Conservative Party. 'We do not need a League to do this. We have got Bill Deedes.'[9] If any lobbying were to be done, Lord Aldington preferred to do it covertly through another group, called the United Kingdom Council of the European Movement.[10]

This was a high-profile, ostensibly non-party organisation, with five Presidents of Honour: Winston Churchill, Konrad Adenauer, Paul-Henri Spaak, Robert Schuman and M.R. de Coudenhove-Kalergi, all of them luminaries in the movement for closer European co-operation. The value of such a body to the Conservatives was that it was publicly considered to be above party politics. The names of the heads of the four main Christian denominations in Britain and that of the Chief Rabbi graced the notepaper to reinforce this point.

With unembarrassed ruthlessness, Aldington minuted Macleod to the effect that this organisation could be suborned.

> If [the United Kingdom Council] wants more money it is in a very good position to get it. My links with [the Chairman] Edward Beddington-Behrens are such—and these were formed at the Prime Minister's request last August—that he will try to do what we want *even though this might involve us in putting him in funds under cover.* (emphasis added)[11]

It seems that nothing came of these disreputable suggestions.

Lord Aldington's political career came to a complete end when he resigned the Deputy Chairmanship immediately Sir Alec Douglas Home was appointed Prime Minister in 1963. Aldington had been one of what Randolph Churchill at the time called the *caballeros* who had tried to block Sir Alec's path, in the hope that "Rab" Butler would be given the job. The whole operation was an abject failure. Iain Macleod, Enoch Powell, Reginald Maudling and Frederick Erroll, then President of the

9   Deedes had been on the staff of the *Daily Telegraph* and was then Minister without Portfolio with special responsibility for co-ordinating government information services. He was the MP for Ashford, a constituency which included Aldington village. He was a close neighbour of Lord Aldington's with whom he played golf. Both men were veterans of the King's Royal Rifle Corps, of which Deedes co-wrote the wartime history with Sir Hereward Wake. In it he described the exploits of the officers (including Major Low) at great length while making almost no mention of any of the other ranks. This author wrote to him to ask if the non-commissioned soldiers had, as the balance of his text implies, been incidental to the fighting. Deedes's only reply was to say, 'The world has moved on since then.' He is now Lord Deedes of Aldington.

10   Co-incidentally, the other ex-Deputy Chairman of the Conservative Party who became a celebrated libel plaintiff, Jeffrey Archer, was a publicist for this organisation in the early 1970s.

11   PREM 11/4415, 11 September 1962.

Board of Trade, met at Powell's house close to midnight on the evening
before the new Prime Minster's name was to be announced. It was
absurdly late to begin plotting. Macmillan's letter of resignation was to
go to the Queen at 9.15 the following morning, and all the major Party
figures were unavailable—most, like Butler, were in bed. The gathering
achieved nothing and the *caballeros* gave up and trickled off home to their
own beds.

Within the week, Lord Aldington had resigned his position and left
the political arena for good.

For all the outward lustre of his reputation, Lord Aldington's career has
a slightly rackety quality to it when examined at close quarters, particularly so after he had escaped the disciplines and restraints of public office.
Controversy had to be smothered in 1963 when Lord Coleraine, one of
his co-Directors at United Power, the nuclear power plant builder which
Lord Aldington chaired, resigned and made allegations of corruption in
the allocation of contracts. These were so grave that Lord Stonham, in
the ensuing debate in the House of Lords, said 'it most certainly was an
abuse of power and a national scandal that must be put right.' Lord
Aldington's response was to try to cover the matter up. 'I think this is not
the right place at this juncture to argue the details of this dispute,' he said.
Lord Carrington supported him: 'The government should not interfere.'
It didn't. Next March, Aldington was appointed Chairman of GEC as
well as United Power.

Lord Aldington's performance at Grindlay's was not tainted by
scandal, so much as by commercial failure when he tried to act the 'go-go
man'—this was his term for one of the bank's favoured clients of the
period, Robert Maxwell. In 1967, Aldington decided Grindlay's should
dust itself off and make its mark on the banking world by making an
acquisition. The target was an old-established but sleepy merchant bank,
William Brandt's Sons and Company Ltd. The unreconstructed City of
the 1960s was not afraid of nepotism, and in this respect Brandt's was
bolder than most. The full list of Directors in 1965 was as follows: W.E.
Brandt, H.A. Brandt, W.A. Brandt, J.M. Brandt and P.A. Brandt. W.A.
was the Chairman; he also sat on the Board of London Assurance with
Lord Aldington. Between the two of them, they agreed that Grindlay's
would acquire a controlling stake in Brandt's. The Chairman of the parent
company naturally wanted to sit on Brandt's board, so, in 1967 Lord
Aldington added another seat to his collection.

Brandt's led Grindlay's to disaster. In a large organisation, like GEC, Lord Aldington's Whitehall-lobbying skills and his smooth committeemanship were assets, particularly if overseen by a strong Managing Director like Arnold Weinstock. But in a small firm, Lord Aldington's lack of aptitude for business could become a major liability. The desire to be liked made him go with the crowd on most issues, only more optimistically than most. He was a bull at the top of the market and a bear at the bottom, the classic recipe for disaster in an investor. Like so many others, Lord Aldington got carried away by Edward Heath's 'dash for growth'. Seeing the rapidly rising prices of land and buildings during the Barber boom, Brandt's invested without restraint. Then, like all trends, this one reversed itself. In 1974 the property market crashed. In 1975 Brandt's crashed. In 1976 Grindlay's crashed.

Amazingly, in the middle of all this, Lord Aldington awarded himself a 35% pay rise, which he excused by saying that it had been agreed by the Board before the losses had become known. One shareholder called it 'immoral and shameful'. Aldington took no notice.

But he could not fail to take notice when he had to ask an American Bank for more capital for Grindlay's and they imposed onerous terms. Soon they—CitiBank—were demanding his head. In December 1975 Aldington was forced to resign. The continuous Low family connection with Grindlay's ended after 120 years. Quickly the bank was re-organised by its new owners. Today Grindlay's is nothing more than a specialist department within the ANZ Banking Group, based in Melbourne, Australia.

The early 1970s were the high point of Lord Aldington's career. His friend Ted Heath was Prime Minister, and all sorts of honours came his way. In April 1970 he had been made a Fellow of the Royal Society of Arts in the same batch as Harold Wilson, Lord Goodman, Anthony Wedgwood (now Tony) Benn and Gerald Nabarro. In October, he was appointed Chairman of the General Advisory Council of the BBC (he had been a member of the Council since 1959). He also took seats on the Management Committee of the Institute of Neurology and the Board of Governors of the National Hospital for Nervous Diseases. His name was mentioned as a possible successor to Anthony Barber as Chairman of the Conservative Party. He was even tipped as a future Governor of the Bank of England by "Albany" in the *Sunday Telegraph*. 'He had political experience in the House of Commons as Toby Low,' the paper said, 'and above all is a tough egg, both mentally and physically.' Nothing came of either of these suggestions. Instead Heath asked him to help spearhead the re-organisation of British industry by taking on the chairmanship of the Port of London Authority.

Lord Aldington had hardly settled into his new job when a national dock strike was called. In the middle of the strike, Heath panicked. He asked Aldington to form a committee with Jack Jones, leader of the dockers' trade union, the Transport and General Workers Union (TGWU), to settle the strike while making recommendations for ways of getting rid of the two thousand dockers for whom, despite their being paid every week, there was no work. Many of them were actually incapable of working due to age or illness, but, due to the power of the union, they could not be made redundant nor could the cost of their upkeep be reduced by passing the responsiblity on to the Department of either Health or Social Security.

'It was a gorgeous committee,' commented Lord Aldington. 'You couldn't get on to it unless both Jack Jones and I agreed.' As the ever-emollient chairman, Lord Aldington did not take long to agree with Jones that paying dockers to do nothing was not a practice which could be stopped. The only solution was to ask the taxpayers for more money which would be used to offer them greatly increased, but still voluntary, redundancy packages. Jack Jones wrote in his autobiography that Lord Aldington 'was on my side'.

In the middle of the strike, *The Times* quoted Lord Aldington as saying, 'Compulsory redundancies are not known or knowable in the docks. It is an industry like no other.' Change had to come, he said, but 'by agreement, not by bludgeoning'. When Lord Aldington finally made an offer which the unions accepted, *The Times* described the scheme by saying, 'If the phrase "protection racket" was not already assigned to the underworld it would fit.'[12]

The attempt to modernise industry by consensus was a failure and Heath was soon out of office. His most recent biographer, John Campbell, writes of the subsequent relationship between the defeated leader and his friend in the City. Lord Aldington, Campbell says, was mainly responsible for encouraging Heath's attitude of querulous disaffection with the new, more radical Conservative Party. Neither man was capable of admitting he was wrong. Like most egotists, they could not be defeated by argument, only overwhelmed by events.

> Most of those who consider themselves Heath's friends believe that Aldington was a bad influence who encouraged him, in 1974 and over the next decade, in his attitude of doggedly self-righteous isolation. In the days after the October [1974] defeat, it was Aldington, more than anyone else, who reinforced his instinct to stand firm and defy his enemies to overthrow him. [13]

Since it became such an important feature of the litigation surrounding the libel trial, it is worth quoting a clear statement of Lord Aldington's belief in the power of behind-the-scenes lobbying. The occasion was a campaign he orchestrated to oppose the construction of an extension to the M3 motorway on a route which was planned to run uncomfortably close to Winchester College, of which he had recently been appointed a Fellow—that is, a member of the board of governors. He argued that the road either should not be built or should be routed through nearby Twyford Down. He wrote several letters to *The Times*[14] and spoke, in April 1973, for the first time in a House of Lords debate on the environment. The adulatory tone which Liddell Hart detected in his wartime correspondence with Anthony Eden was still there.

> I speak with more than usual humility [Lord Aldington said], more than usual diffidence, even greater than the diffidence professed by my noble Leader [Lord Carrington]. For I know that though I feel deeply about conservation and preservation of our national heritage everywhere, I have not the knowledge, nor have I the experience, nor have I the eloquence—not even the elegance—of so many of your Lordships who have made this debate fascinating to someone who is a newcomer to discussions like this in your Lordships' House...

---

13   Campbell *Edward Heath*, p. 656
14   Lord Aldington's frequent resort to self-serving but misleading pedantry was illustrated in the second letter which he began by saying 'some 20 months ago mine was the first name subscribing to a letter protesting against the proposed route.' His name had been first—that was true—but only because the list of signatories was arranged in alphabetical order.

I have always understood that the argument was not really settled until someone at or near the very top said that a road should not go there. Whether or not this is true, it is the kind of firm decisive decision that is required if we are to implement in full the purpose of the Report of Lord Kennett's group. Someone must say, 'A motorway shall not go between St Catherine's Hill and Winchester city.'[15]

In the event it never did. Someone at or near the very top took a 'decisive decision' and the road was built through Twyford Down where it destroyed two Sites of Special Scientific Interest, the remains of an Iron Age village, a Celtic field system, some Bronze Age burial grounds and the prospect which inspired Keats to write his Ode to Autumn.

Lord Aldington had a reputation of never being able to say 'no' to his friends. Like anybody in power, he had made enemies over the years, but he had developed the helpful habit of leaping to the defence of anyone he knew who was attacked in public. His friend Charles Villiers, for example, had been a catastrophic failure as Chairman of British Steel, chalking up the largest losses ever recorded by a British company. (They reached £1,700 million in 1979.[16]) Villiers was hauled up before the House of Commons Select Committee on Nationalised Industries. *The Times* criticised him for being uncandid and treating the committee with contempt. Lord Aldington replied with another of his "friend of both sides" letters. 'I was Chairman of the Select Committee on Nationalised Industries in its early years from 1957-61,' he wrote, 'and I think I can understand their problems and their aims. I know Charles Villiers well enough—since 1933—to be certain that it was never part of his intention to treat the committee with "less than candour".'[17]

---

15   *Hansard*, 11 April 1973
16   The worst of it was that 500 out of British Steel's 2,500 suppliers had gone bankrupt due to the Corporation's policy of making very late payments. After he left British Steel, Villiers became Chairman of the Small Business Research Trust, in which capacity he criticised big business in Britain for being the slowest payers in Europe.
17   *The Times* 24 January 1978. Sir Charles repaid the compliment in 1989 by coming to Court, which he treated with a lack of candour which bordered on rudeness, as will be seen below. Despite his failures as an industrialist, when he died in 1992 Villiers was honoured by the presence of representatives of the Prince of Wales, the Queen Mother and the Duke of Edinburgh at the requiem service held in his honour at the Brompton Oratory in London. Lord Carrington gave an address and Lord Aldington read the lessons.

As the 1970s moved into the 1980s Lord Aldington's name was mentioned less often in the press. He was not a frequent speaker in the House of Lords. Mrs Thatcher took no interest in him: indeed it was precisely his type of person she blamed for the parlous state of British industry. He was by now Chairman of the Sun Alliance and London Insurance company, as well as GEC.

The Sun Alliance pursued its dull and unremarkable way through the dull and unremarkable world of insurance. But GEC was altogether a more interesting operation, and one where Lord Aldington was able to deploy his Whitehall-lobbying skills to great effect. One of GEC's greatest strengths was its ability to persuade the Ministry of Defence to finance the development of exotic and often unusable weapons. This finance was provided on a "cost plus" basis, under which the company simply billed the Ministry—in other words, the taxpayer—for its expenses plus an allowance for overheads and profit. The incentive to be efficient was negligible while GEC's profits rose remorselessly. As Deputy Chairman from 1971 to 1985, much of the credit for this should go to Lord Aldington: he was the Director with the best contacts at the Ministry of Defence.

The list of technical disasters is a long one, even if the period is restricted to that of Lord Aldington's Deputy Chairmanship. One of the more bizarre stories concerns the Spearfish torpedo, which after 15 years development was still not usable. It was supposed to be an "intelligent" weapon, but on trials it behaved very stupidly, setting off purposefully enough, but then doing a U-turn and hurtling back, at 35 knots, towards the launching ship. Luckily it was unarmed at the time.

The total project cost for this weapon was over £1 billion. The Spearfish's predecessor, the Tigerfish, also made by GEC, proved so useless on the only occasion when it was really needed, in the Falklands war, that *H.M.S. Conqueror* had to sink the *Belgrano* with a World War II-type weapon.

Then there was the Foxhunter airborne radar system, which was scheduled to enter service in RAF Tornados in the early 1980s. It never worked properly, and for years the planes had to be flown with concrete blocks in place of the radar to maintain the designed weight distribution. Even during the Gulf war in 1991, after ten years' development, the British Tornados were reputed to have been safe only because the whole Iraqi airforce had fled to Iran.

All these projects were over budget, late and dangerously unreliable.

But the most expensive disaster of all was the Nimrod spy-plane. In 1977 GEC claimed this was going to be the best early-warning aircraft money could buy. Ten years later, after £1 billion of development, the whole project was scrapped and the RAF forced to buy the American AWACs plane, which had been on offer all along, using proven technology and at a lower price per aircraft. It had been discovered that the GEC radar in the Nimrod was still not capable of differentiating between enemy aircraft and lorries on the A1.

Lord Aldington's swan-song as an industrialist produced the greatest failure of his career: at Westland. Here the underlying causes were the same as at GEC: he used his Whitehall-lobbying skills to such effect that the company became progressively further and further divorced from the realities of the international helicopter market. When the Ministry of Defence got a Secretary of State who was determined to destroy the whole flabby court of over-protected contractors who 'billed, ballsed up and billed again', as one observer has put it, the company collapsed. Magnus Linklater and David Leigh have written a book about the Westland saga, called *Not with Honour*. In it, they say of Lord Aldington that 'his connections in the pre-Thatcher Tory establishment were formidable... Aldington's view, understandably in view of his post-war career, was that there were few problems which could not be solved by nudging the right elbow.'[18]

Lord Aldington became Chairman of the company in 1978 and, once again, had his friend Lord Aberconway as Vice Chairman. The Managing Director was a gifted engineer, Basil Blackwell, who unfortunately was no businessman. One of the people who had to pick up the pieces after the company fell apart, has described it as being run, under Lord Aldington, as 'a west country fiefdom'. Certainly Lord Aldington took full advantage of the perks of the Chairmanship, using the company premises in Carlton Gardens as his London base and frequently clattering down onto the playing fields of Winchester in a Westland helicopter for College Fellows meetings. The company also provided him with a Bentley, to which he fitted numberplates he had bought, reading: LOW 1.

The main thrust of Lord Aldington's sales effort in the early 1980s was focused on a civil version of the Sea King, called the W30. It was

18   Linklater and Leigh *Not with Honour*, p. 29

Lord Aldington's pet project and it was a flop from the start. Alan Bristow, Britain's major civilian helicopter operator, described it as 'the wrong helicopter, for the wrong market, at the wrong time.' Bristow was as critical of the company as of its new product: 'I'm red, white and blue to the core, but they can never deliver on time or price.'

The world helicopter market rejected the new aircraft, so rather than redesign it Lord Aldington went back to Whitehall to ask for a grant. He approached the Department of Trade, which gave £40 million in "launch aid", despite the fact that the project had already been launched two years earlier. The purpose of such gifts is not to subsidise failed products but help bring to the market good ones which would otherwise not find the finance. A condition of the grant was that the company put in an equivalent sum of its own, but Westland never did.

When the DTI money had been spent, and the helicopters were still not selling, Lord Aldington needed a new source of money. Still shy of the market, he thought he might try the Foreign Office. He knew the then Foreign Secretary, Geoffrey Howe, very well. Howe was an Old Wyke-hamist whom Aldington had invited onto the board of the Sun Alliance in the 1970s when the Conservatives were out of office. Aldington felt able to ask that the government provide £50 million in "aid" to the Indian government and stipulate to the Indians that they spend it all on Westland helicopters. Aldington was so confident that this was the way to do business—and the company order book was so empty—that he allowed the factory to start manufacturing the aircraft. £42 million of work in progress was standing, unsold, in the factory at Yeovil when the Indian government, to Lord Aldington's dismay, rejected the gift.

Subsequently the British government added another £15 million to the "aid" package, but still the Indians turned the helicopter down. In effect, they would not take it free. The running costs were too high, they suspected its reliability and saw no future in training pilots to fly a machine they would never conceivably *buy* any more of. This left Westland with two major problems: a factory full of unsold helicopters and an almost empty order book.[19]

19   In an unhappy footnote to this episode, the Indian government was put under further pressure by Mrs Thatcher and did agree, shortly after Lord Aldington left Westland, to take the helicopters. Of the 21 machines "sold", two crashed, killing ten people, and the others were 'plagued by technical problems'. (*Daily Telegraph* 21 July 1994) In 1994 the Indian

How did Lord Aldington respond to this? Once again, he avoided the market and dashed back to Whitehall, this time to the Ministry of Defence, about the only relevant Department he had not yet tapped.[20] His idea this time was to persuade the Army to buy the W30 so that the Ministry of Defence would pay for a huge project to redesign it for military use. As the aircraft was originally a naval helicopter, the Sea King, which had been re-designed for civilian use, this ought not to have involved all that much change—give or take some technical advances in the bought-in peripheral systems (most of which would come from GEC where Lord Aldington was still Deputy Chairman). Moreover, this project would be on the old, cosy, "cost plus" and money-up-front terms which Westland so sorely missed during its brief foray into the commercial world.

Unfortunately, by the time this approach should have got down to the serious negotiating stage, the Minister of Defence was Michael Heseltine. Lord Aldington's face suddenly did not fit. The request was turned down flat and Westland was in a state of crisis. *The Times* commented on the 1983-4 results, 'The profit and loss account is not a pretty sight.' A dividend was paid, but only by transferring £11 million from reserves.

Despite this, the management put on a brave face and talked optimistically about new orders for helicopters. But in the three months to the end of 1984, the company received orders for precisely two machines. In February 1985 Lord Aldington resigned, leaving so quietly that it was hardly mentioned in the press. Basil Blackwell, the Managing Director, stepped into his office. He was a loyal servant of the company but, being primarily an engineer, was out of his depth in Aldington's financial slipstream. Blackwell lasted only four months. For Lord Aldington this interval was a godsend. When the company's crisis became public, he was sitting quietly in the House of Lords, his reputation untarnished.[21]

---

government tried to sell the remaining aircraft for £1.9 million, or 3% of their list price. But even at a 97% discount, they found no buyers and have since been broken up for scrap.

20   In the light of the "arms to Iraq" scandal it is perhaps worth noting that the same three departments of state, Trade and Industry, Defence and the Foreign Office, were involved in that case as in this.

21   Westland was rescued by Sir John Cuckney, now Lord Cuckney, who was fresh from his successful re-organisation of the Port of London Authority, after Lord Aldington left that organisation. Within ten weeks Cuckney had fired five out of the nine Directors remaining from the Aldington board. He also told the shareholders, many of them small investors, that they had suffered attributable losses for the previous year, the last of Aldington's chairmanship,

Unembarrassed by unattributed failure, Lord Aldington moved on to chair one of his last public committees, the House of Lords Select Committee on Overseas Trade. In December 1985 he presented the Committee's report on what ought to be done about Britain's poor record as a manufacturing nation. 'Industry has to improve quality control, design, delivery on time, reliability, service.' He went on to say that the nation as a whole had the attitude, 'not my fault—yours', and closed with a call for government to give more financial help to manufacturers.

Like British Steel which, after the disastrous Villiers had left, became the most efficient steel maker in Europe, Westland prospered mightily once Lord Aldington and his board had been replaced by people whose main professional aim was not to sit on committees making recommendations about how industry should be run, but to manufacture, sell and service helicopters. By 1993 Westland had an order book of £1.5 billion, was virtually without debt and was making annual profits of over £30 million.

Lord Aldington bade farewell to the last of his Chairmanships, the Sun Alliance, at the Annual General Meeting on 22 May 1985, 40 years to the day after 5 Corps issued the order to shoot Cossacks who tried to escape forcible repatriation.[22] His successor was to be Henry Lambert, another Old Wykehamist, whom Lord Aldington had appointed a Fellow of the College after he had been appointed Warden. But before Lord Aldington could formally pass control and responsibility to Lambert, a stocky man with a booming voice stood up to ask him what he was going to do about what he said was an unjustly unpaid insurance claim. The man's name was Nigel Watts. Lord Aldington dealt with him quickly and cleanly and left the room for his valedictory lunch, presumably thinking that he had drawn a long and varied career to a very successful close.

His most notable achievement had been to retain his high reputation despite all the disasters and failures he had been involved in. True, there

---

of £98.7 million, and that their company's borrowings were over £100 million. Both these figures were higher than Westland's total market capitalisation. Together they meant that the company was, in Sir John's words, 'perilously near receivership'.

22   Like Villiers, who had in retirement written a book about industrial management called *Start Again—Britain*, Aldington planned to commit the wisdom acquired in his long industrial career to paper in a book, already commissioned by Macmillan's, which would give his solutions to the problems facing British manufacturing industry.

had been costs. Lady Aldington gave evidence at the trial, in rather wistful tones, about the social emptiness of a life-time of elbow-nudging and reputation-building. 'Well, one does see people the whole time, because of the extraordinary life we lead going round and round doing sort of official things. We see an enormous amount of people, but not a lot privately, no, because we want what little time there is to ourselves, you know... We don't entertain.'

Lady Aldington did not mind because she devoted much of her time to her sheep. She had founded the Jacob Sheep Society, and been a long time breeder and exhibitor of these four-horned, "biblical" hybrids. For years she had travelled round the country in a converted ice-cream van, showing her animals at country fairs. She had even written a book about them, *A History of the Jacob Sheep*. In 1965 she donated a prize ewe called Araminta to the Dudley Zoo.

In retirement Lord Aldington found it hard to cut himself off from the world of committees. He carried on as Chairman of the Trustees of Leeds Castle, a position he had been appointed to in 1984, until he was pushed out in a rather undignified way in 1994. In 1986, he took on the Chairmanship of the Independent Schools Joint Council. It was not long after that, that he got down to preparing for the libel trial. In 1989, Lady Aldington told the Court how hard her husband had worked preparing his case, often sitting up till after 2 o'clock in the morning. He no longer had time for golf or gardening on the weekends or for playing cards with her in the evenings. Six-pack bezique was their game and they had played it regularly, keeping a cumulative score, since they were first married. Yet in 1989, despite this pressure on his time, with the trial only six months away, and his head swimming with Situation Reports, Intelligence Reports and Jugoslav Reports, not to mention the changing dates of his own departure from Austria, this strangely driven man could not refuse the offer of yet another public position and so he joined his last committee, the Migraine Trust.

9

The DASHING WHITE COUNT

L IKE MANY A PAIR of well-matched contestants, Count Tolstoy
and Lord Aldington have more in common than would appear at
first sight. Both men seek the approbation of their peers to an
unusual extent and both men can be unusually generous in helping people
they think of as allies. Sir James Wilson, one of the witnesses at the trial,
spoke for many when he told this author that if Lord Aldington has a fault
he finds it too hard to say 'no' to his friends: this applies equally to Count
Tolstoy. Conversely both men can develop an exaggerated hostility to
anyone they think of as an enemy. And slights which most people would
laugh off are quite likely to provoke public refutation by both of them.
Nigel Nicolson, another witness at the trial, has said of Tolstoy that he can
be 'very vindictive'; this applies equally to Lord Aldington. Both are very
litigious.

Both men are intelligent, capable and energetic. Yet both can be very
poor judges of character. Lord Aldington hopelessly underestimated
Nigel Watts, for example, and Tolstoy was completely taken in by Brigadier Cowgill, a friend of Lord Aldington's, to whom he gave a substantial
quantity of his historical material quite unaware of the use to which it was
soon to be put. In both cases, a less self-absorbed character would have
been more canny. Neither man has devoted his life primarily to earning
money. Apart from a conventional desire for quiet affluence, neither is
unduly materialistic. Certainly both disdain the appearance of consumer-
ism, yet both men are quite capable of making ingenious arrangements
for their own pecuniary benefit, although in Tolstoy's case his lack of
business experience keeps his operations to the financial foothills. Both

men are very good at influencing other people, although in quite different ways. Lord Aldington nudges elbows while Tolstoy is a gifted public speaker. Most senior people in the City in the 1970s would have known of Lord Aldington, even if they had not met him, and most browsers in good bookshops in the 1980s would have heard of Count Tolstoy, even if they had not read any of his books. In short, both have been successful, in their chosen fields, at cultivating the reputation which is so dear to them. In both cases, one of their characteristics which allies find so attractive is their perpetual optimism, whether it is Lord Aldington on the British gift industry or Tolstoy on 'very exciting discoveries' which 'throw an entirely new and very revealing light' on, say, McCreery's view of the Selby-Bigge initiative. In both cases, also, the optimism is very much a public mask, as both suffer acutely from depression, although in Lord Aldington's case it seems sometimes to tip into self-pity.

Somehow, also, both men's characters can grate on others. It is not hard to find people who will make deeply unflattering remarks about one or other of them. Lord Aldington was described to me by one of the men who rescued Westland as being 'incredibly stupid'. A neighbour in Kent has called him vain, conceited, cold, xenophobic and arrogant. 'You know those sort of White's Club people?' this man asked, even though he knew Lord Aldington's club was the Carlton. 'I despise them.' Equally unsympathetically, Count Tolstoy has been called an obsessional fanatic by Alistair Horne and has been ridiculed by many for his love of titles, dressing up and pretending to be Russian. In both cases private failings, or eccentricities, attract public scorn because both men are so publicity-conscious.

Both Aldington and Tolstoy have an exaggerated respect for their heroes in the repatriations drama: the former for Macmillan and Keightley, and the latter for Krasnov and Shkuro. Conversely, both men regard the other's heroes as villains of a peculiarly vile sort. Lord Aldington thought the Cossack Generals were war criminals who had worked with a will for the Nazis, and Tolstoy thought Macmillan and Keightley were war criminals who had worked with a will for the Soviets. The common feature of all these opinions is that they are black and white, as if the holders of them are looking at the objects of their gaze not as men, with virtues and faults to varying degrees, but as moral exemplars who either succeed or fail. Neither Aldington nor Tolstoy can see either the human side of their respective villains or the weaknesses of their respective heroes. This mythologising has contributed to the peculiar bitterness of their litigation.

It is typical of both men that they have pushed their views to these unrealistic limits. Tolstoy wants to expose and humiliate Aldington by compelling him to accept publicly the Tolstoyan view of the forced repatriations story, while Aldington wants to crush Tolstoy to the point where he can never again utter any criticism of his military past. Both want the world to see that they were right all along.

Egotism of this sort, the inordinate desire to be liked by the world and, above all, to be seen to be *right,* is as much a characteristic of Tolstoy as it is of Aldington. Neither has the inner self-confidence to accept rebuffs and, on occasion, admit failure. This is not to belittle their motivation: many great men have been unconsciously driven by a similar daemon. Rather it is to seek the underlying causes of the litigation in psychological, as much as in historical and/or legal, factors.

Nikolai Tolstoy was born, on 23 June 1935, son of an English mother and a half-Russian, half-English father, Dmitri Tolstoy, who became a very successful barrister and is known for his still-current reference book, *Tolstoy on Divorce.* Within a few years Dmitri Tolstoy had, himself, divorced. Nikolai grew up in the home of his father and his second wife, a Russian. 'My father and step-mother were very peculiar people,' Tolstoy says today, 'and not very nice parents really. My father is a totally introspective person who has quarrelled with his own father, his grandfather and his own half-brother. My grandfather married a third time and had a daughter, who is my aunt, and my father won't speak to her at all, even though he hardly even knows her. He now lives in Spain, mainly, as far as I can see, to get away from everyone.'[1]

Tolstoy himself was brought up more or less alone. No friends ever called. School holidays were brutally lonely. The young boy had a calendar on which he marked off the hours—not days, hours!—until he could get back to school. 'My father and step-mother,' he says, 'could spend a whole hour discussing which bus they were going to catch that morning, or whether or not they will go shopping at all, or whether it is the day for the dustbins, and that was *all* they talked about.' Occasional relief was to go up to London where one of his aunts lived in Cromwell

---

1   Imperial War Museum, Dept. Sound Records, #10721/9 The tapes last more than seven hours.

Place, and, Tolstoy recalls, 'there were nothing but Russians. We hardly ever saw English people. It was a lovely atmosphere. There were always pictures of the Tzar and icons and hundreds of photographs of Guards officers and so on, and all the people coming and going. So to me the old Russia was very vivid. I was a romantic monarchist. I suppose I still am really[2]—and lived in a strange world of my own where it was all happening in the mind and through books.'

At the same time Tolstoy developed a passionate love of the lore of ancient Britain and started at a young age collecting material on the subject. Living in the west country he could see Lundy Island from his home. He spent many solitary hours imagining life in the ancient Celtic paradise. Now he has an enormous library of Celtic history which he thinks is one of the largest in private hands in England. 'I loved history,' he says today, 'and I loved the past. Actually I just repudiated the whole twentieth century.'

The long history of the Tolstoy family is entertainingly told in Count Tolstoy's own book *The Tolstoys*. But its publication was to have a disastrous side-effect. Tolstoy had described how his father left Russia at a young age, escorted by his English nanny. She had told him to say to the Bolshevik guards at the Soviet-Finnish border that he was English, but he proudly refused. 'What Dmitri had said,' Tolstoy wrote towards the end of his manuscript, 'she never fully discovered, but whatever it was satisfied the Bolsheviks and they were allowed to proceed.' On reading that sentence, shortly before the book was to be released, Tolstoy Senior ordered his son to suppress the whole account. It was too late for that: the book had already been set in print. The result was that from then to the time of this writing, Dmitri Tolstoy has not once spoken to his son, successes, failures, court cases, bankruptcy and illness, notwithstanding.

Nikolai Tolstoy followed his father to Wellington College, in Berkshire, where he became a house prefect. He was a member of the debating society but was not a notable sportsman. In 1953 he left with six 'O' Levels and an 'A' Level (in History). His father did not think these results warranted the expenditure which University fees would involve. Accordingly Tolstoy went into the Army. But he was invalided out of Sandhurst with a serious back injury after eight weeks.

2   Today Tolstoy is Chancellor of the Monarchist League.

Tolstoy's only recourse was primary-school teaching. However, his mother's family were wealthy industrialists from Leicestershire and a relative agreed to support him at University. After failing to get into Oxford, he went to Trinity College, Dublin. This was a happy choice. 'I loved Ireland, and I liked the Irish,' Tolstoy remembers. 'They were everything that the English in those days weren't—and still aren't. They were gregarious; they would talk about anything; they were irresponsible. I still love Ireland.'

As a young man Tolstoy's politics were of the extreme right-wing variety. In 1956, Khrushchev and Bulganin visited Britain. Tolstoy went to Victoria station to protest. There was a small crowd there, including the self-proclaimed fascist, Colin Jordan, Leslie Green of the League of Empire Loyalists, and several Special Branch policemen. As the train pulled into the station, and Sir Anthony Eden stepped forward to greet his Soviet guests, Tolstoy unrolled a poster which said, 'Keep the Red Beasts Out'. A Detective Hodgson, in plain clothes, told Tolstoy to put his poster down. Not unreasonably, Tolstoy refused. Without revealing himself as a policemen, and looking like a typical English busy-body, Hodgson tried to grab the poster, so Tolstoy punched him. A scuffle ensued and Tolstoy was arrested and taken to a lock-up in the back of the station. In court he said that when he saw these 'badly dressed men' he thought they 'were Communist agitators. When they took me off into a dark passage I imagined I was going to get my throat cut and so I struggled.' Tolstoy was fined £10 for using insulting words and behaviour and only £1 for assault, since the magistrate allowed the possibility of a genuine mistake.

In November that year the Red Beasts invaded Hungary. By that time Tolstoy was at university, so he took to the streets of Dublin. Unfortunately, there were no Communists to wave posters at. 'As far as I know,' he says today, 'there wasn't even a single Socialist in the length and breadth of the happy Republic. But still, we all marched dutifully through the streets, myself carrying a photograph of Nicholas II, and there was a wonderful attack on a shop, a newsagent. A rumour had gone round among the Irish contingent that it had supposedly once sold a copy of the *Socialist Worker*, and the windows were broken and I remember seeing men in the streets—a thing which greatly endears the Irish to me—leaning against buildings in raincoats, waiting for the pubs to open. I saw one who had no idea what this march was about, but when he saw a fight break out he rushed to the nearest Gardai and punched him. Then, of course, everybody started having a wonderful time.'

After Trinity, Tolstoy went back to being prep-school master. He wore a brightly-coloured silk waistcoat and sported a silver-topped cane. 'I am ashamed to say I don't think I was a very good teacher,' he says today. 'I just read the boys stories about King Arthur, or made them up. The boys loved it, and I just hope they have all survived their education since.' Since love of the subject is the foundation of all good teaching, Tolstoy was, in fact, an extremely successful master, although his methods would doubtless be prohibited in today's prosaic educational environment. Even more unconventionally, Tolstoy's popularity extended beyond the boys in his forms to their mothers, many of whom are said to have found the dashing white Count irresistibly attractive.

Those were happy days. Outside school, Tolstoy helped form the Sealed Knot, a society which re-enacts Civil War battles for the entertainment of the participants and paying spectators. The cannons fire only tennis balls—'jolly sore if they hit you in the wrong place'—and there is generally a carnival atmosphere. 'Most people turned up for the beer and the girls,' Tolstoy says, 'as no doubt they did in 1642. I threw myself into these battles with great enthusiasm. I met my wife, Georgina, at one of them and proposed to her at the Siege of Warwick Castle.'

For many years it was a turbulent marriage, Georgina often despairing of Tolstoy's unworldly attitude to life. But four children were born and today Tolstoy enjoys the blessing of an extremely happy home. He has always been determined never to treat his children the way his father treated him, and his success has been unqualified. It is all the harder, therefore, to understand why he has been prepared to risk destruction of his domestic security by volunteering to be sued by Lord Aldington.

Tolstoy's preoccupation with the forced repatriations had a long gestation period, but his book on the subject, *Victims of Yalta*, did not, as it were, have a virgin birth. The matter of the cruel fate of the Cossacks at the hands of the British in 1945 was legendary in Russian émigré circles, but no-one seems to have thought that the numbers involved were more than a few hundred. Although he had grown up with these stories, it was only in 1973 that Tolstoy was alerted to the fact that this might have been a very much larger-scale tragedy than was popularly thought. The person who put him onto the trail was a friend, the author Robert Temple. Temple told him about Julius Epstein's recently published book *Operation Keelhaul: the Story of the Forced Repatriations from 1944 to the Present*. Keelhaul applied to Italy and started only in 1946, so it was merely an incident in what Tolstoy later discovered was a very much larger story. Nonetheless, Temple wrote to Epstein asking where he could get further information on the subject. Epstein replied saying that there was much more information in the archives, but these were Anglo-American archives and therefore the consent of both governments was necessary before they could be released. The American government, it seemed, was prepared to allow release, but the British government was not.

Temple was at that time a member of the Royal United Services Institute and at one of their meetings he asked Lord Carrington, then Minister of Defence, about the withheld files. Carrington seemed shocked at the implications of the question and promised to investigate. Temple's recollection is that he was then approached by men from the British security services who asked him if he was 'campaigning' on Operation Keelhaul. He said he was and for the next twenty years he has suffered low-level harassment of one sort of another, much of it using the threat that he might be deported since he is an American citizen. In his reply Carrington stated that the government was prepared to allow release of the files, but *in the United States only*. He also said he would recommend that all the British files for the Second World War be released simultaneously, rather than year by year.

So it was that in 1973, the files for 1944-5 were released as well as those for 1943.[3] Although it was not obvious at the time, this was the real beginning of Lord Aldington's long, and still continuing, nightmare.

Using some of these files, Temple drafted an article on the forced repatriations. But in doing so he came to realise that it was a far bigger subject than he had at first imagined. It needed a book. This would involve a tremendous amount of work, and also a close familiarity with the history of the Second World War. Temple was engaged on another book at the time, and he knew little about the war. Either he dropped or postponed his plan, or he took a partner. He decided to take a partner.

Temple's best friend for many years had been Nikolai Tolstoy, who had been Best Man at his wedding. Being a schoolmaster, Tolstoy had a enough free time to make a start on a book; he also knew a good deal about

---

3   If Temple's claim is correct, that his request was what provoked the release of three years' worth of military records, this surely prompts the question, why? If the records he wanted were to be denied him, except abroad, why would it be helpful to release material that he had *not* asked for?

the war. Not only that, the royalties would be a very welcome supplement to the family's tiny income. Temple's plan was that they would collaborate on a book, which he provisionally entitled *This Other Eden*, in which they would describe the genesis and evolution of the repatriation policy, focusing on what Temple saw as the pivotal role of Anthony Eden. It is noteworthy that the architect of the Yalta policy did not mention a single word about it in his huge, three-volume memoirs.

How *This Other Eden* became *Victims of Yalta*, is a matter on which Tolstoy and Temple differ. Temple alleges that Tolstoy cut him out of his own project, by hanging on to their documents, breaking off contact and signing a contract with a publisher without consulting or involving him. 'I despise that man,' Temple says today. 'I truly despise him.'[4] Tolstoy denies this, saying Temple lost interest in the book so he had to take over. They fell out later over 'a personal matter'. Whatever the truth, the two men were never close again. Today, Temple's position is that he considers Tolstoy an egotist and a fantasist, but nonetheless a highly professional historian whose research is almost always accurate. For this reason, despite his bitterness about the fate of *This Other Eden*, Temple has refused all requests—and surprisingly many have been made, particularly since the libel trial—to attack Tolstoy in print.

Once he started work in the archives, Tolstoy made the uncomfortable discovery that he had a competitor in the field, Nicholas Bethell, heir to the Barony of Romford. Bethell had made the earliest translations of Solzhenitsyn's work into English and was clearly well qualified to undertake the task. Furthermore he was independently wealthy enough to be able to write without the day-to-day financial worries which beset Tolstoy. Partly as a result of this, and partly because his book was shorter and drew on a much narrower range of sources, Bethell had his book, *The Last Secret*, published first.

Though Bethell did not ascribe individual blame for what happened in May 1945, he did say of Brigadier Low's Definition Order that it

> cut across three of the main principles of British justice: that a foreigner who has reason to fear persecution for political reasons is entitled to asylum; that

4   Interview with the author 27 April 1995

an accused man is entitled to the due process of law; and that he is innocent until proved guilty beyond reasonable doubt. Seldom can a British authority have disposed of so many lives so haphazardly.[5]

Bethell's book was published in 1974, long before Tolstoy was ready to launch his own.[6] The publication of Bethell's book was a great help to Tolstoy, whose research was augmented by the many people who came to light only now that the controversy had been made public. In the end *Victims of Yalta* took five years to write. Tolstoy spent a year on Chapter 11 alone, called 'An Unsolved Mystery', which tries to answer the question: why were *non*-Soviets also repatriated by 5 Corps? Amongst the more than two million Soviet citizens handed to Stalin in 1945-7, there is no record of any other deliberate case in which groups of people who did not qualify for repatriation under the Yalta agreement were included. Much of the information now available was still secret. FO 1020/42, for example, was not released to the PRO until 1984. 5 Corps' sabotage of the Alexander-Eisenhower rescue plan was therefore still a secret. More than this, three of the people most intimately involved, Macmillan, Keightley and Lord Aldington, would not talk.

On 6 February 1978 *Victims of Yalta* was launched to near universal acclaim. Since Mr Justice Davies told the jury in the libel trial in 1989 that Tolstoy is 'a self-styled historian', it is worth remembering just how well the book was reviewed. In the *New York Review of Books*, Leonard Schapiro, the famous Sovietologist, wrote,

> Count Tolstoy, a scion of the family which included the great novelist, has written a magnificent book. It deserves this epithet on two grounds. In the first place, he has told a shattering and disturbing story... And secondly, it

---

5   Bethell *The Last Secret*, p. 137
6   Bethell is another professional colleague Tolstoy has fallen out with. *The Last Secret* was re-issued in 1995 to coincide with the fiftieth anniversary of the handovers. Bethell wrote a new Epilogue in which he describes their rift, contrasting what he saw as Tolstoy's egotism and self-promotion with his own, more seemly, pattern of conduct. Bethell's autobiography—rather previous: he was born in 1938—called *Spies and Other Secrets* makes other allegations. He belittles Tolstoy's work, describing *Victims of Yalta* as a 'sequel' to his own book, which is hardly fair. There can be little question that Tolstoy's book will be read long after Bethell's useful but much slighter work has been forgotten.

is so well researched with respect to the documentary evidence and to the scores of participants whom he has interviewed.[7]

Another luminary of the Kremlinological establishment, Edward Crankshaw, wrote, 'Tolstoy's achievement has been to animate a deep perspective with a plenitude of vivid detail... His evidence makes the British case seem in many ways shabbier than before.'[8] Shortly after his review, Crankshaw published a long feature on the book in which he said,

> Anyone who cares for the good name and decency of this country must be deeply grateful to Nikolai Tolstoy for bringing [the story of the forced repatriations] out into the open and documenting it so thoroughly.[9]

Julian Amery, formerly Minister of State at the Foreign Office, said,

> Tolstoy writes with restrained passion but total objectivity. He has no need to exaggerate. The facts speak for themselves... [His] book is a massive indictment of two things: the postwar policy of appeasing Stalin and the evils that flow from setting expediency above principle.[10]

The Economist described Tolstoy as seeming 'to have inherited a gift from Leo Tolstoy for depicting the sweep of world history... Mr Tolstoy has written a full and disturbing account... It is a timely story.'[11] Peregrine Worsthorne talked of 'Tolstoy's monumental book' and called for a public inquiry to be set up. Worsthorne was the first to raise the comparison with Nazi atrocities when he asked how

> high-principled statesmen and outstanding civil servants, at the culmination of a war fought in defence of civilisation, could behave with such savage callousness while in the very act of claiming the moral right to condemn the enemy for not wholly dissimilar acts of barbarism... [These people] were responsible for something so terrible that it makes the blood run cold.[12]

7   *New York Review of Books* 7 December 1978
8   *The Observer* 12 February 1978
9   *The Observer* 26 February 1978
10   *Evening News* 6 February 1978
11   *The Economist* 18 February 1978

Woodrow (now Lord) Wyatt asked, 'Do those gentlemen at the Foreign Office, still alive, who could have saved multitudes from horror, sleep well?'[13] *Newsweek* called *Victims of Yalta* a 'passionate and copiously detailed account' of the repatriations, while Nicholas Mosley in *The Listener* described it as an 'admirable, massive and painstakingly researched book'. David Floyd talked of Tolstoy's 'patience and determination', Hugo Young called for an investigation into the whole affair and Rebecca West observed that those 'who come to the end of Count Tolstoy's volume may find themselves absorbed in grave thoughts; unable, indeed, to do much more than say, "Lord, have mercy on our souls".'

Editorial writers made similar points: for example, the *Daily Telegraph* said it was right that 'Britons should recall such unsavoury historical episodes as our forced repatriation of Russians after the war to face Stalin's terrors.' The *Sunday Express* said that, by comparison with some Foreign Office officials such as Lord Brimelow—he had played a central role in implementing the policy—'there are surely men who have done a 24 hour shift shovelling up the slime from the *Amoco Cadiz* who have cleaner hands.'

Predictably, the Soviet press reacted quite differently. According to the magazine *International Affairs*, the Yalta agreement was 'among the most humane acts ever worked out by the parties to the anti-Hitler coalition.' Tolstoy, it said, distorted the Soviet position, without any factual basis for doing so, in order to destroy détente. The truth was that while the West stalled on repatriations, the Soviet Union 'faithfully honoured its commitments... showing generosity and guiding itself by the humanism inherent in the Soviet system.'

Of all the comment, the most eulogistic came from the author and journalist, Christopher Booker. *Victims of Yalta* was a 'stupendous' book which provoked 'an almost unbearable shame for British behaviour in 1944-5', he wrote in *The Spectator*. Booker drew a moral lesson for the present age:

> One cannot help recognising the way in which so much of what was revealed as craven and despicable in the British at the time has become only too

12   *Sunday Telegraph* 26 February 1978
13   *The Sunday Times* 12 February 1978

characteristic of the way we have comported ourselves since. We see in this story a mirror which provokes self-examination—both collective and individual—of a most profound and uncomfortable kind.[14]

A week later, Booker followed this up with a second article, headed 'The Nation's Shame'. He would understand it if the perpetrators of the repatriations were put on trial for war crimes. 'No review can possibly convey the sickening feeling which is provoked by reading page after page describing what British civil servants and British soldiers actually did in those years.'[15] Booker described the civil service as being 'likely to attract people who would be more than usually ... prepared to abdicate individual moral responsibility in the "higher cause" of doing their "duty".' Booker ended by accusing Macmillan in a way which went far beyond anything Tolstoy had written in his book. This started a hare which was to run for another ten years.

> The silence, or puny attempts at self-justification from Brimelow and Co. have been more damning than anything. And if not one of them is now prepared to speak out, there is only one other senior civilian figure, centrally involved in the events of 1944-7 and still left alive, whose voice would carry sufficient authority to make amends. Harold Macmillan was in Austria in 1945. *It was he who first gave the specific order that the Cossacks should be returned.* He must know a great deal more about the story than he disclosed in his memoirs. (emphasis added)

While one section of the public looked for scapegoats, another called for a public enquiry. The government turned this down point blank. The Foreign Secretary, Dr David (now Lord) Owen made a statement in the House of Commons:

> The decision to publish under the 30-year rule exposes these issues to the public gaze... I think that inquiry and scrutiny are in the public domain. If the people concerned are still alive, they are free to comment, and other people are also free to comment, on the documentation, but it would be a

---

14   *The Spectator* 11 February 1978
15   *The Spectator* 18 February 1978

major step if we felt that every time documents revealed criticism we should set up a formal inquiry.[16]

Since Owen knew that the whole point of the controversy was that most of the people concerned were dead and therefore not 'free to comment', this was a contemptuous answer.

Within months of the publication of Tolstoy's book, a call was made to erect a public monument to the victims. Sir Bernard Braine took the lead and wrote to *The Times* on 26 July 1978 saying that to do so would be 'an act of remembrance and expiation'.

That Soviet citizens [he wrote], who knew only too well what lay ahead of them, were forced to return to Russia at the point of British bayonets, was bad enough; that others who were not even Soviet citizens were included in the transports was even worse; and that the authors of this policy suppressed the truth about its consequences from parliament and the public makes this a crime without precedent in our history.[17]

Signing with Sir Bernard were Jo Grimond, James Molyneaux, Lord Bethell, Rebecca West, Hugh Trevor-Roper and, of course, Nikolai Tolstoy.

The response of the Foreign Office was to try, by every underhand means open to a Whitehall department, to prevent the committee acquiring a site for the memorial. The reason was that it was felt such a gesture would harm détente with the Soviet Union. This was both a feeble echo of Moscow's line in *International Affairs* and a reflection of the reason why the non-Soviets were probably handed over in the first place.

In the end Mrs Thatcher overrode these objections so that today a handsome statue stands in a small garden of remembrance in the Cromwell Road, south-west London, opposite the Victoria and Albert Museum.[18]

---

16   *Hansard*, 22 February 1978. Note that this reasoning was abandoned when the War Crimes Act was passed twenty years later.

17   *The Times* 26 July 1978

18   A fuller account of this is given in Bethell's book, *Spies and Other Secrets*. In fact the original structure was destroyed by persons unknown. What stands there today is a second, quite different and less delicate structure.

Tolstoy's book sold well in hardback, went into paperback and is still in print, nearly twenty years later. Its author was now a recognised authority in his field. Three years later, in 1981, he published another book which dealt, in part, with the same subject, although from the Moscow angle, *Stalin's Secret War*. In this he drew upon an important Soviet account of the handovers, *The Last Six Months* by S.M. Shtemenko, to show that the Soviets had definitely requested the handover of the émigré Generals.

> The Soviet government then made a firm representation to our allies over the matter of Krasnov, Shkuro, Sultan-Ghirey, and other war criminals. The British stalled briefly; but since neither the old White Guard generals nor their troops were worth much, they put all of them into trucks and delivered them into the hands of the Soviet authorities.[19]

Press comment was favourable to this new book, but the public reaction was lukewarm, possibly because the main theme, that Stalin made war on his own people, was not new. Nonetheless, those interested in the repatriations noticed the germ of a conspiracy allegation in the chapter on the Austrian handovers. Once again, the most vocal of the critics was Christopher Booker. For the second time he took aim at someone Tolstoy had not explicitly blamed.

> Now that General Keightley is dead, perhaps the person best placed to tell us is not Mr Macmillan, who merely "flew in", but the "political advisor" on the spot—Brigadier Toby Low, now Lord Aldington.[20]

Why had Booker now targeted Lord Aldington? It was not out of perversity, nor from a misreading of Tolstoy's account. It was, indirectly,

---

19 *The Last Six Months*, p. 420. Shtemenko was Deputy Chief of the Soviet General Staff in 1945, and was a Cossack by descent. In addition to his evidence, Tolstoy has subsequently seen in Moscow the war diary of the Soviet 57th Army, which confirms this account, adding that the handover was to be a mass affair without either individual screening or compliance with Yalta. 'On the basis of agreements with the Allied Military Command [5 Corps] the latter have agreed to hand over in their entirety the 15th Cossack Cavalry Corps, the whole collection of traitors to the Motherland and the White emigrants. Point of handover: Judenburg.'

20 *The Spectator* 29 August 1981

because the historian Alistair Horne was by then at work on the official biography of Harold Macmillan. Coincidentally, the research assistant he had engaged was Christopher Booker's sister, Serena. It was she who had interviewed Lord Aldington. Whereas he had told Tolstoy in 1974, 'I do not myself remember being involved in any matters concerning the Cossack Divisions', he now spoke freely to Horne's assistant.

Serena Booker was nobody's fool and at their first meeting, which lasted only an hour, she managed to disagree with Aldington about most aspects of the forced repatriations. He offered to see her again to try to resolve their differences. At their second meeting Serena stuck doggedly to her view of events and asked him to show her where she was in error. The gap between them widened rather than narrowed. Serena wrote a long memorandum to Alistair Horne setting out her worries about this key figure in the drama.

The first point she made was that Lord Aldington's claim, originally made to Tolstoy in 1974, that he could remember nothing about the handover of the Cossacks was simply not true. He had made the same claim to her when she had first asked if she could interview him. 'Oh well, of course, I know nothing about that,' Lord Aldington said jovially. 'I can't remember anything about that.'[21]

When she arrived to talk to him, Lord Aldington began by making an extraordinary statement. 'I feel no guilt,' he said. 'I've had a long talk with Tolstoy and I'm completely in the clear: so is Charles Keightley.' The fact was, Serena pointed out, Lord Aldington had never talked to Tolstoy on this subject (or any other) in his life. Not only that, as their conversation revealed, so far from having forgotten all about the Cossacks, Lord Aldington was impressively armed with justifications for his own behaviour. But these justifications changed between the first meeting and the second. In her memo Serena gave some examples of these changes.

On the first occasion they talked, Lord Aldington had told her that he knew nothing about Macmillan's visit to Klagenfurt on 13 May but that, despite this, he had drafted the misleading signal which implied that all the Cossacks were Soviet citizens. Serena asked him how, if he had not

---

21   This quote and the following ones are taken from Serena Booker's report. They therefore represent her record of the conversations rather than his.

met Macmillan, he could have done so? 'Ah well,' he said, 'I must have been told about it afterwards.'

Six weeks later, she said, 'I have been told that you *were* at the meeting with Harold Macmillan.'

'Who by?' Lord Aldington asked.

Serena listed several names including Tryon-Wilson's and Musson's. She also mentioned that Macmillan himself talked in his diary of meeting 'Keightley's senior officers'.

'Does he mention me by name?' Lord Aldington asked her.

'No.'

'No. I can't remember being there. Of course I knew about Macmillan's visit. But I didn't know the details.'

A similarly equivocal exchange took place on the question of his presence at the first meeting with Tolbukhin's staff on 10 May.

'I wasn't there,' Lord Aldington said. 'I knew nothing about it.'

'Well, you must have been there, because you sent a report of it to 8th Army,' Serena replied.

'Oh, well, yes I was. Yes, now I remember, we arrived late—about 3 o'clock, and sat drinking masses of vodka. We weren't allowed to eat until the boundaries had been settled.'

Similarly, on the vexed subject of the list, Lord Aldington said at the first meeting, 'I didn't know of any lists. [Tryon-Wilson] says he did, but I didn't.' Six weeks later he had changed his story. 'Yes, I knew of a named persons list. But I didn't know who the people were. I wouldn't have known if they were White Russians or not.'

Serena ploughed on. When she refused to accept that Field Marshal Alexander might have been responsible for the handovers, Aldington asked her, 'Why are you protecting Alexander?' He next suggested that General Arbuthnott at 78th Division had been responsible for the failure to screen the Cossacks.

As she was leaving their first meeting, Lord Aldington said to her, 'I have to protect my friends.' His parting words at their second meeting, were, 'Yes, I will admit that General Keightley *did* know about the White Russians being sent back; so did General Arbuthnott.'

Serena Booker drew the threads of her memorandum together in these uncompromising words.

It is rare that you get the feeling that someone is trying to mislead you and, in total contrast to Tryon-Wilson, Lord Aldington, though outwardly helpful, has been as slippery as a box of eels. He is both a politician and a lawyer, which is, I suppose, in this context a fairly good combination. But after our two meetings, I do not trust him an inch... [I am] quite certain that he knows everything. He will never tell me, so there we are.

When Booker published his article suggesting that the ex-BGS should be more frank about his memories of 1945, Lord Aldington dashed off a note to Serena saying, 'Have you been talking to him? What makes him think I was political advisor?'

Unbeknown to Lord Aldington at this time Tolstoy was working on a second aspect of the repatriations: the recently revealed controversy about the Jugoslav handovers. It is another tribute to the efficacy of British official secretiveness that until Milovan Djilas's views on this subject were published in *Encounter* in November 1979, the general public was completely unaware that 25,000 Jugoslavs had been sent to their deaths by 5 Corps at the same time as the Cossacks were being handed to Stalin. (It prompts the question: what other crimes and scandals have happened which have not come out?) Djilas had been a senior colleague of Tito's in the 1940s, but had subsequently become a fierce critic of the dictator. Now he was speaking out about the morality of the Jugoslav repatriations. Had the British handed over only war criminals and major collaborators, he would have had no criticism, he said, but to have sent back *all* the Jugoslavs was 'profoundly wrong'. But it was more mysterious than that. 'To be frank with you,' Djilas told the interviewer, 'we didn't at all understand why the British insisted on returning these people... This was all the more astonishing because we knew that many Jugoslavs (Croats and others) who found themselves in Britain as prisoners of war were considered safe from repatriation.'

To Tolstoy, the fact of two such handover schemes happening in the same place at the same time, with the same British officers in command, looked like more than mere coincidence. Accordingly he started to investigate the Jugoslav handovers. Despite some of the records having been open since 1972, to date Tolstoy is the only British historian to have done so in depth.

Early on in his research, he wrote to Lord Aldington again. At first, as noted above, the ex-BGS said that he remembered nothing of the Jugoslav handovers, adding only that he did recall 'having to stop a force of Jugoslavs trying to overrun part of Carinthia and seize captured material including tanks, but not any repatriations.'

Before he was ready to publish a book on the subject of the Jugoslav handovers, Tolstoy wrote an article for *Encounter* called *The Klagenfurt Conspiracy*. Published in 1983, its subject is clear from the title. There followed a brief and acrimonious correspondence between the author and Lord Aldington, who was clearly taken aback that someone was prepared to question his veracity and to accuse a British General (Keightley) of being a war criminal. He ended by saying, 'I must state unequivocally that General Keightley was not a war criminal and was not a liar and that statements made so charging him are, in my opinion, grossly defamatory. I will now seek advice as to how best I may secure his good name.'

On 29 August, Tolstoy replied in an unintimidated tone, saying the best way he could secure Keightley's good name would be

> to show that the evidence I have brought forward does not bear the interpretation I have placed upon it, or to produce further evidence causing those conclusions to be revised or proved invalid... I have no desire to see those who blackened Britain's reputation and stained the honour of the British Army by committing these abominable crimes against thousands of defenceless men, women and children 'punished'—it is too late alas for that—but I am exceedingly interested in seeing that the truth of what happened becomes established and widely known. If you can help in bringing that about, I shall be extremely grateful.

Lord Aldington did not reply. Instead he wrote, on 24 August, to Keightley's son, Major-General Richard Keightley, then Commandant of the Royal Military College, Sandhurst, saying

> I am getting increasingly angry with Count Nikolai Tolstoy over his writing about affairs in Austria in May/June 1945, and I am getting increasingly concerned that his quite libellous attacks on your Father are not answered... I am incensed that he should describe your Father as a War Criminal and a liar and not meet with full retribution.

In 1984, Tolstoy took time off from the repatriations to complete a book he had been at work on in one way or another for twenty years. It was published as *The Quest for Merlin* and reflected his other main intellectual interest. His purpose was to show that Merlin had been a real historical personage. Despite the serious aim, the sense of boyish enthusiasm which is such an attractive feature of the best of Tolstoy's writing, was not entirely suppressed. Describing his beloved library, he wrote, 'To this day I feel a tremor of excitement when I open one of these handsomely-bound volumes; for there, written in a mysterious tongue that continues in part to baffle the clearest minds, lies half-hidden the *detritus* of the fragmented lore of the Matter of Britain.'[22]

Once again the critics were warm in their praise. The two most authoritative were Glyn Daniels and Charles Thomas. Daniels was Professor of Archaeology at Cambridge and he wrote in *The Times* that 'No-one interested in our history between the Romans' departure and the 6th century can neglect to read this book with care. The 62 pages of scholarly notes and references reveal the breadth and depth of his reading.'[23] Thomas, the Professor of Archaeology at Exeter University, wrote in *The Times Literary Supplement* that Tolstoy had needed to speculate to construct his theory that Merlin had been a real person but that, by the end of the book, the reader is compelled to agree that the speculation is justified. 'One begins to share Tolstoy's faith that far behind [the sources] stands a historical Merlin personage. There seems to be just that little too much [evidence] for easy dismissal.... Forget the niggles, this is an odd but interesting and worthwhile book and some of its findings ought to stand.'[24] Tom Shippey in *The Observer* called the book 'a labour of love, and the love has made its author read incredibly widely, putting professional academics to shame.'[25]

On 3 January 1985, the controversy which 'The Klagenfurt Conspiracy' article provoked was discussed in a BBC documentary, presented by John Tusa, as part of the Timewatch series. Clearly needled by Tolstoy's allegations, Lord Aldington gave his first ever public interview on the subject. If he had told Tolstoy his memory was very vague, he was much more crisp with Tusa. The purpose of the Deception Order, he said was to 'collect up all Jugoslavs and return them to Jugoslavia'.

Tusa mentioned that the Robertson Order provided for the handover only of those who had been 'serving in German forces' and asked why he

22   Tolstoy *The Quest for Merlin*, p. 25
23   *The Times* 29 June 1985
24   *Times Literary Supplement* 5 April 1985
25   *The Observer* 17 February 1985

had 'cast the net so much wider'.

'I don't think there was any widening,' Aldington replied. 'I think there was just a hurried and loose use of language. It was *not* meant to go further than all Jugoslav nationals who had been fighting with the Germans.'

The whole thing, Lord Aldington said, was just a question of 'administrative arrangements' which he had made with Colonel Hocevar at the same time as the Tito forces announced they were returning to Jugoslavia. Had there been a bargain, Tusa asked?

'No,' Aldington replied. 'There was no need to be a bargain. I was under instructions to do what I said I was doing. That, I have to say, is my recollection. Of course, reading the papers now, it looks as if there may have been a bargain but I do not remember that.'

'What if you had known they were going to their deaths?'

'I would have taken steps to see that they didn't go back to their deaths, of course.'

As before, Lord Aldington's memory had evolved more or less at the speed of public revelations. When, in 1974, nothing had been published on the repatriations, he remembered nothing about them. Now that a certain amount had been published, he remembered those events and the surrounding circumstances, at least so far as they exculpated him. As the rate of revelation increased, so he progressively recovered his memory, including the reasons why he had issued orders whose existence had a year or two previously been forgotten by him. Whatever other conclusion may be drawn from this, it is surely right to say that it is an excellent justification for an inquiry of the sort David Owen turned down.

Shortly before the BBC programme was broadcast, Tolstoy had accepted an invitation from the Winchester College Archivist, Dr Roger Custance, whose wife's family, being Latvian, had suffered at Stalin's hands, to speak about the repatriations to the boys at the school. Lord Aldington was still the Warden and, for the second time, Tolstoy's initiative stung him into making a reply. It was announced that Lord Aldington would address the school on 1 March 1985. Naturally Tolstoy wanted to be there, but Lord Aldington refused permission (though Tolstoy did get a tape made of the proceedings).

Aldington began by assuring the boys that he and Tolstoy were not 'sworn enemies', but that they were both 'engaged in the search for truth'. He went on to describe the background to the repatriations, noting that there were White Russians amongst the prisoners. 'Why did we send the Cossacks back to Russia? The answer is simple. It had been so agreed at Yalta.'

He said he had made provision for the non-Soviets not to be handed over, but it was incompetent subordinates who had misinterpreted his intentions. By implication, he took no responsibility for their behaviour. By further implication, he either disobeyed Yalta, or admitted that there was flexibility in the orders he was later to claim he had no option but to obey. When he moved on to the Jugoslavs, he said that it was junior officers who had invented the lie that the intended victims were being sent to Italy. Finally, to drive home the point that he was not responsible for what had happened, he said, 'the handover in fact took place in the last days of May and the first days of June—and I am not washing my hands of this—by that time I was in England preparing to fight my first General Election. I left Austria on 26th (*sic*) May 1945, the day after my 31st birthday. I did not return because I was elected to parliament the next month for a different form of struggle.' In denying personal responsibility so emphatically, there is surely one point clearly made: something disagreeable happened which a British officer would rather not be associated with.

Four years later in Court, much time was taken up with the content of this speech, partly because of two words Lord Aldington did *not* say. Referring to Tryon-Wilson's list, Lord Aldington said, 'some of these were people who were wanted by the Soviet Russians.' But in a draft which Brigadier Cowgill later gave to Tolstoy, Aldington had described these people as 'distinguished'. Did he know they were distinguished— 'the old boy with the CB' as Tryon-Wilson had referred to Shkuro—or did he not?

The second change was of a similar sort. In connection with the Deception Order, Lord Aldington told the boys that he did not like deceiving people but he thought 'silence was thought better than violence'. The original draft read '*subterfuge* was thought better than violence'. That version implies the knowledge of lies having been told, while the version as delivered does not. When asked about this in Court, Lord Aldington once again blamed a subordinate. 'I think I dictated "silence",' he said, 'but my secretary may have written "subterfuge".'

Winchester College was clearly embarrassed about the allegations being levelled at its Warden. Whereas the *Wykehamist* had devoted four column inches to Tolstoy's talk, it allotted twenty-eight to Lord Aldington's. Not only that, the author of the report embroidered the record. He garbled his account of the Hocevar agreement, for example, and made no mention of the Warden's only compliment to Tolstoy, that he was a 'serious historian'.

Winchester was clearly a weak spot in Lord Aldington's armour of silence, but Tolstoy had no further ideas about how to exploit it. However, he was shortly to meet a man who did. Quite coincidentally, a month after Lord Aldington's Winchester speech, this advertisement appeared in *The Times*: 'Brigadier Toby Low 5 Corps 1945 Klagenfurt 12 May—3 June. Repatriation non-Soviet Cossacks. Researcher urgently requires information relating above.' On 22 April 1985 Tolstoy replied.

Dear Sir

I have been sent a copy of your notice in *The Times*, requesting information concerning Brigadier Toby Low's role in the repatriation of non-Soviet Cossacks in May and June of 1945.

As you may know, I have written on this question in two books, and am about to publish a further book concentrating on this mysterious aspect of the business. I would be interested to learn more of your own researches, and on what aspects you are concentrating.

Yours faithfully

Nikolai Tolstoy

10

The BRITISH PAMPHLETEER

NIGEL WATTS is an old Harrovian who describes his career as having taken him 'from Harrow boy to barrow boy'. His father, the son of a lawyer, was a gifted linguist who achieved "native user" standard of Russian at a young age and went out to Moscow in 1915 as part of the British military mission. He ended up as some sort of spy—Watts knows no more than this—operating behind the cover of an engineering specialist, during the early days of the Revolution. Back in Britain he made and spent a lot of money, dealing in anything and everything that came to hand. He loved social display and, at the age of six, Nigel, to his intense embarrassment, was delivered to his first prep school, St. Bede's, in a chauffeur-driven Rolls-Royce. But with the ostentation went financial instabilty. From as early as he can remember, Nigel hated that whole world. He recalls getting sixteen beatings in his first year at prep school, more than all the other boys put together.

Nigel was equally unhappy at Harrow and left at the age of sixteen. His brother, Richard, who followed him there several years later and enjoyed it, becoming Head of his House, says that Nigel 'has always detested what I would term the Pharisee society'. Nigel preferred a more free-wheeling existence, travelling widely in Europe and North America before settling down as a piano-restorer, and opening two antique shops in Wandsworth Bridge Road, Fulham, in the 1960s. In his spare time he went poaching, amassing a total of 38 convictions. 'I've poached every major estate in this country,' he claims. He says he was once stopped when he had twelve pheasants hooked inside his trousers and was caught when, from the weight of the birds, his braces failed.

On one occasion his activities made the national press. It was his habit to fight every conviction, appeal every sentence and challenge every judgement. He used to spend hours in the British Library looking up the law and precedents and then would represent himself, arriving in court with all his books and notes in a sack slung over his shoulder. He would dress for the occasion in muddy corduroys, one black shoe and one brown shoe and a battered bowler hat. On 13 January 1965 he appeared in front of Lord Parker, the Lord Chief Justice, sitting with Mr Justice Marshall and Mr Justice Widgery, to appeal a £20 fine for trespassing on the Earl of Iveagh's land in search of game and for 'unlawfully pursuing game without a licence'. Lord Parker refused to hear his case unless he appeared more tidily dressed. 'But these are the only clothes I have got,' protested Watts. Nonetheless, the court was adjourned for an hour while Watts went for a shave and hired a collar and tie. 'Scruffy Nigel Stops the High Court', was the headline in the *Daily Mirror*.

Today Watts earns his living producing colourful paintings which he sells from a stall at Covent Garden market. He paints about 20 pictures a week. They are usually 30" x 40", representing an output of nearly 35 square feet of art per day. His business card describes them as, 'Paintings of vibrance retaining the spontaneity of the form in line and colour.' He describes his technique as 'drawing with a paint brush' and himself as 'Artiste Peintre'.

Watts is married with two children whom he will not send to Public Schools (although he was happy to pay the fees of his sister's daughters when she fell on hard times). The family live in an unconventionally elegant Regency house in Tunbridge Wells, escaping from time to time to a farm in France. Both properties are his wife's, which was what saved Watts, unlike Tolstoy, from the fear of losing his home after defeat in the libel action.

Like Tolstoy, Watts is a stubborn individualist, but unlike Tolstoy he has no social ambitions, a fact which makes him much less easy to influence. 'I am not the sort of person who looks around the room before I put my hand up,' he says. 'That's why I would never have been any good in the Army. Probably that's why I am unemployable.'

The only time Watts tried to operate in a purely commercial environment, he nearly went bankrupt. At the same time as Brandt's balance sheet was being turned upside down in the crash of 1974, Watts discovered the pitfalls of property investment. Watts's antique shops had not prospered spectacularly, since the proprietor's skills, apart from his natural flair for salesmanship, were more manual than managerial. Watts's sister's husband, Christopher Bowden, was a chartered surveyor and in the boom years of the property market he had proposed to his brother-in-law that, as so many others were doing at the time, they should buy up old London houses, divide them into flats, renovate them, then rent them out. Watts would run the sites while Bowden ran the business in the spare time he had from his day job at Strutt & Parker, a large London firm of surveyors and estate agents.

As at Brandt's, all went well until property prices started to fall precipitately during 1974. Mortgage rates rose from 8% to 22%, so, consequently, did Watts's and Bowden's outgoings. At the same time the market for rented flats weakened so their income fell. With rising outgoings, falling income and shrinking security for their business borrowings, the company quickly went into liquidation.

Bowden started drinking and, in January 1975, separated briefly from his wife. On 14 April he slipped and fell in the bathroom while slightly inebriated, kinking his throat on the edge of the bath. He died of suffocation. His widow, Sue Bowden, put in a claim on the life policy her husband had held. Fatefully, her insurers happened to be the Sun Alliance. A train of events was started which led to, but did not end with, publication of her brother's pamphlet *War Crimes and the Wardenship of Winchester College*.

Sue Bowden was left without either income or assets. She moved into a council house and went out to work, taking jobs as a typist and in a laundry, despite having three young children to look after. Foolishly, when the Sun Alliance inspectors called to take details of the claim, Sue told them that her husband had been drinking. Instantly, they saw a way of avoiding payment on the policy. Sue was informed that her husband had 'become an alcoholic'. This constituted a material change in his health which, under the terms of the policy, he should have notified to the company. The Sun Alliance repudiated the claim.

While it is true that Bowden's business difficulties meant he had been drinking a lot, he had not become an alcoholic, although he did exhibit some of the symptoms and had twice been admitted to the Priory Hospital in Roehampton. On the night he died his blood/alcohol level was that of a man who had drunk about a bottle of wine. A few years later, in tragic circumstances, it transpired that these symptoms were deceptive rather than indicative. Sue's son, Anthony, developed a very rare condition known as Wilson's Disease, which mimics alcoholism and which is hereditary. Wilson's Disease is incurable and, like a terminal drunk, the sufferer progressively loses control of all his or her faculties. In heart-breaking circumstances, Antony Bowden died in Addenbrook's Hospital in Cambridge in October 1978, at the age of 17.

Although this was four years after the original claim had been turned down, it was clear that Bowden probably had been a sufferer from Wilson's disease at the time of his death. In the light of this a solicitor friend of Sue's wrote to the Sun Alliance, asking for a review of the claim. This was refused. She was invited to sue the company if she disagreed with its verdict on her case. Since this was financially impossible, Sue Bowden wrote to the Chairman of the Sun Alliance whom she assumed set its ethical standards and who might, therefore, be prepared to intercede on her behalf if he were apprised of the full facts. This man was Lord Aldington. He replied saying that, although he had 'sympathy for the difficulties of the policyholder's widow and family, I am satisfied that the decision conveyed to you is the right one. I regret, therefore, that I cannot recommend that any payment be made.'

Sue felt beaten. Her response was to try to put the matter behind her. Her family could offer practical but not legal help. Thus matters stood for five years until, on 25 December 1983, her brother Nigel telephoned her. In his Christmas stocking, he said, he had received a copy of the Penguin *Guide to the Law* by John Pritchard. This is a layman's handbook and Chapter 35 deals with insurance. It begins, 'Few commentators would deny that insurance law is weighted in favour of the insurance companies and against the interests of the consumer.' Watts went on to read the whole chapter straight through, with mounting outrage, then rang his sister. Would she agree to his trying to get the Sun Alliance to change its mind over her claim? She was reluctant to re-open the case, but in the end decided to let him go ahead on her behalf. 'I knew that Nigel's methods would be very different from those of [the solicitor],' she wrote in a witness statement to the Court in 1989. 'Nigel said he would try to discover other people who had been harshly treated by the Sun Alliance with a view to establishing a pattern of conduct.'

Reading Pritchard's chapter, it is easy to understand Watts's reaction. Insurance contracts are exempt from the Unfair Contract Terms Act, 1977 and are interpreted in law as having been made 'in the utmost good faith', *uberrimae fidei*, so that the applicant has to disclose all 'material' facts before a policy is issued, even if the applicant does not realise they are relevant, and, worse still, *even if the applicant is unaware of them.* One example Pritchard quotes should have been enough to persuade Watts that the law was on the side of the Sun Alliance, not his sister.

> Peter Brown takes out life insurance. The proposal form has a question, 'Are you in good health?' Mr Brown, believing himself to be in good health, answers 'yes'. A year later he is killed in an accident at work. A post-mortem discloses that he had a malignant brain tumour which was obviously getting worse and which existed at the time he took out the insurance. The insurance company could then argue that his statement that he was in good health was wrong and declare the policy to be null and void.[1]

Thus Bowden was in breach of his policy by having, unwittingly, contracted Wilson's Disease. Legally, there was no basis for any review of Sue's claim. But Watts saw the Pharisee society at work and his sister suffering as a result of its machinations. He decided to act.

On 27 January 1984 the *Daily Mail* carried an advertisement: 'Unpaid insurance claim with Sun Alliance left widow with three children destitute. If any other persons or companies insured with the Sun Alliance have either not had their claim paid, experienced delay in obtaining settlement, or had their claim reduced would they please contact the above widow's representative on ....'

The next day Watts wrote to the Sun Alliance head office. Not only were his methods to be his own, his style on paper was too.

> Dear Sirs,
>
> 'Extravagant and multifarious' might be an appropriate way of describing those eulogistic commendations which the Sun Alliance advertising communicates to the public, to convey the impression of integrity and security, at the time we are invited to pay the premium for the protection you purport to afford us. However when disaster strikes a radically different approach is pursued. Vacillation, prevarication and any chance of repudiation would appear to be the strategy adopted by your company when

---

1   Pritchard *Guide to the Law*, p. 558. The Law Commission commented on this situation when it reported in 1980. 'The English law concerning non-disclosure and warranties has been strongly criticised by our courts and by our academic writers... It leaves the insurer in the position of judge and jury as to whether or not the full rigour of the law should be applied in individual cases.' *Non-Disclosure and Breach of Warranty*, pp. 100-1

confronted with the prospect of having to pay out money rather than receive it...

It might be of interest to some of your illustrious directors to know that in 1978 a grief-stricken Mother buried her young son Antony. That Mother had been unable to bring the comfort of a home to him during the last three years of his life because the Sun Alliance, who were making millions, saw fit not to pay her. No doubt the noble Baron Aldington, from the security of his baronial seat in Aldington, was not preoccupied exactly with such trivial issues when he endorsed his company's decision and 'regretted, therefore, that he could not recommend any payment be made.' Mrs Bowden will *never forget this* and I propose to make sure that the directors of your company *never forget this*.

Yours faithfully,

Nigel Watts.

Watts copied his letter to, amongst others, the Prime Minister, The Consumer Council, *Private Eye*, the British Standards Institute and all the directors of the company, who included Sir Charles Villiers and Henry Lambert, and Sir Geoffrey Howe, whom he referred to as 'Her Majesty's Foreign Secretary, Ex-Director Sun Alliance, Honorary Vice President of the Consumers Association.'

The response was disappointing. Instead of the flood of replies Watts had hoped to receive, there was just a trickle. He did not see that this altered the justice of his case so he started telephoning Lord Aldington asking for a meeting. None of his requests got past Lord Aldington's secretary. Sue Bowden rang too. Lord Aldington took the trouble to draft a letter to her, but the company's lawyers were nervous of even so timid a gesture. 'Better not to say anything,' they advised on seeing his draft. 'For courtesy say "no purpose in our meeting". Strongly advise not putting anything in writing, especially not the word "evidence".' But the man who had killed 400 Germans on Easter Sunday in the Edhessa Pass thought he could risk a few words. 'I understand how you feel about this matter,' he wrote, 'but I really see no purpose in our meeting.'[2]

Unable to get the Chairman at his office, Watts tried telephoning him at home, sometimes getting Lady Aldington, at others the housekeeper.

He also circulated copies of his correspondence with Sun Alliance to the 7800 insurance brokers in Britain. Tiring of all the reasons he had been given why Aldington could not come to the telephone, Watts wrote once again asking for a meeting.

> I myself have left some eight messages asking for a meeting with my sister and myself. Frankly, I am not the slightest bit interested in your helicopter, your private secretaries, your private cook etc. and all the other propaganda anxiously issued by your representatives to convey the impression of your important status. I am concerned solely that you should rectify the grave injustice that you were instrumental in creating when your company cheated my widowed sister in 1978. Lady Aldington tells me you will not insure her. Judging by the way your company has treated my sister, I can see why. May I suggest that we make a concerted effort to move towards each other's position and that a meeting should be arranged urgently.[3]

The telephone calls carried on until Lady Aldington told her husband that he should 'be efficient, you know, keep a list of them.' Lord Aldington's first list is dated 23 March 1984 and shows that Watts telephoned him at Knoll Farm at 4.00 p.m., 4.15 p.m., 8.00 p.m., 8.05 p.m., 8.06 p.m., 8.10 p.m. and 8.11 p.m. The next day, he phoned seven times in quick succession from about 9.15 a.m. and again from around 4.00 p.m. In all he telephoned 28 times that weekend. Eventually Lord Aldington had to ask the housekeeper to tell all callers that his Lordship was not at home. In Court, Watts explained this approach, saying, 'I regarded Lord Aldington as in the business of avoiding me and I was in the business of making sure he didn't.'

Sue Bowden wrote again, describing her son's illness, but Lord Aldington was unmoved. 'It is really not right in the insurance business to make payments other than in accordance with the terms of the contract and the law.'[4]

---

3   20 March 1984

4   6 June 1984. It is clear from the tone of Sue Bowden's letter that an offer of, say, £10,000—the original claim was for £50,000—would have been acceptable to her as an adequate compromise. To date the Sun Alliance has admitted the case has cost it £530,000, and there have been further, unadmitted, costs, so Lord Aldington's confrontational approach has cost the company far more than a quick settlement would have done.

Overleaf, previous page: Lord Aldington, 1962, shortly after being ennobled (*Times*)
Opposite: Nikolai Tolstoy   Above: Nigel Watts
Below: Lord Brimelow, Brigadier Cowgill and Christopher Booker (*l to r*) at the press
conference for the *Final Report*, October 1990 (*Telegraph*)
Overleaf, next: Mr Justice Michael Davies (*Monitor)*

Watts continued writing his letters and making his telephone calls, none of which Lord Aldington responded to. Instead, he asked the Sun Alliance's main corporate lawyers, a firm called Ashurst, Morris and Crisp, to threaten Watts. They wrote to Watts saying his behaviour constituted 'harassment'.

> In the normal way, tactics of this kind would be ignored. We write to advise you that since there is no outstanding claim nothing will be paid under the policy and no *ex gratia* payment is intended to be made, but if there is a repetition of the conduct which you have recently resumed we shall apply to the Court without notice or delay for the appropriate relief in order to stop you hounding Lord Aldington.[5]

Watts replied saying that he was not 'harassing' Lord Aldington.

> The only reason Lord Aldington received this number of calls [he continued] was because he persisted in replacing the receiver when he failed to accommodate his explosive rage on each occasion that yet another of his inaccuracies were revealed... I think you will agree that if someone keeps putting the receiver down in a fit of rage one is honour bound to keep pursuing the issue until they have contained their temper to some semblance of control. Unhappily with Lord Aldington this has proved something more than a little difficult to achieve.[6]

At this, Ashurst, Morris and Crisp, like so many of the other firms of solicitors in this story, simply gave up.

At the same time, Watts decided to elevate his campaign and write to Mrs Thatcher. He elevated his prose accordingly.

> I am sure you will appreciate that at a time when Lord Aldington seeks to vindicate his behaviour by masquerading to my sister the expedient pretext but unconvincing theory that his duty to shareholders precludes his entertaining the proposition of even so much as an *ex gratia* payment, it is extremely distressing for her to depose to his company's lavish generosity,

---

5   8 August 1984
6   16 August 1984

given without thought to shareholders, in directions more likely to flatter his arrogance... Regrettably Lord Aldington has allowed his preoccupation with power and status to engender the position where he fears that to be seen to climb down from the stand of vicious severity he has adopted might be perceived to reveal weakness rather than strength.[7]

Watts's next recourse was to the venerable practice of pamphleteering. He produced a home-made montage of his letters to the Sun Alliance and "Lettrasetted" a title derived from the company's current advertising campaign: 'The Strength of the Sun Alliance Around You? For or Against the Policyholder?' The document ran to 12 A3 pages. It cannot be said to make compulsive reading. Neither, except by an unusually sensitive soul, could it really be considered defamatory. But Lord Aldington took exception to it, mainly on the ground of the distribution list. Watts posted 5000 copies to Members of Parliament, the press, insurance brokers and anyone else he thought might know of either Lord Aldington or the Sun Alliance. In the light of future developments, the most fateful destination was Aldington village. For a few pounds he had bought a copy of the electoral roll, and all of the Baron's neighbours were sent copies. Lady Aldington described at the trial how this strange publication was received by the villagers.

We live about two miles outside the village and it is quite a long way for our friends to come, but we kept on getting our friends in the village bringing up envelopes with 28p on them and they were horrified that anybody had written to them whom they did not know in a fat envelope which was full of bits of paper from some man they had never heard of and all about Sun Alliance... They were all Mr. Watts's letters to Sun Alliance but with no answer... There was a fat envelope with 28p on it. That is what upset everybody in the village. They said, 'If this man wants money,' which I gather he does, 'why does he not stop paying 28p for thousands of people in the village?' And it was not only our village, it was the village next door. 'Why does he pay 28p?' That was what was worrying the village. I mean, I know it sounds mad, but they said, 'If he can afford that amount of money why does he spend it on us, who he does not know?' You know, simple stuff.

7   16 August 1984

Lord Aldington's response was more sophisticated: he consulted a libel barrister, and then suggested to Henry Silver, the Sun Alliance's Company Secretary (himself an ex-barrister) that he issue what is known as a "gagging writ". This is a popular legal device with people who want to suppress a matter without the embarrassment of having to give reasons, possibly unsuccessfully, in open court and have their opponents put their side of the story in public. Robert Maxwell had nearly 100 writs outstanding at the time of his death, many of them issued for just this purpose. A writ renders any matter *sub judice*, after which mention of it can be a contempt of court. The plaintiff need not have any intention of ever letting the matter come to court. Lord Aldington's response to Watts's pamphlet was precisely this:

> I am still minded to consider the idea of a Writ [he minuted to Silver] which we can publicly announce we have issued without committing ourselves to trial. I know the objections to that course and in particular that we run the risk of increased publicity. On the other hand, the present position is that quite a large number of people, thousands not tens, have been circulated with highly defamatory material to which we have given no response at all. I would not, of course, contemplate the idea of a Writ if that would not silence Watts and certainly if it would not silence the publication by others of Watts's material.
>
> There is no hurry about this. We can discuss it in November when I return from the United States, when I will have had at least ten days without any fear of being rung up by Mr Watts! Please don't give him my U.S. number![8]

Watts's final suggestion for resolving the insurance dispute was to allow the case to be arbitrated by the Insurance Ombudsman. The office of Ombudsman had been set up in the late 1970s, long after the Bowden claim was originally made. In such cases, both sides need to consent to the Ombudsman's involvement. In a letter so brief as to be almost insulting, Lord Aldington refused this offer of an independent judgement on the case.

8   22 October 1984

Not long after John Tusa's Timewatch documentary about the Jugoslav handovers had been broadcast, on 3 January 1985, Watts received an anonymous telephone call from a resident of Aldington village. The caller had received his pamphlet and had also seen the programme, which Watts had not. If Watts wanted to know more about Lord Aldington, the caller said, he should look into the forced repatriations from Austria in 1945. Bombshell!

As it happened, Watts had known Lord Bethell at Harrow. When *The Last Secret* was published he had bought a copy, but it had lain on his bookshelves unread. Now he took it down, and looked up Brigadier Low in the index. He was not mentioned. Watts then went to the newspaper library in Hendon to look for information, but drew a blank there, except that he did discover that a man called Nikolai Tolstoy had written on the subject, and he borrowed his books from the Tunbridge Wells library. On 6 February 1985, he wrote another letter to Lord Aldington, raising the issue of the 'forcible and inhumane repatriation of thousands of Russian prisoners of war, women and children, to Stalin's death camps', saying that 'a few British officers behaved as badly as any Nazi war criminal' and that it was only the thirty-year rule which had enabled them to escape detection.

Lord Aldington did not reply to this so Watts composed the letter in which the connection which was at the heart of the Watts-Tolstoy collaboration is mentioned for the first time.

> Few people could understand how a man who had been raised to the peerage and who had been the deputy Chairman of the Conservative Party could display a condition of such ruthless and vicious indifference to the plight of this widow and then to be so lacking in any modicum of compassion that people who heard of his conduct were left numb. This horrifying situation has perplexed one's mind and then one day I received a telephone call from someone who lives in your village of Aldington who had heard of the case. He was to provide a possible explanation subject to the veracity of his statement being substantiated. He alleged that the somewhat undistinguished fellow resident of his village, who had selected, to the dismay of many, the name of his Parish to raise himself from his family name of Low to LORD, was none other than the man who had played a protagonist role in the participation of one of the most shameful and horrific acts of betrayal and deception ever perpetrated by British citizens. I refer to the perfidious betrayal and subsequent forcible and inhumane repatriation of thousands of

displaced Cossack men, women and children to Stalin's death camps at the end of the Second World War....

There were men of stature and conscience, such as Field Marshal Alexander, who evaded any such participation, and most of the British soldiers with courage and calibre positively mutinied against a policy which embraced such callous indifference to civilised standards of humanity. Regrettably there were others, albeit a minority few, who chose to pursue, some with zeal of application, another direction notwithstanding that they were well aware that they were delivering their captives by trick and deception into Soviet hands to be persecuted and killed.

The question therefore that remains to be asked of The Lord Aldington is whether he can refute these allegations and, if he cannot do so, whether he will concede that the qualities required to participate in such an act and to treat a widow as he has done Mrs Bowden, are not one and the same?[9]

On 11 April the advertisement quoted at the end of the last chapter, in which Watts asked for information on the forced repatriations, was published in *The Times*. Lord Aldington's response was to consider suing *The Times* for libel. Since the advertisement simply conjoins the name Toby Low with the words, 'Repatriation of non-Soviet Cossacks', this shows an extreme sensitivity to the charge—the name 'Lord Aldington' was not even mentioned.

No writ was actually issued because, as he wrote to a friend, he thought that to do so might 'play into the hands of this tiresome man [Watts] and since from my experience he stops at nothing, I prefer to leave this sleeping dog lying!' He added that 'Count Tolstoy has absolved me, certainly in one of his books, of responsibility for the return of non-Soviet nationals to the Russians.'[10]

On the day Lord Aldington wrote this letter, Tolstoy wrote his reply to Watts's advertisement, also as quoted at the end of the last chapter. Watts replied by sending Tolstoy a bundle of documents, in this case other letters he had received in reply to the advertisement, several of which later proved to be of use to Tolstoy's research. Tolstoy sent Watts a copy of his *Encounter* article, The Klagenfurt Conspiracy, which, he said, al-

9   14 March 1985
10   22 April 1985

though outdated, 'may help you to form a still deeper appreciation of the man with whom you have been dealing. But please,' he added, 'do not alert him to my contact with you: he has at last agreed to see me, and I want his guard to be lowered!' Tolstoy concluded with a vituperative flourish which was used against him in court in 1989 to allege malice. He referred to 'Master Low', calling him Macmillan's 'hatchet-man', and said to Watts, 'I wish you luck in your struggle with this evil man. Had he been a German he would have been strung up years ago.'[11] Watts felt he had met a man of his own totem.

The meeting Tolstoy had referred to took place on 8 May 1985, the 40th anniversary of VE Day, at Sandhurst, where General Richard Keightley, was Commandant. Keightley hoped that a meeting might elicit an explanation of the events of May 1945 and remove any suspicions attaching to his father's name. It was the gesture of a sensible and ingenuous man. However, Lord Aldington's way of discussing this subject—a method which he was to use to great effect in Court in 1989—rendered the meeting almost useless. He rejected Tolstoy's propositions but without offering an alternative reading of the evidence. It was purely negative, although the conversation did produce some interesting remarks, such as Lord Aldington's bland assertion that he *had* attended the "shoot the Cossacks" conference on 22 May, a claim he was to deny vigorously in Court four years later.

Tolstoy took this fencing as a form of evasiveness. He wrote in the Introduction to *The Minister and the Massacres* that it increased his suspicions that Aldington knew more than he was letting on. The only important revelation was that Lord Aldington said that Arbuthnott had been against handing over any Cossacks because 'they were just going to be killed.' If Arbuthnott knew the likely fate of the Cossacks before they were handed over, and Aldington knew that Arbuthnott knew, how was it that Lord Aldington could claim, as he did in Court in 1989, that in 1945 it had never occurred to him that they might all be shot? This was put to him in Court. Aldington's answer was that he had forgotten, in 1989, what he had remembered in 1985. 'It is a statement of what I remember Arbuthnott said,' Lord Aldington told the Court. 'I don't remember it

11   29 April 1985

now, but I must have remembered it then.'

As Tolstoy raced to finish his manuscript of *The Minister and the Massacres* by the date agreed with his publishers, new evidence kept surfacing. For the first time he was able to meet Brigadier Tryon-Wilson who told him that he remembered that the list of émigré Generals which the Soviets handed him on 11 May 1945 *did* include Shkuro's name—'the old boy with the CB', were Tryon-Wilson's words. This was a critical point, since it implied that 5 Corps, contrary to everything which was to be argued in Court, knew full well that the Definition order was in flat contradiction to the terms of the Yalta agreement, not to mention 8th Army's standing orders.

Although he had made the admission on tape in late 1985, Tryon-Wilson found that after Lord Aldington had issued his writ this recollection was one which, search his memory as he might, had just gone. In Court he explained this by saying, 'that observation must have been based not on hindsight, but the knowledge I had at that particular moment and of the enormous number of contacts I had had from individuals.'

Another critical piece of evidence came to light towards the end of 1985. A lecturer from Loughborough University of Technology, Dr Robert Knight, whose only other publication concerned post-war Austrian policy for compensating Jews, produced a scholarly paper attacking Tolstoy's conclusions on the repatriations. (To date Knight is the only academic to have done so. In 1989 he came to Court as an "expert" witness for Lord Aldington.) In preparing his paper, Knight used a file which had only been released to the PRO in January 1984 but which was to become central to the later controversy. It is entitled 'Allied Commission for Austria: British element: Jugoslav matters, surrender details, displaced persons'. This was the fateful FO 1020/42—see Appendix A.

Knight delivered his paper at a conference at the School of Slavonic and East European Studies at the University of London in late 1985, just five weeks before Tolstoy was due to deliver his manuscript to his publishers. Listening, it was clear to Tolstoy that Knight had used a very important source, so Tolstoy asked for the reference. Unusually for an academic, Knight refused to give one. A search of all newly released PRO files would be a huge task, for which he did not have the time, but Tolstoy wanted his book to be based on as wide a range of sources as possible. He was worried. It was Watts who came to the rescue.

Watts is no scholar, so his technique was not one frequently used by historians: with a pocketful of five pound notes, he went to the inquiry desk at the Public Record Office and said, 'I don't care what it costs, I want the very best researcher you have got here. We have *got* to find this file.' The file was duly located, Tolstoy looked at it quickly and photocopied some of the 140 documents in it.[12] Given that the file later disappeared into Whitehall for four years, this was to be of immense help to the Defence in 1989. Without it, the Court would have been completely restricted to the documents Aldington selected from the file while it was in the Foreign Office. But Tolstoy might have done much better had he not misused this opportunity. Instead of looking for *any* material which throws light on the mystery of 5 Corps handovers, of which there is a great deal, he looked simply for material which would bolster the case he was about to make in *The Minister and the Massacres*, which was that Macmillan was to blame for what was done. Thus Tolstoy failed to copy many of the documents in the file—which is once again available to the public—which show, to the satisfaction of this author at least, that the forced repatriations were more the fault of 5 Corps than of Macmillan. Lord Aldington did not have to confront this evidence in Court. Tolstoy suffered his catastrophic legal defeat partly as a result of that fact.

Ironically in the light of what was to follow, Knight's conclusion was that the chief blame for the handovers attaches to 5 Corps, although he disfigures his argument by implying that some of the Cossacks were war criminals—although he gives no evidence for this—and that this mitigates the British Army's crimes against the others.[13] Like Alistair Horne, Knight argues that there was no conspiracy by any politicians, just indifference to the fate of the victims on the part of the Army. Although neither historian appears to have assimilated the evidence for the fact that 5 Corps did not simply act as "bad Samaritans", but energetically and secretively forced through the cruellest possible solution to the refugee problem in Carinthia, they are both closer to solving the riddle than Tolstoy was in the book he was preparing. 'The responsibility for going for a "convenient" solution at a time of acute difficulty,' Knight wrote, 'lay primarily with the military commanders concerned.'[14] It is one of

12   This file, FO 1020/42, is the most important of all the public records dealt with in this story—see Chapters 4 to 6 and Appendix A.

13   See *Intelligence and National Security*, May 1986

14   *Ibid.*, p. 251

the mysteries of the way the case was conducted that the Defence lawyers never asked Lord Aldington's "expert witness" why he had come to this important conclusion. Instead they stuck to subjects Knight had never made any formal study of—like the political composition of the Titoist *junta*—and which was irrelevant to Lord Aldington's level of responsibility for what was done by 5 Corps.

Tolstoy made another blunder when he ended *The Minister and the Massacres* with a brief, unsubstantiated smear.

> Perhaps the most disturbing factor, though, concerns not what lay behind the Minister Resident's actions in May 1945, but in what followed. For throughout Macmillan's terms of office as Minister of Defence, Foreign Secretary and Prime Minister, the NKVD (subsequently the KGB) presumably has the best of reasons for knowing the whole of a story which in the West it has taken forty years to unravel.

To accuse a former Prime Minster of having been under the sway of a hostile government without giving any reasons for making the allegation was an act of hubris.

Sensing an *ad hominem* attack, the reviews of *The Minister and the Massacres* were decidedly "mixed". And the attack was *ad hominem*.[15] On a promotional tour of Canada, Tolstoy said that in a comparison with Adolf Eichmann, 'Macmillan comes off worse than Eichmann... He created the policy whereas Eichmann merely implemented policy that had been created by others.'[16] Many condemned Tolstoy as 'a conspiracy theorist'. Moreover, the times had changed. By 1986, the national self-abasement of the late 1970s, when *Victims of Yalta* was published, had given way to a post-Falklands triumphalism and aggressive 1980s talk about 'losers'. John Keegan, the Defence Correspondent of the *Daily Telegraph* caught the changing mood in this brutal passage about the victims of 5 Corps:

---

15 Tolstoy has told this author that the reason he was in such a hurry to publish his book was that at the time, Harold Macmillan, by then Earl of Stockton, was 91 and fading fast. Tolstoy says he was worried that he might be thought a coward if it was not until the great man was dead that his book came out. As it was, publication date was 28 April 1986, eight months before Macmillan's death on 29 December.

16 *Winnipeg Free Press*, 24 June 1986

The losers presented the British with a problem at a time when problems marched in droves, and the British solved it by doing what seemed easiest at the time. No credit to anyone involved. But when Alexander the Great captured Darius's Greek mercenaries after the battle of Granicus, he put them all to the sword. The aftermath of all wars is very nasty and prudent minorities should take care not to be in the wrong place at the wrong time. [17]

In other words, the British Army is as likely to commit war crimes as any other.

One of the few who kept faith with Tolstoy was Christopher Booker who called, once again, for an inquiry. He wrote in *The Spectator* about the stain that the repatriations cast on 'Britain's honour and national character'. Booker's article attracted the attention of Brigadier Anthony Cowgill who was to become the chief apologist for the repatriations. Subsequently, Cowgill paid tribute to Tolstoy's book, at least insofar as it had drawn public attention to what had gone on. 'I only became aware of the repatriations episode after the publication in 1986 of Nikolai Tolstoy's book *The Minister and the Massacres*.' [18]

But most opinion was hostile. The BBC, under its (Old Wykehamist) Director General, Alasdair Milne, banned Tolstoy from discussing his new book. Even Winchester College got its own little kick in. The *Wykehamist* ran another article on Tolstoy, accusing him of displaying 'self-obsession' and 'a lack of humour'. The repatriations were described as

an act of effectively unavoidable military pragmatism... The fact that others, who had left the Soviet Union after the Revolution, were also returned is of course regrettable, but the pressure of circumstances did not make it easy to differentiate between varying types of Russian. Lord Aldington proved himself to be a man of great integrity when he gave his address... At no stage did he actually *lie*, while his enemies, in their relentless witch-hunt, seem keen to suggest he did. [19] (emphasis in original)

---

17   *Daily Telegraph* 2 May 1986. Keegan's authority for this point is considerable. Apart from publishing a host of scholarly books, including *The Face of Battle* and *The History of Warfare*, he was Senior Lecturer in Military History at Sandhurst for twenty-six years.

18   Cowgill *Final Report*, p. vii

1986 was an eventful year for Tolstoy in quite a different field. He started work on the book which was to put him, for the first time in his life, right at the top of the bestseller lists. Before he had even finished writing, a British publisher had offered him quarter of a million pounds for a fictional trilogy about Merlin, and an American publisher the same again for the North American rights. Tolstoy had been commissioned to write a history of the White Armies in the Civil War but he got bored with the project and "bunked off". Without telling anybody, he spent a year, at a high pitch of excitement, writing a book which John Bailey, the Professor of English at Oxford University, later said he preferred to *Lord of the Rings*. This was *The Coming of the King—the First Book of Merlin*.

The *Sunday Telegraph* said 'the saga's re-creation of sixth-century Britain draws on a wealth of research material to tell the story of Merlin, the rune-reading child-man, poet and battling demi-god. The result is complex, poetic and extremely skilful.' Roy Kerridge ended a review by saying

> I felt I could read this book for evermore, so I was pleased to learn that Tolstoy intends to write another two volumes of Merlin's adventures. Who is Merlin's father? Is it Lleu himself? I can hardly wait.[20]

The book shot into the bestseller lists and stayed there for a considerable time. Tolstoy had found his *métier*. If there is one regret he expresses today about the consequences of his subsequent legal entanglements, it is that he has never yet had the time or peace of mind necessary to write volumes II and III. As a result the hundreds of thousands of readers—more than all his other books put together—who bought *The Coming of the King* are still waiting to find out what happened when Merlin attempted 'the Twelve Dire Tasks' and tried to garner 'the Thirteen Treasures of the Island of the Mighty within the House of the Glass lying beyond the portals of Caer Sidi!'

Watts's response to *The Minister and the Massacres* and the resultant

19   *The Wykehamist* 9 July 1986
20   *The Spectator* 21 May 1988

controversy was to produce another pamphlet. In it he collated the passages from the book which mentioned Brigadier Low. It was one of his weakest efforts and there was little response except from a figure who was to play an important part in the libel action, the Earl of Portsmouth. Outraged at the BBC ban, he telephoned to ask Watts what he could do to help, and Watts suggested he phone Tolstoy. Portsmouth also wrote to Alasdair Milne, then Director General, to inquire about the ban. In further correspondence, Milne made what Lord Portsmouth considered a series of fatuously empty and evasive replies, then silence fell. Presumably Milne thought Portsmouth had abandoned the chase. Nothing could have been further from the truth.

At the same time, Brigadier Cowgill responded to Booker's article by buying Tolstoy's book. Within days, he had invited himself to see the author, announcing that his wife had told him that if he did not 'expose that man Aldington' she would divorce him. Cowgill told Tolstoy he had business dealings with Lord Aldington which he intended curtailing if the accusations in *The Minister and the Massacres* stood up to scrutiny. Might he therefore use Tolstoy's address book to get in touch with the still-living witnesses and also see all his files? 'Why not?' said Tolstoy with naive gratitude that somebody else was taking a serious interest in the subject. Cowgill started calling regularly, but it was not long before Georgina voiced her suspicions. Tolstoy pooh-poohed them, but was slightly puzzled when Cowgill announced that he was going to form an unofficial commission of inquiry to investigate the forced repatriations. Cowgill professed to agree with Tolstoy's case, which makes the idea of an investigation even more bizarre. Strangely, Tolstoy did not smell a rat.

Cowgill is a man of nearly Lord Aldington's age. He comes from a north of England, grammar-school background, but affects an ostentatiously "public school" manner, uttering self-consciously "60s" words, like 'trendy', with a smooth imitation of a patronising smile. He even has a verb of his own: 'to bottom', as in 'We're going to bottom old So-and-so', meaning something between 'to de-bag' and 'to shaft', or possibly both in that order. After taking an engineering degree at Birmingham University, Cowgill spent his working life in the Royal Electrical and Mechanical Engineers (REME), from which he was seconded for a while into the Secret Service. Today he is Director of the British Management Data Foundation (BMDF), a one-man body, operating out of his garage in semi-suburban Gloucestershire, which keeps subscribing companies in touch with Downing Street through regular meetings with the Prime

Minister's Press Secretary, then Bernard Ingham.[21] Ingham has described his role as trying 'to keep the BMDF up with government and Prime Ministerial thinking'. Cowgill does not like the term "lobbyist" used about him, preferring to be called an 'illuminator of facts'. Commenting on his approach to Tolstoy, a colleague of Cowgill's who knew him in the intelligence community in the 1940s and 50s—he is now a peer—said to this author, 'I can see him having a hidden agenda.'

Cowgill invited three people to serve on his committee, Brigadier Tryon-Wilson, Lord Brimelow and Christopher Booker. Cowgill thought of asking Lord Aldington to join, but Alistair Horne, for one, tried hard to dissuade him on the ground that his conclusions would not appear independent with such a figure on the committee. But Tryon-Wilson is almost as close to the events under investigation, and in Lord Brimelow, one of the Foreign Office officials who had pushed the Yalta policy through so hard in 1945, Cowgill had a man who so hated Tolstoy for what he had written about him in *Victims of Yalta* that he refused ever to sit in the same room as him. The only member of the committee who had any brief for Tolstoy was Christopher Booker.

On 3 September 1986, just as he was forming his committee, Cowgill gave lunch to Lord Portsmouth, with whom he had been put in touch by Tolstoy. Cowgill told Portsmouth that the BMDF was considering forming links with Lord Aldington but that he was disturbed at the prospect of doing business with a man of Aldington's developing reputation. With respect to his committee's researches, he said he thought the only way to get Lord Aldington to talk was to have him arraigned before an official Army tribunal where, Cowgill assured Portsmouth, Aldington would have no right of silence.

Later that month, Lord Aldington told Richard Keightley in a letter that 'Brigadier Anthony Cowgill ... is helping me with the research on 5 Corps HQ papers and 78th Division files. I have yet to hear the result. Tony [Cowgill] also joined me last week in a dinner-time discussion with Teddy Tryon (Brigadier Tryon-Wilson) where we both refreshed our

21   The companies were, as of January 1993, Allied-Lyons, Allied Steel, Associated Octel, British Coal, British Gas, British Nuclear Fuels, Cranfield Institute of Technology, Ferranti, Greenalls, ICI, ICL, Lucas, Marks and Spencer, National Power, National Grid, Nuclear Electric, PowerGen, Rolls-Royce, Shell UK, Simon Engineering, TI Group and the Wellcome Foundation. (*Financial Times* 19 January 1993)

memories.'[22]

Six weeks later Cowgill wrote to the Ministry of Defence saying he was engaged in an investigation with the two senior surviving staff officers of 5 Corps, Brigadier Tryon-Wilson and Lord Aldington. Writing as he was to a public body, Cowgill now made no claims about personal or business concerns, instead he said that 'this study is being done in the national interest.'[23]

Whatever question marks hung over Cowgill's agenda, there could be no doubt about Watts's. Three months after Tolstoy's book came out, he wrote to Lord Aldington stating his own intentions as plainly as he could.

> Dear Lord Aldington
>   I am preparing a new circular specifying the charges made against you in Nikolai Tolstoy's book *The Minister and the Massacres*. The circular will carry *inter alia* all the recent press articles in the Canadian newspapers [where there was particularly vociferous support for Tolstoy from the émigré Croat community].
>   Before publishing this I would like to afford you an opportunity to put forward any defence you might have against these charges if you feel you have been misrepresented.
>   I would therefore like to come down to see you next week to discuss the issue with you and put some questions to you regarding your particular role in these war crimes.
>   Would Thursday 31st July or Friday 1st August be convenient?
>   Yours sincerely,
>   Nigel Watts[24]

Lord Aldington replied curtly, 'I do not propose to enter into any correspondence with you, or to have meetings with you. In these circumstances, I suggest you save the postage on letters to me.' The die was now cast. Watts started planning what he thought would be his last and greatest pamphlet: the one which would finally bring Lord Aldington to court.

22   25 September 1986
23   6 November 1986
24   22 July 1986

11

The WRIT

WATTS RAN into difficulties with his pamphlet almost at once. He sent Tolstoy a list of questions. But it was immediately apparent to Tolstoy that what Watts needed was not so much answers as a ghost writer. But Tolstoy was hard at work on Merlin, so he relegated the job to an after-dinner occupation. Laying aside his bardic pen for a couple of winter evenings, Tolstoy dashed off two thousand words on Brigadier Low's part in the events described in *The Minister and the Massacres*. Amongst those words were "duplicity", "brutality", "barbarous", "dishonourable", "unauthorised", "savage", "blood", "Massacre of Glencoe", "70,000 men, women and children", "war criminal" and "unrepentant". Forgetting for a moment the Thirteen Treasures of the Island of the Mighty, he included the extravagant phrase, "the worst butchers of Nazi Germany or Soviet Russia". Two related names were repeated several times: "Lord Aldington" and "Winchester College". The last sentence linked them by the words "uniquely honoured". The text ended with a question mark.

These were the last words Tolstoy intended ever to write for publication on the forced repatriations. Macmillan had died a month before, and Merlin was coming more alive with every day Tolstoy spent at his keyboard. His future lay in fiction. Without giving the matter much thought, he printed and checked his draft, re-printed it and posted it to Watts.

Watts was so pleased with what he saw that he decided to publish it unchanged; he did not even have it re-typed. But the artist in him required a few decorative flourishes, so he reproduced the Aldington coat of arms—motto 'Spes'—and included a couple of photographs of the 1st

Baron together with some quotations of his to the effect that he had 'forgotten all about it'. Watts then spread this out on two sheets of A3 paper and gave it a title, *War Crimes and the Wardenship of Winchester College*, which expressed the linkage he wanted to make: was a man with such allegations hanging over him fit to act as a moral exemplar to young people? In a brief covering note, he called on Lord Aldington to resign his position in the school.

Watts ordered 10,000 photocopies, bought 10,000 envelopes and 10,000 first class stamps and started posting the package to everyone he could think of connected with Winchester—masters, parents, Old Wyke-hamists—after which he moved on to Aldington village, the Houses of Commons and Lords, ending up with the Archbishop of Canterbury, the Chief Rabbi, the Prince of Wales and the Queen.

Tolstoy's text made the points and posed the questions which he would have put to Lord Aldington had he been admitted to the Winchester meeting or had Lord Aldington been more candid and in less of a rush at Sandhurst. Tolstoy saw the pamphlet as a direct response to Lord Alding-ton's evasiveness. Historically, there was little to be objected to in the text, given a bit of exaggeration of Low's role and the fact that Tolstoy's information at the time, which had come from Lord Aldington himself, was that the BGS had left Austria on 26 May, not 22 May as he was to start claiming as soon as he had issued his writ. That said, there were two passages which were both abusive and taunting:

> Lord Aldington has been repeatedly charged in books and articles, by press and public, with being a major war criminal, whose activities merit comparison with those of the worst butchers of Nazi Germany and Soviet Russia. He himself professes total innocence of these charges. Is it not a little odd, then, that he has never attempted legal redress for what, if proven false, would be as blatantly defamatory a charge as one could conceive? ...
>
> What is the world to think—what will be the view of coming generations—what must Lord Aldington's few surviving victims believe—if the man proved beyond any doubt to have played a decisive and unrepentant role in the massacre of 70,000 men, women and children is seen to have enjoyed an untroubled term of office as Warden, uniquely honoured by all connected with Winchester College?

From the court record it is apparent that these were the words which provoked the writ. Certainly, they go beyond any evidence which Tolstoy had at the time. Whatever 5 Corps' role in the handovers, there is not a shred of evidence that any senior officers wanted the victims killed, much less actually ordered the killing of any individuals or groups. The worst that can be said—and it is bad enough—was that 5 Corps were utterly indifferent to the fate of the people in their care and were happy, simply for their own squalid administrative convenience, to see them delivered to people whom they should have realised, and by most accounts did realise, would have ill-treated them, if not worse. Moreover, it was absurdly exaggerated for Tolstoy to say that Low had 'played a decisive role in the massacre of 70,000 men, women and children'. The senior officers at 5 Corps had undoubtedly been 'accessories before the fact', as the Scottish legalism has it, but none of them had planned, much less participated in, a 'massacre'. Both paragraphs showed Tolstoy spoiling for a fight; Aldington's response showed him doing exactly the same.

There have been two views expressed on Lord Aldington's resort to law. The first is that a more self-assured character than Lord Aldington would have affected to remain untroubled by these "plainly ludicrous" allegations. He might have made a lofty rebuttal, but, that apart, he would have not dignified the attack by answering it. If Watts's harassment had continued, Aldington could simply have called the police. Issuing a libel writ was a mistake.

The other view is that Winchester College took the association of the war crimes allegation with its Warden very seriously and Lord Aldington came under pressure to 'sue or resign'. Lord Aldington himself claimed this in Court, although, as will be seen below, the evidence he was able to produce was very thin.

In neither view was it *essential* that a writ be issued. It is hard to escape the conclusion that up to a point Lord Aldington wanted to sue Watts. At this point, it must be remembered, he did not know that Tolstoy had written the pamphlet. He assumed that he would be suing only one unknown trouble-maker from Tunbridge Wells. From the heights above Aldington village, Watts must have looked like easy legal meat. Having flown so high for so long, Lord Aldington made the classic mistake of underestimating his opponent.

The writ arrived in Tunbridge Wells on 20 March 1987. Watts was ecstatic. He telephoned Tolstoy who was almost as excited. They met and discussed it. 'I have seen Nigel gleeful on many occasions,' Tolstoy recalls, 'but that was the most gleeful ever.'

The Plaintiff claimed for:

—An injunction restraining the Defendant whether by himself his servants
or agents or otherwise howsoever from doing the following acts or any of
them namely molesting, annoying or otherwise interfering with the Plaintiff
or his family by telephoning or by calling on them at any place whatsoever
or by writing to them or by following or accosting any of them in any place
whether public or private.

—An injunction restraining the Defendant whether by himself his servants
or agents or otherwise howsoever from further publishing to any other
person whatsoever a document headed "War Crimes and the Wardenship of
Winchester College" or any similar defamatory words in reference to the
Plaintiff.

—An injunction restraining the Defendant whether by himself his servants
or agents or otherwise howsoever from publishing any libel or slander
whatsoever in reference to the Plaintiff to pupils at Winchester College or
parents of pupils at Winchester College or staff of Winchester College or
Old Wykehamists or residents of Aldington village.

—Damages for libel contained in a document headed "War Crimes and the
Wardenship of Winchester College" which was circulated by the Defendant
on or about the beginning of March 1987.

Early the following week, Tolstoy took Watts along to see his solicitor
and friend, the defamation specialist Michael Rubinstein. Rubinstein had
read *The Minister and the Massacres* for libel for Century Hutchinson,
concluding that the risk of either Harold Macmillan or Lord Aldington
suing was 'minimal'. 'My impression is,' he wrote, 'that Nikolai has
made special efforts to be fair to Low, quoting him—fairly and accurately
always I trust—in his own defence.' Since the historical charges in the
pamphlet, as opposed to the abusive passages, amounted to little more
than a repetition of those in the book, this seemed an appropriate start to
a legal defence.

After receiving the writ, Watts decided to abandon his campaign of
telephoning Lord Aldington. 'I had achieved my objective,' he explains,
'which was to make sure he didn't think I was the sort of person who
would take this lying down and that I was going to cause him maximum
aggro. Basically, having distributed the pamphlet round Winchester
College, Aldington village, the House of Commons, the House of Lords,
and all the Press I felt that any further phone calls would have been

superfluous.'

At this point, Tolstoy committed an act of hubris equivalent to Lord Aldington's and which was, in the long run, to prove as counter-productive as the Warden's writ. He told Rubinstein Callingham that he wanted to be joined as a Defendant with Watts. It is almost unheard of for a person who owns a house and possesses other assets to volunteer to be sued. This is particularly true if the action to be defended is one for defamation, first, because the burden of proof is always on the defendant(s) as the plaintiff is assumed to be of good character until proved otherwise, and, secondly, because libel juries are well known for being very unpredictable.[1] But Tolstoy's solicitors never made these facts plain to their client.

Tolstoy first asked Lord Aldington to sue him—"join him in the action" is the legal phrase—in May 1987. Lord Aldington refused. Tolstoy then threatened to go to court if Aldington did not agree to make him Co-Defendant with Watts. Aldington still refused, thinking this request so bizarre that it must conceal some ulterior motive. Nothing could have been further from the truth. Tolstoy's motives were quite straight-forward: he just wanted to be attacked in public by Lord Aldington. Only under pressure from Rubinstein Callingham did Aldington finally concede, in August 1987, and amend his writ to add the name of what was now the Second Defendant.

Why did Tolstoy take this extraordinary course, without which his life today, and Lord Aldington's, would not still be blighted by apparently unending litigation? Tolstoy has said that 'honour' compelled him to go to the aid of his friend. But Watts was not in any meaningful sense a friend—they knew each other only slightly, and each other's families not at all—and furthermore Watts had never asked for this kind of help. What Tolstoy, quite honourably, had said he would do is 'own up to authorship'

---

1   Even Winston Churchill at the height of his fame in the early 1950s was advised by his solicitor, Sir Hartley Shawcross, that he would be unwise to defend a libel action, despite the fact that the plaintiff was a disgruntled Army officer who had retired to his estate in Ireland, taken a Gaelic surname and become an active supporter of the IRA. Churchill had slighted this man, Brigadier Eric Dorman-Smith, in the fourth volume of his history of the Second World War. Despite the inequity of their reputations, Shawcross's advice was, '*It is never safe to fight a libel action.*' As a result Churchill conceded, agreeing to correct his book in subsequent editions.

of the pamphlet if the going got rough. But that is one thing; forcing the object of your abuse to sue you is quite another.

Possibly more revealing is a pamphlet which Tolstoy himself published—his first—in June 1987 while he was in the middle of his campaign to get Lord Aldington to sue him. Noting that his request had so far been turned down, Tolstoy wrote that this showed 'how anxious Lord Aldington is to avoid encountering me in open court'. If that was arrogant, what followed was pompous. 'Far more than the veracity of Plaintiff or Defendant is here at stake,' Tolstoy wrote. 'It is historical truth and the national honour which will be examined before the bar of history.'

The first serious warning Tolstoy was given about the risks he was running came from a friend, the distinguished international law expert, the late Professor Gerald Draper, who wrote to him saying:

> You are going to need a great deal of money if Aldington goes ahead with his libel suit... I am somewhat worried by the fact that you seem to place a high level of confidence in the High Court as a place where the historical truth of a complex matter can be fully exposed. I have my doubts about it. The illumination of the historical process is one thing; trial of a libel action in the Queen's Bench is quite another... Juries are not normally good historians, and their capacity to weigh historical data is not always apparent.[2]

Unfortunately, these wise words were not matched by any from Tolstoy's professional advisors.

One of Lord Aldington's first acts after deciding to issue his writ against Watts in March 1987 was to write to the Secretary of State for Defence asking that the Army files he needed to consult to prepare his defence be withdrawn from the Public Record Office and brought to Whitehall. While there, of course, they would also be unavailable to Watts. The Defence Secretary at that time was no longer the awkwardly entrepreneurial Michael Heseltine, whose Cabinet career had been interrupted by the Westland crisis, but George Younger (now Lord Younger of Prestwick). He was an Old Wykehamist and a close friend of the Warden's.

2   27 June 1987

Lord Aldington summarised his dispute, saying, 'He objected to a decision by the Sun Alliance Insurance Group on an accident policy taken out by his brother-in-law ten days before he died.' He also said, 'Being called a war criminal ... is bad for my ego!' He then put his request:

> If [Watts] defends I will have to undergo the whole business of a libel action. He has told the press that he has financial support from émigré groups. I am therefore forced to go through all the relevant documents ... I have no knowledge, except through documents, of what happened after I left Austria on 24th or 25th May. Since Mr Watts accuses me of all kinds of things between then and 29th May, and so does Tolstoy, proof of when I left Austria may be helpful...
>
> I have felt it right to put the situation to you, both because you are a friend who will understand my distress and because you are S[ecretary] of S[tate]. But I shall expect you to pass this letter to others to deal with... If the files can be brought to the Westminster area in a series of bundles, that would be very helpful. In any event I would be very grateful for the advice of your Records people as to how best I can go about this rather tiresome task...
>
> I have seen much of the research work done by Lord Brimelow covering the F.O. sources and some of the AFHQ and 15th Army Group files. I am in touch with Alexander Stockton [Macmillan's grandson] about the Macmillan papers and Alastair Horne's biography of Harold. My researches will be concentrated on the files of HQ 5 Corps, HQ 8th Army and the HQs of 6 Armd, 46 and 78 Divs, and if available the special files of letters or signals from and to the GOCs of these formations; and in particular those of General Keightley and General McCreery.[3]

It is a shock to realise that a private citizen, engaged in what he saw as an essentially commercial dispute felt he could call on the Ministry of Defence to help him simply because the Secretary of State was an old friend. It is an even greater shock to learn that the Ministry swung into action immediately. Within forty-eight hours, an official minuted internally to the effect that they would get hold of the files Aldington wanted and would 'look after him'. On 24 March John Pitt-Brooke, Private

3   8 March 1987

Secretary to the Permanent Under Secretary of the Ministry advised his Minister,

> The MOD has in the past provided Lord Aldington with a sight of the records he now wants to see, all of which are in the public domain. Historical Branch (Army) at the moment hold some of the records and are now obtaining the others. Lord Aldington will be able to examine the records in the Old War Office as soon as those we do not have are received from Kew.

Three days later, the Head of the Army Historical Branch, Miss Alexandra Ward, drafted a reply to Aldington's letter to Younger saying,

> The war diaries covering the formations you mention are now being assembled by the Army Historical Branch, who will be happy to make them available to you in their offices in the Old War Office Building in Whitehall.

In preparing this book, this author wrote to Lord Younger about this.

> I can confirm [Younger replied] that I was certainly never involved in any questions regarding the history or the military documentation of the Aldington-Tolstoy affair. I do not know whether the supporters of either side made direct use of the historical side of the MOD, but I imagine they probably had to. In any event, it certainly never involved me.[4]

A subsequent letter elicited this reply:

> As I already made very clear in my last letter I had no involvement whatever in this matter and that includes the question of being asked to help. I was never approached by either party to this dispute in any way whatsoever.[5]

Fifteen months later, Younger no longer denied involvement. When Tolstoy described Aldington's approach to the Ministry of Defence to Tim Rayment of the *Sunday Times*, Younger was quoted as saying, 'If I had received a letter of that sort from Tolstoy, I would have done the same for

4   10 NOvember 1994
5   21 November 1994

him.'[6]

To have done that would have been equally wrong. Section 4(6) of the Public Records Act 1958 is quite specific about the purpose for which records may be withdrawn from the PRO by government Departments: public business is the only one; nowhere does the Act mention private litigation by friends of Ministers. Once transferred to the PRO, records are supposed to be in the custody of that archive for use by the public.

The effect of Younger's withdrawal of files for Aldington's use was that they were not available to Tolstoy and Watts while they were 'out to Department', in the PRO parlance. Since many were away for a very long time, this was of the highest importance for the forthcoming trial. If the story told so far shows anything, it surely demonstrates that this is a case crucially based on the military documents deposited in the PRO. To have those available only to one side of the Court in 1989 was an open and shut denial of equality of access to the evidence. (Dates and details are given in Appendix B.)

Some of the most important War Office files the defence needed to see were withdrawn in this way. To quote two examples only: first, the 5 Corps war diary itself, WO 170/4241, was withdrawn from 3 January 1989 until late October, half-way through the trial.[7] For this whole period the defence was denied access to what was the most directly relevant military file to the case. Tolstoy made repeated requests to see it, but was never told who was using it or when it would be returned to the PRO. Secondly, WO 32/13749, the file on the disposal of prisoners of war and refugees in the SACMED area (which included southern Austria) was withdrawn on 9 November 1988 and was also returned to the PRO in late October, half-way through the trial.[8] This was possibly the most damaging of the War Office files to the Plaintiff's case since it demonstrates beyond peradventure that both British and American government policy was the opposite of that adopted by 5 Corps. Tolstoy made repeated requests to see this, but was not told anything more than that it was likely to be withdrawn for a long time. In the event he never saw it.

While Lord Aldington was getting War Office files withdrawn from

---

6   *Sunday Times* 7 April 1996
7   Letter to the author from the Head of the Army Historical Branch, 27 August 1993. The source for other dates quoted *passim* of WO (War Office) prefixed file withdrawals is the same.
8   *Ibid.*

the PRO, Brigadier Cowgill was doing the same with Foreign Office files, which were brought from Kew to the Foreign Office Library and Records Department in Stamford Street. This was equally contrary to the spirit and letter of the Public Records Act as Cowgill's committee was very much a *private* enquiry.[9]

By far the most important of the files withdrawn for Cowgill's use, from the point of view of the forthcoming trial, was FO 1020/42. The dates are interesting. Tolstoy was formally joined with Watts as a Defendant in Lord Aldington's action in mid-August 1987. On 28 August, Cowgill wrote to the head of the Library and Records Department asking for that file, amongst others, to be withdrawn for his use, and on 2 September the request was made by the Foreign Office to the PRO.[10] That file did not return to the Public Record Office until November 1991, by which time Tolstoy had not only lost the libel case, but failed in his application to appeal and been made bankrupt. Yet in the meantime, Lord Aldington had submitted two sets of documents to Court, in both of which he included papers from FO 1020/42. It should be noted that this file contains only 140 documents, totalling about 150 sheets of paper. It could have been photocopied in an hour. By its absence, the Court was kept in the dark about, first, the way 5 Corps sabotaged Operation Coldstream and, secondly, General Mark Clark's order to 5 Corps not to make 'signed agreements' with the Jugoslavs two days before Brigadier Low signed an agreement with Colonel Ivanovich. As Lord Aldington's defence against Tolstoy's charges was based on the fact that he had at all times obeyed superior orders, these omissions were of fundamental importance.

The level of importance of these "hi-jacked" files can be gauged from the use Brigadier Cowgill made of them in his committee's *Final Report*. He reproduces 342 key documents. No single PRO file is quoted more than ten times except the 5 Corps war diary, which is quoted *twenty* times, and FO 1020/42, which is quoted *thirty* times. A critic of the forced repatriations would make even greater use of these two files. That they were kept from the Court in 1989, made it impossible for the jury to

9   'In the absence of any official action I decided to initiate a private investigation.' From the Chairman's Foreword, Cowgill *Final Report*, p. vii

10   Letter to the author from the Head of the Foreign Office Library and Records Department, 13 September 1993. As with the WO files, the dates quoted *passim* for movements of FO prefixed files all come from this source.

understand what really went on at 5 Corps in May 1945.

If Watts's pamphlet had a galvanic effect on Lord Aldington, it had surprisingly little effect on the other recipients. Most people either disregarded it, like Sir James Wilson who told this author he threw it unread into the waste paper bin, or they disbelieved it, like Alasdair Milne who says, 'I knew Toby Aldington well. [The pamphlet] did not change my view of him.'[11] George Younger's comment was typical of many: '[the pamphlet] did not in any way affect my opinion of Lord Aldington, who I already knew very well. I, of course, deplored the judgement of the sender, as such a document and the terms in which it was couched was very unlikely to be effective in persuading Old Wykehamists of the validity of the case made.'[12] The Second Master of Winchester College, Mr James Sabben-Clare, spoke for many when he wrote a 'Dear Parents' circular in March 1987 in which he took an opposite line to John Keegan's. 'No Brigadier in the British Army,' Sabben-Clare wrote, 'could conceivably have undertaken what Lord Aldington is accused of doing.'[13]

Since the pamphlet was not mentioned in the press, hardly anyone would have known about it who would not have been in some way connected with Lord Aldington, and most such people seem to have been unmoved either by Tolstoy's arguments or his abuse. In short, Lord Aldington went to Court to defend a reputation which was largely undamaged by publication of the material complained of.[14]

Of the eleven non-supportive letters Lord Aldington received following publication of the pamphlet, the most thoughtful came from Dr Peter Carey, an Old Wykehamist, who was Tutor in Modern History at Trinity College, Oxford. He wrote to say he was 'surprised and somewhat dismayed' at the pamphlet. Why had Lord Aldington kept silent for so long?

11 Letter to the author 18 November 1995
12 Letter to the author 10 November 1994
13 This was a view held by many Army men. Other Armies have similar pretensions. When Field Marshal Keitel was asked at the Nuremberg war crimes trial about the notorious "Partisan Order" of December 1942 which authorised unrestricted combat against civilians as well as soldiers on the eastern front, he replied, 'No German soldier or German officer ever thought of killing women and children.'
14 In Court the Defence made no use of this argument which, though irrelevant to liability, would surely have affected the level of damages?

Attempts to brush off the charges made by Bethell and Tolstoy by Macmillan (and yourself) citing the long passage of time since 1945 and the convenient forgetfulness of memory, look increasingly shallow and mendacious now that new documents are daily coming to light under the thirty-year rule... Frankly, by leaving the charges unanswered for so long you have done both yourself and—more seriously—Winchester College a grave disservice. The time has now come for you to confront the past with courage and integrity and to let the public know exactly what your motives and actions were in this affair.[15]

This saddened Lord Aldington. 'Your letter causes me to wonder,' he replied, 'whether I can rely any longer on the values in which I was brought up and which have governed my conduct.' He went on to accuse Dr Carey of writing 'as if you actually believe what Mr Watts has written... *You seem quite unaware of the fact that I left Austria on 22nd May 1945* before any detailed arrangements had been made about the handover of the Cossacks, and before any massacres had taken place in Jugoslavia.' (emphasis added) Lord Aldington wrote this letter on 27 May 1987, having on 8 March told George Younger that he had left Austria on '24th or 25th May'. Since he had not announced this change of date in the meantime, it was unfair to play on Carey's ignorance of his evolving defence.

Dr Carey was unimpressed.

Although you do not seem to regard the fate which befell the Cossack and Jugoslav POWs as being of much consequence [he replied] everyone I have talked to here feels that it is high time this matter was discussed openly and honestly by those involved... The silence of Macmillan, Brimelow and others in this matter has, I believe, led directly to the disgraceful state of affairs in which rumours and half-truths have flourished and crack-pots with personal grievances like Mr Watts have been able to disgrace the good name of both Winchester and its Warden... You seem to think that the [fate of the victims] does not merit consideration. It must be very galling for you, after a decent, not to say bland, career in public service, to find yourself pilloried in public in this manner. But, frankly, your own insensitivity has led directly

15   10 May 1987

to this state of affairs.[16]

Aldington replied pointing out that Carey had not studied the documents himself, and complaining that he still found 'me and others guilty unless we can prove otherwise. What a reversal of British justice!' Then a self-pitying note crept in. 'You charge me with insensitivity,' Lord Aldington wrote. 'What about your insensitivity to such a charge against a man brought up in the same way as you? If you knew the pain caused to my wife and family by the telephone calls, sometimes in the middle of the night, and by the letters assuming that there is some truth in the charges, you could not charge me with insensitivity.' He wanted Carey, as a historian, to pay more regard to 'justice to individuals'.

Most of the other letters Lord Aldington received were written "more in sorrow than in anger", some saying they were 'ashamed' at having the College associated with such charges. One said simply, 'Dear Toby, Whatever the rights and wrongs of all this, you have my sympathy.' Only two correspondents were angry, and one of those was angry with Watts rather than Aldington. Charles Jewell, of Alresford in Hampshire, wrote a colourful letter saying he knew nothing of the Warden, and did not want to. But that, he said to Watts—he copied his letter to Lord Aldington—was irrelevant:

> What you have written is *prima facie* an uncommonly poisonous libel: and of course you are an uncommonly poisonous little man. That is the case whether or not any or all of what you have written is true since, even if it is, going about bringing Lord Aldington to book in this manner is cowardly and various other disagreeable things to a degree. There are very adequate legal steps which you could take to deal with this matter. I can't make up my mind whether I would find you nastier if you can't substantiate your accusations but haven't the guts to take the matter to the courts; either way, you stink to high heaven![17]

Gordon Nimse, a retired Army officer from Ewell in Surrey, wrote the only seriously hostile letter Lord Aldington produced in Court. In fact

16   14 July 1987
17   15 March 1987

it should have been ruled out of Court since it related solely to *The Minister and the Massacres* which was not the subject of the action. Unaccountably, Tolstoy's lawyers did not object. This is important as the text caused Lord Aldington to weep in front of the jury, which his Counsel made play of in his closing speech, as did the Judge who asked them not to forget the ordeal which the Plaintiff had been through in taking action against Watts's pamphlet. Nimse wrote:

> If, as I do, you believe in some form of life after death you must be dreading meeting all those men and women you betrayed in '45. What you did brought disgrace upon yourself, the army and the country. Your actions are now widely known and the peerage that seems to have been your "reward" cannot offset the utter contempt that is now your due.
>
> In personal contempt,
>
> Gordon Nimse.[18]

Lord Aldington replied saying, 'I am surprised that you should have condemned me without hearing my side—most unBritish.'

Watts received another hostile letter, from a Fellow of Winchester College, Mr A.R. Taylor, of Alresford in Hampshire:

> Your behaviour is utterly shameful. The matter is *sub judice*. I very much hope that your latest load of filth will enlarge the damages when the matter comes to court. It certainly tells us what manner of man you are. The course of action you have pursued is beyond comment: it is utterly despicable.[19]

Watts replied with his usual *sang-froid*.

> You protest that [the pamphlet] is "a load of filth". I take it that this is your way of expressing that the facts are inaccurate... It would be helpful and constructive therefore if you would now identify any inaccuracy relating to those charges against Lord Aldington.

He received no reply.

18   12 September 1987
19   6 July 1987

There was one serious factual inaccuracy in the pamphlet: the underlying assumption that Lord Aldington had left Austria after 25 May 1945. But Tolstoy can hardly be blamed for that, since that was what he had been told by Aldington himself. The evolution of the ex-BGS's memory of the date of his departure from Austria is interesting. Since this date was one of the central issues of the trial, it is worth summarising Lord Aldington's shifting claims:

Before 1987:
- 1974: Lord Aldington does not remember anything about the handover of the Cossacks but says in a letter to Tolstoy that he left Austria **'on or about May 29th'**.
- 1981: Lord Aldington discusses the repatriations in detail with Serena Booker, saying, **'I left on 25th May.'**
- 1983: Lord Aldington writes to Tolstoy saying he has no memory of Jugoslav handovers and that **'I left on 25th or 26th May'**.
- 1985: Lord Aldington tells boys at Winchester: **'I left Austria on 26th May, the day after my 31st birthday.'**
- 1985: Lord Aldington tells Tolstoy at the Sandhurst lunch, **'I left on 25th or 26th [May].'**
- 1986: *The Minister and the Massacres* is published in April. Tolstoy says Brigadier Low left Austria on 29 May, quoting the 1974 letter noted above and discounting the 1983 one.

During 1987:
- Beginning of March: Watts publishes his pamphlet. No departure date is mentioned but Lord Aldington is held responsible for events at least up to 25 May.
- 8 March: Lord Aldington writes to George Younger saying he is suing Watts and that he left Austria on **'24th or 25th May'**.
- 20 March: **Lord Aldington issues his writ.**
- 30 March: Lord Aldington writes to Patrick Gale saying he left Austria on **'22nd or 23rd May.'**
- 6 May: First withdrawal of FO 1020/42 to Foreign Office (before Cowgill). This file shows clearly that whoever it was who was BGS on 23 May was the chief culprit in sabotaging the Alexander-Eisenhower plan to save the Cossacks by sending them to SHAEF.
- 27 May: Lord Aldington writes to Dr Carey stating emphatically that he

'left Austria on 22nd May'. This is the date he has stuck to ever since. It is the earliest possible one he could claim, having signed the Definition Order at 5 Corps HQ on 21 May.

After the trial:
* 1990: The only British Army signal giving a date for the departure of the BGS comes to light: it says he left on 23 May.

Although there can be little doubt that Aldington's earlier claims were a genuine mistake—and an understandable one, given the length of time that had elapsed—this evolution does call into question his claim at the trial that, on the matter of the date of his departure, the jury should rely on his memory.

Tolstoy's use of the information he had been given is not above criticism either. In *The Minister and the Massacres* he accused Brigadier Low of pushing through the handover policy until his departure *on 29th May* (p. 296). Tolstoy noted that the British attitude moderated after that date and commented,

> It is hard not to believe that [in Low's departure and succession by de Fonblanque] we have the factor which brought about so sudden and revolutionary a change in policy.

The violence and trickery, he implies, lasted only so long as Brigadier Low was in Austria. In a footnote to that passage Tolstoy gives brief authority for his date: 'Letter from Lord Aldington to the author, 25 June 1974. Much more recently, on 14 February 1983, Lord Aldington altered the date of his departure to "25th or 26th May". This is certainly too early.' Tolstoy gave no further reason for making this damaging, and incorrect, assumption. Neither did he mention the fact that at Sandhurst a year before he published those words he had said to Lord Aldington about the kidnapping of the Cossack officers on 27 and 28 May, 'I know you did leave before it actually took place, didn't you?' 'I left a long time before,' Lord Aldington replied, mentioning once again '25 or 26 May'.

Having made arrangements about the evidence, Lord Aldington turned to witnesses. In the event, his list was surprisingly weak, but there may have been tactical reasons for this. For example, he recruited Dr Knight as his "expert" on Jugoslavs and Cossacks rather than the vastly more authoritative Sir Fitzroy Maclean. Sir Fitzroy had travelled extensively in the Soviet Union in the 1930s and had, during the war, fought with Tito inside Jugoslavia for two and a half years. He was an old friend of Lord Aldington's from the time they had been Members of Parliament for neighbouring constituencies in Lancashire in the 1940s and 1950s. And Sir Fitzroy was *par excellence* the sort of man whom juries regard as speaking with authority. Why did Aldington not ask him? Possibly because of what he would have said about the likely fate of those to be handed over. 'I should certainly have said that any Chetniks or Ustache handed over to the Partisans would have been likely to receive short shrift (just as Partisans would had it been the other way round).'[20]

Another authoritative witness who did not testify for Lord Aldington was Nigel Nicolson, though in this case it was because he refused when asked. The two men had known each other for a long time, although never particularly well. 'Would you come here to lunch one day and talk to me about it all?' Lord Aldington wrote to him in July 1987. 'If you would prefer to lunch at Leeds Castle, of which I am Chairman, you only have to say so!'

Nicolson was happy to eat, though not necessarily to deal. As he was already in touch with Tolstoy over his research about 1945—this was before he had been joined in the action—Nicolson imposed two conditions on any discussion. First, for the avoidance of any future legal dispute, he wanted a third party present (he suggested Bill Deedes, a mutual friend) and, secondly, he insisted he be free to repeat to Tolstoy anything that was discussed. Lord Aldington would not agree to these conditions, so the lunch never happened. In the event, Nicolson testified for Tolstoy.

There are three things necessary to fight a court case: evidence, witnesses and money—and the greatest of these is money. Lord Aldington's third job was to secure financial backing. At some as yet undisclosed point in these proceedings Aldington asked the Sun Alliance Chairman, his friend and fellow Fellow of Winchester College, Henry Lambert for money. A deal was done, though what the terms were, both sides have consistently refused to disclose, though Lambert's successor as Chairman, Sir Chris-

---

20   Letter to the author 29 July 1994

topher Benson, said at the 1994 Annual General Meeting, 'We simply paid the legal bills, penny for penny.' In the meantime, however, the agreement was kept completely secret, even from shareholders—which Tolstoy alleges constituted a breach of Lambert's fiduciary duties in terms of the Companies Acts. The admission that money had changed hands was made only after all the main litigation had finished.

The Sun Alliance money paid for one of the most expensive firms of City solicitors, Allen & Overy, and one of the best known libel barristers, Charles Gray QC. Allen & Overy handle a good deal of the Sun Alliance's corporate litigation.[21]

For his part, Tolstoy had problems with evidence, witnesses and money. Much of the main evidence he needed was secreted in Whitehall, and much of the rest that he now began assembling concerned the legally irrelevant issue of the fate of the victims of the handovers, rather than the degree of Lord Aldington's responsibility for what 5 Corps had inflicted on these people.

To a great extent this was also true of the Defence witness list. Most of them had no knowledge of events at 5 Corps headquarters. Tolstoy has told this author that one of the reasons he asked so many victims to come and testify was that this helped with his fund-raising. But part of the blame must be laid at the door of his Counsel who advised in February 1989 that the case would be strengthened 'if we are able to place before the jury a significant number of witnesses to, and victims of, the British actions.' But what was needed was evidence that British troops knew the likely fate of the intended victims. Sir Ian Fraser, for example, who had been

---

21   Allen & Overy, based opposite St Paul's, have 99 partners; Rubinstein Callingham, based in Lincoln's Inn, have 16. Allen & Overy indulge in corporate public relations by undertaking *pro bono* civil liberties cases for Liberty; Rubinstein Callingham do not. Allen & Overy have recently seen a senior partner the subject of well publicised writs for fraud and deceit from a former non-corporate client (the issue was the sale at Sotheby's in 1990 of the Sevso Roman silver hoard); Rubinstein Callingham have not. The equity partners at Allen & Overy share profits which averaged at £344,000 per partner in 1992, while at Rubinstein Callingham the figure was closer to a third of that. Essentially Allen & Overy are corporate businessmen who happen to be involved in the law, whereas Rubinstein Callingham are lawyers who happen to get involved in corporate litigation from time to time. One prominent client of Allen & Overy's was Lady Baillie, who bought and restored Leeds Castle. On her death she gifted it to the Leeds Castle Foundation of which Lord Aldington was, until recently, Chairman.

Intelligence Officer in the Scots Guards in northern Italy at the end of the war, says, 'I knew, and many hundreds of officers must have known, that 5 Corps units were being required to ship POWs of various kinds to their deaths at the hand of the Russians and Jugoslavs. Tolstoy's defence team was quite inadequate. They could easily have collected dozens of witnesses like me.'[22]

Despite these difficulties, Tolstoy's biggest problem was actually money. He formed the Forced Repatriations Defence Fund and enlisted some distinguished figures as Patrons. Most of them had been involved in the events of 1945. Three were British officers, Nicolson, Major Barre, the commandant of Viktring Camp, and Colonel Murphy-Palmer, the Commanding Officer of the Royal Irish Fusiliers. Others had seen events from the Cossack side: Count Aripand Thurn, the owner of Bleiburg Castle and the witness to Alexander's fury at hearing about the handovers, Count Leopold Goëss, an officer in the 6th Terek Regiment, Prince zu Salm, Commander of 2nd Division of the Cossack Cavalry and Zoë Polanska-Palmer. Four other figures in Britain added their names too, Sir Bernard Braine MP, the former diplomat Sir Nicholas Cheetham, Professor Gerald Draper and the Earl of Portsmouth. The list was completed by four prominent White Russians and Sieghard von Pannwitz, General von Pannwitz's son.

Rubinstein Callingham produced an estimate of the trial costs: about £250,000 and Tolstoy set about raising this huge sum. He travelled round the world speaking to émigré groups of Croats here and ex-Cossacks there. An appeal brochure was prepared and mailed. Money came in, but much too slowly. They thought they had about 18 months until the trial, so the Fund had to take about £14,000 per month. Even in the early period of initial enthusiasm, it took less than half of that. After that, receipts began to decline.

It was not long before Tolstoy began to realise that he had involved himself in a personal financial nightmare. Fund-raising and evidence collation became so time-consuming that he had to stop work on the second volume of the Merlin trilogy, while, as is normal, his royalties from

---

22   Letter to the author, 19 November 1993. Sir Ian, as ex-Chairman of Lazard Brothers and Rolls-Royce Motors, had known Lord Aldington in the City. 'His record of corporate achievement had not passed me by,' Sir Ian commented. 'Indeed to many of my generation it was something of a joke.'

his previously published books slowly declined. He had anticipated making money from the paperback edition of *The Minister and the Massacres* which was due out in October 1987. But in August 1987 Lord Aldington took proceedings against Century Hutchinson, publishers of the hardback edition, alleging that the book was libellous.

At the trial it was suggested that he did so only because Tolstoy had forced his way into the proceedings. In fact Aldington could hardly have gone to Court arguing that the pamphlet was libellous when the book on which it was based was circulating freely (and probably selling very well as a result of all the trial-related publicity). This had always been Aldington's intention. 'I have had to start proceedings [against Watts],' he wrote to Richard Keightley on 9 March 1987, immediately before service of the original writ, 'and inevitably I will have to follow up with a writ against Tolstoy's publishers.'

Late in September 1987 Lord Aldington made his formal Reply to the Defence which had been submitted. Now the legal juggernaut really started to roll. After digesting this, Rubinstein Callingham requested from Allen & Overy Further and Better Particulars of Lord Aldington's Reply to the Defence. Watts and Tolstoy then submitted Particulars of Justification. Allen & Overy responded with a request for Further and Better Particulars of the Particulars of Justification. Consultations with Richard Rampton QC, the barrister Rubinstein Callingham had recommended, were now held to decide on the subject of all these Defences, Replies, Particulars and Particulars of Particulars. Soon Fee Notes of £1,000, plus VAT, started moving from the Temple to Lincoln's Inn, to be incorporated in much larger invoices moving from Lincoln's Inn to Court Close, Southmoor.

In the light of this, it might be asked why Watts and Tolstoy kept going. The fact is that they had the considerable evidence gathered by Tolstoy over the years and did not know that they were to be denied access to the main files they needed for their defence. They had an impressive roster of possible witnesses which seemed to be approved of by their Counsel. And they had at least the hope of raising almost enough money to pay their lawyers. On each of these matters they were, sooner or later, to be in for a shock.

But before that, they were to get another surprise, which came from a quite unexpected quarter: Cowgill's committee produced an *Interim Report* which had the result that Tolstoy would enter Court with his reputation as a historian in tatters. Was this mere coincidence, or were there reasons for thinking that Cowgill was in some way co-operating with Lord Aldington?

12

The INTERIM REPORT

IN MAY 1988, nine months after Tolstoy had been joined in the action, he went to Allen & Overy to inspect the documents Lord Aldington was submitting in evidence. This is a routine stage in pre-trial preliminaries. Amongst the papers was an item, not itself of critical importance, but which should not have been in Lord Aldington's files as Tolstoy owned the only extant copy in Britain and had lent it to Brigadier Cowgill, before the pamphlet was published, on the strict understanding that it was to be kept confidential. The document in question was the daily engagements diary of General Weir, Commander of 46th Infantry Division, which had been kept by his aide-de-camp, a Captain Norrie. Like Weir, Norrie was a New Zealander, and a White Russian friend of Tolstoy's who lives in New Zealand, Mrs Natasha Templeton, had known Norrie in later life and had been presented with a copy of the diary. It is typed and looks much like a military document, except that it has marginal jottings, both by Captain Norrie and, crucially, by Natasha Templeton herself. Tolstoy had given Cowgill a photocopy of this in 1986 and now it appeared in Lord Aldington's bundle of papers.

With surprising diffidence Tolstoy mentioned this to Booker, with whom he was still friends, and Booker mentioned it to his Chairman, whom Tolstoy still imagined to be conducting an independent inquiry. Cowgill responded in bluff terms, saying he was 'most concerned to learn that a copy of General Weir's Diary has turned up in legal documents received by you and that you believe it is a copy of the one you gave me in confidence. Knowing your wishes in this respect we had not included any reference to it in our working papers, and I was certainly not aware of it being passed to anyone outside my study group. If, indeed, the copy is, through some unwitting mischance, from my files I can only offer my sincere apologies.'[1]

This was a straw in the wind, but Tolstoy said nothing further. Watts, however, did.

'You wouldn't answer on this Norrie diary how Aldington got hold of that,' Watts said in a later telephone conversation. 'What do you say to that, Brigadier?'

'I'll say nothing further than what I said in the letter I wrote to Nikolai,' Cowgill replied.

'Yes, but you didn't reply to his second enquiry where he actually remonstrated with you that you hadn't given him adequate response to it.'

'Well in his view I haven't given an adequate—'

'Well, how did Aldington get hold of it then, Brigadier?'

'Uh, I've nothing to add to my letter.'

'How did Aldington get hold of something which was shown to you in confidence by Nikolai?'

'I've nothing to add to my previous letter.'

'You did give it to him then?'

'No I didn't.'

'Well how did he get hold of it?'

'Uh, I've nothing to add to my previous letter.'

'All right, Brigadier. You didn't give it to him?'

'No, I'm-I'm-I'm saying "no comment" and I'm making no addi-tion—'

'Brigadier, I'm not asking you to make a comment; I'm just asking you this: did you give him a copy of the—'

'I'm adding nothing to my previous letter which was quite precise.'

'Yes, but hold on, Brigadier. Nikolai was very disappointed over this and he said that you hadn't responded adequately to it and, in fact, you really haven't given him any answer to his question as to how Aldington got the copy at all. What do you say to that, Brigadier?'

'Well, I've apologised to him for whatever way it happened.'

'What have you apologised for? You've apologised to him for giving it to Aldington?'

1   7 July 1988

'No. I've apologised for the fact that it, in one way or another, got to Lord Aldington.'

'But you didn't actually give it to Lord Aldington?'

'I will say nothing further than what I've said.'

'You must know whether you gave it to Lord Aldington or not, Brigadier?'

'Many things,' said Cowgill, speaking very slowly, 'can happen, um, which are not, ah, ah, answered by a straight yes or no.'

At the beginning of September 1988, with the trial now scheduled for June 1989, Tolstoy learned that Cowgill intended to publish a preliminary booklet stating in advance of the completion of their research what the committee's findings were going to be. The committee was going to put out what they called an *Interim Report*. This is a conventional practice in bureaucratic circles when practical matters are under investigation. It is usually sensible to adopt the broad outlines of future policy in advance of detailed recommendations which might take some time to formulate. However, this is a self-evidently absurd procedure in a scholarly context. One piece of evidence can change the view of a whole subject. The *Interim Report* was to make two points: there had not been any "Klagenfurt conspiracy" and Tolstoy, who had suggested there had been, was a bad historian.

Though both points were tenable in a scholarly context, they were much more dubious in the legal one which now obtained. Once an action has been set down for trial, as this one had, it is *prima facie* a contempt of court to publish material which might sway a jury. But when Cowgill let Tolstoy's lawyers know he intended to publish, they reacted with extraordinary nonchalance. Instead of immediately demanding to see the text, the solicitor involved wrote Cowgill a letter of sweet emollience saying, '*from what you have told me*, I consider it unlikely that my clients would have or indeed could have any legitimate objection to publication in September.'[2] (emphasis added) It is astonishing that Rubinstein Callingham were happy to rely for evidence on the likely damage to their client on the man who was possibly going to do it.

On Thursday 22 September 1988—when he knew Tolstoy himself

2   6 September 1988

would be in Chile—Cowgill presented his booklet to the press at the Royal United Services Institute in Whitehall. The full title was: *Interim Report of an Enquiry into the Repatriation of Surrendered Enemy Personnel to the Soviet Union and Jugoslavia from Austria in May 1945 and the Alleged "Klagenfurt Conspiracy"*. It was a cheaply bound typescript, written in a dense bureaucratese which was clearly not designed for direct public consumption. In the event only the press consumed it, and in doing so they seem to have ignored the arguments and concentrated solely on the conclusions, which Cowgill presented in an easily digestible summary. Since the press coverage was the main result of publication, there is no point in rehearsing the arguments very few people have ever read.[3] There are two other reasons for not considering Cowgill's arguments here. First, they bore an uncanny similarity to those advanced in Court by Lord Aldington, which will be considered in detail below. Secondly, Cowgill's arguments vary with time and circumstance.

The most glaring example of this is the thorny matter of Tryon-Wilson's list of émigré Generals. Three years earlier Tryon-Wilson had told Tolstoy that he remembered 'the old boy with the CB'. In the *Interim Report*, Cowgill says the Soviet List *did* include 'several names picked out in capital letters whom Brigadier Tryon-Wilson believes included the "White Russian" heroes of the Civil War, Generals Krasnov, Shkuro and Sultan Khelich-Ghirei.'[4] Next year Tryon-Wilson swore on oath in Court that this was a recently acquired memory, not one dating from 1945, and so, in the *Final Report*, which was published after the trial, Cowgill amended this sentence to read, '[The Soviet List] included several names picked out in capital letters. Brigadier Tryon-Wilson no longer recalls the identity of these names, nor was he aware at the time of their significance.'[5]

Cowgill ignores uncomfortable arguments like that surrounding Operation Coldstream. Though FO 1020/42 was withdrawn to the Foreign Office specifically for his use, it is not even hinted at in his booklet. In fact he says the exact opposite: 'It is clear that the decision in

---

3   The curious reader can write for a copy to Brigadier Anthony Cowgill, British Management Data Foundation, The Garage, Highfield Villa, Longridge, Sheepscombe, Stroud GL6 7QU. Tel: 0171 839 2798 (this number will be answered in Stroud)

4   Cowgill *Interim Report*, p. 22

5   Cowgill *Final Report*, p. 61.

principle to repatriate the Cossacks (the great majority of whom were Soviet citizens) was entirely in accord with Allied policy.'[6] Since this is a point of fundamental significance to the entire controversy—and, of course, to the forthcoming trial—and one which was completely untrue, questions arise over the quality of the analysis Cowgill was presenting. If the clearest evidence that Allied policy was *not* to repatriate non-Soviet Cossacks is, in the military sphere, in FO 1020/42, in the political sphere it lies in WO 32/13749. There is no doubt Cowgill saw that too, since he actually reproduces the front cover of the file in facsimile in an appendix to the *Interim Report*. It is an even smaller file than FO 1020/42 and it includes documents which show that the 5 Corps description of all the Cossacks as being Soviet nationals was received as fact in government circles—in other words, that 5 Corps' deception of 8th Army and AFHQ in the 13 May signal—'cannot see any point in keeping this large number of Soviet nationals'—soon became accepted fact in government circles in London. The file also shows how, at the end of May, Alexander's decision to send the Cossacks north to SHAEF was ratified by both British and American governments. In the light of this it is nonsense to say, as Cowgill did, that the decision to hand over the Cossacks, Soviet and non-Soviet alike, 'was entirely in accord with Allied policy.'

It is also of fundamental significance to the way the trial was undermined that this file was kept out of Court by the Ministry of Defence who had let both Cowgill and Lord Aldington use it. Tolstoy had used WO 32/13749 in the 1970s when writing *Victims of Yalta*, although at that time it had a different reference number. He had tried to use it more recently but could not find it under the old reference number. Neither could the Ministry of Defence, who did not know that the number had been changed and assumed, therefore, that it had been lost. Tolstoy noted this in *The Minister and the Massacres* (p. 344), saying the file had 'vanished some time between the early part of 1974, when I inspected it, and the beginning of 1977. The file number has been transferred to another file.' Cowgill printed a facsimile of the front cover of the file under its new reference number and translated Tolstoy's report of what the Ministry of Defence had told him into an allegation by Tolstoy that the file had been 'deliberately destroyed', putting those words in quotation marks to make them look as if Tolstoy had written them. In fact he had never done so. Tolstoy wrote to the Ministry of Defence to ask how it was that they had not been able to find the file for him, but had been able to find it for Cowgill. The predictable answer was that it was an unaccountable clerical error for which they apologised but for which they did not propose to make amends.

It is also noteworthy that as soon as it was known that Tolstoy was raising this matter, the file was withdrawn from the PRO and brought to Whitehall. This was done on 9 November 1988, and the file stayed there until 19 October 1989.[7] Also returned by the Ministry of Defence on that day were the 5 Corps war diary and the 6th Armoured Division war diary. The result was, by the time the file actually reappeared on the shelves of the PRO (there is lag of a few days between a Department releasing a file and its being available to the public in the PRO) Tolstoy had finished giving evidence, which he did on 27 October.

Cowgill's other main point was that Tolstoy was not a credible historian. Cowgill devoted the whole of one of his seven chapters to this, listing eight points on which he said the allegation of the Klagenfurt conspiracy rested and then apparently refuting them all. 'We have considered each of these allegations with great care,' Cowgill wrote, 'and in no instance has corroboration been found for any of them.'

Within hours of the journalists filing out into Whitehall, the *Evening Standard* was on the streets carrying a story under the headline 'Inquiry clears Macmillan of war crimes'. An 'independent inquiry,' the paper said, had cleared up 'one of the last great mysteries of the war'. Cowgill was reported as saying, 'We all went into this believing there was a conspiracy. But viewing all the facts we have changed our minds.'

The following morning, 23 September 1988, *The Times* ran the headline 'Macmillan "no conspirator"'. The *Daily Mail* had 'Macmillan cleared of war deaths plot', and said the committee had 'unearthed vital missing documentation' which showed that 'the men (*sic*) were handed over in compliance with the agreement between Churchill, Roosevelt and Stalin at Yalta to repatriate all Soviet citizens. And at the time there was nothing in Allied policy stating that émigrés should not be sent back.'

---

7   See note about file movement dates in Chapter 11.

John Keegan wrote in the *Daily Telegraph* on the same day that 'an independent committee of inquiry' had refuted allegations against Macmillan. He quoted from *The Minister and the Massacres* at length and then concluded that the handover of 'some "White Russians"'... [was] the consequence of confusion during a highly stressful situation.' This was not, in fact, what Cowgill had said. Cowgill argued that the Cossacks were handed back because, first, there was not enough time to screen them and, secondly, because it was not appropriate to dispose of such primitive people on an individual basis as they prefer to do everything in groups.[8] (The implication is that Cowgill believes it would actually have been kinder to the non-Soviet Cossacks to have allowed them to go with the others to 'slavery, torture and probably death' rather than to have forced them to survive. The evidence of the riot in the barrack square at Peggetz on 1 June 1945 points strongly to the opposite view.)

Keegan repeated Cowgill's invented quotation about the 'deliberately destroyed file' commenting that the committee had been 'able to trace or reconstruct all the documents that [Tolstoy] alleged had been removed, destroyed or altered.' This, too, was completely untrue. Of the eight documents listed in *The Minister and the Massacres* as having been 'removed, destroyed or altered', the only one which Cowgill had successfully traced was WO 32/13749, as described above.

In a follow-up article the next day, Keegan twisted the knife. 'Had Tolstoy found all the documents which the committee subsequently searched out, his charge against Macmillan could not have proceeded. But he did not.' As a result of this, Keegan wrote, Tolstoy 'must now retract or risk losing his scholarly credibility.'

Over three million people would have read the papers containing Keegan's two articles, and several millions more the others. It is not inconceivable that some of those were amongst the twelve selected for the jury a year later. Yet Rubinstein Callingham did nothing about this. Allen & Overy's approach, however, was completely different.

On 25 September 1988, three days after Cowgill's press conference, the *Sunday Telegraph* published the only article to appear anywhere that

---

8   In an interview with this author in 1991 Cowgill commented, 'A lot of those Russians were very primitive people, from outer Mongolia and God knows what.' This echoed Macmillan's point that the Cossacks were 'practically savages'

showed the writer, Peter Millar, had read carefully the whole of Cowgill's booklet, rather than just the summary. Not only that, Millar had clearly put it together with *The Minister and the Massacres*. The result was an article which provoked legal action from Allen & Overy. The complaints were all of detail. For example, Millar had written, quite correctly, that the Distone Order was intended to go to 5 Corps. 'The true position is different,' David Mackie, Lord Aldington's solicitor at Allen & Overy, wrote. 'The order issued by Alexander was *not* addressed to 5 Corps in which our client was then Brigadier General Staff.' (emphasis in original) Echoing Cowgill's language, he went on, 'We have found no evidence to suggest it was ever received by 5 Corps.' As this article was to cost the *Sunday Telegraph* £15,000 in an out-of-court settlement, it is worth emphasising that even Cowgill, in the *Final Report*, published in 1990, asserts that the Distone Order *was* intended for 5 Corps. Allen & Overy ended with a warning: 'Lord Aldington's action has already been set down for trial and it is most unfortunate that a reputable newspaper like the *Sunday Telegraph* considers it appropriate to publish an inaccurate article potentially prejudicial to our client's action. In the event of any further inaccurate and prejudicial publications by your newspaper our client will have to consider taking further action.'[9]

Booker now joined the chorus rubbishing Tolstoy in the press. No longer the eulogistic supporter moved by shame at his country's misdeeds, he published an article in *The Spectator* entitled 'The Conspiracy that Never Was'. Tolstoy, he said, had misrepresented some documents, failed to find others and made an entirely baseless attack on Harold Macmillan. His sources were interesting: 'We have been greatly assisted,' Booker wrote, 'by discussions with a number of senior officers in Austria at the time, including Lord Aldington.'

Alistair Horne, near completion of *Macmillan Vol I*, had private reservations. 'The nub of the Cowgill/Booker case,' he wrote to a friend, 'is that HM is almost purer than the driven snow, now! ... Although they regard their new conclusions to be both as successful as Newton's discovery of gravity and as infallible as the Pope, new developments might yet occur in the forthcoming months to change that picture again.'[10]

9   30 September 1988
10   Letter to Sir Philip Goodhart, MP, 21 June 1988. Note that this was written three months before

Despite these private reservations, Horne wrote eulogistically of Cowgill's *Report* in public.

> Well done the Brigadier and his men! I used to dread the lengthy telephone calls from him, usually prefaced with the, I thought rather droll, expression, 'We're about to bottom old So-and-so', asking for special access to the Macmillan archives of which I was, temporarily, the sole beneficiary. But the results, the minute by minute review of May 1945 signals, including many declared by Tolstoy "missing" or "destroyed" are a tribute to British Army doggedness—and all, apparently, financed out of Cowgill's own pocket.[11]

Horne got so carried away, that he even described Cowgill's booklet as reading 'like the most exciting kind of Len Deighton whodunnit'.

The occasion for Horne's article was the publication, on 6 October 1988, of the first volume of his official biography of Macmillan. Cowgill had noted in his Introduction that 'close liaison has been maintained with Alistair Horne so that the results of the enquiry can be taken into account in the official biography *Macmillan* to be published in October 1988.' The effect is obvious when comparing the two texts.

Horne differs from Cowgill mainly in that he is too experienced a historian to be able to describe something as horrific as the forced repatriations and conclude that no-one was to blame. It had to be either Macmillan, 5 Corps or both of them. Horne considered that responsibility lay with 5 Corps. In support of this view he quoted Lord Aldington, as has already been mentioned, to the effect that whatever Macmillan's advice, 5 Corps would have turned the Cossacks and Jugoslavs over to the Communists. 'Lord Aldington's admission,' Horne concluded, 'was fundamental to the case against Macmillan, *and, if it could have been made several years earlier, the old statesman would have been saved much distress in his last years.*'[12] (emphasis added) Horne used a similar

---

Cowgill published.

11   *The Spectator* 8 October 1988

12   Horne *Macmillan*, p. 275. There are conflicting opinions about the exact degree of distress caused by Tolstoy's allegations. Booker wrote in an early draft of an as yet unpublished manuscript *The Looking Glass Tragedy*: 'Although [Macmillan] tried not to show his distress

passage to end his article in *The Spectator*. Lord Aldington was now accused of self-seeking silence which, by its indifference to the suffering of a former superior, had led to unnecessary distress. Lord Aldington responded by threatening a writ. Horne was invited to take tea with him in the House of Lords. 'I was fairly robust about it,' Horne says today. But he was not so robust that he did not alter his text for the paperback edition. From the sentence quoted above, the italicised words have been cut out. It now reads simply, 'Lord Aldington's admission was fundamental to the case against Macmillan.'

Tolstoy's response to Horne's book was entertaining. He wrote the author a letter which started with a page of almost obsequious compliments: 'I would like to tell you how fair-mindedly and civilly you have conducted your account in my view, and to reflect how much better it would have been if all (including myself!) had entered the controversy with a similar approach.' He said he did not agree with Horne's conclusions, but regretted his own insinuation in the closing sentence to *The Minister and the Massacres* that 'Macmillan may have been acting under covert NKVD pressure.' His regret was not because he thought the charge unfair, but because exploration of motive should await definite proof of the alleged crime.

Tolstoy went on to say he would like to add 'a minor carping note to what is generally an admiring view of a lucidly-written and fascinating book.' This ended up as a 3,500 word discussion of everything in Horne's chapter on the repatriations which he disagreed with, even though, Tolstoy said, he was 'deliberately restricting' himself 'to matters which you raise'.

Six weeks after publishing the *Interim Report*, Cowgill interviewed for the first time one of the best-known eye-witnesses of the controversy they were supposed to have just settled, Nigel Nicolson. Nicolson recalls that the committee gave him lunch—'one of the nastiest I've eaten,' he said—on 16 November at Cowgill's invitation at the Carlton Club. This

---

to the outside world, according to his family and close friends he several times broke down completely at the horror of it all, bursting into tears and confessing it was the most awful thing that had ever happened to him.' Macmillan's grandson, the current Earl of Stockton, has told this author that 'Booker's account of my grandfather's emotional outburst is totally fictitious.' (letter 29 April 1994)

was an odd choice since not one of the committee was a member. Lord Aldington is, though. Tryon-Wilson did not come as he was 'tending sheep in Cumbria', but Nicolson gave his impressions of the other three to Tolstoy. 'Cowgill was as you have described him: bluff, ruddy, not very sharp: Brimelow rubicund, civil-servanty, anxious not to commit himself, referring difficult questions to Cowgill, soft more than wet. Booker chirpy, the cleverest, pleased with his recent TV encounter with the Prince of Wales. Brimelow was the only one who expressed actual hostility towards you.'[13]

The committee told Nicolson that in due course they were going to publish a fuller version of their report with document facsimiles. Would they incorporate the objections raised to the *Interim Report*, Nicolson asked? No, that would only blur their conclusions, Cowgill said. 'I got the impression that they were unwilling to modify anything they had previously concluded. I pointed this out and they were embarrassed by the question.'

Pointless though it was, Nicolson pulled out the collection of documents he had brought with him, including his writings about the 1st Guards Brigade operations and his contemporary manuscript log book. He said he thought it quite unfair of them to make such a play of Tolstoy's allegation about missing documents, when seven of the eight he said were missing were still missing. 'They could not deny this,' Nicolson noted. He tried to persuade them that there was no "chaos" in Carinthia which would justify the forced repatriations. There was no fighting, the refugees and prisoners did what they were told and the military situation was so unthreatening that 1st Guards Brigade was never deployed for battle. The threat from Tito receded on 19 May, the day they started to send the Jugoslavs back. Thus the subsequent handovers were unnecessary. 'Tito had not demanded them and Yalta had not even considered them,' Nicolson pointed out. 'All this I argued to Cowgill. They had no adequate response.'

In a subsequent interview Nicolson told this author that a note of farce had crept in when, amongst the papers he had brought, he produced a map of southern Austria. The committee members were hungry for relevant documents, they said, and asked him eagerly where and when he had

---

discovered the map. 'Stanford's of Long Acre,' Nicolson replied, 'about an hour ago.'

All this would be simply trivial were it not for the fact that the British government has taken the findings of this ostensibly private committee as established historical fact. When a relative of some of the Jugoslav victims of 5 Corps wrote, in 1991, to the Crown Prosecution Service asking for an investigation into the treatment of his people by the British Army in 1945, a Senior Crown Prosecutor wrote to him, saying, 'This matter was the subject of a very detailed report by Brigadier Cowgill... No evidence has been found to support a criminal offence (*sic*) against any named person. If you have evidence ... then I am sure the police would be willing to investigate your complaint.'

At the beginning of 1989 Rubinstein Callingham gave an upwardly revised forecast of the likely cost of the trial: £299,210, up from £225,687 a year before. Not only that, the new figure excluded large additional disbursements which had not yet been estimated, like 'substantial photo-copying' costs (eventually they billed over £5,000) and travel expenses. These were necessary as solicitors had to visit the witnesses, from Austria to Australia, to take sworn statements from them, and then they had to be brought to London to testify at the trial. Since little of these witnesses' evidence was relevant to the issue of Lord Aldington's responsibility for the handovers, this was money wasted. But no-one raised a caution.

The Forced Repatriation Defence Fund had taken about £90,000 in its first year, but was now faced with raising between £200,000 and £250,000 in the six months remaining before the trial opened, an ob-viously impossible task on current form. Moreover, Michael Rubinstein wrote to Tolstoy to stress how unreliable all his firm's cost estimates of necessity were, given the unpredictability of all serious litigation. He added that his partners were concerned that the Fund did not look remotely as if it might be able to cover their costs. 'It is this Firm's practice in all proceedings to be secured prior to going into court, for our costs and Counsel's fees and all other disbursements (plus VAT of course) up to the end of the trial.' Rubinstein was holding a terrifying gun to Tolstoy's head: unless the FRDF took donations from now until the trial in June at more than five times the rate it had achieved through 1988, the Defendants might find themselves unrepresented in Court.

Tolstoy decided on a second appeal, which he launched with a document describing the urgent necessity for money to fight the trial.

There was little else he could have done, except prepare himself to appear as a litigant in person. Watts seriously considered this course but Rubinstein wrote him a letter saying that he would 'have no chance at all as a litigant in person to defend the issue of malice, bearing in mind the complexity of the law as it is now.' As will be seen below, the course the trial was to take suggests the opposite.

Aldington's response to Tolstoy's second appeal document was to claim that it misrepresented his position to such an extent that a jury trial could not possibly be fair. Though the press coverage of the Cowgill Report must have done infinitely more harm to Tolstoy, Aldington still went ahead and applied for a judge-only trial. Considerable further expense was incurred by the FRDF in defeating this application, first in the High Court and then in the Appeal Court. It was a 'classic jury trial' the judges in both trials said. Since the shareholders of the Sun Alliance were paying Lord Aldington's costs he was not seriously worried by the escalating cost of the litigation.

It was at the earlier of those hearings that the parties had their first sight of the man who was eventually to try the case, Mr Justice Michael Davies. Like Cowgill, Davies is a grammar-school boy who graduated from Birmingham University. He prides himself on his understanding of the type of people who serve on juries. Opinions vary on his performance on the Bench. Some barristers have said he is a fair judge, if a little over-fond of his own jokes. Others think he is a snob and that it is a lucky Lord who gets him to try his case. One barrister, who had lost a particularly high-profile case in front of him, has described him as 'a loud-mouthed braggart: not High Court material'.

Certainly *gravitas* is not part of Davies's stock-in-trade. The journalist Mark Lawson once telephoned him for an interview but made the mistake of asking for 'Judge Michael Davies'. 'There is no such chap,' said the voice at the other end of the line. There was a '*Mr Justice* Michael Davies', though, would Lawson like to speak to him? Yes, Lawson said, he would. 'Speaking!' said His Lordship brightly.

After the Appeal against the application for a judge-only trial, Rubinstein Callingham sent Tolstoy a bill for the previous seven weeks' work and expenses: £32,708. This was more than the balance in the FRDF. Were there any more funds on the way, Rubinstein Callingham wanted to know? The truth was, not much. After the second appeal for funds had gone out, towards the end of February 1989, the money which Tolstoy had anticipated just did not arrive. The FRDF needed to bank at least £50,000 per month from then until the trial, a quite impossible task since in the whole of the first two months after sending out the second appeal document, only £20,000 had come in. After that initial flush, the rate of contributions dropped.

To add to Tolstoy's problems, Rubinstein Callingham revised their estimate of anticipated costs upwards again. The grand total, given prudent allowance for all expenses, now approached the staggering figure of £500,000. Of this, approximately £75,000 had been paid, leaving a balance of £425,000 still to find. A reasonable estimate in April of likely future fund-raising, based on past performance, would have counted on no more than about £50,000. The trial date had recently been moved back from June 1989 to October and recent receipts had averaged about £10,000 per month. Taking this together with the money already banked, the £425,000 required would be undershot by a figure approaching £350,000. With the best will in the world, there was no conceivable likelihood of even a small fraction of this huge sum being found. Tolstoy and Watts might, it seemed, be going into Court undefended after all.

Then one of the quieter supporters of the FRDF stepped in. After Alasdair Milne's dismissive letters following his inquiries to the BBC about the ban on Tolstoy following publication of *The Minister and the Massacres*, the Earl of Portsmouth had offered to finance advertisements in the national press to draw public attention to the case. Tolstoy had said he thought that would not achieve much and that the most effective way of helping would be to contribute to the Forced Repatriation Defence Fund. After a period of deliberation, Lord Portsmouth said, 'Well, I think that is what I will do.'

One day in late April 1989, Tolstoy was out in the garden at Court Close, unable to concentrate on his preparations for the trial from worry over money. Pottering about, he noticed a familiar white Bentley Continental gliding sedately up Town Pond Lane. The car swung into the drive of Court Close, and out stepped Lord Portsmouth's chauffeur. 'His Lordship has sent you this message, sir,' he said, handing an envelope to Tolstoy. Puzzled, Tolstoy opened it. There, to his utter amazement was a cheque, made out to the Forced Repatriation Defence Fund, for a six-figure sum which made the difference between the trial proceeding and not. Appended to the cheque was a note saying,

I would like to put on record the reasons why I am making this gesture:

(a) This is probably the last opportunity to find out what happened and why.
(b) It would appear that there has been a cover-up. Hopefully it will emerge during the trial who ordered it, who connived at it and why there has been no government inquiry.
(c) In protest at the hypocrisy and double standards of the British government and certain sections of the media over the issue of war crimes in the light of the Forced Repatriations of 1945.[14]

I do not expect to be repaid. In the event of a successful defence, any surplus remaining in the FRDF should be applied to assist those who have suffered as a result of this tragedy and also charities dealing with suffering as a result of war or as a result of man's inhumanity to man.

Stunned, Tolstoy could only reply with 'a feeble letter of thanks. I don't think I need say what a load it has taken off my mind, nor what a difference it makes to ensuring the success of our cause. All I can say is that it will not be just me, but whole peoples who will in time come to hold your name in honour.'

Within a week of Rubinstein Callingham becoming aware of Lord Portsmouth's donation, Allen & Overy turned their attentions to the Patrons of the FRDF in an attempt to frighten them off. They wrote a letter to each of them individually asking them to 'confirm to us or otherwise that you are indeed a Patron and that you associate yourself with the claims made in the Appeal document and leaflet'. Behind this

---

14   Subsequently Lord Portsmouth has explained this paragraph by saying to this author, 'I was referring to the All-Party Parliamentary War Crimes Group which was then inquiring into whether or not there was a case for enacting legislation to enable certain categories of British citizen to be tried for war crimes in this country albeit that they had been committed abroad. That legislation is now on the statute book in the form of the notorious War Crimes Act. It was very much with that in mind that I wrote the cheque. Here was Lord Aldington, who was alleged to have committed war crimes, or crimes against humanity, by giving or carrying out orders which evidence strongly suggests he knew would result in atrocities and the laws which would enable him to be tried in this country on such charges were already on the statute book, yet neither he nor any other of those involved had ever faced so much as an Army inquiry. Nonetheless, the All-Party Parliamentary War Crimes Group was recommending retrospective legislation to the effect that people who were not British citizens at the time they allegedly committed these offences could be deemed to have been British citizens at that time in order that they could now be tried in this country, and that, further, it was being proposed that the laws of evidence acceptable in this country be changed so that evidence collected abroad by such as Stalin's secret police would be acceptable in a British court of law.'

apparently innocuous request was the threat that the Patrons might be found by a court to have "maintained" Tolstoy's action. If Tolstoy were to lose, any "maintainers" might find themselves liable for Lord Aldington's costs, which a few months later Allen & Overy denied the Sun Alliance were paying.[15]

None of the Patrons gave Allen & Overy any cause for hope. Sir Nicholas Cheetham described it as a 'grotesque letter' and wrote to Tolstoy, saying, 'If that is the best they can do to intimidate the Patrons, I think we may be sure to win in October.' Professor Draper called Allen & Overy's letter 'a confused tangle of rubbish'. Colonel Brian Clark consulted his solicitors about what he called 'Allen & Overy's attempt at an intimidating letter', and they expressed surprise that a firm like that would write 'such a useless and meaningless letter'. Nigel Nicolson thought the approach 'extraordinary and panic-stricken'. Many of the other Patrons simply ignored the letter, although Sir Bernard Braine replied saying that, even at this late stage, it would better for Lord Aldington to abandon his suit and 'join in a demand for a full judicial enquiry'.

The Prince of Liechtenstein's secretary wrote to Allen & Overy saying

> I have been authorised to give you the following information.
>
> H.S.H. the Prince has consented to become a Patron of the Forced Repatriation Defence Fund as the tragedy of forced repatriation which took place in the south of Austria in 1945 is a historical fact which has remained a vivid memory with him, the more so as the Prince and his government at the time gave asylum in Liechtenstein to about 600 Russians including their families, in the face of strong pressure from the Soviet repatriation authorities.
>
> By giving his patronage to the Forced Repatriation Defence Fund, the Prince supports the endeavour of Count Tolstoy to make known the truth of these events which brought death and suffering to thousands of innocent people, without taking a stand about individual responsibilities.

---

15 On 14 August 1989, David Mackie wrote to Rubinstein Callingham saying, 'There is no agreement between our client and the Sun Alliance for the company to discharge our client's costs.'

Princess Tatiana Metternich replied on 22 May, the anniversary of the "shoot the Cossacks" order.

> I happened to be in Austria when the "forced repatriation" you refer to took place and am well-informed of these events. My father's close friend, General Krasnov, an émigré since the Revolution, was among those lured by false promises to a meeting, from which he was forcibly handed over to the Soviets and hanged in Moscow. Apart from the many thousands who suffered a similar fate, this alone would ensure my sympathy for Nikolai Tolstoy's efforts to establish individual responsibility for this iniquitous measure.

Lord Portsmouth replied that, though he did associate himself with Tolstoy's cause, he would be happy to meet Lord Aldington to see if any common ground could be established. Soon afterwards, they lunched at the Carlton Club where Aldington complained that all his actions were being judged with hindsight. In 1945 he had had no idea, he said, that those handed back to the Jugoslavs and Soviets would be killed. He thought they might be 'punished', but no more than that. Nonetheless, Lord Portsmouth also remembers Aldington saying that General Shkuro in particular had been a major war criminal and deserved anything that might have been coming to him in the Soviet Union. Portsmouth was not impressed with either assertion. 'I felt I was being patronised and lied to,' he says today.

Over lunch, Aldington hinted to Portsmouth that the purpose of Allen & Overy's letter was to put all the Patrons of the FRDF 'on notice' that if Tolstoy and Watts lost their case and could not meet his costs bill, he would look to the Patrons to make up any shortfall. Since Tolstoy and Watts did lose and paid nothing towards Lord Aldington's costs, and he never pursued this course, it seems more likely that the purpose of the letter was rather to deter people from paying, with a view to putting the two Defendants in the position of having to represent themselves in Court. This possibility is confirmed by the fact that those Patrons who were clearly not rich appeared not to get such a letter. Zoë Polanska-Palmer, for example, wrote this to Tolstoy:

> I did not get a letter from Lord Aldington's lawyers, but I did get a very strange telephone call, asking if I will be going to the trial as a witness. My answer was: I will be there come what may! To the next question, asking if

I was involved in the repatriation, I said I could not talk about it because my telephone is tapped. Their telephone was then promptly replaced! [16]

Lord Aldington's next pre-trial manoeuvre was one of his most important and effective. Responding to the Particulars of Justification which Tolstoy had lodged some time before, Aldington submitted to the Court a document entitled 'Admissions'. In it he formally admitted everything Tolstoy alleged about the brutality toward the handover victims. The purpose of doing so was to prevent this matter being discussed in Court, since it is an absolute rule of procedure, for the avoidance of wasted time, that matters agreed between the parties becomes inadmissible. Accordingly, Lord Aldington admitted:

—that a substantial number of the Jugoslavs handed back to the Titoists between 14th and 31st May, alternatively 4th June, 1945 were tortured, brutally treated and massacred and that the overwhelming majority were killed ... and that they had not been told their destination
—that violence was used by British troops to facilitate the repatriation of the Cossacks [and] that the log book of the Intelligence officer for the First Guards Brigade noted that the Division had been ordered: 'Shoot to kill [the Cossacks] if it becomes necessary.'

Added to both of these were specific admission of every act of violence or deception put forward in Tolstoy's Particulars of Justification. Tolstoy was now very vulnerable. Without the evidence of slaughter and brutality by the Soviets and Titoists, and brutality and killing by the British troops enforcing the Cossack evacuations, the 'Nazi butchers' taunt would be very hard to justify.

There was another flurry in June when Tolstoy heard that Century Hutchinson had settled with Lord Aldington over *The Minister and the Massacres*. The book, Lord Aldington said in his writ, made some very serious allegations.

16   26 May 1989. Although Zoë simply invented this claim to disconcert the caller, Tolstoy started having unusual problems with his telephone at about this time. He claims to have evidence that his phone was actually tapped.

The Plaintiff as a serving officer in the British Army in Austria in May 1945 had, by means of elaborate deceptions of his superior officers and in deliberate disobedience of his orders and in defiance of British and Allied government policy, procured the brutal forcible repatriation of many thousands of Cossacks and Jugoslavs to face what he knew would be torture, slavery and death and that in consequence he was responsible for the ensuing massacres and was guilty of a major war crime and that he has repeatedly lied about his role in the same.

Since this was a clear summary of the case Tolstoy was about to argue in Court in the pamphlet action, it was important that this not be conceded now. Why had his publishers caved in? It is possible the reason was commercial rather than legal. Century Hutchinson was about to be sold to the large New York publisher, Random House. Outstanding litigation might have jeopardised a very lucrative deal for the vendors. Whatever the truth of the matter, Tolstoy was never told. Yet one clause in the settlement bore directly on Tolstoy: the terms were to be kept secret until after the trial. The damages paid by Century Hutchinson to Lord Aldington were £30,000. Had the jury known this they might have thought differently about awarding the same man £1.5 million for a pamphlet which made, if anything, fewer substantive allegations and which had been circulated far less widely.

On 30 June, with the trial now only three months away, Lord Aldington placed a final bomb under Tolstoy's position when he served a 'Supplemental List of Documents' on the Defence. This contained many items that illuminated issues relevant to the trial, but a disturbingly high proportion of them came from archival sources now effectively closed to the Defence. Tolstoy was unable to check the context of any of them, nor to see if any of the files they came from contained answers to the points raised by the documents Aldington had chosen—see Appendix C.

The list contained 150 documents, 73 of them dated between 7 May and 1 June 1945. Taking, for simplicity, those 73 only, *no less than 40% of them came from sources available to Aldington only*. The list breaks down as follows:

Kirk Papers	4
Birch Grove Archive	1
PRO—FO 1020/42	11
WO 32/13749	5

5 Corps and 8th Army war diaries   8
Total   29 (out of 73)

The Kirk Papers were a Cowgill discovery, in America, consisting of Alexander Kirk's archive. He made it available to Aldington but not to Tosltoy. Of the Birch Grove archive, the current Earl of Stockton, one of the Trustees of the archive, has stated, 'Lord Aldington was given access by my grandfather... Brigadier Cowgill was given access in order to refute the wilder allegations of, amongst others, Nikolas (*sic*) Tolstoy. Nikolas Tolstoy at no time had access.'[17] If this policy was understandable out of family sentiment, the Ministry of Defence and the Foreign Office have no such excuse. FO 1020/42 had been out of the PRO for nearly two years now, and WO 32/13749 for almost as long. Even the 5 Corps "G" and 8th Army war diaries had been withdrawn to Whitehall since January. All of these Tolstoy needed desperately—how desperately is only apparent today now that the files are available again. A quick glance at chapters 3-6 of this book will show how many of the documents which tell the story come from one or other of these files.

But Whitehall malpractice did not stop there. In the autumn of 1988 Tolstoy had written to the Ministry of Defence specifically asking for access to WO 32/13749. He received no reply for nearly six months until Mr J. Oliver, then head of Common Services (Records), wrote, on 18 April 1989, saying that the file was unavailable. 'If you wish to examine WO 32/13749,' Oliver wrote, 'you should be aware that it has been called for from the PRO ... and it may take some time to return it to Kew.'

Thus the Ministry of Defence was denying access to one party in a major court case while making it available to the other. Almost unbelievably, its partisanship went farther than that. On 29 March 1989, Lord Aldington had written to Lord Trefgarne, an old friend, who was at the time Minister of State for Defence Procurement, asking for help in getting hold of evidence he needed for the case.

> My Counsel, Charles Gray QC ... wants to be absolutely sure that he can put the best evidence of my departure from Central Mediterranean Force to the Court... It is the BEST evidence Charles Gray wants. (emphasis in original)

17   Letter to the author, 27 September 1995.

On 10 April Lord Trefgarne replied to Aldington's letter saying,

> I am sure you will appreciate that the Records of former Members of the Armed Forces are held in confidence as between the Crown and the individual...
>
> However, as the two papers in question are, in themselves, fairly innocuous, I am happy to provide the attached copies. I must ask that they be treated in strict confidence, for use by yourself and your Counsel only and that the source of the documents (i.e. your Personal File) should not be revealed.

What is quite chilling is to realise that this reply, sent just a week before Tolstoy was denied access to WO 32/13749, was drafted by Mr J. Oliver, *the same man who turned down Tolstoy's request.*

As if that accommodation were not enough, Trefgarne appended a handwritten note to his formal reply to Aldington saying:

> Dear Toby,
>
> We spoke on the telephone. If your Counsel feels that it is essential to use these documents in Court, I shall be happy to consider the matter further.
>
> David

Predictably, Lord Aldington's Counsel did feel it would like to use the documents in Court, so on 29 June, Aldington wrote to Trefgarne again.

> My senior Counsel is very firmly of the view that copies of the two documents are necessary for the purposes of the Action. I enclose a letter from my solicitors Allen & Overy about the matter.
>
> I would therefore be most grateful if you would allow the documents to be put in under the Civil Evidence Act in the way suggested in my solicitors' letter.

Mr Oliver, once again, wrote a note, in which he gave a warning:

> By producing the two documents, Lord Aldington's lawyers will effectively be admitting that they have been supplied by the Department and whilst it will be self-evident that they have originated from MOD records, it is still important that their precise source (i.e. the personal file) should still not be

revealed.

Trefgarne then gave Aldington permission to use the documents, provided he kept completely quiet about their source.

Remarkably, while all this was going on Tolstoy was corresponding with Oliver about WO 32/13749. All he now asked for was some sort of written acknowledgement that Cowgill's baseless allegation that he had falsely claimed the file had been destroyed be refuted by the Department. This had, he said, done great harm to his professional reputation. Oliver refused to help. On 31 July, a fortnight after he drafted Trefgarne's accommodating reply to Aldington's most recent request, he wrote to Tolstoy:

> I note what you have suggested about restitution, but it is not the practice of the Ministry of Defence to approach third parties in the way you propose. You are, of course, quite at liberty to write to Brigadier Cowgill yourself.

There, perforce, the matter rested.

Tolstoy was completely unaware of the legal ambush he was walking into. Despite the problems of fund-raising and witness gathering, he was still very optimistic about the outcome of the trial. He told Chapman Pincher, for example, that given the evidence he had he did not see how he could possibly lose.

Tolstoy could see only one problem still looming: money. Incredibly, despite Lord Portsmouth's huge contribution to the FRDF, Rubinstein Callingham's bills looked set to outstrip the £500,000 which they had, in April 1989, estimated to be the total cost. Although Tolstoy did not learn this until some time later, Rubinstein Callingham was to submit an invoice for costs and disbursements for the ten weeks leading up to the trial which came to the almost unbelievable figure of £128,721. It is true that a solicitor had had to visit Canada, the United States and Australia to take witness statements during this period, but still Rubinstein Callingham's own share of the bill, excluding air fares, expenses, Counsel's fees and VAT was £98,600, or *nearly £10,000 per week for labour only!* Half of the Portsmouth donation had been spent before the trial started. The total left in the Fund was down to £167,456.

Previously uncosted expenses kept cropping up, the most bizarre of which was the £5,310 premium which was paid to insure Mr Justice

Davies's life for a period of four months beginning on 1 September. The sum insured was £500,000 and this was intended to cover the costs of a retrial in the event of the Judge suddenly dying.

Despite his very thorough behind-the-scenes preparations, Lord Aldington was less confident than Tolstoy. He, too, was burning the midnight oil in preparation for the trial. In Court, Lady Aldington lamented the loss of her husband's company. Since issuing the original writ, 'he became more and more involved,' she said, 'with bits of paper every night. We used to play cards in the evening quite often, and the result of this was that I got rather fed up because I could never get him to play cards or do anything—he was always far too busy... For over 2 years [he did] nothing every evening, probably until 2 o'clock in the morning, except work on bits of paper. I knew that there were all these bits of paper and he kept on working every night on bits of paper, but I wasn't actually conscious of what was happening. I just was bored that he wasn't playing cards with me. Do you see?'

All this work was undermining her husband's health, Lady Aldington said. 'He's getting extremely—I don't know what the word is quite— fragile, I think, is a good word, very—oh, dear, how do you say it?—nothing one says is absolutely correct—I'm sure otherwise I understand these things—whereas normally everything is perfectly all right, but whatever one says is not absolutely right. It's very difficult to live with somebody who is 75, although I've never thought of him as 75, and I'm sure he'll bob back, but he has undermined his health. There's no two ways about it.'

Nigel Nicolson told Tolstoy that in Kent the word was that Lord Aldington expressed confidence in the outcome of the trial, but that he said so 'in rather the tone of voice that Bruno used about Tyson before their fight'. Nicolson also said, 'the general Establishment opinion seems to be that Toby and you are both a bit eccentric (you in raising the matter so long after the event, and he in not confining his protest to a dignified rebuttal) but they are fascinated by the approaching fight.'

Part III

The

TRIAL

'We are a country without censorship in any form that
would stop the free expression of truth.'

—Mr Justice Michael Davies
Court 13, Royal Courts of Justice, October 1989

13

LORD ALDINGTON'S EVIDENCE

O N THE MORNING of Monday 2 October 1989, Tolstoy
approached the Royal Courts of Justice in an optimistic frame of
mind. In an unpublished memoir he has described his feelings
inside the huge and rather rambling building:

> The High Gothic architecture appeared to me a wholly appropriate reflexion
> of Victorian grandeur. Here it was not hard to picture justice impartially
> administered to high and low by detached olympian arbiters, unswayed by
> personal preference or outside influence.
>
> The antiquarian in me approved also the quaint ranks and robes of the
> court officers, which smacked so strongly of the eighteenth and nineteenth
> centuries. The mock-medieval setting seemed unconsciously to reflect a
> Victorian pseudo-historical confidence in the belief that modern English
> justice, fairest and finest in the world, represented the ultimate perfection of
> those frank and manly institutions by means of which our remote Anglo-
> Saxon forebears ordered the tribal kingdoms of the Heptarchy.

He was surprised and disappointed at the size of Court 13. He had
imagined the trial would take place 'in a large hall, with a fair-sized
audience'. The room is more or less cuboid, possibly thirty feet each way,
with the walls covered in drab and slightly tatty oak panelling. There are
two pews of twelve seats each for the public, and three pews for the parties,
their lawyers and assistants. There were at all times more officers of the

court, if that number includes the jury, than members of the public in Court 13.

The Judge, Sir Michael Davies, was a familiar face in the libel world, as were the two barristers. Richard Rampton QC, Tolstoy's Counsel, who would be representing Watts as well on all issues not related to the Sun Alliance, is the co-author of the most recent edition of *Duncan and Neill on Defamation*, one of the standard reference books. He has also been involved in affairs outside court; for example he served, with Lord Windlesham, on Thames Television's inquiry into their controversial programme *Death on the Rock*. More recently he represented the McDonald's corporation in their titanic struggle against the unemployed gardener and postman who had leafletted outside one of their restaurants.

Charles Gray QC, for Lord Aldington, has won a string of well-publicised cases, including those brought by Bill Roache, the television star who was awarded £50,000 for being called 'boring', and Jason Donovan, an actor who won £200,000 for being called 'gay'. He has also lost a few cases, including the celebrated one in which Ms Jani Allen, a South African journalist, sued a television broadcasting company over allegations that she had had an affair with the right-wing politician Eugene Terre'Blanche. On that occasion Gray made the news when he brandished a fabricated keyhole in front of the jury, by way of illustration of his client's claim that a defence witness could not have seen Terre'Blanche's 'large white bottom' in the copulative posture in the way she claimed to have seen it.

The tone of the proceedings was set right at the start by Mr Justice Davies, who said, 'This is a trial of an action for libel and not an historical commission, or some sort of inquisitorial process; this is not an inquiry into what happened in May 1945 over the Jugoslavs and the Cossacks.'

In legal argument before the trial proper started, the Judge gave a hint of his attitude to the Second Defendant.

'While you are on your feet,' the Judge said to Rampton, 'your last sentence reminds me of a question nothing to do with this point. What are we going to call your client? Is he really, as far as this Court is concerned, a Count, or is he Mr Tolstoy?'

'Your Lordship might be inclined to regard it as a courtesy title,' Rampton replied.

After watching the jury being selected and sworn in, Tolstoy thought them 'a not unrepresentative bunch, including what I took to be motherly housewives, an Asian shopkeeper or businessman, two cheerful young labourers, an attractive if vacant-looking girl in a pleasingly short skirt, and a young black man who seemed uncertain of the purpose of his arrival among us. To outward appearances, they seemed decent, honest people, to whom I was happily prepared to entrust the fate of our cause.' Tolstoy was happy despite the fact that one of the jurors, the uncertain young black man, was unable to read the oath, and had to be helped through it, phrase by phrase, by a Court official. Considering there were ten files of documents in the Court Bundles, excluding the Defendants' Witness Statements, running to nearly 2,000 pages, this might have seemed a serious handicap to the proceedings. But Tolstoy is an optimist. In any case, he says, this juror spent the whole time chatting up the very pretty girl in the short skirt whom he sat next to throughout the case, paying no attention to the proceedings whatever. Tolstoy thought, 'Well, we have an eleven man jury, what's the difference?' By contrast, he remembers that there was an Indian juror who followed the case with rapt attention, on one occasion giving a thumbs-up sign to the jurors behind him when Rampton scored a major point against Lord Aldington.

Georgina is less of an optimist by nature, and she remembers the unsympathetic impression made by another of the jurors. He looked like 'a retired colour sergeant': cold and unemotional, she thought. One observer noted that he made notes only when Lord Aldington was talking. In the event, this man was to be the foreman; it was he who announced the jury's verdict.

The following day, the proceedings started in earnest. Nigel Nicolson arrived to sit next to Tolstoy as he did for the rest of the trial, giving him personal support as well as what legal/historical advice he could. Nicolson noted that the jury 'looks alert, all upper working class.' He described the Judge as 'a homely old soul, [who] speaks kindly to the jury as if about to offer them a cup of tea, and when he wants to go out for a pee, he pretends he is rising for the jury's sake.'[1]

The first salvo of the trial was Gray's opening speech. He spent a day and a half on his feet outlining Lord Aldington's case against the pamphlet. It was an unremarkable performance except for his slighting reference to Tolstoy as a person 'who describes himself as a writer of books on the

---

topic [of the repatriations] and who I think is going to tell you he is a historian by calling.'

Right at the start Gray was able to make use of the material Trefgarne had supplied his client. Referring to the controversy over Brigadier Low's date of departure from 5 Corps, Gray pointed to his Personal Record and said there was no longer any doubt. 'Happily, the contemporary documents clarify the picture beyond any possibility of doubt... It is happy that this document has survived because it makes clear beyond any doubt that Lord Aldington did arrive in the UK on 24 May.'

There was one moment of excitement during these preliminaries, though. On Day 3 Tolstoy arrived in Court to be told by a solicitor from Rubinstein Callingham in a whisper, 'The Eden diaries have arrived!' A hurried conference was conducted on the polished wooden bench outside Court 13. It will be remembered that Lord Aldington had, after issuing his writ against Watts, changed the date of his departure from Austria from '25 or 26 May' to early in the morning of 22 May, just before the Corps Commander's conference at which it was ordered to 'shoot at Cossacks' if necessary to enforce the evacuation plan. Tolstoy was suspicious, but without hard evidence either way could not respond. Two weeks before the trial started, Tolstoy had received a copy of the Plaintiff's Witness Statements. For the first time, Lord Aldington gave his opponents details of his evidence about the date of his departure from 5 Corps. This included the claim that he had dined twice with Anthony Eden in the Foreign Office, on the evenings of 25 May and 26 May, when the Foreign Secretary tried to persuade him to stand for parliament. Lord Aldington wrote that on the first night 'he half persuaded me, but not fully. The next day, 26 May, I had dinner with him again and he did persuade me to stand.'

Submitting this story so late meant that it was very difficult for Tolstoy to research it adequately before the trial began. He quickly contacted the Ministry of Defence to see if they might have any record of Low's movements, but, on 28 September, the Wednesday before the trial began, the MOD replied it had not, despite having gone to such lengths on behalf of Lord Aldington. At the same time Tolstoy had been in touch with one of Eden's biographers, David Carlton, who told him Sir Anthony had kept a personal diary which was held with the rest of the Avon papers in the Birmingham University library. That might confirm or refute Tolstoy's suspicions. Rubinstein Callingham instantly sub-poenaed it. Now, half-way through Gray's opening speech, it had arrived.

Tolstoy flicked through the material: it contained a bombshell! At 4 p.m. on 25 May, Eden left London for his home at Binderton in Sussex, where he had remained throughout 26 May. On neither evening had he dined in with Brigadier Low. Tolstoy took his place in Court in a state of excitement. One of the pillars of the Plaintiff's departure date claim had, he felt, now been demolished.

While Tolstoy had had one success, there was another, much more serious, failure. During the frantic last months of preparation for Court, he had employed a research assistant to keep applying for the files he needed at the PRO, principally, the 5 Corps war diary, WO 32/13749 and FO 1020/42. Shortly before the trial began, they were still 'out to Department'. Now, to Tolstoy's dismay, he discovered that he could not even ask for them as the PRO had closed on Monday 2 October, the first day of the trial, for its two-week annual stock-take. By the end of that period, Lord Aldington would almost certainly have left the witness stand.

During his opening speech, Gray rubbed salt into this wound by using the absence of parts of FO 1020/42 to good effect. He quoted Alexander's signal of 16 May to Churchill saying that he was trying to get SHAEF to accept the prisoners in Carinthia 'but so far without much success... My administrative problem is a big one... I must clear the decks in this area.' This was the germ of Operation Coldstream. Considered in isolation it looked like corroboration for any plan to get prisoners out of Carinthia. Of course, as even a cursory glance at FO 1020/42 shows, this is not true. Alexander *did* want to 'clear the decks', but by moving the Chetniks to Italy and the Cossacks to SHAEF, which is exactly the plan 5 Corps successfully sabotaged. But with this file still in the Foreign Office, this point could not be made.

Gray ended with what, for him, was the main point: his client's character. Lord Aldington did not deserve the attack the Defendants had made on his integrity, particularly not at the age of 75. 'He is a man,' Gray told the jury, 'of whom I think it can be fairly said that he did more for this country in war-time than most of us can aspire to do in our life-time, and you perhaps can picture for yourselves without much difficulty the effect on him as an individual, and not just on him but on his family as well, of this vile attack on his honour and integrity.'

Mounting the witness stand to give evidence, Lord Aldington was clearly nervous. He confused his name and his title, giving the former as Lord Aldington, and when asked his address he gave his age. But he quickly pulled himself together and was soon well into his stride, describing his career in the Army, right up to the time he left for England.

'What happened when you got back to England on 24th May?' Gray asked him.

'I was asked to ring up the then Foreign Secretary and go and see him about his idea that I should stand as a candidate in the General Election. I wasn't certain whether I was fit to do so—a fit person to do so—because I really didn't know much about what was going on in Britain, and nor, quite frankly, was I certain that I wanted to go at once into the hassle of an election and politics because I hadn't had a holiday for a long, long time.'

'Did he persuade you?'

'He did not persuade me the first night, he did persuade me though, the second night.'

Tolstoy grinned inwardly at this hostage to fortune.

Nicolson wrote in his diary, 'Toby affects a jolly Jack manner, but his attitude is not off-putting.'

Lord Aldington's answers to Gray's questions were, as is usual when a witness is being examined by his or her own Counsel, intended to be uncontroversial. But even so, a few of them do read rather sourly as he consistently refused to take any responsibility for anything 5 Corps did. The deception aspect of the Jugoslav handovers was 'imposed by me, *at my Commander's instructions of course*'. (emphasis added) Equally, the handover of the German and Austrian officers in the Cossack Cavalry was not his fault, but that of incompetent subordinates for whom Aldington refused to take responsibility since he was in England by the time his order was carried out.

Gray ended his examination-in-chief[2], as he had his opening speech,

---

2   The stages of a trial are: first, the opening speech by the Plaintiff's Counsel in which he states his client's case; secondly, the examination-in-chief in which the Plaintiff's Counsel elicits the evidence his client wants the jury to hear. This is followed by cross-examination by the opposing Counsel, which in turn is followed by re-examination by the Plaintiff's own Counsel when any new points raised in cross-examination can be dealt with. The examination-in-chief, cross-examination and re-examination are then repeated for all of the Plaintiff's witnesses. Then this whole process, from the opening speech onward, is repeated for the Defendant(s) and his, her or their witnesses. Finally the Defence Counsel makes a closing speech summarising the evidence brought (no evidence may be introduced at this stage which has not already been given by witnesses or in documents previously examined and, if necessary, cross-examined upon). This is followed by a closing speech by the Plaintiff's Counsel. Then the judge gives legal direction to the jury and sums up the evidence. The jury retire to consider

with the issue of his client's character and Watts's campaign. Lord Aldington told the Court that he had at first ignored Watts because he thought him too unimportant to bother with. But the pamphlet changed that, for two reasons.

'Its wording and the charges,' Lord Aldington said, 'but more importantly because of the people to whom it was addressed, as it were, to all the most sensitive parts of my then life. To the school I was Warden of. To the parents of the boys. Can you imagine that? To all my old colleagues and all old Wykehamists. To the masters and staff and to my (*sic*) villagers. To MPs and members of the House of Lords. I think in those political circles, people are used to having nasty things circulated to them about their colleagues but not, I think, anything like this and that hurt me too. It got about that this kind of charge was being made, and get about it did because we began reading in the newspapers about war crimes accusations.[3] Here I am being accused, I suppose, for the first time anybody in a small way in public life has ever been accused, of being a war criminal—worse than the Nazis. Yes, it upset me.'

Lord Aldington's other concern was for his family. 'I thought it was monstrous that my family should have to carry this stigma of having at their head a war criminal worse than the Nazi butchers.'

That was bad enough, as far as the Plaintiff was concerned, but when Gray moved on to the critical letters his client had received after Watts had circulated his pamphlet, Lord Aldington gave way to tears. The incident was rendered farcical by the Judge's blundering attempt to be sympathetic.

'Did you receive correspondence shortly after this pamphlet was put into circulation by these defendants?' Gray asked his client.

'Yes I did, and I have disclosed all those letters to the other side.'

'Well, we are going to have to look at some. Bundle F.'

'I wonder if you could give me just a moment, please?'

The transcript records: 'The witness was upset.'

---

their verdict. After the jury announce their verdict, the judge incorporates it into his judgement, which is the official word of the court.

3   This should have been a very important point for the Defence. In fact Watts's charges were *not* written up in 'the newspapers'; the charges did *not* 'get about' in the way Lord Aldington suggested, which is one of the reasons why some of his friends suggested he confine himself to a rebuttal and then drop the matter. Rampton never asked him in which papers the charges 'got about'.

'Yes, of course,' the Judge said. 'Would you like a short break?'

'No, I want to pull myself together.'

'Well, do say, any time. Any witness who feels under stress, just say so. I cannot do what one newspaper apparently said I ought to do. They likened me to the Radio Doctor where you have to keep your bowels open!'

'I do not think that would help, just at the minute!' said the Lord Aldington.

Nicolson noted that, after the Judge's inept remark, 'both QCs looked down at their papers, expressive of their contempt. The jury are far better than I expected... I like them for not laughing at the Judge's jokes.'

After his client had mopped his brow and blown his nose, Gray took him through the letters, including the one from Gordon Nimse. Nimse, it will be remembered, said that if Lord Aldington believed in life after death, he must be dreading meeting 'those men and women you betrayed in '45'. The former Brigadier broke down again as he choked his way through his answer, 'It is not a very nice letter, is it?'

This was an illegitimate question, as has been mentioned earlier, because Nimse was responding to *The Minister and the Massacres*, not the pamphlet. But Rampton made no objection.

Gray made one more point before he sat down, namely that the anguish his client had suffered was not confined to an emotional response to hostile letters: he had had the pleasure of his retirement ruined by his decision to sue Watts.

'Things like the two rounds of golf at a weekend that I used to have even when I was working very hard,' Lord Aldington said as if the writ had been issued by the Defence and he was a reluctant litigant, 'have become two rounds of golf a month. Things like gardening a lot, which I like doing, to look after my garden, I hoped to be able to do that because it is quite a nice garden, I have had to neglect that and get the help of some boys for my garden. Reading very little. Not being able to go to family functions overseas. Not being able to travel about amongst friends as much as I would have liked. Yes, I have had the last two and a half years properly messed about.'

After Gray sat down, it was the turn of Edward Garnier QC whom Watts had, on Rampton's advice, hired (at the FRDF's expense) to deal with the Sun Alliance aspect of the case. Garnier is a Member of Parliament. In 1996 he piloted the reforming Defamation Act through the House of

Commons.

On this occasion, he made little impact on the Plaintiff. He did not make a single point which struck home. Watts was appalled. Nicolson wrote that evening in his diary, 'The Sun Alliance bit bores the jury.' In all, Garnier was on his feet for less than three hours. Apart from that, his contribution to the case amounted to sitting in Court until Day 13 when Watts decided to dispense with his services, thinking he could do better himself. Including his brief fee (for preparing his questions) Garnier's bill for this work was £23,400 plus VAT, another substantial chunk out of the rapidly shrinking Forced Repatriation Defence Fund.

The first time the proceedings really came to life was when Richard Rampton stood up to cross-examine Lord Aldington. Rampton started with one of the most controversial issues of the case: if Lord Aldington claimed, as he did, that he had no knowledge of the likely fate of the people he ordered handed over, what did he think they were all doing trekking in such huge numbers into Carinthia?

'I don't think I can positively know,' Lord Aldington said, 'but I thought it was absolutely natural that people in the Baltic (*sic*) world who had lost the struggle should at first—well, not wish to surrender to the person who had defeated them. But it wasn't for me to make decisions about whether they were political refugees or not. I have to tell the Court that. That is not the role of a subordinate headquarters. That was the role of the War Office in London or Field Marshal Alexander, the Commander in Chief. Brigadiers and Chiefs of Staff do not make political decisions.'

This answer was true in theory, but could not be challenged in this instance without access to FO 1020/42 and WO 32/13749. Without being able to adduce evidence of 5 Corps' sabotage of the intentions of the War Office and Field Marshal Alexander, Rampton had to move on to the subject of Communist brutality. Lord Aldington said he had known about it, but he did not at the time think their brutality 'extended to massacring'. But did he not know that Tito had eliminated all opposition?

'You have asked me what I knew,' Lord Aldington replied. 'That is hindsight. We are importing hindsight now into what Tito was. I did not know that. How could I know that?'

'Is it hindsight to suggest that you knew at the time that these different groups of Jugoslavs in your hands had been fighting bitterly against the Titoists for some years?' Rampton asked. 'Is that hindsight?'

'What we knew was that the groups—you are moving me about a

bit—we are moving now from Titoists to the Serbs and the Croats. We knew they had been fighting with the Germans against Tito and prolonging the war. That's what we knew.'

'So one did not really have to feel sorry for them whatever their fate might be. Is that it?'

'That's not what I said. You are trying to put words into my mouth. What we knew was that they had been fighting for the Germans and had prolonged the war. That's what we knew.'

Lord Aldington had started as he meant to continue—and did continue—by trying to negate Rampton's points rather than establishing a different and more plausible view. The onus of proof is on the defendant in libel cases, so all he had to do was make Tolstoy's arguments look either wrong or so complex as to be incomprehensible to a jury fresh to the subject and the Defence would have failed to persuade. The Plaintiff does not have to convince the jury of his case, only prevent the Defence from doing so.

However, Lord Aldington cannot have helped his cause by getting tetchy with Rampton, as he often did, for example when pressed on the deception of the Jugoslavs.

'What I am putting to you is this,' Rampton said. 'It was entirely predictable that when a British soldier or a British officer was asked by a Croat, let us say, who feared what was going to happen to him when he went to Jugoslavia "Where are you sending us?"—when they got on to the train to go to Rosenbach and then to Jugoslavia—"Where are you sending us?" "Oh, I can't tell you that," it is entirely predictable that the man will infer, quite rightly, that he is going to Jugoslavia, is it not?'

'It may be predictable to you, Mr Rampton,' Lord Aldington replied. 'I don't know what knowledge you have of how soldiers behave, but I can only tell you what is recorded as having happened, and that I have tried to do. If you want me to speculate, then I suggest you get me out of this box where I am not subject to an oath and we can have a little conversation. But, subject to an oath, that is the only thing I know, and I do not agree with your ideas of predictability. It may come from great knowledge which I don't happen to have. I merely fought through the war for five years.'

'Do you ask this jury to accept,' Rampton continued a little later on, 'that the method you put in place—"do not tell them where they are going"—is equivalent to persuading them that they should return to Jugoslavia?'

'It is equivalent. I think you want to break this down. If they do not know where they are going, they are more likely to get into the transport presented to them.'

'That is to persuade them to go to Italy. You have had them persuaded of that,' Rampton said. 'Very well done–'

'I will not be charged by you over and over again that I did do something, particularly when I said on oath over and over again, I did not. I cannot understand how a man in your position can do that.'

'It may be at the end of the day and this is not the first time I am going to have to remind you of it, that the jury may decide that what you have said in this Court is not true.'

'I know you think I am a liar, but I tell you I am not and I find it very difficult to keep an equable temper with a man who behaves in Court to me when I have on oath said things to him and said things to others. I find it very difficult to go on answering questions–'

At this point the Judge intervened. 'The comparison is not exact, but in a sense Mr Rampton is a soldier on a particular side. He has a job to do. You may rest assured if he steps out of line, as I would with any Counsel, it is my job to intervene, but unless I do so, I am afraid I shall have to ask you to listen patiently to his questions even though to you they seem to contain certain things that are untrue, repetitive, boring, loathsome. I am not implying that, but you have to answer them just as you, no doubt, will be sitting there listening to Mr Gray with a slightly different style, asking questions of Mr Watts and Count Tolstoy. This is the way this particular contest has to be dealt with. It may not be the best way; it may be. So, let us get on.'

This homily had only a temporary effect. 'I am not used to dealing with people who accuse one over and over again of being a liar on oath,' Lord Aldington said, not long afterwards. 'I regard giving evidence on oath as being something sacred and I am very sorry but I was brought up that way.'

Ignoring the Plaintiff's protestations, Rampton pressed him on the allegation that he had known the likely fate of the Jugoslavs he ordered handed over to Tito. Aldington's first response contained a note of self-pity. 'What I do not understand,' he said, 'is why, if everybody knew it, and that must be true of colonels in command of battalions, company commanders, brigade commanders and the generals in charge of divisions as well as myself, why are they not charged with being war criminals as well as me?'

The simple answer, of course, was that they had not issued libel writs. But Rampton had to stick to his line of questioning. He asked Lord Aldington why, if he had no inkling that a dark fate awaited any anti-Tito Jugoslavs handed over, they had fled 'in panic' towards the British lines. 'The reason to any sensible, normal person as to why they are fleeing in panic is because they fear slaughter, and you knew that too.'

'I never said that they did not have those fears,' Lord Aldington replied. 'One man's fears is not necessarily what is going to happen to him.'

'You did not believe, then, that to return these groups of people to the Titoists might be "fatal to their health"?'

'What does that mean?' Lord Aldington asked. 'I did not believe that they would be massacred, no.'

'What do the words "Might be fatal to their health" mean?' Rampton asked incredulously.

'I do not know,' Lord Aldington carried on. 'They were not used in front of me, and indeed anybody could work out what those words mean. It may be it was meant that they would be imprisoned. It may be that they would be tried and hanged. That is what happened to traitors (*sic*).'

Rampton asked Lord Aldington about the fact that women and children had been handed to Tito as a result of the Deception Order. Was this not a breach of the Robertson Order which provided for the repatriations of those who had been 'serving in German forces'? Lord Aldington answered that, by including women and children in those to be delivered to Tito, he had in fact made a 'humane gesture' which would avoid splitting up families. Rampton pressed him on this incredible answer. If that had really been the case, surely his order should have read, 'Such civilians of Jugoslav nationality as can be classed as their camp followers *and wish to go with their men*'? (The italicised words were not in Low's order.)

'No,' Lord Aldington replied, 'it might have done if it had been drafted in your chambers, but it was drafted in an operations room or probably in an operations caravan just north of the Wörthersee, and we didn't have the benefit of either Mr Rampton or Miss Sharp. [Rampton's Junior Counsel]'

'I do wish you would de-personalise this discussion,' Rampton said. 'For what it is worth—'

'I find it personally very offensive that you keep on going over and over the same ground. I know you have to, but I do find it personally offensive.'

'For what it is worth, Lord Aldington, you were a lawyer by qualification, you have done some time as a pupil in chambers, you have a law degree from the University of Oxford, I dare say you were fairly used to the use of precise language, were you not?'

'Yes, I was quite used to precise language and I think that I used precise language which would be precisely understood by staff officers, even though it is not precisely understood by you.'

'So do we read into this order of the 18th some sort of qualification "But ignore this order if the camp followers do not want to go back"? Is that what it is?'

'Where do you get that from?'

'This order compels or obliges the troops to send back all the camp followers, does it not?'

'Yes.'

'How does that lie with your suggestion that this was a humane gesture or humane concession so as to allow families not to be split up? What of the families that wished to be split up because the soldiers did not want their wives and children to be slaughtered by the Titoists? What of them?'

'I am afraid I don't know... I have done my best to reconstruct the reasons and I hope you will think—perhaps you don't—that I have done it honourably and honestly. If you don't think that then you had better say so too because I might as well stop answering your questions.'

At this, the Judge decided it was time to mitigate the severity of the cross-examination, something he was never to do when the Defence was under pressure. 'I am not here to protect Lord Aldington,' Mr Justice Davies said to Rampton, 'but do remember that you are cross-examining a man—if he will forgive me saying so—of 75. You have got to do your duty but I think to impose unnecessary strain by repeating the same questions over and over again with hourly intervals is not really the proper way to do it.'

Already by this stage in the trial Nicolson was remarking in his diary that he had doubts about the Judge's complete impartiality, although, he noted, 'there is no drooping in Nikolai's confidence. He thinks he is going to trip Toby up on his departure date which I do not.'

As the Court rose for lunch one day towards the end of Lord Aldington's time in the witness box, Nicolson went to the Gents lavatory where he found the Plaintiff. He noted the encounter in his diary.

'"You're keeping wonderfully cool, Toby. Isn't it a great strain?" "Well, it is a bit. By the way, I love reading your Situation Reports, so free of all the military jargon." And so on. Very amicable. We were quite alone, like two cows in a milking parlour.'

In the witness box, Lord Aldington continued to be less than amicable with Richard Rampton, particularly so when he sensed the Defence Counsel was implying he was not telling the truth. 'Are you accusing me of telling you an untruth?' Lord Aldington asked at one point when the issues of the Distone Order (Alexander's order, issued on the same day as the Deception Order, to send the Jugoslavs to Italy) and Low's departure date came up.

'I shall be reproached for repeating myself if I do,' Rampton said, 'but may I put it like this: certainly I do not accept your answer as being truthful, no, because, as you know, on our account of the matter you were not out of Austria by the morning of the 22nd, not by any means.'

'But this is the morning of the 24th, we are talking about.'

'What I am suggesting to you is this: that it is quite apparent from these documents that your statement that 5 Corps never received a copy of Distone, that Distone did not apply to and bind 5 Corps, is untruthful.'

'It is nice of you to accuse me once again of being a liar,' Lord Aldington said. 'I hope we can make some record of these clashes.'

'It is all being recorded both mechanically and by the shorthand writer,' the Judge said.

'Have no doubt, Lord Aldington,' Rampton continued, 'that if the ladies and gentlemen of the jury accept what you are telling them and reject what I am suggesting then they will reflect that as best they can in an award of damages at the end of the case. Have no doubt of that. It may be small compensation to you if you are telling the truth.'

'I have the problem, and I am sorry that it is a problem, it may be personal to me, of having to confront a man who over and over again says I am a liar—and I find it very difficult.'

'Look at it another way, you have accused my client, Count Tolstoy, of being a liar.'

'I haven't. I have accused him of accusing me of being a war criminal and I am not. If that is a lie then—'

'You said that he has made false statements about you which he says are not false, he says they are true.'

'But he hasn't made them in the box yet. Perhaps when he makes them in the box then—'

'Forgive me,' the Judge said, intervening again, 'but there is a slight difference, Mr Rampton. The difference is that Count Tolstoy is—and I do not say this in any sneering sense—a *self-styled historian*. [emphasis added] He is not talking in anything he writes about anything he has experienced himself. Lord Aldington is accused of being a liar in relation to events in which he played a part, you say a major part. Count Tolstoy may be accused by Lord Aldington of being quite wrong about history but not about the part he himself played. I think that is the distinction.' Why 'self-styled' historian? The point the Judge wanted to make was about the difference between historians and historical figures. The Second Defendant's status within his profession was not relevant to that in any way at all.

When he moved on to the part of the case which related to the Cossacks, Rampton started with a question which ought to have been uncontroversial, but, typically, proved to be just the opposite.

'Do you agree,' Rampton asked, 'that in order to achieve the repatriation of Soviet citizens it was necessary that the ex-Russian forces in Allied hands must be screened to see who was a Soviet citizen and who was not, in accordance with that definition?'

'Do I agree that they must be screened? No, I do not think I do agree that they must be screened,' Lord Aldington replied. 'If you mean by the word "screening" exactly what was done in civilian terms in England, about which there is much written, in America, about which there is some written, in Germany, in Austria and in Italy with civilians, through a proper screening process by a military government and other people, that is certainly one detailed process. I do not agree that such a process would have been appropriate in a fighting formation such as 5 Corps in Austria.'

Since the question of screening was central to the whole controversy, it is unfortunate that Rampton did not ask Lord Aldington on whose authority he asserted that the individual screening which had been clearly ordered by 8th Army on 13 March should no longer be undertaken. Instead, Rampton moved on to Lord Aldington's state of knowledge about the likely fate of the Cossacks if they were sent back to the Soviet Union. Surely he had had an inkling of the fact, as so many other people at 5 Corps did, that their fate would be dire? No, Lord Aldington said, he had not.

'What would happen to these people,' Rampton put to him, 'is exactly the same as it was with the Jugoslavs, is it not? What would happen to these people was a matter of common knowledge throughout 5 Corps, and if you did not know it, or did not believe it, you must have been the only person.'

'Well, you're sort of sneering at my inability to be an ordinary competent officer,' Lord Aldington replied. 'You can go on with the sneer. We've had it very often, and your knowledge of what happens in an army has been put to me several times—it's not evidence, you must have picked it up somewhere—but it's not the same as mine, and I am trying honestly to put before the Court what I knew then, not what I know now.'

Once again, the Judge intervened. 'I think, Lord Aldington, Mr Rampton's point is slightly different. It may be equally or more offensive. I think his point is not that you are not efficient or competent enough to learn what was going to happen to them, but that you did know what was going to happen to them, but have not been frank with the jury in Court about your knowledge. That is his point.'

'Oh, yes, I didn't realise that it was quite as offensive as that,' Lord Aldington said.

'That is your point, is it not, Mr Rampton?' the Judge asked.

'Yes, my Lord, that he knew—just as everybody else knew.'

'Well, I didn't, is the answer to that,' said the Plaintiff.

Rampton pointed out that Alexander, for one, knew, having described repatriation of both Cossacks and Jugoslavs as being likely to be 'fatal to their health'. Do you remember that signal, Rampton asked Lord Aldington?

'Yes, I do, whatever that might mean.'

'"Fatal to one's health", what does it mean?' Rampton repeated in amazement.

'Tried and executed.'

'"Fatal to one's health" means death, does it not?'

'Tried and executed,' Lord Aldington repeated, forgetting that two days earlier he had said he thought the phrase might have meant "imprisoned". 'What you are saying is that I knew they would not be tried. There is no actual evidence that they weren't that I've seen. What we have admitted we have admitted, and I'm not going back. What I say is that I expected them, like to any other Allied country, to go back and be tried. You may not have liked the way they were tried, you may not have liked the punishment that they were given, but that's what I expected.'

But other people suspected the worst for the Cossacks, not just

Alexander. Rampton reminded the Plaintiff that Robertson, for example, had told Kirk on 14 May that he 'could not bother at this time about who might or might not be turned over to the Russians and Partisans to be shot.'

'It appears,' Rampton asked, 'that if Mr Kirk is right about what General Robertson said, General Robertson thought that the Cossacks who were turned over were likely to be shot?'

'Yes,' Lord Aldington replied cockily, 'but it doesn't say whether he expected them to be tried before they were shot, or afterwards, or not at all.'

Tried *after* they were shot...? The contempt in that answer was exceeded only by Lord Aldington's assertion shortly afterwards that, despite his own unhappiness at the forcible repatriation of the Cossacks, he had to carry the policy through because, he said, 'we had made an agreement and we had *the honour of Britain's name to defend.*' (emphasis added)

'Did you know that General Shkuro was one of the old émigrés—what elsewhere you have described as White Russians with French nationality or something like that?' Rampton asked him.

'I think I must have known that, but it is difficult for me to say yes or no to that. I knew that General Shkuro was there, obviously. How much I knew, I am not sure.'

'Did you know, for example, that he had fought under General Denikin for the White Russians against the Red Russians in 1918-19: did you know that?'

'No, not so far as I remember, but if you tell me that there is a document which shows that I was told that, or could have been told that, then I will accept it. It does not seem to me to matter.'

Rampton would not accept this dismissive answer; but neither would Lord Aldington change it.

'I do not know if this jogs your memory about General Shkuro or not—the fact that he was awarded the Companionship of the Bath by King George V in 1919. Does that jog any memory?'

'No, and I am sure it would have done. If I had known that I would have thought it rather extraordinary that somebody who was the Companion of the Bath had taken up arms against the country and the King who had awarded him that. So that I would most certainly have remembered.'

'Do you say that General Shkuro fought against the British?'

'Well, he was fighting for the Germans, and if that is not fighting against the British I don't know what is. I don't know whether you have ever been in a war—if you have allies, if somebody is fighting against an ally, he is fighting against you.'

'It will not improve the temperature or the atmosphere of this Court,' Rampton said, 'if we engage in confrontations of that kind. He was not fighting against the British: I think the answer to my question is you agree he was not?'

'Yes, but my answer is that anybody who was fighting against the Russians was fighting against the British.'

'By an indirect route I suppose one could reach that conclusion, I accept. Do you know how old General Shkuro was at this time?'

'No.'

'You did not know that he was in his seventies?'

'No.'

'He was something around your present age: and do you still say that he was fighting against the Soviets?'

'He was in command of groups,' Lord Aldington said. 'I have read in some other documents rather opprobrious comments, in German archives, about him, but I won't repeat them. He was there in command of troops under German Army Command, yes.'

Here the Judge chimed in, offering evidence in support of Lord Aldington's point. 'The French in 1940 had commanders in their eighties, if I remember rightly—so I have read!'

'This is the trouble, Lord Aldington,' Rampton carried on, ignoring the Judge's intervention. 'You seem to have assumed that General Shkuro fought in World War II.'

'I didn't know anything about General Shkuro,' Lord Aldington repeated, 'other than that he had a unit called General Shkuro's whatever it was. That is what I knew about General Shkuro. I don't know what you think we did all day.'[4]

'Well, one of the things you were supposed to do before you composed the lists of people to be repatriated—if indeed any such list existed—was to find out who was who, who had been fighting for the Germans, who was a Soviet citizen. You assert that General Shkuro was fighting—'

'I was not supposed to find out who was—'

---

4   This assertion is contradicted by Lord Portsmouth's recollection of his quite detailed discussion of General Shkuro at his lunch with Lord Aldington three months earlier (see p. 188).

'I beg your pardon, Lord Aldington, you have asserted as a fact that General Shkuro first was fighting against the British. That is not so, you now accept. You assert that he was fighting against the Soviets. That is not so. Do you now accept that too, or must I prove it?'

'What I know was he was fighting for the Germans. I have read about that unit: they started off in some part in the Ukraine somewhere and they were then moved into Italy, they were fighting against the Italian partisans who were most definitely part of the British attack in Italy.'

'So you now say. If I am able to establish that not even that is so, will you accept it?'

'No, not until I have heard it,' Lord Aldington said. 'I am not going to answer a hypothetical question.'

'Let me return to General Shkuro himself–'

'Does it matter, if I may say so?'

'*Does it matter*?' repeated Rampton, aghast. 'General Shkuro, a 76-year-old human being–'

At that point Rampton gave up and turned to other aspects of the Cossack story. But he got no further there. Did Lord Aldington know about the presence of the émigré Generals in 5 Corps immediately after the surrender? No. But had he not written in the draft of his Winchester speech, 'Amongst [the Cossacks] were officers who belonged to what has become known as the White Russian community, many of them living in France and other parts of Western Europe. Some of these were distinguished—and the word "distinguished" is crossed out—people who were wanted by the Soviet Russians'? Yes, Lord Aldington did remember that. Then why had he crossed out the word 'distinguished'? That was something Lord Aldington could not remember. Did he remember Brigadier Tryon-Wilson's trip to Voitsberg on 11 May (when he was given the list of wanted men by the Soviets)? No. Did he remember the list? No. Did he remember it being discussed at the time? No. Did he remember, as he told Tolstoy at Sandhurst, that Arbuthnott had warned him that if the Cossacks were handed over they would all be shot? No, he may have remembered that in 1985, but he did not remember it now. Could the Plaintiff explain, having a military background, what the words 'operational manner' meant in connection with a document at the time? No, he could not: he could tell the Court what he now thought it meant but not what he thought at the time as he had not seen the document in question at the time.

Moving back to the issue of screening the non-Soviet from the Soviet citizens amongst the Cossacks, Lord Aldington was equally obtuse. He had a duty to return Soviet nationals, but no-one told him *not* to return non-Soviet nationals. Asked if he should have ordered that the Cossacks be screened into Soviet nationals and non-Soviet nationals, he replied: 'I do not recognise that I had any such duty. I had a duty to see that Soviet nationals were repatriated. That was my duty.'

By the time Rampton got onto the issue of the signal 5 Corps sent to 8th Army on the night of Macmillan's visit to Klagenfurt and which Brigadier Low either composed or helped compose, depending on whether Lord Aldington's 1985 or 1989 version is accepted, the Plaintiff clearly felt that he had Rampton beaten: he no longer needed to give answers that were even logical. The signal says of the Cossacks, it will be remembered, 'can't see any point in keeping this large number Soviet nationals'.

'This suggests,' Rampton said, 'that all the Cossacks were Soviet nationals. You now tell us that to your knowledge only some of them or the majority of them were. That is right, is it not?'

'It certainly does not suggest anything of the sort.'

'"This large number Soviet nationals"?'

'There *were* a large number of Soviet nationals,' Lord Aldington said.

'"This large number... Cossacks should be returned to Soviets at once",' Rampton repeated. 'I am sorry, I simply do not understand.'

'I suppose you do not understand it because you do not understand that in the Army we were in the habit of obeying orders. We had an order then which defined what a Soviet national was. At that time the order was a little ambiguous, but the only people in this sort of formation who were most definitely not Soviet nationals, were those who came from areas to the west of the 1939 border. I cannot tell you how many of those there were, but it was known in divisions—that order was known in divisions. As they began looking around they obviously raised some questions with me. That is why—and we are now going on to the 21st order—I had the conference and gave some rulings. That is that. Those words really do not mean what you say they mean. They do not say that all Cossacks are Soviet nationals.'

Rampton suggested that the 5 Corps description of the Cossacks as all being Soviet nationals might have been what prompted Robertson to order that "all Russians" be handed to the Soviets. Was that not the case?

'I do not know,' Lord Aldington replied. 'I was not in General Robertson's mind.'

If the Army was in the habit of obeying orders, Rampton asked, and the orders were to screen Soviets from non-Soviets, would not most people understand the wording of the Definition Order—"following groups will be treated as Soviet nationals"—to imply that the groups referred to had all been screened?

Lord Aldington replied by saying that if his order had not been in accordance with 8th Army instructions, McCreery would have objected. The fact that he did not, meant that everything was approved. Since this argument depended on the assumption that 8th Army had not been deceived by 5 Corps' description of the Cossacks as being all Soviet nationals, Rampton pressed the point.

'I wonder about that,' he said. 'Would it not have meant to 8th Army, to whom a copy of this Definition was sent, what they had been told on the 14th May, that these people were Soviet nationals? "Cannot see any point in keeping this large number of Soviet nationals."'

'Mr Rampton, you do go on and on. A "large number of Soviet nationals": there most certainly *was* a large number of Soviet nationals in the Cossacks.'

There was only one occasion, when a group of 60 Cossacks officers was reprieved, that the "individuals" part of Low's Definition Order was applied. Lord Aldington pointed to this as an example of how screening worked in practice, but when Rampton said, fine, we'll look at it then, Lord Aldington replied, 'I do not see why we need to.' His embarrassment was obvious because there were thousands of non-Soviets amongst both Cossack groups and to save 60 did not show an impressive screening record. Not only that, this group was saved by accident and as a result of a very resolute protest by the Cossacks concerned, who asked to be shot on the spot and would not move into the British trucks under any provocation.

This was dangerous territory for the Plaintiff. Suddenly the Judge called the afternoon adjournment. Nicolson noted in his diary, 'I overhear Rampton say to Gray, "If this goes on we'll find ourselves in the Court of Appeal." Gray calls Rampton "Richard".'

After tea, Rampton asked Lord Aldington why he had not reflected the spirit of the 8th Army order of 13 March in the Definition Order—in other words, why was the order to screen disregarded. The Plaintiff replied that 5 Corps had 'time constraints'. He went on: 'The purpose of their going back [was] to clear the decks, get them out of our area. In those circumstances this kind of adjudication and thorough screening simply was not possible nor even entertained by anybody.'

'What need was there at that stage to clear the decks?' Rampton asked.

'That is a judgment to be made by Field Marshal Alexander, who gave us the order. I thought we had been over this problem yesterday. It is not for us to overrule the orders of the Army Commander or the theatre Supreme Commander. That is a judgment for him, and I would not be so impertinent as to say: "Well, the answer to your question is..." You must put it to somebody who can give evidence of what Field Marshal Alexander thought at the time.'

In fact, there was ample evidence of what Alexander thought, namely that the Cossacks should be sent north to SHAEF, as he had arranged with Eisenhower. The point on which there was no evidence in Court was why that plan had failed and who was responsible for its failure. The answer to that lay amongst the documents within FO 1020/42 which Lord Aldington had chosen not to submit as part of his evidence. With the file held in the Foreign Office, the Defence could not tell its side of the story.

Since Lord Aldington's case was so firmly based on the proposition that Alexander had intended 'clear the decks' to mean 'hand over to the Soviets', it is important to be clear just how much evidence there is in FO 1020/42 to the contrary. Lord Aldington submitted thirty-five of the 142 documents in FO 1020/42 for inclusion in the Court bundles. These are some of the ones he omitted: (numbers indicate the file index numbers within FO 1020/42; for the full list, see Appendix A)

- *#123: 21 May, 0930 hrs—15th Army Group to 8th Army:* Copying a SHAEF message to 12th Army Group saying: make ready to move south into 5 Corps area and evacuate Cossacks.

- *#129 21 May, 1415 hrs—12th Army Group to 15th Army Group, copied to 8th Army and to 5 Corps:* Reports plans already made for an initial reconnaissance into Carinthia by SHAEF troops. The formations, routes and tasks are detailed, one of which is removing the 150,000 prisoners of war, as part of which were 45,000 Cossacks, including 11,000 women, children and old men, to SHAEF.

- *#125 21 May 2250 hrs—8th Army to 15th Army Group:* 5 Corps report the arrival of 800 vehicles, but asking that the main bodies do not move yet. 5 Corps refuse to hand over until the position has been 'clarified'.

- *#126 21 May 2340 hrs—15th Army Group to 8th Army:* Operation Coldstream is triggered, including the move south by SHAEF troops and the removal of the Cossacks.

- *#131   22 May, 1645 hrs—5 Corps to 20 US Corps (part of the SHAEF forces):* Do not move your main bodies south yet, only reconnaissance parties. 5 Corps say they understand 'higher authority' is planning a delay. With regard to the Cossacks, 5 Corps is awaiting orders from 8th Army.
- *#134   22 May, 2130 hrs—15th Army Group to 12th Army Group:* Clark signals Bradley to the effect that he has just visited McCreery at 8th Army who, since receiving 5 Corps' messages, wants to slow down the move south, on account of 'congestion'.

These signals should be taken together with one other which was also unavailable to Watts and Tolstoy, being held within the Ministry of Defence. At 1715 hrs on 22 May, between #131 and #134 above, 5 Corps sent a message to 8th Army saying, 'Do NOT now consider it necessary to be relieved up to boundary suggested... as situation in Lienz now in hand and can be organised by one unit.' (emphasis in original) This was in the 8th Army war diary which had been in the Ministry of Defence from January to September 1989. It was not in Court, even though it is headed: 'Confirmed conversation, Chief of Staff - BGS'

It is clear from all this that it was 5 Corps which sabotaged Alexander's plan, and it is equally clear that whoever was BGS at 5 Corps on the afternoon of 22 May was the person who played the principal role in that act of insubordination. With the Defence prevented from using this material, the jury were kept in complete ignorance of these critical facts.

Nonetheless there were a few documents from FO 1020/42 not entirely favourable to the Defence which were in Court. These were ones which had been quoted by Tolstoy in *The Minister and the Massacres* and so were public knowledge. The most dangerous for Lord Aldington was the signal which Eisenhower sent to the Combined Chiefs of Staff in Washington and the British Chiefs of Staff in London in which he described how the move was to be made. But the most important fact about this signal was a manuscript addition in the top right-hand corner which said, '*Copy sent to 5 Corps by G(Ops)*'. The signal was sent to AFHQ on 19 May and forwarded to 5 Corps on 21 May.[5] This was potentially a very serious point for the Plaintiff as it clearly showed that,

---

5   This is another signal which should appear in the 5 Corps war diary but which has disappeared.

before he left Klagenfurt, 5 Corps was simultaneously being informed of Alexander's plans and, for the first time, was moving to try to frustrate them. The signal read as follows:

> [SHAEF] understand the enemy personnel urgently required to be moved into 12 Army Group area consist of a maximum of 150,000 surrendered enemy of which approximately 105,000 are Germans not repeat not yet totally disarmed and 45,000 are Cossacks still fully armed... The Cossacks may be expected to move more or less as organised bodies intact... In order further to assist any possible operations by AFHQ Forces in Austria against Jugoslavs, we [SHAEF] are willing to accept the enemy personnel mentioned above in the status of "disarmed enemy forces".

Presented with this signal, Lord Aldington responded by making detailed queries about irrelevant issues. When asked whether he would not deny that 5 Corps had seen this signal, Lord Aldington avoided answering. Instead he questioned the signal's provenance: he could not comment on it until he knew which file it came from.

'What I do not know is the provenance of this signal,' Lord Aldington said, moving the discussion away from the date Rampton had just asked about. 'It has no War Office file number on it. I don't know which copy this is, whose it is, whether it is 8th Army's copy or what.'

'If it is of importance,' Rampton said, 'I believe it is a Foreign Office document. One copy I have is marked FO 1020/42.'

'I can't at the moment say whether that is General McCreery's files in Austria, in the High Commission or where,' Lord Aldington replied, pretending to a complete lack of familiarity with FO 1020/42, from which he had submitted nine documents just three months earlier.

Lord Aldington also questioned the instructions at the top of the signal, which said it was for 'Action AFHQ ... 8th Army.' 'It couldn't be action 8th Army,' he said, 'because it is from SHAEF, and 8th Army didn't accept orders from SHAEF... This is a very odd copy, this is what worries me, it is not the original.'

Without the rest of the file being available, in particular the signals quoted above, Rampton could not press Lord Aldington on the most important issue arising: why was it that the Field Marshal's orders were never implemented? Out of context the signal above looked like an inexplicable anomaly. Rampton tried simply asking what happened next. Lord Aldington did not help him. The danger passed.

Nicolson's comment that evening was, 'Dull day; Rampton tiring. Toby standing up well and making a good impression on the jury.'

There was one further crisis to come, though, before Lord Aldington stepped down from the witness box. That concerned his date of departure from 5 Corps. At issue was his participation in the "shoot the Cossacks" conference on 22 May, otherwise known as the Corps Commander's conference. The Plaintiff had a difficulty in that, before the writ had been issued and he had revised that date, he had written to Brigadier de Fonblanque saying that he thought he *had* been at the conference. Lord Aldington explained that his memory then was wrong: 'At that time I thought I had attended because at that time I thought I had left the Corps Headquarters on the 25th and *it would have been inconceivable for me as BGS not to have been at the conference.*'(emphasis added) He had written in the same sense to Brigadier Tryon-Wilson on another occasion. He had also told Tolstoy at Sandhurst that he thought he had attended. Now he knew differently, although he readily conceded there was no evidence for his new knowledge beyond his own memory. Since he was arguing that his memory was unreliable, it was brazen of him to ask the jury to take its current state as being reliable.

'There is no document which tells us that you left 5 Corps on the 22nd,' Rampton said.

'Absolutely right. There is no document which tells you that I flew from Klagenfurt first at 9 and then at 10.30. No, there is no document. You rely upon my memory.'

'Correct. We rely upon your evidence to that effect, your oral evidence in this Court.'

'Yes, and the oral evidence, as I have told you, is based upon my memory, and I shall hope to persuade everybody. I hope they will believe I am telling the truth about my memory, but I hope to persuade everybody that my memory is correct.'

'We will come to that, because that, of course, is what it depends on, whether the evidence you have given on this topic is accurate or not, to use a neutral word. I say that without any sarcastic note in my voice.'

Rampton was moving slowly towards the production of the Eden diary evidence. But he had another high card to play first: meteorological evidence which Tolstoy had uncovered. Rampton reminded Aldington of what he had said to Gray about the weather on the day he flew south. 'Lord Aldington, you told us on the fourth day of this trial that it was a clear day. You mean it was a clear morning?'

'Yes.'

'That was your impression. It was an occasion which has stuck in your mind?'

'That's what I remember. Are you going to tell me I was quite wrong?'

'Yes, I think I am. Would you turn to page 166 of bundle C. It is the last document in bundle C, and it is the operations record book kept at Klagenfurt airfield.'

Lord Aldington read out the entry for 22 May with evident surprise. 'It says it was raining all day.'

'Yes, it does: "Klagenfurt, 22.5.45."'

'It could have been raining all day except the time when I took off, couldn't it? That's all I remember.'

'You see it about a third of the way down,' the Judge added. '"22nd, eight American aircraft nightstopped, crews' accommodation in marquee. Rain all day".'

Lord Aldington continued reading: 'The next day was: "Heavy rain all day, airfield unserviceable." Good gracious.'

This was the first time the Plaintiff had given the impression that the evidence he now had before him confounded his argument. It was a moment of gigantic opportunity for Rampton. He had ten minutes to go until the Court rose for the day. He wanted to press his advantage before the Plaintiff had time to consider this line of argument and evolve the defence he clearly did not yet have. He had timed his attack perfectly.

Then the Judge intervened. He said he was suspending the proceedings ten minutes early to settle some procedural matters. Lord Aldington now had until the morning to think about this new evidence. The importance of the issue had already been emphasised by the Judge himself, who had said earlier in the trial that, in his opinion, 'the date of Lord Aldington's departure from 5 Corps is to put it at its lowest, a very, very critical part of the evidence in this case.'

It was at this point in the trial that Georgina Tolstoy, who had been in Court almost every day, first thought that the Defendants were likely to lose. On a bench outside the Courtroom, she was approached by a solicitor from Rubinstein Callingham.

'I was sitting there,' she remembers, 'and I just said to him, "Simon, we have just lost." I was almost crying and he said, "Why on earth did you say that?" I said, "Rampton had the best opportunity of the trial and

he couldn't make any use of it. There is no doubt about it, we have lost."
He said, "Oh no, come on, come on," and I said, "Well, I am just going
to get in there and stand up and tell that Judge what I think of him." He
said, "Oh you won't." I said, "No, you're right. I'm far too English. I
won't.""

The final day of Lord Aldington's cross-examination was Friday 13
October, the last day of the PRO's annual stock-taking closure fortnight.
Rampton began by reminding the witness of his evidence of blue skies on
the day he flew south, then quoted several eye-witnesses' diaries. Jane
Balding, a Red Cross nurse, wrote of 22 May, 'Very cold and pelting rain.'
Dennis Conolly, a Friends Ambulance Service officer, wrote in his diary,
'Rain and wind, cold.'

'Lord Aldington,' Rampton said, 'it is clear, is it not, that from
Klagenfurt in the middle or east to Villach in the west, Tuesday the 22nd
was a cold, wet and windy day? A depression had settled over the whole
area. It is clear, is it not?'

'Well, yes, it's clear from there. It's clear from my memory—and
this is what I want to say—my memory tells me how bright it was over
the top of the Karavanken. There is nothing inconsistent with having rain
on the ground and bright sky well up, and everybody knows that who's
flown in an aeroplane. That's what my memory tells me. Everyone
knows, don't they—I don't have to get a meteorological expert to prove
that—that if there is rain on the ground and you're in an aeroplane when
you go up in the air you ordinarily get through and into the sunny uplands.'

'That, Lord Aldington, may be so if the cloud cover is low and thick.
If, however, as very often happens, the reason why it is raining all over
the adjacent countryside is that the clouds have banked up over the
mountains?'

'Well, you don't know that, do you, nor do I. All I can tell you, quite
honestly, is what I remember about these things, and I remember this
incident very, very clearly.'

'Lord Aldington, may I put it like this: would you agree with me that
one very likely explanation of your account in relation to these contemporaneous accounts of the weather on that day is this, is it not: that if it
was the bright clear day that you remember on the morning of 22nd May,
then that day which you remember so clearly was not the 22nd May at all,
but some other day?'

'Well, it is a possibility, and of course I've thought of that, but, as
I've told you on a number of occasions—I don't think you've believed a

word I've said—but I've told you that over two and three-quarter years I've done my best to reconstruct my memory and to try and avoid—I think I used this phrase in answer to Mr Gray—getting anything wrong. I didn't want to mislead the Court here, and I remember this very, very clearly.'

Rampton moved on to the lack of evidence for Lord Aldington's version of events. 'There are no documents recording your presence in Naples on the evening of 22nd May, the day of the 23rd or the evening of the 23rd?'

'Absolutely, and my memory, to be quite clear, Mr Rampton, so that you understand the way my memory works, does not say that when I arrived in Naples I saw a calendar which said 22nd May. My memory does not say that. My memory says that I left Klagenfurt as I have told you, and there was this incident over the Karavanken. I arrived at Naples. I did not get on the plane until the day after next. I, therefore, had to spend two nights in Naples and I took a plane the day after. The documents show that the day after was the 24th, so on that basis I have reconstructed my memory to say why it was the 22nd. Now, that's what I say and there's nothing that anybody has shown me—because I've been trying to check up, my legal advisers have been trying to check up, for two and a half years.'

After further coming and going, Rampton moved finally onto the new evidence of the Eden diaries. He started by reading through all the entries until he came to Saturday 9 June, when 'Toby arrived in time for luncheon' (at Eden's home at Binderton, in Sussex). That was the first mention of the candidate for Blackpool North in the diary. There was no mention of any dinners on 25 or 26 May. Lord Aldington replied that Eden was a busy man and would not necessarily have recorded every encounter in what was, anyway, not an official engagement book but 'very much a sensitive, feeling diary'. He said they must have met before 9 June, otherwise how could the visit to Sussex have been arranged? 'Well,' Rampton replied, 'there is a telephone, is there not, even in 1945?' But that would have required preliminary contact, Aldington said rather weakly, implying that he would have had to meet Eden in order to make arrangements to telephone him in order to arrange a meeting.

'Well, that is what you tell us,' Rampton said, sceptically.

'Well, why should I not tell the truth? You sneer at everything I say.'

'I do not sneer. The contemporaneous document shows no sign of you before the 9th June and that is why I challenge your answers.'

'Yes, because you do not understand people writing their personal diaries which you have used for your own purposes here. It is ridiculous to say that this diary proves that I did not see him, and I am surprised that you should even venture to suggest such a thing.'

But Lord Aldington was clearly rattled by this. Rampton pressed on: 'You told us that the way you reconstruct your memory is by reference to documents; and if you pore over them long enough then things come flooding back?'

'I have told you that was not the only way,' Lord Aldington replied. 'I have told you there were events and I was asked about some of them, the vodka incident, the Karavanken incident, the return to London, seeing my mother, then going round to the Foreign Secretary and deciding whether I was going to alter the whole career of my life and go into politics. Those sort of events stick in anyone's mind. The dates may not be right. That I quite see, and I have always said I have to reconstruct dates from documents.'

'Lord Aldington, I put it to you that there is another way of looking at the way you deal with documents, the relationship between the documents and dates. This is the point at which I put my case so far as the credibility of your evidence is concerned: the evidence you have given on this topic is not true. This is a point at which you and I, if we are not careful, are going to get cross with each other–'

'It will be about the hundredth time you will say what I say is a lie, and it is the hundredth time you make me very angry.'

'Perhaps we could get that out of the way first, as it would be better for everybody. First of all, the date you say you left Austria is 22nd May. Until the pamphlet is published in March, 1987 and until you start researching the documents consequent upon receiving that pamphlet or learning about it, the dates you have consistently given are 25th, 26th May?'

'Yes.'

'Is this right, that upon researching the documents and reading the pamphlet, you realised that it is essential that you should not be found in Austria during the 22nd, 23rd, 24th May?'

'That is not the way my mind works, Mr Rampton. It was essential to get the right date because the date suddenly becomes important. It was not important before for reasons I explained to you. It suddenly becomes important when charges against me are pushed to this length. So, I have to bestir myself and find out the date and the proof of it and as I understand, despite all you have said this morning about lies, you now accept that I left the Central Mediterranean Force on 24th and reached London on 24th.'

'You cannot have left Austria before the 21st because we have seen a document with your signature on it,' Rampton said.

'On the 21st, that is correct. I have never said—may I repeat what I have said consistently. I have said that it took, in my recollection, two days from the time when I left Klagenfurt to the time when I left Naples. I said I had to find out when it was that I left Naples. I found out when I left Naples, and so it follows I left Klagenfurt on the 22nd and, for reasons we have not gone into today, I can prove to you I was not present at the Corps Commander's conference on the 22nd; and if I had been in Austria at that time, I most certainly would have been. That is the way I have constructed those dates. I have not tried to invent false dates in order to counter these outrageous charges, I have tried to counter these outrageous charges all over the period and I said to you yesterday, even if I was in the place for the next three days, I would still challenge and refute altogether the gross libel against me that I am a war criminal.'

'You see, you have expressed it yourself, that is exactly what I do say, that you do invent dates in order to suit the story. When challenged by incontrovertible evidence such as the Eden diaries, you change the story. Between 19th September, 1989 and let us say today in Court, the story has been changed. A full account of dinner with Mr Eden on the 25th and again on the 26th and the reasons for it?'

'Well, I have told you that my memory told me, because it was quite a significant thing, that I saw Mr Eden on the 25th, the day after I got back and that I had dinner with him twice. What I do remember and I was wrong in thinking, I had no documents to help me, that I dined with him on the 25th. It is clear that I was wrong. I apologise for that but it is a lapse of memory. It does not seem to me to alter the date on which I arrived in England, and I do not imagine you are saying the Army records have been falsified also?'

'No, in the Army records, Lord Aldington, there is a gap identifying you one way or the other between 21st May when you signed the definition about the Soviet nationals and the document which shows you left CMF on 24th. On their face, the military documents are silent about where you were, what you were doing and all we have to fill that gap is your account. Do you follow me?'

'Because you are a suspicious guy, you never believe what anybody says, ever.'

'It is important you understand—'

'I do understand,' Aldington interrupted.

'I do not want it said later that I have not put it to you—'

'You have put it a hundred and fifty times.'

'If the jury should conclude that it is the fact that the dinners with Mr Eden were an invention to give colour to your account, if they should conclude that, that casts a certain light, do you not agree, upon the account of the time when you left Austria?'

Suddenly the Judge intervened once again. 'I think I know the answer, but is there any dispute—and I am thinking of the Pleadings—that by 24th or on 24th, Lord Aldington arrived back in England?'

'No, none at all,' Rampton said, trying to conceal his fury. 'There cannot be in the light of the documents.'

'That is what I thought,' the Judge said.

Lord Aldington continued, 'What we have been talking about now, as I understand it, is proof that I am always a liar because I lied about some dinners with Mr Eden. That is as I understand that. I have told you that immediately I saw these documents which were introduced late after I completed my story, immediately I saw these documents I accepted that my memory was wrong. I told you it was memory and we all know we have fallible memories. I told you that and I told you that the memory of my journey back from Klagenfurt to Naples was based on this great incident over the Karavanken, was based on my recollection of two nights in Naples, on the documents that showed I left Naples on the 24th and based on the documents which showed (*sic*) that I was not at a Corps Commander's Conference on the 22nd. That is how I reconstruct my memory on that occasion.'

'Thank you.'

Nicolson noted about this exchange, 'Toby gets into one of his simulated rages.' Since the trial, there has been controversy about the words: 'I am always a liar because I lied about some dinners with Mr Eden.' Did they amount to an admission by the Plaintiff that he had lied to the Court? This became a key issue in the Appeal Court when one of the Judges said he considered 'Lord Aldington's veracity' to have been the basic question in this trial.

Nonetheless, Rampton had finished. The old soldier had survived his self-imposed ordeal. After a brief re-examination by Gray, he was able to descend from the witness box and limp across the well of the Court to be comforted by his wife and daughter.

14

LORD ALDINGTON'S WITNESSES

IN THE LIGHT of the abrupt way in which he was later to prevent Tolstoy's witnesses from digressing from the precise subject at issue, it is worth noting how much latitude Mr Justice Davies gave Lord Aldington's witnesses, most particularly the first one, Brigadier Tryon-Wilson. Tryon-Wilson started his evidence with a long description of how he won a DSO at the battle of Monte Cassino. The crossroads were heavily mined... troops in the citadel could only be supplied by mule train... the Germans shelled the road every night, sometimes five shells would fall, sometimes fifty... 400 troops on 100 mules were stuck because of the shelling... Tryon-Wilson listened to the fall of shot, decided there was a pattern to it and trotted the mules across the danger zone in groups of ten, in between the salvos. However praiseworthy, none of this had anything remotely to do with the matters at issue.

The next subject he was invited to address the Court on, the Cowgill committee, had almost as little relevance.

'Brigadier Cowgill,' Tryon-Wilson said, 'had apparently felt pretty unhappy about the allegations that had been made, not only against individuals but against the British Army and he rang me up one day, I think it was in Scotland and he called in and stayed the night and talked it over with me and said would I like to join him in looking into this matter—'

Unable to listen to this irrelevance any longer, Rampton stood up. 'I apologise, Brigadier.' Turning to the Judge he said, 'I can see the relevance of Brigadier Tryon-Wilson's involvement in the research that was done for that report but I see no relevance in the reasons why the body was formed or what, in due course, it might have said.'

The Judge had to agree with Rampton, but said to the witness, 'Your research is obviously worth mentioning to us because it shows you were not just looking back on your memory of 1945 without having taken part in research.'

But Rampton could not accept that either. A witness is expected to tell what he knows of an incident, not what he has learnt at second-hand by research. The courts have a precise role for such people, who are called "expert witnesses". They are allowed to venture opinions about matters. Dr Knight was to be Lord Aldington's "expert", so Tryon-Wilson should have been confined to matters of relevance of which he had personal knowledge. Once again, the Judge was compelled to agree with Rampton, but it seemed to make little difference to the latitude Tryon-Wilson was actually given.

Nicolson's impression of Tryon-Wilson was of 'a spare, elderly man, with a certain dignity, wishing to please Toby'. In the main Tryon-Wilson repeated the conclusions which Cowgill had reached in the *Interim Report*. However, he seems to have learned very little about the history of the forced repatriations during his time on the committee. At one stage in the witness box, he confessed he did not know whether the Isonzo river flows through Carinthia. Since Tito's claim in Italy was 'all land east of the Isonzo', this was an extraordinary lapse for a member of a committee which was going to set history to rights.

Why was this old man in Court? The answer came when the subject of camp-followers was raised. Since not even the Robertson Order, Aldington's main plank in defence of his own two orders, mentioned civilians—arguably it specifically excluded them—it was important to establish that no distinction is normally made by the British Army between "enemy" soldiers and civilians in cases like this one. Tryon-Wilson mentioned his service in the Army in India and ran through the categories of people, bearers, cleaners, cooks, who were considered "camp followers".

'That was in India,' Mr Justice Davies said, taking over the examination from Gray. 'In Jugoslavia was there an additional group of people in camp followers other than helpers?'

'Yes,' Tryon-Wilson answered, 'apparently there was.'

'Well, I think we have heard from Lord Aldington, perhaps you would

like to tell us as well. Tell us yourself what other types of person apart
from helpers and so on, aides, they had?'

'Well, they had wives, but they did not come under the heading, as I
understood it, of normal civilians because they were part of the unit. They
were certainly looked after and maintained by the unit. They were not
maintained by civilians or true civilian organisations.'

'Maintained by the army?' the Judge asked.

'Yes,' Tryon-Wilson answered.

'In which the husbands were serving?' the Judge asked.

'Yes, my Lord.'

In cross-examination by Rampton, Tryon-Wilson expanded his definition of "camp followers" to the point where the distinction between
combatants and non-combatants was completely lost. He remembered all
sorts of surprising categories of people who could be classified as camp
followers, including priests, a category specifically excluded by both the
Geneva Convention and the British Manual of Military Law.

Rampton was handicapped in his questioning by the poor quality of
Tryon-Wilson's memory about certain things. He remembered nothing
of the civilians in Viktring camp. How was the camp organised? Rampton
asked. 'I know nothing about that I am afraid.' Did the witness know
that the Jugoslavs in Viktring were divided into a civilian and a military
camp and that the majority of the civilians were Slovenes? 'I don't
honestly remember,' Tryon-Wilson said. 'I'm here on oath and I don't
remember that.' Was it right that the military camp was administered by
5 Corps under a Lieutenant Haines? 'You may be right. I don't remember.' And was the civilian camp administered by the Allied Military
Government under Major Johnson? 'If that is what you say, yes.'

By contrast, Tryon-Wilson's memory for a couple of matters directly
connected with the charges against the Plaintiff was very clear indeed. He
was 'absolutely sure' that Low had *not* attended the "shoot the Cossacks"
conference on 22 May. He had realised instantly, when shown the signal
for the first time a few years previously, that the controversial 'As a result
of verbal directive Macmillan' signal of 23 May, in which permission was
requested for the use of force against the Cossacks, could not have been
composed by Brigadier Low as it was not the sort of phraseology Low
would have used. (On 13 May, Low had helped draft a signal which
started 'On advice Macmillan'.) Tryon-Wilson also said he could 'honestly' not remember hearing, before 24 May, that returned Jugoslavs were
being 'shot, massacred or tortured'.

When it came to the identity of the people on the list he had brought back from the Soviets on 11 May 1945, Tryon-Wilson's memory once again failed. Although he had told Tolstoy in 1985 that he remembered Shkuro's name being on the list—'the old boy with the CB'—Tryon-Wilson now realised that that had been a false memory. In 1985 he had not realised that what he was "remembering" for Tolstoy's benefit was only something someone had subsequently told him, although he could not now remember what that might have been.

Rampton produced evidence that subordinate formations knew that Yalta was to be ignored in the forthcoming handovers. The war diary of 2nd Battalion of the Lancashire Fusiliers, part of 36th Infantry Brigade, for example, recorded that the Soviets 'were particularly keen on the return of the officers, many of whom were Tsarist émigrés.' If such junior officers knew all that, Rampton asked the witness, why was it that someone as senior as Tryon-Wilson was so ignorant? Because, Tryon-Wilson said, those people were dealing with the matter directly. At Corps headquarters, the senior officers would not necessarily have known what the inferior formations knew. Tryon-Wilson did admit that General Keightley might have known too. But as for himself, he remembered quite clearly that he had not known.

Tryon-Wilson went on to tell the Court that, personally, he liked the Cossacks. He had known about them in the First World War and felt that 'they were a jolly fine crowd of outfits.' He did, in 1945, know that they had committed 'crimes', and, slightly to the detriment of Lord Aldington's argument that the Cossacks were a nuisance, said, 'They were no problem at all.' But he knew, he said, from the Robertson Order that they all had to 'go back'. Nonetheless, as a 'a caring officer', he had made a protest, though in the feeblest imaginable terms: 'If it was possible at all,' he told the Court he said, 'it would be very nice if the Cossacks did not have to go back.'

Tryon-Wilson was firm on one point: that the handovers were necessary 'to carry out General Alex's instructions which were to clear the area because he had given instructions that we should be ready to fight [the Titoists] by 1st June.' In fact, every statement in that sentence is wrong, as the presence of FO 1020/42 in Court would have shown. The 'clear the decks' plan involved *saving* the Cossacks and Jugoslavs from their enemies by moving them, respectively, north into SHAEF and south into Italy. Neither was there any operational plan which called for preparations to attack anybody on 1 June—Brigadier Low, it will be remembered, had cancelled 5 Corps' plan to eject the Titoists from Carinthia, Operation Beehive, on 20 May. After the success of General Clark's push on Trieste on 22 May, there were no more plans developed anywhere to fight Tito.

Tryon-Wilson was asked why the Alexander-Eisenhower plan failed. 'What I do not follow and have never followed,' Rampton said, 'and perhaps you can help us, is this: it being the case that Eisenhower had agreed to accept all the 45,000 Cossacks into the American zone, what was the pressing need to hand over Jugoslavs and Cossacks to their enemies, the Communists, from 22nd or 23rd May?'[1]

'Quite frankly, at this time I can't tell you, and I'm not hedging that question in any way at all.'

Despite this unambiguous assertion, made on oath in October 1989, Tryon-Wilson had a full understanding of why the Alexander-Eisenhower plan failed in April 1990 when he recorded his memories of the handovers for the Imperial War Museum Sound Archives. As mentioned above (p. 51), he told the researcher that it was Brigadier Low who, 'at the *moment critique*, decided that he didn't want [the American] help.' This version is corroborated by the FO 1020/42 documents kept from the Court and is the diametrical opposite of Lord Aldington's case in 1989.

If Tryon-Wilson is right in accusing Brigadier Low of frustrating the Alexander-Eisenhower plan to save the Cossacks, this might explain the fact that Lord Aldington has prevented the tape he made for the War Museum at about the same time to be made public. Recently, he justified his decision to embargo his own words in these revealing terms: 'I do not want to complicate affairs by having on record for the public any statements different from those I made on oath in the courts.'[2]

Lord Aldington's second witness was an Old Wykehamist friend, General Sir James Wilson. Nicolson described him as 'cheery, rubicund'. He was not able to add much to the historical evidence as he had been only a 'very

---

1   This was the only document in FO 1020/42 which Tolstoy had copied in 1985 which related to the Alexander-Eisenhower plan to save the Cossacks. He had submitted it to Court. Lord Aldington had not submitted any of the others, which was why Rampton could not go any further with this absolutely central line of questioning. See also Appendix A.

2   Letter to the War Museum, 26 August 1993. Subsequently he has had the tapes embargoed until his death. They have even been removed from the War Museum Sound Archive's Index, though they are still within the building.

junior Company Commander' at the time. His only significant contribution was to say that he thought Keightley an ambitious and unlikeable man, neither trusted by many of his subordinates nor interested in them. 'Likely to jump at a chance to ingratiate himself with an influential superior,' was the note Tolstoy had made of their interview. Sir James did not resile from this in Court.

Another old friend of Lord Aldington's now took the witness stand, Sir Charles Villiers. As he did so, Nicolson whispered to Tolstoy, 'He beat me when I was at Eton.' Villiers made the worst possible impression on the Court. He swaggered up to the witness stand and treated the proceedings as a monstrous intrusion on his valuable time. That week he was, he said, hosting a conference for young entrepreneurs in Brighton, so Mr Justice Davies allowed him to break his testimony into two parts separated by several days.

When Villiers 'condescended' to return to Court—the word was used by the Judge—his answers were brief and uninformative to the point of rudeness, particularly under cross-examination by Rampton. Did the witness know when the Allies first recognised Tito? No, Villiers 'barked' (as Nicolson put it). What sort of a government was it? He didn't know. Were there legal institutions in place capable of giving a fair trial to returning Jugoslavs who were alleged to be war criminals? 'I do not know.' Were the Titoists under Soviet influence? He had no idea. Given all the various groups in Jugoslavia, could he say whom the Titoists were engaged in combat with? The Germans. What did he know about Stalin at the time? 'I do not remember.' He had never known the difference between Slovenian Domobranci, Croat Ustache and Serbian Chetniks: 'In my mind they were all the same people who were working with the Germans.' For a member of the Special Operations Executive (SOE) who had worked for some time inside Jugoslavia, this answer was hardly believable.

Villiers was almost as rude to the Judge. As he stepped down from the stand, Mr Justice Davies said to him, 'Thank you very much for coming back, Sir Charles, and I hope it has not been unduly inconvenient.' The witness ignored him.

It is impossible to say what Villiers thought he had achieved by this boorish performance. Tolstoy dismisses the suggestion which has been made that it all might have helped the Defence by alienating the Bench. 'The Judge,' he says, 'looked like the sort of person who wished he was being beaten by Villiers as well.'

The Plaintiff's next witness was hardly more forthcoming. Finlay Lochhead had worked with Villiers as part of SOE inside Jugoslavia. 'Brisk,
grim, superior grin, ex-Managing Director of Glasgow firm,' Nicolson
noted. Lochhead had witnessed the Jugoslav handovers, acting as a
liaison officer with Tito's forces. What was his role, he was asked? 'I
presume I was an observer,' he said. He might have carried messages, he
added, but he could not remember anything about them. He remembered
no 'nastiness' at the stations, and no suicides. He saw no mistreatment of
prisoners, and no looting. He 'got on very well' with his Titoist contact.

Lochhead's time on the witness stand was remarkable only for the
single occasion on which the horrific reality of the repatriations intruded
into the proceedings. Rampton read out the Todorovic memorandum (as
used by Krek when he complained to Alexander in July 1945—see p.
69ff). In describing the deceit at the time of handover and the brutality
afterwards, Todorovic mentioned Lochhead by name, saying that he *had*
been present when looting and beating of prisoners had taken place.
Nonetheless, Lochhead denied it.

Gray responded to Rampton's cross-questioning by pointing out that
Todorovic was not British. 'As a piece of paper, [the Todorovic statement]
is worth nothing,' Gray said. 'Mr Rampton says that it comes, in some
sense, into the same category as the war documents but that is plainly not
so. Simply because it got on to a Foreign Office file at some stage does
not render it into the same category as a war diary or a record compiled
by a British officer in pursuance of his military duties.'

The Judge sympathised with Gray, saying he thought the introduction
of this evidence amounted to an attempt 'to upset the jury by going over
and over matters which it is not possible or may not be possible to connect
Lord Aldington with, but, more importantly, which incontrovertibly are
admitted. That is something I am determined to stop.'

It was beginning to become apparent that Lord Aldington's witnesses did
not make a very strong team. The next one, Mr John Shooter, did not even
pretend that his evidence was relevant. Shooter was a retired civil servant
who had read about the case in the press in late September, just before the
case opened. 'I felt that Lord Aldington perhaps would welcome a letter
of moral support,' he told the Court, 'and I wrote to him with [some
detailed material], thinking it was too peripheral to this case to be of any

use. To my surprise, I found it was of interest and I readily agreed to come along and give evidence.'

Shooter had been a junior officer in the Rifle Brigade and his only contribution was to describe conditions in Carinthia immediately after the German surrender. It was 'a melting pot'. At the end of May 1945, a week after the Plaintiff had left for England, his unit helped ferry Cossacks to Judenburg, and he witnessed some of the suicides along the way. That completed Shooter's evidence.

Lord Aldington had only one other witness who had any experience of Austria in 1945, and that was Major John Taylor, now Judge Taylor. Nicolson thought him, 'squeaky, nervous but endearing'. Unlike Shooter, he did have something to contribute on the subject of 5 Corps headquarters' activities, as he had been head of the "A" branch under Tryon-Wilson. Taylor dealt with the human side of the logistic train, from courts martial to chaplains, while the "Q" side, also under Tryon-Wilson's overall control, dealt with matériel.

Although he had not been involved with operational matters at 5 Corps, Taylor gave evidence on the military situation. The Titoists could have 'overwhelmed' 5 Corps if they had chosen to invade Carinthia, and of course, their allies, the Soviets, were menacingly close. Neither was there enough food for all the refugees who threatened to irrupt into the British occupation zone from Jugoslavia. That, in turn, impinged on the military capability because 'if you can't feed a prisoner then you need four or five more guards.'

Like Lord Aldington's other witnesses, Taylor had been entirely ignorant of the likely fate of the Jugoslavs. 'All that I heard at the time,' he said, 'was that there was a scuffle in one of the border towns in which I think one Montenegrin got killed or something of that sort. That is all.' Taylor described as 'balderdash' the idea that Lord Aldington was the only man in 5 Corps who suspected nothing untoward would befall the victims. Tito was fighting the same 'evil things' as the British were, Taylor said. He had not heard any evidence that Tito was involved in massacres. These must have been the work of 'a wicked local man'.

Taylor told the Court that 5 Corps could not have received the Distone Order, because to have obeyed it would have created 'the biggest traffic block you could imagine' on the roads back to Italy.[3] Rampton did not press him on Tryon-Wilson's claim to have supervised the transport of 70,000 Italians to Italy. With fewer than 30,000 Jugoslavs at Viktring, they could presumably have been moved without 'traffic blocks'—if, that is, the will to obey Alexander had existed at 5 Corps headquarters.

Likewise, when Rampton asked him about the plan to send the Cossacks north to SHAEF, Taylor said he could not understand how they could be got across the mountains. Here again, had the Defence been able to make use of the 8th Army war diary, they could have shown Tryon-Wilson himself making arrangements at this time for the movement north of the 105,000 Germans who, with the 45,000 Cossacks, were the object of the Alexander-Eisenhower plan to clear the decks in Carinthia. On 29 May, while the first of the Cossacks were being herded at bayonet point over the bridge at Judenburg, Tryon-Wilson sent this message to the American forces receiving the Germans (only): 'Route designated by 3 US Army ... unsuitable and blocked by snow. Possible that arrangements can be made for percentage of surrendered personnel [to be moved to] your area via Radstadt (Bruck route unserviceable).' If this file had been in Court, the Defence could have confounded Taylor while making the devastating point that in sabotaging Alexander's plan, it was only the Cossacks 5 Corps were preventing from moving north. Tryon-Wilson himself, as shown in the signal just quoted, had been making arrangements to move the 105,000 Germans. The fact that no problem was encountered with this move, casts an even harsher light on 5 Corps subversion of the Alexander-Eisenhower plan.

Nonetheless, Rampton did have the signal which gave the initial orders for the movement, since it had been quoted by Tolstoy in *The Minister and the Massacres* (p. 216) It comes from 15th Army Group (General Mark Clark) and was sent for information to 12th Army Group (General Omar Bradley) and 3rd US Army. The latter formations were those from which the units to be sent south as part of Operation Coldstream were to come. The signal was sent 'for action' to all units in northern Italy and southern Germany, including 5 Corps. It is dated 22 May, the day when the 800 vehicles arrived suddenly in 5 Corps area, apparently for the purpose of moving the Cossacks north.

For 5th Army: 150,000 surrendered enemy now in British 5 Corps sector

---

3   When Cowgill wrote a year later in the *Final Report* that 5 Corps *had* received the Distone Order, he considered Taylor's reasoning so light-weight that he did not bother to refute it.

are to be moved to United States 3rd Army sector. Route designated for movement is LIENZ—VIPITENO—INNSBRUCK. Desire arrangements for movement over portion of this route in your sector to be directly with 8th Army. 3rd US Army is dealing directly with representative 15th Army Group now at 5 Corps HQ [i.e. Colonel Gerrett] on details of movement.

For 8th Army: when details of movement worked out deal directly with 5th Army movement over portion route in that sector.

For Colonel Gerrett, 5 Corps: keep 8th Army informed plans for movement to enable prompt movement arrangements to be made with 5th Army. Include in your daily sitrep numbers moved.

'So, Judge,' Rampton said to Taylor after he had finished reading, 'would you agree that it looks as if at that stage, the 22nd May, not only had Eisenhower agreed to accept all those people, including the Cossacks, but that a route had been worked out?'

Shaken, Taylor could only gasp, 'It certainly looks like that.'

'It does, does it not?'

'Yes.'

This signal came from FO 1020/42, but with the rest of the file in the Foreign Office, Rampton could go no further.

That evening saw a dramatic development in the story of FO 1020/42. On the previous day, Monday 16 October, the PRO had re-opened after the annual stock-take. A representative of Rubinstein Callingham had visited with the urgent request that this file be made available to his firm for use at the trial. But he was refused: the file was still 'out to Department'. So the firm had contacted the Foreign Office directly. The next morning, Tuesday, an official handed over the file. But it was not the full file, it was a thin folder with a few photocopies in: the actual file, Rubinstein Callingham were told, had been unaccountably 'lost' within the Department while on loan from the PRO and this was the best they could do.

Tolstoy was aghast, but there was nothing he could do, except study the eviscerated document he had been given. Very quickly he realised that most of the photocopies he had been given were of documents *already disclosed to the Court*. In other words, everything he needed to see—all the documents which Aldington had chosen not to submit in evidence—were not there. He was immediately suspicious.

It will be seen in Appendix A that the whole of FO 1020/42 consists of 166 numbered entries, of which 25 had been removed before the file was sent to the PRO in 1984. Thus there were 141 documents (almost all of them single sheets) in it which Knight and Tolstoy had seen in 1985. Between the Plaintiff and the Defendants 43 of those had been submitted to the Court and were in the Bundles of evidence. This represented just under a third of the whole file. The Foreign Office produced photocopies of 27 documents, out of 141. Had the photocopies been made randomly you would expect just under a third of the 27 to have corresponded to those in the Bundles and just over two thirds not. Thus of the 27 papers handed to Rubinstein Callingham, chance or accident would have meant 8 should have been copies of those already in the Bundles and 19 not. In fact the proportion was so different from this it is hard to avoid the suspicion that the photocopies were deliberately selected to keep the important papers away from the Court. Instead of 8 out of 27 photocopies being documents already disclosed, it was 25 out of 27. Only two were new to the Court. Might someone have been trying to suppress what they thought, quite rightly, was some very important evidence? Given the complexity of the case, only a handful of people would have had the knowledge to have made this selection correctly; even fewer stood directly to benefit from what had been done.

Lord Aldington's last historical witness was his "expert", Dr Robert Knight. In his examination-in-chief, Gray asked one major question from a variety of different angles: were all the people at Viktring accurately describable by Robertson's phrase 'serving in German forces'? The answer he wanted—and got—was, 'Yes.' But the evidence was almost laughably unconvincing. For example, Gray produced a photograph of the Slovenian General Rupnik standing next to the German General Roessner and sought to deduce that therefore all Slovenians were Nazis. The reasoning was that as Rupnik was the pro-Axis leader of Slovenia during the war, all Slovenians were citizens of a state which supported Germany, and had all, by extension, been 'serving in German forces', including the civilians. *Ergo* Low was obeying Robertson by handing them all over to the Titoists. On that type of evidence, this argument could have been applied with equal force to the Jews in occupied Europe.

The point which Knight wanted to make was that 'in order to understand the handovers one has to put them in their historical context.' This was fair, but it was also irrelevant as Aldington's plea was not that he had acted with compassion informed by historical understanding but that he had been obeying superior orders. Knight had little else to say, and soon stepped down. Nicolson thought he 'would make a very dull lecturer'.

Lord Aldington's last two witnesses were purely personal. The first was General Richard Keightley. He testified to the effect that the Sandhurst lunch was not accurately described by Tolstoy in the Introduction to *The Minister and the Massacres*. Rampton observed that none of what Keightley said helped the Court with any of the matters in contention. This was not entirely true: Keightley's evidence corroborated the 'self-styled historian' jibe.

The final witness for the Plaintiff was his wife. Nicolson described Lady Aldington as, 'stout, in white jersey, gray hair, bright eyes, upper-class talk like calling "crying" "boo-ing"'. Tolstoy's recollection is harsher. 'She spoke,' he says, 'in an amazing caricature of what people imagine as the way in which upper-class people once spoke. It was the sort of characteristic guff you hear if you go to the wrong sort of dinner party.'

Gray started with Watts's telephone calls, quoting from the notes Lord Aldington made which were collected in Bundle E, 'Harassment'.

'Do you see: "6th August",' he said, 'I think it is 1984, "N. Watts rang," and then "10 times"? Does that jog your memory as to what was happening at about this time?'

'Well, yes, I think I said to him, "For goodness sake, keep a list." I mean, I got so bored with having to get up to answer the telephone.'

'"Get up"—you mean out of bed?'

'The telephone is actually on my side of the bed so I was getting extremely angry, as you can imagine because we have two telephones, one downstairs and one up—you know, you have to get up to answer the telephone.'

The main subject on which Lady Aldington could help the Court was the effect that the pamphlet had on her family and circle. It had none on her directly for the simple reason that she never read it. The effect she said it had on "the village" has been quoted above. Gray asked her about the effect on her husband.

'Well, to start with,' Lady Aldington said, 'I knew he had a pamphlet, and I think there were one or two—to start with I think he looked upon it as a nutcase, you know—my father had a file called "crooks, cranks and maniacs", and I think it would have gone into that—so we weren't terribly worried about it. We knew of this incident of the village, and all that.

What really, I think, made my husband extremely worried was the effect on Winchester College, that every Old Boy, which included our son and our son-in-law, and all the children's parents who were there at the time when he was Warden had all been issued with this amazing bit of paper, and I think that it worried him most dreadfully.'

'How did he feel about the copies of this pamphlet going to Members of Parliament and peers?'

'I think he was very worried. I think peers and Members of Parliament are fairly used to curious bits of paper coming through their door, and they don't probably pay all that much attention to it, but when it gets down to one's personal friends and particularly the boys at Winchester and that kind of thing–'

'Do you remember any comments being made about these charges contained in the pamphlet—comments made to you, I am talking about?'

'Nothing derogatory, no, but I don't think one does hear derogatory things about oneself, do you?'

'Now, what about the effect on your husband of these proceedings? I am talking about the trial going on for two and a half weeks?'

'Well, that has—I suppose you could call it an age thing, but he's very resilient, so I'm sure he will bob up again, but, you know, it obviously has detrimented his health and family life, you know.'

'During the period when he was being cross-examined, which went on for some time, you were with him, were you, every evening?'

'When he was being cross-examined here, now?'

'Yes?'

'Oh, Lord, yes. Yes.'

'How was he feeling during that period?'

'Well, we had tears three nights, I think, and two we didn't have tears, but I think that's his safety valve. I mean, I was brought up rather differently. I was brought up not to boo, but I think his family have got Celtic blood. I was very glad that he had a safety valve. Why not?'

That was the end of Lady Aldington's evidence. Rampton did not cross-examine her, so, for the first time, Watts stood up and addressed the Court. He had, that morning, dismissed his Counsel, Edward Garnier. For the rest of the trial he would speak for himself. Since he was a separate party to the action, he was given an opportunity to cross-examine the witness.

'Your Lordship,' Watts said, bowing to pressure from the Defence lawyers to say something to Lady Aldington, 'can I say to you right away that I have no wish to ask Lady Aldington any questions, but just to take this opportunity of saying that I very much admire Lady Aldington and everything she has said this afternoon, and I am most desperately sorry for any distress that the telephone calls, which I also have lost count of, caused Lady Aldington. I am most sorry for any distress caused to her, and very much regret that Lady Aldington got caught in the course of my altercation with her husband. I can obviously see that Lady Aldington is a wonderful wife to Lord Aldington, and I have nothing but regret for any distress that she has been caused, and I would like to offer that apology to Lady Aldington in Court, and I hope she will accept it.'

Nicolson wrote that night in his diary, 'She does not even acknowledge [Watts's] apology with a glance. Quite right too.'

The witness stepped down, and Gray stood up. 'That is the Plaintiff's case,' he said.

15

NIGEL WATTS'S EVIDENCE

WATTS'S DISMISSAL of Garnier clearly came as a shock to the Judge. The First Defendant had behaved impeccably to date and Davies gave the impression of almost having come to like him, despite his habit of appearing casually dressed in a polo-necked sweater and sporting what Tolstoy calls 'upstanding hair'. Watts's decision introduced an element of unpredictability into the proceedings. It meant that he would from now on be acting for himself as a litigant-in-person. Davies tried to dissuade him from taking that course. Litigants-in-person are much harder to manage in court being, inevitably, ignorant of the rules and customs which keep lawyers under control. Nonetheless, the fiction that the law is accessible to all, regardless of money, requires that they be tolerated. The biggest danger in a trial such as this was that Watts might inadvertently say something which so prejudiced the jury that it had to be discharged and a re-trial ordered. There is nothing so bad for a Judge's reputation as aborted trials.

'Mr Watts,' said Mr Justice Davies before the jury came into Court, 'am I to understand that you wish to dispense with the services of your Counsel?'

'Yes,' Watts replied. 'I am obliged to your Lordship.'

'I do not follow that. In my experience in other cases in which litigants have decided to do that it has usually turned out to be a complete disaster for them. So I want you to be quite sure, because if you do decide to do that then various consequences follow. You will presumably, as you say in your letter, represent yourself and of course you will be bound by all the same rules and prevented from asking the same questions, if improper or irrelevant, or giving evidence which was improper or irrelevant as you would be if represented by Counsel.'

'I quite understand.'

'In other words, in this Court if people choose not to be represented they are entitled not to be, but they play the trial by exactly the same rules. Has that been explained to you?'

'Yes, it has, and I quite understand that.'

Watts then told the Court why he had taken the decision. First, Garnier was costing the Defence several thousand pounds for every day he sat in Court saying almost nothing, and secondly, when he had spoken, while cross-examining Lord Aldington, he had done so 'inadequately'. Watts told Mr Justice Davies that Garnier had told him '"it would not have been prudent to continue that cross-examination on account of the mood of the Judge." That is no disrespect to yourself at all, your Lordship, but that is the position that prevails. I am not prepared to be represented on that basis and, therefore, whatever your Lordship says, I totally respect everything you say and I have high regard for your opinion, your Lordship, but I am sorry—'

'I am not running in the popularity stakes, Mr Watts. As long as you behave yourself, which so far you have, and play the trial according to the rules, that is all I require. You can hate me for all I am concerned.'

'I do not hate you, my Lord.'

'In most cases somebody hates the judge—usually the side that loses. But, you do understand that first of all you are bound by all that your Counsel, when representing you, has done. That cannot be undone and secondly, you will be bound by the same rules.'

'I totally accept that.'

'There is one very important matter which I hope you understand which I have made clear. You may not have been in Court. But it has been accepted by Mr Garnier, your Counsel, that this Court is determined not to allow clients to debate as to whether the Sun Alliance Insurance Company were right or wrong in rejecting your sister's claim. You understand that?'

'Well, I read the transcripts of that, your Lordship, and I can only say to you now that it is my personal view that it is unfortunate in the extreme that the issue of the Sun Alliance who are funding Lord Aldington's action, have come into this—'

'You are making wild statements and if you start saying that in front of the jury when there is no evidence of it, I shall shut you up. Lord

Aldington was not asked about that. This, fortunately, is non-reportable, but this is just the sort of thing and if you persist in front of the jury in saying things you have no business to say, I shall shut you up. Let there be no misunderstanding about that, Mr Watts. I do not want any tears—I do not mean literal tears, metaphorical tears—later on. You are not going to debate in this Court the rightness or wrongness of something the Sun Alliance did. I am only speaking firmly now because you are taking a step which seems to me to be extremely ill-advised and if you make statements such as you have just made of which there is no evidence and which are wholly irrelevant, I shall shut you up and if necessary, I shall have you removed from the Court. You have to obey my ruling. On that basis, you have every opportunity, of course, to deploy your legitimate and sensible defence as pleaded on your behalf but that is all.'

The Judge was clearly right to insist that the procedures of his Court be respected, but Watts, equally clearly, had a point about the introduction of the Sun Alliance material. In his opening speech, Gray had, in effect, accused him of trying to blackmail the Sun Alliance through Lord Aldington. It would be completely inequitable if that charge could be made but not answered, particularly as Watts's malice, or lack of it, might well become an issue for the jury, which it would do if the pamphlet were held to contain statements which were comment rather than fact. Defamatory comment is not libellous if it is "fair" and based on true facts, and, importantly, not actuated by malice. Gray's argument implied malice on Watts's part. Watts felt he had to be allowed to refute that.

'In Mr Gray's opening address, to put it mildly,' Watts said, 'he was extremely critical of my conduct, as to how I came to be raising the issues of Lord Aldington's character as the final arbiter in determining claims as head of Sun Alliance Insurance company and the person who is, as Lord Aldington has admitted in his evidence, responsible for dealing with the ethical ways of that Company. Therefore, raising the issues of whether a man of that constitution was worthy of being the final arbiter in determining such claims, I was seeking, legitimately in my submission, to raise the issue of his character.'

Watts offered to forgo his right to lead evidence on all this if Gray would withdraw his remark about blackmail. 'I would then be in a position of not having to raise these peripheral issues,' he told the Judge. 'I simply say through the offices of your Lordship's great wisdom, that if you could seek to intervene and let commonsense prevail—it is going to take an awfully long time to go through all this evidence and I am loath to do it, I am loath to exasperate you, I am loath to exasperate the jury.'

'I like things to get on,' the Judge said, 'but I am paid to sit here and if I was not doing this matter I would be trying another one. I shall not be exasperated but I think it is a great pity if unnecessary time is taken.'

It was over to Gray now. Putting on an expression which Tolstoy has called his 'Winchester prefect face', Gray replied with contemptuous brevity. He was not, he said, 'instructed to enter into some sort of bargain' with Watts. That was the end of that.

Watts had a second submission to put. This concerned his suspicion that the Sun Alliance was funding Lord Aldington. His argument was as ingenious as it was logical: could it not be, Watts suggested, that the whole issue of the Sun Alliance, and therefore Gray's formal rubbishing of him in his opening speech which Watts now wanted the opportunity to refute, was inserted by the Plaintiff only so that he could claim that this case arose directly from his dispute with the Sun Alliance? After all, if there were no connection, would not a gift of what was later disclosed to be over half a million pounds have been completely unjustifiable, if not illegal? Watts asked permission, 'as a matter of equity', to be able to lead evidence of the company's involvement by way of explaining Gray's motive for calling him a blackmailer in his opening speech.

Gray countered this, not by denying Sun Alliance involvement, but by saying that the issue of who was funding Lord Aldington did not 'go to any of the issues' in front of the jury. The Judge agreed with him and disallowed Watts's request.

With the legal arguments settled, Watts was free to address the jury. Would he be able to do better than Garnier? Certainly he had made a good impression so far. Nicolson noted in his diary, 'Watts is crazy, but in the dock he gives a better impression.' Tolstoy, on the other hand, was annoyed. Watts was rocking the legal boat which he was still hopeful might bring him a famous victory over Lord Aldington. Watts felt liberated, and, as an old High Court hand from his poaching days, wished he had never allowed himself to be persuaded to let a barrister speak for him.

At noon on the fifteenth day of the trial, the jury returned to Court to hear Watts address them. Walking back down to his seat at the front, in the well of the Court, Lord Aldington tripped and fell over. He hit the back of his head hard and lay moaning on the floor of the Court. A juryman— Georgina's 'retired colour sergeant'—leapt to his feet, swung over the rail of the jury box and, despite the fact that he had been further away from Lord Aldington than almost anyone in the room, was the first to reach him. Nicolson noted: 'Wigged QCs bent over the prostrate body and clerks rushed to him with tumblers of water while the press rushed to telephone the news. Toby gets up, bleeding head in a towel, and calling across to the reporters, "I didn't do it on purpose."'

After this flurry, Watts stood up.

'Your Lordship, ladies and gentlemen of the jury,' he said, 'I don't think there has been a case in English libel history where the Plaintiff and the Defendant are exactly bosom pals, but I would like to say right away that I regret that Lord Aldington has had this most unfortunate accident, and I hope he has a speedy recovery.'

'Thank you very much, that is very proper and good of you to say so, Mr Watts,' said the Judge.

After a few further preliminaries Watts walked up into the witness box and was sworn. He started his opening speech by describing to the Court how he got into the property business with his brother-in-law and how the Sun Alliance policy came to be taken out but not paid when Christopher Bowden died. He went on to draw attention to Lord Aldington's claim in evidence that, as Chairman of the Board of Directors of the Sun Alliance, he was responsible for 'seeing that the management is working properly in financial and ethical ways'. The way his sister's claim had been dealt with was, he felt, an example of these ethics. He replied to Gray's point that if Sue Bowden were dissatisfied with the Sun Alliance's behaviour, she should have sued the company.

'You can appreciate,' Watts said, 'that having lost a husband, having been in a situation where she had no money at all, trying to provide for a family of three children, she was not in a position when Lord Aldington made his decision, to take on an organisation such as the Sun Alliance with their vast financial strength. How could a lady in those circumstances, who had lost her husband, was shortly to lose her son, and was totally grief-stricken on account of this, be supposed, as Mr Gray suggested, to take on in a legal battle, the Sun Alliance?'

Nicolson thought Watts 'unexpectedly articulate' and that he 'put a boring, unconvincing case well.' But he also thought the jury were impatient at the insurance issue. Despite Watts's 'wide, confident gestures', they had, he thought, 'already decided he was guilty of blackmail—which he undoubtedly is.'

After lunch Watts told the jury how and when he had been given what he called 'the Layman's Penguin Guide To The Law' and how he had initiated his campaign to have the claim re-examined. 'I am sure, ladies and gentlemen of the jury, and I am the first person to say to you candidly—not being a professional person and not being a professional negotiator—that I have probably gone about it the wrong way and I have probably been far too belligerent about it.'

The phone calls were the main evidence of Watts's behaviour which the Plaintiff had raised. 'Mr Gray has made big play of the God knows how many phone calls I have made,' Watts said, 'but I have to say this to you: I doubt if during all these phone calls I have had more than six or seven conversations with Lord Aldington. I can say to you that had he agreed just to meet the widow and to accord her a little of what he purports now to be the sympathetic treatment that he did accord her, all would have been well and we could have discussed the issue. I basically thought that Lord Aldington was in the business of avoiding me and I was in the business of making sure that he did not.'

Watts described how Lord Aldington consistently refused to let the claim go to arbitration. 'You can appreciate what that does to you when you are fighting for justice, ladies and gentlemen of the jury, and the impression that you get of Lord Aldington. First of all, he would not meet the widow, then he would not allow the matter to be reviewed by the Ombudsman. I have to say frankly, without being unduly offensive, that not only did I think at that point of time, before I ever heard of the forced repatriations from Austria in 1945, my opinion—without being offensive because Lord Aldington is not here—was that he was ruthless, he was callous, he was cunning and he was extremely evasive.'

The suspicion of evasiveness was confirmed in Watts's mind after he learned of the forced repatriations and spoke to Lord Bethell about them. 'I telephoned Nicholas Bethell and I said, "Look, I have read your book with great interest and I have been told that Lord Aldington was involved in this ghastly business of repatriations from Austria and I cannot find any reference to him in your book at all." He said to me what was at the time a very interesting comment, he said to me, "Well, Lord Aldington was definitely involved, but when I asked to interview him, when I asked to go and see him about this, he said he could not recall anything about the repatriations at that time and would not give me an interview". Now, you can appreciate, ladies and gentlemen of the jury, that I had already found Lord Aldington evasive on one count, in dealing with my sister's claim, and so, therefore, you can appreciate what was going through my mind:

was there a possibility that he was being evasive on another count?'

Then Watts explained how he came to suggest the pamphlet which eventually materialised as *War Crimes and the Wardenship of Winchester College*. 'I felt that Lord Aldington's stature, a man of irreproachable integrity, was a false stature—that's what I felt and that everything Nikolai Tolstoy had said was absolutely right. I felt that Lord Aldington should be exposed for the falseness of his position.

'I have no hesitation or embarrassment in saying to you,' Watts continued, 'what my policy was. I telephoned Count Tolstoy on 15th February 1987, and I said: "The only thing to do, if he goes on being as evasive as this—he's never answered any of your charges at all, not properly and not adequately, and I had had the same business with my sister, that he wouldn't address himself to the issue—is to winkle him out of his shell, take the most sensitive area that you can which would embarrass him to come forward and give an explanation." That was Winchester College. I will tell you why it was Winchester College. It is the only venue that he had felt it appropriate before to come down and answer any question over these issues at all, apart from a couple of earlier radio or telephone interviews where he had given no information at all.'

Watts wound up by saying, 'That's an outline, ladies and gentlemen of the jury, of my explanation of what happened. I have some difficulty here. It's a nerve-wracking experience being in the witness box to start off with, unless you are a professional in these courts; and, secondly, because I'm conducting my own examination-in-chief, I have to keep on prompting myself with all the things I want to say to you. I'm sure that half the things I'm supposed to say to you, or want to say to you, I've forgotten, but they will come out in the documents.'

For the next four hours Watts conducted a "self-examination-in-chief", as it were. He took the jury slowly and carefully through the documents, mainly his letters to, and occasionally from, Lord Aldington, his correspondence with Tolstoy and his portfolio of pamphlets. The basic theme was that Lord Aldington was a fraud. 'I felt that he was purporting to be a man of perfect uprightness whose stainless soul was free. That was not the position and he masqueraded behind a facade of false integrity and respectability.'

Watts denied that his campaign constituted "blackmail", as Gray had alleged. 'If Lord Aldington really thought that there was any case of blackmail, in the terms of the criminal way that we know it and regard it, Lord Aldington and Sun Alliance did not even have to put their hand in their pocket. They could have gone straight down to the police, put the matter in the hands of the Director of Public Prosecutions and they would not have had to bother about dealing with the matter, they would have had the whole matter dealt with for them. I think that the whole suggestion there is as absurd as it is erroneous.'

The Judge made few interventions, but in general allowed Watts to make his case as fully as he thought fit. When he came to the pamphlets, Mr Justice Davies drew him out. 'Then Prince Charles gets a letter from you,' the Judge said, in an amused tone of voice.

'Oh, yes,' Watts said. 'I wrote to Prince Charles because I had a photograph of Prince Charles reading *Victims of Yalta* and I said: "I enclose a copy of two letters to the Headmaster of Winchester College whose Warden is The Lord Aldington. It is unfortunate for our Country that those people with the power and influence to help rectify this shameful blot on our National honour, by having the courage to demand the truth however unpalatable, are those who elect to do nothing."'

'And then Princess Michael,' the Judge said.

'Yes, what happened on that was that Princess Michael, some time previously, your Lordship, had been subjected to enormous publicity in all the papers over her father and the most tenuous links of being associated with some undesirable party at the outbreak of the war. I was just illustrating the paradox of the situation, that here was a book with well documented charges and no publicity had been given to it at all.'

By the time Gray stood up to cross-examine Watts, the First Defendant undoubtedly had the Court on his side. Gray put on the look of a senior man irritated that he has to take valuable time to swat a junior who will not recognise the hierarchy. He opened aggressively by accusing Watts of attempted extortion. Watts coolly described this as 'fanciful', pointing out that he had only started his "war crimes" campaign after Lord Aldington had left the Sun Alliance. 'If I had wished to extort money, as you suggest, the last person I would be writing to would be Lord Aldington, because Lord Aldington was not in a position to, in actual fact, pay out any money because he had nothing to do with the Sun Alliance at all.'

Gray got no further when he tried to suggest to Watts that the whole Sun Alliance business was irrelevant to the case anyway. 'I want you to understand,' Gray said, 'that my position will be that the rights and wrongs of the claim on the Bowden accident policy is not a matter which is of concern to this jury. You understand that, Mr Watts?'

'Well, I don't understand that,' Watts replied, quite unintimidated by Gray's condescension. 'If the rights and wrongs of the actual policy on the Bowden case were as peripheral as you suggest, and, indeed, his Lordship has suggested, and, indeed, I suggested yesterday in submissions in closed Court, you would not have raised the issue in your opening address, and, of course, the purpose of your raising the issue in your opening address was for the sole purpose of blackening me. That is exactly what your purpose was: to represent the interests of your client by blackening me in the most misleading way. That is what you have done.'

Needled, Gray became increasingly patronising. 'I am going to ask you about the contents of this letter and then I am going to pass to other topics. Do you understand, Mr Watts?'

But Watts was unaffected by any of this. At one point Gray tried to show that the Sun Alliance's solicitors had a different view of the merits of Sue Bowden's case from her own. He started to read out a letter where they said, 'We have once more reviewed the position arising out of the death of Mr Bowden on 14th April–'

'Hold on a second, Mr Gray,' Watts said. 'I would like to just interrupt you. I would like to submit to your Lordship that if the memorandum which was prepared by Stephenson Harwood, which goes into the details of the very rights and wrongs of the issue that Mr Gray seeks to avoid in this action, your Lordship quite properly directed me yesterday that the rights and wrongs of that memorandum could not be discussed in front of the ladies and gentlemen of the jury, and here is Mr Gray seeking to do so.'

'Mr Watts, you are quite right to make that point,' the Judge said. 'There is no reason why we should go into the arguments they put forward to their side when I have not let you put forward yours. As they say on the other side of the Atlantic: "Your objection is sustained."'

Gray was forced back on his original suggestion that Watts's campaign was a 'lever' to get money out of the Sun Alliance. But he did not get very far here either. 'Do you follow what I am putting to you, or about to put to you, Mr Watts?' Gray foolishly asked this very alert witness.

'I can't follow what you are *about* to put to me,' Watts replied with a grin.

Eventually Gray backed off, and started phrasing his questions more respectfully. 'I want to make it very clear to you what my suggestion is, Mr Watts, and it is this: from the very start, from January 1984, everything you did was dictated by a determination to bring pressure to bear on the Sun Alliance to make payment on this policy?'

'I think you're a remarkable advocate,' said Watts, 'and I think your advocacy is formidable.'

'Will you answer?'

'I am totally convinced, Mr Gray, that anybody taking industrial action against an employer would be condemned as a blackmailer on that account.'

Gray put the basis of his case in two questions. The first one was this: 'Was the object of all these telephone calls to Lord Aldington, his family, his office and so on to harass the Sun Alliance into making payment on the accident policy?'

'It was to bring pressure on the Sun Alliance,' Watts replied, 'and indeed Lord Aldington, to address themselves to the issue which, as I have said in my previous answer to you, they had failed to address themselves to.'

The second question was this: 'Precisely the same purpose was intended by you when you, as you do in February 1985, seek to make use of these accusations of war criminality which you had been told by some anonymous informant on the telephone. Am I right?'

'Of course, Mr Gray—'

'Please answer the question and then make any comment.'

'It is not a question,' Watts said, 'because you are not asking a question, you are making a statement and this is where you are so misleading. I have already given you an answer to that question—if it is a question because in fact it is a statement with a question mark at the end of it—I have said to you that what I was doing with regard to those allegations, which were inspired by a totally independent source, was to raise the character of Lord Aldington and put a question mark over the character of Lord Aldington as an appropriate person to be the final arbiter in determining the case.'

At one point, Gray became quite flustered. Watts had just described the trip he made to the newspaper library in Hendon after reading Lord Bethell's book.

'Did you see any newspaper cuttings referring to Lord Aldington?' Gray asked.

'Yes,' Watts replied.

'Oh, really, and what did they say?'

'*The Times* newspaper 1978: "Perhaps a fuller and franker account from those personally involved would convince a nation and quieten a growing sense of collective guilt. Alternatively, it might show that we were wrong, that we were accomplices in a massive crime. Then we should have to think seriously how best to make restitution. But in either case the nation now needs all the available evidence."'

'Mr Watts,' Gray said, 'we are going to get on much better if you listen to my question and attempt to answer it. My question was, did you find any cutting in the Hendon newspaper library that referred to Lord Aldington? How is it an answer to that question for you to read out what you have just read out?'

'Because Nicholas Bethell in the article refers to Lord Aldington and his evasiveness.'

'What has that got to do with what you found at the Hendon newspaper library?'

'Because that article came from the Hendon newspaper library.'

'Which article?'

'The article in *The Times*.'

'Does that refer to Lord Aldington?'

'Yes, it does.'

Watts scored another victory when Gray tried to suggest, for the umpteenth time, that his "war crimes" campaign amounted to an attempt to get money out of Sun Alliance. The exchanges got so confused that the Judge had to intervene with his own paraphrasal of Watts's point. 'I am writing down: "I don't agree that this letter means: Agree to arbitration or I will give publicity to the events."'

'That is absolutely what I say,' Watts confirmed. 'The only difference is that your Lordship explains in ten words what I have failed to explain in a thousand.'

'And your evidence on oath,' Gray said, 'is that you never uttered any such threat with a view to obtaining money on this insurance policy?'

'I wasn't asking for money, I was asking for an independent review.'

'Would you now answer the question?'

'I have answered it.'

'Is your sworn evidence that you never threatened to use these allegations of war criminality in order to obtain money on that insurance policy?'

'Never.'

'Never?'

'No.'

Since Tolstoy has been criticised for attacking Lord Aldington without having any financial motive—the implication being that it is pure malice to attack somebody without the prospect of monetary gain—it is worth stressing that the suspicion that you *do* have something to gain can equally easily be used against you to allege malice.

Having failed to dislodge Watts with bluster and aggression, Gray tried the polite approach. 'You are being very fair, Mr Watts, at this stage. You are saying as at the date of this letter, 14th March, 1985, that you had this telephone call but that you needed to have the veracity of these allegations made to you by the anonymous caller substantiated before you could take the matter further. Is that what you are saying to the jury?'

'I am always suspicious of statements which come from you,' Watts replied, 'which you then pose later on as a question. What I say to you, to put it more accurately, is that manifestly if you had heard from a person in Aldington village with regard to the allegation that Lord Aldington was involved in the most shameful and treacherous betrayal in British military history, you would wish to seek more information on the subject to satisfy yourself that those allegations were correct and I think it is further manifest that I did just that.'

'I think the answer to my question is just, "Yes"?' Gray said.

'You did not ask a question,' Watts countered. 'You made a statement.'

Gray quickly reverted to his earlier approach. He also reverted to his earlier line of questioning. 'What, may I ask you, have these unsubstantiated accusations against Lord Aldington made to you by your anonymous informant, to do with the subject of this letter which I remind you was the Unpaid Sun Alliance Claim, Mr C.C. Bowden deceased?'

'Well, first of all,' Watts replied, 'I quarrel with the word "unsubstantiated"–'

'I thought we agreed a moment ago–'

'Hang on a moment,' Watts said. 'I am just answering your question, Mr Gray. By this time we have got to the 14th March. When I told you with regard to the letter of 6th February that I was not sure at that point of time whether I had telephoned Lord Bethell, I am convinced that by 14th March that I had done so and, therefore, since Lord Bethell was the author of that book and he had indicated to me that Lord Aldington had refused to give an interview when he was writing this book and indeed had been extremely evasive, I was satisfied that Lord Aldington had played a protagonist role in the matters alluded to. Therefore, when you make the statement they were unsubstantiated, they were not unsubstantiated.'

'I will try again, Mr Watts. What had these allegations, substantiated as you now say they were in your mind, to do with the subject matter of this letter which was according to its heading: Unpaid Sun Alliance Claim Mr Bowden deceased?'

'I will repeat the same answer which I have now given you, I should think, about 15 times and the nexus, the exact nexus which you seek to elicit is that it was reasonable and legitimate for anybody placed in my position to take the view, as indeed I did, that if those allegations were correct it was wholly inappropriate for a man of Lord Aldington's constitution to be the Chairman of a £2.5 billion insurance company and so be the final arbiter in determining the claims of the man in the street who had not sufficient muscle to fight the iniquity of the insurance company's vast strength.'

The Judge got fed up with Gray's repetitive questioning and asked him, much as he had asked Rampton when cross-examining Lord Aldington, to accept that the answer he had been given by the witness was the only one he was going to get.

Gray was gasping now, and had to fall back on trivial points like objecting to Watts's self-description as "researcher" in the 1985 advertisement in *The Times* which Tolstoy had answered. 'Anyone reading this advertisement in *The Times* would take it, would he not, that the person who wanted information was a historical researcher?'

'Well, to be frank,' Watts said, 'I think you have got a point there, but the context of that did not strike me as being so when I put it in, but I certainly think that you have got a point there, Mr Gray. I can only say that if I had a rub of Aladdin's lamp I think that I would have made it more clear that I meant researcher in an amateur capacity.'

Finally Gray started quibbling about words. At one stage he asked Watts about a letter he had written to a Mr Stewart who had replied to one of his advertisements.

'You refer to your own manuscript,' Gray said.

'Yes,' replied Watts.

'What is that document?'

'The one I showed you.'

'Which document?'

'*This* one,' said Watts, pointing to a typewritten sheet in Bundle E.

'That does not look like a manuscript to me,' said Gray.

'Well, it is obviously a misuse of the word "manuscript".'

'Where is your own manuscript, Mr Watts? You know the difference between "manuscript" and "typescript", do you not?'

'Well, if there is a misuse of words, *that* is the manuscript which I eventually prepared.'

'Are you telling his Lordship and the members of the jury that there never *was* a manuscript, *despite* what you wrote to Mr Stewart?'

'Well, *there* is the manuscript and, in that context, I think that is the manuscript insofar as it is a matter where I have written the central part of it, where it starts, "I have researched" and ends up with, "cruel injustice".'

This had gone too far for the Judge. 'Mr Gray, is that quite a fair question? Do not authors get things back, "Your manuscript returned herewith"? It may well be typed, it might have been printed. A manuscript does not necessarily have to be written.'

The last substantial point Gray made was to ask Watts what he meant by the term "reputable historian" as he had applied it to Tolstoy. The context of that question was the waspish comments Tolstoy had made in his letters to Watts. Gray was trying to suggest that Tolstoy had pre-judged Lord Aldington.

'Would you agree with me that the qualities you would look for in a reputable historian include objectivity?' Gray asked.

'I certainly think that would be a fair statement.'

'Fair mindedness?'

'Fair minded, yes.'

'A person who finds out the facts first and then makes comment and not the other way round?'

'With one exception,' Watts said.

'What is the exception?'

'That when a man of integrity, such as Nikolai Tolstoy, had been trying to find out the facts and had been met with evasiveness—I under-stood that to be the position—that indeed was the position—and, therefore, the imbalance which you imply in your suggestion did not effect itself in my mind in that regard.'

'So you are saying there is nothing in this letter which in any way cast doubt on your opinion of Count Tolstoy as being a reputable histo-rian?'

'Since I had been investigating the character of Lord Aldington since January 1984,' Watts said, 'and had first-rate experience of the fact that he was a callous and ruthless and cunning and devious individual, it didn't surprise me in the least to receive a letter like this from Nikolai Tolstoy.'

Apart from some concluding odds and ends, that was the end of the Plaintiff's case against Nigel Watts. Gray had signally failed to make a dent in his position. It is hard to believe that Garnier could have done anything for Watts which Watts could not have done for himself. Furthermore Garnier's presence on the Defence team early in the trial robbed the Court of what would undoubtedly have been the most entertaining spectacle this case could have thrown up: Watts cross-examining Lord Aldington on the Sun Alliance aspects of the case. Watts had performed above expectations without a lawyer; the next question was how would Tolstoy perform with so many lawyers that he could hardly concentrate on the issues for worry about the cost of them all?

16

COUNT TOLSTOY'S
EVIDENCE

TOLSTOY mounted the witness stand dressed in a blue blazer with
gold buttons and what Nicolson described as 'sort of Simpson's
slacks' and looking 'young, British, like a naval officer facing a
court martial. His manner is calm, well-informed; very different from the
crazy Cossack the jury expected.'

Tolstoy felt confident. 'I didn't think Gray could trip me up because
I felt I knew what I was going to talk about. I was confident in the Court
procedures, and went on being so—although my distaste for the Judge
grew and grew, but I thought the jury might correct the imbalance.'

Georgina felt 'anxious, but proud'.

Earlier in the day, in his brief opening speech—it was about a tenth
as long as Gray's—Rampton had made the basic point that the Defendants
did not accuse Lord Aldington of having 'some insane blood-lust that he
wanted to satisfy by sending people back to their deaths'. Their case was
that the Plaintiff had been aware of the likely fate of the victims but was
indifferent to it. However 'his overwhelming obligation as a human being
and indeed as a British officer was to do everything he could within the
scope of his orders to prevent it from happening and, if he could not, to
protest against the orders and try and have them changed.'

In the absence of FO 1020/42, Rampton was making quite the wrong
case. The forced repatriations were a result of 5 Corps *dis*obeying orders,
by ignoring Alexander and obliging Marshal Tolbukhin. After a few
preliminaries, including an injured response from Tolstoy to the 'self-

styled historian' jibe, Rampton asked his client how it was that he had first become suspicious of Lord Aldington.

'I recall two officers serving at 5 Corps,' Tolstoy replied, 'who both independently said: "Well, the man you ought to see is Lord Aldington." One was General Sir Geoffrey Musson, commanding the 36th Infantry Brigade and the other was Colonel Sir Andrew Horsbrugh who is now dead, who commanded the 27th Lancers. When I said: "I have written to him and he does not remember", they gave a cynical snort and I remember General Musson, I think it was, said: "Well, he is a politician, he would say that, would he not?"'

Tolstoy described how, by the time he came to write his *Encounter* article, he had identified in his own mind the "guilty people". Keightley was near the top of the list, he said. 'What I heard seemed to me to confirm that, though he was an excellent and admired officer in the field during the war, he was something of a bully, rather arrogant as described to me by one person who saw a great deal of–'

At this, Gray rose to his feet. 'My Lord, there does come a point when one must intervene. This evidence is objectionable on half-a-dozen scores.'

The Judge agreed with him. 'One of the questions you will be asking, no doubt—if you do not then I shall—of this witness is: does a careful, unbiased historian swallow everything that people say, who may have motives for saying unpleasant things?' Had Mr Justice Davies read Keegan's attack on Tolstoy's scholarly credibility in his *Daily Telegraph* articles following publication of Cowgill's *Interim Report*?

It was 'really going a bit far' for Tolstoy to criticise Keightley from the witness box, the Judge went on, when he 'is not here to defend himself'. This was extremely ominous for Tolstoy. If any criticism of Low's superiors was ruled out of Court, Tolstoy would be left with the argument that Lord Aldington was a lone "criminal", which was not his case at all. On this basis he could not even criticise Macmillan. The absurdity of this assumption is demonstrated by applying it to the Nuremberg trials in 1946. On that occasion, Hitler was not in court. But would it really have been 'going a bit far' to forbid criticism of him on the basis that he was not there to defend himself?

The Judge allowed Gray's objection. He said that the comments of Musson and others were not necessarily 'the sagacious views of other officers, [they] might have been just jealous tittle-tattle... It is all this attempt, which you pooh-poohed when I said it earlier, of trying to turn this case, as certainly some journalists in articles which have been drawn to my attention have tried to do, into a historical inquiry or a war crimes trial. It is nothing of the sort.'

Rampton protested, but the Judge was adamant: 'You see, if that had been put to Wilson he might have said, I do not know, "Well, that fellow Tolstoy was such a pest, he wanted me to say something nasty about Keightley, I wanted to play golf and so I agreed, to get rid of him." That may be fantastical but this is one of the reasons for the very good Rules of Evidence. Unfortunately authors, and this is not a criticism of Count Tolstoy because I am sure that all historians are the same, they are not always concerned with real evidence.'

Rampton would not accept this astonishing assertion. 'Count Tolstoy must be allowed to say why it is that he has not singled out Lord Aldington and why it is that he believes that General Keightley was involved and why that is credible.'

'I do not know how it will strike the jury,' the Judge replied, 'if we follow it up. They may say, "What a useless historian, who acts on tittle-tattle from other people." All I can say is that I am probably less intellectual about this, but I know what my reaction would be if somebody came asking me to pass comment on a Judge who had sentenced people to death, and they thought that they had been wrongly sentenced to death: I would boot them out. However, there we are. That is just a personal view, and sometimes a Judge's personal view might affect the jury.'

'I do not deny that for a moment,' said Rampton, painfully aware that the jury had listened to the whole exchange.

The Judge pitched in again when Rampton raised the issue of the Plaintiff's moral responsibility for the repatriations. What about people like Tryon-Wilson, Mr Justice Davies asked? 'The mere fact that he did not, for want of a better word, protest might make almost everybody a war criminal,' he said.

'It is really a very simple case,' Rampton replied. 'He disobeyed orders, he knew that they would probably suffer something like this and, therefore, he is responsible for what happened.'

'That is perfectly clear, perfectly proper, but it is this moral responsibility that is worrying me.'

'My Lord, I am not interested in responsibility under military law; I am not interested in responsibility under the law of England. That is not what I am concerned with. I am concerned with moral responsibility, that a man should, morally speaking, be answerable for the consequences of his deliberate acts; nothing more and nothing less.'

'As long as they are deliberate acts or omissions I can understand that,' the Judge said, 'but the idea of "moral responsibility" seems to me rather like saying that we are all morally responsible for the things that teenagers do because we do not bring them up properly.'

Possibly here the Judge had tacitly revealed the basis of his determination to prevent this case turning into a "war crimes" trial. The Nuremberg trials turned on the question of moral responsibility. It was that which enabled the Allies to reject the defence of superior orders. Lord Aldington's case was that he obeyed superior orders at all times. There was no moral dimension to that. If issues of morality were allowed into Court, Mr Justice Davies would have a "war crimes" trial on his hands. Having said that, it should be remembered that he had allowed Dr Knight to make points of precisely this sort about both the Cossacks and Tolstoy. Knight had not been stopped when he said that the Cossacks 'were in no sense morally-speaking innocent and they had a very black record.' Knight went on to apply this point. 'I think it is important, firstly, to expose Tolstoy's deliberate blurring of the moral issues with the legal issues and show that he is really concerned with the former: secondly, that the conduct of the Cossacks (and Croats, etc.) in the war is very relevant to the moral issues involved.' Incidentally, Mr Justice Davies did not object to this criticism of dead people on the ground that they were not in Court to defend themselves.

When Tolstoy began to deal with the military history, he started doing himself considerable damage. Early on, Rampton asked his client if his view of the Definition Order had changed over the years.

'There have been shifts in my interpretation of this document,' Tolstoy said, 'which is absolutely crucial to the whole issue, as I see it, since I first saw it. I think that in earlier days—it is quite clear from my books—I always thought that it was a cover document and it is quite clear that it was not intended as a real screening document. My earlier interpretation of this was that it was intended, on the face of it, to be more genuine than it is, but having considered the matter and other matters very carefully over the last two years in preparation for this case, I think that I was wrong and I think that my general import was right (there is no question of that), that no screening was intended to take place and no screening did take place.'

First, this answer is so confused as to be almost incomprehensible— the interpretation has, apparently, changed from thinking no screening was really intended to no screening was intended. Secondly, for Tolstoy to have admitted to uncertainty about his interpretation of one of the two most important documents in the case, was a catastrophic mistake. The Plaintiff may have been unconvincing at times, but he was never uncertain. Thirdly, it is hard to believe that the Court was interested in the subtle shifts of the Second Defendant's view: this can only have made it harder for the 'upper working class' jury to have understood the case Tolstoy was trying to make. He should have been explaining the basics of his argument, not dilating on the subtleties of his own evolving, and contradictory, interpretations of historical documents. Finally, if they had been listening carefully to what he said, they would surely have been dismayed by the admission that the view he was now putting forward was arrived at *after* he had forced Lord Aldington to accept him as a Defendant in this case.

Today Tolstoy says he feels angry with himself that he gave so many answers like this. 'What I ought to have had in the forefront of my mind was that I was addressing twelve people who were not historians.' But Georgina remembers pointing this out at the time. 'You must stop qualifying your answers,' she said to him at an early stage. 'Just say what you think in one sentence and leave it at that.'

Tolstoy did not help himself either when Rampton brought up the subject of the rather aggressively worded letters he had written to Watts about Lord Aldington. 'Looking back now, Count Tolstoy, to those words: "... handed over by Low and butchered in circumstances of indescribable brutality ...",' Rampton asked him, 'do they seem now to you to be, in any sense, an exaggeration?'

Instead of saying a blunt "No", as he eventually did, Tolstoy talked round the issue. 'I wouldn't say they are an exaggeration,' he said, 'but certainly what I wrote in a private letter rather hurriedly to someone who is not a fellow historian, I certainly wouldn't have phrased it like that if I were expecting anybody else to read it except the recipient.'

'I am asking you about the flavour of it?' Rampton persisted.

'The flavour of it, I would stand by, yes.'

The Judge pressed him on this answer. Did he still stand by it?

'I'm glad you raised that,' Tolstoy said, 'because, in fact, I think it's what Lord Aldington, himself, described in another context as "loose and hurried phraseology". As I say, in a private letter I have elided things, which would certainly give a false impression. For example, I say there was a camp for Jugoslav and White Russian refugees at Viktring. That is correct, but when I go on to say that most of them were handed over, that is incorrect, because the White Russian refugees—that is the Russkii Korpus—were evacuated from Viktring, so, of course, I am being sloppy in my language, because I am referring only to the Jugoslavs, of course. When I say: "handed over by Low", again that is rather sloppy, because it means literally that he went up to the tunnel—accompanied them—with a revolver in his hand, which, of course, didn't happen. So, if I am asked, is the flavour of it correct, do I still hold Lord Aldington responsible for what happened? Yes. Do I say that all that I have written in that sentence is literally true? I certainly don't, because it is very sloppily written as many of my letters are.'

Why did Tolstoy not simply answer the Judge's question, "Yes"? After all, "most" of the people at Viktring *were* handed over: in round figures, 4,000 were members of the Russkii Korpus, who were not handed over, and 25,000 were Jugoslavs who were. Thus 84% of the inhabitants of Viktring on 14 May were handed over: that, surely, is "most"? As for responsibility, it was Low who issued the Deception Order which initiated the handovers. Tolstoy was picking holes in his own case.

Reading another of Tolstoy's letters to Watts, Rampton unintentionally allowed his client to ensnare himself yet again. '"I wish you luck in your struggle with this evil man. Had he been a German he would have been strung up years ago."' Rampton read out. 'You will no doubt be invited to say whether or not you retract those two sentences?'

'Well, now,' Tolstoy replied. '"I wish you luck in your struggle with this evil man." Well, I knew that Mr Watts had a private difference with him. I didn't know very much about it beyond the fact that it existed. So that was simply like saying: "Yours sincerely".'

At this point Mr Justice Davies intervened to ask Tolstoy whether a historian is a person who is 'anxious to speak out and record the truth of past events'? Yes, said Tolstoy. 'Well,' said the Judge, 'would you say that this letter, taken as a whole, bearing in mind that it was a private letter, was written by a historian who was within the definition which you have just given?' Tolstoy replied that it was not a letter he would publish, but the Judge did not want to leave it at that.

'I am not pressing you,' he said. 'I am just asking you again: would you describe it, bearing in mind it is a private letter, as coming from a historian seeking to discover the truth?'

Naturally, Tolstoy said it was, adding that 'If you read the letters, say of Gibbon or Macaulay, or many other historians of eminence—vastly more eminent than me—you will find many intemperately worded letters about matters which they feel are more or less resolved to their satisfaction.'

Tolstoy's reply was 'quick', Nicolson commented in his diary. 'But we are all shocked at the Judge's partiality.' Nicolson's impression of the start of Tolstoy's testimony was good: 'not vituperative or exaggerating; instant recall of every fact, name and date; wise, calm and above all interesting.' Alistair Horne was in Court and Nicolson noted that he felt the same way.

When he was allowed to give a straight-forward account of the relevant history, Tolstoy spoke convincingly and very interestingly, as he usually does. Moreover, he clearly enjoyed mocking Knight's contribution to the academic debate about the Cossacks.

'I was present at the conference at which Dr Knight read extracts [from the diaries of a German officer with the Cossacks] and they excited a certain amount of ridicule, at any rate, in certain quarters of the audience because, in fact, whilst in some cases they described reprehensible acts which no-one could defend, generally speaking there was nothing like the "shock, horror" massacres which Dr Knight described in the witness-box; some of the events seemed quite inappropriate to what he was arguing. For example, he read an account of a burning village during the fighting in which a Cossack dashed into a house which was on fire, went into an upper room and rescued a baby and brought it out. I do not know if that was an atrocity or what. Another atrocity which I can well believe from what I know of the Cossacks and from what I have been told by those who were with them, was when, as a result of an order for relaxation from the fighting, they were apparently shown a French pornographic film and, having drunk a vast quantity of vodka before they went into the film, they celebrated by destroying the cinema. However, again, I find it hard to see this as a major war crime.'

Amusing though this was, it was off the point, which should have been that Knight's material was irrelevant. Even if he was right and hundreds of the Cossack Cavalry, say a thousand, were war criminals (which in Britain means that they had been tried in court and convicted, which not one of them had been), that does not justify sending the other twenty-four thousand to 'slavery, torture and probably death'. Tolstoy has many times made this point elsewhere, but it escaped him now. Unlike Aldington and Watts, Tolstoy was turning out to be rather ineffective in the witness box.

He was much better when allowed to make a speech. He ended his evidence-in-chief with a statement of his view of Lord Aldington's continuing obligation to the victims of 5 Corps. 'He has never,' Tolstoy said, 'expressed any contrition, repentance or regret. He has never attempted, although he is a man of considerable wealth, to help any of the people, many of whom are still living in appalling conditions of penury and suffering. I do not think he ever even subscribed to the erection of the memorial to these victims. By any standard, even if we accept every single word of the Plaintiff's case, Lord Aldington played a major part in the handover of these people. I do not think he, or anyone else, disputes that. Yet, far from expressing any regrets whatever, that I have heard anyway, for the suffering that these people went through, he is at great pains to blacken their reputations—people who have no means of answering except perhaps through me—by suggesting that people were war criminals, Nazis, vicious people who prolonged the war they had been fighting against the British for six years; that General Shkuro had been actively engaged in fighting in the German Army; and that the Cossacks were raised by the SS. All these things he must know are completely untrue and are simply designed to blacken the reputation of these poor people who have already suffered such unspeakable horrors. Such a man, it seems to me, not only on the evidence that he did perpetrate a war crime, is the sort of man one would expect to do so.'

'Would you accept from me that the charge you have made against Lord Aldington is the most terrible charge that could be brought against a public man?' Gray asked, soon after he stood up to start his cross-examination.

'Yes,' Tolstoy said, 'because I think it is probably the worst thing that I can think of that has happened in recent British history.'

'One of the things you said when you were giving evidence earlier on was that it was very damaging to be referred to as a self-styled historian. Do you remember that?'

'Yes, I do.'

'That charge, if that is the right word, pales into insignificance, does it not?'

'Of course it does because it is in quite a different context. Here it is designed to damage me in the context of this case within the Court, which is quite another matter. Of course it pales into insignificance but it is a different charge in a different context and it does not seem relevant.'

It was not long before Gray moved on to the war crimes aspect of the case.

'You have made abundantly plain that you regard General Keightley as a war criminal?' Gray said.

'Yes, Corps Commander in charge of the operations,' Tolstoy replied. 'Yes.'

'Including the Knight of Grand Cross of the Bath?'

'Yes. Just one rank below General Shkuro whom he sent back to be hanged.'

'Do you want to reconsider that answer, one rank below?'

'Well, I am not an expert.'

'If you attach importance to the fact General Shkuro had the CB, perhaps you will accept from me that is several tiers below the KCB General Keightley had?'

'Well, I cannot say it worries me much.'

'Keightley was also a GBE and had the DSO, is that correct?'

'Yes,' Tolstoy said. 'Does that mean he cannot be a war criminal?'

'Did you know he was Commander-in-Chief of the Army on the Rhine?'

'Yes.'

'Did you also know he was Commander-in-Chief of the British Forces in the Far East?'

'Yes.'

'And in the Middle East?'

'Yes, and of the Suez operation.'

'And Governor of Gibraltar?'

'Yes.'

'Did you know when you were saying what you said about him the other day in open court, that his widow is still alive?'

'I did not know she is today. She may be.'

'Do you accept from me she is?'

'Yes, if you say so.'

'Do you spare any thought for the feelings of someone like her hearing what you had to say about her dead husband?'

'Obviously, but I have to spare a great deal more thought for the victims.'

'Did one simple solution not occur to you that those officers, including Lord Aldington, who were involved in this sad exercise of repatriation, were not war criminals at all, they were doing what in the exigencies of the time had to be done?'

'Well, that is something advanced on behalf of Field Marshal von Manstein on the Eastern front in relation to Ukrainians, Russians and others. Most of whom with certainty would have been starved or liquidated by the SS. There are duties and duties, some of which one should not undertake. So, I do not accept that view at all. It is a very sinister one. When you say I should not believe General Keightley was a war criminal because he obtained high distinction—if Germany had won the war, there would be people with very high distinctions who would have been war criminals.'

However true, and valid, such observations may have been, they were off the point, which was that what had been done by 5 Corps on May 1945 was the *opposite* of what had been ordered by Alexander. What 'had to be done' was that the Cossacks should have been sent to SHAEF and the Jugoslavs to Italy. Even without FO 1020/42 in Court, Tolstoy had enough evidence of that to have answered without introducing von Manstein, of whom the jury probably knew next to nothing.

Tolstoy's reply gave Gray an opening which he took immediately and, later on, was to exploit mercilessly. Was General Murray a war criminal, he asked? Well, Tolstoy replied, he had participated in a war crime, although fairly peripherally. Did Captain Nicolson participate in the commission of a war crime? 'To a lesser extent down the line,' Tolstoy said, with Nicolson sitting about ten feet away. 'I think that is what he would say. I cannot speak for him.' Was Tryon-Wilson a war criminal? To some extent, Tolstoy replied. This could have gone on all day, so he asked to be able to state his view in general.

'I believe,' Tolstoy said, 'that all the people who were there (or most of them) knew that a terrible war crime took place. The question of blame is not entirely for me, or indeed particularly for me, to assign. That is not my role as I see it. I am not a judge and I am not proposing there should be a trial. I wish the truth to be known at this long stage after the war. It seems to me that it is too late for trials. What we need is for the truth to come out and for responsibility to be assigned, with a general view, I hope, to inform the public. It is my view that the public should decide; and where officers and soldiers have been full and frank with me, I have never attempted to level any accusation at them other than what the public might infer by reading my books.'

The Judge's response to this was surprising. 'I think you would agree, would you not,' he said, 'that if there had been a means of obtaining an enquiry which was an historical enquiry, which could have ranged over perhaps a wider field and certainly in a more investigative manner rather than a libel action, you would have probably preferred it?'

Tolstoy's reply was even more surprising, at least in retrospect. 'I think I would before, my Lord, but I do have to say that now I think this is actually preferable: the adversarial method seems to me preferable.'

'Well, one of you is not going to think much of the adversarial method—either you or Lord Aldington—and we shall see at the end!'

The only enquiry so far had been a 'private' one, Tolstoy said to Gray when he resumed his cross-examination, and that had not produced a wholly satisfactory solution to the repatriations riddle, to put it mildly. Its main function seemed to have been to discredit him. It was, he said, 'a truly absurd, and I think now generally discredited, report by a self-styled committee which was issued last year and, without any attempt to find out from me or anyone else whether an alternative view existed. It utterly discredited everything I had ever written, for ever.'

'What are you referring to when you say that?' Gray asked.

'A thing which calls itself the Cowgill Report.'

'When you say "calls itself the Cowgill Report", is it the report prepared by a committee of which Brigadier Cowgill is the chairman?'

'It is not a committee, at least Brigadier Cowgill now says it isn't a committee, though earlier the committee members—I think he now says he never called it a committee—have denied it is a committee.'

'Whether it is a committee or a group or a band or anything else, shall we run through its members? Brigadier Cowgill is one, is he not?'

'Yes.'

'Is another Christopher Booker who you were talking about in very flattering terms I think yesterday?'

'Was I? I would be very surprised if I was. He's a complete idiot—an amiable one.'

'Lord Brimelow, also an amiable idiot or not?'

'Not an idiot and not amiable either. He is one of the Foreign Office officials who bore major responsibility for implementing the Yalta Agreement in its most inhumane aspects. He so loathes me for exposing his role in it in *Victims of Yalta* that Brigadier Cowgill himself told me that Lord Brimelow would never ever enter the same room as me. I am not sorry.'

'Why do you feel so strongly about the conclusions arrived at by the Cowgill Committee?'

'Well, it was totally phoney. For a start it was not a committee, it simply consisted of a businessman with no understanding or knowledge or experience of historiography whatever.'

'You are now talking about Brigadier Cowgill?'

'Yes. Who are the members of this so-called committee? It isn't a committee anyway. All I have to do to make myself a committee presumably is put the milkman and my wife on the front page of my books and I become a committee.'

'Let's not get bogged down with the word "committee"—a group,' said Gray, using Cowgill's own preferred word.

'It's quite important,' Tolstoy said, 'because the word "committee" and the issuing of a report were designed to pull the wool over the eyes of the public. Had it been issued as what it really was, which was a cyclostyled jumble of selective British documents—most of which had already been published—published privately by a businessman under his own name, no newspaper would have noticed it. So it is the phoney aspect of the committee which is all-important. The fact, for instance, that he didn't give his own address but the address of the Royal United Services Institute, of which he is presumably a member, so that it would have some sort of fake official imprimatur. This is really just the tip of the iceberg: if you really want to know what I think of it, I have at home in my computer a 90-page file showing from beginning to end how it was filled either with ludicrous errors or deliberate misrepresentations. Even documents quoted have been doctored so as to make them say the opposite of what they do say.'

'Do you level the accusation against those three gentlemen—namely, Brigadier Cowgill, Christopher Booker and Lord Brimelow—of distorting and suppressing the evidence?'

'I don't think Christopher Booker, because I asked him—we were on fairly friendly terms at that time—I asked him what his part in the so-called Cowgill Report was, and it amounted to nothing. I said to him: "How many documents did you actually discover?" "None." "How many witnesses have you interviewed?" "Three." "Have you ever entered a public repository of archives in your life?" "No." That seemed to be the end of his participation.

'Brigadier Tryon-Wilson,' Tolstoy continued, warming to his theme, 'is obviously, very much like Lord Brimelow, *parti pris* in this, seeing, as you yourself have pointed out, he was very much involved in the handovers in 5 Corps area. According to Christopher Booker, he was asleep during most of the sessions and didn't attend many of them anyway because he was busy shooting grouse. So it ended up with Lord Brimelow who has a personal grievance against me—justified, I would say—and Brigadier Cowgill, who knows nothing about history or historical methods whatever. But I don't object to that—people can send out circulars wherever they like. What I object to is the misrepresentation— well, two things: first of all, the misrepresentation. Second, the extent to which they were able to manipulate sections of the media into accepting that it was something other than what it was. Thirdly, the use that was made of it in Alistair Horne's biography of Harold Macmillan, but that is another matter you may or may not wish me to go into.'

Not surprisingly, Gray declined the offer. Tolstoy had the Winchester prefect on the ropes for the first time. Tolstoy has gifts for both witty repartee and persuasive public speaking. Thus he makes an excellent interviewee. But the technique of the successful media interview is quite different from that required to defeat skilful cross-examination. In the witness box, the art is to say the minimum necessary, and in the simplest possible terms, while conveying the appearance of "trying to help the court". Tolstoy was talking cockily in an arena where either schoolboyish self-effacement or, more riskily, measured aggression, Lord Aldington-style, would have worked better. Nonetheless, Horne said that day to Nicolson, 'One cannot help admiring Nikolai for his guts.'

Gray tried to take advantage of the fact that the pamphlet had been written on the assumption that Lord Aldington had, as he told Tolstoy and others between 1981 and 8 March 1987, left Austria on '25 or 26 May' (see p. 165). Tolstoy, Gray said, had 'got it wrong'. Did he now wish to apologise to Lord Aldington for falsely accusing him on the basis of the wrong departure date?

Certainly not, said Tolstoy. 'You asked me why I had the impudence to write such things in the pamphlet, when you know very well that I had what seemed to be the best of authority for believing that I could write that and be factually correct.'

'Count Tolstoy,' Gray said, 'you may have various excuses–'

'There is no excuse, that is the fact.'

'Please let me complete my question. You may have various excuses for having got it wrong, but the plain unvarnished fact is that you did get it wrong.'

'Lord Aldington got it wrong: and I got it wrong because I believed Lord Aldington. It was a mistake, was it not?'

'Do you wish to apologise for your mistake, as you describe it?'

'No, I am afraid I do not; because if I was misled by Lord Aldington, and acted in good faith accordingly, how can you say that there is anything to apologise for?'

'I think Count Tolstoy would say that Lord Aldington ought to apologise,' the Judge said, to Gray's astonishment.

'Exactly. He misled me,' said Tolstoy.

Clearly unimpressed with Gray's line of argument, the Judge went further. 'He says, "I thought that he was responsible for that one because I was acting on what he said, about the date that he left." That is the only point. He agrees that he is wrong now because, undoubtedly, Lord Aldington left at the very latest, he says, on the 27th. That is Count Tolstoy's point.'

'I think my client would probably decline the invitation to apologise to Count Tolstoy,' Gray said.

Moving on to the Jugoslav handovers, Gray changed tactics. Now he allowed Tolstoy's volubility free rein, hoping he would take enough rope, if not to hang himself, then at least to confuse the jury to the point where they could not understand the Defence argument.

Gray asked the witness about the third paragraph in the Robertson Order ('All surrendered personnel of established Jugoslav nationality who were serving in German forces should be disarmed and handed over to Jugoslav forces'). 'Can I make sure,' he said, 'that I have understood your case correctly? You say that that order only applies to Jugoslavs of established Jugoslav nationality actually serving in a German unit, wearing German uniform and so on?'

'Well, I take it to mean exactly what it says,' Tolstoy replied, 'and Lord Aldington can only be expected to understand what it says.'

'Can you answer my question?'

'You added some words which are not in the order and that is why I said that.'

'I am trying to understand your case. Do you take that to mean Jugoslavs serving in German units and wearing German uniforms?'

'I think it is fair to say that one should look at it as an officer receiving it would have looked at it and "serving in German forces" means that you are serving in units, yes, of the German Army; if you are serving in the British forces then you are in the British Army.'

'Thank you. Now, that would not cover, you say, Chetniks?'

'No, not for the most part. No, it would not; I do not think it covered any of them.'

'Would it cover Slovenes?'

'No, they were not in the German forces.'

'It would not cover White Guards?'

'I am not absolutely certain who the White Guards were at this stage.'

'Well, if there were any they would not be covered either?'

'I do not think I can answer that because if there were such people they could be anything you chose to call them.'

'It would not cover the Nedics?'

'They were not serving, as I understand it, in the German Army. However, I do not want to be too categorical on this because it would really need an expert on Jugoslav history. I am very happy to answer your questions to the best of my knowledge but, to my knowledge, the Nedic forces were not serving in the German Army.'

'It would not cover Domobrons?' Gray asked.

'Slovenian or Croatian or both?'

'Both.'

'Well,' Tolstoy replied, 'they are very different but I do not think that it covered either.'

'Well, then, it does not matter, does it? Would it really come to this: that the only grouping which, on your interpretation of the Robertson Order, would be covered by it are the Ustache?'

'Well, I do not think that even they were, though I would not like to swear on this because, again, it is a matter for an expert. I do not think that the Ustache, reprehensible though they were, were serving in the German Army; they were serving in the Croatian Army.'

'You say, do you, that paragraph three of the Robertson Order did not in fact apply to anyone at all?'

'Not taken at face value, I do not think it did,' said Tolstoy, confusingly. 'Again, I have to preface this throughout and say that I am not an expert on it and this is my understanding. An expert might argue differently but my understanding is that, no, it would not, strictly speaking, apply to any of them.'

'So, General Robertson was wasting his breath when he dictated this order, if that is what he did, and a whole lot of cipher clerks were wasting their time when they coded and decoded paragraph three because it did not apply to anybody in 5 Corps area at all?'

'Well, now we are looking at it differently,' Tolstoy said, 'because we were talking, first of all, of the literal interpretation of the wording of the order and now we are moving to what was the intention of the order. If I may say so, with respect, and as I think I can show, those are two different things. What General Robertson is referring to, and, of course, he could only issue his order like anybody else on the basis of information received—what General Robertson knew, as it seems to me the evidence indicates, at this stage, and had only learned within hours of issuing—almost an hour—was that this vast hoard of 200,000, maybe half a million, Croatians—or Jugoslavs as they were sometimes described—was approaching the 5 Corps area and it was indeed believed for a short period that they had actually surrendered. So if you are saying it was to clear the decks of these people, then, of course, I fully accept what you are saying, but if you're saying that it included—it was a reference, a direct reference, a conscious reference, to those units—I don't know how many—30,000, 50,000, who had already surrendered before that from about 12th May, then I don't accept it. That's my qualification, and I think it's a very important one, because it is about the second grouping that all these subsequent orders were concerned.'

'And you are really suggesting,' Gray asked with some justice, 'that what Lord Aldington had to do was to take out his crystal ball, gaze into it, look at the Robertson Order and say to himself: "Oh, well, that can't really mean what it says, it only applies to the Croats who were approaching Bleiburg"?'

'No, we are discussing—I accept that we have to discuss things in separate points and try to establish them and move on—what we have been discussing is what, conjecturally, on the evidence, was in General Robertson's mind and what he intended by that order, and I have already said that I accept that Lord Aldington and General Keightley, on the ground, would have had other considerations and they had to interpret the order. And I think that anybody can see that the Robertson Order, all the way through, is a very loosely, one might say poorly phrased, order, even from so talented an administrator, when we are reflecting the chaos.'

Unbelievably, more than four hours of Court time was devoted to Robertson-related wrangling. Between Tolstoy's superior knowledge of the facts and Gray's mastery of the tricks of the advocate's trade, they were quite evenly matched. But the contest had very little to do with extracting "evidence".

As a result of all this Gray slowly began to get the better of his opponent. Without noticing it, Tolstoy was being induced to render his own argument incomprehensible. The more they cavilled about details, the harder it became for the jury to see the main outlines of the Defence case. However negative, it was subtle and undeniably effective advocacy.

It was no accident that the Robertson Order got the lion's share of the historical debate as it was the most ambiguous document in the case. Despite, or possibly because of, the hours of debate devoted to it, its real meaning was never elucidated. The jury must have become totally punch-drunk. 'Do you accept...?' Gray would ask. 'No, I do not,' Tolstoy would reply. 'Why have you changed your mind?' 'I do not think I have...' 'Another 180° swing?' 'No. I did not know then that paragraph 2 of the Robertson Order...' 'There cannot be any new evidence...' 'Yes, there is.' 'I am content with that.' 'That is not what you said... I think we are in danger of getting into a real fog of war and I cannot even remember what it was relevant to and how it arose.' 'Can we forget about it or not?' 'I think for the moment, yes.'

After nearly a whole day of this, Mr Justice Davies intervened. 'This is Day 20,' he said, 'and I do not know if I speak for any of the jury, but I think for the first time in the last ten minutes I am completely lost.'

'I apologise,' Tolstoy said.

'I am completely and utterly lost,' the Judge said to Gray about the witness. 'I do not know what he is talking about.'

'I am trying to make–' Gray started to say, but his words were drowned in a general hubbub.

'It is not irrelevant but I think it has been a bit of a digression,' said Tolstoy by way of attempted clarification.

'Try and put your point if you could,' the Judge said, 'so that we can take it on board, but we have been darting from signal to signal and we do not really know quite which is relied on. I do not know where we are. So, I put down my pen. Let us try and see if you can explain to us–'

'I apologise,' said Tolstoy once again.

'There is no need for apologies,' the Judge said, 'but the point is we do want to get to know what is happening.'

'I think the historian ran away with the litigant just then.'

There was a break for tea, followed by a brief interval of comparative clarity, then the fog descended again. Gray had made the apparently uncontroversial point that whatever it was that 5 Corps had to do in obedience to Robertson was something they had no option about.

'Yes,' Tolstoy replied, 'I think it implies that, but what that implies, in turn, is of course another matter.'

'I beg your pardon?' said Gray, mystified.

'What that implies in turn is another matter,' said Tolstoy, 'but I accept, yes, that that is the implication.'

With that, they were off again.

'Could I just look at that because you have asked me about it?' Tolstoy asked.

'I thought I had your answer,' Gray said.

'Oh, no, I have not given my answer at all.'

'Well, what does it mean, this paragraph, if it does not mean what I have just said?'

'Well, it just means what it says. Unfortunately, it's so ambiguous—well, not ambiguous, but cloudy—that I don't think from that one can really tell at all.'

And so on, *ad soporem*.

With FO 1020/42 unavailable to the Court, Gray had the opportunity to engage in some spectacular logic-chopping. Predictably he took it. He argued, for example, that Brigadier Low had never disobeyed the higher command, with regard to the Jugoslav handovers, because, until 23 May, only Croats were repatriated, and even Tolstoy conceded they were possibly covered by the Robertson Order, and after that date, the "no force" order was applicable, which covered *all* Jugoslavs. (This had been one of Keightley's answer's to Alexander's 'war crimes' inquiry in June 1945—see p. 70ff) Since the Serbian and Slovenian handovers were, like the Croat ones, accomplished by subterfuge rather than violence, the "no force" order was not violated unless those words be taken to mean "not against their will", which Lord Aldington had denied ('My Goodness me Mr Rampton! If you do not understand the Queen's English we cannot get much further'). In short, Low's Deception Order of 17 May, which covered all three groups, was rendered correct by a subsequent coincidence that the Croat handovers took six days, and therefore happened to finish on the day 5 Corps received the "no force" order.

In a question-and-answer format it is almost impossible to make headway against this kind of argument. Gray used this limitation on the investigative power of the Court very skilfully. Even if he did not persuade the jury of Lord Aldington's argument, he demonstrated that Tolstoy's case was at least debatable. He devoted two hours to the Distone Order, apparently trying to 'understand' the Defendants' case, but in reality simply confusing Tolstoy's presentation of it. Soon the jury must have been thirsting for simple, easily understood points.

The simplest issue in any libel trial is that of character. Whatever the evidence, each member of a jury has a view, if only on a 'cut of the jib' basis, of the parties as people. If Gray could bamboozle the jury on the Defence arguments, he would stand a good chance of getting a verdict for the old war hero against the self-styled historian. There was no need to win the argument about the history; a draw would be adequate there, since he could be confident of a win on the personalities of the parties.

Gray tackled both simultaneously when he moved onto the subject of Brigadier Low's motive for what he was alleged to have done. This combined issues of character with further possibilities for evidential confusion. 'If you do not have a motive,' Gray said, 'the whole thing is a nonsense.'

Tolstoy's answer was that he could only guess at what the motive might have been and was not inclined to do so. Rampton objected that his client should not be made to guess. The Judge said he did not have to, but said that if Tolstoy did not do so in his evidence, Rampton could not do so in his closing speech for the Defence. Accordingly Tolstoy took a guess.

He said Low's motives were probably inseparable from Keightley's and that his actions were almost certainly bound up with what was discussed when Macmillan visited 5 Corps on 13 May. At the mention of Macmillan's name, Gray interrupted him. 'Count Tolstoy, my question was about the motivation of Lord Aldington. I was not intending for you to make this a platform for you to malign General Keightley and Harold Macmillan–'

'I thought you would say if I did not provide a motive for General Keightley I had no motive at all,' Tolstoy replied.

'We want to know, at least I think the jury may want to know,' the Judge said, 'the question you are being asked, is if you care to advance any theory or speculation or guess—it is up to you whether you do—as to what motivated Lord Aldington to do what you say. So far you have told us in effect, I think—tell me if I have it wrong—he did what he did because he was told to do it by General Keightley?'

'My Lord, this is where I feel so apprehensive. I did not say it happened because of that. I said this is very likely.'

'Well, very likely. Beg your pardon.'

'I am very worried about being misinterpreted,' Tolstoy said. 'You have to take the two things separately. Take the Jugoslavs. It is possible Lord Aldington took the more brutal and cruel of the two alternatives presented and there are other alternatives we have not discussed in this cross-examination; for example, the Jugoslavs need not have been sent to Italy or to Jugoslavia. They could have stayed put in the camps where they were, but he took what seems to me an unnecessarily and excessively brutal and inhumane attitude.'

'Can you confine yourself please to the question?' the Judge said tetchily.

'The motive, as I see it, quite possibly included wishing to get rid of these people. Nothing I have seen of Lord Aldington, and I have seen vastly more of him in this Court than ever before, suggests he would have been worried about the fate of all these insignificant people. They were in his way. He has never expressed any great remorse or desire for restitution or anything like that and it does not seem to me, and his friend Sir Charles Villiers too, they neither care very much at all. All Lord Aldington's efforts have been directed to blackening the reputations of the people he sent back rather than suggesting–'

'Were you listening to my opening?' Gray cut in abruptly.

'I am answering your question. He does not strike me in this instance a particularly humane man who would draw the line much at an order and, therefore, could push ahead with something very harsh and unnecessary as I see it, in large part, as a result of his own character, and another officer in the same position would not have done these things.'

At this point suddenly Gray went off the rails and started introducing evidence himself, something Counsel are explicitly forbidden from doing. He was obviously rattled by the way Tolstoy had seized the opportunity to get off the complex historical issues and make a smooth speech about Lord Aldington's character.

'What do you think is the penalty under military law for deliberate disobedience to important orders coming from above?' Gray asked.

'I am afraid you must ask a soldier,' Tolstoy said. 'I do not know precisely.'

'I will suggest an answer and put it to any soldier you care to call. He is shot in wartime?'

'I think he is court-martialled first. We are not talking about the kind of justice Lord Aldington is talking about.'

'And if found guilty, he is shot under court-martial military law?' Gray asserted.

'You are telling me.'

Gray's "evidence" was complete nonsense, even ignoring the fact that mid-May 1945 was not, in the Europe theatre, 'wartime'. In fact, only one Briton was shot as a result of a court martial during the Second World War. In the 1930s the death penalty in the Army had been abolished even for such serious offences as desertion in the face of the enemy. A case with some similarities to that of a humane officer in 5 Corps refusing to implement the forced repatriations policy was the well-known one of a junior officer, William Douglas Home, who, in September 1944, had refused to obey an order to attack Le Havre because, he said, it would result in large numbers of unnecessary civilian casualties. He was court-martialled and given a year's hard labour.[1]

'I knew you were laying a trap for me by moving into a completely different area,' Tolstoy said. 'Lord Aldington has not confided in me his motives and you are trying to trap me, having got me to speculate on a reasonable assumption he acted on the orders and full knowledge of his Corps Commander. Therefore, the Corps Commander is primarily re-sponsible, but you are now asking me to say he should be sentenced to death and make a whole series of claims I have no intention of making.'

'One final suggestion,' Gray said before sitting down, 'I suggest to you that you and Mr Watts have done Lord Aldington a great and irredeemable wrong, both by publishing the libels as you did in that pamphlet and by persisting throughout this long and very public trial in claiming that those libels are true, after the evidence has shown they are and always were utterly baseless.'

'Well,' Tolstoy said ('pale as a candle', as one observer described him) 'if it is correct that Lord Aldington did send all these tens of thousands of men, women, children and babies to certain death or tor-ture—to be sent to the Pit at Kocevje, or massacred in their thousands in the tank traps at Teharje, off to the slave labour camps of Siberia—and has lived easily with this ever since, has no regret or care: I do not regret it, no, and the fact he could not play bridge (*sic*) in his retirement is different from the fate of the people whose fate he settled in 1945. I do

1   See Douglas Home *Sins of Commission*. Le Havre was under siege and contained thousands of civilians. The German commander offered to send the civilians out if allowed three days to do so. The British commander refused the offer. Despite this, it was four days before the British commander ordered the attack. Douglas Home refused to obey, commenting, 'It's quite unnecessary to attack the foul place. It's purely to allow some politician to say all of France has been liberated. As a port it will be useless for some time.' The whole affair was well publicised in the press at the time.

not feel any regret.'

Rampton re-examined his client with more hope than confidence. He spent a day correcting the evidence given on innumerable points of detail, and then the following morning, before he could complete this process, Gray made a dramatic intervention. A critical new document had turned up, he said, which bore on the date of departure issue and, before the jury were admitted to Court, he wanted to address the Judge about it.

'When my instructing solicitors got back to the office last night,' Gray said, 'there was a message from Brigadier de Fonblanque's son. He has got two sons, one of whom lives in Belgium and has been following the case in the newspapers there, as many other people have. He then, a few days ago, I think, came back to this country to see his mother who lives in Lyndhurst. Having had his interest aroused in the case by the report of it, he went through his father's papers with his mother and came across a document which I have had faxed to Mr Rampton about an hour and a half ago and of which he has seen the original; and I hand the original to your Lordship, if I may.

'As your Lordship will see,' Gray continued, 'this is a manuscript document, and I think it is accepted this is Brigadier de Fonblanque's handwriting and it appears to be a document made up by him. It has other passages of interest, but the relevant one is at the top of the second page and it is the second entry. This is obviously taken from a much longer journal or chronicle. Entry of 21st May. We would wish to put this document before the jury.'

The entry in question reads: '21 [May] Toby Low departed on leave not to return and I became BGS. Jugs started to evacuate Carinthia.' That was the only sentence of relevance to the case. As not even Lord Aldington claimed to have left until 22 May, this document was clearly not accurate. Neither can it have been written at the time to which it referred as de Fonblanque could not then have known that Low was never to return to Austria. Finally, 21 May was the day the Jugoslavs *completed* their evacuation of Carinthia, not started it. All in all, it was a document of questionable value, being so clearly inaccurate. Why it was produced at this time and in this way has never been established.

It is hard to see what purpose Brigadier de Fonblanque's son can have seen in claiming that it was his father, rather than Lord Aldington, who had been involved in issuing the order to shoot escaping Cossacks. It is also odd that de Fonblanque Jnr. has consistently refused to allow

Tolstoy (or this author) to see the document. Tolstoy wanted to have the hand-writing checked to see if the entry for 21 May was not inserted later.

Most observers present at the trial feel that the production of the de Fonblanque journal was a turning point. From then on, the atmosphere was defensive in the Tolstoy camp and optimistic on Lord Aldington's side of the Court. Nonetheless, with hindsight, it was far less damaging to the Defendants than the absence of FO 1020/42, WO 32/13749 and the war diaries. This can now been seen when re-reading Tolstoy's closing remarks to the jury. He could have gone so much further had the most important evidence not been kept from him.

'The Cossacks could very, very easily have been disposed of in another and humane way,' Tolstoy said in his concluding statement, referring to Operation Coldstream. 'As a result of the negotiations between Eisenhower and Alexander, it was suggested that the SHAEF boundary should be extended into 5 Corps boundary in order to release 5 Corps for possible operations against Tito. At the Corps Commander's Conference on 22 May—and I am setting aside the matter of whether Lord Aldington was at that conference completely—it was pointed out the Americans were suggesting taking over Lienz and Spittal which included most of the old émigrés and women and children. *In the first five minutes it says in no circumstances are we to give up Spittal and Lienz to the Americans. That is quite extraordinary.* They could, by one stroke, accepting the American suggestion, have rid themselves of more than half the Cossacks, especially the ones most difficult to screen, especially those whom humanity would suggest one would be most reluctant to return—I mean the women and children, thousands of them—and this is what 5 Corps desperately wanted to avoid. *They wanted the responsibility and wanted to hand them back to the Soviets.* That does not seem to spring explicably from a desire to obey orders.' (emphasis added)

All this was true as the withheld files show, but Tolstoy had no means of proving it in Court. He was forced to leave the matter there and move on to the vexed question of motive. Why had 5 Corps sabotaged the humane option in disposing of the Cossacks? 'I think the reason would be,' Tolstoy said, 'first of all, that he [i.e. Lord Aldington] does not appear to have been a man who wished to take any risks with his career whatever, even if that involved sacrificing the lives of many thousands of people. He was not a man who would do what others did then, and on other occasions: to question the commander, demand reconsideration or refuse to obey an order which any humane officer should have implemented at that level. Instead he went along with them and, indeed, participated in the deception. I can only think this was because he was in a rather different position from General Keightley, who was rather lazy—not lazy in the field but lazy as far as administration goes, from my information.

'Lord Aldington,' Tolstoy continued, 'a budding politician, did, as we know, fly straight back to contest a safe seat in a time when seats of Conservative politicians were extremely unsafe, and won that seat and subsequently rose to all the eminence we know, and became ennobled. I cannot help thinking that, in some degree, he had his eye on the main chance, if I may use the pejorative colloquialism. He knew, whether or not he was present at the meeting between Keightley and Macmillan, that Macmillan was flying in; he knew these were Macmillan's wishes and he did not see any reason to jeopardise his political career by not fulfilling the last comma and semi-colon of what he took to be Macmillan's orders. That second part is speculative, but since I am invited to give a motive I believe that is as likely a motive as any for what would otherwise seem to be quite motiveless conduct.'

That concluded Tolstoy's evidence. He had tried to be balanced and fair, and at least one observer thought the jury had liked him, being surprised at his lack of pomposity. He had come across as sincere and upright, and much more even-tempered than Aldington. More than this, Gray had not tripped him up on the facts. But what Gray had done, which was infinitely damaging, was to have prevented Tolstoy giving a clear exposition of his case in language and with arguments the jury might have been expected to be able to follow. This was critical: Tolstoy stepped down from the witness box with his case still utterly opaque.

The only hope remaining for the Defence was that their witnesses would be able to engage the sympathy of the jury. But since the first twenty-three of them—Ljotic, Miletic, Prvulovich, Vlahovic, Stankevich, Dernulc, Dejak, Kozima, Zajec, Pavlovich, Plesko, Zivkovic, Abjanic, Kristof, Pinoci, Lishchenko, Bratjakin, Platonov, Somoff, Polanska, Kudrenko, Protopopov and Vierkorn—were all foreigners, and the jury were all English, this was likely to be an uphill struggle.

17

WATTS'S AND TOLSTOY'S WITNESSES

O NE OF THE TWENTY-THREE foreigners, Joro Miletic, has spoken of how he and his fellow Slavs felt they were viewed by the Court: 'We were wogs, just as the black is: foreigners, jetsam, nobodies, second-class people who never had an Empire.'[1]

The Defence called twenty-eight witnesses, who took up ten days of Court time. Only one of them, Nigel Nicolson, was in a position to address substantially and authoritatively the issues in front of the Court. This was no worse than Aldington, whose only significantly relevant witness had been Brigadier Tryon-Wilson. The difference was that, whereas the Judge had treated the Plaintiff's whole team politely, he made no effort to conceal his irritation at the irrelevance of many of the Defence witnesses, particularly the foreigners.

First up was Vladimir Ljotic, a retired accountant living in Lancashire. He had served in the Serbian Volunteer Corps and Rampton asked him to tell the Court what sort of a body it was.

'The Serbian Volunteer Corps was formed by General Nedic,' Ljotic said, 'who was the head of the Serbian Government which was formed towards the end of August 1941 because Partisans were killing the village people and they also started actions in the towns and the Germans started

---

1   Interview with the author, 7 April 1993

retaliating. The retaliations very soon became very drastic–'

'What has that to do with the issues in the case, Mr Rampton?' the Judge interrupted. 'We have had ten minutes, it is all very interesting, about his life story—I do not mean to sneer—but we must get to the point. I have indicated that matters relating to the issues in the case of course we must hear about.'

'Unless we know who was serving in the Serbian Volunteer Corps–' Rampton said.

'He told us that,' said the Judge, cutting him off. '"I joined the Serbian Volunteer Corps formed by General Nedic."'

Rampton had to abandon this line of questioning, even though Gray had been allowed to pursue it, for example with Tolstoy whom he asked about Nedic's men (had they been 'serving in German forces'?). Rampton tried another approach, aiming to demonstrate that people like Ljotic, who were part of the SVC regiments camped at Viktring, had not been fighting for the Germans and therefore were not repatriable under the Robertson Order. But he could not get very far with this either. Tito's Partisans, Ljotic told the Court, had been cleared from Serbia in late 1941 and did not venture back again until late in 1944. 'Then at the end of 1944—I would say September 1944—part of the Jugoslav territory was invaded by the Soviet forces, that was north-east and eastern parts of Jugoslavia—which was actually Serbian parts strictly—were invaded by Soviet forces, and of course they were not only a superior force but–'

'I am not going to go on warning you, Mr Rampton,' the Judge said. 'You are dealing with matters that are not at issue in this case and are not within the ruling I have made. You have had a quarter of an hour and not a word of it has been relevant to the issues.'

'It has,' protested Rampton. 'The witness has told us about the officers in his Serbian Volunteer Corps and what contact he had with the Germans.'

'That is when they were fighting the Partisans. Couldn't we get somewhere remotely nearer the time we are concerned with?'

Ljotic tried to edit his account of his time in the SVC, but he had not got himself over the Karavanken mountains and into Austria before the Judge intervened again, this time with a loaded question. 'Did you know by that time that the Partisans were—how shall I put it?—on the side of the British and Americans fighting the Germans?'

From a Serbian perspective, it was the British who had changed sides in the Jugoslavian civil war. Surely the Judge did not want Serbian witnesses to give evidence from a British point of view?

Rampton tried to ignore this and moved on to the moment of handover to the Titoists. 'You went, I think, to a place called Maria Elend?'

'That was the station,' Ljotic replied.

'Did you know what it was called then or is it something you discovered subsequently?'

Once again the Judge butted in. 'What is the relevance of that?'

Rampton was visibly annoyed now.

'Do not put your pen down like that to me,' Mr Justice Davies said angrily. 'Please stick to my rulings. I do not want to have to order a new trial.'

This was the ultimate threat. Judges have the freedom to do that; Rampton knew that the Defence could not afford another trial. He had no option but to defer.

In cross-examination, Gray concentrated on accusing Ljotic's father of being a 'quisling' on the ground that he had been part of the Serbian government during the war. The Judge did not reproach him for this distant area of interest, nor did he say that it was 'really going a bit far' to impugn the honour of a person who was 'not here to defend himself'. Gray's purpose was to suggest that anyone in the SVC had been 'fighting in uniform with the Germans', as Low had put it in the Deception Order, and that this wording was functionally equivalent to Robertson's phrase, 'serving in German forces'. He was allowed to do this, while Rampton was prevented from making the opposite case.

When the second witness, Joro Miletic, pointed out that those elements of the SVC which had marched into Austria had been commanded by the non-German Colonel Tatalovic, Gray objected, saying that the last witness had made the same point. But Rampton refused to concede. 'Each of these witnesses tells the same story,' he said to the Judge. 'If my learned friend is, as it were, to say that these people were serving in the German forces then it is entirely necessary that they should make clear that they were not and the reasons why not.'

'Mr Rampton, you know, as well as Mr Gray and I,' the Judge said, 'that there is a rule that if you wish to challenge any evidence you have to ask about it and cross-examine. I know that sometimes people make a mistake and do not, but there was no cross-examination on this. If we are going to hear a whole stack of these gentlemen, then it is taking our minds off the real issue. Mr Gray did not cross-examine the previous witness on this aspect.'

'I cannot guarantee that he is not going to cross-examine this witness. This is a different witness.'

'You and I have completely different ideas of how trials should be conducted,' said the Judge, 'and I happen to think Mr Gray is right.'

'The evidence of the previous witness is not contradicted by Mr Gray. That stands and it is unchallenged, but it does not apply to this witness.'

'He says the same,' the Judge said.

'We do not know what he is going to say until we have heard him,' Rampton insisted.

The Judge was forced to back down and Rampton continued. Nonetheless it was Nicolson's impression that about this time the Counsel for the Defence began to lose hope. Nicolson also thought the Defence tactics flawed. 'Endless repetitions of the same story will bore the jury and irritate the Judge,' he confided to his diary. Despite this, the Jugoslav witnesses made a favourable impression on him. 'They have rotund faces [and are] merry, rubicund, stout in figure, working class but alert.' They had 'no bitterness', Nicolson thought, and were 'truthful'.

The Judge gave an indication of the extent to which matters of race influenced him in a question he asked Miletic just before he stepped down. 'You were sent to Jugoslavia,' Mr Justice Davies said, 'and you describe it as an act of deception—Mr Ljotic chose a similar or stronger word—now, when you escaped (and all these years later I am sure you are very, very glad that you did) you gave yourself back to the English—maybe there was nowhere else to go—but this race that had deceived you, it seems that you and Mr Ljotic came and lived in this country and lived ever since. You must have felt rather uncomfortable with all us deceivers, the English, did you not?'

'No, my Lord, we bear no malice to the English people. We are talking about politics which are sometimes dirty business.'

'I understand the answer. You held nothing against the English people, that is why you were happy to come here, but you do not like politicians particularly or the politics.'

'I wouldn't generally say that I don't like politicians—I am myself interested in politics–'

'I am sorry, I did not mean to be offensive.'

'–but sometimes there is an ugly aspect or an ugly face of politics.'

'It was a matter of politics, you say, not the English people who caused you to go to Jugoslavia, so you are quite happy for that reason.'

'Yes.'

Tolstoy's next witness was Dr Zvojin Prvulovich. An Oxford PhD, Prvulovich has written a book about the repatriations entitled *Serbia Between the Swastika and the Red Star.* He has an acute understanding of both the forced repatriations and English law. But he was treated with no more respect than the others. When he offered to explain how the SVC came into existence, the Judge interrupted him. 'The point is that we are not conducting an historical enquiry, nor an enquiry into the history of the SVC. What may be important is the relationship of the SVC with the Germans, in particular any question of the command structure. So if you would be kind enough to listen carefully to Mr Rampton's questions and then answer them, it would be better.'

This was a wholly prejudicial intervention. The Judge was quite right to confine the witnesses to the facts and issues in dispute, but he was quite wrong to assert that the only facts and issues in dispute about the SVC concerned its command relationship with the German Armed Forces. Why, for example, had its members been so willing to believe that they were being sent to Italy?

Gray exploited the Judge's attitude. 'We are now getting from Dr Prvulovich a lecture on the political composition of Jugoslavia,' he said at one point, 'and the activities of the various groups through 1941, 1942 and up to 1945. My understanding is that there is an order for experts, so that this should be dealt with by the experts. Of course these individual witnesses can give such evidence as they can usefully give on the issues in the action, but each is not going to give us a lecture on Jugoslavia throughout the last war.' The bizarre implication was that Dr Knight was more "expert" on a subject that even he admitted he was not an expert on than a mature academic, from the country in question, who had lived through the events under discussion, spoke the languages of the relevant written authorities and who had himself published a book about the controversy.

'What Mr Gray said is surely right,' the Judge said. 'It was agreed the jury would need to know about the constituent parts of the Jugoslavian nation at the time, but that it would be a matter for expert evidence.'

Rampton countered by saying that Prvulovich had direct evidence to give, whereas an expert witness was, by definition, one speaking from 'hearsay'.

'Would you just heed my plea?' the Judge retorted. 'This may be looked at by witnesses as an opportunity to get off their chests something they have had on their chests for forty-five years but unfortunately, this is not a place where we provide a soap box. Please keep your witnesses under control.'

'I accept that,' Rampton replied, 'but may I remind your Lordship of the latitude that was given to some of the Plaintiff's witnesses. Brigadier Tryon-Wilson told us—it was extremely interesting and without interruption from myself or your Lordship—at considerable length of his experience in Italy when he won his DSO.'

'If you thought it was irrelevant, I hope you would have objected.'

'It was plainly irrelevant. Nothing to do with the case at all.'

'It is a great pity you did not get up and say so.'

'I believe witnesses should be allowed the indulgence to some extent of establishing themselves as individuals when they have important evidence to give, as this witness does, which is why I did not interrupt Brigadier Tryon-Wilson.'

Gray got more than he bargained for when he asked Prvulovich about his claim that the finger of blame for collaboration with the Germans could equally be pointed at the British where they were forced to live under Nazi occupation, for example in the Channel Islands. 'Can you explain how the British collaborated with the Germans?' Gray asked the witness, holding up a copy of his book.

'It is very simple,' Prvulovich replied. 'In the Channel Islands, where the Germans were in occupation for several years, according to the reliable historians and people who have documented this, three-quarters of the Channel Island population collaborated or worked for the German Army. I will add something more. When this information was passed on to the late Sir John Colville, he displayed quite an amazement anybody could talk about a collaboration of the British in the Channel Islands. When I collected the material and sent him chapter and verse, all based on British historians, the late Sir John Colville wrote back to me and said: "Of course, I did not know things had gone so far." Sir John Colville was Mr Churchill's Private Secretary. Later on he agreed that there was a great deal of collaboration there and the people in Guernsey, in his own words, "had gone too far". But later on he also tried to draw a distinction between the words "collaboration" and "co-operation", which would be an interesting issue to consider since many of us here seem to be accused of collaboration but in a very one-sided way, if I may say, my Lord.'

In re-examination, Rampton took up this point.

'Nothing was done about the collaboration in the Channel Islands,' Prvulovich said. 'But when at the end of the war Mr Morrison, who was the Home Affairs Secretary, went to the Channel Islands and when some people there wanted to raise the question of collaboration, Mr Morrison said: "No, we will leave this now," and everything was hushed up. And in a very few weeks, the leading collaborators were given the highest honours, including three peerages and many other decorations and titles which were duly reported in *The Times*, I think some time in December of that year.'

'Is that what you mean by a double standard or double morality?' Rampton asked.

'Yes. According to this, General Nedic should have been also given a life peerage for what he did for his country which was in a much more difficult condition than the Jersey Islands, because not one Jersey Islander was killed or shot—a number of them were sent to concentration camps. Even Jews were put on the persecution list in the Channel Islands. General Nedic, although he was accused as a collaborator, never issued—Serbia was the only little country which never issued—an edict against the Jews. In fact we sacrificed thousands of our lives to protect Jewish refugees. Often people who were caught were shot as accomplices.'

'What you are saying can be put very simply,' the Judge said. 'It comes to this, does it not? If somebody has got a loaded pistol and points it at your heart and says: "Give me a cigarette," even though he may be your enemy you will probably give him one.'

'Wouldn't you, my Lord?'

'That is what it comes to, does it not?' insisted the Judge.

'Wouldn't you?' repeated the witness.

'Fortunately I do not have to answer, but the answer is yes, if you want to know, though I might slip a bit of poison into his cigarette.'

'But you may not have time to do that because he is still watching you.'

'The jury knows what you are saying,' said Mr Justice Davies, 'that of course there are forms of collaboration which are absolutely despicable, but there are some which are understandable and even forgivable. That is what you are saying, is it not?'

'That's why I—'

'Don't any Jugoslavs say "Yes" or "No"?' interrupted the Judge.

'Not if they can help it!'

'That is very fair.'

Prvulovich's evidence was supported by Milovje Stankevich, a retired teacher of Old Church Slavonic, the archaic language used in

Orthodox Church services. Gray once again concentrated on the suggestion that the Serbian Volunteer Corps was a pro-German "quisling"
formation simply because it had fought Tito's communist Partisans.

'Tito and the Allies,' Gray said, 'had effectively won the war, had
they not, by the time you got into Austria?'

'Effectively, if you say so, yes,' the witness said. 'But Tito as an ally,
I cannot accept it. I would like to put a boot on the other foot, Mr Gray.
What was King Peter II of Jugoslavia who was here at the time? Was he
an ally or not?'

'I am not quite sure I caught the question,' Gray said.

'King Peter II of Jugoslavia, with all the prerogatives of a King, was
still here in England. Was he manipulated or was he deceived, or was he
ignored, Mr Gray? That was more important for us than Tito.'

Gray still looked baffled, so the Judge intervened. 'I think his point
is, if Tito was an ally how could an enemy of Tito be an ally as well? I
think that is the point, but how it has anything to bear on this case, I do
not know.'

'I am not sure it does,' said Gray.

'I can elaborate on that,' said Stankevich.

'No, I am going to stop you doing that,' said the Judge.

He allowed Gray, though, to make his point that the SVC, by
supporting the King of Jugoslavia consistently and not changing sides
when the British did, were 'defeated soldiers'. Britain won the war and
the Royalist Jugoslavs lost it, he said. Would Stankevich agree, Gray
asked very rudely, that 'defeated soldiers, if they can, play down the extent
to which they have been involved in fighting on the losing side?'

Stankevich was followed by France Dejak, France Kozima and Milan
Zajec, the three Slovenians who had escaped from the pit of Kocevje, as
described above (see p. 65ff). It is illustrative of the extent to which the
jury was given the impression of an almost victimless crime that Rampton
was forced by the Judge's repeated interventions to say to them all, 'Do
you understand that it is accepted in this Court that you were taken to the
pit at Kocevje and that you suffered appalling experiences and that we do
not wish you to describe that in this Court?'

"Yes", was the only word they were allowed to utter about this
incredible atrocity which they were so lucky to have escaped.

When France Dejak said he was willing to tell the Court about his
escape, the Judge intervened immediately.

'I do not know if you were here this afternoon,' Mr Justice Davies said, 'when one of the witnesses, in answer to my question, "Cannot Jugoslavs answer a question yes or no?" said, "Not if they can help it". Mr Rampton knows what has to be proved in this case and what is not admitted and, so, if you would just answer the question. The answer to the question, "Did you escape?" is "Yes". That is right, is it not?'

'Yes,' said the witness.

Their combined evidence lasted less than twenty minutes.

As he sat behind Lord Aldington after giving his own evidence, Sir James Wilson formed the impression that the Court did not want to hear what these witnesses had to say.

> The jury tended to switch off when you had these Jugoslavs from America coming back and telling them the appalling stories of what had happened to them when they got back [he has said subsequently]. I don't think the jury were frightfully sympathetic to that, quite frankly. Most of them were quite prosperous and I don't think the jury liked that—what's that language they all speak? Serbo-Croat—I don't think they liked the Serbo-Croat supporters club at the back of the Court. Again, I think that led to the damages being increased. I think there is a certain xenophobia on the part of British people. I am not saying that is admirable, I am just saying it exists. I don't think they like, again, seeing what they regard as respectable people being, as they would see it, unfairly attacked by people who have come from the United States apparently specially to do this. My feeling is that that evidence was probably counter-productive from Tolstoy's point of view.[2]

The next witness, Milovje Pavlovich, was once again asked about the consequences for the Serbs of Britain's change of sides. Why had he, after the British abandoned the Royalists, continued fighting the Communists? 'It is the case,' Gray said, 'is it not, that Tito and his Partisans were the allies of the British and the Americans?'

'Since 1943,' replied Pavlovich. 'Since English politics have changed. Until that time King Peter and Jugoslav Government were the real allies.'

---

2   Interview with the author 21 May 1993. Sir James, an Old Wykehamist, read law at New College, Oxford before entering the Army. Lady Wilson is a magistrate. Sir James sat through the whole trial. He said that when he read *The Minister and the Massacres* he did not think it libellous.

'But,' said Gray, 'in 1943, 1944 and 1945 Tito was the ally of Britain and America. Is that right?'

'He could be ally of St Peter as far as we are concerned. It was not our intention ever to be with Communists.'

After Gray sat down, the Judge added his own unofficial cross-examination. 'Just help me about this, Mr Pavlovich,' he said. 'The jury might be thinking along these lines—I do not know—you and the SVC hated and fought against the Partisans, did you not?'

'We did,' said the witness.

'And the Germans hated and fought against the Partisans. Is that not right?'

'The Germans' motives—motivations—were different from ours,' explained Pavlovich.

'Different motives for hating, but for different reasons from yours they also hated the Partisans, did they not, the Germans?'

'That was their own affair. I wouldn't go into the Germans' affairs, sir.'

'Did they fight the Partisans?'

'They did, yes.'

'What people might think now—may have thought then—and I want you to explain this to the jury—that might put you and the SVC on the same side as the Germans, do you see, both fighting Partisans for different motives?'

'To this question of yours I say that Germans fought Allies on all fronts. They fought Russians on the eastern front, and on the western front they fought British and Americans, but we were fighting exclusively Partisans. We never fired a shot at any of the other Allies. We never did.'

'Nothing in my question suggested that you did,' said the Judge. 'I will just ask it once more; I am not going to cross-examine you. Do you not agree that it would be reasonable for people to think that you and the SVC fighting Partisans were also on the same side as the Germans who were fighting the Partisans?'

'Somebody to form that opinion had to be quite sure that Serbian Volunteers and the Germans had the same ideas and same ideals, which was not the case.'

'I shall not ask you again,' the Judge said with heavy emphasis.

The next witness, who had travelled from Tasmania, was Dusan Zivkovic. Tolstoy has described him as 'merry, a sort of Serbian Nigel Watts. He was a combination of fiery Serb and laid-back Australian: no rudeness, but no awe for the Court either.'

Zivkovic, too, tried to describe the Serbian strategy. 'It wasn't as easy to drive Germans out, as it is for you to drive London fog out,' he said. 'You just have to wait until sun comes out. The whole idea was to wait until Allies land, like they did in Greece, and you know that in Greece British troops actually fought Communist Partisans. We were glad that Germany was losing war. If you were a Serb, or a Pole or Slovenian, for that matter, and Germany won the war—or Jews of course—you'd be finished. There was not a minute in our minds that if Germany won the war we would survive as a nation, or as individuals. He over there,' Zivkovic said, suddenly gesturing towards the Plaintiff, 'saw that we didn't survive anyway.'

Zivkovic explained that remark. His daughters were born in Britain, he said, and when Tolstoy asked him for help in this action, 'they said: "Look, you've got to go and try to clear this thing up, because unless it's cleared up and these BRs—you know what Australians say—unless these BRs are nailed, it will be a mar on British people and British Army and they don't deserve it"—and I *do* mean they don't deserve it. When I came here, this was a country—how would I say—that I found my feet. The British were polite, they loved animals—I'm a great supporter of the RSPCA—they loved animals. They treated me fairly. They were not only discriminating, they were friendly. They were always trying to help. They were a bit shy, but at that time—you may not believe it—I was shy. I like this country except the weather.'

Gray started his cross-examination aggressively, without any pre-liminaries: 'What did you say you came here to do?'

'Pardon. Speak up, please?' Zivkovic said in what Gray seemed to take as an offensively egalitarian tone.

'What your daughter said?' the Judge said.

'They said I should come here and help to clear this thing, to find who really did this, because unless it's done the history will be saying that we were sent to our death by Britain—that is British people and British Army—and they don't deserve that, because it's out of character. When I was getting naturalised—let me point out to you—the examining officer asked me about my past, and when I said this he dropped his pen, and said: "I don't believe this, the British would never do anything wrong, and be careful, don't tell fibs, because you may hear from us again." I never heard nothing; I got my naturalisation papers.'

'Did you use the phrase in your evidence just now: "Nail the BRs"?'

Gray asked.

'Did I use that? Did I?'

'I will ask the question again: did you use the phrase: "Nail the BRs"?'

'I might have. Do you say I used it?'

'I am asking you if you used it?' Gray said.

'I don't know, I can't remember. Don't you listen to what I am saying?'

'Be polite,' Mr Justice Davies said. 'They are very polite in Australia. I do not know about Tasmania. I am told the weather in Tasmania is very like it is here. Mr Gray is not talking about something you said in 1945. He is talking about something you said ten minutes ago, or less. Do you remember?'

'I think I meant—yes.'

'I think you were mentioning a conversation you had with your daughter, and that you came here to "nail the BRs",' said Gray.

'Yes, to help clear this matter, yes.'

'No, I am asking you what phrase you used. Did you use the phrase "nail the BRs"?'

'Yes, I did. All right, I did. So?'

'What does "BRs" mean?'

'Bastards,' Zivkovic said.[3]

'Who are the bastards?'

'Well, those who sent us to our death.'

'And you have come here, have you, to nail the bastards?'

'Well, help to discover the truth.'

'Well, which is it?' Gray asked in a tone of voice which implied he had scored a major point.

'Are you telling me that I wasn't sent to my death, that I walked over?'

'Do you follow the distinction between seeking to ascertain the truth and coming here to nail the bastards. Do you follow that distinction?'

'Well, to help to nail those who did it—to find the culprits, if that is possible.'

'You are giving evidence in a libel action, are you not?'

---

3   That is the word in the transcript, and as reported in the *Daily Telegraph*. However Nicolson's clear recollection, from his diary written that evening, was that the word used was 'buggers'.

'Yes, yes.'

'You know who the Plaintiff is?'

'Yes.'

'Are you saying that you came here to nail Lord Aldington?'

'I don't know—is he guilty? Does he feel guilty?'

'Could you please listen to my questions and answer them. Does that mean pointing your finger in the direction of Lord Aldington? Do you understand me? Are you saying that you came here to nail Lord Aldington?'

'Well, I think he's guilty.'

'Right, you think he is guilty, you tell me on what evidence?'

'Well, I have read the book, there's documents there.'

'Which book?' Gray asked.

'Tell me—was he Chief of Staff of the 5 Corps?' said the witness.

Once again, the Judge intervened on Gray's behalf.[4] 'Mr Zivkovic, what Mr Gray is asking you—and in view of what you have said it is a perfectly fair question—on what evidence do you think he is guilty?'

'I think he's guilty because he was Chief of Staff of the 5 Corps at the time of handing over. Somebody must have signed the orders, I can't see that his corporals had done it. It's as simple as that. That's how I see it.'

'Very well,' said Gray, 'in the light of that answer—I have not done this with any other Jugoslav witness—I am going to ask you to look at a British military document. Would you look at bundle B, page 123. This will not be a familiar document to you so we will take it slowly. This is a signal—and I am not tricking you, you must accept my word for that–'

'I believe you, I believe you,' said Zivkovic.

'–sent by Allied Forces Headquarters to Main Eighth Army on 23rd May 1945. It reads: "Agree that all Jugoslav Nationals in Eighth Army area should be returned by you [5 Corps] to Jugoslavs unless this involves the use of force in which case they should be dealt with in accordance with" another order.'

'What is the other order?' Zivkovic asked. 'What does the other order say—shoot them?' In fact it was the Distone Order, by which Alexander

---

4   It is worth noting that there was not a single comparable occasion when he intervened with one of the Plaintiff's witnesses to assist Rampton's cross-examination.

ordered all the Jugoslavs be sent to Italy.

'You are suggesting, are you, that there is another order which says shoot them?' Gray asked, hoping, presumably, that the witness did not realise that the Welsh Guards had been ordered to 'shoot to kill if it becomes necessary' in handing the Jugoslavs to Tito.

'You've just read it,' Zivkovic said.

'Did you just say, "Does the other order say shoot them"?'

'Yes, what does the other order say?'

'Are you seriously suggesting,' Gray repeated, 'that there is an order which says, "Shoot them"?'

'No, I don't think so.'

'Do you want me to show you the other order?'

'Tell me what the other order says.'

'All right, I will,' said Gray. 'Turn to page 43 in the bundle.'

'Your Lordship, I must apologise,' Zivkovic said, turning to the Judge, 'I might be a bit quick but remember my life was at stake.'

'We understand that but–' the Judge replied.

'I also lost 28 men that have never heard of Karl Marx or Toby Low and, you know, they were all massacred.'

'What did you say a moment ago?' Gray asked. 'I am sorry. You are making remarks which I do not always catch. You had never heard of Karl Marx? You had never heard of Toby Low?'

The Judge explained. 'He said, and he can tell me if I am wrong, that he lost so many men (he gave the number) and none of them had ever heard of Karl Marx or Toby Low. What it has to do with anything I am not quite sure.'

'They were simple peasants and they were sent to their death,' Zivkovic added.

'Is what you are saying that you feel you want to find a victim or scapegoat or something like that?' Gray asked.

'No, I don't want to find a victim or scapegoat.'

'There you are; there is the other order,' said Gray. 'I have shown it to you now and can we go back to the relevant order which is the one I showed you before?'

'Yes.'

'Do you understand that that is an order that is coming from the Allied Forces Headquarters?'

'Yes.'

'That is a General (*sic*) called Alexander,' said Gray.

'Yes.'

'It is being sent to 8th Army and it is being copied to 5 Corps.'

'Mmmm.'

'Do you see the date of it, 23rd May?'

'All right.'

'What date did you go back to Jugoslavia?'

'24th.'

Zivkovic was the only witness for the Defence who put the Jugoslav aspect of the case plainly, and it is noticeable that he was able to do so only by ignoring the etiquette of the Court. For the rest, the Judge tried to keep this kind of exchange off the record. For example, he told one witness, France Kristof, that he had 'never known a case so plagued by witnesses who will not listen to the question and answer it. We all understand your feelings and I am sure that every Jugoslav here would like to talk for a day to the jury about what happened, and I sympathise with them. However, unfortunately, from that point of view, this Court is not set up to make that sort of enquiry. If you would only listen, peacefully and quietly, to the question, by very experienced Counsel on both sides, and answer it—not you particularly but any witness—we would get on a bit quicker.'

This exchange took place just before the Court rose on day 25, and the witness clearly thought about it overnight. Next morning he came back to complete his evidence and started by saying to the Judge, 'I was sworn in to tell the truth, the whole truth, but yesterday I was cut short–'

'The whole truth,' Mr Justice Davies said, interrupting him, 'means the whole truth in answer to questions you are asked. It is not the whole truth about your life-story or any other witness's. Please, sir, I beg you, do just listen to the question and answer it. This is not a platform or a soap-box, as I have said before. You just listen to the question and answer it and, if possible, answer it shortly, "Yes" or "No". We all realise that a lot of questions cannot be answered "Yes" or "No", but we do not want speeches. I have to be blunt and say that to you, we do not want speeches, we want the answers to questions, evidence.'

That completed the Jugoslav witnesses. As the first Cossacks mounted the witness stand, Gray's tactics changed. Cavilling was exchanged for near-total silence. Gray had no questions for two of the first four witnesses and only one for the other two: when had they run away from Peggetz camp? Beyond that, he objected to the presence of these Cossacks in Court at all.

'What concerns Lord Aldington—and I make no bones about it—and he was exceedingly upset, I repeat, *exceedingly* upset,' Gray said to the Judge in the absence of the jury, 'is that the manifest purpose of putting those [Cossack] ladies in the witness box is to convey the impression to the jury that in some way Lord Aldington is responsible for what happened. That is, as your Lordship knows, although the jury may not have their eye on this particular ball at the moment, a mile away from the true facts. One has the rulings on 21st May [the Definition Order] which relate only to formations and individuals in those military formations, and that is the end of it—and the implication of this procession of witnesses is as prejudicial as it is possible to get.'

'I think you underrate the jury,' the Judge said. 'I will speak quite bluntly. I think the jury cannot understand what on earth all the relevance is of all this evidence. I think they thought the whole of yesterday was a waste of time, looking at their faces, but I would not say that in their presence—this is non-reportable. But that is the view I formed, and I know a little bit about juries.'

'That is consoling to hear,' said Gray.

'But I may be completely wrong.'

'That is the worry. One does not know. That is the problem with prejudicial evidence.'

'I quite understand how Lord Aldington feels as a party to the case,' said the Judge, 'but in the end everything comes out in the wash and I do not think the jury in the end will be left in any illusion about the situation. What I do regret and I know Mr Rampton thinks I am harsh and unjust in saying this, but I do rather regret what seemed to me to appear on several occasions when Mr Rampton seemed to feel it was necessary to allow the witnesses to ramble on simply to justify their trip from the far corners of the world.'

Rampton ignored that jibe, but did reply to Gray's point. 'The idea that I am leading evidence in order to prejudice the jury,' he said, 'is resented on this side of the Court. We believe this evidence is relevant because what happened to these people or did not happen, more particularly—namely they should have been reprieved, many of them, from repatriation—was a direct consequence of Lord Aldington's order. These witnesses prove three things. First, no screening took place. Secondly, it could have done, and, thirdly, that if it had done, a whole lot of people would have been saved who ought never to have gone back.'

If the foreign witnesses did not make a good impression on the jury, what impression did the jury make on the foreign witnesses? Zoë Polanska-Palmer was one of the Cossacks who gave evidence. 'I was so mad I wanted to throw my knickers at the Judge,' she says today. She has put her feelings in writing in words which stand for most of the Slavic witnesses.

It was set in comic opera style where the legal establishment were presenting much of trivia evidence, conniving and smiling to each other, the jury nodding off, yawning or laughing.

Mr Rampton was asking me irrelevant questions which was most insulting to someone like myself who had been at the centre of the forcible repatriations. He should have been recalling the human tragedy, the murder of innocent women and children and the frail and the sick—and only by the grace of God, I was not murdered too.

I should have been telling the jury about the beautiful summer day in Peggetz camp, how the British soldiers who, under orders, were clobbering innocent people with pickaxes, rifle-butts, bayonets and machine-guns.

Is a massacre of this nature not a War Crime?

This account was not admissible to the jury. The jury had not read my book *Yalta Victim* nor Count Tolstoy's two books. Perhaps if they were acquainted with such horrendously evil murders by the British soldiers, then they would not have been yawning and nodding off, and the outcome of the trial might have been different.[5]

Outside the Court, Nicolson witnessed the Plaintiff's reaction to these people's evidence. 'Toby comes out,' he wrote in his diary that evening, 'while a Cossack woman is describing what awful things she endured, and is on the verge of tears. Toby indifferent.'

The last of the foreign witnesses, Ivan Kudrenko, a Jugoslav citizen who had been an officer in the Cossack Cavalry, described how, by chance, a Major Ostrovski and 60 other non-Soviets were saved from repatriation at Weitensfeld (the only occasion this happened). Before Kudrenko stepped down, the Judge cross-examined him about this incident.

'There was just one loose end which I think you had better clear up,'

5   Letter to the author 5 March 1993

Mr Justice Davies said, 'although it has not really got a lot to do with the case, it may be thought, but you left the unfortunate Major Ostrovski—you told us he was taken away to be shot and I think we ought to know whether he was or whether you ever saw him again?'

'Would you like me to explain?'

'No, I would not. I would like you to answer the question. Did he get shot?'

'No, he did not get shot.'

'Did he come back to you?'

'Yes, sir.'

'Did he remain at the camp with you?'

'That is correct.'

'Still in command?'

'Still in command of who was left, yes.'

'I would not like anybody to think that the unfortunate man got shot. He may not have had a very nice time but eventually he came back. He was not sent back to Russia, was he?'

'No, sir, but do you want to know why he was not shot?'

'No, I do not want to know, quite honestly. It was quite irrelevant, in my view, that you even told us that he was taken away, but he did not go in the end, so that is all right.'

Nicolson noted in his diary that night, 'The Judge is getting more and more biased.'

That concluded the Slavic witnesses. Would the Judge treat the others any better?

First up was Philip Brutton, an Englishman now resident in France who had, in 1945, been a junior officer in the Welsh Guards, part of 1st Guards Brigade. He had kept a diary at the time which shows that he and his fellow-officers all thought that in Balkan wars 'the loser did not live'. They thought anyone handed back would be shot, as the Titoists were 'purely brigands and looters'. He thought the 'extradition of the Chetniks and Croats most nauseating'.

Gray's response to this, in cross-examination, was to suggest that 5 Corps had a motive for the handovers in that there was a real threat from Tito. That argument was quite irrelevant because Lord Aldington had argued that he ordered the handovers in response to superior orders, not as a form of blood-sacrifice to the Communists out of fear of having to fight them.

There were a couple of other witnesses who filled in gaps in the testimony—most saying mainly that they knew that anyone handed over to Tito or Stalin would be badly treated—and they were all dealt with perfectly properly by the Judge.

The Court then broke up for the sixth weekend of the trial. The Defence was so short of cash that Tolstoy had to fly to Canada on an emergency fund-raising trip. Georgina was left alone at home with her increasingly pessimistic thoughts. There was no-one locally to whom she could talk about the case and so she telephoned the Defence's most staunch supporter, Nigel Nicolson, at Sissinghurst Castle. 'I feel so confident when Nikolai is here,' she said, 'but when he is away I feel a terrible misgiving. I have a certain feeling that we are going to lose— mostly from the feeling that Gray is better at it than Rampton. I have just been hanging on Nikolai's personal enthusiasm.'

On Monday Karl-Gottfried Vierkorn was called. Most of his evidence concerned the behaviour of the British Army in connection with the handover of the Cossack Cavalry and had already, by virtue of Lord Aldington's Admissions, been rendered inadmissible. Gray must have had an unusually hectic weekend because, for once, it took him a while to focus on the business of the day. Early on he asked some amazing questions. For example, he wanted to know if the Cossacks had been equipped by the Germans. They had, said Vierkorn; they were in the German Army.

Rubinstein Callingham had not thought to provide Vierkorn with an interpreter and, although his English is much better than most English people's German, he still had difficulty expressing himself as he would have liked. By playing on Vierkorn's inadequate English, Gray was able to extract evidence which enabled him to say in summing up, quite wrongly since that is not what Vierkorn intended his words to mean, that the Cossack officers went to the Soviet Union because they did not want to be separated from their men.[6]

---

6   This was one of Cowgill's arguments and it had no authority other than Tolstoy, who wrote, on page 44 of *The Minister and the Massacres*, 'Neither General Krasnov nor any other old émigré was seeking to extricate himself from sharing whatever fate attended those of their comrades who were in the equivocal position of being Soviet citizens.' However, on page 234, Tolstoy also wrote: 'About 23 or 24 May General Peter Krasnov sent a second letter to his old acquaintance Alexander, drawing attention once again to the Cossacks' plight, emphasising

'You have described how a good many officers of the Cossacks, including yourself, went back to Russia,' Gray said to Vierkorn, 'and you had appalling experiences yourself, I know. Did that come about as a result of General von Pannwitz speaking to the Cossack officers?'

'General von Pannwitz didn't speak to the Cossack officers to stay with their troops,' the witness replied. 'He spoke only to the German officers in the last part of this dramatic scenario, because the Cossacks had been separated from the Germans in the middle of May 1945.'

'Tell us what General von Pannwitz said to yourself and the other officers?'

'There was a small group, I suppose it had been 15 or 20 officers, maybe, at the 20th May—15th/20th May—that he said to us that the war is over and: "You are not standing on oath to swear—that's also not relevant, you can go wherever you like, but I spoke to your responsibility against our comrades in the war, to our Cossacks until the British troops have decided where the Cossacks have to go." He said—I heard that they shall come to Canada and another answer was to Australia. So *we decided to stay with our men until the British troops decided what going on with them in the future.*' (emphasis added)

'That was really what General von Pannwitz wanted you to do?'

'That was really General von Pannwitz said to us who were standing

---

that he and many others were not Soviet citizens and were in consequence owed protection as refugees in international law.' These two statements are contradictory: either Krasnov sought to share the fate of the Soviet citizens amongst the Cossacks, or he did not. Cowgill uses the first quote in his *Final Report* in order to justify the Definition Order in its abandonment of screening (p. 97). He did so earlier, in the *Interim Report* (p. 40): 'The vast majority of the Cossacks were to continue to see themselves, regardless of their individual status, as a collective entity.' This otherwise unsupported assertion implies the bizarre conclusion that, if Low *had* ordered individual screening, the non-Soviet Cossacks would have resisted it, clamouring to be allowed to leave for Siberia with their Soviet comrades and accusing the perfidious English of 'betraying' those they forced to remain at liberty. Obviously, this is complete nonsense, but it is revealing how often this argument has been repeated. Alistair Horne, for example, quoted Tolstoy's first remark in the paperback edition of *Macmillan* (p. 268)—it is not in the hardback edition—but ignored the second. This enabled him to comment, completely erroneously given Tolstoy's account of the petitions, that 'Krasnov and Shkuro had, very honourably, not come forward to be treated differently from their unit or their fellow Cossacks.' Not for the first time, Tolstoy's occasional tendency to overstate his case—here by whitewashing the émigré Generals beyond even his own evidence—gave his opponents a weapon with which to attack his fundamentally valid argument.

round him.'

'He said: "Stay with your men"?'

'"Stay with your men," yes.'

'Did you at some stage, as a group, the German officers, explain this to the British, that you wanted to stay with your men?'

'Of course, so the British allowed us to have our pistols.'

'So, great credit to all the officers who did this, *your return to the Soviet Union was as a result of your deciding to follow what General von Pannwitz asked you to do?*' (emphasis added)

'Yes, in the one side and in the other side, I said that I was thinking that it would not be happening what happened.'

The second italicised passage does not follow from the first. Vierkorn's words were misused, but Gray needed to get this admission in evidence, however unintentional given the witness's incomplete grasp of English, or he could not argue in his closing speech that the Cossack officers went 'voluntarily' to the Soviet Union. Suspecting this might be the case, Rampton tried to put the record straight in re-examination.

'If, on the 25th or 26th May,' he asked Vierkorn, 'the British had said to you: "We are going to give you Germans over to the Soviet authorities", what would you have done?'

'Not one would stay longer in this camp and all would be escaping in the near mountains and the forests,' replied Vierkorn.[7]

Tolstoy's last and most important witness was Nigel Nicolson. Nicolson's knowledge of the military history, his first-hand experience of the handovers and his air of social distinction made him the ideal person to speak up for Tolstoy's view of events in a London court. What is so impressive about Nicolson is that he did so thinking that the pamphlet was libellous, and that if he had been on the jury he would have found for Lord Aldington (although he says he would have awarded contemptuous damages). Nicolson objected to the 'Nazi butchers' insult and to Tolstoy's assertion that Brigadier Low had 'issued every order and arranged every detail of the lying and brutality which resulted in these massacres'. Nicolson's

7   It should be noted that both Cowgill and Horne published the 1990 editions of their books *after* attending the trial, and hence after Vierkorn made this statement. It is significant that they both ignore it completely.

view is that a war crime was undoubtedly committed in May 1945—four war crimes, he will say: against the German officers of the Cossacks Cavalry; against the women and children of the Kazachi Stan; against the non-Soviet Russians in both Cossack camps; and against all the Jugoslavs—but that Low was far from being solely responsible. During the trial, Nicolson was in the habit of lunching with the Tolstoys in the Law Society dining hall. Shortly before he was called he told them what he would say if asked about the pamphlet itself. 'Georgina looks at me as if I am Judas Iscariot,' Nicolson wrote in his diary, 'but Nikolai takes it well.'

Right away, Nicolson started making points very dangerous to the Plaintiff's case. He described the surrender of the Russkii Korpus and the arrival of the ten-mile-long column of Jugoslavs at Viktring, stressing that they were *not* under German command.

'They did not come marching in threes down the road,' he said. 'They were muddled up as women and children, carts, even camels. There were three camels I remember well, in this train. They had their cooking pots, and all the other apparatus and stores, and of course they were armed, the military element, and we disarmed them. As the German element was the leading element under this German colonel, we thought that he had total control over the whole column. It turned out of course that he did not. It was impossible for him to have control over the whole lot because they did not recognise his command.'

Were they all Nazi sympathisers who had been fighting the Allies? Rampton asked him.

'These Jugoslav dissidents had in many cases been fighting with the Germans, but never *for* the Germans,' Nicolson said. 'I make the distinction in this way: we had to ask ourselves whom, which side, in the second World War did these dissident Jugoslavs want to win the War? There was no question at all what their answer would be, except perhaps a few extremist fascists. They wanted the British and the Americans to win, but they had been obliged by the civil war which was going on in Jugoslavia contemporaneously with the international war to accept German arms and to fight alongside them against the same enemy: Tito. It made them, in other words, sometimes co-belligerents of the Germans, but never their allies.'

Ironically, as Nicolson pointed out, the Russkii Korpus, who were *not* repatriated, were far more amenable to German authority than the Serbs, who were.

Rampton read from Nicolson's Situation Report of 13 May, the day

Macmillan visited Klagenfurt, 'None of these can be repatriated except to almost certain death at the hands of Tito.' Who were 'these'? he asked.

'Slovenes, Serbs, Chetniks and Croats,' Nicolson answered.

So what was the reaction at 1st Guards Brigade when they heard rumours that the Jugoslavs were to be handed back to Tito?

'Consternation,' Nicolson said. 'We thought someone must have blundered. It cannot be true.'

On 17 May the Deception Order was received at Brigade headquarters. What was the reaction then?

'We considered it to be one of the most disgraceful operations that any British troops had ever been ordered to undertake,' Nicolson said, loudly and clearly. He had been waiting years to say that in public. He has felt ashamed of the part his unit played in these operations ever since they happened, and has long regretted that he obeyed the order. As he said these words, the Court was hushed. He noticed that Lord Aldington buried his head in both hands.

Pressing on, Rampton asked him who he meant by 'we'.

'The immediate recipients,' Nicolson answered. 'That is, the officers of the Brigade Headquarters; the battalions when they were told of it, and right down to the ordinary guardsmen who had to execute it, and I should like to say here that it was not only officers with tender consciences who felt like this. It was all of us, particularly those who had to carry the order out at the railway stations.'

'That seems a very strong reaction,' Rampton said. 'Can you tell us the reason for it?'

'The reason was that we were being ordered to hand over to what we considered was almost certain death, thousands of people, including men, women and children, and civilians, who had surrendered to us, refugees who had appealed to us for asylum, and which we had granted to them. Men, women and children who had come to trust us, who we had come to like through our contacts with them, and now we were to betray their trust, and send them back to their arch enemies.'

This was strong stuff, and it immediately became clear that the Judge was not amused. For the first time since the Slavic witnesses had left the stand—he had been quite polite to Vierkorn and the other non-Slavs—he told a Defence witness to stick to the subject when answering a question, although he did so in amusingly obsequious terms.

'It would help us if you would be so gracious as to conform to our procedure,' said King Edward's School, Birmingham, to The College of

Our Lady of Eton Beside Windsor, 'which is that when a question is asked, one does try to answer it and not simply in effect make a speech, however strongly felt. Would you put your question again, please, Mr Rampton?'

Two minutes later the same thing happened again, but this time the Judge was less fawning in his phraseology. Rampton had asked the witness whether he had ever told 'a dissident Jugoslav or dissident Jugoslavs a lie about their destination'.

'I can give you an example if his Lordship will allow me,' Nicolson replied.

'I would much rather you answered the question first,' Mr Justice Davies said. 'You can start with a yes or no and then qualify it by all means. The question was, did you ever tell a Jugoslav a lie about where he or she was going?'

'My Lord,' Nicolson said, 'if you would listen to my answer I think you will see it cannot be answered yes or no, even that question. May I go on?'

'Yes, go on,' the Judge said testily. 'But it is really up to Mr Rampton to control you. It is very invidious for me to have to intervene. The jury will judge whether that question can be answered yes or no, plus any addition, of course. Nobody expects a witness to say yes to a false question.'

'It may have been a false question—' Rampton started to say.

'Do not start backtracking and sidetracking,' said the Judge, interrupting him. 'Let the witness then answer the question in his own way to see if he can answer it yes or no. My opinion is in the end that it does not matter tuppence.'

Finally Nicolson gave his example: 'A Serbian officer who could speak some French came up to me on the platform at Maria Elend station when we were embarking many of his men and women into the trains, and said to me, "Is it true that we are going to Italy?", and I said to him, "I am going to turn my back on you for thirty seconds, and if when I turn back you are still there you are going to Italy." When I turned back he was not there. He had escaped.'

'The answer then to my question is yes and no, is it not?' said Rampton.

'Mr Rampton,' the Judge interrupted, 'you give more evidence than any of your witnesses. I really wish you would not. It is a bit too clever for me, but then I am a simple soul.'

When Gray stood up to cross-examine Nicolson, it was immediately apparent that, unlike the twenty-three foreigners, he took this witness very seriously. He was aggressive from the start. It was imperative that Nicolson be prevented from making the case Tolstoy had failed to get across. But first, Gray had to belittle him.

'Mr Nicolson, may I ask you to try and find, in the witness box, this little bundle of plans and maps? What I want to start by doing is finding you in the command structure or in the hierarchy. Will you turn to page 6 please?'

Gray worked his way down the hierarchy to Keightley's headquarters. '5 Corps is underneath 8th Army. Is that correct?'

'It says 5 Corps Field Units; 5 Corps Structure. I am turning backwards now.'

'Listen to my question, Mr Nicolson, and it will be quicker. Underneath 8th Army comes 5 Corps. Is that correct?'

'I understand. I hear your question, Mr Gray, but I am not certain which page you are referring me to.'

'Do not worry about pages, just answer the question,' Gray said, rather rudely considering the question he had asked related to what was on the pages Nicolson was trying to find. 'I do not think it is really contentious. Underneath 8th Army comes 5 Corps?'

'That is correct,' said the witness.

'Underneath 5 Corps, there come a number of field units and you see those at page eight of the bundle. The relevant one for present purposes— that is to say, your purposes—is 6th Armoured Division. Is that correct?'

'Correct.'

'Then we can go to page nine, I think, where we find 6th Armoured Division; commander, Major General Murray?'

'Yes.'

'If we follow down the line, we get 1st Guards Brigade and that is your Brigade, is it not?'

'Yes; 1st Guards Brigade.'

'That was commanded by Brigadier Verney?'

'Yes.'

'Serving under him was Colonel Rose Price?'

'He commanded the 3rd Battalion Welsh Guards in that brigade.'

'Then, there is you, Intelligence Officer, Captain Nicolson, as you then were?'

'Yes.'

'Is that a fair description of where you fit into the overall picture?'

'Yes.'

Gray then settled down to a lengthy attempt to prove that Nicolson's impressions at the lowly level of 1st Guards Brigade were different from those at the rarefied altitude of 5 Corps headquarters and AFHQ—even the War Cabinet. What would a 28-year old Captain in the Grenadiers, who featured no earlier than page nine in Gray's schematic representation of the Mediterranean Theatre command structure, know of these high concerns? The fact that Captain Nicolson had not felt the Titoists a threat did not mean that the Supreme Commander did not have reason to fear them, Gray said.

'I agree there was anxiety,' Nicolson conceded after a particularly intense bombardment of high-level notes and minutes. 'All these messages reveal it, but I think it is rather strange that, if there was a continuing anxiety after about 18 May, more preparations were not made, for instance, by reinforcing 5 Corps, which never received its armour even. It was still, I think, south of the Po until June, and our thin line in Austria was never deployed in such a way that we could engage in combat with anybody. We had not got our artillery with us.'

'I am sure you have been listening carefully to the evidence, Mr Nicolson, and you probably remember Lord Aldington explaining how an important part of Operation Beehive [5 Corps' plan to eject the Titoists from Carinthia] was indeed to call up the armour which was still in Italy. That was something that he was arranging for, as part of Operation Beehive. Do you remember that evidence?'

'I remember him saying that, but it did not arrive.'

'The answer to that, of course, is that there was an agreement on 19 May.'

'Exactly. You are simply altering it by one day, which I do not dispute. I said on the 18th the crisis was over; you are saying the 19th. So Beehive was off.'

The thrust of Gray's argument was that until 21 May, 5 Corps was still legitimately worried about the intentions of the Titoists. Thus both of Low's main orders, the Definition and the Deception Orders, were issued under threat of action from Tito. It has already been remarked that this line of argument should have been irrelevant as the Plaintiff's case was that he was acting under orders, not making political decisions about which groups of people should be sacrificed to appease Tito. Lord Aldington had said: 'It was not for us to overrule the orders of the Army Commander or the theatre Supreme Commander.' Quite so. Disastrously, the Defence did not try to simplify, and therefore clarify, the argument by disentangling these two mutually contradictory pleas. The resulting confusion played directly into the Plaintiff's hands.

As he had done with Tolstoy, Gray displayed his tactical finesse by arguing exhaustively with Nicolson about the Robertson Order, without any clear result, yet without giving the impression of quibbling. It was notable that once Gray was putting the questions, the Judge largely stopped interrupting the witness. Nonetheless, at one point, Nicolson came dangerously close to simplifying things.

'The only order which we can attribute on this subject directly to Lord Aldington,' Nicolson said, 'is the one which says that all people of Jugoslav nationality in the Corps area must be returned. That must include civilians as well as soldiers and camp followers.' But, as the Robertson Order referred exclusively to people 'serving in German forces', Low's Deception Order cannot be said to derive authority from it.

It was a simple and powerful point. But, as the person asking the questions, Gray was in control. Instead of trying to put a different view, he suddenly produced a mountain of tenuously related documents and started jumping from Bundle to Bundle, like a goat with a sore hoof, until the point was suitably obscured again.

Relaxing, Gray moved on to the irrelevant question of the witness's motive for lying in his Situation Report of 18 May, when he had noted that the Jugoslavs were 'kindly and efficiently handled [by the Titoists] and provided with light refreshments before continuing their journey into Jugoslavia.'

'Were you ordered to include that false information in this summary of the activities of the 1st Guards Brigade?' Gray asked.

'I did not like doing it,' Nicolson said. 'but if I had told the whole truth, as I am telling it in this box, at that time, I would not have been very popular.'

'You are not saying you were ordered to do that, but you felt that, if you told the truth, you would not have been very popular?'

'That is right. I wish I had not.'

At this point the Judge intervened. 'Would that have mattered, really? To you, I mean? You were not a career Army officer; the war was over, in the sense that it was not a fighting situation and one wonders—I only invite you to deal with it—if these were lies, as you say, why you were much bothered about being popular?'

'My Lord,' Nicolson said, 'I have often thought of these events since and one thing I feel now is that I should have disobeyed General Murray. I would probably have been court-martialled, but, as you suggest, what would that have mattered? I was not a regular soldier. I might have gone to prison for a year. I would not have been shot, as Mr Gray once suggested in this court, and I would have emerged with credit, but that is hindsight. I wish I had done it that way.'

That was more or less the end of Nicolson's evidence. 'I step down from over 5 hours in the witness box,' he noted that evening in his diary, 'having quite enjoyed it and made only one gaffe—over Hocevar. People congratulate me and Jugoslavs almost weep when shaking my hand.'

With his case completed, barring Rampton's closing speech, a period of depression set in for Tolstoy. The opportunity he had engineered for himself and his twenty-six witnesses to speak publicly about the forced repatriations had produced neither a wave of public sympathy for the victims nor any significant new historical evidence. Not only that, Nicolson noted: 'Nikolai hints for the first time, that he expects to lose the case owing to the Judge's bias, and has actually taped an interview with the press to be published after the verdict saying so. I beg him not to risk impeachment for contempt of court. He's rash in that way.'

The last submission before the closing speeches was made in the absence of the jury. It was by far the most dangerous for the Plaintiff, and threatened by its simplicity, its relevance and its force to turn the case upside down. Dr Christopher Greenwood, of Magdalene College, Cambridge, had agreed to come to Court to help Rampton with his argument on points of international law.[8] Strangely, in all the Defence pleadings there was no specific allegation that Lord Aldington had committed a war crime. Yet the pamphlet called him a war criminal. In order to justify that, the Defence had to be able to show that Brigadier Low had violated the Geneva Convention. Greenwood had come to help Rampton argue that point.

Gray immediately objected on the ground that the Geneva Conven-

---

8   Greenwood is University Lecturer in the Faculty of Law. He is joint editor of *International Law Reports* and he also lectures to the Royal Naval Staff College, the Joint Services Defence College and the Royal College of Defence Studies.

tions dealt exclusively with the position of prisoners of war and the victims of 5 Corps had not been prisoners of war but surrendered enemy personnel. It is true that many of them were referred to as SEPs rather than POWs in the documents of the time, but this distinction was a purely administrative one. SEPs were people who, after surrender, were allowed to retain their own internal organisation and discipline to make them easier to handle by the Allies in the early days of peace, when millions of surrendered Wehrmacht troops would make the individual recording of prisoners, a specific requirement of POW status, impracticable. Nothing in this was intended to remove the obligation on the capturing power to treat their captives humanely. Quite the opposite in fact, as POW status was still insisted upon for members of the SS, for example, who were to be interrogated individually with a view to possible prosecution for war crimes. As has been pointed out above, the Cossacks and Jugoslavs would have had a better chance of survival if they had been members of the SS than gullible and co-operative captives of 5 Corps.

Nonetheless, Gray proceeded to state the definition of a prisoner of war which, in his words, was 'a person who has been taken captive during hostilities'. But the victims of 5 Corps had, mostly, surrendered *after* the cessation of hostilities, therefore maltreatment of them was not outlawed by the Geneva Convention, he argued. Gray further confused the issue by asking the silly question, what is a captive? He had, he told the Judge, consulted the Shorter Oxford Dictionary on this point.

'"Capture",' Gray said, 'means to take forcibly or by stratagem. That is of significance because as your Lordship will remember, all these Jugoslavs and all the Cossacks marched over the mountains voluntarily in order, as has emerged from witness after witness, to surrender and/or to seek asylum from the British.' In fact this was another nonsensical point, since every surrender is a voluntary act.

The Judge got stuck on the concept of voluntariness. 'Supposing you have trench warfare, with no-man's-land, Mr Gray, and a dozen men on one side decide they have had enough, and they walk across no man's land and knock (*sic*) on the wall (*sic*) of the trench (*sic*) and say, "We have come to surrender". Are they not prisoners of war?'

'My Lord, it would appear not from the Definition Section. But it may be that when hostilities are continuing–'

'I want help on that,' the Judge said. 'I am thinking whether it makes a difference, if hostilities are concluded—it may well do. But supposing they are still continuing?'

'My Lord, I take that point. If you are driven to a position, as your Lordship puts it to me, in no-man's-land, where you feel you have no option but to surrender, then it may be that that would be covered by the Geneva Convention.'

'A deserter. Is a deserter a prisoner of war?'

'I would have thought not, but again, I do not know.'

'I am not posing any concluded view; I am just seeking for help.'

Rampton's case was that the handover of the German officers in the Cossack Cavalry to the Soviets was a cut-and-dried breach of the Geneva Convention, since Article 2 provides for humane treatment of all prisoners and to have handed these men to Stalin was, indirectly but still culpably, to have mistreated them. They were German citizens, and were sent to the Soviet Union, which 5 Corps had no right to do. The relevant passage in the pamphlet was this:

> Were all that Lord Aldington claims to be true he would still stand arraigned in gross violation of the laws of war and humanity. The deliberate inclusion of German and Austrian officers of the 15 Cossack Cavalry Corps for example was authorised by Lord Aldington in flagrant contravention of the Geneva Convention on prisoners of war.

Greenwood's case was brief and cogent. The English courts, he said, accept that for all practical purposes international law is part of British law[9], and that gives rise to three propositions. 'First of all, there was a duty on the part of the United Kingdom to treat members of the German armed forces humanely whenever the members of those armed forces came into the power of the United Kingdom. Secondly, that duty of humane treatment includes a duty to protect captives from inhumane treatment by anybody else, and that the duty to protect from inhumane treatment would be violated if members of enemy armed forces were handed over to another state in circumstances where it was known or suspected that they would be massacred or in any other way ill-treated.

---

9   Greenwood quoted Lord Denning in Tremtex v Central Bank of Nigeria (1977). Lord Denning held that international law is binding on British subjects. Thus Lord Aldington was vulnerable to the charge that he had committed acts which were crimes *in Britain*. This was why it was imperative that Gray get the Court to accept that none of the victims of 5 Corps were covered by the Geneva Convention.

Thirdly, if it is found that the Plaintiff was in some way responsible for a breach of that kind, then as a matter of international law he would be guilty of a war crime.'

Greenwood answered Gray's point that the Geneva Convention on Prisoners of War did not apply to surrendered enemy personnel by saying, 'The Defence had submitted in the Nuremberg trial, my Lord, that the ill-treatment of Soviet prisoners of war by German troops was not a war crime because the 1929 Prisoners of War Convention was not binding between Germany and the Soviet Union, the Soviet Union never having been a party. The Tribunal rejected that argument and it based its rejection on the fact that the principle of humane treatment of prisoners of war reflected the general principles of international law applicable to captives in wartime.'

Greenwood then quoted Admiral Canaris, head of the *Abwehr* (the German Secret Service), by way of explanation: 'Since the 18th century the rules of war have gradually been established along the lines that war captivity is neither revenge nor punishment, but solely protective custody, the only purpose of which is to prevent the prisoners of war from further participation in the war. This principle was developed in accordance with the view held by all armies that it is contrary to military tradition to kill or injure helpless people.' The Nuremberg Tribunal not only sought to apply these principles, but quoted Canaris's words in describing its function.

Greenwood emphasised that 'the war crimes trials held at the end of the Second World War clearly indicate that there is individual criminal responsibility on the part of those members of armed forces or civilians who, knowingly, played a part in the commission of violation of the laws of war.'

This seemed to leave no way out for Lord Aldington. So, in his reply, Gray concentrated on the procedural point that the war crimes allegation had not been made in so many words in the original pleadings, and could not therefore, under the Rules of the Supreme Court, be introduced now. The pamphlet had mentioned 'war crimes', but not the pleadings. That was the key point in technical legal terms.

The gravity of the situation from Aldington's point of view was that if Greenwood's evidence were admitted it would not be very hard to prove that the handover of the German officers of the Cossack Cavalry was a breach of the Geneva Convention, and it is a principle of the law of libel that for a defence of justification to succeed, the defendants have to prove only one of the several charges if they are all of approximately equal gravity. If you call X a murderer, saying he has killed A, B and C, but you can succeed only in proving he has killed A, you will win your case: X is still a murderer, even though he did not murder B and C. The gravamen, as lawyers like to call it, of your charge is justified. Everything, therefore, hung on whether the Judge would accept that the original Defence pleadings made in 1988, the Particulars of Justification, and the Further and Better Particulars that followed them, included allegations of war crimes because they mentioned breaches of the Geneva Conventions.

Mr Justice Davies decided that they did not. He gave no reason for his decision. In his ruling, he rehearsed the submissions from both sides and then said: 'What I have to decide is whether the assertions made now come within the pleaded case. Having heard the argument at some considerable length, I have no doubt at all that they do not. Of course it is open to the Defendant to urge those matters which are in his pleadings, specifically about the behaviour alleged to have been undertaken by the Plaintiff, that he was responsible for the torture, etc. But in the light of the particulars given of that, it is not open on the pleadings, in my judgment, that the assertions which it has been sought today to make, are open to be urged. That is my ruling.'

The Defence could have applied to "re-re-amend" the Particulars of Justification, but this would have taken time, the Plaintiff would then have to be given the opportunity to produce an expert to counter Greenwood, which would have taken more time, and then there would still have been argument about these submissions. All this would have been very expensive. On the day the trial started there had been £167,456 left in the Forced Repatriation Defence Fund. Since then, in thirty-two days of Court time, £300,469 had been spent. Thus a deficit of £132,993 had already accumulated, without the still considerable costs for the rest of the trial. A serious prolongation was unthinkable, at least if the lawyers were to be paid. Thus no application was made.

The result was catastrophic for the Defence. Direct allegations of war criminality could not now be made. The next stage of the trial was the barristers' closing speeches, starting with Rampton. He now had to try to justify the wording of a pamphlet called *War Crimes and the Wardenship of Winchester College* without using the term "war crimes".

18

The CLOSING SPEECHES

THE FIRST to make his closing speech was Watts. Before the jury filed in that morning, the Judge complimented him on the way he had behaved in Court. 'I would like to say now and I hope I shall remember to say it to the jury, that if you had not behaved properly during the trial—I do not mean by not making noises, but if you had not followed the same rules that lawyers would have done, or tried not to, this case would probably have taken a great deal longer and been much more bad-tempered. The Court is grateful to you for the way you have approached matters.'

In the event the Judge did not repeat this handsome compliment in front of the jury. The only comment he made which bore in any way on Watts's conduct was to describe him as 'articulate', by which, he said, he meant that, like Tolstoy, he 'finds it easier to start a sentence than to finish one.'

Watts did not speak for long. Early on he made a point which was uppermost in the mind of everyone associated with the Defence: the cost of litigation.

'What possible chance,' Watts asked the jury in connection with Gray's assertion that she should have sued the insurance company she was in dispute with, 'does a widow in those circumstances have, of taking on an organisation such as the Sun Alliance, with their vast financial strength? Lord Aldington ruthlessly exploited his legal and financial position against this widow in her situation and circumstances. We are sure of one thing: ethics, morality, compassion and any form of humanitarian feeling came a long way down the list, as indeed it did in 1945.'

Nicolson noted in his diary that this connection between the Plaintiff's behaviour in 1945 and when Chairman of Sun Alliance 'makes Toby squirm, but it undoubtedly has an effect on the jury.'

Watts made a further point about his methods. 'I think the word "harassment" is really a ridiculous concept,' he said, 'when you have regard to the vast financial strength of the Sun Alliance and the vast influence and power that Lord Aldington, because of his position, wields. More of a David and Goliath situation I could not imagine.'

Watts then dealt with the charge that because he was not a historian, he had no business inquiring into Lord Aldington's military past.

'I ask you, ladies and gentlemen of the jury, if you were fighting for justice for a close member of your family, in the circumstances that I was, and evidence is produced from a person, an historian of Count Tolstoy's standing, that this was one of the most devious and cunning war criminals in Europe, would you not be disturbed by the fact that the same man, who claimed to have dealt with a widow with sympathy, was a final arbiter in determining insurance claims? Would you have a man of this distinction determine the claim of a close member of your family? That is not a grudge: that is a legitimate concern and it is my legitimate right to raise the question of his character, and that is what I was doing.

'The purpose of the publication was to winkle Lord Aldington out of his shell of silence so that he would come forward and give an explanation. He had manifestly been totally evasive and I was totally convinced that not only was he a ruthless and callous character but he was devious, cunning and evil with it.

'I ask you, ladies and gentlemen of the jury, to imagine this scenario. Had a man of the calibre, standing and integrity of Nigel Nicolson been in the position of Lord Aldington in 1945, could you not reasonably conclude that thousands and thousands of lives would have been saved? That is the difference between a ruthless and callous man, devoid of any compassion and humanitarian feeling, and a man of stature and integrity. I ask you, members of the jury, to use your insight, judgment and perspicacity to penetrate the truth in this action. I think it is a marvellous thing that we have a jury and that this case is not being tried by one individual.

'I come from a very, very close family indeed. When I started to fight for justice for my sister I had no idea what this was going to cost me. I've spent every penny of capital I possess but I have no regrets about doing it, because, as a family, we believe in standing up against injustice. Thank you very much for your attention.'

Watts sat down, having taken just about an hour. The Judge thanked him 'for keeping within the time'.

It was an impressive performance, marred only by the false heroics of the last paragraph. In fact, Watts's capital was next to nothing. The only person whose domestic security was threatened by the cost of participation in this case was Tolstoy, yet in Court he never mentioned money, neither did he instruct his Counsel to do so on his behalf.

Nicolson thought Watts had spoken 'very well indeed, with eloquence, courtesy, logic, grace and conviction. I am really coming to like him quite a lot.' He congratulated him outside the Court. Garnier was now a distant and, for the FRDF, expensive memory.

Rampton spoke next. He, too, started with the Plaintiff's character. 'You have seen him give evidence,' he said. 'He is alert, intelligent, vigorous and, one might even say, at times over-bearing. Certain it is, that he does not take easily to being challenged or questioned about his conduct. Does his present-day demeanour, his present-day appearance, the way he gave his evidence, give you any sort of clue as to the sort of person he was in May of 1945? What are the particular qualities you would look for in a person faced with the sort of decisions which Lord Aldington had to take in May 1945 in relation to these Cossacks and Jugoslavs? Compassion, understanding, sympathy to the plight of the many thousands of people who delivered themselves trustingly into the hands of 5 Corps in May 1945. Are those not the sort of qualities which you ought to be looking for?'

Rampton then rehearsed the history of the repatriations, up to the three possible dates of Brigadier Low's departure: 22, 23 and 24 May. But, he said, the moral responsibility for the handovers does not rest on any particular view of his departure date. Rampton devoted nearly an hour to that issue, concluding with the accusation that Lord Aldington's key evidence on this point, the two dinners he said he had with Anthony Eden, on 25 and 26 May, were inventions. 'Like the two days in Naples, they were designed to give colour to this account of the Plaintiff of when he left Austria.' Why was this so important? 'If we are right about the date,' Rampton said, 'there is one thing about it which may help you to an overall decision in the case. It is not the fact of the date of his departure but, if we are right, the light which it throws upon the credibility of his evidence in general. If you think that we are right about the date that he left, then quite clearly the account he has given to you cannot be relied upon in any aspect at all.'

At that point, Nicolson noted, 'Toby murmurs with indignation.'

Rampton then showed how many senior people in the Mediterranean command were aware of the likely fate of the victims. 'Is it credible,' he asked the jury, 'that the Plaintiff did not know what might happen to the losing side in that civil war if they fell into the hands of the victors, that is to say Tito's men? He was General Keightley's right-hand man and he was at the centre of everything. He was well educated, intelligent and able. He was the protegé of Mr Eden, the Foreign Secretary. He was given the remit, by General Keightley, to deal with the Jugoslavs.'

Low had been 'in something of a black hole,' Rampton said. 'Those below know and those above know so why is there this black hole at 5 Corps?'

Yet maybe this hole was not quite so black, Rampton went on. Lord Aldington had known that the people he was sending back to Jugoslavia were so scared that they would resist, possibly desperately, and so he had decided it was necessary to trick them. Worse than that, Rampton added, was the way Lord Aldington had tricked the victims' families too by the camp followers "concession".

'Where is the concession, as I think Lord Aldington described it, in allowing the families—the camp followers—to join their men on what they believe is a happy family trip to Italy, but which is, in fact, a journey to slavery and death in Jugoslavia? What is compassionate about that? The effect of this trick is to shepherd these people just like cattle into the slaughterhouse. They do not know where they are going and when they find out it is too late. No wonder that Mr Nicolson thought it one of the most disgraceful operations that any British troops had been ordered to undertake.'

At that point the jury left Court for their morning coffee. But before the Judge would let Rampton out for his break, he ticked him off for having been too friendly to the jury that morning.

'You will think I am a silly old fusser,' Mr Justice Davies said, 'but I have certain rules in this Court. It is not the practice for Counsel to say to a jury "Good morning", "Good night", "How are you?" It just is not the way we work. The next thing that happens is that we are going to have some bright young Counsel who gets up and says, "Hello, my darling". You may think that is fanciful, but it is not. I am not going to have it, and if you start saying "Good morning", "Good afternoon", "Good day", either Mr Gray follows the example or they think he is a snooty, stuffy old fellow. In forty years—and this is awful reminiscence—as man and boy, barrister, Queen's Counsel and Judge, in a serious case I have never heard anybody say that to a jury, and I hope they never will. And they *will* not in my Court. What happens if Mr Gray does not do it? Then we will all be saying, "Hello, how's your foot?" or, "You do look pretty this morning", or something like that. We have got rules, and the rules are that you exchange pleasantries if you meet somebody in the street, but you do not in the course of what is a very serious case.'

After coffee, Rampton moved on to make the same point about the Cossacks that he had about the Jugoslavs: everyone knew they would be seriously mistreated if handed over to the Soviets. Rampton read out the evidence. From Corporals who had written to Tolstoy up to the most senior Generals he had interviewed in the course of his researches for his books, they all said the same thing, most succinctly put by General Arbuthnott, whose forces had to kidnap the inmates of Peggetz at 5 Corps' behest: 'They are just going to be killed.' And where did that quote come from? *Lord Aldington himself* at the Sandhurst lunch! 'One had to harden one's heart,' Lord Aldington had gone on to say. 'We had been fighting against the Germans for six years, and we weren't awfully sorry for people who'd been fighting for the Germans.'

'The question in this case,' Rampton went on, 'is whether the Plaintiff was responsible, in part at least, for disobedience to orders which determined the fate of thousands of people.' With FO 1020/42 retained in the Foreign Office and other key files held in the Ministry of Defence, Rampton could not follow this point up with hard facts about 5 Corps' sabotage of the Alexander-Eisenhower plan to save the Cossacks. Neither could he point to the orders to 5 Corps *not* to make signed agreements with the Jugoslavs.

But Rampton was able to argue that 5 Corps had not even obeyed the Robertson Order. He pointed out, for the umpteenth time, that it had provided for the handover only of those Jugoslavs who had been 'serving in German forces'. Did 5 Corps have the means of finding out which of the non-Croats in Viktring came within that category? 'Quite obviously they did,' Rampton said. 'These people lived there from the 12th May onwards until they were sent back variously from the 24th to the 28th and 29th. They lived unguarded and largely self-fed in peace and good order in their different identifiable groups with interpreters available. Who asked them whether they had been serving in the German forces? No-one did. They were never asked.'

The Plaintiff's contention that, because the Jugoslavs had marched over the mountains from Jugoslavia at the same time as the retreating Germans, they were under German command, and therefore 'serving in German forces', was simply a 'fiction'. Nicolson's evidence made that clear, Rampton said.

Likewise, 5 Corps had concealed what it was doing from the gaze of those higher officers whose orders the Plaintiff now claimed to have been obeying. 5 Corps did not respond to Alexander's "no force" order of 23 May by reporting that they had avoided the use of force by the use of lies, trickery and deception.

'So what is behind this extraordinary series of events?' Rampton asked the Court. 'Why, from the 19th onwards, until the end of the month, were these thousands of Jugoslavs handed over? We do not know. We cannot see into the mind of the Plaintiff, and certainly we cannot, alas, ask General Keightley. You may think that it is some kind of bureaucratic insanity. General Keightley, it appears, was, at any rate according to some views, a rather rigid sort of person, and he and the Plaintiff obviously worked very closely together.

'After all, nowhere else in 8th Army area were Jugoslavs returned in this way lock, stock and barrel to Jugoslavia. You will remember that there were two whole regiments, the 1st and the 5th of the Serbian Volunteer Corps—exactly the same outfit, army or corps as the 2nd, 3rd and 4th that were in 5 Corps—in Italy. If the Robertson Order applied to the Serbian Volunteer Corps in 5 Corps area—they arrived, you remember, three days before Robertson was ever received at 5 Corps—if it applied to them it certainly also applied to the 1st and 5th Regiments of the SVC in Italy, yet none of them were sent back.

'What then do you think was the Plaintiff's motive for this? Human nature is odd, and you have to go back to the sort of person he was at the age of 31 in May of 1945. Perhaps it is not very difficult to see after all. He is a young and very successful soldier. He is a very brave soldier. He has won the DSO on the way up through Italy (*sic*). He is a very good administrator. He is much liked and admired by his commanding officer and, it appears, that for some reason known to them they agreed that it was necessary to get rid of the Jugoslavs in a hurry. So they went ahead and got rid of them.

'Perhaps—one does not know—perhaps they felt it did not matter all that much because, after all, in their eyes these Jugoslavs had been fighting on the wrong side and perhaps did not deserve very much consideration. If that be right, it is, as Count Tolstoy wrote in the pamphlet—for these Jugoslavs alone, never mind the Cossacks to whom I am coming—"an indelible blot on the history of the British Army".'

Moving on to deal with the Cossacks, Rampton started with the Low/Keightley signal sent to AFHQ on the evening after Macmillan visited Klagenfurt ('cannot see any point in keeping this large number Soviet nationals who are clearly great source of contention between Soviets and ourselves'). Surely, he asked, that was 'where the Cossacks' seed of destruction is sown?'

The Plaintiff claimed Robertson had authorised what subsequently happened to the Cossacks. But had he? Had his order been properly taken together with the 8th Army standing order about who was and who was not a Soviet citizen, Low could never have produced the Definition Order. Robertson ordered 'all Russians' handed over, and 8th Army had defined Russians in terms of the Yalta agreement. This implied screening into those eligible and those not eligible. Far from ordering screening, Brigadier Low had forbidden it in the operative paragraph of the Definition Order. True, the second paragraph had defined a screening procedure, but that paragraph was preceded by an order not to concede individual screening except under pressure from the victims. Since the order as a whole was kept secret from those to whom it applied, this can only have been meant as a piece of bureaucratic cover.

Rampton tried to put this point simply to the jury. 'No-one,' he said, 'went round the Cossack groups in 5 Corps area saying, "Look, if anybody particularly wants to press his case, I am the person to speak to. If you want to satisfy me that you are not a Soviet citizen, now is the time to say it".'

Moreover the rules Low had laid down were different from those ordered by 8th Army. The last clause was the exact opposite of the 8th Army instruction, which was that if there was any doubt about nationality the individual would be sent to Italy. 'What happens under the Plaintiff's definition?' Rampton asked. 'No such chance is offered to them. "Oh well, you are a doubtful case, you are going off to the Soviets."'

In discussing the Definition Order, Rampton was crippled by the exclusion of the Geneva Convention. Article 20 states: 'Regulations, orders, announcements and publications of any kind shall be communicated to prisoners of war in a language which they understand.' Not only should the Definition Order have been communicated to all prisoners of war, but *in German*. In addition, Article 26 states: 'In the event of transfer, prisoners of war shall be officially informed in advance of their new destination.'[1]

'The nationality of all these unfortunate Cossacks in 5 Corps area,' Rampton went on, 'people who are in fact Latvian, Jugoslav, French and Belgian and German, the nationality of all those people is predetermined by this order. They will be treated as Soviet nationals. How is a German, for example, to know that he has been classified as a Soviet national? Nobody ever tells him. Where in the Plaintiff's definition of the 21st May do we find any provision for adjudicators or examining officers as was plainly contemplated by AFHQ and Eighth Army? Nowhere. Why not? Because—and this lies at the heart of this part of the case—the reason is that the whole intention and effect of that order or definition of the 21st May was to ensure as far as possible that the whole lot went back to the Soviets, including the German officers of the 15th Cavalry. Lock, stock and barrel.'

Shortly after that Rampton wound up for the day. Nicolson noted that evening, 'Toby says, "Phew" once or twice. But Rampton did marvellously.' Nicolson now thought a 'moderate victory' for the Plaintiff was likely. Tolstoy's spirits, partly restored by Watts's performance, had been kept up by Rampton's. Georgina's foreboding, however, remained unrelieved.

The next morning, 22 November (Day 35), Rampton rose to conclude his speech. Within ten minutes, his argument was once again crippled by the lack of FO 1020/42. He had noted that Alexander wanted to 'clear the decks' in Carinthia and that Eisenhower had agreed to take the

---

1   There were two other serious breaches by 5 Corps. Article 25 covers Arbuthnott's barbaric order to include 'lying sick and expectant mothers' in the handovers: 'Unless the course of military operations demands it, sick and wounded prisoners of war shall not be transferred if their recovery might be prejudiced by the journey.' Article 42 covered the petitions from the Cossack Generals which Tryon-Wilson thought were destroyed at 5 Corps headquarters: 'Prisoners of war shall have the right to bring to the notice of the military authorities, in whose hands they are, their petitions concerning the conditions of captivity to which they are subjected... Such petitions and complaints shall be transmitted immediately.' Of course, if, following Gray, the people concerned were not prisoners of war, then, either as refugees or surrendered enemy personnel, they were entitled to more humane treatment than that laid down by Geneva, not less.

Cossacks into the SHAEF area at Alexander's request. But there the evidence dried up. Why had the Supreme Commander's plan failed? The answer to that lay at that moment in the Foreign Office. Rampton could not show that 5 Corps was directly involved in subverting superior orders. This would not necessarily have inculpated Aldington—he might have been able to show, for example, that Keightley had ordered him to issue the orders he did—but it would have completely destroyed his argument that 5 Corps at all times obeyed superior orders.

As a result of the absence of the most important evidence, Rampton was forced back on the confusing approach of posing nine questions in connection with the Cossacks' handover which he invited the jury to answer for themselves before arriving at their verdict. For the same reason he had to adopt a similarly confusing approach to the Jugoslav handovers, in that case posing *fourteen* questions which he felt the jury needed to answer.

As Rampton read out his questions, he was asked by a jury member to speak more slowly so that the questions could be copied down. At that, the Judge intervened. 'Members of the jury,' he said, 'if you tried to write everything down that was said we would be here until Christmas. If it is a help to you, Mr Rampton is asking the same question about each of the orders... It is one of my jobs, members of the jury, not to go through Counsels' speeches again—that would be tedious in the extreme—but [in summing-up] to point out to you the main planks of their argument. You may rest assured that I shall be reminding you of it. It is not quite insulting to suggest Mr Rampton should speak at dictation speed, but you need not worry if you do not have that in mind.'

In the event, the Judge did not restate Rampton's twenty-three questions. Since they established a connected argument, the result was that Rampton's attempt to clarify the Defence case was lost to those on the jury who did not have shorthand. Since the whole of Rampton's list of questions totalled 646 words—about a page and a half of this book—it was a grotesque exaggeration to threaten the jury with a four-week extension of the trial if they tried to copy them down.

Rampton concluded his speech by going through the pamphlet. 'The law in this area,' he told the jury, 'is remarkably sensible. It says if you take a detailed pamphlet of this kind—a detailed piece of writing like this—the Defendants, to succeed in proving that it is, in essence, true, do not have to prove the truth of every single thing they say, nor do they have to prove that every allegation they make is true if, when you have looked at the evidence overall, you believe that it proves, *in essence*, a solid case against the Plaintiff.'

Rampton ended with an observation about Lord Aldington's behaviour in Court. 'You will have seen,' he said, 'all through this case, when he was giving his evidence, and as he sits and listens to the witnesses and listens to me, that he gets angry and excited and upset. One cannot fail to notice it.[2] There are two possible explanations for that. One, and it is an obvious explanation, is that what has been said about him, which he has had to sit and listen to rehearsed day after day, week after week, in this Court, said about him repeatedly, is false. That he has been gravely and cruelly wronged by what has been said. That would be enough to upset anybody.

'The alternative explanation is this: do you think that it might be because perhaps for the first time since May 1945 he has had to face up in public to the full extent of his responsibility for the fate which befell these people? If you think that, then for all that he has had his family in Court, for all that he has quite clearly, as I say, been distressed and upset by these proceedings, then you may think there is no room for sympathy. If he did in essence what the pamphlet says he did, well then that is the decision you have to make. Do not decide for him; do not give him damages, just because you feel sorry for him. Do it only if you think that the defence fails, that he was not responsible for what happened.

'Perhaps one can sum up what one means by true responsibility in the circumstances of this case by reminding you of that injunction from Admiral Lord Nelson's prayer before Trafalgar, which was quoted by General Murray: "In victory, humanity".

'My Lord, I have finished.'

After lunch that day, which was a Wednesday, Gray stood up to begin a speech which was to last the rest of the week. He started with Lord Aldington's 'Why me?' protest. 'You may think,' Gray said, 'that plainly war crimes of the most awful kind were committed. They were committed

---

2   This was a fair point. Many observers noted the latitude the Judge gave Aldington to mutter, talk, gesticulate and fulminate. However, as soon as Tolstoy did so, the Judge warned Rampton, 'You must warn him [Tolstoy] that he must not give evidence by nodding or shaking his head. I have noticed it once or twice. Would you ask him to control his features as much as possible.' (Day 8)

by the Soviet Russians. They were committed by Tito's henchmen, if you like, but not the Plaintiff. It is Lord Aldington who is the Plaintiff.'

At the end of the war, in many of the countries of recently occupied Europe, 'there were collaborators or, as they are called, quislings.' This was 'not an English phenomenon', he said sanctimoniously. The Robertson Order was designed to deal with such people in 5 Corps' area, and all Brigadier Low's actions, Gray said, had been designed to implement that order. 'Dr Knight, the only expert who has been called before you, says that all categories could properly be regarded as having been serving in German forces; certainly could properly be regarded as having fought under German command.'

Gray then quoted from *The Minister and the Massacres* in which Tolstoy described the Robertson Order as being 'inclusive enough to apply to virtually all uniformed Jugoslav refugees'. Since then, in the light of the papers released by the US National Archives, Tolstoy's view of the order had changed. Gray made full use of this.[3]

'You first of all get *The Minister and the Massacres*,' he said, 'where Count Tolstoy, before he is involved in this libel action, says: "Oh, well, it applied to all uniformed Jugoslav refugees. It would mean that Croats, Serbs, Slovenes, all should go back under the Robertson Order". You then get him trying to maintain in his written evidence that it did not apply to anyone at all because it only applied to members of the German forces. You then get him conceding in cross-examination that it was proper for the Croats to be returned.

'It now emerges, does it not, pretty clearly, that it is accepted that the Croats who were returned during Lord Aldington's time in southern Austria were returned properly under the Robertson Order. Not only was there no deliberate breach, there was no breach at all. That is one of the questions that Mr Rampton invited you to ask when he was making submissions to you this morning. It is not just a change of the Defendant's case on a crucial aspect. It is a collapse of the Defendant's case on a crucial aspect.'

There was justice in the allegation that Tolstoy has shifted the aim of

---

3   It is surely fair to observe that there was something deeply inequitable in Rampton's being prevented, on a legal technicality about the scope of his client's pleaded case, from mentioning 'war crimes' in his closing speech, while Gray was free to use *The Minister and the Massacres*, which did not form any part of Aldington's pleaded case, as evidence against Tolstoy?

his historical wrath over the years, but Gray did not mention the fact that Tolstoy had *never* suggested that a legitimate interpretation of the Robertson Order included women and children, as Gray was now implying. Since Rampton had already spoken, Gray was safe from correction. This is one example of the way the forensic advantage lies with the Plaintiff, since his or her Counsel always closes after Counsel for the Defence.

Gray exploited his position once against when he came to the subject of the Bleiburg Croats, whom he lumped in with the Viktring ones, as if orders applying to one applied to the other. As a result, Nicolson wrote in his diary that evening, 'It is now clear that Counsel can ignore whole chunks of the opposing argument when there is no chance of being interrupted or corrected because the opposition has spoken first.'

Gray sarcastically characterised the Deception Order as 'an order to lie'. He described Nicolson's evidence on the subject and then said, 'There is a mile of difference you may think between saying, "Do not tell the Jugoslavs their destination" and saying, "Lie to the Jugoslavs about their destination". The two are simply not the same.' Brigadier Low, he said, had *not* ordered any lies to be told, simply that the truth be withheld.

'Members of the jury, you may think that someone in the position of Lord Aldington, who receives the Robertson Order—and orders have to be obeyed, members of the jury—then has to think to himself, "How am I going to achieve what Robertson has told me must be achieved?" And Lord Aldington decided that the right way to do that was to say that they would not be told of their destination. I commend that to you, members of the jury, as being a perfectly proper, sensible, honourable course for a British officer to have adopted.'

The Deception Order was issued by Low on the same day that AFHQ promulgated the Distone Order which Tolstoy maintained (and Cowgill now maintains) was intended to save the Jugoslavs by sending them to Italy. Gray's client's view was quite different. 'The plain fact is, members of the jury—and really all the evidence points this way—that Distone had nothing whatever to do with 5 Corps. It was not addressed to them. They did not receive it and it did not apply to them. Where, I ask you, is the copy of the Distone Order that 5 Corps received, if indeed they did receive a copy? The answer is it does not exist, members of the jury. There is not one. You can look in vain through all these thousands of pages. There is no such thing.'

Several of Lord Aldington's witnesses remembered clearly that no such order as Distone had ever arrived at 5 Corps. Brigadier Tryon-Wilson, for one, remembered its non-arrival 'with extraordinary clarity', Gray said. 'I just mention that simply to remind you of the man he was. Straight as a die.'

Major Taylor was equally clear about the fact that the Distone Order did not arrive at 5 Corps because had it done so he would have been the person it would have come to and he 'was sure he would have remembered it if it had.' Gray added that Taylor was not the sort of person who would come and lie to the Court: 'He is a Judge.'

Finally, Gray reminded the jury, Lord Aldington had not remembered receiving the order. 'Members of the jury, all the evidence is one way, is it not, on this?'

Gray was not content with that. He went on to consider what the effect would have been on 5 Corps if it *had* received the order. It would have meant that Low's agreement with Ivanovich would have been 'a total breach of Distone Order'. Since that was exactly what the Defence *was* arguing (and, in effect, what Cowgill concluded ten months later in the *Final Report*), this was a circular argument. Was Gray carefully judging his arguments according to his estimation of the jury's ability to assess them?

Gray produced the "no force" order and said, 'That is irreconcilable, members of the jury, with the proposition that there was a total change of policy at AFHQ and everybody had to go back to Italy.' That sounded like a point for the Plaintiff, unless the jury remembered that the Defence had never argued that there was a 'total change of policy at AFHQ'. From at least the date of the Distone Order, 17 May, possibly earlier, the orders emanating from AFHQ had been entirely consistent, they had argued, in wanting to protect 'dissident' Jugoslavs from Tito.

Gray told the jury that they should not believe the Defence argument that Brigadier Low was well aware of the likely fate of the Jugoslavs when he issued the Deception Order. 'Shall we test that,' he asked, 'by reminding you of the evidence you have heard in this case? Like every other issue, it has to be decided according to the evidence.' What was that evidence? Major Taylor thought they would be tried fairly; so did Sir Charles Villiers. Did either witness know of any massacres? No. There you have, Gray said, 'two responsible, honest witnesses telling you that they did not know'. Sir James Wilson did not know, nor did Lieutenant Lochhead. The latter was 'a wholly honest witness' and so, when he said that Todorovic was wrong to say that he had told him at the time about massacres on the other side of the border, 'you can only come to one answer': Lochhead had not been told.

Evidence for the Defence supported his client's case, Gray said. In at least one of his Situation Reports (SitReps), Nicolson had expressed reservations about the moral legitimacy of the handovers. 'But they do not go to 5 Corps,' Gray said. 'So although Mr Rampton is entitled to read them, they do not really help very much, do they?, on the question of what Lord Aldington knew, because Lord Aldington knows what the Division SitReps tell him—*different* SitReps. It is very important to have that distinction clearly in mind.' This was true, although it was possibly significant that Gray chose not to draw the jury's attention to the content of those SitReps.

Moving on to the way the Robertson Order was translated into the Deception Order, Gray took up the issue of whether or not it was right to describe all the people handed over by 5 Corps to Tito as having served 'in German forces'. Not only was there the evidence 'from Mr Knight, the expert', but also 'from a whole series of Serbs and Slovenes'. Mr Ljotic said the Serbian Volunteer Corps was armed by the Germans. Mr Miletic said they had German liaison officers and Gray had shown the Court a photograph of 'what I think is accepted as a German officer undoubtedly forming a Nazi salute.' This German was marching at the head of a platoon. 'Members of the jury, liaison officers do not march at the head of platoons, you may think.' Another witness, Gray said, had given evidence of the nature of the salute in Domobranci units. Their uniforms had been made from cloth 'provided by the Germans'. Their weapons came from German sources. The three men who survived the pit of Kocevje had, Gray said, agreed with this. Accordingly, Gray argued, Low had obeyed Robertson in ordering that every Jugoslav national at Viktring should be considered a member of the German armed forces.

Jumping about a bit, Gray took the issue of the departure date next and its concomitant controversy: had Low been at the "shoot the Cossacks" conference on the morning of 22 May? Brigadier Tryon-Wilson, 'whose honesty as a witness must be beyond doubt', had told the Court that the Plaintiff 'could not have been there'. Then the de Fonblanque journal had suddenly appeared and, Gray said, clinched the point. 'It is accepted, members of the jury—and I say plainly rightly—that that entry for 21st May is based on a contemporary diary or record being kept by Brigadier de Fonblanque.'

In fact, it was never accepted by the Defence that the de Fonblanque document was contemporary. Almost the only thing both sides agreed on was that it was *not* a contemporary document. Neither had the Defence accepted that the journal was 'based on' a contemporary document. But, speaking second, Gray could conclude without fear of challenge that, 'on the basis of this document any doubt that there may have been up until that moment about the date when Toby Low left southern Austria is utterly dispelled.'

On what evidence had the Defence relied for their contention that Low left later than 22 May? Three things only, Gray said: the weather argument, which was 'all rather tedious', the notes of the Corps Commander's conference on 22 May, which were ambiguous, and letters from Lord Aldington and Brigadier Tryon-Wilson in the mid-1980s. True, those showed that before the writ in this action was issued, Lord Aldington did think he would have attended the conference, believing he had left on 25 or 26 May. Referring to the papers Lord Trefgarne had provided from his client's Personal Service Record, Gray said, 'Certainly Lord Aldington had not seen the documents showing him quite clearly that he got back to England on 24th May. There is no doubt about that now. We have got documents. He did not have those documents then. He was doing his best to recollect. It is obvious that he was wrong. He now knows what the position is because he has been helped, as so often happens in a case of this kind, by a document.' The bizarre implication of this was that if FO 1020/42 had been in Court, Aldington would have remembered all sorts of other things which he was clear had never happened.

Finally on the issue of his client's departure date, what about his apparent admission that he had lied about the Eden dinners? 'If Lord Aldington is really going to invent things and tell you lies,' Gray said, 'you would think that he would invent things and tell you lies which helped his case. The Eden diaries are irrelevant for this reason: the dinners that Lord Aldington thought he had with Eden were on the 25th and 26th, but everybody agrees that he was back in England by then, even Count Tolstoy and Mr Watts. So what does it matter? It is wholly beside the point. I am not going to take time on that because it does not assist either way.'

With Robertson's 'armed forces' apparently including women and children, the Distone Order disregarded, and 15th Army Group's 'no signed agreements' command hidden in the Foreign Office, the departure date mattered to the Plaintiff in connection with the Jugoslavs only insofar as he was accused of having violated the AFHQ "no force" order of 23

May. That was easily disposed of: Lord Aldington was back in England by then. 'Can it possibly be fair or justifiable,' Gray asked the jury, 'to blame Lord Aldington for any deception which continued to be practised, if there was any, after the 23rd because of what he had done on the 17th May?'

At that point the Court rose. 'I go to the men's loo,' Nicolson wrote in his diary that evening. 'There is Toby Aldington. Only us two. I had to say something, so I say, "How are you bearing up under all this?" He answers, "It took me ten hours to get over being called a murderer."' Aldington turned on his heel and walked out, leaving Nicolson talking to his disappearing back.

After the recess, Gray moved on to the Cossacks. 'The striking fact,' he said at the outset, 'is that Lord Aldington had very little to do so far as the Cossacks were concerned.' Gray went through the history chronologically. With regard to the 'can't see any point in keeping this large number Soviet nationals' signal, he said no more than this: 'Members of the jury, if you see a false implication there, that all the Cossacks are Soviet nationals, then you are way ahead of me.'

The main charge related to the Definition Order—except that Gray did not call it an order, but 'rulings or guidelines'. His client, apparently, had been more of an umpire than an Army officer. As with the Robertson Order, Gray played on the fact that Tolstoy's view of the Definition Order has evolved. This was fair: his view *has* evolved. But so had Gray's client's views, as new documents changed the way he remembered events.

'How can you find a charge justified that this is an order which prevents screening,' Gray asked the jury, 'when the order has remained in the same terms since May 1945, and for ten years Count Tolstoy, the man who is making the charge, regarded it as being the very opposite: an order which requires screening to take place? It is a desperate attempt to salvage some sort of a plea of justification in relation to this disgraceful charge that Lord Aldington deliberately procured the return of these Russian émigrés, is it not?'

With FO 1020/42 in the Foreign Office, Gray was able to make his biggest and most important historical statement unchallenged. 'May I deal with what was a recurrent theme in the Defendants' case?' he asked. 'Lord Aldington, it is said, frustrated—countered—Field Marshal Alexander's wish that the Cossacks should be returned to General Eisenhower at SHAEF. Members of the jury, the impression may have been given that if these Cossacks had been sent back to SHAEF to General Eisenhower, the impression may have been given to you that then they would have had, if I can paraphrase what Mr Rampton said at one point about Italy, some sort of family holiday. Members of the jury, that is simply not right.'

Of course the Soviet citizens amongst the Cossacks would have been repatriated by SHAEF, but that was not the point. The whole group would have been screened, just as 5 Corps had been ordered to do on 13 March. Rampton tried to object, but got nowhere.

On the last day of Gray's summing-up Georgina Tolstoy did not come to Court. She could no longer bear the feelings of foreboding and was too upset by what she saw as the Judge's bias. Tolstoy mentioned this to Nicolson as they took their seats at 10.30 a.m. 'I say she has supported him marvellously,' Nicolson wrote in his diary, 'and never hinted that he ought to put his family before his duty to expose injustice. He expects defeat and will have to sell his house. He is a little nervous and has that silly laugh, which is really his modesty.'

Certainly the skies were darkening for the Defence. Gray chose, for sound tactical reasons, to end on a personal rather than a historical note. After all, this was not a war crimes trial, as the Judge had repeatedly emphasised, but a libel action. It was, in the end, a matter of individual character.

Was Tolstoy's letter to Watts wishing him luck in his struggle with 'this evil man', Gray asked the jury, written by 'an objective and fair-minded historian'? The Second Defendant appeared to consider anyone connected with the forced repatriations to have been, to some extent, a war criminal. 'He said of Brigadier Tryon-Wilson, one of our witnesses, that he was an untruthful man,' Gray said. 'Count Tolstoy called Sir Charles Villiers a liar. He called Lochhead, the Scots Lieutenant, a liar. He conceded, rather surprisingly, that Major Taylor (Judge Taylor) was quite possibly telling the truth. He was about the only one who received that acquittal. He said that General Murray told lies in two documents. He said that Field Marshal Alexander was an idle man. He made this charge against Brigadier Tryon-Wilson: that he had been "got at" by Brigadier Cowgill. He then said that General Robertson, the author of the order of the 14th May, about which we have talked a good deal, forgot that he had issued that order. He accused General Keightley of being lazy.

'He then made the charge that General Keightley was a war criminal, a liar and an arrogant bully,' Gray went on. 'He said that Brigadier

Tryon-Wilson was "to some extent a war criminal". He said there were hundreds of 5 Corps soldiers he regarded as war criminals. He said that Harold Macmillan was a war criminal and he said General Murray was on the borderline, but in some respects he was a war criminal. He said that Captain Nicolson, to a lesser extent, was a war criminal. He said of Sir Anthony Eden that he was definitely a war criminal. He finally said, on Day 19, "If we had lost the war the whole of the War Cabinet would have been charged as war criminals".[4]

'Members of the jury, what is the significance of all that? May it not be this: Count Tolstoy is the only man in the platoon who is in step. Does it not suggest to you that what he has accused Lord Aldington of being is yet another instance of a man making accusations, having totally lost his grip on reality. You may find that list I have read out to you is some help in deciding whether the claims he has made about Lord Aldington can be well founded.'

It was a powerful piece of advocacy, though largely inaccurate as a summary of Tolstoy's evidence as he had been much more measured in his assessments of guilt. But it was effective in depicting Tolstoy as the querulous outsider whose judgement should not be trusted. Lord Aldington, by contrast, had been 'a brave, loyal and dedicated young Brigadier, 31 years old, serving under an experienced, professional soldier, Lieutenant-General Sir Charles Keightley'.

What motive, Gray asked, would there have been for his client to do the 'horrific things that these Defendants say he did? Why, you would want to ask yourself, would he deliberately rephrase orders to send 6,000 Slovene civilians to their death? Why would he do the other things of which he is accused in the pamphlet? We say, in summary, that the charge that Lord Aldington is a war criminal to be compared with the worst Nazi butchers, is a grotesque one. We say that the claim that he disobeyed orders or countered what AFHQ wanted is insulting nonsense. We say, finally, that the notion that Lord Aldington issued orders deliberately in order to send Slovenian civilians or Russian émigrés, or anyone else, to their death is bunkum. I ask you, members of the jury, to reject the defence

---

4   In fact Tolstoy had said, on Day 19, something rather different: 'If the Germans had won the war... I think most of those [in the War Cabinet] who accepted the implications of the Yalta Agreement and were instrumental in pushing it through in the full knowledge of what it would result in [would] possibly have been charged.'

of justification.'

Gray then asked the jury to reject the defence of fair comment. The words in the pamphlet made factual accusations. They were not comments, fair or otherwise. But, as an alternative argument, Gray said that for comment to be "fair", it had to be based on correct facts. This case was not. But even if the facts were accepted, 'could any fair-minded person honestly express those opinions on the proved facts? I ask you to say, even supposing for one moment that it is a comment to compare Lord Aldington's activities to those of the worst butchers of Nazi Germany, that no fair-minded person could possibly arrive at such an opinion on the facts as we now know them.'

But even if that defence were allowed, Gray went on, and the jury could imagine a fair-minded person thinking as Tolstoy did, this defence must also fail as the comment was actuated by malice. The pamphlet was a product of the 'disgraceful way Mr Watts seized gleefully on the malicious gossip that some anonymous telephone caller relayed to him as he embarked on his campaign against Lord Aldington'. After Tolstoy got in touch with Watts, the two collaborated in their campaign of vilification. Not only was Watts actuated by malice, so was Tolstoy. 'You will ask yourselves, in relation to Count Tolstoy, whether his claim to be an honest, objective, fair-minded historian, giving the benefit of the doubt to Lord Aldington, can possibly be right. We say that that claim is a far-fetched and ludicrous one.

'It is one thing, members of the jury, to write a work of history. It is quite another to embark on a diatribe—as Mr Rampton called it—sent where it will hurt most. You may think that the dominant motive of both these Defendants was to inflict the maximum hurt on Lord Aldington, and for all those four reasons I ask you to dismiss as an irrelevance—a sort of smoke screen—this defence of fair comment. It is not a fair comment case.'

Finally, Gray came to the question of damages. 'I suggest to you that your award of damages should reflect three separate elements, and may I please list them for you: firstly, there should be an element of compensation for the damage done to Lord Aldington's reputation. That is the first one. Secondly, there should be an element of compensation for the intense distress caused to Lord Aldington by the publication and by all that has gone on since. Last, and perhaps you may think in this case, the most vital element of all, the award should be of a sufficient size to vindicate Lord Aldington's reputation, by which I mean to demonstrate to all and sundry that he has been falsely accused.'

The means of the Defendants was irrelevant, Gray said. The jury should, however, consider the 'agony' Lord Aldington had endured since publication of the pamphlet and the 'ordeal of being cross-examined for 30 hours, facing an attack—a public attack—of being a war criminal at the age of 75.' Gray invited the jury to remember the 'eloquent words' of the transcript, 'The witness was upset.'

'Remember, too,' Gray went on, 'what Mr Watts said when he was making his closing speech to you earlier this week. He called Lord Aldington ruthless, callous, evil, guilty of atrocities worse than those by the Nazis convicted at Nuremberg. He said that he was one of the most devious and cunning war criminals in Europe. Imagine the feelings of Lord Aldington when that is being said.

'Remember, too, that there was a procession of ladies from various countries who were, I think without exception, Soviet citizens, and do you remember that they all gave their evidence and I did not cross-examine any of them? Why do you think the Defendants put those ladies in the witness box? Was it in order to make you feel that in some way Lord Aldington was to blame for the ordeals each one of them had experienced? How do you think Lord Aldington felt when they were processing into the witness box?'

Nicolson remembers that the Court was hushed as Gray wound to a close. 'It is for you, members of the jury, to award a sum of sufficient size by way of damages to demonstrate to the world at large—because this case has been followed not just in this country, but in many other countries besides—clearly that these charges have been rejected by a British jury which has heard and examined in great detail all the evidence, so that if, members of the jury, at some future time this libel is resurrected then Lord Aldington or indeed his son or indeed his grandchildren will be able to say: "My father, my grandfather, sued on that libel in 1989, there was a trial lasting nine weeks, the jury found the libel untrue and they awarded substantial damages."

'Members of the jury, I have finished my closing speech to you now. Thank you for listening patiently to me. I now leave the honour and the reputation of Lord Aldington in your hands.'

19

The SUMMING-UP

IN HIS AUTOBIOGRAPHY, the barrister and creator of Rumpole of the Bailey, John Mortimer, said that 'summing-ups in court are thinly disguised attempts to persuade twelve honest citizens to agree with you.'[1] The Judge speaks last and therefore has tremendous influence on the jury. Many people think there is no reason why the Judge should speak at all, beyond reminding the jury of points of law. The evidence has been produced and examined by both sides, and the barristers have had their respective turns at drawing the threads of their cases together in the closing speeches. Critics of the existing court practice say that judicial summing-ups give judges the freedom to manipulate the outcome of important cases while still retaining the public illusion that cases are disposed of even-handedly. Defenders of current practice point to precedent and to the desirability of reminding the jury of the evidence after the inevitably partial accounts they will have heard from the two barristers. Either way, by going over evidence the jury has already heard, the judge should be telling the jury something it already knows. If he tells them something new, he should not be speaking. In short, a good case can be made for the proposition that a judicial summing-up is either prejudicial or redundant. Neither is useful.

In legal argument before he started his summing-up, Mr Justice Davies made it clear that he did not want to be bound by the precise words

---

1   Mortimer *Murderers and Other Friends*, p. 260

that the witnesses had actually used in giving evidence. He said he thought transcripts were more of a hindrance than a help.[2] He was trying a 'serious civil case', he said, not 'having an intellectual debate' and the transcript made it possible to go through the words uttered 'with a nit-picking comb'. The result was that the case ended up being tried 'not on the evidence but on the transcript,' Davies said mysteriously. 'I think they are a pest, myself, for a fair decision.'

What did this mean? The distinction between oral evidence and the words spoken in giving it is new to jurisprudence, unless the Judge was proposing a return to the nineteenth century criminal practice of 'condemning an action because the agent appeared to him a cad'.[3] But Davies was determined. 'Mr Rampton, if you think I am going to spend the rest of the day nit-picking through a whole bundle of transcripts, you are quite wrong.'

'They are not, I hope, nit-picked,' said Rampton. 'I hope I have combed out all the nits.'

Rampton tried to raise what he saw as legal or evidential misstatements by Gray in his closing speech. But he was soon interrupted. 'You are beginning to make me think I had better emigrate,' Mr Justice Davies said. 'What you will think about my summing-up, Mr Rampton, I dread to think.'

Rampton pressed on, but he only succeeded in exasperating the Judge. 'Have you ever summed-up a case like this to the jury?' Mr Justice Davies asked him.

'No, my Lord, of course I have not.'

'If I start going through all these the one certain thing is that the jury will get completely befuddled, bemused and are unlikely to do justice. This really is transcript mania gone mad.'

---

2   This part of this book is, of course, based on the transcript. Since the parties have to pay for them, and the cost of having a transcript made can be as much as £1000 per day, few cases are recorded. It is arguable that serious legal criticism by non-lawyers is rendered impossible as a result. For justice to be seen to be done, it is essential that the methods, thinking and conclusions of the courts be accessible to the nation at large. For this a proper record of all important trials is necessary. It would be easy to do, simply by having tapes running during all High Court proceedings. The recording apparatus is already there, being used when transcripts are made. It would cost next to nothing to switch it on regularly and archive the resulting material on a routine basis.

3   Harding *A Social History of English Law*, p. 362

'No, my Lord, it is not.'

'I am telling you that in my view it *is*,' said the Judge.

For three days, starting on the morning of Monday 27 November, the jury listened to the Mr Justice Davies's summing-up. Tolstoy had recovered his optimism. The previous evening he had written to Lord Portsmouth, 'Now it is the Judge versus Tolstoy, but thank goodness the jury has the last word. They at least appear sensible and unbiased, unlike his Lordship.'

Davies started by expressing his intentions: 'I shall do my best in an impartial way, a neutral way, to summarise the facts on both sides. I often say to juries: if at the end of Mr Rampton's speech you think: "Well, this plaintiff has no case at all", he has done his job well. If at the end of Mr Gray's speech you think: "Well, there's no defence to this case", he has done his job well. If at the end of my summing-up you say to yourselves: "Well, we really don't know which side the Judge thinks should win", then I have done my job well.'

The Judge's first point concerned the wider controversy about the forced repatriations. 'Members of the jury,' he said, 'there may have been speculation as to whether your decision in this case, whatever it may be, will put at rest a debate which has raged for years. It would be very nice to think that it would, and that one side or the other, or preferably both, would shut up about it all once you had given your decision.'

He described the parties briefly. Lord Aldington was a 'tough nut', Nigel Watts was 'a property developer', and Count Tolstoy was, for the second time, 'a self-styled historian', he said. 'There is no sneer about that. He is a self-styled historian, in the sense that he calls himself an historian. Whether he is an impartial, balanced, unbiased historian is entirely a matter for you to decide.'

At greater length, Davies described the jury to themselves. 'You have concentrated intensely on the case,' he said. 'I know some of you have had a cough, or a cold; some of you have had various matters which I am sure concern you about your everyday life, but it has not stopped your faithful attendance. It has been perfectly obvious to me that you have often been ahead of me, and ahead of Counsel, in getting to the right document, and matters of that kind. It is right that the public should know in this case that it is being tried by a plainly highly intelligent jury which is a representative cross-section of society.

'Out of the twelve of you, I know that ten are in full-time employment,' he went on. 'One is in half-time employment and the twelfth has duties which fully occupy that juror. So much for the criticisms that sometimes appear that you only see unemployed people sitting on juries.' More than that, the Judge said, he knew that seven of the twelve could be described as 'professional' people. 'So much for the libel on jurors that juries are not only unemployed but ignorant people.'

After these preliminaries, Mr Justice Davies went into the law applicable to the case. The jury had to judge on the civil rather than the criminal standard of proof, that is on 'the balance of probabilities' rather than 'beyond reasonable doubt'. Had the Plaintiff been libelled by what the words of the pamphlet conveyed in their 'natural and ordinary meaning' in the spring of 1987? Every citizen has the right to an unblemished reputation unless a defamer can prove to a jury that his allegedly libellous words are true or fair comment on a matter of public interest and, in that case, not actuated by malice. Thus the burden of proof is always on the Defendants, the Judge said. But if the words published are found to be true, then no matter what the damage to the Plaintiff's reputation, feelings or material interests, the jury must find against him. Furthermore, in finding for the Defendants, it is not necessary that every word of the pamphlet be proved literally true; it is enough that the substance of the charges be proved—the "sting" of the libel, as it is called. But against that, the more serious the charge, the more solid the proof has to be. 'Grave charges require grave evidence in order to support them.'

At the end of the first morning, the Judge dealt briefly with the Plaintiff's formal Admissions. 'There are the Admissions of the Jugoslav handovers between the 19th May and the end of May, a total number of about 35,000, the overwhelming majority of whom were killed and others were tortured, brutally treated, and massacred.' The Cossacks were dealt with almost as briefly. It was admitted that 50,000 were sent to the Soviet Union, and that, in carrying out the handovers, British troops had been ordered to 'Shoot to kill if it becomes necessary.' It was also admitted that 'considerable violence' was used by British troops on the Cossacks and that as a result of their handover, a substantial number of them 'were tortured, executed or condemned to lengthy periods in Soviet labour camps'. These were 'undoubted facts', the Judge said, and were 'of the highest importance' to people who had an interest in these matters. 'But they must not dominate this case. The question in this case is not what happened to the Jugoslavs and what happened to the Cossacks but, accepting what happened to them, what part if any is Lord Aldington to be held responsible for? That is what you have to decide.'

'Lunch with Georgina and Nikolai alone,' Nicolson wrote in his diary. 'They are not feeling hopeful.'

After lunch the Judge started on the evidence. He said he would do it in three stages: first, he would go through the documents in chronological order; secondly, he would deal with the oral evidence; finally, he would review the pamphlet. The result of this scheme was that the documents were divorced from the testimony to which they related. This made the arguments harder to follow. The historical debate receded into the background and the characters of the parties were thrown into starker relief. Nicolson noted in his diary, 'After lunch, the Judge delves into the documents and visibly tires. Turning over all the pages bores the jury and his comments are neither true nor sharp.'

'If you would get out bundle A,' the Judge began wearily. 'If you would be kind enough, in order that we can set the scene for what happened, to look first of all at page 14 in bundle A. That is a letter of 24th August 1944 from Mr Grigg (I think he was "Mr" then) who was Secretary of State for War, to Anthony Eden, who was the Foreign Secretary, and he was writing on the subject of Russian prisoners, as he says in the beginning. He discusses the pros and cons, and then at page 14 you will see he says this: "If the choice is between hardship to our men and death to Russians the choice is plain." And, of course, what was being discussed was the idea of the Soviets handing over any Allied people they had, particularly prisoners of war—perhaps exclusively prisoners of war—and the Allies doing the same, and there is Mr Grigg expressing that view.

'If you then go on to page 17—you will notice Mr Grigg said, "I should like a Cabinet ruling as to its solution" at page 14 — then at page 17 you get the War Cabinet considering (at the top of page 17) a memorandum by the Secretary of State for Foreign Affairs (that is, Anthony Eden). If you look near the bottom of page 17, paragraph 5...'

And so he droned on, document by dreary document. It was the dullest presentation possible.

'So there was this discussion about Soviet prisoners of war and the War Cabinet...

'So that is, so you may think and so it seems to me, a starting point of these later events...

'Turn on, please, and we are getting nearer to the time with which we are concerned. We are now plunging into the military documents them-selves...'

And so on it went. But once Mr Justice Davies started dealing with documents on which the parties placed different interpretations, it became clear there was more to the developing pattern of the afternoon's dreary monologue than pure dullness. Early on, he dealt with one of the most important documents in the repatriations story, the 5 Corps signal, sent on the night of 13 May, which arguably described the Cossacks as Soviet nationals: 'Cannot see any point in retaining this large number Soviet nationals who are clearly great source of contention between Soviets and ourselves.' The Defence argument was that this was deceptive as the Cossacks were not all Soviet nationals and 5 Corps wished to deal with them as if they were; Lord Aldington's argument that it was not deceptive as a large number of them *were* Soviet nationals.

This is how the Judge summed up the two arguments: 'Mr Rampton said to you, "Well, that must mean Soviet citizens and not any other meaning given to the words used there." Mr Gray says that it does not say Soviet citizens in this document, and that is an unreasonable assump-tion to make, that made by Mr Rampton, and, says Mr Gray, there is no suggestion in that document that the Russians had not asked for the return of the Cossacks, and that it was the Cossacks that returned that they were expecting. Well, that is page 127, members of the jury. If you would now go on to page 131...'

That was all. It is surely legitimate to say three things about that gloss. First, it does not illuminate the issue at all; if anything the opaque language confuses it. Secondly, it conveys the whole of the Plaintiff's case while omitting most of the Defence's which was that if this signal had been candid it would have mentioned the Soviet request for the émigrés (Tryon-Wilson's list) and that, as a result, the higher command would have been aware that 5 Corps was 'going beyond Yalta' (to use Macmillan's phrase) in handing over the Cossacks *en bloc*. Finally, in suggesting that there was some distinction between Soviet nationals and Soviet citizens, the Judge was making a point which had nowhere been argued by either of the parties. In sum, the Judge was obscuring rather than illuminating the clash of evidence on this vital document.

Next Mr Justice Davies considered the Robertson Order. This is the whole of what he said about the Jugoslav aspect of it. (He said very little about the Cossack aspect.)

'I think it is right to say that Count Tolstoy accepts—and it is accepted on his behalf—that that order was apt to cover Croat troops but not Croat camp followers, and, of course, we shall have to consider camp followers in due course. If you remember from the agreed Admissions that I mentioned to you this morning, the Croat handover—I think I have got this right—began on 19th May and no Serbs or Slovenes were handed over until the 24th. Mr Gray, on behalf of the Plaintiff, says that if it is right that Count Tolstoy, who I think at first said in the witness box, said that, literally speaking, this order did not technically apply to anybody, then there was no breach of that order as the Plaintiff, who is alleged to have been in breach of it, by the handing over of the Croats—and no Serbs or Slovenes were handed over until Lord Aldington had disappeared out of the picture completely. That is the submission made on his behalf and, of course, does require you to give it earnest consideration. If you think it right, obviously it will affect your view.'

There are many detailed problems about this passage. Tolstoy, for example, would argue that the word 'accepts' in the first sentence implies a reluctantly held view, when in fact the argument that the Robertson Order covered only Croats and none of the other categories mentioned in Low's Deception Order was at the heart of his case. But the main point is that the Defence argument is never mentioned. According to the Judge, Tolstoy had told the Court nothing more than that he 'accepted' a simple point about the Croats, whereas Lord Aldington's case was cogent and deserved the jury's 'earnest consideration'.

Mr Justice Davies's approach became clearer in his comments on Kirk's memorandum recording his alarm at his conversation with Robertson on the evening of 14 May (immediately before the Robertson Order was issued). 'It is said that the importance of this document from Lord Aldington's point of view is that here is General Robertson, according to Kirk—and this document has been admitted into evidence—saying what had got to be done, and what he had suggested, he would do it whether the Americans agreed or not, and with the problems of these hundreds of thousands he could not bother at this time about who might or might not be turned over to the Russians and Partisans to be shot.

'If General Robertson were the Plaintiff in this case, certain arguments would follow, but what is said here is: "Look at this, this is General Robertson saying this, and yet Lord Aldington was accused in the pamphlet of not only not doing what he was instructed to do but actually deceiving his superiors as to what he was doing."

'I am not making that point as a Judge's point, of course. I am telling you what is said on behalf of the Plaintiff on that point, and you will have to give it consideration.

'Now, if you would go on to page 147...'

Once again, Lord Aldington's case is described in some detail but Tolstoy's is entirely omitted. The Defence submitted that document in order to show that Lord Aldington's claim that he could not be expected to know what would happen to the people he handed over was nonsense. If Robertson, in Naples, knew, Low, who was on the spot, should surely also have known. Tolstoy's allegation was that Low had simply not cared what happened to these inconvenient foreigners so long as he was able to leave Austria with his reputation for military efficiency unblemished. None of this was even hinted at by the Judge.

Next Mr Justice Davies considered the 8th Army transmission of the Robertson Order down to 5 Corps. He told the jury, 'As Mr Gray said, one of the points you have to consider is...' But there was no, 'As Mr Rampton said...'

After tea, Mr Justice Davies moved on to Bundle B and it was not long before he came to the Deception Order. All he said for the Defence was that this order was not, 'as Mr Rampton put it, "within miles", or was "miles outside", of the Robertson Order. That, of course, you have got to consider by comparing them, and it is said that here was the first sign, in the documents we have looked at, of the subterfuge, or silence—whichever you like to say—whatever word the Defence would say you apply.'

This was a hopeless understatement of the Defence case which was that the Deception Order was an act of lethal insubordination as well as being a cowardly blood-sacrifice to Tito made easy by the way the victims put their trust in the honour and honesty of the British Army. Worse still, the Judge did not even say why the Defence made the limp allegation he did mention.

By contrast, Mr Justice Davies put the Plaintiff's argument on this critical document much more fully. He was concerned that the jury understand Lord Aldington's problem. 'When he was asked about that on "Timewatch", a television programme—this came out in the course of Lord Aldington's cross-examination—he said: "Well, I agree this was loose and hurried use of language." Members of the jury, I think, although there was no fighting going on at this time, we must try and put ourselves in the position of somebody like Lord Aldington. He was not sitting in solicitors' offices, or a barrister's chambers, with all the time in the world with which to consider—go next door and consult somebody else—what he should put in an order and then polish it up. Here he is—and the same applies to others—under the constraint of somebody in the field. That is one side.

'The other side of it is that when a barrister or a solicitor is sitting there drafting a document in calm and coolness it may affect his client as regards the sale of a house or an investment or, in a criminal case, something more serious. He is not dealing with the shifting of large bodies of people who may be exposed to hardship, whose wishes may not always be consulted. So you have got all considerations like that. They are not all on one side. They are not all on the other, you may think.'

The mass murders at Kocevje, then, were nothing more than the Jugoslavs being 'exposed to hardship' as a result of having their 'wishes not always consulted'.

Moving on to Alexander's 'fatal to their health' signal, the Judge emphasised, quite correctly, that this was not a document Brigadier Low would have seen. But he avoided mentioning the real relevance of this signal to the Defence case, which was that it constituted further evidence of the widespread fear that if the refugees in Carinthia were handed to the Communists they would very likely be killed. If Alexander knew, why was Low so disastrously ignorant? This was the main question the Defence posed, but the Judge ignored it completely and made quite a different point. That Alexander's signal was the germ of the plan to rescue the Cossacks, was something that only someone with access to FO 1020/42 would have known. Nonetheless, the Judge's comment misses even the points the Defence had been able to make.

'It is so important,' Mr Justice Davies said, in steadily more tortuous language, of Alexander's message, 'that you disentangle the involvement of Lord Aldington, established by evidence, from documents, however important, which cannot be and are not brought home to his responsibility—not merely that he did not write them, but his evidence, and there is no evidence to the contrary, is "I did not see this. I did not see this reference to 'fatal to their health'." That is why it is so extremely important in this case—and I am sure Mr Rampton for the Defendants would not dissent from this—that we must look at what is, bearing in mind the burden on the Defendants, brought home to Lord Aldington, if anything, as his being responsible for.'

On the Distone Order, the Judge said it was 'undoubtedly true' that it had not been addressed to 5 Corps. He ignored the Defence argument—since shown by Cowgill to have been correct—that it was meant for 5

Corps. This was fundamental, because if it had been accepted that 5 Corps had received the Distone Order, then the handover of the Jugoslavs was, on Lord Aldington's evidence, an unambiguous act of insubordination. Of course, this could have been shown by producing the 15th Army Group prohibition on 'signed agreements' with the Jugoslavs which was sent to 5 Corps on the same day, but that was lying in the Foreign Office.

On Tuesday morning Mr Justice Davies started with the report of the Low-Ivanovich meeting, on 19 May, at which Low signed the agreement to hand over to Tito all the Jugoslavs in 5 Corps area. Once again Lord Aldington's was the only argument described. Furthermore, the Judge broke his own rule of not intermingling documents with testimony when he quoted the Plaintiff's words from the witness box, 'If this agreement had been wrong I would have been told. That's the way the Army works.' This would have sounded good if the jury had forgotten the Defence argument that there is no evidence that this agreement was ever formally reported to 8th Army. The Judge did not remind them of that.

On the subject of the Definition Order, Mr Justice Davies quoted Gray, who said it was 'an honest, conscientious and successful attempt to apply the Yalta treaty'. For the Defence, all the Judge said was that 'Count Tolstoy describes this as a crucial document'—no mention of *why* he said it was crucial.

The Judge then read out the text of the first half. 'Paragraph 1 was not dealing with individuals but with formations,' he commented, 'and Lord Aldington says that that was a fair and proper way in which to deal with the problem.' Once again, no mention of why Tolstoy said it was not fair and proper: because it contravened the Geneva Convention, the Yalta agreement, the standing order from 8th Army to 5 Corps (13 March) and the wishes of both the Supreme Allied Commander and the British government.

Mr Justice Davies then read out the second half of Low's order, the part concerning the individual cases which were not to be considered unless particularly pressed. 'By and on behalf of Count Tolstoy it is said that really the purpose of this order was to get rid of what I think Mr Rampton called "the whole boiling"—"send the whole boiling back"'. [Actually Rampton never said this.] It was not a genuine screening order, or a genuine attempt to carry out policy which had been laid down insofar as it had been laid down by higher authority, or to take a proper course where there was any discretion left to 5 Corps.

'Well, members of the jury,' Davies went on, 'you have got to make up your minds. You cannot look at this document in isolation, of course. You have got to look at it in the context of the whole, and in the end—we shall come to the pamphlet—say: "Does this document, with other documents, come anywhere near supporting—justifying—the charges made against Lord Aldington?"'

This was the first time that Tolstoy's case had been discussed, although it was hardly a helpful discussion. But, Nicolson noted, even when the Judge made a point for Tolstoy, he did so in a tone of voice which made it sound dull. At one point Rampton handed Tolstoy a note, which Nicolson, sitting next to him, saw. 'Overall this is a complete disgrace,' it said. In his diary that evening Nicolson commented, 'It's all so biased that it's funny, and possibly the jury will turn against the Judge and Toby, but I doubt it.'

There was one document on which the Judge did comment only from Tolstoy's point of view. Unfortunately for the Defence, it was not a document of any central significance to the case. It was a signal from a Colonel Barsdorf at AFHQ in Caserta to another officer on the General Staff side there, reporting a conversation between him and a Colonel Jackling. As this was an internal minute, exchanged between two officers four hundred miles from Austria, and which was never sent to 5 Corps and which was, in any case, accepted as being wrong and therefore irrelevant, it did little to correct the imbalance.

Coming on to 22 May, the Judge said, 'We are now entering the period when Lord Aldington says he was no longer there.' Amazingly, he made no mention of the Defence's central argument that he was still there throughout that day, possibly the most critical in the whole story of the forced repatriations.

Commenting on the "no force" order of 23 May, the Judge had this to say: 'You have to remember two things, members of the jury, when you are looking at this order not to use force: one, as the Admissions that I mentioned yesterday show, force was, in fact, used; but secondly, there is no suggestion that force was used towards the Cossacks before Lord Aldington left—indeed, I think it is right, you can check the dates, no Cossacks were sent back at all until after he had left. There is nothing, you may think, to suggest that Lord Aldington in any way directly contemplated, let alone authorised, the use of force towards the Cossacks.

'What is said on the other side, however, is, well, that is true in the sense that he did not do anything directly to authorise force, but because he knew or should have known quite clearly what the attitude of the Cossacks would be—that they would never go without the use of force or deceit—then what happened was a necessary consequence of the orders that he did, in fact, participate in issuing. That was a necessary consequence to his knowledge, because, as well as force, you have to consider the element of deceit. You will remember the Cossacks were told, it is said, that they were going to a conference on the day when many of them were, in fact, returned. The same applies, as I have said, in relation to force, as to whether that can possibly be brought home to Lord Aldington in the circumstances, as it does to deceit.'

This summary of the Defence argument was utter nonsense. The whole of Tolstoy's case hinged on the fact that Brigadier Low had been at the "shoot the Cossacks" conference and had participated in a decision, not just to use force, but to *kill* the Cossacks if they would not submit to 5 Corps' kidnapping scheme.

When the Judge considered 5 Corps' request to be allowed to use force against the Cossacks, despite AFHQ's prohibition in the "no force" order, his summary of the two arguments was equally one-sided. This was all the Judge said about the Defence case on this critical point: the signal 'was drafted, or at least approved, by Lord Aldington'.

By contrast, this is how he described the Plaintiff's case: 'Lord Aldington says no such thing, that he was in Naples, I think it was, when this occurred on his way back to England, and he would never have used the words in the second or third line: "As a result of verbal directive from Macmillan". That is not a phrase, he says, he would have used, and he disagrees with the suggestion made to him—you may like to make a note of the reference—on this document, that there was a similarity with the wording of A127. He says there was what he describes as a sharp difference. Brigadier Tryon-Wilson also thought that this was not the sort of phraseology which Lord Aldington would have used, and the Plaintiff's case is that the BGS there was Brigadier de Fonblanque and not him. So that is what is said about that. Now 126, please...'

That difference in emphasis was typical of the issues which were contested. But even when the Plaintiff had no point of substance to make, the Judge often made a comment against the Defence. On 26 May 1945, for example, the Foreign Office gave its views to the Chiefs of Staff, for consideration by the Cabinet on the disposal of the Cossacks and Jugoslavs in the Mediterranean Theatre. The Chetniks, the Foreign Office suggested, should be disarmed and interned, and the Croat soldiers handed to Tito, unless the Americans complained, in which case they would be treated the same way as the Chetniks. By 26 May 5 Corps had already handed over to Tito all the Croats, soldiers and non-soldiers alike, and nearly 10,000 Chetniks. Given that in Britain the Army is always subordinate to the government, this surely suggested that something was wrong? Not in the Judge's view. All he said to the jury was that this letter 'shows that the politicians, having regard to the history of the matter that we have looked at together, *are rather behind the march of events.*' (emphasis added)

One of the last documents the Judge considered was the report General Murray prepared in June in response to Dr Miha Krek's "war crimes" allegations which had been submitted to Alexander and which AFHQ had passed down to 8th Army for investigation. The Judge read Murray's report in full. The last paragraph stated: 'The Tito troops to whom these anti-Allied Jugoslavs were handed over accepted them formally and correctly, and this HQ has no reliable evidence of their subsequent treatment in Jugoslavia.' How was such a comment to be taken? Was it true or false? The Judge said if this document were true, then it favoured Lord Aldington, but if it were false, it was irrelevant. These were his words: 'If it is a true and honest account, then you may think that it is of support to the Plaintiff's case, as indicating how the orders were, in fact, implemented. If it is untrue and dishonest then, of course, it does not assist the Plaintiff's case. Whether it harms it at all is another matter. It may simply become a nonentity as far as the Plaintiff's case is concerned, because, of course, nobody can suggest that he was responsible for this. He had been gone certainly over a month by then. Then if you would be kind enough to go on to 102...'

The Defence argument was that this document was evidence of the beginnings of a cover-up of the forced repatriations which was corroborative evidence of the fact that 5 Corps knew at the time that what it had been doing was wrong. The Judge did not even hint at this.

The last group of military documents to be considered was the Bundle containing the various war diaries. When he came to Captain Nicolson's Situation Reports at 1st Guards Brigade, Mr Justice Davies drew attention to their sympathetic tone in these words: 'Whether you think—if he will allow me to say so, and I am now going to use modern, ordinary vernacular language—he was rather a "wet" is a matter entirely for you. I am not for a moment suggesting that you should so think, but you have got to face these facts. Was he rather too over-sensitive for a soldier? That is what I mean by was he rather "wet". Please do not think that I am suggesting that he was at all, but you are bound to have to face that when you are considering what he said.'

The Judge seems to have thought he had gone too far, because, with a nod to the Press benches, he added, 'Any headline referring to this part of the summing-up on these lines: "Judge asks if Captain Nicolson was a 'wet'" would be a malicious misrepresentation of what I have said.'

Dealing with the Report in which Nicolson retracted his first, truthful statement about the British soldiers' dislike of the deceit involved in handing over the Jugoslavs and "placing on record" that the Jugoslavs had been 'kindly and efficiently handled' by the Titoists after handover, the Judge said, 'Mr Nicolson told you that [the previous day's SitRep] was a lie: "I deliberately set out those untruths because I had been reprimanded as to the previous day's SitRep and I was ordered by General Murray to put in something on those lines to contradict what I had said the other day." He pointed out—and this may be too clever—it is too clever for me, I am not sure I follow it enough to do justice to the point—but he says: "Well, the reference to light refreshments"—provided them with light refreshments before they continued their journey—"was a coded message to anybody who read this SitRep, it is all a lot of balderdash"—to use a Judge Taylor expression. Well, you have got to make up your mind about that.'

Though Nicolson had 'lied', Lord Aldington had not, even though he had used that word himself in connection with the two phantom dinners with Anthony Eden on 25 and 26 May 1945. Instead, the Judge recounted the version the Plaintiff gave in his pre-trial affidavit, and then said, 'Now, that is what Lord Aldington said he believed to be the truth when he signed his statement [in September 1989]. In fact, some diaries—some papers of Anthony Eden—came to light, and I shall not need to refer you to them; and, when his attention was drawn to those, Lord Aldington accepted that he could not have had dinner with Anthony Eden on those nights. Anthony Eden was not in London, and he did not meet him until a little bit later. He says that he did have dinner with him, as he described, but it could not have been on those particular dates. Well, that just shows, you may think, assuming you find Lord Aldington to be doing his best to assist you about that, just the sort of situation which arises when one tries to take one's mind back 40-odd years.'

Once again, the Defence argument was completely ignored, namely that if Lord Aldington could admit to lying about one thing, how could he be believed on another, in particular his date of departure about which the Court had no evidence beyond Lord Aldington's own word? Even if the Plaintiff's *bona fides* were accepted and he was only accused of forgetfulness, how could the Court accept so much of his other evidence, such as his not having attended the "shoot the Cossacks" conference, which depended solely on the reliability of his memory?[4]

Having dealt with all the military documents, Mr Justice Davies moved on to the letters between the three litigants, starting with Tolstoy's inquiry about the Cossacks in 1974. Lord Aldington had said he remembered nothing about the Cossack handovers.

'You will remember,' the Judge said, 'that Lord Aldington's involvement with the Cossacks was, you may think, very limited: one document. You may think—it is a matter for you—it is not surprising that, not having done any research into it, which, of course, he later did, he should make that reply to Count Tolstoy.'

Soon the Judge was on to the correspondence between Tolstoy and Watts. '"I wish you luck in your struggle with this evil man,"' he read. '"Had he been a German he would have been strung up years ago." Well, members of the jury, I pose a question to you, and I am not suggesting an answer: is that the letter of a balanced historian, or is it the letter of a fanatic? You must consider that.'

'Now, what do you make of that letter?' the Judge asked rhetorically of one of Watts's earlier communications with Lord Aldington about the Sun Alliance claim. 'Is that a threat? Is it undue pressure? Is it the beginning of something tantamount to, resembling, if not in criminal law, blackmail? That is a matter for you to consider.'

Once again, there was no mention of Watts's answer to the charge of blackmail. On the Defence benches, the tension created by this one-sided summing-up was becoming unbearable.

The Judge moved on to deal with Watts's letter to Lord Aldington on

---

4   On the military documents, a crude indicator of the respective weight given to the two sides of the argument, is the number of times the Judge mentioned the two main parties in the course of dealing with the contemporary documentary evidence. Lord Aldington's name crops up 76 times in the transcript and Tolstoy's 23 times. Given the difference in tone and context in which these two names were mentioned, this ratio substantially under-estimates the different weight given to their respective cases.

14 March 1985. '"Few people could understand,"' he read, '"how a man who had been raised to the peerage and who had been the deputy Chairman of the Conservative party could display a condition of such ruthless and vicious indifference to the plight of this widow and then to be so lacking in any modicum of compassion that people who heard of his conduct were left numb." Then he goes on a little further down to say that this was "none other than the man who had played a protagonist role in the one of the most shameful and horrific acts of betrayal and deception ever perpetrated by British citizens." Here was Lord Aldington receiving from Mr Watts, really you may think, simply a broadside prepared by Count Tolstoy. Mr Watts, I do not think, had done any research himself. He does not suggest he had. He had simply swallowed what he was told–'

Suddenly there was commotion on the Defendants' benches. Watts stood up, shaking with fury, his face flushed. 'On 14th March I had not met Count Tolstoy!' he shouted.

The Judge looked up, astonished. 'I beg your pardon, Mr Watts.'

'Your Lordship, this summing-up of yours is so prejudiced and biased I think you have–' He tailed off, lost for words. 'You should disentangle yourself from a situation where you are purporting to represent the facts to the jury. It is an absolute disgrace, and everybody in this court thinks so.'

There were a couple of cries of 'Hear! Hear!' from the public benches.

'Mr Watts, sit down,' the Judge said sharply. 'And if there is any more interruption the Court will be cleared.'

'I will leave.'

Suddenly the Judge looked apprehensive. Tolstoy noticed that Lord Aldington did so too. Might this mean a re-trial?

'Mr Watts, I have told the jury over and over again,' the Judge said, suddenly more emollient, 'that the matter is entirely–'

'Keep your British justice!' Watts roared at him.

'–for them to–'

'Keep your British justice!'

'Do not lose your temper. Control yourself, sir.'

Watts pushed his way out of his crowded bench. At the door he turned round and bellowed up at the Bench, 'You are a disgrace to the legal profession!'

Then he was gone.

There was a short but significant hush. But Davies quickly pulled himself together.

'Members of the jury,' he went on, 'we have to face facts, and not prejudice. I am doing no more than drawing your attention to documents in these files. You have got them all. And if Mr Watts expects this court to favour one side or the other he is completely wrong. In this summing-up I have illuminated over and over again, and I shall do until the end of the summing-up, the matters which are put forward in criticism of Lord Aldington, and you have them well in mind. When I am in error on a question of fact, and in a complicated matter like this, it is absolutely right that I should be interrupted to correct me on fact—if it be a case of fact, as I accept it is, that on 14th March 1945 Mr Watts had not met Count Tolstoy—and as I say I think that is right—then of course you must bear in mind what I have said in the light of that. If it suggested to you that I was saying they had met and he had fed Mr Watts with this material, then of course that would be, if they had not met—as I accept they had not—incorrect. But I repeat, and I am not withdrawing what I said in any way, that Mr Watts does not suggest that he had himself done any research and what he had gained which enabled him to write this was surely, was it not, from what he must have learned and read of what had been found out by others, and in particular by Count Tolstoy, and I do not resile from saying that.'

Georgina remembers that the women jurors looked shocked that anyone should have shouted at the cosy, avuncular figure of the Judge. But it was a cathartic moment. 'In a way it was a sort of release for me,' she remembers. 'I thought, good for Nigel, he said exactly what we all wanted to say. You can't imagine the feeling of being restrained; it's like being in a straightjacket. You hear all these lies going on and you can't say or do anything. That's what I couldn't stand about the court. It had nothing to do with justice, or even the real world. You sat in this closed room, you couldn't see daylight; you didn't know what season it was, what day it was, what time of the day. It was all grey, all monotonous. You knew it had no real bearing on what really happened, yet you were caught up in it, and you had to fight it according to its own stupid, petty little rules which seemed to be created to frustrate the truth rather than help it.'

Watts went home to Tunbridge Wells, and got back to his painting. He never returned to Court.

For all the Judge said about not resiling from anything, he certainly modified his approach after Watts left. For the first time, he gave the Defence's case equal weight to the Plaintiff's. He dealt quite even-handedly with Watts's dispute with the Sun Alliance, as he did with the evidence Lord Aldington gave from the witness box. Rampton, who had been doodling for the past two days, was seen to draw a cartoon of a judge on a bicycle, peddling backwards at high speed.

That ended Day 39, and the next day, the last of the summing-up, Nicolson noted that the Judge 'is less hostile today, obviously affected by Watts's outburst'.

Mr Justice Davies moved uncontroversially through Lord Aldington's evidence, and on to Tryon-Wilson's. He had earlier said he would deal with the "camp followers" issue in detail at this point, but now he gave no prominence to that highly questionable testimony. He droned on through the other witnesses for the Plaintiff without saying anything remarkable, although he laid emphasis on a few rather surprising points. He was keen, for example, that the jury should appreciate that when Dr Knight said that Tolstoy's scholarship was not respectable, this did not apply to Tolstoy personally, only to his scholarship. Equally, he wanted the jury to know that Lady Aldington had 'made it quite clear that she was not in the habit of crying, whatever happened, about anything'.

When he came to the Defendants' evidence Mr Justice Davies was a little more controversial at times, but not much. Running through Watts's evidence about his dispute with Lord Aldington, he mentioned the accusation of blackmail once again, but this time, he quoted Watts's answer, 'If I was a blackmailer, Lord Aldington could have gone to the police.'

Before leaving Watts's evidence, the Judge made a statement. 'I think it is right that I should say a word to you about Mr Watts's outburst yesterday. It is not basically to criticise him but it is to warn you as to the notice, if any, that you should take of it. That it was rude, there is and can be no doubt. If Mr Watts or his supporters thought that he or they by any behaviour in court could influence a judge or jury, I hope you will agree with me that he and they were utterly wrong. It was a misconceived outburst, members of the jury—I do not hesitate to say so—in so far as it was inspired by any error of fact that I may have made—and he alleges I have made—in the summing-up.

'Mr Watts's outburst was also misconceived,' the Judge went on, rebutting a charge which Watts had not levelled at him, 'if he thought that more time ought to be devoted to his case, as it were, against the Sun Alliance. If he had had the patience to control himself and remain in Court, by the end of the summing-up he, and anyone else, would I hope have seen that you will have been reminded not only of the Plaintiff's case but of his case, in so far as it is relevant, and of Count Tolstoy's case of course, which is adopted by Mr Watts, in some considerable detail. Whether at the end of the summing-up, members of the jury, it is impartial and fair, taken as a whole, is in the first place for you to decide and judge and not in this Court for Mr Watts or his supporters.'

The Judge dealt with Tolstoy's evidence reasonably fairly and then moved on to the last body of evidence he had to consider: that of the Defence witnesses. 'You will remember them,' Mr Justice Davies said. 'Jugoslavs, Cossacks and, of course, others, and a good deal of evidence was read, and it is no disrespect to their evidence, which Mr Gray says is largely irrelevant.'

The Judge said he would deal with them briefly. 'Of course, one does not need to be humane, or sympathetic, or clever, to realise that these witnesses—most of whom were ones who in one way or other escaped the fate that befell so many people, but who can blame them? we would all feel the same—welcome the opportunity of being able to tell in public, irrespective of whether they assist anybody or not, their experiences: no criticism of them for that. But in some respects, at least, to decide the issues in this case, which is not an historical enquiry, their evidence may be of limited value, but I would not be doing my job, as I see it, if I did not touch on their evidence.'

In the event Davies dealt with these witnesses' evidence so briefly that he rendered it almost meaningless. For example, France Kozima's entire story, which in his pre-trial statement included his escape from Kocevje after the Partisans dynamited the mouth of the pit full of bodies, was reduced to this: 'There was Mr Kozima from Slovenia, who joined the Domobranci, and he said that he took orders from the Slovene, not from German, officers. He was told by his Jugoslav commandant that they were going to Italy, not told anything or asked any questions by the British. He was taken to Jugoslavia, but escaped.'

That was all. Most of the other Slavs were dealt with at similar length. Once the Judge got onto the non-Slav witnesses, the length of the summaries increased dramatically. On average, the word-count quadrupled. The summary of Nicolson's evidence was nearly half as long as the Judge's summaries of all 22 Jugoslav and Cossack witnesses put together.

The Judge ended his summing-up with a short homily on damages. They must be compensatory only, not punitive, he said. The means of the parties were irrelevant. The award should compensate for damage to reputation and for hurt feelings, but in computing an appropriate amount, account must be taken of the gravity of the libel. 'This is obviously a very serious libel indeed, in effect, being party to mass murder. So that is a factor that you are entitled to take into account.'

The sum awarded must not be unreasonably high, nor unreasonably low, neither must it be arrived at from consideration of other awards, nor by judicial direction. 'I hope and pray,' he said, 'for the sake of our law and our court, we never get the day when judges dictate to juries so that they become rubber stamps. I am, however, allowed—indeed encouraged—by the Court of Appeal just to say a little bit more. I say it not perhaps in the words of the Court of Appeal, but in my own way, which may be too homely for some, but I say to you that you must remember what money is. You do not deal in Mickey Mouse money just reeling off noughts because they sound good, I know you will not. You have got to consider money in real terms.'

Subsequently controversy has attached to the use of the phrase, 'Mickey Mouse money'. Was this a hint that a high award would be appropriate, or the opposite? Certainly most people understand the phrase "Mickey Mouse" to imply something small. Brigadier Cowgill, for example, described the British Management Data Foundation to the *Financial Times* as a 'Mickey Mouse outfit' because he runs it from his garage with a staff of one (himself). But 'reeling off noughts because they sound good' implies the opposite.

'Also remember,' the Judge continued, 'that this is a case in which, although the damages have to be large, it is accepted, if the Plaintiff succeeds, you are not doing a Plaintiff a favour if you give a figure which is grossly too much, because it leads to appeals and further litigation, and so on. Equally, of course, if you go in a case much too low—ridiculously down—that may lead to further litigation as well, and I am sure that the one thing that the parties wish, and I hope that they do wish, certainly I am sure that you do wish for them, is that this case, if it does not end the debate about the matters you have been looking into, will at least end the litigation between them.'

Shortly before 11 o'clock on the morning of Thursday 30 November, the jury retired to their room and the Court rose.

Georgina remembers she had "butterflies". The Second Defendant, followed by several supporters, pushed through an immense crush of photographers and made his way across the Strand to Benjamin Stilling-fleet's wine bar. It is the haunt of litigants rather than lawyers and has seen many a nervous party passing the hours over a glass of wine while a jury decided his or her fate. Georgina remembers feeling her whole life was hanging in the balance. Michael Rubinstein had said to her pre-viously that if the jury are out for a short time, the news is likely to be good, but the longer they take, the less rosy the prospect becomes.

At 1 o'clock lunch was called for from the jury room. The Tolstoys, accompanied by their second, school-age daughter, Anastasia, who had been given an exeat to allow her to attend Court as an educational experience, finished a tense meal and went for a wander in Lincoln's Inn Fields. Homeless people were camped in the shrubberies. Might this family soon be joining them? It would be handy for appeals, Tolstoy joked. With every lap of the gardens, Georgina's apprehensions rose. At about 3.30 p.m., they returned to the wine bar for a cup of coffee. Then shortly after four o'clock a runner from Rubinstein Callingham came over the road to tell them to get back into Court quickly: the jury had reached its verdict.

At 4.15 p.m. the doors of the Court were unlocked and everyone filed in. No longer were there just the usual six sleepy-eyed occupants of the Press bench: now there were twenty-five excited-looking reporters. The Judge came in and took his seat. At 4.24 p.m. the back door of the Court opened and the jury filed in. Two of the more elderly women were red-eyed, and clearly in a state of deep distress. Lord Aldington still had the back of his head bandaged from his fall in Court a month ago. Next to him sat Lady Aldington, holding his hand. A few feet away, also on the front row of benches, sat the three Tolstoys and Nigel Nicolson. Watts was at his easel in Tunbridge Wells.

The Clerk of the Court asked the jury who their foreman was. The 'wartime NCO' stood up. 'At that moment,' Georgina remembers, 'I knew we had lost. I just looked down and listened.'

'Mr Foreman,' the Clerk said, 'are you all agreed upon your verdict?'

'We are.'

'Have Count Tolstoy and Mr Watts proved that the statements of fact in the pamphlet are substantially true?'

'No.'

'Does the pamphlet contain expressions of opinion?'

'Yes.'

'Have Count Tolstoy and Mr Watts proved that those expressions of opinion are fair, in the sense that they are such as a fair-minded man could honestly make on the facts proved to be so?'

'No.'

'Do you find for Lord Aldington or for Mr Watts?'

'Lord Aldington.'

'Do you find for Lord Aldington or for Count Tolstoy?'

'Lord Aldington.'

'What sum in damages do you award Lord Aldington?'

'£1.5 million.'

There was a momentary hush. The Judge smiled at the jury. Lord Aldington took off his glasses, dabbed his eyes and mouthed a silent 'Thank you' at them. A sob burst from Anastasia. Georgina's eyes moistened. But she was determined not to give the Plaintiff the satisfaction of seeing her cry. 'I must get out of here right now,' she thought. Nicolson put his hand on her knee and gave it a comradely squeeze. Tolstoy went pale and put his arm round his daughter's shoulders. Fifty miles away, Watts slapped another dash of colour onto his canvas.

Some legal words were mumbled in a world the Tolstoys were no longer fully conscious of. They did not stay to hear the end of them but fled the Court, Georgina to look for sanctuary in Michael Rubinstein's office, and Tolstoy, bravely, to face the cameras in the Strand and give the Press the statement it wanted.

Nicolson stayed in Court to hear the closing formalities, including the award of costs and the imposition of injunctions. None of this took very long. The Court rose at 4.45 p.m. 'Then the Judge retires,' Nicolson noted in his diary. 'I bow to his biased back.'

Part IV

A TARNISHED

VINDICATION

'I do not want to complicate affairs by having on
record for the public any statements different from
those I made on oath in the courts.'

 —Lord Aldington
  Letter to the Imperial War Museum, 1993

20

COUNT TOLSTOY APPEALS

O UT IN THE STRAND Lord Aldington told the Press of his feeling
of 'tremendous relief that my reputation and the name of my
family have been fully and wonderfully vindicated. It is a relief
such as I could never have imagined having.' He looked tousled rather
than triumphant, as if this was not a fight he had sought. He disdained
anything more flamboyant than a hint of a smile and a brief flourish of
his hat.

Tolstoy gave a short interview too. He looked wintry and almost
wobbly, as if he had run across the road to help an old lady and been hit
by a truck. 'We are ruined,' he said, 'completely and utterly ruined. The
Establishment has got its way and can now go and repatriate the Viet-
namese in the same way. They want to shut me up. I hope the honour of
Britain is satisfied. Presumably they will take my house, my library and
everything.'

On the issues, Lord Aldington said that if he had lost, 'it would have
meant I was the only man in Britain to be charged with such a crime.'
Tolstoy was asked whether he now regretted having written the pamphlet.
'Perhaps it would have been better to have left everyone in their graves
and the story untold,' he said, 'and certainly in this country there would
have been a lot of people who wish that I had done that. But you have to
do what you think is right.'

Immediate public reaction was that that the size of the award was out
of proportion. Tolstoy went further and said it was meaningless. 'If it
was a hundred thousand, I couldn't pay it.' From behind his easel in
Tunbridge Wells, Watts was more down to earth. He told reporters that

he owned no significant assets, so would have to pay out of income. He reckoned he could manage between £3 and £6 per week, depending on the state of the art market. On this basis, he said, he would have the debt discharged within about 6,500 years.

Outside the Court, Lord Aldington missed the best opportunity he was ever to have of winning the moral as well as the legal high ground by announcing that he would forego the damages he knew he would be very unlikely to see.[1] All he would say was that if he did get the money he 'would like to think' he would pass some of it on to his favourite charities—no mention of the victims of 5 Corps. He then made what the papers called 'a Churchillian gesture' to the crowd outside the Royal Courts, gathered up Lady Aldington, climbed into his son's Mercedes and disappeared into the evening traffic.

That night, the Aldingtons celebrated at the Carlton Club. The victorious Plaintiff told one reporter that if the Defendants appealed, it would be 'very unfortunate', but he would rely on 'British justice' and 'let the law take its full course'. They drank champagne, Lord Aldington said, but 'there was none of this racing-driver carry-on, spraying it all around. It tasted too sweet to waste.'

In Michael Rubinstein's office, Georgina had broken down completely. 'How do you ever get rid of a sum like this?' she sobbed. 'It's going to be with us for the rest of our lives. However hard Nikolai works, however much he earns, we will always be ground down.' It is not as bad as a death in the family, Rubinstein pointed out. Then Anastasia spoke up. They must all 'be brave for Papa, who is coming round now and he must feel awful having brought us to this.'

Tolstoy arrived and Rubinstein produced a bottle, appropriately enough for his Jacobite client, of Drambuie. After several hefty swigs, they watched the 6 o'clock news on the television. The outcome of the case was the first item. The mood swung dramatically. Soon they were laughing, feeling a heady sense of unreality. The more they thought of the size of the award, the more absurd it seemed.

Georgina wanted to get back home, but Tolstoy insisted that they

---

1   Lord Aldington wrote to Richard Keightley on 12 August 1989 saying, 'Watts and Tolstoy are not by any means certainly going to be able to pay my costs, even though they will be ordered to do so.' How much more so for a vast award of damages?

spend the night in London with friends and have a sort of litigatory wake. They went to the Polish Hearth Club in Kensington where the atmosphere is refreshingly un-English. The feeling of support combined with the drink to make a strangely fortifying evening. Everyone expressed the view that the award was so monstrous that it could not be allowed to stand. 'In a way it was *so* big,' Georgina remembers, 'that we began to feel quite important. We were on a high, all laughing hysterically.' Tolstoy's main memory of the evening is that one guest at dinner asked a Polish waitress for a dish of 'Judge's Balls' and was amused when she returned from the kitchen with a plate containing a long Polish sausage flanked by two meatballs, artfully arranged to suggest, well... Ha! Ha! Have another vodka!

The next morning, before setting out for his home in Southmoor, Tolstoy rang his neighbours to say that if any journalists appeared they should... But he could not finish his sentence. 'Any journalists! Town Pond Lane is *crammed* with them already,' he was told.

When they arrived and saw the numbers, Georgina, for the first time, had the thought that there was some hope. Their fate was now a matter of public interest.

That morning, Friday, 1 December, the press was full of the verdict. The most extensive coverage, as it had been throughout the trial, was from the *Daily Telegraph*, which quoted Lady Aldington as saying of her husband, 'He did it for the Army really, and I hope they thank him for it.' Bill Deedes, on another page, said that Lord Aldington 'went to Court to defend his honour.' Lord Aldington himself said he did it for his family. The only person for whose benefit the case was *not* said to have been mounted was the man who had been awarded the damages.

Lord Aldington gave an interview to John Keegan. He had not minded what Tolstoy and Watts had said about him—a remark which provokes the question, why had he sued them?—but 'hearing the charges repeated by Rampton, that hurt. When you first get accused of being a liar, a war criminal, a murderer, it doesn't hurt. But when it goes on and on it forms a bruise. It hurts. You cry.'

In a statement made before the verdict, Tolstoy was quoted as saying that if he lost he would be unable to continue living in England and would probably emigrate to France. 'It would be a frightful wrench, but setting aside any consideration of Lord Aldington, the dirty tricks the British Establishment has used is such an outrage that I could not go on living in a country where it is allowed to happen.' He was not worried about bankruptcy, he said, which is 'not necessarily a bad thing for an author'.

The *Daily Telegraph* leader-writer was of the opinion, broadly, that the verdict was right, but the size of the award made a mockery of the judicial process. This was a theme repeated elsewhere although Bill Deedes said that no amount of money would compensate Lord Aldington for the loss of his peace of mind. 'Happiness stolen from youth may eventually be regained; tranquillity stolen from old age is much harder to retrieve.' Deedes was typical of the press comment which nowhere gave a thought to what had been stolen from the victims of 5 Corps, some of them, including Generals Krasnov and Shkuro, even older than Lord Aldington. The historical dimension to this case, Deedes continued, made it quite unlike the normal run of defamation actions. Therefore the shock at the size of the award should not be a trigger for a change in the law, but rather be seen as an appropriate response to a unique libel.

The Times called for judges to decide the awards in defamation actions, leaving the jury only with the job of reaching a verdict. The *Independent* pointed out that a man recently left mute and paralysed after a road accident at the age of 16 had received little more than half the damages awarded to Lord Aldington.

In the *Guardian* Richard Norton-Taylor wrote a background article saying that 'the huge award makes the reform of the libel laws a virtual certainty.' The paper also published an article by Robert Knight in which he jeered at Tolstoy's aristocratic pretensions. 'His title has no more historical validity than Count Basie's.'

The *Daily Mail* adopted a more serious tone, saying the case 'should stand as a warning to all historians about the danger of judging people and their actions in the past by the usually quite different standards of today.' Lady Aldington was quoted as saying that her husband had virtually collapsed during the Judge's summing-up. 'The doctor said it was stress,' she said. 'But I only understand about sheep. When they're under stress they get fleece-break.' Lady Aldington also thought her husband was, in general, too sympathetic to opponents. 'Toby says I'm Old Testament, black or white, blood and thunder, right or wrong. He's much too Christian to be like that. He's New Testament. He says you have to look at the other person's side, but I think that takes up too much time.'

In the *Daily Express* Michael O'Flaherty described Lord Aldington as 'the epitome of a distinguished British military gentleman'. Tolstoy, by implied contrast, had 'left Court a broken man'. This was no more than he deserved. Whereas Lord Aldington had once been 'a tall, proud, marching soldier'—actually he stands about five foot eight—in Court he had moved with 'a slow, stooping gait. Now the ghosts called at him, screamed at him, cried at him, claiming he was a monster, a war criminal.' After the trial 'the ghosts that have haunted Court 13 will disappear. But the memories, dark and excoriating, will remain.' Despite this lurid fictionalising, even the *Express* thought the size of the award made 'a mockery of British justice'.

The most succinct comment was in the *Sun*. The award was 'totally potty', the paper said simply. 'How many legs, arms and other bones would Lord Aldington have had to lose in a car crash to get that kind of money?'

The *Daily Mirror* made a similar point though at greater length. 'The law is not just an ass, it's gone loony.' In two large, adjacent boxes, Lord Aldington's luck was compared with the way the families of 95 soccer fans, who had been crushed to death in a recent accident in the Hillsborough stadium in Sheffield, were treated. 'Lord is awarded £1,500,000 for a slur hardly anyone noticed,' said one box. 'But just £50,000 average payout for Hillsborough,' said the other. The editorial, headed 'Obscene Lottery', said 'an elderly man who does not need the money is given a fortune because allegations—admittedly very grave—were published in a pamphlet with a circulation of only 10,000. On the other hand, the families of those who were killed at Hillsborough will get vastly less. In Britain, not for the first time, the loss of a life is worth a lot less than damage to a reputation.'

Back at home at Court Close, Tolstoy was immensely encouraged by the press interest, both domestic and international. For the first time in his life, he was on all the front pages. Georgina, however, was less affected by the media fizz and could not forget the reality of the debt. She told reporters how she 'did not relish' the thought of swapping the children's private schools for comprehensives. She commented bitterly to the *Daily Mail*, 'We have learned it doesn't pay to be honest.' Her house, she said, felt 'so safe, so secure that I simply can't believe they will take it away from me.'

The reaction of the participants in the trial naturally depended on which side they had supported. Nicolson spoke for most of the Defendants' witnesses when he said simply, 'Everyone thinks the jury mad and the system must be changed.' Tryon-Wilson's view was different, but equally trenchant. 'Myself I think it was the most diabolical trial that I have ever been in,' he told the Imperial War Museum some months later.

'It really is appalling to think that our legal system is such that an individual like Count Tolstoy is allowed to bring such misery not only on the head of one individual but onto families galore, including his own, by making these appalling statements for which, really, there is no substance, entirely due to the fact that he feels that he wanted to draw attention to himself and because he was part of the Tolstoy family and he thought he was doing good. He absolutely crucified poor Harold Macmillan and very nearly crucified Toby Low. The fact that the lawyers on Tolstoy's side were allowed to ask these really disgraceful questions and tried time and time again to suggest that he was telling lies, it's awful to think that you've got to protect yourself to that extent. The pressure on Toby in the court was tremendous. The atmosphere was very trying. It has pulverised his family.'[2]

It was not long before letters started arriving at Court Close by the sackful. Ludovic Kennedy wrote in despair; Roger Scruton expressed amazement at the verdict; Sir Richard Body wrote to say how glad he and others were that the story of the repatriations was, as a result of the trial, now widely known. Michael Rubinstein wrote about 'transparent injustice' and Giles Gordon, Tolstoy's literary agent, said that it was 'impossible to over-estimate' the 'power and weight of the Establishment'. A senior solicitor in Belgravia, who had been particularly helpful in the background, wrote that he felt 'ashamed to be British and ashamed to be a British lawyer'. A retired Major sent some money because 'you will be light on the housekeeping, especially after m'learned friends have dined'. Sir Bernard Braine offered to help Tolstoy in any way he could and a man from Edinburgh wrote to say that 'Butcher Cumberland would have got the verdict over Saints Peter and Paul from such servile scum.'

Many of these people enclosed money, usually on condition that it be banked only if it was certain not to fall into Lord Aldington's hands. The architectural critic Gavin Stamp expressed a very common sentiment. 'The only worthwhile honour comes after admitting mistakes, not covering them up.' He added: 'As for Macmillan, I have long maintained that a man who could demolish the Euston Arch was capable of anything.' A Dutchman wrote offering a house he owned in Norfolk for Tolstoy's use

---

2   Imperial War Museum, Dept. Sound Records, tape 11738

should he be evicted from Court Close. The survivor of Siberia, Karl-Gottfried Vierkorn, said, 'though the battle has been lost, the war goes on'. Some of the correspondents thought that Aldington's plea about having to obey orders (*sic*) was fair, but sent money anyway, in one case, 'because Lord Aldington expressed no regrets and because some of your witnesses were not allowed to give evidence.'

The journalist Harry Phibbs expressed another common view when he wrote that, 'there seems to be some muddled thinking from a few people that you have been right to point out a crime took place but awfully beastly actually to blame anyone for it.'

A spinster from Canterbury proposed a 'pilgrimage of reparation' and a man from Dartford sent £50, saying mysteriously, 'I know how you feel, as I brought my ex-wife out of Poland and she went off with a window-cleaner!!!'

The most frequently expressed sentiment, though, was put into words by a man from Bedford. 'I'm afraid there are certain cases where British prestige appears to be at stake—Guildford, Birmingham, the Londonderry business, Belgrano, Iranian Embassy, etc.—when the result of a trial or inquest is nearly always predictable and utterly wrong.'

There was one aspect of the judgement which did not make the headlines: the three injunctions which the Judge granted on the nod immediately after the verdict had been delivered. The first restrained Watts from harassing Lord Aldington, which was not unreasonable, given the verdict. The second was more controversial. Mr Justice Davies ordered both Defendants

> whether by themselves their servants or agents or otherwise howsoever from publishing or causing or permitting to be published or assisting or participating in or conniving at the publication whether within the jurisdiction of the Court or elsewhere to any other person whatsoever... any words or allegations (however expressed) to the following or any similar effect namely that the Plaintiff in connection with the [repatriations] was guilty of disobedience or deception or dishonourable or inhumane or other improper or unauthorised conduct...

This **staggeringly wide injunction** has become known as the "gagging injunction" because it has had the effect of turning the jury's view of the evidence into "official history". No new evidence can be allowed to affect the jury's verdict. Most importantly of all, the documents suppressed at the trial, the contents of FO 1020/42, for instance, can never be discussed in print by Tolstoy. History has, in effect, been frozen.[3] It might perhaps be added that Mr Justice Davies told the jury early on in the trial that 'we are a country without censorship in any form that would stop the free expression of the truth'.

The third injunction Mr Justice Davies granted froze the Forced Repatriation Defence Fund which could not now dispose of the money raised to pay for the trial, even for the purpose for which it had been collected. Neither could it be used for any appeal. Tolstoy was helpless.

But there was one bright patch on the horizon: cheques soon started arriving from sympathisers in very large quantities. They were credited to a new fund, the Georgina Tolstoy Family Fund (GTFF). The three Trustees were Nigel Nicolson, Ludovic Kennedy and Sir Bernard Braine. The Patrons were a mixture of English media or Establishment-fringe folk and titled Europeans.[4] Most of the Europeans were friends of Tolstoy's but many of the English names were not known to him personally. They agreed to act as Patrons because of a threat they perceived to freedom of speech. When asked by this author, only one (Alan Watkins) mentioned the size of the award as a reason. Lord Vinson said, 'Throughout the whole matter, I sense the wet, clammy hand of the Foreign Office—always more anxious to please our enemies than support our own.' How horribly true that was, only came out some years afterwards. Some noted how much sympathy there was for Lord Aldington in Establishment

---

3   In the light of the injunction, it might be worth noting that when General Sir David Fraser, the noted military historian and biographer of Alanbrooke and Rommel, was asked what he thought the trial had contributed to historical knowledge, he replied, 'I cannot comment on what the trial "proved". Certainly nothing factual I would have thought.' Letter to the author, 12 November 1993

4   The full list (there were some changes over time) was: Peter Ackroyd, Lindsay Anderson, Jonah Barrington, Sir Nicholas Cheetham, Colonel Brian Clark, Lord Courtenay, Viscount Cranbourne, Sir Nicholas Fairbairn, General Sir David Fraser, Sir Ian Fraser, Dr Leopold Graf Goëss, Countess Casimir Grocholski, Prince Dmitiri Galitzine, Richard Ingrams, Hon. John Jolliffe, Lord Kingsale, Norris McWhirter, Princess Tatiana Metternich, James Lees-Milne, Lady Olga Maitland, Zoë Polanska-Palmer, Colonel "Murphy" Palmer, Chapman Pincher, Fr. Michael Protopopov, Prince and Princess Lew Sapieha, Philipp von Schöller, Prof. Roger Scruton, Alexander Solzhenitsyn, Gavin Stamp, Lord Sudeley, Lord Thomas of Swynnerton, Colin Thubron, The Duke of Valderano, Lord Vinson of Roddam Dene, Alan Watkins, Auberon Waugh and Michael Wharton ('Peter Simple').

circles, in particular at the Carlton Club. Despite this, John Jolliffe spoke for many others when he said Lord Aldington 'was a bully and a "Pukka Dud", good at spotting who would be useful to him and making himself useful to them'.[5]

Substantial press interest did not last beyond the Sunday after the verdict when some longer articles were published in the broadsheet papers. Alistair Horne said that the trial had 'cleared' Harold Macmillan—an odd view on two counts: first, Cowgill was supposed to have done that a year earlier and, secondly, Macmillan was never mentioned other than in passing. Christopher Booker wrote cattishly of 'the sad little pamphlet, riddled with factual errors', but also said that the only certainty to emerge was that a court was not the place to settle such historical controversies. Simon Jenkins was more neutral, saying the Judge seemed to have been under 'some cosmic edict to protect the Establishment from some of the murkier recesses of its past'. Nigel Nicolson wrote the only piece sympathetic to Tolstoy, criticising the summing-up, but saying, to the astonishment of anyone who has read the transcript of the whole trial, that the quality of debate in Court had been far higher than was normal when he was in the House of Commons!

The last prominent article was in the following week's *Spectator* when Auberon Waugh criticised the legal profession.

> If anyone so much as whispered the old nursery adage to the effect that 'sticks and stones will break my bones but words will never harm me' within the gothic confines of the High Court, the whole edifice would collapse, leaving all those cocky young barristers and preposterous judges to go begging for their next pair of silk tights.[6]

To maintain the momentum of his fund-raising, Tolstoy needed to stay in the public eye. But the "gagging" injunction proved a major handicap. He wanted to hold a press conference, but Michael Rubinstein persuaded him that would be unwise. He wanted to launch the Georgina Tolstoy Family Fund with a public appeal document, but Rubinstein advised against that too. He was told he had to be very careful about what

5   Letter to the author, 31 January 1994
6   *Spectator* 9 December 1989

he said. He should never mention Lord Aldington's name in print unless a few words were appended to the effect that the jury had 'exonerated' him.

Meanwhile, Allen & Overy set to work to seize the Defendants' assets. Watts was immune, personally owning little more than his brushes and easel, but Tolstoy was not. He owned a half-share (with Georgina) in the family home, though he had few other substantial assets. He had two basic courses of action open to him. The first was to admit legal defeat, declare himself bankrupt and accept the not unduly onerous conditions this would impose on him and get back to his highly profitable work on Merlin. He could almost certainly have retained his computer equipment, and probably his library, as tools of his trade and lived off the Georgina Tolstoy Family Fund while he wrote Volume II. Within three years he would have been discharged from bankruptcy, whether he had payed his debt in full or not, leaving Lord Aldington with little more than the memory of a heroic victory in the High Court and the sweet taste of Carlton Club champagne.

The second possible course of action was to fight the verdict by appealing. There was no telling where this would end, but since it would involve putting himself in the hands of the courts again, it was for Tolstoy, at best, a very uncertain approach. The optimum result would be to have the whole judgement and all its effects, including the injunctions, reversed. That would represent a major victory, but the chances of achieving it were minimal—at least that was the advice both Rampton and Rubinstein Callingham gave him.[7] Anything less than complete victory would do little more that delay the inevitable moment when he had to bow to the judgement of the Court and surrender all his assets either to Lord Aldington or, if he had died by then, to his estate. The risk was that the longer this took, the further Tolstoy would be from the source of his inspiration about Merlin. Might it not vanish forever, like Coleridge's of Kubla Khan after the man from Porlock rapped on his cottage door?

The Defendants had until 28 January 1990 to lodge any appeals. Watts decided against doing so as he was about to undergo heart surgery.

---

7   Amazingly, at the conference at which this advice was tendered, none of Tolstoy's legal advisors could give him any detailed information on the consequences of declaring himself bankrupt. He was offered the name of an accountant who might advise, but he did not take up the offer.

Tolstoy was initially inclined to take his lawyers' advice, until, over the New Year holiday, he met the journalist Harry Phibbs at a party. Was he going to appeal or not? Phibbs asked him. Tolstoy said he thought he would probably not, though many supporters were urging him to. But what did Phibbs think? Well, put yourself in Aldington's shoes, Phibbs replied. Would you rather hear that Tolstoy was taking you to the Appeal Court or that he was not? The answer to that question was obvious. On the spot Tolstoy changed his mind and decided to appeal.

If Lord Aldington made a future bed of thorns for himself in not making a magnanimous gesture immediately after being awarded £1.5 million in damages, Tolstoy did the same when he took the decision to appeal partly on the basis of what would most harm Lord Aldington rather than what would most help himself.

When Tolstoy formally lodged his appeal he gave eight grounds for doing so. One was that the damages were 'unreasonable and excessive' but all the others related to the Judge's behaviour. Mr Justice Davies had 'displayed overt animosity' towards the Defendant, Tolstoy alleged, and had tried to discredit him and his witnesses by 'continual interruption, sarcasm and abuse of Counsel'. He had also allowed Dr Knight to be called as an expert on matters on which he was 'manifestly unqualified to speak'. Aldington had 28 days in which to respond.

He made two responses, the first of which was to ask for security for costs in the action. Allen & Overy wrote to Tolstoy using his own public statements to demonstrate that if he lost he would be unlikely to be able to pay Lord Aldington's costs. Accordingly they had costed a likely appeal and asked him to lodge that sum in Court as security. Their total bill would be £188,179, they said.

It is customary for impecunious plaintiffs (confusingly, in an Appeal Tolstoy would be in the position of Plaintiff—called the "Appellant"—and Lord Aldington in the position of the Defendant—called the "Respondent") seeking access to the Court of Appeal to be asked by the Defendant to put up security for their costs before being allowed to proceed. The court will usually order this if it feels the plaintiff's grounds for appeal have little or no merit. If the case appears very strong, then the court will rarely make such an order.

Aldington's second response was made four days later, on 2 February. Allen & Overy wrote an open letter to Tolstoy saying that, though £1.5 million was, 'in the unique circumstances of this case, a proper sum for the jury to have arrived at and that it was in no way an unreasonable award', Lord Aldington was old and therefore reluctant to become involved in a lengthy appeal hearing and to that end would accept £300,000 plus his costs. Tolstoy immediately saw this made no practical difference to his position, and felt it was simply a stunt. As a real offer of a reduced settlement it was too little, too late. Tolstoy rejected it out of hand.

Aldington could not now get down to his golf and gardening, much less his book on the problems of British industry. He was back once again to affidavits and conferences with solicitors. David Mackie was still his *chef de cabinet* at 9 Cheapside, and on 8 February he swore an affidavit testifying to his client's wish to avoid further litigation. The libel trial had been

> a severe and visible strain upon the Plaintiff, so much so that owing to stress and injury to his back caused by a fall in Court, he was at times nearly unable to rise from his seat at adjournments or to walk. He is normally a fit and ebullient man. The strain was particularly intolerable during the several days of the trial when the Defence called as witnesses a succession of Jugoslav survivors of *Jugoslav* atrocities and Cossack women who had escaped *Soviet* atrocities, to give evidence about whose relevance the Judge expressed grave reservations and who certainly could and did give no evidence of anything done by Lord Aldington. (emphasis added)

On 21 March Mr Registrar Adams heard Lord Aldington's application for security for costs in Tolstoy's appeal. The hearing was *in camera*, and conducted without wigs, gowns or silk tights. Mr Registrar Adams was a dapper man in a dark suit, and he conducted the proceedings in a business-like rather than a theatrical manner. Aldington did not attend. He wrote to Richard Keightley on 24 March saying, 'I was NOT present on the instructions of my advisors, for fear I would get much too angry.'

What Adams had to decide was whether Tolstoy's case was sufficiently strong to over-ride the presumption that security for costs should be required, on appeal, from a clearly impecunious Plaintiff. The hearing lasted four days, and his judgement was not delivered until 18 May. In it he said he thought five of Tolstoy's seven points about Mr Justice Davies's summing-up had 'just enough strength to lead me to conclude that security for costs should not be awarded in this case'. Furthermore he took the view 'that Count Tolstoy has reasonable prospects of establishing on appeal that the award is so large that it should be set aside, notwithstanding the very grave and damaging nature of the libel'.

Aldington had lost. Tolstoy could now proceed to the Court of Appeal without lodging any security. Not surprisingly, Tolstoy thinks highly of Adams. 'He was absolutely marvellous from beginning to end. He was utterly impartial, and obviously had a very acute brain, unlike the bewigged buffoon, Davies.'

But Tolstoy's joy was short-lived. Lord Aldington immediately appealed against Mr Registrar Adams's judgement. Now he and Tolstoy would be facing each other in the Appeal Court, not to hear Tolstoy's appeal against the libel judgement, but to hear Lord Aldington's appeal against Adams's verdict in Lord Aldington's application that Tolstoy's appeal against the libel verdict should not go ahead until Tolstoy had put up £188,179 be disallowed. It was feeding time in the lawyers' pool.

While these manoeuvres were in progress, there was a dying flutter of press interest in the litigants. Hugh Trevor-Roper, a retired Oxford history Professor, took up Knight's theme about titles and wrote rather bitchily in The *Independent* that Tolstoy was a 'bogus' Count. 'I am sure that Mr Tolstoy would make an excellent count [Trevor-Roper's lower-case] as counts go, if he were one; but he isn't.'[8] More nastily, Alistair Horne invoked the issue of race in an American magazine. He talked about the 'tangled cobweb of truths, half-truths and downright inaccuracies woven by Tolstoy', saying, by way of explanation, that 'in his writing, [Tolstoy] came to reveal a fanatical obsessiveness that was more Slav than Anglo-Saxon.'[9]

But Aldington came in for rougher treatment than Tolstoy. Lord Lambton, the millionaire Old Etonian who had served in Edward Heath's government when Lord Aldington had been at the pinnacle of his career, but who had been forced to resign in humiliating circumstances over a sexual scandal, wrote a rumbustiously vituperative article about the victorious Plaintiff in the *Literary Review*. Lambton called Lord Alding-

---

8   The Tolstoy Countship dates from 1930. It was retrospectively backdated to 1910 when the Tsar is said to have declared his intention of honouring the family with elevation to the Russian peerage. The Tsar never got round to it, but one of his self-proclaimed "successors", the Grand Duke Kyril Vladimirovitch, did so in exile on the Tsar's behalf, posthumously. Tolstoy's father has never used the title. For a fuller account, see Tolstoy's *The Tolstoys*, pp. 374-5

9   *National Review* 5 February 1990

ton 'a previously forgotten little man' and a 'perennial schoolboy', and described him in the 1950s as 'a spring-heeled jack following Anthony Eden around, self-satisfied, ingratiatingly anticipating his master's demands... [later] a keen, earnest adorer of Mr Harold Macmillan, [who] walked around with the look of a praised fag on his face.' He talked of his 'fawning manners to the great' and said that 'whenever he entered the smoking room, he used to glance round to see who had noticed the entrance of a rising star. I always noticed him by a flash at the door for he wore spectacles which somehow or other reflected the light, causing a surprising lighthouse-beam effect.'

Lambton's story concerned a letter which Eden had mistakenly sent in the late 1950s to Low rather than Lambton, and which the ex-Prime Minister advised Lambton to get back from Low. But Low would only allow the real addressee to copy it out, not have it. Lambton did so 'with the little spring-heeled jack's feet fidgeting about beneath his desk, nervous that I might demand the original, which he has by now probably presented to Winchester College'. Lord Avon later recommended he ask for the original, but Lambton did not do so. 'Somehow or other,' he wrote, 'I felt that would have spoilt a perfect joke and it would have been sad to see the look of disappointment on Lord Aldington's schoolboy face. He might even have burst into tears as he did in the recent court case. I have often noticed bumptious little men crack easily.'[10]

Central to the security for costs issue was the role of the Sun Alliance. Would they be paying for Lord Aldington's appeal? If they were going to, then it was unlikely that the Court of Appeal would allow Aldington to demand security for costs against Tolstoy as he would have no costs to secure. In order to find out what the Sun Alliance were up to, Nigel Watts went with his brother, Richard, to the 1990 Annual General Meeting. It was held in the company boardroom at 1 Bartholomew Lane on 16 May and Henry Lambert was in the chair, looking very nervous.

Few of the shareholders displayed any signs of life until Richard Watts stood up and asked how much of the Group's resources had been 'used, or pledged to assist, or underwrite' Lord Aldington's '*private* legal action'. Lambert flailed around for a few moments, saying nothing of substance, but eventually admitted that the Company was providing 'some help'. But then he thought of a way out. 'It appears that this case may now go to Appeal, and therefore is, I suppose, *sub judice*. We shall cross this particular bridge when we come to it.'

'So: an open-ended commitment to fund the private legal action of an erstwhile director?' said Richard Watts.

'We are–, we are–,' stumbled Lambert in reply.

'An open commitment to fund–'

'It's *not* an open commitment.'

'Well, what commitment is it, Mr Lambert?'

'There is no commitment. We shall do what we think appropriate when the time comes.'

'Well, how much has been spent to date?'

'A very small amount indeed. I mean, something absolutely–'

'I hadn't asked your opinion about the size of the amount; I asked what it is.'

'That is a question entirely for the management, but in terms of–'

'It's a question for the shareholders. The shareholders answer–'

'Hear, hear!' boomed Nigel Watts. 'Answer the question!'

'As I said, it is actually, in terms of legal expenses, an infinitesimal amount.'

'What is it? Could you not just give us an honest answer to this question?' said Richard Watts.

'I've given you an honest answer.'

'Well, you haven't given us an honest answer: you're filibustering, Mr Lambert. Will you tell us how much you've been spending, how much you've been underwriting?'

'In the last year we have spent nothing.'

'Have you underwritten anything, or pledged anything?'

'No, we haven't—we haven't.'

'You are planning to do so?'

'We have made no pledge whatever. I have said: we will provide what has to be done when the time comes. And that is all.'

'I think where Lord Aldington is involved in this may be that you were also at Winchester,' said Richard Watts. 'And I must remind you that you're meant to be running a public company, and you're accountable to the shareholders. We're not running some Old Boys' club for the benefit of ex-Wykehamists. And let us have some proper facts. What do you plan to do in this respect?'

'I've told you all that I'm going to tell you for today.'

'It is not open to you to decide what you account to the shareholders for,' Richard Watts continued. 'If you're not prepared to be honest and open about a relatively small matter like this, how much less are you going to be honest and open about large matters? How do the shareholders not know that large sums are not being filched away to the Conservative Party? There's an important point of principle here.'

'I'm not going to—I'm not going to say any more. And I think that the shareholders on the whole are tired of hearing any discussion of this-'

'They're not tired of hearing it: we want the answer! Let's have the answer! They'd be a lot less tired if you stopped filibustering and gave us a few facts.'

'Now let's have another question, shall we?' said Lambert, looking hopefully round the room.

'Will you answer the *last* question?' shouted Nigel Watts, to laughter from the company.

'You've heard all that I'm going to say, Mr Watts.'

'Well, Mr Chairman,' the recently defeated litigant continued, 'the shareholders are entitled to an honest and open answer with regard to the level of funding which you accorded Lord Aldington, or which you have pledged to Lord Aldington with regard to an Appeal which has nothing to do with this Company *whatsoever*. Will you now state whether you can confirm or deny the veracity of Lord Aldington's statement at a City banquet earlier this year that his costs in this case have been over a million pounds, and that they have been underwritten by this Group? Will you confirm or deny that statement?'

'I will deny that statement.'

That was easy because Aldington's actual costs were considerably less than this.

'Will you then state what level of support you have given to Lord Aldington,' said Watts, speaking loudly, slowly and angrily, 'and what you have pledged to give him?'

'We pledged no sum to him: I have said that three times already.'

'Well, that is in contradiction to what you said last year, Mr Chairman, isn't it?'

'We have pledged no sum. We have said that we will give help, and when we know what help Lord Aldington needs, we will decide what, if anything, we will do.'

'Well, that's an open-ended answer, and we'd like a specific statement as to what is the level of funding that you have accorded him over the last year?'

'It is a minute figure.'

'Well, if it's so minute, then you've got nothing to hide. Let's have it out! What is the level of the funding which you've given to Lord Aldington over the last year?'

'What difference does it make?'

'Because it's our funds.'

'Yours? What shares–'

'The shareholders of this Company—our funds. Can we now know what level of funding you have–'

'I'm not going to accept your–'

'Well, let's have—in that case, you've got nothing to hide, Mr Chairman: let's have the amount!'

'I'm not going to reveal that. I'm not going to talk about what we've spent on anything in particular.'

As a result of Lambert's stonewalling, the Appeal Court sat, on 9 July, without Tolstoy being able to point to the fact that Lord Aldington had had all his legal bills in the main trial paid for him. More importantly, Tolstoy did not know whether they were going to be paid in the Court of Appeal. This was clearly a sensitive matter because Lord Aldington did something which he had not done before: he started a disinformation campaign on the subject of his own financial arrangements.

In June, during a television programme about the Aldington reservoir in Kent he said he had not been paid 'a sausage by anybody'. 'I did not fight the case to enrich myself and my family,' he said in injured tones, 'but I have to say that I did not fight it to impoverish us either. I have got to get my costs paid, which were very considerable.'

In fact Aldington had had his bills paid by the Sun Alliance. Further-more, Century Hutchinson had paid him £30,000 plus costs in the action against *The Minister and the Massacres* and, now that the trial was over, he was proceeding against the *Daily Telegraph* in connection with the Peter Millar article of 25 September 1988. He was eventually to be paid £15,000 for this.

Tolstoy, by contrast, was saddled with huge legal bills, quite apart from what he owed Lord Aldington in damages. Rubinstein Callingham had submitted a final invoice for the period 18 November 1989 to 9 January 1990 in the sum of £40,746—generously, the disbursements did not include a bottle of Drambuie. This pushed the total bill, from the date the firm started representing Watts to the date they ceased representing Tolstoy, up to the fantastic figure of £619,248. (The original estimate had been £225,000; Allen & Overy's bill to Aldington was £350,000.) The total raised by the Forced Repatriation Defence Fund had been £460,266, leaving a shortfall of £158,982. Where was that going to come from, Rubinstein Callingham wanted to know? Soon an acrimonious correspondence had broken out, with Tolstoy accusing his solicitors of treachery, betrayal and dishonourable conduct. In the end, Rubinstein Callingham wrote the whole sum off.

On 9 July it was back to wigs, gowns and tights as Tolstoy stood up to address Sir Stephen Brown and Lord Justices Russell and Beldam in the Court of Appeal. There was cause for hope since Lord Justice Russell had, just nine months earlier, been one of the judges of Appeal who, for the first time in 25 years, had reduced a jury award in a libel case purely on the ground that the amount was excessive. Sonia Sutcliffe, the wife of the "Yorkshire Ripper", had won £600,000 damages against *Private Eye* in the High Court but the Appeal Court changed that to £60,000.

The proceedings did not have any of the drama of the libel trial. Lord Aldington did not attend—though Brigadier Cowgill did—and there were few people in the public gallery. Gray spoke for Lord Aldington and set the tone by making the distasteful pedantic point that Tolstoy had talked of 70,000 deaths when in fact only about 35,000 people had perished.

Tolstoy tried to begin by drawing attention to the fact that the Sun Alliance was supporting, to an unknown extent, the legal campaign of Lord Aldington. He was immediately told this was irrelevant and that the Court was interested only in the alleged misdirections by Mr Justice Davies in his summing-up. That would have been true in the Appeal proper, but in a security for costs hearing, it was surely relevant? Tolstoy felt beaten from the start.

He tried to focus on what he felt were the misdirections in Mr Justice Davies's summing-up, but Lord Justice Russell pointed out that he had followed most of them by saying, 'It's entirely a matter for you [the jury]'. 'You cannot be fairer than that,' said Russell. Later on he said: 'Rampton prepared 23 questions for the jury. Could there be anything more fair?' Remembering that Davies had effectively prevented the jury copying them down, Tolstoy's gloom deepened.

Towards the end of the hearing, Russell put his finger on the key issue. 'You could not hope to have got a verdict,' he said to Tolstoy, 'unless the jury disbelieved Lord Aldington.' With FO 1020/42 still held in the Foreign Office, he could not respond to that. The Judges were not impressed by the few submissions Tolstoy could make.

Three days later, on Thursday 19 July, their Lordships delivered their judgements. Sir Stephen Brown took the lead. As far as the summing-up was concerned, he said, 'all the major matters were, in my judgement, dealt with fully and fairly. The Judge clearly left to the jury the decision on the facts of the case.' Nonetheless, he did say that he had read only 'the transcript of the summing-up and the transcripts of the addresses of Counsel'. Since a careful perusal of the whole trial takes about a month, it is understandable that he had not done so. Still, it is surely impossible to assess the impartiality of a summary without reading the material to which that summary relates.

Lord Justice Russell gave no indication of having read anything beyond Davies's summing-up either. Nonetheless, he was extremely impressed with it. 'Far from being critical of it,' Russell said, 'I want to pay tribute to it. Count Tolstoy has singularly failed to persuade me that it was in any way biased, prejudiced or unfair... There is not in my judgement the remotest chance of a Court of Appeal interfering with the jury's finding.'

Russell did, however, give one very large hostage to fortune when he said, presumably unaware of the whereabouts of FO 1020/42, 'This case and the jury's verdict depended essentially upon the veracity of Lord Aldington. No document or documents were produced which on their face could destroy Lord Aldington's credibility. If the jury had disbelieved Lord Aldington there would have been an end of the case.'

Lord Justice Beldam spoke third. He seemed to have completely misunderstood the whole of the Watts/Tolstoy case against Lord Aldington when he summarised the argument in the pamphlet by saying they 'sought to justify an allegation that the victims of Yalta were in truth the victims of the respondent [Lord Aldington].' Since the whole case was that Lord Aldington had *disobeyed* the Yalta guidelines, which anyway applied only to the Cossacks and not the Jugoslavs, it was odd of Beldam to observe that, in his appreciation of the trial documents, Tolstoy 'in many instances lacked intellectual objectivity and reasoned impartiality.'

Like the others, Beldam thought there was no merit in Tolstoy's submission that the level of damages was excessive. One comment of Beldam's showed the wisdom of Aldington's offer to accept only £300,000 in damages. 'Even if [Tolstoy] persuaded the Court to grant a retrial on the issue of the amount of the damages, I would regard as negligible the prospect of any jury, doing their judicial duty, awarding the respondent less than the sum which he has already offered to accept in compromise of this appeal.'

The Judges were unanimous: Lord Aldington's appeal against Mr Registrar Adams's judgement had succeeded, Tolstoy would have to put up £124,900 (reduced from £188,179) by way of security for costs if his appeal against Mr Justice Davies's judgement were to go ahead. Furthermore he had to do so within fourteen days. Such a sum would take time to find, so Tolstoy asked for an extension. It was refused on the ground that it might upset Allen & Overy's timetable for the preparation of Bundles for the Appeal proper. He was also ordered to pay Aldington's costs in this and the Adams hearing to a total of £22,000.

With the legal wind now blowing fresh at his back, Aldington turned his attention to the main outstanding publication in which he was mentioned, *The Minister and the Massacres*. He had already forced Century Hutchinson, the book's publishers, to withdraw any unsold copies from the bookshops and pulp them, together with any left in their warehouse. (In fact there were very few as the first impression of 10,000 had almost completely sold out.) The final step was to get all the public libraries in Britain to remove the book from their shelves.

Since there was no legal basis for such an initiative—no injunction prohibiting re-publication of the book, for example, had ever been granted—Allen & Overy had to be more "creative". David Mackie authorised the despatch of a document which gave the impression that the libel case related to the book, not the pamphlet, and that any Chief Librarian who continued to lend it out might lay his or her local authority open to a claim for £1.5 million in damages. Obviously this was a fearsome threat to direct at local authority employees, and all the more likely to succeed because of that.

The document was in three parts: a covering letter, a copy of the Statement in Open Court which described the agreement between Lord Aldington and Century Hutchinson and a backing sheet for the Statement which falsely linked the pamphlet case with the book action.[11]

---

11   A backing sheet, incorporated in all such legal documents, summarises the names of the parties

The letters, dated variously in July 1990, said,

> *The Minister and the Massacres* by Nikolai Tolstoy seriously libelled our client...
>
> As we are sure you will appreciate, by continuing to loan the book out, the libraries under your control are republishing the libels contained in the book and by doing so are themselves libelling our client. We should be grateful if you would confirm that you will arrange for all copies of this book within your libraries' possession to be withdrawn from circulation.

This was complete nonsense. No court had ever found for Lord Aldington *versus* Century Hutchinson. Watts and Tolstoy have called this document a forgery. Speaking for Allen & Overy, David Mackie says it was 'a mistake—certainly not the first clerical error this firm has made'.[12]

The whole package was sent to the head of every library authority in the United Kingdom, and in almost every case it had the desired effect. It was not long before libraries throughout the country were withdrawing *The Minister and the Massacres* from their shelves. In 1991 the magazine *Topical Books*, which had interviewed Tolstoy and was under threat from Lord Aldington for having done so, undertook a survey of library response to Allen & Overy's 'mistake'. Questionnaires were sent to each of the 120 library authorities in Britain. 40% of those who replied said they had never received Allen & Overy's letter. Of the libraries who had received it and who did have the book in stock (quite a few said they had not bought it), all but two said they had done what Allen & Overy demanded. Perth & Kinross was the only authority who saw things clearly: 'As far as I am aware,' the Depute District Librarian wrote, 'the libel action only referred to the pamphlet and not the book. I have no plans to take the book off the shelves.'

---

to the action and the date the case starts. Allen & Overy typed one which said 'Between The Right Honourable Toby Low Baron Aldington and Nigel Watts and Count Nikolai Tolstoy Miloslavsky: Statement in Open Court'. Thus the impression was falsely created that the book action, which was concluded by a Statement in Open Court, was connected with the pamphlet action, which it was not. £1.5 million damages had been awarded in the pamphlet action, in which the parties had been Aldington, Watts and Tolstoy, as opposed to the book action in which the parties had been Lord Aldington and Century Hutchinson, and the damages agreed at £30,000.

12   Interview with the author, 13 August 1991

Birmingham City Council Library Services, by contrast, though perfectly aware of the circumstances of the case and the distinction between the pamphlet and the book, felt that they just could not take the risk of keeping this material on their shelves.

The most robust reply came from the National Library of Scotland whose legal deposit unit in Edinburgh said they had not received Allen & Overy's letter but even if they had, they would not have paid any attention to such threats. 'A libel in England is not necessarily a libel in Scotland,' they said.[13]

The most feeble reply, in view of its high reputation, came from the Bodleian Library in Oxford. Dr David Vaisey, Bodley's Librarian, seems to have taken Allen & Overy's threat as disinterested advice: 'The law of defamation is an exceedingly expensive area,' he said, 'and the publishers of the book having acknowledged in open court that the charges made in it were "entirely untrue", it seemed to me that I would be unwise not to heed the warning from a law firm of repute that I would be libelling their client if I made the book available.'

At the beginning of August 1990, with Tolstoy having failed to post £124,900 security, his appeal against the libel judgement automatically failed. Mackie wrote to him asking for payment of £300,000 within seven days. 'If you believe that you are not in a position to pay this sum in full,' he said, 'we should be grateful if you would give us full details of your assets and the income which you currently receive and expect to obtain in the immediate future.'

Tolstoy replied that his only assets were his half-share in Court Close and his library. The house had recently been valued at £325,000, but between his mortgage and bank overdraft, he said his net asset value was £16,750. He would pay that if Lord Aldington accepted it in full and final

---

13   This is, of course, quite true. But in most circumstances it is irrelevant because if even a single copy of a book from, say, a Scottish publisher (or one from any other European country) is distributed in England, that publisher can be sued in London where the awards are, on average, ten times higher, case for case (see *Carter-Ruck on Libel and Slander*, p. 370). However, the National Library, like the English copyright libraries, does not lend. Since books cannot be removed from the premises, it is physically impossible for their stock to be "disseminated" in England. To take the book off their shelves, Lord Aldington would have to start a new action in the Scottish courts, a much riskier enterprise.

settlement of all claims. Otherwise he would petition for his own bankruptcy, as he had, he said, no income and 'no prospect of earning enough to make any payment to your client'. He was going on holiday to Portugal for a fortnight and required acceptance of his proposal on his return at the end of August.

Lord Aldington proceeded against Watts at the same time. To him there had been no offer of £300,000 plus costs—there had been no need: Watts never threatened to take him to the Appeal Court. Thus, on 17 August, the full demand was issued: 'The Creditor, the Right Honourable Lord Aldington, claims that you owe him the sum of £1,500,000 and that it is payable immediately... The Creditor demands that you pay the above debt or secure or compound for it to the Creditor's satisfaction.'

Watts did nothing, waiting for the legal mills to grind at their own deliberate and expensive pace. Tolstoy, however, returned from holiday in September, found no letter of acceptance of his offer to Lord Aldington and, on 20 September, petitioned for his own bankruptcy.

That autumn, Brigadier Cowgill made his final bow on the historical stage when he launched the committee's *Final Report* with another press conference in the reading room of the Royal United Services Institute in Whitehall. Cowgill had spent a great deal of what he says is his own money having a thousand copies of a large, two-volume edition printed and cloth-bound.[14] It is not worth describing as it is much the same as the *Interim Report*, only longer.[15] The only important difference is that, as mentioned above, Cowgill had, by 1990, concluded that the critical Distone Order, by which Alexander sought to save the Jugoslavs from Tito, *was* intended for 5 Corps, contrary to what Lord Aldington had argued in Court a year earlier. Although Cowgill was not so indelicate as

---

14   His BMDF salary was £35,000 per annum (*Financial Times* 19 January 1993) and he claims no other substantial source of income apart from his Army pension. Given the size, quality and print-run of the two *Reports*, their production costs (i.e. excluding research expenses, time etc.) must have been close to £20,000. Brigadier Cowgill says this all came out of his own, apparently rather shallow, pocket.

15   It is in two volumes, one narrative and the other a collection of facsimile reproductions of what Cowgill calls the 'Key Papers'. This is, in fact, a very useful collection for anyone seeking to understand this incredibly complicated subject. There are important (and highly significant) gaps, but a couple of dozen photocopies from files like FO 1020/42 and WO 32/13749 will fill most of them.

to point it out, this implied that almost all the 5 Corps handovers of Croats, and all the handovers of Serbs and Slovenes, were carried out in defiance of the wishes of the Supreme Commander. Had Cowgill published a year earlier, Lord Aldington's defence of obeying superior orders would, as far as the Jugoslavs are concerned, have collapsed completely. Had Tolstoy published the same conclusion as Cowgill, he would have been in breach of the injunction and liable for a jail sentence for contempt of court. Similarly, if Cowgill had arrived at the same conclusions as Tolstoy, he, Brimelow and Booker would also have rendered themselves jailable.

Compared with the 1988 launch, the whole affair was something of a damp squib. The press coverage was much less favourable. Daniel Johnson, for example, ended a piece in *The Times* by saying that Macmillan could not have been a war criminal because he believed in God. Basil Davidson, who had been an SOE operative with Tito during the war, wrote an article in which he made this artlessly revealing statement:

> The purpose of the Cowgill-Brimelow-Booker volume is to lay bare the real circumstances of the handover, and thereby to exonerate from taint of guilt those who made it.[16]

Robert Harris came to a similar conclusion about the purpose of the *Report*, but from a less sympathetic angle. He called it 'a masterpiece of bureaucratic self-justification'. He went so far as to say that before Saddam Hussein faced a war crimes court, as many people expected him shortly to do, he should get a copy of Cowgill's book and read it. The sub-editors at the *Sunday Times* gave the article the headline: 'Here's a way out for every war criminal'.

Christopher Booker wrote a long article in the *Sunday Telegraph* in the course of which he abused Tolstoy. The libel trial had made him

> more of a celebrity than ever, so that he and his family appear regularly in the pages of colour magazines like *Hello!* and are presented as battling bravely on after having suffered some frightful injustice. Tolstoy continues to be taken seriously... Tolstoy, in short, still has no lack of admirers... Lord Aldington [on the other hand] will have to spend the rest of his life paying

off his legal bills, while the man who levelled the farrago of charges against him assiduously drums up sympathy from the media and floats on as if nothing very much had happened.[17]

Booker went on to say that the real 'Victims of Tolstoy' (as the headline called them) were the media who 'are still prepared to take Tolstoy even half-seriously as a "historian"'. He had, Booker said, turned a historical tragedy into a

> cheap and pretty nasty work of semi-fiction. The sufferings of the victims of Yalta became harnessed to the ambitions of an author who had in many respects ceased to be able to distinguish fact from fantasy... The whole subject is now in danger of being degraded by its identification with one man's ego.

Despite Booker's efforts, the report sold only a handful of copies. But publication did have one very important consequence. So keen had Cowgill been to bury any criticism of 5 Corps beneath a mountain of documentary references—many of them were quite irrelevant; one concerned the state of the telephones in Italy—that some documents were published which came from files which neither Tolstoy nor any of his supporters had ever consulted. One in particular provided exactly the ammunition Tolstoy needed to call into question Lord Aldington's 'veracity'. In a blundering attempt to deliver the *coup de grâce* to Tolstoy's campaign, Cowgill had inadvertently injected new life into it, just when it looked on the point of collapse.

17   *Sunday Telegraph* 21 October 1990

21

NIGEL WATTS
MAKES A DEAL

A SOURCE OF STRENGTH for Tolstoy in his long campaign has been the large number of people who have come to his aid, over historical research as much as money. One such supporter, a dogged, determined Slav who prefers to remain anonymous, took Cowgill's *Final Report* as the cue for a thorough examination of each one of the more than three hundred PRO files quoted in Cowgill's accompanying volume of documents. Since these contained close to 100,000 separate papers, this was a gigantic task. But it quickly yielded very important results.

The researcher had not been at work more than a month before he summoned a file which, it might almost be said, gave Lord Aldington a further six years of litigatory misery. The file in question is WO 218/248, the "Phantom" file. WO 218/248 is the war diary of the 2 GHQ Liaison Regiment, Central Mediterranean Force, for May 1945. This was the unit (see Chapter 5 above) known as "Phantom", which provided direct intelligence for the Army or Army Group commander from all the divisions under his command. It takes the form of a log, filled in hour by hour. The signals are numbered consecutively and are dated and timed. Above each one is written the identity of the source, the formation whose Phantom unit had made the report. (All of them went to General Mark Clark's headquarters, 15th Army Group.) WO 218/248 is not a big file, although, being handwritten, some entries are more legible than others. But it is easily used because of the way it is organised. Only a few pages relate to each date, and within those pages the signals from each unit are grouped together and clearly differentiated from those of other units.[1] One of the most clearly legible entries in the whole file, is a note which, at first sight, turns the whole trial on its head: 'BGS left 5 Corps for England on FLIAP on 23rd May.'

Mr Justice Davies had said of Lord Aldington's date of departure from Carinthia that it was 'to put it at its lowest a very, very critical part of the evidence in this case'. Lord Justice Russell had said that a document which 'at its face' could disprove one of Lord Aldington's major contentions—and his claim to have left 5 Corps before the "shoot the Cossacks" conference was surely one of those?—would have meant 'the end of the case'. With FO 1020/42 hidden in the Foreign Office, Tolstoy had not been able to produce such a document. Now, he felt, he had one. He lost no time in giving Watts the sensational news. Watts, in turn, lost no time in putting this new discovery to use. Without a Court hearing in progress, he chose the next best option and fired off a new pamphlet. This was sent to the Directors of the Sun Alliance. It raised the issue of the company's support for Lord Aldington's 'private' legal battle. In doing so, he referred in general terms to the new evidence which called into question Lord Aldington's sworn testimony about his departure date. Watts being Watts, he leapt straight to what he saw as the conclusion, describing Lord Aldington's departure date issue as the one 'which determined the verdict of the trial' and his evidence on this subject as a 'most grave perjury'.

This was an open provocation, and intended to be. On 14 January 1991 Allen & Overy moved against Watts, accusing him of contempt of court by a breach of the "gagging" injunction. They could not do this on the allegation of perjury, which was a new charge and one which did not relate to his conduct in 1945. It was therefore not covered by the injunction. Instead they focused on the fact that Watts had included in his bundle of papers copies of Serena Booker's 'slippery as a box of eels' memorandum to Alistair Horne, arguing that it implied similar charges to those dismissed by the Court in 1989 and that it consequently came within the scope of the gagging injunction. In quoting Serena, Watts had 'repub-

---

1   Despite the fact that, for the crucial days in Carinthia, it is possible to read all the entries relating to 5 Corps in a few minutes, Cowgill says he 'did not see' the signal which has caused all the controversy (letter to the author, 8 February 1994).

lished' the libel. He should be committed to prison.

The case was heard on 25 January 1991 in front of Mr Justice Macpherson. Lord Aldington was not in Court, but Watts was. He knew that he risked jail and so had brought a bag containing his pyjamas and toothbrush. An apology might save him from prison, but he was determined that in no circumstances whatsoever would he make any apology. With two tipstaffs standing in front of him, ready to arrest him if the Judge gave the nod, Watts spoke on his own behalf. He went through the evidence, concentrating on his contention that it was entirely legitimate to refer to the conclusions of a respectable researcher, even though her conclusions had, from Lord Aldington's point of view, been 'particularly damaging'. He ended by saying that the man who should be walking out of Court with his head bowed with shame was not him but Lord Aldington.

Watts's advocacy worked. Mr Justice Macpherson, although finding him in contempt, decided that a custodial sentence was not appropriate. He awarded costs to Lord Aldington, but nothing more. But Watts would not accept even that: he immediately gave notice of appeal.

At the same time, Watts got a second case running by applying, as he was entitled to do, for a variation in the terms of the gagging injunction. This application was heard by a judge in chambers, but failed. Watts then appealed that decision too.

He started a third case when he made an offer of settlement to Lord Aldington for the debt of £2,029,888 which he had recently proved against Tolstoy's estate in bankruptcy.[2] Watts offered £10,000 'in full and final settlement' of all indebtedness between them. The £10,000 would be paid by his widowed and elderly, but wealthy, mother who wanted to avoid the 'shame' of having a bankrupt in the family. Watts had first made this offer nearly a year before, but Lord Aldington had rejected it out of hand, saying he was not prepared to take money from someone like Watts's mother. Now, in late 1990, he rejected the offer once again and continued pursuing Watts into bankruptcy. It is clear from the correspondence that Lord Aldington thought Watts was concealing assets which might be uncovered

---

2   Lord Aldington's aggressive approach is revealed in the way he made up that sum. He withdrew his offer to 'limit his recovery' to £300,000 and now went for the full damages of £1,500,000. He asked for *untaxed* (important later) costs of £350,000. Finally, and despite his oft-repeated assertion that he is not interested in the money, he claimed interest (to 20 September) on both sums, amounting to £179,888. Total £2,029,888.

by a formal bankruptcy investigation.

Watts equipped himself for battle with a second-hand copy of the official Rules of the Supreme Court (the so-called "White Book"), and, in December 1990, swore the first of what was to be a long series of affidavits. He did so in his highly personal style, combining legal precision with the rhetoric of outrage.

> I oppose this petition [for my bankruptcy] brought by Rt. Hon. Toby Low, Baron Aldington, and submit that this is a proper and justified case for the Court to employ its wide discretionary powers under Section 271 sub-section (iii) and Section 266, sub-section (iii) of the Insolvency Act 1986 to look behind the judgement debt of £1.5 million which arose out of a libel action in which the Plaintiff, now the Petitioner, was successful on 30 November 1989, and awarded damages of this eccentric proportion. I was not able to appeal this judgement as I was facing imminent heart surgery and in any event I had no funds with which to do so. Even Magna Carta made provision for a man not to be fined beyond his means... Notwithstanding this, Lord Aldington by his petition seeks to pursue into bankruptcy for £1.5 million a person with no other debts whatsoever and who has made a totally reasonable offer [of £10,000] to settle... If this order were granted I believe I would be the only person in British legal history to be made bankrupt by a plaintiff's petition as creditor as a result of a libel action, which, in my submission, is outside the spirit, purpose and acceptable propriety of the administration of this Court, having regard to the fact that I have taken every reasonable and responsible measure within my power and means to accommodate a unique liability, out of all proportion to what an ordinary person could pay.

Watts's application failed and he was adjudged bankrupt. But he appealed this decision too. He now had three appeals pending. By this time he was becoming a familiar figure at the Civil Appeals Office in the Royal Courts of Justice and on helpfully chatty terms with some of the senior clerks. As a result of advice they gave, he decided to put in his fourth and biggest appeal: he applied for 'leave to appeal out of time' against the original libel verdict on the ground that he had new evidence referring to the central issue of the trial, the Plaintiff's claimed departure date from Austria in 1945.

On 8 February 1991 he swore an affidavit which contained the following explosive clause:

[In the autumn of 1990] vital new evidence was discovered by an historian and a researcher which undermined the entirety of Lord Aldington's position which he maintained at the trial... The effect of this new evidence is that it establishes beyond reasonable contention that Aldington was BGS throughout 22 May, contrary to what he categorically stated at the trial and on which his case relied. Therefore he was responsible for the minutes of the Corps Commander's Conference which decided on the policy to shoot at Cossacks and furthermore makes apparent his failure as BGS to fulfil his duty to advise his commander that the use of force had not been authorised.

More than this, Watts described other evidence which had not been considered at the trial but which another supporter of Tolstoy's had shown pointed to the fact that Operation Coldstream had been subverted by 5 Corps, although, with FO 1020/42 still in the Foreign Office, the conclusions were inevitably provisional. The new evidence demonstrated, Watts wrote, 'the extent of Aldington's deception and disobedience and refutes entirely the contention that there was no possibility of the Cossacks being taken over the mountain route [north to safety in SHAEF].'

Lord Aldington reacted to this with what looks like panic. After having repeatedly rejected Watts's offer to settle a £2 million debt for £10,000, within a fortnight of seeing this affidavit he changed his mind and accepted it, even though he was still going to be paid by Mrs Watts Snr.—somehow or other that no longer seemed quite so distasteful. In accepting the money, Lord Aldington abandoned all claims on Watts and agreed that the £10,000 was paid 'in full and final settlement of the judgement and orders and any liability howsoever arising before today's date which could involve any payment by [Watts] directly or indirectly to Lord Aldington'. Not only that, Aldington agreed that he would not oppose Watts's appeal against his bankruptcy, the hearing of which was scheduled for 20 March in front of Lord Justice Hoffman. Thus Watts was in the clear completely, and all apparently due to the threat of producing the Phantom signal and the evidence about Operation Coldstream in court.

It was a good settlement for both men. The second term of the agreement was that Watts 'undertake that [his] campaign against Lord Aldington is at an end.' Watts agreed he would never again communicate with or comment on Lord Aldington. Lord Aldington accepted that Watts really did not have any assets worth the cost of seizing. In return, Watts was to abandon his other appeals. Thus, with the handing over of the

£10,000, all litigation between the two of them would cease. The pre-
amble to the agreement said, 'You [i.e. Watts] have proposed to Lord
Aldington that a settlement of the issues between them is to their mutual
benefit on account of the disruption to their lives and the expense and
work involved in continuing litigation and Lord Aldington has agreed.'

Watts appeared before Mr Justice Hoffman on 20 March 1991, as
previously arranged, but clutching the settlement agreement. On the basis
of that document Hoffman annulled Watts's bankruptcy. Watts's mother's
solicitors handed over £10,000 to Lord Aldington and that, Watts supposed, was the end of the matter. Over a period of eight years, he had
fought Lord Aldington to what might be described as a messy draw. In
the end both had agreed that further conflict was pointless. It was the
settlement of two apparently sensible and practical men.

But that still left Tolstoy. He was determined to keep up the pressure on
Aldington, if nowhere else then on the historical front. On 11 January
1991, BBC television broadcast a documentary called 'A British Betrayal'. The film told much the same story as *The Minister and the
Massacres*, but it began by showing Tolstoy and Aldington emerging from
the High Court on 30 November 1989, and it concentrated on the 'emotional' evidence about the actual fate of the Cossacks and Jugoslavs which
had been excluded from the trial. It is almost true to say that it was an
hour-long audio-visual tutorial on the Admissions. It is a powerful work,
and pulls no punches when describing the dishonesty and thuggery of the
British Army. Cowgill gave reasons for this. He was shown leafing
through the *Final Report* and saying, with the hint of a stammer, that 5
Corps had been under such pressure in May 1945 that 'at one stage people
thought [conflict with Tito] was likely to be the first battle of World War
III.' In the closing sequence Tolstoy was shown sitting in his library,
discussing the court case. However much he had suffered as a result of
trying to publicise the events of May 1945, he said, it was nothing by
comparison with the fate which had befallen the victims of 5 Corps. The
truth must be told, he said. As the credits rolled, the viewer noticed that
the 'research consultant' was Nikolai Tolstoy.

The one notable absentee from the film was Lord Aldington. He had
been invited to appear, but had declined. When he saw the write-up in
the *Radio Times*, he tried to stop it being broadcast. 'The title alone is
emotive,' he told the press. 'I know my way round the BBC and I assure
you [the programme] can be stopped if need be.'[3]

Unfortunately for Lord Aldington, the man he had to deal with was not the amenable Wykehamist Alasdair Milne, who had by then retired, but the sturdily independent-minded Managing Director of BBC Television, Sir Paul Fox. Aldington and Cowgill went together to see him, after which Cowgill said, 'We're putting maximum pressure on the BBC and may yet seek an injunction. At the very least, if they do not let us see the film, they are running a grave risk of a court action which could result in aggravated damages of the kind Tolstoy was ordered to pay.'[4] Cowgill also demanded that his contribution be suppressed. Even Booker joined the hue and cry, writing in the *Sunday Telegraph*, 'It might be prudent for [the BBC] to show their film to Aldington's lawyers before it is broadcast.'[5]

Fox ignored all these threats and they all came to nothing, which prompts the reflection: what would have been the fate of *The Minister and the Massacres* if the English libraries had had the courage of Sir Paul Fox?

Three months later, Lord Aldington wrote to the BBC asking for an apology and 'proposals for compensating' him for the damage to his reputation. The BBC refused to make any so, three years later, just before the limitation period for libel actions expired, Lord Aldington lodged a writ.[6] In it he complained that 'by reason of the publication of the words and visual images [he] has been caused acute distress and anxiety and his reputation has been gravely damaged.' The BBC still refused to settle. As of this writing, no case has been set down for trial. It is unlikely the case will ever come to court. For once, Lord Aldington's bluff had been called.

For Tolstoy the episode had its amusing side as the film provoked another surge of letters volunteering support, including one or two strange ones. Quite the weirdest came from a lady in Glastonbury who claimed to have applied astrology to the case and arrived at the conclusion that Macmillan had been bisexual, with tendencies towards sadism, and that the KGB discovered this during the trip he made to the Soviet Union in 1932. Not only that, he hated England partly because, being a Celt, he

3   *Daily Express* 8 January 1991
4   *Ibid.*
5   *Sunday Telegraph* 30 December 1990
6   *Broadcast* magazine, 14 January 1994, reported, 'Aldington said he had not served the writ, but by lodging it, he was securing his right to sue in the future.'

came from a culture which worshipped the pig, an animal which was the result of a foul genetic experiment between a human and an animal. Darkly, the lady added that she had 'suffered terrible experiences with pigs to obtain this awareness.'

As a bankrupt, Tolstoy now had an official "Trustee in bankruptcy" who managed his estate on behalf of his creditors (bank, building society and Lord Aldington), collecting all monies due and distributing them according to well-established rules. Creditors are forbidden from dealing directly with a bankrupt, so Allen & Overy started badgering the Trustee. They had heard that Alexander Solzhenitsyn had sent $5,000 to the Georgina Tolstoy Family Fund. Why had the Trustee not seized it? And what about an article in the *Tatler*, for which Tolstoy had been paid £30? And what about the single share, worth about £3.50, which Tolstoy had acquired in the Sun Alliance Group. What steps was the Trustee taking to seize that 'asset'?

Since Allen & Overy charge £10.50 per letter or telephone call, plus £225.00 per hour of partners' time, all this was costing vastly more than it was ever likely to recoup. Tolstoy wondered if Lord Aldington really were paying. Might this be coming out of the Sun Alliance shareholders' funds? Tolstoy decided he would try to find out. On 15 May 1991, he accompanied Watts for the first time to the company's Annual General Meeting so that he could put that question to the Chairman, Henry Lambert.

In the Chairman's Statement in that year's Annual Report, Lambert had already admitted the Sun Alliance's involvement in the libel action.

> In 1989 [the report stated] a jury rejected allegations against the Group's former Chairman, Lord Aldington, and awarded him record damages together with his legal costs. In 1990 he successfully resisted an appeal. The campaign of harassment against Lord Aldington arose directly from his duties as Chairman, as I reported at the last AGM. Distributing the libellous pamphlet was designed to put pressure on him (and hence the Group) to pay an insurance claim which had been declined some years earlier. Any employer must in fairness assist any official who is under pressure from a third party relating to his duties. The Group assisted Lord Aldington to terminate the defamatory campaign by an advance towards his legal costs of approximately £500,000.[7]

Lambert's admission about the level of assistance was helpful, but the rest of the statement was not. Why had Lambert agreed to fund a libel action concerning Lord Aldington's behaviour as BGS of 5 Corps in 1945 when the dispute related to his conduct as Chairman of the company in the 1970s and 80s? While Lord Aldington was Chairman, Watts's pressure was designed to get the company to submit his sister's case to arbitration—there was never any request for payment. In any case, the pamphlet which gave rise to the libel action was published nearly two years *after* Lord Aldington had left the company, when he was in no position to influence its policy on claim payments. The admission of the grant of £500,000 was odd, too. Lord Aldington had recently sworn an affidavit to the effect that his untaxed (i.e. full) costs were £350,000.[8] What had the other £150,000 been spent on? Might it be, Tolstoy wondered, that it was still being spent, for example, on the harassment of the libraries, or Allen & Overy's letters to his Trustee in bankruptcy, or even supporting the production of Brigadier Cowgill's two *Reports*?

At the meeting, Tolstoy's first question was whether the 'advance' to Lord Aldington was a loan or a gift. It was a loan, Lambert said. 'Anything he can get back, he will of course pay to us.'

'Oh good!' said Tolstoy, 'So he has already repaid the £10,000 he has recovered from Mr Watts? Because what you don't mention in [the Statement], among other things, is that Lord Aldington has made a complete and final settlement with Mr Watts. Mr Watts owes Lord Aldington *nothing*. You say your dispute is with Mr Watts, but why has Lord Aldington settled with Mr Watts completely, but is pursuing me and attempting to drive me and my wife out of our home?'

Lambert answered that Lord Aldington's arrangements were his own business. 'Let me remind you,' he said, 'that there is absolutely no reason why the directors, if they so choose, should not simply pay Lord Alding-

---

7   Sun Alliance Group plc *Report and Accounts 1990*, p. 7

8   Costs in legal actions are generally paid by the losing side, but in order to prevent the winner presenting inflated bills there is a process known as "taxation" by which a court official, known as the Taxing Master, will arbitrate on the proper size of a bill if the loser does not accept the winner's estimate of his costs as fair. Costs are initially computed "untaxed", and then if disputed are reduced "on taxation"; that is, on the invoices being re-examined by the Taxing Master. Thus Lord Aldington's statement that his "untaxed" costs were £350,000 sets an upper limit on his claim.

ton's - um - er - expenses.'

'"In 1990 Lord Aldington successfully resisted an appeal,"' Tolstoy said, reading from Lambert's Statement. 'Can I ask you who was conducting that appeal?'

'I assume that it was you,' Lambert replied hesitantly.

'It was me? Had it anything to do with Mr Watts?'

'N-n-no.'

'Mr Watts didn't appeal but he applied for leave to appeal out of time. What happened then? Was that application "successfully resisted"?'

'That's got nothing to do with it–'

'*Nothing to do with it!*' repeated Tolstoy, clearly enjoying being, as it were, barrister rather than witness. 'What in fact happened when Mr Watts applied in the courts for leave to appeal out of time, *this* year, which you carefully omit to mention? Lord Aldington immediately capitulated, didn't he? He did *not* resist the appeal. He made a settlement in a hurry. You may think it rather odd that he did. It is very odd! I don't know if it has anything to do with a certain document,' Tolstoy said, brandishing a copy of the Phantom signal.

Tolstoy got no answer to his basic question, but Lambert did admit certain relevant facts—for example, that up to that moment the Sun Alliance had actually disbursed no more than £26,000 to Allen & Overy. He also admitted he knew that the Watts settlement had been for £10,000, and he claimed loudly that the company had not made any contribution towards Lord Aldington's costs in the Court of Appeal.

By the middle of 1991, there were quite a few people working in one way or another on Tolstoy's behalf. One of these, the historian Peter Gwyn, set in train the events which were to lead to the discovery of the hi-jacking of FO 1020/42. Gwyn had been a history master at Winchester, and had served as the College archivist. He is the author of the definitive modern biography of Cardinal Wolsey. He is as much at home in a historical archive as anyone, and he had taken a deep interest in the events of 1945. Gwyn was the first to concentrate on Operation Coldstream. Why had Alexander's plan to send the Cossacks north failed? Who was responsible for frustrating the Supreme Commander's wishes? Tolstoy had not mentioned Operation Coldstream in *The Minister and the Massacres*. But Gwyn now thought a serious attack on the associated records might just yield something of interest. He was not sure what, but he set to work anyway.

It was obvious that FO 1020/42 was one of the most important files he should look at. Wondering if it was still 'lost', Gwyn requested it at the PRO on 8 April and again on 5 August 1991. It was *still* 'out to Department', he was told. Tolstoy remembered that Sir Bernard Braine, then Father of the House of Commons and now Lord Braine of Wheatley, had said soon after the trial that if there was anything he could do to help Tolstoy he would be happy to. Tolstoy asked Braine if he would raise the matter of the whereabouts of FO 1020/42 with the Foreign Office—as a Privy Counsellor, he might be able to get an answer. But Tolstoy was not hopeful that anything would be achieved. 'I did it simply to oblige Peter,' he remembers. 'I myself thought for certain that all that would come out of it would be a bland, "Oh yes, it was out to Department" and they would return it, because *I didn't realise how much there was of importance in the file.*' (emphasis added)

Thinking this a perfectly routine matter, Braine wrote on 13 August 1991 to the Foreign Secretary, Douglas Hurd, asking why his department had held on to this file for so long. The reply Braine received fell like a bombshell onto his desk at the House of Commons. He telephoned Tolstoy immediately, interrupting his breakfast. On Hurd's behalf, the Foreign Office Minister, Lynda Chalker, now Baroness Chalker, had replied, saying that the file had been recalled in 1987 *for the use of Brigadier Cowgill*. The file had been retained for him for 'more than a year', Chalker said, until in 'late 1989... another enquirer' asked for it, whereupon the Library and Records Department discovered the file was 'missing'.

The was the first time that Cowgill's name had been associated with the withdrawal of PRO files. Braine consulted Tolstoy who drafted a reply to Chalker. He put seventeen questions, the main ones being: who authorised the help to Cowgill? Why was that help authorised, not at the time the committee started work (summer 1986), but after Lord Aldington issued his writ against Tolstoy (in August 1987)? Was there any connection between Cowgill's work and Lord Aldington's litigation? In other words, had the Foreign Office contributed to the suppression of vital evidence in a major court case? 'I would like to have your full assurance,' Braine wrote to Chalker on 8 October 1991, 'that the fullest investigation will now be undertaken into this whole sorry business.'

This being Whitehall, though it was Chalker who had replied to Braine's letter to Hurd, it was Hurd who now replied to Braine's letter to Chalker. He had, Hurd said on 29 November 1991, made 'the fullest investigation' into the serious charges and discovered that the loss of the file had been purely accidental. Furthermore, Foreign Office help to Cowgill 'amounted to no more than making available some Foreign Office papers already in the public domain for consultation at the FCO'. This completely missed the point, which was that by making the papers available to Cowgill *in the Foreign Office* the papers were taken *out* of the public domain, just when Tolstoy needed to consult in preparation for the trial.

But the file was still unavailable. Then, by coincidence, a Thames Television producer, Margaret Gilmour, who was working on a film about the way PRO files are used and misused by Whitehall, asked about FO 1020/42. Suddenly the public spotlight was on this document. Amazingly, within a matter of days, the file was found!

Hurd wrote to Braine on 4 December 1991 saying, 'Since signing my letter to you at the end of last week, I have learnt that the missing file has been found. It had been misfiled. It has been returned to the Public Record Office, where it is again available to researchers.'

The implication in Hurd's letter was that the recovery of the file should be the end of the matter. But since that missed the main point, which was the denial of access to the file by the Defendants during the libel trial, Braine tried again. 'Many of the questions I put in my letter of 8 October were in my view answered either not at all or else obliquely and inappropriately,' he wrote on 17 January 1992. He repeated his questions. He also added a new and very significant one: it was agreed that the Foreign Office knew in late 1989 that FO 1020/42 was "missing"; why had they not informed the PRO of this? Braine also repeated with emphasis his questions about Cowgill. Why was he considered a 'fit person' to be given such special treatment? 'There is no disputing the fact that before, during and after the trial he was actively working in Lord Aldington's interest,' Braine said. 'Their collaboration started in 1986... During the trial Brigadier Cowgill sat almost every day next to Lord Aldington, acting openly as his adviser. (Lord Brimelow likewise frequently attended in the same capacity.)'

Braine now had a total of 24 questions and his letter ran to fifteen typed pages. For the avoidance of doubt, he put the basic issue unambiguously: 'Do you think it was proper for a Department of State to lend extensive secret aid to one party in such a dispute, while denying the other access to public documents which officials concerned must have been well aware he required in order to defend himself? What do you think

would have been the Court's reaction had the true nature and extent of the
FCO's withholding evidence from the Defence and their assistance to the
Plaintiff's advisers become known?' Braine ended by saying he wanted
a 'full, impartial and urgent inquiry, and the very least I expect are frank
answers to the questions asked in this letter.'

Hurd replied with a letter of contemptuous irrelevance. He ignored
all Braine's questions, and the only relevant point he made was transpar-
ently illogical. 'There was no question of denying access by others to
these papers while they were marked out to the Department. Neither we
nor the PRO now have any record of the PRO requesting their return
during this period.' Since the whole point was that access *was* denied,
the question of PRO requests was irrelevant to the undoubted fact of denial
of access.

More than this, the implication that the PRO had not requested the
file is false. In fact, the PRO keep very careful records of the movements
of their files. All those "out to Department" are checked every four
months and are requested routinely every October at the time of the annual
stock-take. Thus on *five* annual stocktakes, the Foreign Office would have
been asked for the file and would have given reasons for retaining it. This
is the PRO's account:

> FO 1020/42 was out to the FCO in 1987 and the document reference was
> included on a print-out of documents requisitioned by the FCO and was
> retained by them until 1989 when they informed us that the file had been
> mislaid. Comprehensive searches were then undertaken *by both depart-*
> *ments* to track it down. Checks were also made of subject related files and
> of other files returned from requisition over a four year period in case FO
> 1020/42 had been enclosed in another file jacket. These searches were
> unsuccessful and the document's status remained in doubt until the file was
> found in November 1991 at the FCO. It was then returned to us.[9] (emphasis
> added)

In his final letter to Braine, Hurd made one important admission: 'We

9   Letter to the author from R.A. Blake, Head of Repository Services at the PRO, 22 February
     1995. The system is that every government department has a Reader's Ticket number, just
     like an ordinary researcher. Full records of the dates of withdrawal and return of each file are
     kept, going back to 1977, indexed both by ticket number and by file number.

do not know when [FO 1020/42] was lost. From papers found with it in November last year it appears that it was incorrectly put away with other papers *in early 1988.*' (emphasis added)

If this was true, why was the PRO not notified of the loss until late 1989? But more than this, if that date was accurate, how was it that Lord Aldington had been able to compile his second list of documents, in mid-1989, which contained nine papers from FO 1020/42? Had the Plaintiff used a "lost" file? And was there any connection between that and the fact that the file had apparently been lost, in early 1988, at about the time Aldington had compiled his first list of documents, which also included papers from it? This being Whitehall, no answers to these questions, of fundamental importance to the conduct of the 1989 trial, have yet been given.

22

LORD ALDINGTON GOES BACK TO COURT

E ARLY IN 1992 Lord Aldington told the press, 'I am disappointed
that this hasn't ended and that I haven't had any money. I am
getting short of money. I have won every legal action but legal
costs have continued to occur.'[1] More than this, he felt a sense of injustice.
'If you look at the social pages,' he said, 'it seems that Tolstoy is leading
the same life as he was before this action.' A 'Volvo estate car' sat in the
drive of his '£300,000 Jacobean farmhouse', while he, the winner in
Court, had exchanged his 'company Bentley for a two-year-old Ford
Escort'.

The article was the opening salvo in yet another court-room battle,
one which carried with it the possibility that Tolstoy's bankruptcy would
be discharged as a direct consequence of Lord Aldington's settlement with
Watts the previous March. The background was Tolstoy's acquiring a
new firm of solicitors, the young, Baker Street firm of Schilling & Lom.
Their first act, on hearing about Watts's settlement with Aldington, was
to write to Allen & Overy saying that he had therefore settled with their
client as well, and would they confirm that Aldington accepted that fact?
The legal logic was that all debts incurred by joint defendants in civil
actions are, in the words of the law, "joint", in which case, if Lord

Aldington had settled with Watts he had automatically and simultaneously settled with Tolstoy. There was only one debt and Watt's mother had discharged it. Furthermore, if Tolstoy owed Lord Aldington nothing, he should no longer be bankrupt. Schilling & Lom asked for David Mackie's formal 'confirmation that our client and his estate no longer have any liability to your client pursuant to the Judgement.'[2]

Mackie would give no such confirmation. Indeed he said that Lord Aldington had not "settled" with Watts, but merely agreed to 'limit his recovery' to £10,000. Since there had not been any settlement, it followed that Lord Aldington was still at complete liberty to proceed against Tolstoy, which he certainly intended to do. If this was uncomfortable for Tolstoy, it was much more so for Watts, who really thought he had heard the last of Lord Aldington. But if it was the case that Tolstoy was still bankrupt, Watts would still be vulnerable to Aldington, though indirectly. The reason lay in the complicated legal concept of "contribution" which governs the position of two joint debtors in the event that one of them pays more of the joint debt than the other.

The idea behind contribution is simple and fair: if one debtor is forced to pay more than "his share" (a term open to a variety of interpretations as the law lays down only that such contribution shall be 'just and equitable' in the circumstances[3]) of a debt owed by two people jointly, he can claim part of what he has paid from the other. For example: A and B owe a joint debt of £20 to X; A pays X £10, but B pays nothing; A is more conveniently suable than B (say B lives much of the time abroad), so X, quite legally, proceeds against A for the remaining £10 and is awarded it; A can then claim "contribution" of £10 from B. In this case, if Tolstoy's Trustee in bankruptcy were able to get, say, £20,000 from the liquidated estate and pay that to Lord Aldington, the Trustee could proceed against Watts for (probably) £10,000. That would also go to Lord Aldington. The result of all this was that, though Watts thought he had made, in the words of the settlement agreement, a 'full and final' settlement of 'any liability howsoever arising before today's date which could involve any payment by [Watts] *directly or indirectly* to Lord Aldington', he was still vulnerable to claims from Tolstoy's Trustee for part of anything he could realise from the estate. Watts had paid Lord Aldington £10,000 and agreed to abandon

2   12 April 1991
3   Civil Liability (Contribution) Act 1978.

all his appeals, so that he would no longer be pestered for money by Lord Aldington, only to find that he could still be pestered by the Trustee, operating as the agent of the main creditor, who was none other than Lord Aldington. Nobody at Allen & Overy had said a word about "contribution" while the settlement was being negotiated. It is hardly surprising that Watts felt he had been tricked.

Mackie gave Schilling & Lom the reasoning behind their position. The question was whether the Aldington-Watts agreement constituted a 'full release' or merely a 'covenant not to sue'. If it was a release, then the debt had been paid and Tolstoy owed Lord Aldington nothing. If, on the other hand, the agreement amounted only to a covenant not to sue for so long as Watts observed certain conditions, like not attacking Lord Aldington in public, then the debt had not been paid, merely suspended. In that case, the existence of the debt was unaffected and Lord Aldington was still free to proceed against Count Tolstoy. In *Duck v Mayeu* (1892), an analogous case, Mackie continued, the court held that the answer depended on the intentions of the parties. In the present case Lord Aldington's intention had not been to release Watts, so the settlement was therefore correctly viewed as a covenant not to sue. 'The reservation of rights against a joint tortfeasor or debtor,' Mackie wrote, 'need not be express but will be implied if it appears from the agreement and the surrounding circumstances and the evidence that, to the knowledge of the parties to the settlement, the Plaintiff intended to proceed against the other tortfeasor or debtor.'

This still did not answer the commonsense point that Lord Aldington had agreed not to do anything which would involve Watts in any payment 'directly or indirectly' and that by continuing to go after Tolstoy, Lord Aldington was doing just that. Mackie's answer to that would have been incomprehensible to anyone but a specialist. He quoted *Bryanston Finance v De Fries* (1975), *Apley Estates v De Bernales* (1947) and *Cutler v McPhail* (1962). He 'adopted the language of Jessel M.R. in *Ex Parte Good*' and rehearsed 'the headnote to *Re Wolmershausen* (1890)'. He referred to *Re EWA* (1901) but said that it 'is a case of doubtful authority as a very strong Court of Appeal in *Re Tuchmann* (unreported, 1961) doubted its correctness'. Nonetheless he did quote 'Collins L.J.'s judgement in *Re EWA*' as it explained Jessel's decision in *Ex Parte Good*. Moreover, Mackie stressed Lord Denning's comment, in *Bryanston Finance v De Fries*, to the effect that the whole argument about releases and covenants not to sue was 'an arid and technical distinction without any merits' and should be completely discarded. 'In the light of the considerations set out in this letter,' Mackie ended by saying, 'I trust you will on reflection agree that there is nothing further to be gained, except the expenditure of legal costs, by pursuing this matter.'

This was indeed true, and even more so because it was becoming rapidly clear that Lord Aldington would never actually receive any money from Tolstoy. On 11 April 1991 his Trustee in Bankruptcy had told Allen & Overy that, after reviewing the status of Tolstoy's business loan, the realisable asset *before the Trustee was himself paid*, was 'of the order of £45,000'. But this was based on an increasingly fictitious valuation of Tolstoy's house, the only concrete asset that could be set against the liabilities. The market for expensive country properties was in sharp decline throughout 1991. A 15% decline from the valuation date, September 1990, would wipe out the whole asset. But it was worse than that. Interest rates were high throughout the period and unpaid interest on Tolstoy's bank and building society loans was mounting rapidly. Moreover, by early 1992 the Trustee's costs had reached about £10,000. The result was that the asset had contracted and the first-charge liabilities increased to a point where, probably in the autumn of 1991, there was nothing left for Lord Aldington. But, for reasons he will not disclose, he continued to pursue Tolstoy, trying to get him evicted from his house and having his library seized.

Watts wanted to have nothing to do with these battles, and the only way he could be sure to be rid of the threat of further legal action from Lord Aldington was to ask the High Court for a declaratory judgement on his settlement agreement. Watts hoped that this would formally bar Aldington from any action which might affect him. This was the case in prospect when Aldington spoke publicly about the injustice of the outcome of the libel action. Tolstoy was involved because he had decided to ask the same court to adjudge that, as a result of the Watts-Aldington settlement, he was no longer bankrupt.

Schilling & Lom did not accept the thrust of Mackie's long letter about releases and covenants not to sue, and instead wrote back asking for a statement of just how much money Aldington was claiming from Tolstoy? The damages figure was clear, but what about the £350,000 'untaxed costs' which the Plaintiff claimed? As the Sun Alliance had recently admitted they were paying for the libel trial, Aldington could hardly claim these costs from Tolstoy. To assess the situation Schilling & Lom asked to be given full details of the arrangement between Lord

Aldington and the Sun Alliance. When this was not immediately forthcoming, they made a formal application to the Court for 'discovery', or
compulsory disclosure, of all documents relating to this transaction. Lord
Aldington reacted in a most extraordinary way. Rather than produce the
paperwork, he dropped his claim for costs entirely. This was to be only
the first of a long series of similar retreats when this subject has been
raised. Clearly it is a very sensitive issue.

Tolstoy's Trustee in bankruptcy was formally notified on 28 April
1992 that Aldington's claim for costs had been reduced from £350,000 to
£36,302. The new figure represented the expenses incurred in resisting
Tolstoy's appeal against Aldington's security for costs application at the
time of the libel appeal in the summer of 1990 (even though the figure
claimed at the time was £22,000).

At the same time, Aldington took a very surprising step: he initiated
legal action against Allen & Overy, asking for recompense for the expenses incurred in defending his view of his settlement with Watts. Even
more bizarrely, if Lord Aldington's affidavit of 5 November 1996 is to be
believed, it was Mackie who suggested that Aldington take action against
his own firm. Aldington selected another large City firm, Herbert Smith
and Co., and they agreed with Allen & Overy that Aldington should not
have to bear the cost of the new litigation with Watts. Once again,
Aldington found himself going to court without having to worry about
costs, although he says in his affidavit that he did so 'with reluctance'.
Most bizarrely of all, he was about to be represented by the firm with
whom he was in dispute since, but for their inadequate drafting, the case
would never have come about.

On Thursday 7 May 1992, the three parties and their lawyers came to
Court. This time the venue was a modern courtroom in a new annexe to
the Royal Courts of Justice. The Judge was Mr Justice Morritt, a very
different, and altogether more formidable-looking, figure than Mr Justice
Davies. An owlish and sharp-featured Old Etonian of Scottish ancestry,
he is the same age as Watts, and therefore younger than Tolstoy by two
years and Lord Aldington by twenty-five.

Morritt opened the proceedings in an unusual way by declaring that
he already knew Lord Aldington. He said that he had met him on two
occasions, both on a 'non-professional' basis.[4] If Watts and Tolstoy
preferred that the case be heard by a different judge, they were free to
apply now. This was such an unexpected development they were non-

plussed. One supporter present said optimistically that if Mr Justice Morritt were going to find for Lord Aldington, he would never have made such an admission, so it was probably a good sign. Another supporter, a retired American lawyer, said, 'Stop the trial, dammit. Get a judge who knows *none* of the parties.' After a quick huddle, Tolstoy and Watts decided they would not object.

That was almost the last excitement in the two-day hearing. If a libel trial is a dull affair, a case in Chancery, with two barristers droning on about the sort of references Mackie quoted in his letter to Schilling & Lom, is sheer torture. Lord Aldington seemed to think so too as he spent much of the time with his head resting on his hands, apparently asleep. Incidental details assume disproportionate importance. From this author's notes: 'Lord Aldington: gold pen, gold watch, gold cufflinks. Lady Aldington: does the *Telegraph* crossword (slowly); not wearing a ring.'

Only once was there a hint of drama. Watts was determined that the Court be made aware that the 'consideration' which had 'moved from' him to Lord Aldington under the settlement was not just the £10,000, but the abandonment of his appeals, in particular the one against the libel verdict on the ground of new evidence such as the Phantom signal. 'While it was a good settlement for me,' Watts said, 'it was a *very* good settlement for Lord Aldington.' Gray had argued that Lord Aldington would not have given away £1.5 million for £10,000, so it was obvious that he intended to get money out of Tolstoy; following *Duck v Mayeu*, this intention should be decisive. Watts wanted to demonstrate the opposite, namely that his appeal against the libel verdict had been very solidly based and its abandonment was a major concession to Lord Aldington. Without mentioning the Phantom signal directly, Watts said that a new document had been discovered at the Public Record Office which showed that 'Lord Aldington did not leave on the date [he told the Court he did] and consequently committed a most grave perjury at the trial.'

At the word 'perjury' Gray shot out of his seat as if his gown had caught fire. This new evidence, he objected, had been considered by the Court of Appeal and discarded as worthless. Not so, said Watts loudly, this was newer evidence than that. Before things could liven up, Mr

---

4   It is possible that this was provoked by the fact that Watts had recently been making public play of the fact that both Mr Justice Davies and Lord Aldington played golf at the 'exclusive' Rye golf club in Kent.

Justice Morritt said firmly that he was not going to allow such issues to be ventilated in his Court. Watts was forced to leave Gray's riposte uncorrected. Gray sat down as ordered but continued to shuffle about angrily for some time. Had he not made his misleading interjection and Morritt not then curtailed the discussion, presumably thinking it a red herring, he (Morritt) might have learned just how valuable a 'consideration' Lord Aldington had received by Watts's dropping his application for leave to appeal the libel judgement. But he never did.

The proceedings ground to a dreary close half-way through the second day. The Judge thanked the two barristers, said, 'Judgement reserved', then stood up and swept out of Court.

A fortnight later, on 22 May 1992, Mr Justice Morritt gave his judgement. He accepted Tolstoy's and Watts's twin arguments that, first, the agreement between Watts and Aldington constituted 'accord and satisfaction', as the law calls it, meaning that Lord Aldington had no further claim over Watts, and, secondly, that there was only one debt. This seemed to imply that Lord Aldington had no further claim over Tolstoy either. Morritt went further and rejected Gray's twin arguments, first, that the provisions of the Civil Liability (Contribution) Act of 1978 meant that in this case the liability was not 'joint', and, secondly, that Tolstoy's bankruptcy severed any joint liability there might have been so that when Lord Aldington subsequently made his agreement with Watts, he legitimately ignored Tolstoy's position. In short, Lord Aldington had lost the argument. But he still won the case as Morritt said that the main clause of the agreement 'can, and in my judgement must, be construed as an agreement to accept £10,000 in full and final settlement of the judgement only for so long as Mr Watts observes the continuing obligations undertaken by him.' Thus, the settlement was "final", but at the same time also "temporary" so Lord Aldington got the verdict he wanted.[5]

Having won the action, Lord Aldington asked that he be awarded costs, severally, against Watts and against Tolstoy's estate in bankruptcy. He

---

5   Since the whole case arose from ambiguity in the settlement agreement, it is relevant to observe that Morritt ignored the *contra proferentem* rule: any agreement whose intention is unclear should be construed *against* the party which drafted it, and so construed even more strongly if the drafting party was advised by lawyers and the non-drafting party not, as in this case. Watts made this point in Court but Morritt ignored it in his judgement.

did so knowing that he had not incurred any costs, thanks to Allen & Overy's agreement with Herbert Smith. Lord Aldington went further: he wanted Mr Justice Morritt to order that Tolstoy be forced to disclose the name of the person or persons who had paid his lawyers—his "maintainer" in legal terminology—so that he could proceed against him or them for the costs which he had just claimed. This would have the effect of warning anyone minded to support Tolstoy that in doing so they risked not only the money they gave him but also any money Allen & Overy declared publicly they had spent on Lord Aldington's behalf.

Although Aldington never succeeded in discovering the fact, the maintainer had been Lord Portsmouth. Portsmouth resisted disclosure because, as he puts it today, 'I believed in the rightness of my cause and I did not trust the law to make what I considered the correct decision.' In the event, this mistrust was amply justified, partly because Lord Aldington was being so uncandid about who was paying his lawyers. The reason Portsmouth had financed this action was quite simple: 'I had continued to follow the litigation which flowed from the original libel judgement,' he says, 'and I was incensed by Lord Aldington's grotesque idea of what constituted decency and fair play in letting off Watts yet continuing to pursue Tolstoy, simply because Watts was successful as a gadfly and a barrack-room lawyer.'

Gray had come equipped with a long argument, complete with authorities, to justify his client's request, clearly hoping to take it at a rush while the Judge was still smiling down at his side of the Court. Tolstoy's Counsel objected to this and asked for the matter to be dealt with fully, properly and, therefore, on another occasion. Gray objected to this, saying the law was clear, can we not dispose of it right now? But Mr Justice Morritt was not to be rushed, and he ordered the matter heard later.

In early June, a junior solicitor at Allen & Overy, Simon Watson-Jones, swore an affidavit in support of Lord Aldington's application, saying that unless Tolstoy's maintainer were disclosed, Lord Aldington would be 'out of pocket'. As yet unaware of the agreement that Allen & Overy were paying for the case, but still suspicious of Aldington and his costs claims, Tolstoy opposed this application, suggesting that it was entirely possible that the Sun Alliance had paid Lord Aldington's costs, possibly out of the £150,000 difference between Aldington's untaxed costs in the libel trial and the £500,000 Lambert had said the company had paid. Accordingly, Tolstoy asked for "discovery" of the paperwork relating to the Sun Alliance agreement.

Once again, Lord Aldington seemed prepared to disclose anything other than the documents relating to this deal. Accordingly a partner at Allen & Overy, John Kendall—he had recently replaced David Mackie on the case—swore an affidavit in July saying, 'The position is that my firm has agreed to bear the costs of this work.'

This flatly contradicted Watson-Jones's sworn testimony. But it was not long before Tolstoy and Watts discovered that not even this claim was true. Actually a body called the Solicitors Indemnity Fund had agreed to pay.[6]

Kendall swore his affidavit, to the effect that Allen & Overy would be bearing Lord Aldington's costs, eight weeks *after* he, Kendall, had received a letter from Lovell, White, Durrant, another large firm of City solicitors who represented the Solicitors Indemnity Fund, saying that the Fund would be paying. The chronology is this:

- on 5 May 1992 Kendall is informed that Lord Aldington's costs would be borne by the Solicitors Indemnity Fund
- on 7 May he writes to Lord Aldington telling him this
- on 7 and 8 May, Mr Justice Morritt hears the case described above
- on 22 May Morritt delivers judgement and Lord Aldington asks that "his" costs be paid by Watts and Tolstoy, and that Tolstoy's maintainer be disclosed so that he can be forced to pay Tolstoy's share
- on 11 June Simon Watson-Jones swears that Lord Aldington would be 'out of pocket' if the maintainer were not identified
- on 7 July John Kendall swears that Lord Aldington would not in fact be out of pocket if no payment were forthcoming, since Allen & Overy had agreed to bear the costs of the action
- on 9 July Mr Justice Morritt hears the action intended to force disclosure of Tolstoy's maintainer
- in August, Kendall tells both Watts and Tolstoy that Allen & Overy had paid for the Morritt hearing, but that the Solicitors Indemnity Fund would be paying for any appeal

---

6   The Solicitors Indemnity Fund is an "incompetence insurance" fund, constituted under the terms of the Solicitors Act (1974), but instituted in 1987 under the auspices of the Law Society. All practising solicitors have to contribute to it and they can claim from it if a client alleges negligence leading to financial loss. Other types of negligence allegation are dealt with by the Solicitors Complaints Bureau.

- in November Watts and Tolstoy discover that neither Watson-Jones's nor Kendall's affidavits, nor Kendall's letter in August, are true and that it was actually the Solicitors Indemnity Fund which had agreed, *six months earlier*, to pay Allen & Overy's fees at the Morritt hearing.[7]

The costs and maintainer hearing, on 9 July 1992, was relatively brief. Gray said that Lord Aldington was not now asking for 'his' costs, but those which 'he had incurred'. As far as both Tolstoy and Mr Justice Morritt were aware, Gray was trying to avoid a situation in which Allen & Overy would be out of pocket. (The truth of course was that it was the Solicitors Indemnity Fund which would be, if Aldington lost.) With a row of law books lying spine upwards on the bench before him, Gray tried to give legal substance to the distinction between costs 'of' and costs 'incurred by' a party. He quoted *Singh v Observer* (1989) and *Regina v Miller* (1983) which, in turn, referred to *Adams v London Motor Coach Builders Ltd* (1921). Once again Tolstoy was well represented, by a distinguished Chancery barrister, and he was having none of this. He drew himself up to his full height and boomed back with *Gundry v Sainsbury* (1910) in which the Master of the Rolls 'adopted the words' of Baron Bramwell in *Harold v Smith* and which had been 'binding on' Mr Justice Lloyd in *Regina v Miller*, which had formed the basis of Gray's argument. The libel specialist looked out of his depth in Chancery.

Mr Justice Morritt found for Tolstoy. As between the costs 'of' Lord Aldington and 'incurred by' him, Morritt said, 'I confess that I cannot see any relevant distinction.' In the circumstances, he said, there was no likelihood of Tolstoy's maintainer ever being ordered to compensate Lord Aldington for costs which he (Lord Aldington) had never incurred. Thus there was no reason to order the disclosure of the maintainer. For the first time, Lord Aldington had lost. Costs of £6,807 were awarded against him.[8]

---

7   It is possibly also worth noting that Lord Aldington did not put his name to any of these claims, although they were all made on his behalf.

8   Ironically, if Kendall had revealed to the role of the Solicitors Indemnity Fund in his affidavit of 7 July, Lord Aldington would probably have won. In his judgement, Mr Justice Morritt said that if Lord Aldington had been in the position of, say, a member of a trade union whose union's funds were supporting him in the action, then he would have had every chance of claiming costs from Tolstoy. In that case there would have been a good reason to order disclosure of any maintainer. A trade union is different from a firm of solicitors acting free of charge for a

A footnote to this case was that Allen & Overy now asked the Solicitors Indemnity Fund, not just to pay for their own work in resisting Watts, but also to cover Herbert Smith's costs in advising Lord Aldington to proceed against them! Amazingly, the Fund agreed to do this. Even more amazingly, the cost of Herbert Smith's advice to Lord Aldington and of the brief correspondence on his behalf was £12,000.

The truth about who was ultimately bearing the cost of Lord Aldington's defence of the settlement case emerged later, and only because of another legal ploy. When Watts and Tolstoy both lodged appeals against Morritt's judgement, Allen & Overy asked the Solicitors Indemnity Fund to pay Lord Aldington's costs in that case as well. Lovell White Durrant wrote back suggesting a plan which would 'put pressure on Count Tolstoy not to pursue the litigation any further'. The Fund's view was that the best 'commercial option at this stage would be to apply for security for costs against Count Tolstoy and Mr Watts'. Lovell White Durrant added mysteriously that 'the Fund recognises that Lord Aldington is governed by considerations other than the need to take a commercial view.'

No solicitor can apply for security for costs in an action of which it is bearing the costs. So it was that Allen & Overy revealed the involvement of the Solicitors Indemnity Fund. An insurer could legitimately ask for security for the costs, so Allen & Overy did this, though they did so in an affidavit in which they gave the impression that the Fund had agreed to pay only for the forthcoming hearing, and that Allen & Overy had itself borne the cost of both hearings before Morritt. On this basis, Allen & Overy now asked that Watts and Tolstoy lodge £13,378 in advance of their appeals.

The admission of the role of the Solicitors Indemnity Fund set Watts thinking. By the time of the settlement hearing in front of Mr Justice Morritt in May, he and Tolstoy had learned that the libel trial had been financed by the Sun Alliance. By the time of the "maintainer" hearing

---

dissatisfied client as it is an outside body which can justly ask for its costs in any case which it supports. The Solicitors Indemnity Fund is an equivalent outside body. Thus if Morritt had been told that it was the Fund rather than Allen & Overy which had borne the costs of the hearing in May, it is highly likely that he *would* have ordered the disclosure of Tolstoy's maintainer, with incalculable consequences for the further course of this litigation. John Kendall had, as it were, shot his client in the foot.

in front of Morritt in July, they had been told that the settlement hearing had been financed by Allen & Overy. In both cases Lord Aldington had at first claimed 'his' costs, then abandoned that claim when a story closer to the truth had been forced out. Now a new source of funds for Lord Aldington's litigation had been revealed, Watts was immediately suspicious. He put two and two together and decided that the Fund had financed the original case before Mr Justice Morritt and had tried to conceal that fact in order to get the costs of the action which they might otherwise not have been awarded. As far as he was concerned, this was fraud, and he said so. He wrote to Kendall on 17 August 1992 saying the earlier claim for costs 'exposed your client's outright dishonesty in seeking a costs order against me when there were, in fact, no costs to pay.'

Watts also wrote, on 2 December 1992, to the Solicitors Complaints Bureau drawing attention to Allen & Overy's tactics over what he called the 'fraudulently obtained costs order'. They replied saying that they could not do anything because their brief was restricted to investigating complaints made by clients against their own solicitors and Allen & Overy had not been acting for him. So Watts wrote to the Professional Conduct Committee of the General Council of the Bar in connection with Gray's submissions in Court. He assumed Gray had known who was ultimately paying the lawyers on his side of the case, particularly as the entire maintainer hearing concerned who was ultimately paying the lawyers on Tolstoy's side of the case. Watts, as usual, did not mince his words. He alleged 'Criminal conspiracy: fraudulently obtaining a costs order'.

The Bar Council wrote to Gray asking for his side of the story. Gray denied that he had known who was paying Allen & Overy. 'I was entirely unaware of any reason why application should not be made for Lord Aldington's costs to be met by the unsuccessful parties.'

The Bar Council asked for a response from Watts. He posed seven questions, through the Bar Council, to Gray, including asking how he had reconciled Watson-Jones's affidavit in June (Lord Aldington would be out of pocket) with Kendall's in July (Allen & Overy were paying).

The Secretary of the Bar Council refused to pass Watts's questions on, saying he was 'not in a position to act as an intermediary for the purposes of an exchange of questions and answers between you and Mr Gray'.

Watts also wrote to Lord Mackay the Lord Chancellor on the basis that Gray has, since 1990, been a Recorder. This is a part-time position, usually in a Crown Court, and is the first step on the judicial ladder. Gray has ambitions to be a judge, and Watts thinks they are misplaced. He wanted the Lord Chancellor to investigate.

But the Lord Chancellor refused, saying he could not deal with the matter as Gray had been acting as a barrister at the time of the alleged offence, not as a judge. On 11 December 1992 Watts replied that Gray

> is nonetheless a judge whom you have appointed. My purpose in promulgating these issues for the public warning is because I sincerely believe that it is wrong for the misdeeds of those privileged in the hierarchy of the administration of the law to be protected by the accommodation of an iniquitous cloak of silence from fellow members of their circle who effect a pretence of formal integrity. I remain most unhappy about this state of affairs on which I am proposing to publish a pamphlet.

This was no idle threat. Watts wrote letter after letter to both Allen & Overy and to Charles Gray, hardly ever receiving a reply. In one he accused Allen & Overy of 'taking the view that if you do nothing and say nothing you will be able to extract yourselves from having to answer for this fraud.' Still he got no reply. He wrote once more suggesting that both Allen & Overy and Gray had 'retreated to bury their heads in the sand, desperately entertaining the hope that either Providence or the Establishment will intervene.'

Watts decided he would postpone publication of his pamphlet until after the Bar Council had adjudicated. This they did not do until 9 June 1993, nearly a year after the case was referred to them.

> After a very full discussion [the Secretary of the Professional Conduct Committee said] the Committee decided that there was no evidence of professional misconduct on the part of Mr Charles Gray. The reason for the Committee's decision may be summarised by saying that Mr Gray denied your allegations. Having considered the matter carefully and taking into account all available evidence, the Committee could find nothing to support your allegations or to cast doubt upon that denial.

There is no appeal against a decision of the Bar Council, so Watts referred the matter to the only other possible adjudicating authority, the Legal Services Ombudsman, who operates outside the charmed circle, from offices in Manchester. Six months later, on 13 December 1993, the Ombudsman produced a report which took no view on Gray's conduct but which was critical of the way the Bar Council had conducted its investigation. The Ombudsman suggested the Bar Council should take evidence from James Price, Gray's "Junior", who had advised on the settlement agreement. The Bar Council did nothing for three months (the full period allowed for their investigation), then wrote to Watts saying they had put the request 'to Allen & Overy'. Watts was aghast but could do nothing. Furthermore Allen & Overy refused to reply to the Bar Council. Finally, in October 1993, *two years* after the complaint had been made, the Bar Council told Watts that Price had denied any knowledge of the way the action was being funded. They were now 'satisfied that the original decision was justified and [would] be taking no further action on your complaint.'

That closed the last door to action through the established channels of justice. Watts had two options: resign himself to the fact that Lord Aldington's lawyers had successfully got off the hook or take his complaint to the general public through a pamphlet. Predictably, Watts chose the latter course.

In the middle of 1994 Watts published an eight page 'brochure' as he now started to call his pamphlets, entitled 'The Darker Side of Lord Aldington, Sir Christopher Benson [Lambert's successor as Chairman of Sun Alliance], Allen & Overy and Charles Gray QC'. It is a lurid work, in which Gray got his share of the abuse. For good measure, Watts published details of Gray's messy divorce in 1988, as well as details of his efforts to keep it out of the press. But this achieved no more than all his references to the legitimate complaints bodies.

While all this was going on, the campaign to establish the truth about Sun Alliance's funding of the libel action had not been abandoned. Both Watts and Tolstoy attended the 1992 Annual General Meeting in May. It turned into a shouting match with one newspaper referring to 'the incredibly angry Mr Watts'. Lambert was in a weaker position than usual because he had to report losses of £466 million for the previous year which, combined with a loss of £181 million the year before and another big loss which he forecast in the current year, was to bring the total deficit in the last three years of his Chairmanship to about £700 million. Shareholders were not mollified by the fact that, in the middle of this, he announced an increase of his own salary by 25%. Thus Lambert was on the defensive when Tolstoy asked him to explain the difference between the £500,000 which had been 'advanced' to Lord Aldington—Lambert still maintained it was a loan—and the £350,000 untaxed costs which Lord Aldington had claimed he had incurred. What had the other £150,000 been spent on?

'He had a great many other expenses,' Lambert said, looking very nervous.

'Such as?' Tolstoy asked.

'Research.'

'Research?'

'Research.'

'Can I ask you a very simple question?' Tolstoy went on. 'Do you know, and if so how do you know, whether this research money was used to fund a certain Brigadier Cowgill who published many attacks on me before the trial and afterwards and was entirely discredited as a result? His connection with Lord Aldington is very close.'

'I think,' Lambert replied, 'his connection with Sun Alliance is absolutely nil.'

After many diversions, Lambert said, 'We have lent Lord Aldington some money, which was asked for by his solicitors for their expenses.'

Well, what were the terms of the loan, Tolstoy asked? He could get no answer, beyond the assurance that if Lord Aldington did recover anything he would repay Sun Alliance. But he had already been paid £55,000 by Century Hutchinson, the *Sunday Telegraph* and Mr Watts, Tolstoy said. Had he paid that back? No answer again.

Lambert tried to shift the discussion to less controversial matters and called on David Mackie to speak about Lord Aldington's legal expenses. Mackie told the meeting that the £150,000 was accounted for by the difference between Lord Aldington's taxed and untaxed costs. But the £350,000 was his *un*taxed costs, Tolstoy objected: Lord Aldington had sworn an affidavit to that effect. 'Please, Count Tolstoy, let me answer important questions as quickly as I can,' Mackie said, 'so this meeting can continue.' With that the proceedings meandered off into less controversial areas, like the company's gigantic trading losses.

Tolstoy's response to the Solicitors Indemnity Fund revelation was different from Watts's: he swore an affidavit in early December 1992 opposing Lord Aldington's application for security for costs on the ground that there was no reason to believe that the deal with the Solicitors Indemnity Fund was anything other than a cynical stitch-up tailored to suit the conditions Mr Justice Morritt had said were those in which an order for disclosure of his maintainer might have succeeded. Tolstoy accordingly asked the court to order disclosure of all the documents relevant to this deal.

This request had the same effect as the one asking for disclosure of the Sun Alliance deal: suddenly the whole idea of applying for security for costs was dropped. Now Allen & Overy were 'of the view that the appeal should be brought on as quickly as possible, rather than delayed by the security for costs application'.

Now that speed was apparently the goal, Allen & Overy applied for an expedited hearing of the appeal. On 29 January 1993, Kendall wrote a long letter to the Civil Appeals Office giving reasons why Lord Aldington should jump the queue of litigants. The main one was that Tolstoy's Trustee in bankruptcy had refused to order the sale of Tolstoy's house and library while there was any doubt that he owed Lord Aldington what was claimed. Kendall also said that Lord Aldington had been 'embroiled in this litigation since 1987' and wanted an end to the 'considerable and continuing strain and distress'.

In the event, Kendall's application was turned down and the appeal was scheduled for November. But, reading Aldington's words, Watts decided he should try for another settlement. If Aldington really wanted an end to the litigation, there might be scope for agreement. Watts wrote to Allen & Overy proposing they draw a line under the whole matter. 'In the circumstances,' he said, 'I offer to your wretched client one penny in contempt and full settlement of any liability howsoever arising from Count Tolstoy and myself.'

This was ignored, but still, soon afterwards, Lord Aldington gave another interview in which he said he had paid £300,000 out of his own pocket. For some reason he added, 'Eighteen months ago I was in despair. I laugh about it now.'[9] This enraged Watts and he wrote to Allen & Overy on 7 December.

Is your client quite incapable of telling the truth? The deplorable mendacity of this vulgar little man—'slippery as a box of eels'—is placing beyond salvage the remnants of Allen & Overy's compromised standing in the arena of legal affairs. Fraud, criminal conspiracy, perjury, shifty prevarications, subterfuge and now ever more atrocious lies. How much longer can this

9   *Kent Today* 26 November 1992

outrage continue? It is an affront to any civilised standard of decency and integrity. Even Macchiavelli would have been embarrassed by this sort of conduct.

Early in 1993, the preparations for the appeal against Morritt's judgement in the settlement case received a major legal boost. Once again, it was an unguarded statement on oath by a junior solicitor at Allen & Overy which provoked it. In an affidavit sworn while Lord Aldington was still asking for security for costs, a solicitor from Allen & Overy argued that when Lord Justice Hoffman annulled Watts's bankruptcy, which he did on the day Watts made the settlement with Lord Aldington—that settlement was the pre-condition of the annulment since it meant Watts was no longer indebted to Aldington—he did so under section 282(1)(a) of the Insolvency Act 1986, not section 282(1)(b). The significance of this arcane distinction was considerable. The former clause provides for bankruptcies to be annulled if a court, for any reason, holds that they should not have been declared in the first place. The latter clause provides for annulment in the event that the debt leading up to a correctly declared bankruptcy has been paid. If Watts's annulment had been allowed because the debt had been paid—paragraph (b)—Lord Aldington could not go after Tolstoy since the debt no longer existed. But if Watts's annulment had been allowed under (a), as Allen & Overy contended, Tolstoy would still be vulnerable. That much was common ground.

But Watts had been made bankrupt in December 1990, and the annulment on 20 March 1991 was as a result of the settlement between him and Lord Aldington. As that settlement had not existed at the time of the original bankruptcy, and the annulment was a direct result of the settlement, it would seem that the bankruptcy had been correctly declared in the first place and was being annulled on the ground that the debt had been paid in full—in other words, (b), not (a). Thus the chronology suggested that Allen & Overy's contention was wrong and that in consequence Lord Aldington had been paid in full. If that were so, both Watts and Tolstoy would be free.

Watts would never have thought of this, but for Allen & Overy's attempt to gild their legal lily for the security for costs application by making an issue of it. However, once the issue had been brought to his attention, Watts had a bright and sensible idea: why not simply write to Lord Justice Hoffman and ask what he had in mind when he made the annulment order? This Watts did.

In January 1993 Hoffman replied saying he could not remember his thoughts at the time, but he agreed with Watts that the chronology must have meant that 'I was not so much allowing an appeal as exercising an original jurisdiction to annul an earlier order... I agree that section 282(1)(b) would appear more logically the basis for the annulment.' This meant that Lord Justice Hoffman felt that the debt had been paid in full by the settlement and that Watts was released, which was the opposite conclusion to Morritt's. The prospects for the appeal began to look very good.

Despite this fillip, Watts still thought the best course of all would be to persuade Lord Aldington to abandon his financially fruitless litigation and settle the whole matter. In February 1993, he wrote once again to Allen & Overy. 'If your client wishes to make a realistic and reasonable assessment of the situation, I am prepared to be modest about my costs [which was all Watts was asking for by way of settlement]. This proposal, if accepted, would terminate litigation which would produce no benefit to your client.'

Allen & Overy did not reply. Neither did they reply to seven other letters Watts wrote to the same effect in March. Watts wrote an eighth time saying, 'If you are no longer acting for Aldington would you please have the courtesy to say so.'

Still no reply. But Watts was not to be put off. In May, he restated his offer.

The plain fact is that Tolstoy has no equity against which to proceed. Your client will be 80 this month. The proposals I have put forward are reasonable. I have no more wish than Aldington has to be embroiled in this continuing fiasco for the rest of my days. If you choose to reject this offer or again fail to respond, I sincerely hope I will hear no more suggestions from your side that I bear any responsibility for subjecting a man of Aldington's age to the stress and strain of this interminable litigation, the continuation of which is entirely of his own making.

This time Watts did get a reply. But it was brief: 'Our client still opposes your appeal.'

23

The SUN ALLIANCE TURNS NASTY

IN MAY 1993 Watts and Tolstoy went once again to the Annual General Meeting of the Sun Alliance to follow up the questions they had put in 1992.

'Was the agreement with Lord Aldington evidenced in writing?' Watts asked Henry Lambert.

'It doesn't have anything to do with you,' Lambert replied.

'Has Lord Aldington paid back the £55,000 he has received from litigation which *our* members have paid for, from *our* money?' Watts persisted.

'I told you before that we are going to deal with this at the end of the matter—'

'No, we are going to deal with it now. We've had eight years of your prevarication. You have never answered a question from any member yet,' Watts said, as a general murmur spread though the hall. 'Will you now tell us if you have required him to repay the £55,000?'

A voice called out, 'The shareholders have a right to this answer.'

'I have told you before, at previous meetings,' Lambert said, 'that until this whole affair is wound up—'

'Why have you not required him to pay it now over the last four years?'

'—because he has had a whole lot of other expenses.'

'And what were those other expenses, Mr Chairman?'

Other voices started calling out, 'And what are they to do with Sun

Alliance?' and 'Why are you paying our money?'

'We are not paying your money,' said Lambert, clearly hoping to avoid answering Watts.

'You *are* paying our money,' one voice shouted, while another one added, 'Well whose money is it?' 'This is an outrage,' said a third. 'This Lord Aldington, you are paying him to assist in attacking this man in court with the shareholders' money.'

'As everybody well knows,' Lambert said, looking very worried by the number of people yelling at him, 'this arose from a claim on the Sun Alliance and action the former Chairman took in the service of the company.'

'Hold on a second,' Watts boomed over the din. 'You were saying in 1991 that you hadn't made any commitment to Lord Aldington. Aldington left in 1985. Correspondence about the claim has since 1985 been with you. How could there be any improper pressure on Lord Aldington? It's a total fraud, isn't it?'

'I am not going on with this—'

'It's a total fraud,' Watts repeated. 'You've doled out £500,000 of shareholders' money to your old school chum. We want some answers.'

Another voice called out, 'Shareholders have got only one chance to face you and ask you these silly questions—as you say silly—and we are entitled to the answers.'

'They have been answered before,' said Lambert.

'They have never been answered before,' shouted Watts.

Yet other voices said, 'If they had been answered we wouldn't keep on asking them, but you never answer them.' And: 'Even if shareholders write to you, you never answer them in writing.' And a third: 'Neither you nor your directors answer any enquiries.'

'You have never responded to the questions I have put to you in writing about this,' said Watts, 'so now is the time to give us your answers.'

'I have given you the answers.'

At this point a tubby man in a middle-management suit stood up. 'I am very sorry that our annual meetings always break up into these very unpleasant situations. I hope I can lower the temperature and ask you a direct question. The Corporation of Lloyds is allowing corporate capital to become Members of Lloyds for the first time. Is this a window of opportunity?'

Some shareholders laughed, and one said scornfully, 'What a sycophant!'

Lambert visibly relaxed and talked for several minutes about Lloyds. Then another suited figure stood up. 'What is the Sun Alliance's view on the environment? Particularly, does the Sun Alliance have an environmental policy?'

With the colour returning to his face, Lambert explained that the company insisted on using lead-free petrol and re-cycled paper. 'We have a keen interest in ensuring high standards of waste disposal,' he added.

Then Tolstoy took the floor. He asked about the £150,000 which Lambert had said the previous year had been spent on Lord Aldington's research. 'Do we know what that research was? Or was it just money that dribbled through your fingers?'

John Kendall from Allen & Overy answered that one, saying the difference between the £500,000 the company had spent on Lord Aldington and the £350,000 Aldington himself claimed the libel trial had cost was represented by the difference between taxed and untaxed costs. Lord Aldington could expect to recover only three fifths of his total expenditure after taxation, he said. Few people at the meeting had seen the affidavit in which Aldington swore that his *un*taxed costs had been £350,000. Lambert adjusted his explanation accordingly

'I didn't say he spent £150,000 on research–'

A loud, angry voice said, 'You *did*. I was there. Last year you said £150,000 on research. Let's get that absolutely clear.'

'No, the £150,000 extra was–'

'You said £150,000 on research, Mr Chairman. I was here. You *did*.'

'No I didn't.'

'Mr Chairman, you are lying.'

'No I'm not lying.'

'You *are* lying. You said £150,000 quite clearly.'

This went on for a few more minutes until another suited gentleman got to his feet and said, 'Mr Chairman, reverting, please, to the operational performance of the group: could you tell us a little more about how the group is taking advantage of the significant increases in prices being charged currently within the general insurance market frame?'

Evidently relieved at the familiar sound of a commercial cliché, Lambert tried to divert the meeting from the awkward subject of Lord Aldington's legal offensive. But he did not get far. 'Excuse me, Mr Chairman, you said last year that £150,000 had been spent on research.'

'I said, amongst other things on research,' Lambert retorted.

'You said £150,000 for research last year. Well, we now want to know about this research.'

'No I didn't.'

'You *did*, Mr Chairman. Did you or did you not mention research last year?'

'I certainly mentioned that his expenses included research, but not £150,000.'

'Well, what has happened to the research, because Mr Kendall appears to deny that there was *any* of it now?'

This of course was the logical implication of Kendall's new claim. Lambert could see that and was completely stumped. He looked about the hall at a loss for words. After a pause he said, 'Lord Aldington's total costs must be well beyond half a million pounds.'

The loud, angry voice was not satisfied. 'Excuse me, Mr Lambert, Mr Kendall has just said that the legal costs were £500,000. Is that not correct? Now what has happened to this research that you talked about last year which was what made up the £500,000?'

'No I didn't say that,' wailed Lambert, looking almost frightened.

'Excuse me but you *did*,' said the loud and angry voice.

'I said he had costs for research which had actually taken his expenses far beyond £500,000.'

'Count Tolstoy asked you last year what the difference was between the £350,000 and £500,000 and you said "research". What we want to know now is what has happened to that "research"?'

Lambert simply could not bring himself to speak any longer. He looked close to tears. There was a pause before he pulled himself together and bought the questions to a close. 'Another Lambert lie,' shouted Watts. 'That is what it is: another Lambert lie.'

This was Lambert's farewell meeting, as he was going into retirement two years early. So he ended by introducing his successor, Sir Christopher Benson. He then fled from the room to the Directors' lunch. Before joining them, Sir Christopher mingled with the shareholders. Watts button-holed him and asked when the company would answer the very serious questions which hung over the arguably illegal arrangement with Lord Aldington, and would they not agree to outside arbitration on his sister's claim? Benson said he would look into both matters and respond.

Although Watts was sceptical, there seemed no reason to doubt this assurance. Benson had joined the Board after Lord Aldington left and might well not be under the obligation to him which seemed to have crippled and embarrassed Lambert. Neither does Benson have any connection with Winchester. In contrast to Lambert, who gives the impression of being a cultivated but weak man who has been put in an uncomfortable position by Lord Aldington, Benson has the dull but aggressive look of the successful professional manager that he is. Such a man might want to establish his independence from the old regime by ridding his enterprise of the taint of corruption.[1] That, at any rate, was Watts's best hope.

Watts wrote to Benson as he said he would with brief details of his sister's case—he tactfully made no mention of Lord Aldington's loan at this stage—saying, 'if you make some reasonable proposal to rectify the severe injustice involved, then an end may at last be reached in this unhappy saga. If you consider a meeting would be helpful to this end, one can easily be arranged.' But he might as well have saved the stamp. All he got was a four line reply, six months later, from the Company Secretary who said that the Board was unanimously of the opinion that the company had behaved correctly and that 'this correspondence should therefore be closed.'

But Watts was not to be put off. He was given another opportunity to put his question in September 1993. Due to the massive losses of the Lambert years, the company was forced to raise more capital and so called an Extraordinary General Meeting on 22 September 1993 to ask the shareholders to approve a £300 million rights issue.

Hardly anybody turned up for what was supposed to be a "rubber stamp" meeting. But Watts did, taking a friend along with him. His main question was this: if the company needed money so badly, why had it not started by recalling the "loan" to Lord Aldington?

Benson reacted quite differently from Lambert. Impatiently, he told Watts to be quiet. Watts refused. 'Will you now state,' he said loudly, 'whether you have recalled the half million pound loan to Lord Aldington?

---

1   After school in Worcester, Benson started his professional life as an agricultural auctioneer, having failed to get into Dartmouth as he had wanted to. He moved into property, eventually rising to be development director of MEPC, then managing director. At the time of writing he is Chairman of Boots and Costain, as well as Sun Alliance. He sits on a large number of charity boards, including the Royal Opera House and the Cancer Relief Macmillan Fund. He is married and has two sons, both of whom are barristers.

You are trying to raise £300 million and a large percentage (*sic*) of that can be raised by recalling the loan that your predecessor, whom you were so vociferous in supporting, has lent by way of an arm's length transaction to his old school chum Lord Aldington. You have got something to hide, otherwise you would state whether you have recalled the loan.'

A timid voice from the floor said to Watts, 'Why don't you write to the Chairman?'

'He never replies to letters,' Watts said quietly before raising his voice to the pitch he thought appropriate for a meeting with as many as fifteen people present. 'I want to see a manifestation that the rot has stopped,' he boomed. 'There is not one scintilla of evidence that it has stopped. An act of good faith by the present Chairman would be to recall [the] bogus loan made to his predecessor's old school chum, Lord Aldington.'

Once again, Benson asked him to be quiet. Once again, Watts refused. So Benson called a vote to have him excluded from the meeting. Benson got a majority (8-2, with 5 abstentions), but still Watts refused to leave. He had a right to raise such issues, he insisted. What, otherwise, was the purpose of the meeting?

Benson called a recess. He disappeared from the room and, fifteen minutes later, reappeared with two members of the City of London Police. Trotting along behind them was the Sun Alliance head of "security" who, for form's sake, asked Watts once more to leave before the meeting recommenced.

Watts refused, saying, 'I am here to cast my vote. This is a civil issue. It has nothing to do with the Police.'

He was told that if he did not leave he would be arrested for a breach of the peace.

'I won't be arrested,' said Watts. 'The Police are here to keep the law, not administer it.'

'If you resist arrest, you will be arrested,' said the security officer, clearly flustered at the gravity of the situation.

'I am here to cast my vote in respect of a £300 million–'

'Sir, for the last time, will you please leave?'

'Don't mention the last time, I am not going.'

'You are going to resist, are you, Sir?'

'I am going to resist.'

'Then I am afraid there is nothing more I can do.'

'Sir, you have been asked to leave the premises,' said one of the policemen, Police Constable Minichiello.

'I am here by invitation with my ticket to exercise my vote–'

'I have heard you,' said Minichiello, interrupting him. 'Now you listen to me. You have been asked to leave the premises. You refused to leave the premises. I will have to arrest you.'

'You are arresting me?'

'Listen to me. You are now under arrest for a breach of the peace.'

'Right.'

'You do not have to say anything unless you wish to do so but whatever you say may be used in evidence. Do you understand that?'

'Yes.'

'Right. I would like you to stand up and I will search you before I remove you from the premises. You are now under arrest.'

Watts was handcuffed and marched out of the Sun Alliance board-room to a waiting Police van. He was taken to Bishopsgate Police station where he was told he had done nothing wrong and was free to leave. By that time, Benson had received majority approval from the fourteen remaining shareholders for the rights issue, in strict accordance with the legal requirements of the Companies Acts, and closed the meeting.

This incident had two sequels, one of which was that Benson was told at the next AGM, by an elderly shareholder who had been present at the EGM and was outraged by what he had witnessed, that he had acted 'like a petty dictator' by introducing 'practices of a Police state to shareholder meetings'. He should apologise to Watts and resign. Benson laughed.

The other consequence was more serious: Watts sued the City of London Police for wrongful arrest. The Police defended the case on the ground that there had been an imminent danger of a breach of the peace by Watts. They submitted, by way of evidence, the notebooks of the two arresting officers. PC Minichiello's description of the events in question was the main one and turned out to be quite different from that quoted above. But the one quoted above has been transcribed from a covertly-made tape-recording. It was produced in court and accepted as authoritative. But Minichiello did not know this was going to happen at the time he composed his own account.

Watts became agitated and began shouting [Minichiello wrote], I then said to Mr Watts, 'You have been asked to leave the premises and have refused. I am therefore asking you to leave the premises.' Mr Watts said, 'I will not leave, you will have to throw me out.' I then said to Watts, 'I am going to escort you from the premises.' I took hold of Mr Watts and asked him to stand up. He said, 'No,' and pulled his arm away. He began shouting and said, 'I am not moving.' I again took hold of his arm and tried to stand him up. Watts began struggling and shouting. I said to Mr Watts, 'I am arresting you for [in Minichiello's manuscript the word 'for' is crossed out and 'to prevent' is substituted] a breach of the peace.' I cautioned him to which he stated, 'You will have to drag me out.' With the help of PC Symons, who had by now joined us, and due to his struggling, PC Symons applied quickcuffs to his wrist to restrain him. Watts was then escorted from the premises.

As a result of comparing the tape recording with the Police notebook, Watts accused Minichiello in court of fabricating evidence. The Police account gave the impression that there was a scuffle followed by the threat of violence, which is entirely absent from the tape recording. In the witness box, Minichiello went so far as to say he had feared for his own safety. The two accounts are simply incompatible.

In the event, the jury believed Watts, rather than PC Minichiello, and awarded him £5,090 damages for wrongful arrest, plus costs.

Watts's costs were not great but those of the Police, who were represented by Herbert Smith & Co., were reported to have been £150,000. Despite this, they were happy to finance an appeal, at which the verdict was reversed. They could afford to do so: they were insured by the Sun Alliance.

Before issuing his writ, Watts had written to the Police Complaints Authority (PCA). When he decided he should take legal action, he asked the PCA to suspend their investigation pending the outcome of the case. The PCA ignored Watts's request and completed their investigation, but without taking evidence from him. Not surprisingly, they therefore found for the Police. The PCA wrote to Watts, saying their investigation had 'not produced any evidence to show misconduct by any officer. The Authority have carefully studied all the papers and have decided that no disciplinary action should be taken.'

Watts learnt about this in March 1994, four months before his case came to court. He wrote to them, referring to his request to suspend their inquiries and, in the light of what they had done, asking them to re-open the investigation so that his evidence could be considered. A procedural detail was invoked to give the PCA grounds for refusing. In April 1994 the Deputy Chairman (Discipline), Peter Morehouse, wrote to Watts saying that in circumstances such as that of his complaint, 'the Police are empowered to apply to this Authority for a dispensation from the need to make further investigations under The Police (Dispensation from Requirement to Investigate Complaints) Regulations (1990).' The Police had applied for that dispensation and the Authority had granted it. That was the end of Watts's complaint.

Watts's resistance, though, had one positive result: at the 1994 Sun Alliance AGM Benson was not able to use the Police inside the hall. Instead he had security men inside and the Police waiting in a van in the street outside. Resisting the security men would constitute a breach of the peace, *per se*, enabling Benson, quite legally, to summon the Police to "prevent further violence".

Benson started the meeting by making a long statement about the loan to Lord Aldington. He said that it totalled £530,000 and that the company had now 'made provision in our accounts' for £450,000 of it. 'The loan is still outstanding,' he said. 'It has not been repaid.' Sun Alliance had paid Allen & Overy's invoices, 'penny for penny', he said. That statement sounded candid but in fact it entirely avoided the main questions still unanswered from the previous year: what had happened to the "missing" £150,000? Why had more than £500,000 of company money been spent fighting a case which basically concerned Tolstoy, and why had the support been kept secret while the case was in Court?

For once, Watts sat and listened while a friend, Martin Gwynne, put these questions to Benson. 'Go and ask Lord Aldington,' said the Chairman with mingled anger and contempt. But Gwynne insisted that it was for the company to account for how it spent shareholders' funds, not the recipient of that money. Impatiently, Benson asked Gwynne to sit down and keep quiet. Gwynne refused. Benson called another "exclusion vote", and ordered him out of the hall. Gwynne stood still and repeated his question. Benson signalled to his security men, and three of them grabbed Gwynne, one hissing in his ear, 'You're going to get hurt, mate.' The awkward shareholder was bundled out into the street and the subject of Lord Aldington's loan was thus disposed of.

For the 1995 AGM, Benson proposed two amendments to the company's Articles of Association which showed just how far Watts and Gwynne had got under his skin:

—To include additional powers for appropriate searches and other security arrangements to be used at general meetings

—To give the Chairman power to adjourn a general meeting without obtaining formal consent in cases where ... the conduct of persons present prevents the orderly continuation of business, and to give the Chairman the power to take appropriate action to promote orderly conduct at general meetings.[2]

There would be no more tape recordings and no more awkward questions. (One wonders what now is the purpose of such a meeting? The company will not publish the transcripts it makes of the proceedings.) To help divert attention, the whole event was choreographed by a public relations company. Shareholders entered the Insurance Hall to the sound of loud Wagnerian music and the sight of a huge picture—possibly twelve feet square—of Benson's face which was beamed onto a nine-section screen behind the Directors' table. The Benson visage gave way to an advertisement for the Sun Alliance which ended with the punch-line, 'Whatever life throws at you, you are not alone with the Sun Alliance.' Not alone, indeed! There was a van-load of police outside in Aldermanbury, and no less than twelve security men inside the hall, excluding those checking bags and pockets.

It all turned out rather farcically. As the music swelled to an almost Nuremberg-style crescendo, a door to the left of the high table opened and the Directors marched in. With eyes front, they passed at slow-march pace under the huge screen onto which the icon of the Chairman was being projected. The music, the grey suits, the dark blue background behind the screen and the ranks of security men on either side of the stage, combined to produce an effect which was almost comic. The same was true of Benson's big moment. When he called for 'Any other business' he was met with a deathly silence. His eyes roamed round the room, looking, almost hopefully, for an obstreperous shareholder to justify these ludicrous preparations. Nobody even raised the issue of corporate waste-disposal strategy. Benson's expression relaxed into a smirk. He could afford to: by that day, 3 May 1995, as will be seen below, Watts was in jail.

2   Sun Alliance *Notice of Annual General Meeting 3 May 1995*, p. 5

24

LORD ALDINGTON
TRIUMPHS

O N TUESDAY 16 November 1993, the appeal against Mr Justice Morritt's judgement in the Watts-Aldington settlement case came to court. Why did Lord Aldington bother to defend the case? By now it was obvious that the defeated litigants in the libel trial would never be able to pay anything towards his costs or the award, and therefore also would never be able to pay his costs in the pending appeal, even if he were to win. Eighteen months before he had complained about this in the press. He told an interviewer that he had a net worth of about £900,000. He said the fight with Watts and Tolstoy had already cost him personally £160,000. 'That is one's life savings,' he commented. 'I wasn't a rich man when I started. I haven't had to sell my home yet and I hope that I won't have to. I always ask myself whether it is worth the expense and time. What was it we were taught when we were young? That we mustn't feel sorry for ourselves and, if we did, we mustn't show it.'[1] Yet the case about to start, in November 1993, was to cost over £50,000, none of which he was to recover from his opponents. His motivation remains a mystery.

At 10.30 a.m. on 16 November three red-robed and white-wigged figures, two grey-faced, and one red-faced, filed into Court 2 in the Royal

---

1   *Evening Standard* 1 June 1992. This piece was printed a week after Lord Aldington had failed
    to compel Tolstoy to disclose the identity of his 'maintainer', if any, in the Morritt action.

Courts of Justice and took their seats behind a long desk elevated perhaps six feet above the well of the Court. These three Judges were Lord Justices Neill (presiding), Steyn and Simon Brown. Neill was the co-author of the earliest editions of Rampton's textbook *Duncan and Neill on Defamation*. He had the grave mien popularly associated with senior judges, unlike Steyn (pronunced "stain"), a rubicund Afrikaner who smiled from time to time and made ostentatiously down-to-earth comments about the law in lightly accented though fluent English. Brown was much the youngest of the three, and looked more like a colourless company director than one of Her Majesty's Lord Justices of Appeal.

Lord Aldington was not in court when it assembled, but Tolstoy was, looking rather drawn. Watts looked his usual cheery self. Formally Watts was the Appellant as he had been the signatory of the settlement whose meaning and effect the Court was assembled to determine. He was represented by a young, clever-looking and approachable barrister called Jon Turner, the only member of the legal profession present who was not wearing spectacles. Gray, by contrast, looked baggy-eyed and sour, like a senior and once-bright Latin master going slowly to seed: images from *Mr Perrin and Mr Traill* sprang to mind.

The proceedings were dull and at times slightly farcical. One of the main issues was whether or not Watts would, in terms of the Civil Liability (Contribution) Act, actually have been vulnerable to a claim from Tolstoy's Trustee. Was it the position that Watts would have to "contribute" half of everything Tolstoy's estate paid to Lord Aldington, or would he just have to recompense the estate for everything paid over and above half of the *total* debt? If the position was the latter, the whole issue of contribution was academic as there was no conceivable chance of Tolstoy's estate being worth half of £1.5 million (or over £2 million, including costs and interest). This was what Gray had been arguing in opposition to Watts's important point that he could not, in justice, be held to an agreement which purported to be 'full and final' but in practice was not.

'This is all governed by statute,' Steyn said to Gray. 'Can you tell us which section of the Act you are relying on?'

'I'm not sure about that,' replied Gray. There was a long pause while the defamation barrister dredged his memory for commercial references. Eventually he said lamely, 'It sounds like the commonsense position.'

'Speaking for myself I would be astonished if the statute applies as you say,' Brown said.

This was too much for Neill. He insisted the proceedings go no further until the issue was clarified. What would happen, he asked Gray by way of example, if Lord Aldington decided to compromise with Tolstoy and accept £100,000 in full settlement? As that would then be the *whole* debt, Watts would, on Gray's argument, be liable for half of that, so the issue was far from academic, as Gray was trying to argue.

'I have to say,' replied Gray, reddening, 'that, in commonsense, you are right. I am merely making my submission.'

To add to the impression he gave of a Queen's Bench barrister floundering in Chancery, Gray said, 'My Lord, this is a case in which one hesitates to venture into the real world.'

Steyn summed up what seemed to be the feeling of the Court. 'The problem is that the law in this area is in a preposterous state.'

As a result of all this, the Tolstoy-Watts camp was optimistic about the result when, after three days, the Court rose to write its judgement. Four weeks later that judgement was delivered and, like Morritt's, it managed to find against Gray but in favour of his client.

Lord Justice Neill, who wrote the main part of the judgement, squared the circle by deciding that the settlement was *neither* a full release *nor* a covenant not to sue. This was a surprise, since Morritt had said it must be one or the other. It was a release, Neill said, which was 'subject to an implied term that Lord Aldington's rights against Count Tolstoy would be reserved'. He said he thought 'the right approach is to try to ascertain the presumed intention of the parties.' This is a tenable view, if applied even-handedly. But Neill did not do this. He inferred, correctly, that Lord Aldington wanted to proceed against Tolstoy after settling with Watts, but he did not infer Watts's intention, which was to put an end to all litigation. Neill concluded that there was an implied condition in the settlement: but it was Lord Aldington's. The only reason he gave for this view was that, 'I consider that any other result would offend commonsense.' With this one sentence, and without a single word about any conditions Watts might have thought were implied, Lord Justice Neill dismissed the whole case for the appeal.[2]

Steyn concurred. He, too, disagreed with Morritt and held that

---

2   For a summary, see the Law Report in *The Times*, 16 December 1993. The full Judgement (as in all the other cases in this story) is available from the official transcript writers who can be contacted through The Mechanical Recording Department, Room WB11, Royal Courts of Justice, Strand, London WC2A 2LL.

Watts's settlement did amount to a release, even though it should not, in practice, release him from liability. Morritt had held that the release of one joint debtor meant the release of the other, but Steyn disagreed. 'There is no inexorable march of logic,' he said. Whether Tolstoy was or was not released was 'a policy issue', to which 'good sense, fairness and respect for the contracting parties' should apply. Applying 'policy' to this case, Steyn, like Neill, argued solely from Lord Aldington's point of view. He concluded that there was an implied condition in the settlement by which Lord Aldington reserved his right to continue suing Tolstoy. 'It is the equivalent of an express reservation,' he said, completely ignoring the question whether Watts would have signed the contract, surrendering £10,000 and abandoning his appeals, if it had contained a clause stipulating that he would still be liable to a claim for contribution. Steyn's premiss was that abandoning the old rule that a debt is indivisible enabled the law to escape 'the absurd consequences of applying the rule of logic'.

Like Neill and Steyn, Lord Justice Simon Brown disagreed with Morritt and held that the Watts-Aldington settlement was a full release and not merely a covenant not to sue. He called the dichotomy a 'juridical relic'—an odd phrase as the whole basis of the common law is that prior decisions bind later courts; the law is, it might almost be said, a collection of juridical relics which can be disposed of only by statute—and said he thought the courts could take a 'more direct' approach. Simon Brown thought that the law as it strictly stood did not produce a 'just' conclusion, so he decided the settlement was a release 'subject to a condition subsequent'. In strict legal terms, this was a slightly different view of the settlement from Neill's and Steyn's, although it had the same effect. Simon Brown then asked the question, 'Is a conditional release of this nature sufficient for the Appellant's purpose?' His answer was, 'No'.

Why? Because 'the crucial question is ... was Lord Aldington reserving his position under the settlement agreement with Mr Watts, to pursue his judgement further against Count Tolstoy?' Clearly Lord Aldington *thought* he was doing so, but equally clearly Watts thought that a 'full and final settlement of any obligations howsoever arising' meant that he would not be able to. Like Neill and Steyn, Simon Brown simply posed the question from Lord Aldington's point of view, and completely ignored Watts's. 'It is nothing short of absurd,' Brown said, 'to suppose that the parties were intending by their agreement that Lord Aldington would receive a total of [only] £10,000... Such a conclusion would be both unjust and unreal.' Watts would have answered that when, in 1990, he offered

Lord Aldington only £10,000, the victorious Plaintiff turned it down, but when, in early 1991, he offered the same sum *plus the abandonment of his appeals* (one of which was based on the Phantom signal), Lord Aldington signed immediately. Nonetheless Brown ended by saying he rejected Watts's appeal 'without regret'.

Taking the Morritt hearing together with that in the Court of Appeal, the result was that four Judges had arrived at three different views of a two-page document, all of which views favoured one litigant: Lord Aldington. The Judges could not agree on the law, only on who it favoured.

This seemed to be the end of the legal road. Watts applied for leave to appeal to the House of Lords. That was refused, so he applied to the House of Lords directly for permission to appeal to them. Lord Aldington opposed this application and so it, too, was refused. Since no higher tribunal exists, Lord Aldington had won. He had kept the Phantom signal out of court and retained his freedom to pursue both Tolstoy and, indirectly, Watts, while pocketing Watts's mother's £10,000. After a year of further acrimonious correspondence, Allen & Overy sent Watts a bill for his 'moiety' of the costs of Lord Aldington's defence of the appeal: £25,603 for the Neill-Brown-Steyn hearing and £603 for the failed House of Lords application. The total was £26,206. Adding the money he had paid Lord Aldington, Watts was nominally out of pocket to the tune of £36,206, and yet without any greater protection from financial demands than he was while his appeals were still live.

Furious at what he saw as trickery, Watts wrote to Allen & Overy in November 1994 offering £500 by way of settlement of Lord Aldington's costs claim, to be paid over two years, adding angrily, 'On reflection, I feel my offer was far too generous. You must tell your despicable, devious and cunning little war criminal, who perfidiously sent thousands of defenceless refugees to their deaths, that he will have to pursue me as he will.'

Allen & Overy rejected the offer on the ground that it was 'too little over too long a period'. But Watts, in his rage against the obtuseness of the legal world, was moving onto dangerous ground. His use of the phrase 'war criminal' in connection with Lord Aldington was the first clear breach of the gagging injunction since it had been granted. The danger was compounded by the language he was now using in the pamphleting campaign he had started in late 1992 after realising what had gone on behind the scenes of the Morritt hearing. His first production had been headed: 'Lord Aldington's Perjury: 7 July 1992'. Watts assumed that calling Lord Aldington a perjurer in public would force him to take action, in the course of which he could demand discovery of the documentation Lord Aldington relied on to deny the allegation. But Lord Aldington's response was quite unexpected: he did absolutely nothing. Watts was amazed. The only solution he could see was another pamphlet making a further allegation, 'Lord Aldington: From Perjury to Forgery'. The latter accusation referred to the suppression of *The Minister and the Massacres*. This, too, produced no response. So Watts issued a third "brochure", entitled 'Lord Aldington at Law: Perjury, Forgery and Trickery'. The trickery allegation was one Watts then made subject of a separate publication. It dealt with the settlement case, and had a long, explanatory title: 'Lord Aldington's Cheating of Disabled Widow of Nearly Eighty Years Old, and Others, by Worthless Agreement, 20 March 1991'.

After that, Watts returned to his original theme with an eight-page production headed, 'Lord Aldington: the Perjurer of Leeds Castle and the House of Lords'. Finally, when Lord Aldington was suddenly, and in rather mysterious circumstances, relieved of his position at Leeds Castle—ostensibly, but improbably, due to a dispute with the management over the advertising budget—Watts added a fifth epithet and put out a pamphlet gleefully headed, 'Lord Aldington's Resignation from Leeds Castle: Perjury, Forgery, Fraud, Lies and Trickery'. In this he taunted the ex-Chairman for his failure to reply to the other accusations. 'The plain fact is,' Watts wrote, 'that you have chosen to remain silent in order to avoid confronting the truth. Members of the public are outraged at the way you have been able to nudge the shoulders of your highly-placed influential friends to extract yourself from the consequences of the catalogue of dishonesty in which you have indulged.'

This material was sent to Leeds Castle, naturally, but also to Aldington village, the press, the House of Lords, and anywhere else Watts thought Lord Aldington might be known. One copy reached Barron Hilton, Chairman and President of the Hilton Hotel chain. On "personalised" notepaper from the Waldorf-Astoria in New York, Hilton wrote to Watts on 8 October 1993 saying he felt sorry for him:

Your document shows up its author as such an unhappy man: at times a self-important, whingeing loser, at others a demented wasp courting the fly-swatter. Self-pity, the mark of a bad loser, is hard to shake off. Try doing something wonderful, unasked, each day for someone worse off than you. Gradually let yourself and those you love forget about this sadness and come alive again. Compassion, even for a victorious adversary, is the key.

Despite all this, Lord Aldington still did not respond. Watts was feeling both exasperated at his opponent's silence but also encouraged by his own apparent freedom. Once he sensed this, he started talking to the press. 'Why doesn't Aldington make a statement answering my allegation?' Watts asked the *Evening Standard*. 'I'm inviting him to go ahead and sue me. I'll even go up to London to collect the writ myself.' Allen & Overy were quoted in reply: 'We've had Mr Watts up to our neck. Watts is a plague. His pamphlet is untrue and selective. We are not going to take action over it. Lord Aldington has wasted enough time on Mr Watts.'

Lord Aldington told the press, 'Tolstoy has ruined part of my life. I just wish it would all stop.' Lady Aldington's reaction was more robust. 'One learns to live with these things,' she says. 'We are hardy perennials. It is Life, with a capital "L". We're quite capable of dealing with Life.'[3]

Nonetheless, she was vexed by the way the law works. 'We imagined that once the injunction [had been granted], that would be the end of it. The law is so extraordinary. You can take anything, as far as I can see, I mean anything quite cuckoo, and it has to then give the person a chance to prove that it's right, which of course he has never been able to do. You can say anything. It seems curious to me that when a Judge gives an injunction, it's not maintained. I think it is strange. I just don't understand the law.'

Lady Aldington also had views on Tolstoy. He had, she said, an 'Achilles heel' in that 'he has been proved to be a very bad historian.' By way of example, she pointed to her evidence in court about how preparation for the trial had meant the end of evening card games with her husband. '[During the trial] Tolstoy took this up and said, "I really can't think what it has to do with Lady Aldington and her bridge parties." Well, I can't play bridge. I dislike bridge. I'm not nuts on people who play bridge. And that is absolutely *typical* of him, imagining—he's got a very good imagination—that I was sitting playing bridge. I was not. I was playing SIX PACK BEZIQUE!'

3   Interview with the author on 15 December 1993 (as following quotes).

By contrast with Lady Aldington's vexation, and Watts's rising anger, Tolstoy response was to fall into a mood of depression. He became ill with worry, and could not sleep at night. Outwardly he was cheerful, but Peter Gwyn thought him 'dangerously optimistic'. The situation was aggravated by a continual shortage of cash. The Georgina Tolstoy Family Fund had taken rather more than £150,000 during 1990 and 1991, after which the donations more or less dried up. Within three years this sum had been spent, approximately a third of it on paying the mortgage for Court Close—'maintaining Aldington's asset for him', as Watts puts it—and the rest on living expenses. 'Nikolai has lived off the *capital*,' says Nigel Nicolson, a Trustee of the GTFF. Inevitably "compassion fatigue" set in amongst well-wishers, and by early 1993 the family was living off 'the jars at the back of the cupboard', as Tolstoy put it. Salvation came in the form of the immensely rich Prince of Liechtenstein, who took over where the Fund left off.

Throughout this period Tolstoy tried to work on the second volume of the Merlin trilogy, by far the most promising project as far as earning potential was concerned. But, like Lord Aldington's gardening and golf, this suffered from the fact that he simply could not devote enough time to it. Time was not the only problem: Tolstoy also felt he did not have the peace of mind he needed to write imaginative fiction while slowly sinking into the legal and financial quagmire. This is not hard to understand: there can be few activities more deadening to the poetic spirit than the composition of endless affidavits, memoranda for Counsel and commentaries on judicial decisions.

To sympathetic outsiders, the only solution seemed to be to try to get the two parties to compromise and declare the whole contest a draw. Nicolson repeatedly urged that Tolstoy content himself with a moral victory and leave it at that. Lord Portsmouth took the most practical step when he tried to broker a settlement through a family connection, but the idea foundered, almost as soon as it had been suggested, on the mutual intransigence of the two antagonists. 'Nikolai's reaction was, frankly, hysterical,' Lord Portsmouth says. Lord Aldington's reported demand was for a full apology from Tolstoy to him, as well as for acceptance of the 1989 judgement in its entirety, including the injunctions. This would not have been an armistice, but capitulation. Not surprisingly, no deal resulted.

The litigation ground on, with Aldington trying to get Tolstoy evicted from Court Close and Tolstoy trying to delay, and hopefully halt, the process by initiating a late appeal against the original libel verdict. Equipped with the Phantom signal, a full copy of FO 1020/42 and Tryon-Wilson's evidence to the War Museum which, as described in Chapter 13, flatly contradicted what he had said in Court a few months earlier in 1989, the chances, Tolstoy felt, were quite good.

Not so, said Rampton. His informal opinion was that Tolstoy did not have 'a snowball's chance in hell' of being allowed to appeal the original verdict. After considerable prevarication, Tolstoy's lawyers eventually decided that a better way of getting all the new evidence into Court would be to sue Lord Aldington for fraud on the basis that the 1989 verdict had been achieved by perjury. Accordingly, on 21 February 1994 a writ was served, followed by a long Statement of Claim. This concentrated on the Phantom signal, but, in the course of the nearly 200 pages of argument and documents, mentioned not only FO 1020/42, but also the de Fonblanque journal, the weather argument, Low's letters to Anthony Eden and a host of other matters, all of which served only to diffuse the light Tolstoy was trying to shine on the relationship between the full body of evidence of what happened in 1945 and that presented to the Court in 1989. The connection he was trying to suggest—that Aldington had knowingly given false evidence in 1989—was completely lost in the welter of subsidiary arguments.

On 29 March Lord Aldington replied with an application to have the case struck out as 'vexatious'. In support of this, he swore an affidavit on 10 May 1994. It was one of the longest he has composed in all this litigation, yet it ran to less than seventeen pages, a much more "Judge-friendly" length than Tolstoy's monster production. Lord Aldington's reply was to the effect that the Phantom signal was simply wrong.

> I still verily believe that I left Austria from Klagenfurt airfield in the morning of 22 May... I have not been in any doubt since I first acquired a copy of the [Phantom] Log in June 1992 that it did not establish that I left Austria on 23 May; in these circumstances, so I respectfully submit, any rational person would say that the log entry can safely be disregarded as evidence of my having left Austria on 23 May, given that otherwise I would have had to have made up (and perjured myself about) [evidence of my departure] for no readily comprehensible reason.

Aldington's argument was circular. Tolstoy had said the Phantom signal showed Lord Aldington had perjured himself: Lord Aldington replied that the Phantom signal must be wrong because otherwise he would have perjured himself. Aldington concluded his affidavit by ignoring the charges relating to the hi-jacking of FO 1020/42.

> If, in a case of this sort, the matter can be re-opened simply because the losing party has found on the open shelves of the Public Record Office *material which was there throughout*, it is difficult to see how there can be any finality in this litigation, now or in the future. (emphasis added)

Since Lord Aldington had himself used FO 1020/42 in the Foreign Office during the period referred to, he would have known the file had not been in the PRO *throughout* the relevant period—see Appendix B.

Tolstoy countered with an affidavit saying that FO 1020/42 had *not* been available at the time of the trial. Lord Aldington then swore a further affidavit in which he tried to justify his earlier assertion by saying, 'I do not recall any complaint during the trial by Count Tolstoy or his legal advisers that access by them to either file had been prevented.'

There was a final flurry before the case came to Court, concerning Tryon-Wilson's War Museum tapes. It will be recalled that he had said that it was Low who had taken the decision to prevent the Americans rescuing the Cossacks from 5 Corps' plan to deliver them to the Soviets. At the last minute, Tryon-Wilson swore an affidavit saying that the '*moment critique*' he referred to was actually on 18 May. Thus Brigadier Low was said to have prevented the saving of the Cossacks before the operation to rescue them had been set in motion. Not only was this a chronological absurdity, it was also irrelevant to the main point which was that whatever had been done had, according to Tryon-Wilson, been done *on Brigadier Low's initiative*.

All of these arguments seemed so transparent that Tolstoy went to Court in a relatively confident frame of mind. But a warning bell sounded when he learned that the Judge was a new-boy on the Bench, Mr Justice Collins. Collins is a soft-featured Old Etonian who, Tolstoy learnt with dismay, had been severely criticised in the Scott Report for allegedly withholding evidence from a court while still a barrister. Collins, while acting as prosecuting Counsel in the Ordtech case (about the sale of artillery fuses to Iraq) was alleged to have maintained that the government had no documents relevant to the Defence case when in fact it had several. Shades of FO 1020/42, Tolstoy thought.

Tolstoy's gloom deepened when he learned that the case was to be heard 'in Chambers', that is with the public excluded, rather than in open court. Tolstoy could have objected, but he was advised not to as the Judge might take that as evidence that he had issued this writ purely for publicity purposes, and strike his action out. In a sense he *had* done that, because, since the gagging injunction, a court is now the only forum where he can present the new evidence he has gathered without risking jail.

Preferring to lay the main emphasis on the Phantom signal rather than the material contained in FO 1020/42, Tolstoy's basic argument was that Lord Aldington had invented the account of his departure to lend colour to his claim that he had not been at 5 Corps headquarters at any time on 22 May, thereby, amongst other things, missing the "shoot the Cossacks" conference. But Tolstoy's barrister for this case, Alun Jones QC, could not get very far with his evidence before the Judge interrupted. 'Are you suggesting the Lord Aldington cynically *made up* the details of his journey home?' Since that was precisely what Tolstoy was suggesting, this was a bad sign.

Jones did not get far on the Phantom signal before the Judge gave it as his opinion that it was of no greater evidential value than the de Fonblanque journal. It was 'hearsay', the Judge said, and, for all he knew, there may be other entries in the Phantom file which support Lord Aldington's case. Mr Justice Collins did not say why, if that were the case, Lord Aldington had not produced them in evidence. Neither did he explain why the messages of the most secure communications unit in the Army should be considered hearsay, while those of less élite formations should be taken as being infallibly correct. 'The documents saying Lord Aldington returned [to Britain] *must* be right,' the Judge said, 'because we know they are. This does not apply to Phantom.'

Mr Justice Collins also said that he thought the Phantom signal would not have had the slightest effect on the jury.

'If the Phantom signal had appeared at the trial,' said Gray, 'Lord Aldington would have said, "It's ridiculous" and the jury would have believed him.'

'That I have no difficulty with,' the Judge replied, adding, 'The jury would already have believed Lord Aldington was telling the truth by the time Phantom would have been produced at the trial.' There was a perfectly 'innocent' explanation for the fact that the Phantom log contradicted Lord Aldington's testimony, he said: the Phantom signal was wrong.

Mr Justice Collins delivered his Judgement on 16 December 1994.

'The law sets its face against permitting the reopening of issues already decided by a competent court,' he said. For new evidence to be admissible, it has to have been something which could not 'with reasonable diligence' have been produced in the original trial. 'There was much material available in the Public Record Office,' the Judge said, presumably accepting Lord Aldington's mendacious assertion in his affidavit that FO 1020/42 had been available to Tolstoy 'throughout'.

Collins also said that the Definition Order did not 'breach the Yalta guidelines', even though much of Lord Aldington's case amounted to a defence of a breach of Yalta on the ground that screening would have been impossible with the time and resources available to 5 Corps. Collins, in other words, was making a case more favourable to Aldington than even Aldington himself had.

Collins dismissed the argument about Tryon-Wilson's War Museum evidence. 'It is quite impossible,' he said, 'for Count Tolstoy to place any reliance on the Tryon-Wilson interview as an indication, let alone possible proof, of perjury.' He also refused Tolstoy's request to *subpoena* the long tape Lord Aldington had made for the War Museum at the same time. This, it will be recalled, was the one Tryon-Wilson referred to when he said, 'When you spoke to Brigadier Low he would have told you that at the *moment critique* he decided that he did not want [American] help.' When the War Museum asked, in August 1993, for Aldington's permission to make his interview publicly available, he had turned the request down (see p. 234), saying, 'I do not want to complicate affairs by having on record for the public any statements different from those I made on oath in the courts.'

Tolstoy considered this a highly suspicious formulation, but Collins turned his request down, saying, 'You're going to listen to the tape and analyse it. No, I'm certainly not going to let that happen.'

Dealing with the legal force of the submission Tolstoy had been able to make, Collins noted that in Scottish law a judgement can be set aside on the basis of new evidence, while in English law this can happen only if fraud can be proved. He added that he would narrow that condition further by insisting that the fraud had to relate to a central aspect of the case. He said he had come to the conclusion that Low's departure date from Austria was not a decisive issue, and so he had no trouble in reaching the further conclusion that any fraud Lord Aldington may allegedly have committed by inventing evidence about it was irrelevant. 'For the reasons I have given,' Mr Justice Collins said in conclusion, 'I propose to grant the relief claimed by Lord Aldington and strike out Count Tolstoy's claim.'

The proceedings ended with a very unusual application from Gray. Tolstoy's case, he observed, had been adjudged so flimsy that it should clearly never have been brought. It was just a tactic to delay the seizure of his assets and showed he *still* did not accept the verdict of Mr Justice Davies's Court. Since he could plainly not pay Lord Aldington's costs for this action, Tolstoy's lawyers, Schilling & Lom, should, Gray argued, be made to pay, 'in order to prevent any other firm of solicitors from representing Count Tolstoy'. Mr Justice Collins agreed with this and ordered that they pay 60% of them.

Gray went further and asked that the judgement, including the costs award, be made public. The Judge allowed this too. As a final triumphant act, the transcript of the trial, in which was disclosed all the evidence Tolstoy had tried to deploy, was ordered to be destroyed. Due to the "gagging" injunction, this meant that, as far as the public record was concerned, Tolstoy's new evidence did not exist.

The only repercussion was that Schilling and Lom appealed the "wasted costs order" as it was formally called. Aldington had applied for this on the basis of two arguments: first, that Schilling & Lom had behaved 'improperly' and 'unreasonably' in conducting the case for Tolstoy without charging him and, secondly, that by acting without charging, the solicitors had put themselves in the position of 'maintainers' of the litigant. Collins rejected the first argument, but accepted the second, and made his award on that basis. On appeal, Lord Justice Rose, supported by Lords Justice Roch and Ward, said that Collins was wrong on the law but right on who it favoured. Schilling & Lom had not put themselves in the position of maintainers, but they had acted 'unreasonably' since the action they initiated amounted to an attack on the judgement of a court of competent jurisdiction.[4] The order against Schilling & Lom was upheld.

With Tolstoy silenced and denied access to court, Lord Aldington turned to the final threat he faced, Watts's pamphleteering campaign. So long as Watts had confined himself to calling him a perjurer, a forger, a fraudster,

4   *Times Law Report* 27 December 1995

a liar and/or a trickster, Lord Aldington had done nothing. But as soon as Watts revived the war crimes allegations, he acted. On 4 January Watts started distributing his last and most aggressively worded "brochure". The text went beyond the limits of both truth and legality, not to mention fair comment. He headed the document 'War Criminal In The House Of Lords' and cast the narrative in the form of an affidavit.

> I hereby state as follows because it is the truth. Lord Aldington left Austria on 23rd May 1945. He has consistently lied about the date of his departure. This financial adviser to the late Robert Maxwell is a perjurer, a trickster and a fraudster. Until he left Austria he was at the centre of arranging, with abhorrent duplicity, the most perfidious and treacherous war crimes of all time. He is totally despicable and had escaped any form of condemnation for his appalling war crimes because his close colleagues and associates held high office in the judiciary and other establishment posts.

Watts faxed this to members of the House of Lords, almost at random. This was a challenge Lord Aldington could hardly ignore. On 2 February, Allen & Overy wrote to him pointing out that this represented a breach of the "gagging" injunction. 'We are now instructed to institute proceedings against you for contempt,' Mackie wrote.

Watts responded to this with his most blatant provocation yet: he designed and had printed what he called his 'war crimes notepaper'. Where most people have the details of their address, and possibly some small personal device or picture, Watts put a large picture of Lord Aldington, surtopped by his coat of arms and surrounded by extracts from the original pamphlet as well as a new paragraph linking Lord Aldington's practices in litigation with those of Lord Archer—'both are ex-Deputy Chairmen of the Conservative Party'—and commenting, 'The judiciary are wilfully blind to any other view than that which is favourable to them.' At the bottom Watts added this clarion call, addressed to no-one in particular: 'Do not waste your time pursuing, against such pillars of the British establishment, issues which come before the British judiciary. Just have the courage to speak up and speak out the *truth* loud and clear.' For good measure, Watts covered the reverse side with another photograph of Lord Aldington surrounded by further quotes from the libellous pamphlet and headed, 'War Criminal in the House of Lords'.

The space left for the text of any correspondence was small, but just large enough for letters like the following, addressed to Mr Justice Davies:

Dear Sir Michael

Nigel Watts -v- Corruption in the British Judiciary

When I walked out of Court during your wholly prejudiced summing-up of the libel trial in November 1989, I told you that you were totally biased and a disgrace to the legal profession. Over five years on, I reflect how right I was. It is on account of your corruption that one of the most perfidious and treacherous war criminals in Europe is now able to effect the pretence that he is an angel of innocence who has been vindicated.

I propose to expose this vipers' nest of iniquity in which you and some of your unsavoury colleagues operate.

Yours sincerely

Nigel Watts

Davies ignored this, but on 14 March Mackie wrote to Watts saying, 'We shall shortly be serving you with our Notice of Motion to commit [to prison] for your contempt in breaching the injunctions contained in the judgement of 30 November 1989.'

On 29 March the Notice of Motion was served. The motion was for an order that 'Nigel Watts be committed to prison for contempt of this Court' on the grounds that he had 'published' a letter on 24 January 1995 in which he breached the 1989 order that he never again allege that Lord Aldington was 'guilty of disobedience, deception, and/or criminal, dishonourable, inhumane and/or other improper and/or unauthorised conduct.' The evidence of Watts's contempt was contained in four affidavits, one each from Lord Aldington, his son-in-law, Lord Boardman and Sir Edward Heath.

Lord Boardman, an ex-Chairman of the National Westminster Bank, swore that he 'was both horrified and distressed' by Watts's letter, sent on his war crimes notepaper, and he 'informed Lord Aldington of the position'.

Sir Edward Heath's affidavit was almost as brief. 'I was disgusted by the contents of [Watts's] letter, so much so that I tore it up and threw it in the bin. I informed Lord Aldington of the position.'

In addition to this evidence of Watts's contempt, a supporting affidavit from a junior solicitor at Allen & Overy drew attention to Mr Justice Davies's comment at the time he imposed the injunction: 'I think the verdict of the jury has made it quite clear that it would be their view, as it is mine, this matter having been thrashed out over 40 days, that Lord Aldington is entitled to a rest from this matter being pursued in future.'

The hearing had been set down for 7 April 1995, only 8 days after Watts received the Notice. This left him no time to seek legal aid, much less to work out his defence. Accordingly, when Watts appeared on 7 April in front of Mr Justice Garland he asked for a 13-week adjournment. Gray appeared for Lord Aldington and opposed this. The Judge was minded to grant Watt's request, provided he undertake to observe the injunction in the meantime. Otherwise, he said to Watts, 'you will be inside so fast your feet won't touch the ground. Will you accept an adjournment on these terms?'

'No,' said Watts, who began packing his books and papers into his plastic holdall.

'Are you leaving us, Mr Watts?' the Judge asked.

'Yes, sir.'

'Your liberty is in peril,' said the Judge.

Watts looked unperturbed. At that, the Judge caved in and granted a three-week adjournment. But that might not be long enough to get legal aid organised, protested Watts. Garland then offered to write to the Legal Aid office himself asking that an emergency certificate be granted 'in the interests of justice', if that would help. Watts asked when he would do so. 'I will sit here and write it now,' Mr Justice Garland said tiredly, 'if someone will give me a piece of paper.'

On 27 April Watts reappeared in the High Court, this time in front of Mr Justice Morland. This was quite a different affair. Morland looked in no mood for leniency. Watts did not help matters by interrupting Gray's opening speech to ask for a declaration from the Judge that he had never met Lord Aldington on any occasion, particularly at any ceremonies of secret societies like the Freemasons. Smiling wryly, Morland said he was not a Mason, never had been one and had never met Lord Aldington.

Once again, Gray tried to start his opening speech, but Watts interrupted again saying he wanted to argue that this Court had no jurisdiction on the ground that the European Court of Human Rights, which was hearing a case between Tolstoy and the United Kingdom government, was about to give judgement on, amongst other things, the validity of the injunctions.[5] Without looking up from his notes, Morland dismissed this

---

5   This case (8/1994/455/536) had been initiated in 1991 in response to the libel verdict. The
     basic claims were that the gagging injunction was an inhibition on freedom of speech, and that

application saying he would apply only English domestic law.

Gray was then free to make Lord Aldington's case. 'It would appear that Mr Watts is intent on inflicting maximum distress and anguish on Lord Aldington and his family by the repetition of libels found after a long trial to be wholly unfounded,' he said. The trial had been 'a horrifying ordeal' for Lord Aldington, Gray added, so 'the point has been reached in this particularly unhappy case where a drastic penalty is called for.'

After Gray had finished, Morland asked him if there was any limit to the sentence he might impose. Gray did not know and looked up the 1981 Contempt of Court Act. Two years, was the answer he eventually found.

Watts then mounted the witness box and was sworn. His case was, basically, that the injunctions did not apply since they had been subsumed in the settlement agreement, which Lord Aldington had later repudiated. Gray cross-examined Watts in a short exchange which was notable mainly for the volume at which Watts shouted at him. Gray tried to look tauntingly unconcerned by this while he quietly repeated his questions. But it did not work and eventually he had to give up.

Watts stepped down from the witness stand and, almost before he had regained his seat, Mr Justice Morland began reading out the judgement which he looked as if he had started composing before Watts had finished his argument. The injunctions were not affected by the settlement agreement, Morland ruled. Watts's letters, Morland said, 'manifestly indicate that he has an obsessive intention to continue his general campaign against Lord Aldington and, in particular, is intending to continue his campaign,

the size of the award was a punishment so large as not to be 'necessary in a democratic society', the phrase used in the European Convention on Human Rights for maximum permissable punishments. On 13 July 1995, the Court found against Tolstoy on the former, but in his favour on the latter, though no order was made for any sort of restitution against the British government. Though Tolstoy, for all practical personal purposes, lost the case, the consequence has been that the English courts must now have regard to this judgement in libel cases. This was translated into legal precedent by Mr Justice Bingham, then Master of the Rolls and now, as Lord Justice Bingham, the Lord Chief Justice, in his judgement in the appeal in the *Elton Hercules John v Mirror Group Newspapers* case in late 1995. Bingham stated that 'it is not healthy if any legal process fails to command the respect of lawyer and layman alike, as is regrettably true of the assessment of damages by libel juries... It is in our view offensive to public opinion, and rightly so, that a defamation plaintiff should recover damages for injury to reputation greater, perhaps by a significant factor, than if the same plaintiff had been rendered a helpless cripple or insensate vegetable. The time has come in our view when judges, and counsel, should be free to draw the attention of juries to these comparisons.'

which he may believe to be true, that an injustice was perpetrated upon him when judgement was found against him as long ago as 30 November 1989.' The pamphlets Watts had sent out were clear breaches of the injunction. 'In my judgement,' Morland continued, 'the manifest determination of Mr Watts to continue his campaign against Lord Aldington, and in particular that Lord Aldington was guilty of the gravest of war crimes, forces me to the conclusion that no sentence would be appropriate in this case other than a custodial penalty. Having regard to the gravity of the breach of the injunction and the whole background as displayed by the conduct of Mr Watts, in my judgement the appropriate sentence, the penalty I impose, is one of 18 months' imprisonment.'

Three tipstaffs escorted Watts from Court. He said to the waiting reporters, 'That's British justice for you.' He was led through the main hall of the Royal Courts, then down into the basement where a steel-reinforced door was opened from the other side. As it closed heavily behind him, Watts was taken through into a holding cell from where he was to be transferred to Pentonville Prison.

EPILOGUE

A CONVICTION for civil contempt does not automatically carry remission. Though one of the tipstaffs who escorted Watts to the cells said to him, 'Don't worry, mate, you'll be out in nine months', Watts's solicitor thought that he had been given a fixed term sentence. Uncertain of his position, Watts spent a frightening week in Pentonville Prison, during the course of which he lost nearly a stone in weight. Still without any word on the effective length of his sentence, Watts was transferred to an open prison, Standford Hill, near Sheerness in Kent. There he had a cell to himself and could at least get on with his painting. He volunteered for a job as 'main camp cleaner', since it meant he could earn an extra £4 per week which he could spend on phone cards. These he needed for contact with his solicitor as he was determined to appeal his sentence.

'I am here with people who have stabbed their opponent to death and multi-million pound fraudsters,' he wrote in a letter from prison. 'Their sentences range from nine months to two years, of which, due to remission, they will serve half. They will be out before me.' It was six weeks before the Official Solicitor to the Supreme Court removed the uncertainty. You will be released early, Watts was told, only 'if you satisfy the Court that you are genuinely sorry for your disobedience'. In other words, Watts was to be given no remission, only the opportunity to 'purge his contempt' by an appropriate apology.

Watts was further upset by the reaction of the people around him. Apart from the understandable distress of his family, he was also distressed to realise that Tolstoy was largely ignoring him. He did not attend any of Watts's Court hearings; he wrote to him only once; and he never went into print about his ex-co-Defendant's plight.

The fiftieth anniversary of VE Day came and went in a blaze of British self-congratulation. The historian Richard Overy published a book called *Why the Allies Won,* in which he stressed the moral element. From 1939 to 1945, Britain had suffered 60,000 civilian casualties, mainly in the Blitz. This gave popular justification to the fight, Overy noted. Throughout May 1995, the British media relived the glories of the crusade against the Nazis. But the victims of 5 Corps numbered 70,000, possibly half of whom sooner or later died in captivity. When the anniversary of that tragedy came around two weeks later almost nobody mentioned it. The single exception was Nigel Nicolson who wrote a long, sympathetic piece in *The Spectator* during the course of which he said, 'I do believe that what took place was a war crime.'

On 22 May 1995, the fiftieth anniversary of the "shoot the Cossacks" conference, Watts was brought before Lord Justices Russell, Millett and Ward to appeal his sentence. Watts apologised to the Court for breach of the injunction, as his solicitor advised him he should, but would not extend the apology to Lord Aldington personally, though he had been advised to do this too.

This was not good enough for their Lordships. In his Judgement, Lord Justice Russell began by saying that Watts 'contended, and I suspect still contends, that in 1945, to summarise the matter in a sentence, Lord Aldington was party to a very grave war crime involving the loss of thousands of lives.' Watts had, Russell said, 'demonstrated beyond any peradventure that over the years he has persisted in an orchestrated campaign to vilify Lord Aldington by the publication of scurrilous allegations against this distinguished former Brigadier in the British Army.' When he came to deal with the sentence, Russell said that, although Mr Justice Morland had been 'manifestly in error in imposing so heavy a term', he did 'not accept that at this date there is any genuine contrition on the part of the contemner.' Russell said he thought Watts's apology was not 'a genuine and sincere one' and so, although he quashed the sentence of 18 months' imprisonment, he imposed one of nine months.

In the late afternoon, at almost exactly the time as, fifty years before, 5 Corps had signalled the American troops who had come to rescue the Cossacks that, 'in view of improvement in local situation', their help was no longer needed, Watts was led in handcuffs to the prison van in the yard behind the Royal Courts for his journey back to Standford Hill. His teenage son was ill with vexation at his father's imprisonment, and was shortly facing important exams. Watts's wife pleaded with him to make the apology the Court demanded. She was utterly uninterested in either her husband's campaign or the man it was directed against. Alone in his cell, Watts contemplated the bitter fact that he was now forced to choose between his family or the fight he had waged for the past twelve years. He concluded his family was more important.

Thus, on 23 June, Watts was back in the High Court, having made a new application to purge his contempt. His solicitor laid before the Judge, Mr Justice Latham, the following letter:

Dear Lord Aldington

I wish to apologise to you for my breach of the injunction in this matter. I wish to express my regret for any embarrassment that my breach has caused to you or your family. I wish to offer to you and the Court my assurance that I will respect the rule of law in the future and will not breach any of the injunctions granted at the end of the libel action in 1989.

Yours sincerely

Nigel Watts

Despite this evidence of the humiliation of his opponent, Lord Aldington still fought to keep Watts in jail. He would not agree to his release unless Watts formally and publicly accepted 'the validity of the 1989 judgement' and also stated that the allegations 'which he refers to as "perjury, forgery and trickery" are entirely unfounded'.

Family pressure notwithstanding, Watts would do neither. Fortunately for him, Mr Justice Latham was more sympathetic that the previous Judges. Latham remarked in connection with Lord Aldington's first stipulation that, as a Judge, he could control Watts's actions but not his thoughts, and in relation to his second that these were not matters covered by the injunction and were therefore irrelevant. Latham dismissed Lord Aldington's objections, found that Watts had, by his apology, purged his contempt and accordingly released him from jail.

Is there anything to say by way of conclusion? From the point of view of the people involved, the first thing is that none of the parties, neither winners or losers, has found that the courts operated the way they assumed they would before embarking on this litigation. The second is that, paradoxically given the final outcome, it is probably Watts who has come closest to achieving his declared aim: 'I felt Lord Aldington was in the business of avoiding me and I was in the business of making sure he didn't.' Lord Aldington sought peace and quiet in his retirement, which he has, for all his legal victories, signally failed to achieve, and Tolstoy sought public recognition of his detective work on the war crimes of late May 1945. Instead he has seen his considerable reputation damaged, possibly beyond recovery, and his blossoming career as a novelist brought to a sad and quite unnecessary end.

Neither man need have become embroiled in this litigation. Lord Aldington could with very little ill-effect have ignored Watts; Tolstoy could have confined himself to appearing at the trial as an expert witness. But both have been inwardly driven to go much further than commonsense and ordinary prudence might have dictated. Both men are classic libel litigants, at least as described by Michael Rubinstein, Tolstoy's and Watts's lawyer, in his book about defamation law in practice.

> The psychology of libel-prone authors might usefully be the subject of expert study. No less interesting, however, would be an examination of the psychology of libel claimants... [Most display] an outmoded Victorian hyper-sensitivity relying on a concept wholly at variance with contemporary understanding of social psychology, to say nothing of the teaching of the Bible. Are those who most easily take offence also in some way more vulnerable?[1]

It is not necessarily to criticise either man to observe that the import-ance which they place on their public reputations, higher even than their own families' domestic tranquillity, is at least in part a product of the peculiarities of their upbringing. This case was more about reputations than repatriations. Arguably, Lord Aldington needs counselling more than compensation; and Tolstoy, paternal affection rather than public acclaim.

From the point of view of the public interest, there are surely three main points to be made. First is the obvious undesirability of keeping public records secret for so long. How much healthier would it have been if the whole issue of the forced repatriations could have been ventilated ten years or so after the event? For one thing, Brigadier Low would have had his actions judged by the standards of the time in which they were carried out. For another, his role might have seemed less central if the truth about Macmillan's and Keightley's actions could have been dis-

---

1   Rubinstein *Wicked, Wicked Libels*, p. 143

covered by means of a proper judicial inquiry. Ironically, it is Lord Aldington who has been worst served, in the long run, by the British habit of extreme administrative secrecy.

Secondly, and much more importantly in the shorter term, there is the undoubted fact that the 1989 libel trial was conducted without some of the most important evidence needed for a fair decision. Had FO 1020/42 and the other hi-jacked files been in Court, there is no question that the Defence would have been able to deploy completely different, and far more formidable, arguments. Who can say that the jury would necessarily have seen the facts in the same way if they had, for example, been able to look at evidence suggesting that 5 Corps, far from obeying superior orders, had probably *dis*obeyed them? In the light of that, the verdict can no longer be regarded as either legally safe or historically satisfactory. A re-trial is urgently called for.

Finally, and as a separate issue from any re-trial, there should be a full official investigation into the way the 1989 trial was conducted, focusing on three central questions:

1. Did Lord Aldington have any contact, either direct or indirect, with Mr Oliver in the Ministry of Defence before that official wrote to Tolstoy in April 1989—the month in which Oliver recommended that Lord Aldington be given privileged access to Crown records—saying WO 32/13749 would not be made available to him? And if not, on whose authority did Oliver, who knew about the case, act to keep that file from Tolstoy when he needed it in Court?

2. Since Lord Aldington told Lord Trefgarne less than six months before the trial opened that the Army Historical Branch had co-operated with him in every way it could—'[Alexandra] Ward continues to help me to the full, whenever I call upon her for help'—was it true that this help included withdrawing both the 8th Army and 5 Corps war diaries from the Public Record Office for over six months immediately prior to the trial, thus rendering them unavailable to the Defence; and was this a consequence of Lord Aldington's earlier, personal appeal to the then Secretary of State for Defence, George Younger?

3. Most importantly of all, was Lord Aldington the last person to have used FO 1020/42 before it was "lost" within the Foreign Office and was there any connection between his, and/or Brigadier Cowgill's,

use of the file and its "loss"? And how was it that Lord Aldington was able to produce a second selection of documents from it, just before the trial, but eighteen months *after* Douglas Hurd, then Foreign Secretary, said it was lost?

Behind these particular questions lies the larger, more general one: does official Britain interfere with the courts in politically sensitive trials? If it does, then the "British justice" which the Cossacks and Jugoslavs sought the protection of in May 1945 is as much an illusion today as was the Communist goodwill which 5 Corps sought, fifty years ago, to buy with the lives and liberties of 70,000 tragically trusting foreigners.

Appendix A
FO 1020/42

THIS FILE, the most important of those missing from Court in 1989, has an index which runs from 1 to 166. However 25 are missing from the file, that is they are not listed in the index, which skips numbers 9, 14, 17-19 and so on. Paper 1 is dated 24 April 1945 and paper 166 27 May. Most of the missing papers are dated earlier than 7 May, and therefore are probably not relevant to this story. The following pages list all documents from the file which are still within the folders in the PRO, and which are dated after 7 May.

Entries with details in *italics* are important ones which were in Court. Those which were NOT in Court in 1989, but which would have had a significant impact on the Defence case if they had been, are outlined in heavy boxes.

heavy type for important papers which were kept OUT of Court

From left to right, the columns are as follows:

Index	this is the number in the PRO file index
M&M	page numbers of all papers from this file referred to in Nikolai Tolstoy's book *The Minister and the Massacres*
In Court	YES means it was in Court; NO means it was not in the Court bundles
LA/'lost'	YES means that this paper was submitted by Lord Aldington in his controversial 'Supplemental List of Documents', made on 30 June 1989 (see p. 190-1), just three months before the trial opened and, much more importantly, eighteen months *after it had been lost*

	within the Foreign Office (see p. 399)
FO copy	**missing** means it was not in the photocopied file which was given to the Defence on 19 October 1989 (see pp. 239-240)
	copied means that this paper was included in the FO set of copies
CowBook	All papers quoted by Cowgill, Booker and Brimelow in their *Final Report, Volume II.* This is a list of what they call the Key Papers, hence the designation 'KP233', for example, which means Key Paper #233. These are all, they claim, that are needed to understand the whole story, so the omissions are of significance.
Description	This details the content of the paper. Only those of possible relevance to the case have been included. They are in the form: unit of origin; unit sent to ('-' represents and order, '~' a signal for information); date; brief description of contents (note abbreviations of units at top of page). Particularly important papers which were in Court are described in *italics*; important ones which were NOT in Court are described in **bold**. Page numbers on right refer to the main text.

Index	M&M	In Court	LA/'lost'	FO copy	CowBook	Description (15AG = 15th Army Group; 8A = 8th Army; 5C = 5 Corps)
56		YES	YES	missing	KP53	15AG - 8A: 7 May: German surrender
57		NO		missing		
58		YES		missing		8A - 5C: 8 May: Now negotiating with Tito; get to Klagenfurt first
59		YES	YES	COPIED	KP55	15AG - 8A: 8 May: Advance on Klagenfurt; no casualties
60		NO		missing		
61		NO		missing		
62		NO		missing		
63		NO		missing		
64		NO		missing		
65		YES		COPIED	KP59	5C - 8A: 10 May: Must be able to shoot Partisans
66		YES	YES	COPIED	KP69	AFHQ - Chiefs of Staff: 11 May: Report of Morgan's meeting in Belgrade with Tito
67		YES	YES	COPIED	KP70	8A - AFHQ: 11 May: May we eject Partisans from Carinthia by force?
68		NO		missing		
69		YES		missing	KP67	13C - 8A: 10 May: Dispositions in Venezia Giulia
70	-	-	-	-	-	Missing from PRO file
71		YES	YES	COPIED	KP71	8A - 15AG: 11 May:Situation in Venezia Giulia
72		NO		missing		

Index	M&M	In Court	LA/'lost'	FO copy	CowBook	Description (15AG = 15th Army Group; 8A = 8th Army; 5C = 5 Corps)
73		YES	YES	COPIED	KP72	AFHQ - 8A: 11 May: Macmillan coming to explain about Partisan problems
74		NO		missing		
75		YES		missing		
76		YES		missing		
77		YES		missing		
78		YES	YES	COPIED	KP77	15AG - 8A: 12 May: Copy of Alexander's message to London about Venezia Giulia
79		YES		COPIED	KP86	5C - 8A: 13 May: Situation in Carinthia: Soviets quiet, Partisans a problem
80		YES		missing		
81		NO		missing		
82	p. 75	YES		missing	KP93	5C - 8A: 14 May: *'On advice Macmillan... this large number Soviet nationals...'*
83		YES		missing	KP95	5C - 8A: 14 May: German surrender matters
84		NO		missing		
85		YES	YES	missing	KP96	8A - 15AG: 14 May: copy of 'On advice Macmillan...'
86	p. 80	YES	YES	COPIED	KP97	8A - 15AG: 14 May: Macmillan suggested we hand Cossack troops to Tolbukhin
87	p. 113	YES		missing	KP102	8A - 15AG: 14 May: German surrender details; suggest Croats handed to Tito
88		NO		missing		
89		NO		missing		

Index	M&M	In Court	LA/'lost'	FO copy	CowBook	Description (15AG = 15th Army Group; 8A = 8th Army; 5C = 5 Corps)
90		YES		missing	KP106	8A - 5C: 14 May: Tell Partisans, Carinthia is in British zone
91		YES		missing	KP103	A list of POW in 5C area
92	p. 91	YES		COPIED	KP113	8A - 5C: 15 May: *Robertson Order*
93		YES		missing	KP114	8A - 5C: 15 May: copy of AFHQ - SHAEF: 5C area refugees problematic
94		NO		missing		15AG - 8A: calls 8A to conference: germ of Coldstream
95		NO		missing		
96		YES		missing	KP111	5C - AFHQ: 15 May: Partisans still penetrating Carinthia
97		YES		missing	KP116	AFHQ - 15AG: 15 May: Arrestable categories of Germans
98		NO		missing		
99		NO		missing		15AG - 8A: 17 May: No signed agreements with Jugoslavs—see p. 33
100		NO		missing		8A ~ 5C: 17 May: No signed agreements with Jugoslavs—see p. 33
101		NO		missing		
102		NO		missing		
103		NO		missing		
104		NO		missing		
105		YES		missing	KP146	AFHQ - SHAEF: Refugees in Carinthia a problem, can you take Cossacks?
106		YES		COPIED	KP156	AFHQ - SHAEF: 17 May: Please take over northern sector of 5C area

Index	M&M	In Court	LA/'lost'	FO copy	CowBook	Description (15AG = 15th Army Group; 8A = 8th Army; 5C = 5 Corps)
107		YES		COPIED	KP157	AFHQ - London: 17 May: Report on Morgan trip north, Partisans will not co-operate
108		YES		COPIED	KP166	8A - 5C: 18 May: Copying #106, #107
109		NO		missing		
110		NO		missing		
111		NO		missing		
112		NO		missing		**5C - 8A: 19 May: Report of Ivanovich dinner, omits "signed agreement"**—see p. 33
113		YES		COPIED		8A - 15AG: 20 May: copy of 112
114		NO		missing		
115		NO		missing		
116	p. 122	YES	YES	COPIED	KP154	AFHQ - 8A: 17 May: *Distone Order*
117		NO		missing		
118		NO		missing		
119		NO		missing		
120		NO		missing		
121	-	-	-	-	-	Missing from PRO file
122	p. 216	YES		missing	KP184	SHAEF - AFHQ: 19 May: (SCAF 399) Will take Cossacks into US area
123		NO		missing		**15AG - 5C: 21 May: Full details of Operation Coldstream**—see p. 47

Index	M&M	In Court	LA/'lost'	FO copy	Cow Book	Description (15AG = 15th Army Group; 8A = 8th Army; 5C = 5 Corps)
124		NO		missing		
125		NO		missing		8A - 15AG: 21 May: 5C say 800 US vcls arrived, 5C will NOT hand over—see p. 50
126		NO		missing		8A - 15AG: 21 May: Warning of Coldstream codeword; action imminent
127	-	-	-	-	-	Missing from PRO file
128		NO		missing		
129		NO		COPIED		12AG ~ 5C: 21 May: Coldstream boundaries; prepare to remove POW
130	p. 216	YES		COPIED	KP216	15AG ~ 5C: 22 May: Move 150,000 Germans (incl. Cossacks) north to US sector
131		NO		missing		5C - 20 US Corps: 22 May: STOP Coldstream movements for now — see p. 53
132		NO		COPIED		
133		NO		missing		
134		NO		COPIED		15AG - 12AG: 22 May: 8A say Coldstream moving too fast for 5C—see p. 52
135	p. 216	YES		COPIED	KP224	AFHQ - 8A: 22 May: Cossacks may go to Russians but "no force" to be used
136		NO		missing		
137		NO		missing		
138		NO		COPIED		Break up German Command
139		YES		missing	KP226	8A - AFHQ: 23 May: Consider 5C Jug handovers in accordance with Robertson Order
140		NO		missing		

Index	M&M	In Court	LA/'lost'	FO copy	CowBook	Description (15AG = 15th Army Group; 8A = 8th Army; 5C = 5 Corps)
141	p. 217	YES		COPIED	KP229	5C - 8A: 23 May: *"Verbal directive Macmillan... verbal agreement with Soviets"*
142		NO		missing		
143		NO		missing		
144		NO		missing		
145		NO		missing		
146		YES	YES	COPIED	KP233	8A - AFHQ: 24 May: Telephones not working very well
147		NO		missing		
148	p. 215	YES		COPIED	KP208	8A - AFHQ: 21 May: Send rep. to sort out refugee and POW problems
149		YES		COPIED	KP230	AFHQ - 8A: 23 May: Precise orders about Jug repatriations
150		YES		COPIED	KP240	AFHQ - 15AG: 24 May: Further to #148, rep. coming
151		NO		missing		
152		NO		missing	KP241	AFHQ - 8A: 24 May: Partisans may help themselves to German war material
153		NO		missing		
154		NO		missing		
155		YES		COPIED	KP228	AFHQ - 8A: 23 May: No force in Jug repatriations, otherwise send to Distone
156		NO		missing		
157		NO		missing		

Index	M&M	In Court	LA/'lost'	FO copy	CowBook	Description (15AG = 15th Army Group; 8A = 8th Army; 5C = 5 Corps)
158		NO		missing		
159		NO		missing		
160		NO		missing		
161		NO		missing		8A -AFHQ: 26 May: Improved political situation makes Coldstream unnecessary
162		NO		missing		
163		NO		missing		
164		NO		missing		
165		NO		missing		
166		NO		missing		

Notes:

1. The signals quoted in *The Minister and the Massacres* relate mainly to Macmillan's role. Due to the "hi-jacking" of this file, the gaps in the book could not be filled for the trial, in which Lord Aldington rather than Macmillan was under scrutiny.

2. Lord Aldington, in his choice of documents from this file, omitted everything relating to Operation Coldstream and the attempted rescue of the Cossacks from 5 Corps except what Tolstoy had already published in *The Minister and the Massacres*, see pp. 220-1.

3. The Foreign Office copies followed very closely the documents already submitted to Court, and therefore added almost nothing new.

4. Cowgill followed very closely the Aldington/Foreign Office selection of papers, and omitted most of the crucial ones needed to show that Operation Coldstream was Field Marshal Alexander's plan to save the Cossacks, and to understand how it was subverted.

5. Lord Aldington, the Foreign Office and Cowgill all omitted the 'no signed agreements with the Jugoslavs' order, #99, #100.

Appendix B
PRO–Whitehall file movements

THE MAIN REASON for retrospective concern about the conduct of the libel trial in 1989 is the fact, which has only emerged fairly recently, that much of the most important evidence needed to support the Defence case was kept out of Court, being in either the Foreign Office or the Ministry of Defence for part or all of the period of preparation for the trial. Inquiries at the Public Record Office at the time elicited the reply that the files in question were "out to Department". Apparently, nothing further could be done. Critical arguments—principally about the insubordination of 5 Corps, which was vital since the basis of the Plaintiff's case was that he was only obeying orders—could not be properly put. *The verdict was, therefore, arrived after considering evidence which was incomplete in fundamentally important ways.*

It is not known who was using which files and when, since neither the Foreign Office nor the Ministry of Defence will comment on the use made of their documents by outside researchers. But it is known that Lord Aldington asked the then Secretary of State for Defence, George (now Lord) Younger if he would arrange for War Office (WO series) files he needed for the preparation of his case be moved from the PRO to the MOD for his use (see pp. 156-7). It is also known that Younger's Ministry agreed to do that (see pp. 157-8). It is, further, known that Brigadier Cowgill requested the Foreign Office move FO series files from the PRO to the Foreign Office for his use, and that it did so (see p. 160). Finally, and from the point of view of the deployment of evidence in Court, most importantly, it is known that Lord Aldington made use of at least one of those files, the 'lost' FO 1020/42, during the period it was in the Foreign Office and, it would seem, during the period it was said to have been 'lost' (see Appendix A).

The extent of the co-operation between Brigadier Cowgill and Lord

Aldington is not known though there are grounds for thinking it was very close. Partly this is because of the very extensive use made by Cowgill of the "hi-jacked" files (see pp. 159-60) and partly it is because of the close identity of their cases (see pp. 175-7; Appendix C); Aldington produced Cowgill's *Interim Report* as a document in his Supplemental List and Cowgill quoted Aldington as a major source for his conclusions in his *Final Report*[1] and elsewhere. There would have been nothing exceptionable about any of this, had not the question of the withholding of critical evidence from the jury in a major High Court action been raised.

The authority for the dates given in this table is as follows:

FO files   Letter to the author from Richard Bone, then Head of
                 Library and Records Department, Foreign Office,
                 13 September and 4 October 1993, and 11 January 1994
WO files   Letter to the author from Miss Alexandra Ward, Head
                 of Army Historical Branch, Ministry of Defence,
                 28 June and 27 August 1993, and 8 February 1994

The main files which were withheld from the Court for all or part of the period of preparation of the trial and which contained important evidence are FO 1020/42, WO 32/13749, two of the 8th Army War Diaries (WO 170/4183 & 4) and two of the 5 Corps War Diaries (WO 170/4241 & 3). (Note: they are all back in the PRO now, where they may be consulted by researchers.)

Listed below are the file numbers, their titles (in *italics*), the dates they were in Whitehall, and some of the main evidence which they contain.

FO 1020/42   *Allied Commission for Austria: British Element; Jugoslav*
              Matters; Surrender Details; Displaced Persons
              Details: This file contains all the most important material
              explaining the failure of Operation Coldstream, and the
              insubordination of 5 Corps as regards the handover of both
              the Cossacks and the Jugoslavs against the wishes of the
              higher Allied command.
              Dates: Withdrawn from PRO on 6 May 1987 and returned

---

1   Cowgill *Final Report*, p. xi. Aldington's is the first name in a short but non-alphabetical list
     of 'surviving Army Officers' from whom 'the fullest co-operation was received'.

on 3 August 1987. On 28 August 1987 Brigadier Cowgill
wrote to Dr P.M. Barnes, then Head of Library and Records
at the Foreign Office asking for this file and six others
(including FO 1020/2838, see below) to be moved from the
PRO to the Foreign Office for his use. FO 1020/42 was
withdrawn four days later, on 2 September 1987 and was
held for the next four years in the Foreign Office, being
returned to the PRO on 28 November 1991.

Cowgill: Cowgill reproduces 30 papers from it, out of a
total of 342, in his *Final Report*, though he omits many
important ones (see Appendix A).

WO32/13749   *Disposal of Surrendered Enemy Personnel and Refugees
in Central Mediterranean Force by SACMED*

Details: This file provides evidence that the Chiefs of Staff
in London and the Combined Chiefs of Staff in Washington
were misled into thinking the Cossacks were all Soviet
Nationals and the Chetniks were all being sent to Italy.
It also contains the signal (see p. 34) in which the American
government makes clear that, in addition to the above, it
does not condone the handover to Tito of even the Croats
'until our relations with that government are clearer.' This
message was sent on the same day as Brigadier Low signed
an agreement to hand over all the Jugoslavs, Chetnik and
Croat alike, to Tito. That message was not in Court.

Dates: This file was used by Tolstoy in preparing *Victims of
Yalta* but was then recatalogued and apparently mislaid by
the Ministry of Defence, who could not find it for him in
1982 when he asked to see it again. Nonetheless, Cowgill
was given sight of it (he reproduced the front cover in the
Interim Report, and used that to criticise Tolstoy's
scholarship, see pp. 176-8). When Tolstoy wrote to the MoD
in early 1989 asking to be allowed to consult the file in
preparation for the trial, he was told it was in the MoD and
therefore could not be made available to him (see pp. 191-3).
In his Supplemental List of Documents, prepared in June
1989, Aldington quoted five papers from this file. It was
sent back to the PRO on 19 October 1989, probably being
available again about a week later. By then Tolstoy had
nearly finished giving evidence, and it was of no possible

use to him at the trial.

Cowgill: In the Final Report, Cowgill quoted eight papers from this file, though he omits the one quoted above.

WO 170/4183   *Main HQ 8th Army, War Diary May 1945*

Details: Contains the crucial message from 5 Corps to the American forces sent to rescue the Cossacks that they should not move south (see p. 53). This signal was not in Court. The file also contains much other material of obvious relevance since 8th Army was 5 Corps' superior formation.

Dates: It was withdrawn from the PRO by the MoD on 19 January 1989, and sent back on 8 September, being available again possibly a week later, or just a fortnight before the trial began.

Cowgill: reproduces seven papers in the *Final Report,* though he omits the one mentioned above

WO 170/4184   *Main HQ 8th Army, May 1945: Messages*

Details: As above. Contains the crucial message from 5 Corps saying the Americans should not take over Spittal and that 'situation in Lienz well in hand' (see p. 53). This signal was not in Court.

Dates: It was withdrawn from the PRO by the MoD on 17 January 1989, and sent back on the same date (8 September) as WO 170/4183. Despite this, Aldington used it in preparing his Supplemental List of Documents in June 1989, including in it three documents from this file.

Cowgill: reproduces ten papers in the *Final Report,* though he omits the one mentioned above.

WO 170/4241   *5 Corps War Diary G* [Operations] *May-October 1945*

Details: Of obvious relevance (includes both Deception Order and Definition Order), though interesting more for what it omits than what it contains since most of the material was in Court.

Dates: The Defence was not able to use it for more than ten months since it was withdrawn from the PRO on 3 January 1989, and not returned until 10 October 1989, well into the trial. Despite this, in June 1989, Aldington used the file in preparing his Supplemental List of Documents, including in it three documents from this file. Despite the MoD's claim to have returned it on 10 October, Gillian Hughes, Tolstoy's researcher was told, on 8 November, that the file was 'out to Department', i.e. unavailable.

Cowgill: reproduces twenty papers from this file in the *Final Report*, the second highest of all these files, after FO 1020/42, illustrating its importance to the case.

WO 170/4243   *5 Corps War Diary AQ* [Logistics] *May-October 1945*
Details: As for WO 170/4241, though less so, since logistical matters were less controversial than operational ones.

Dates: It was withdrawn from the PRO to the MoD on 12 June 1989. On 30 June, Aldington finalised his Supplemental List of Documents, and included two papers from this file in it. It was not sent back to the PRO until 19 October, apparently becoming available again about the time Tolstoy finished giving his evidence. In fact, Gillian Hughes asked for this file on 8 November, at the same time as for WO 170/4241, and was told that it, too, was 'out to Department'.

Cowgill: reproduces six papers from it in the *Final Report*.

Apart from these files, there were others which would have been required for a properly conducted Defence that were kept away from the PRO for long periods of time. FO 1020/2838, for example, (subject: *Carinthia: Prisoners of War and Displaced Persons repatriation*) was out for eight months after Cowgill asked for it in August 1987, and for a further five months, straddling the trial, in 1989. Aldington had included a document from it in his Supplemental List of Documents, prepared in June 1989.

Of War Office files, 6th Armoured Division's War Diary (WO 170/4337) was called from the PRO on 24 April 1989, and not returned until 19 October, once again becoming available to the public only after Tolstoy had completed his evidence. Finally, mention should be made of WO 204/10449, entitled *Evacuation of Cossacks and Caucasians from 36th Infantry Brigade,* which Lord Aldington quoted from but which was kept out of the PRO from 18 February 1988, to 31 October 1989, becoming available again only after Tolstoy had finished giving evidence. Not only did Lord Aldington use it during this period (see p. 73), but Cowgill reproduced material from it in the *Interim Report*, published in September 1988.

Appendix C
Aldington-Cowgill
co-operation?

THE QUESTION of whether Brigadier Cowgill assisted Lord Aldington in the preparation of his case touches on several important aspects of this story. These are some of the main ones:

1. To what extent was the Cowgill Inquiry an independent undertaking?
2. Is there any truth in the allegation that some of the unaccounted-for £180,000 of the Sun Alliance payment to Lord Aldington was used to finance Cowgill's research?
3. Most importantly, what facilities did the Foreign Office and the Ministry of Defence afford Cowgill in his researches, and was there any connection between his use of files in those Departments of State and their unavailability as evidence when needed in Court?

It is perhaps relevant to these important questions to note two things: first, that Lord Aldington submitted the whole of the Cowgill Committee's *Interim Report* as a document in his Supplemental List of Documents on 30 June 1989. Secondly, there is a close correlation between the documents submitted by Aldington at that time and those quoted by Brigadier Cowgill in his list of Key Papers (*Final Report, Volume II*). It should be noted that these documents were in many cases taken from files which at that time were unavailable to the Defence. In the case of those taken from FO 1020/42, it is also relevant that the Foreign Secretary said in 1991 that the file had been lost in early 1988, that is *eighteen months before this list was prepared* and about nine months before Cowgill published his *Interim Report*. They stayed "lost" until November 1991, *over a year after* publication of the *Final Report* in which they are reproduced in facsimile. Had Brigadier Cowgill completed his research by 'early 1988'? If so, why did he not release his final conclusions until after Tolstoy's appeal had failed in July 1990? (It will be remembered that Cowgill concluded, crucially, that the Distone Order had in fact reached 5 Corps, contrary to what Lord Aldington argued in Court.) The only other possibility is that Cowgill used FO 1020/42 during the period it was "lost", which would raise questions of involvement with keeping that file and its crucial evidence of 5 Corps' insubordination out of Court.

Therefore it seems worthwhile to list the documents submitted by Lord Aldington on 30 June 1989 (restricting, for convenience, the period to 7 May–1 June 1945) and noting how many of them were used by Cowgill in his list of Key Papers. At the same time, it is important to note which files those papers came from and which of those files were unavailable to the Defence for all or part of the period of preparation of the Court action—see Appendix B and above pp. 190-1.

Number in Lord Aldington's Supplemental List of Documents	Number in Cowgill's list of Key Papers (if used)	Source of document if from file or archive unavailable to the Defence (see Appendix B)
30	KP53	FO 1020/42
31	KP55	FO 1020/42
32	KP56	
33	KP58	
34	KP68	
35	–	
36	KP60	
37	KP69	FO 1020/42
38	KP70	FO 1020/42
39	KP71	FO 1020/42
40	KP72	FO 1020/42
41	KP74	
42	KP76	
43	KP75	
44	KP77	FO 1020/42
45	KP80	
46	KP83	
47	KP87	WO 170/4241

Number in Lord Aldington's Supplemental List of Documents	Number in Cowgill's list of Key Papers (if used)	Source of document if from file or archive unavailable to the Defence (see Appendix B)
48	KP92	
49	KP96	FO 1020/42
50	KP97	FO 1020/42
51	–	
52	KP116	WO 170/4184
53	KP112	WO 170/4241
54	KP120	
55	KP125	
56	–	
57	KP120 (copy)	
58	KP126	
59	KP136	
60	–	
61	KP132	
62	KP131	
63	–	
64	KP144	
65	KP154	FO 1020/42
66	KP149	
67	KP161	WO 170/4243
68	KP147	WO 170/4243
69	KP178	Birch Grove Archives
70	KP165	WO 32/13749
71	KP172	
72	KP189	
73	KP187	
74	KP195	
75	KP180	
76	KP192	
77	KP199	
78	KP214	WO 170/4241
79	KP213	Kirk Papers
80	–	
81	–	
82	–	
83	KP218	WO 170/4184

Number in Lord Aldington's Supplemental List of Documents	Number in Cowgill's list of Key Papers (if used)	Source of document if from file or archive unavailable to the Defence (see Appendix B)
84	–	
85	–	
86	–	
87	KP231	
88	KP233	FO 1020/42
89	KP240	Kirk Papers
90	–	
91	KP250	Kirk Papers
92	KP252	WO 170/4184
93	KP260	WO 32/13749
94	–	WO 32/13749
95	KP257	
96	–	
97	KP259	WO 32/13749
98	KP267	
99	KP266	
100	KP269	Kirk Papers
101	KP272	WO 32/13749
102	–	

The totals are as follows:

Of the 73 papers submitted by Lord Aldington, 58, or 79% were used by Cowgill. Of Cowgill's Key Papers for this period, exactly a third (73 out of 219) were submitted to Court in Lord Aldington's Supplemental List, three months before the trial opened.

Of the papers submitted in that list, and for the period taken above, *40% of them came from files which were closed to the Defence for all or part of the period of preparation before the trial.* (See Appendix B and above pp. 190-1)

Acknowledgements

ALISTAIR HORNE has described the story of the forcible repatriations as a 'staggeringly complex topic, *the* most complicated I have ever encountered as a historian.' The story of the libel trial and the litigation it gave rise to is, if that is possible, even more complex. On top of the events of 1945, there is what might be called 'the war of evidence' which has been waged, on the one hand, between the parties and, on the other, between Whitehall and the British public, at least insofar as it makes use of public records. Therefore, though this book is the product of my pen alone, the material on which it is based is the product of the labours of a great many people, to each of whom I owe a great debt.

The greatest debt, by far, is owed to Nikolai Tolstoy, and I would like to have acknowledged this in conventional, straight-forward terms. However the "gagging" injunction (see pp. 367-8) means that I must be very precise. Specifically, I should like to emphasise that while Tolstoy placed the whole of his vast archive at my disposal—just as he did for Brigadier Cowgill—he did so without any agreement or understanding of any sort as to how I should use it—just as he did with Cowgill. In the end (see p. 43), I came to conclusions closer to Horne's (the Army did it) than either Tolstoy's (Macmillan did it) or Cowgill's (nobody did it). But that does not mean that I acted as Tolstoy's 'servant or agent' in my use of his material any more than Cowgill did. It is an amazing, and shameful, fact that such a point as this has to be made by an independent writer in a country which purports to afford its citizens freedom of enquiry, thought and expression.

The injunction notwithstanding, I do not want to down-play Tolstoy's contribution to this book. For nearly three years he allowed me free access to his unique collection of documents, correspondence and tape-recordings, and made himself available for comment or discussion. It should be stressed, though, that he acted as "tutor" rather than "research assistant", just as he did for Cowgill. Also, in common with Cowgill, I read all the books, looked up all the sources and talked to all the available people myself. My working copy of FO 1020/42, for example, did not come from Tolstoy but was purchased in the normal way from the Reprographics Department of the Public Record Office. Those original documents used in my research which were copied from Tolstoy's archive all related to the period after 1974 (when he started work on *Victims of Yalta*) and relate solely to the story of the litigation, which is not covered by the injunction.

Lest there be any remaining suspicion that Tolstoy was in any way involved in 'causing, permitting, assisting, participating in, or conniving at' publication of this book, I should emphasise that from the time he read the first draft of it, in May 1995, he has tried hard to *prevent* its being published.

One wider point should be made: without Tolstoy's pioneering work on the forced repatriations the horrible likelihood is that the surviving eye-witnesses to the tragedy would have gone to their graves with their evidence unrecorded by historians and even, in some cases, disbelieved by their own families. 'The British Army doesn't do that sort of thing,' Zoë Polanska-Palmer was told again and again by her Canadian husband, even though she had the lacerated legs to prove it. Though other writers have worked in this field, it is to Nikolai Tolstoy that credit must be given for drumming it into the public consciousness that the British Army has, on at least one occasion, done 'that sort of thing'. Thankfully, no amount of injunctions can ever stuff that particular cat back into the bag.

Next in order of indebtedness, at least as far as historical elucidation goes, must be Brigadier Cowgill. Though Cowgill was, with one exception, consistently unhelpful to me personally, his efforts to shine his own exculpatory light on the issue of responsibility for the handovers have provided an essential foil to Tolstoy's accusations. As his co-author Christopher Booker told me in an interview, 'Everything that happened had a perfectly simple explanation and, on the whole, everyone [in the British Army] behaved extremely honourably, efficiently and decently.'

I would also like to acknowledge a third major source of assistance, this time in connection with the litigation of 1987-97 rather than the events of 1945: Nigel Watts. If Nikolai Tolstoy and Brigadier Cowgill have provided thesis and antithesis on the historical issues, it is Nigel Watts's single-minded refusal to be defeated by what he saw as gross injustice which provoked the original writ and which kept the litigation alive after the libel trial was so catastrophically lost in 1989. Since nothing spurs historical research so much as the prospect of a major trial in which history is at issue, it is true to say that without Watts's fighting spirit, much of the material which informs our present understanding of the forced repatriations would still lie undiscovered in the archives. I should add that Watts has also been an invaluable tutor to me on what might be called the "street" aspects of the law: one-man, cut-price litigation—the legal equivalent of unarmed combat.

It is, in this unusual case, possibly relevant to mention that when I wrote to Christopher Booker, as part of the Cowgill team (13 November 1995), and to Lord Aldington (15 November 1995) offering them sight of my manuscript, with the opportunity to reply and to suggest any corrections they thought proper, neither answered my letter. In Booker's case this was unexpected since he had already given me three courteous and informative interviews, as well as letting me read an early draft of his version of this tale, *The Looking-Glass Tragedy* (which Tolstoy also tried to suppress). Lord Aldington, by contrast, had consistently refused to be interviewed since my first request in October 1991. In his last letter to me (14 April 1995) he said, '[I want to] take no part in any publication you are preparing.'

Of the two major surviving officers who issued important orders in May 1945, Brigadier Edward Tryon (now Tryon-Wilson) and Brigadier (now General Sir Geoffrey) Musson, both turned down all requests for an interview, Musson even refusing to reply to my letters on the ground that they did not include a stamped, addressed envelope.

Further down the ranks, where there was no significant responsibility for what was done, the reaction was completely different. Nigel Nicolson kindly allowed me to quote from the daily diary he kept of the trial in 1989, at which he was a major witness. General Sir James Wilson, like Nicolson, both a witness at the trial and also a junior officer in Austria in May 1945, was also helpful.

Other witnesses of the events of 1945 who kindly helped me were Theodore Abjanic, Paul Barre, Philip Brutton, Lt-Col Brian Clark, Sir Ian Fraser, Dr Leopold Goëss, Franz Kristoff, the late Sir Fitzroy Maclean of Dunconnel, John Marley, Bernard O'Sullivan, David Ovens, Dr Eli Pinoci, John Pinoci, Stanislav Plesko, Father Michael Protopopov, Philipp von Schöller, Peter Speakman, Stanisa Vlahovic and three whose experiences set them apart: Milan Zajek, who survived the pits of Kocevje, Karl-Gottfried Vierkorn, who survived eight years in Siberia, and Zoë Polanska-Palmer, who survived Auschwitz, Dachau and 5 Corps.

I have also had a great deal of help, whether in the form of correspondence, interviews or the loan of material, from researchers into the events of 1945 and informed commentators on them. They include the late Lord Brimelow, Richard Davenport-Hines, Peter Gwyn, Alistair Horne, John Keegan, Dr Robert Knight, Ivan Marinov and Professor Norman Stone. I am grateful to all of them, including those whose views I do not share.

I would like to make special mention of Major-General Richard Keightley, son of the late Lieutenant-General Sir Charles Keightley, GOC 5 Corps in May 1945, who was, in my view, the man chiefly responsible for the forced repatriations as they finally happened. It must be a heartbreaking business to have your father accused of being, in effect, a war criminal by a well-known historian like Nikolai Tolstoy, and on grounds which you have neither the time nor the expertise to investigate and reply to. Despite this, Richard Keightley not only tried to bring Aldington and Tolstoy together twelve years ago to try to find some way to reconcile their different views of his father's role, he also agreed much more recently to my request to see General Sir Charles's papers and anything he had of his own which was of relevance to the story of the trial (at which he was a witness for Lord Aldington). When I visited him in Dorset, he gave me lunch in the local pub, showed me his bee-hives then left me alone in his study for the rest of the day with a copying machine and a pile of papers nearly a foot high. It would be hard to imagine a more frank and, if I may say so without impertinence, manly approach. If more of the people involved in this ghastly drama had had the same courage, the truth would have emerged much earlier and less painfully.

The heart of my story is the libel trial in 1989, and the main issue, in retrospect, is the withholding of evidence from the Court. It is therefore of the highest importance that I have been able to get exact dates for the movement of each of the main files in question. In the case of the Foreign Office, the late Richard Bone, Head of Library and Records Department, was both friendly and extremely helpful; in the case of the Ministry of Defence, Miss Alexandra Ward, Head of the Army Historical Branch, provided the crucial dates, and I.D. Goode, Deputy Departmental Records Officer at the Ministry of Defence, helped with the background to releases and retentions. Gillian Hughes, a freelance researcher who worked for Tolstoy in the period leading up to the trial, gave me the dates she was unable to consult key files and R.A. Blake, Head of Repository Department Services at the Public Record Office, gave me details of the measures taken to locate FO 1020/42 during the four years it was 'lost'. I would also like to thank Mike Rogers, the Repository Manager at the Public Records Office, for taking me "hands-on" through the back-office computer system and showing me how it is possible to trace the movement of every file and the use made of their files by any government department, and which files each one has at any time called for and how long they are 'out to Department'. As a result of all this help, the guesswork has been removed from my main conclusions.

I was given a great deal of help in the tricky business of defamation law, past and present, and of European law as it has recently impacted on this branch of English law by a great many people, including Lord Bingham, now the Lord Chief Justice; the late Sir Nicholas Fairbairn QC; Edward Garnier QC MP, sponsor of the 1996 Defamation Act; Lord Lester of Herne Hill QC; Richard Rampton QC and Richard Sykes. Judy Slim helped me on the background to several of the solicitors firms involved in this case, all of whom, without exception, were either totally unhelpful or actively hostile to me. Beverley F. Nunnery & Co. kindly allowed me to quote at length from their transcript of the libel trial (laboriously put into machine-readable form by Nikolai Tolstoy). I am particularly grateful to the late Charles O'Neall, a retired American lawyer and the initiator of Tolstoy's case before the European Court of Human Rights, who was unstinting with his assistance and encouragement. I hope something of his spirit survives, if nowhere else, in the incredible sub-story of the use of the costs weapon in all this litigation.

Other people who have helped with background information, or with their version of the myriad small events which make up this huge story and to whom I am grateful are Lady Aldington, Lindsay Anderson, Sue Bowden, Lord Braine, Nicky Byam Shaw, Francis Carr, Sir Nicholas Cheetham, Joan Cooksley, Lord Courtenay, Lord Cuckney, Mark Deavin, Sir Paul Fox, General Sir David Fraser, the Hon. John Jolliffe, Lord Kingsale, Richard Lamb, James Lees-Milne, Kathy McGrath, Sir Carol Mather, Alasdair Milne, Princess Tatiana Metternich, Gordon Nimse, Harry Phibbs, Harry Chapman Pincher, Rhona Rimmer, Rt. Rev. Edward Roberts, Professor Roger Scruton, Martin Short, Gavin Stamp, the Earl of Stockton, Lord Sudeley, Robert Temple, Colin Thubron, Countess Tolstoy, Lord Thomas of Swynnerton, George Urban, Lord Vinson of Roddam Dene, Alan Watkins, Richard Watts, Auberon Waugh and Lord Younger of Prestwick.

The custodians of four archives central to this story were also helpful in important ways: Margaret Brooks, Keeper of the Imperial War Museum Department of Sound Records; Christopher Hunt, Deputy Keeper of the Department of Printed Books at the Imperial War Museum; Glen Lougher, Librarian at what is now the *Blackpool Evening Gazette*; and Dr

Roger Custance, Winchester College Archivist.

Several people have put themselves to the trouble of reading one or other version of my slowly evolving manuscript. Amongst those who have commented and also helped with facts or background, I would like particularly to thank John Campbell, the biographer of Edward Heath; Dennis Conolly, who was a member of the Friends Ambulance Unit in Austria in May 1945; Dr Benita Cox, a dear friend; Robert Harris; Sir Ludovic Kennedy; Richard Lamb; Max Morgan-Witts; Andrew Melvin, a solicitor and friend; Mark Stephenson, who has also gone through the Cowgill report with the ultra-fine toothcomb one would expect of a senior Winchester history master in retirement; and Nigel Nicolson who, amongst other encouraging observations, said, 'You are quite right to call Arbuthnott a butcher.' Naturally, I must emphasise that, despite all the generous help I have had from these people, as well as from my other informants—most particularly from Nikolai Tolstoy—the views expressed are my own, and the responsiblity for any mistakes or omissions rests solely with me.

I am also grateful to those people who have helped turn my manuscript into a published artefact. Pavel Marek helped with the proof-reading; Andrew Fisher drew the maps; Dr Jean Knowles and her staff at the Port Ellen surgery provided reprographic services; Toby Roxburgh proof-read and commented on two early articles on the Aldington-Tolstoy litigation and no fewer than three drafts of this text; and my brother, Gordon, produced a proper (i.e. not computer-generated) index. Finally, I would like to remember my Father, who sadly died before seeing this book in print, but who gave much more fundamental help over many, many years. Also, as a publisher, he followed the evolution of my manuscript with close attention. His laconic comment on finishing reading it distilled so much of the reaction I have had: 'The law's up to maggots.'

Lagavulin
Isle of Islay
August 1997

Bibliography

Where a book is of interest to the story, but has not been directly quoted in the text above and its relevance to the subject is not immediately apparent from the title, a brief description is given in brackets. All published in London unless otherwise noted.

Adoko, Dr Akena *The Libel of the Century* London Truth Publishers 1989 (about the Jeffrey Archer trial)

Aldington, Lady *History of the Jacob Sheep* Geerings, Ashford 1989

Alexander, Earl, of Tunis *Memoirs* Cassell 1961

Aris, G.R. *Story of 46th Division* Aldershot 1948

Army Council *Manual of Military Law* (7th ed.) HMSO 1929

Avon, Earl of, *Memoirs* (3 vols.) Cassell 1960-5

Beljo, Ante *Yugoslavia: Genocide* Northern Tribune, Sudbury Ontario 1985

Bethell, Nicholas *The Last Secret* Deutsch 1974—reissued with a new Epilogue, Penguin 1995

Bethell, Nicholas *Spies and Other Secrets* Viking 1994

Blaxland, Gregory *Alexander's Generals* William Kimber 1979

Bower, Tom *Maxwell, the Outsider* Heinemann 1991 (Aldington, Maxwell and Brandt's)

Brutton, Philip *Ensign in Italy - A Platoon Commander's Story* Leo Cooper 1992

Campbell, John *Edward Heath* Jonathan Cape 1993

Carlton, David *Anthony Eden: A Biography* Allen Lane 1981

Carter-Ruck, Peter *Carter-Ruck on Libel and Slander* (4th ed.) Butterworth 1992

Cawthorne, Nigel *The Iron Cage* Fourth Estate 1993 (the story of British PoWs who fell into Soviet hands in WWII)

Cesarani, David *Justice Delayed: How Britain became a Refuge for Nazi War Criminals* Heinemann 1992 (accuses Lord Brimelow and others of facilitating what Tolstoy accuses them of obstructing)

Churchill, Randolph *The Rise and Fall of Sir Anthony Eden* MacGibbon and Kee 1959

Churchill, Randolph *The Fight for the Tory Leadership* Heinemann 1964 (Lord Aldington and the 'caballeros' for R.A. Butler)

Cowgill, Anthony; Booker, Christopher; Brimelow, Lord *The Repatriations from Austria: The Report of an Inquiry* (2 vols.) Sinclair-Stevenson 1990

Cowgill, Anthony; Booker, Christopher; Brimelow, Lord; Tryon-Wilson, Edward

Interim Report on an Inquiry into the Repatriation of Surrendered Enemy Personnel to the Soviet Union and Jugoslavia from Austria in May 1945 and the Alleged 'Klagenfurt Conspiracy' Cowgill, Sheepscombe 1988

Crone, Tom *Law and the Media* Heinemann 1989

Davenport-Hines, Richard *The Macmillans* Heinemann 1992

Denikin, A.I. *The White Army* (tr. Alan Wood) Jonathan Cape 1930

Dixon, Norman *On the Psychology of Military Incompetence* Jonathan Cape 1976

Douglas Home, William *Sins of Commission* Michael Russel, Salisbury 1985

Dubcek, Alexander *Hope Dies Last* HarperCollins 1993 (mentions Soviet lists of wanted people, similar to Tryon-Wilson's list, in 1945 in Slovakia)

Foot, M.R.D. *S.O.E. The Special Operations Executive 1940-46* Mandarin 1993

Gilbert, Martin *The Road to Victory: Winston S. Churchill 1941-45* Minerva 1989

Gilbert, Martin *Never Despair: Winston S. Churchill 1945-65* Minerva 1990

Graecen, Lavinia *Chink, A Biography* Macmillan 1989

Hamilton, Nigel *Monty, The Field Marshal 1944-1976* Sceptre 1987

Hills, Denis *Tyrants and Mountains - A Reckless Life* John Murray 1992 (includes a first-hand account of the refugee camps in Italy after WWII)

Horne, Alistair *Macmillan Vol. I: 1894-1956* Macmillan 1988

Hutchinson, George *Edward Heath: A Personal and Political Biography* Longman 1970

Huxley-Blythe, Peter *The East Came West* Caxton Printers, Caldwell, Idaho 1964

James, Robert Rhodes *Anthony Eden* Weidenfeld & Nicolson 1986

Karageorgevich, Peter *A King's Heritage: the Memoirs of King Peter II of Jugoslavia* Cassell 1955

Keegan, John (ed.) *Churchill's Generals* Weidenfeld & Nicolson 1991

Kinley, David *The European Convention on Human Rights: Compliance without Incorporation* Dartmouth, Aldershot 1993

Knight, Robert 'Harold Macmillan and the Cossacks: Was there a Klagenfurt Conspiracy?' *Intelligence and National Security*, May 1986

Krasnov, Nikolai *The Hidden Russia: My Ten Years as a Slave Labourer* Henry Holt, New York 1960

Krasnov, Peter *From Double Eagle to Red Flag* George Allen & Unwin 1928

Laing, Margaret *Edward Heath: Prime Minister* Sidgwick and Jackson 1972

Law Commission *Insurance Law: Non-Disclosure and Breach of Warranty* HMSO 1980

Lees, Michael *The Rape of Serbia* Harcourt, Brace, Jovanovich, New York 1991

Lewis, Philip (ed.) *Gatley on Libel and Slander* (8th Ed.) Sweet & Maxwell 1981

Linklater, Magnus; Leigh, David *Not With Honour: The Inside Story of the Westland Scandal* Sphere 1986

Luckett, Richard *The White Generals: An Account of the White Movement and the Russian Civil War* Routledge and Kegan Paul 1971

McDermott, Geoffrey *The Eden Legacy and the Decline of British Diplomacy* Leslie Frewin 1969

Maclean, Fitzroy *Disputed Barricades* Jonathan Cape 1957

Maclean, Fitzroy *Eastern Approaches* Jonathan Cape 1948

Maclean, Fitzroy *Tito: A Pictorial Biography* Macmillan/McGraw-Hill 1980

Macmillan, Harold *The Blast of War* Macmillan 1967

Macmillan, Harold *Tides of Fortune* Macmillan 1969

Macmillan, Harold *War Diaries: The Mediterranean 1943-5* Macmillan 1984

Malcolm, Col. Alex *History of the Argyll and Sutherland Highlanders 8th Battalion, 1939-45* Nelson 1947

Mantle, Jonathan *Jeffrey Archer: In for a Penny* Warner 1993

Marnham, Patrick *The Private Eye Story* Deutsch 1982 (describes Christopher Booker chummily as half-way between Gussie Fink-Nottle and Walter Pater)

Martin, David (ed.) *Patriot or Traitor? The Case of General Mihailovic* Hoover Institution, Stanford 1978

Mather, Sir Carol *Aftermath of War 1945: Why Everyone Must Go Home* Brassey 1992

Neill, Sir Brian; Rampton, Richard (eds.) *Duncan and Neill on Defamation* (2nd ed.) Butterworth 1983

Newland, Samuel *Cossacks in the German Army 1941-1945* Frank Cass 1991

Nicolson, Nigel *Grenadier Guards in the War of 1939-45, Vol II* Gale & Polden, Aldershot 1949

Nicolson, Nigel *Alex: The Life of Field Marshal Earl Alexander of Tunis* Weidenfeld and Nicolson 1973

Nicolson, Nigel *Long Life* Weidenfeld and Nicolson 1997 (includes a long section on Carinthia 1945 and Court 13 1989)

Nicolson, Nigel *Operations of 1st Guards Brigade in Northern Italy and Southern Austria, April-May 1945* unpublished

Nork, Karl (alias Karl-Gottfried Vierkorn) *Hell in Siberia* Robert Hale 1957

Overy, Richard *Why the Allies Won* Jonathan Cape 1995

Pavlovich, Stevan *Tito: Jugoslavia's Great Dictator: A Reassessment* Hurst 1992

Polanska-Palmer, Zoë *Yalta Victim* Mainstream, Edinburgh 1986

Pritchard, John *The Penguin Guide to the Law* Penguin 1983 (the book which stimulated Watts to take up Sue Bowden's insurance claim)

Prvulovitch, Z.R. *Serbia Between the Swastika and the Red Star* Z.R. Prvulovitch, Birmingham 1986

Rosenberg, Norman *Protecting the Best Men: An Interpretive History of the Law of Libel* University of North Carolina Press 1986

Rowe, Peter (ed.) *The Gulf War 1990-1 in International and English Law* Routledge 1993 (legal aspects of the forcible repatriation of Iraqis unwilling to return home: 'contrary to the general principles of international law')

Rubinstein, Michael *Wicked, Wicked Libels* Routledge and Kegan Paul 1972

Shephard, Robert *Iain Macleod* Hutchinson 1994 (Lord Aldington was the first to declare Profumo had lied to Parliament about Christine Keeler)

Shtemenko, Semyon *The Last Six Months* William Kimber 1978

Shukman, Harold (ed.) *Stalin's Generals* Weidenfeld and Nicolson 1993 (describes

Shtemenko)

Taylor, Telford *Nuremburg Trials: War Crimes and International Law* Carnegie Foundation, New York 1949

Taylor, Telford *Guilt, Responsibility and the Third Reich* Heffers, Cambridge 1970

Tolstoy, Nikolai '"Victims of Yalta"—an Inquiry?' *Encounter,* June 1980

Tolstoy, Nikolai 'The Klagenfurt Conspiracy: War Crimes and Diplomatic Secrets' *Encounter,* June 1983

Tolstoy, Nikolai *The Coming of the King: The First Book of Merlin* Bantam 1988

Tolstoy, Nikolai *The Minister and the Massacres* Century 1986

Tolstoy, Nikolai *The Quest for Merlin* Hamish Hamilton 1985

Tolstoy, Nikolai *The Tolstoys: Twenty Generations of Russian History 1353-1983* Hamish Hamilton 1983

Tolstoy, Nikolai *Victims of Yalta* Hodder and Stoughton 1978

Tyson, Geoffrey *100 Years of Banking in Asia and Africa 1863-1963* National and Grindlay's Bank 1963

Wake, Sir Hereward; Deedes, William *Swift and Bold: the story of the King's Royal Rifle Corps in the Second World War 1939-1945* Gale and Polden, Aldershot 1949

Warlimont, Walter *Inside Hitler's Headquarters 1939-45* (tr. R.H. Barry) Weidenfeld and Nicolson 1964

Wrangel, Peter *Memoirs* Williams and Northgate 1929

de Zeyas, Alfred *The Wehrmacht War Crimes Bureau 1939-45* University of Nebraska Press 1989

Index